THE OFFICIAL ENCYCLOPEDIA OF
Manchester United

THE OFFICIAL ENCYCLOPEDIA OF

Manchester United

Written by Ross Biddiscombe

Patrick Curry and Jonathan Hayden

**SIMON &
SCHUSTER**

London · New York · Sydney · Toronto · New Delhi

A CBS COMPANY

Simon & Schuster UK Ltd
1st Floor
222 Gray's Inn Road
London
WC1X 8HB
www.simonandschuster.co.uk

Simon & Schuster Australia
Sydney
Simon & Schuster India
New Delhi

A CIP catalogue for this book is
available from the British Library.

ISBN: 978-1-84737-918-4

Printed and bound in Spain by
Graficas Estella

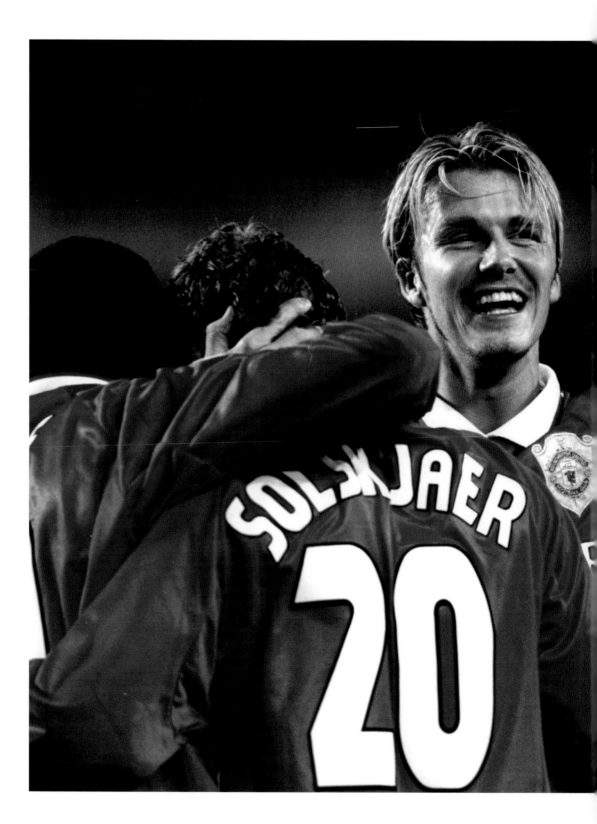

Contents

Foreword

FOR ME, IT'S history that sets Manchester United apart from every other football club.

I'm incredibly proud to be associated with the club, and to have represented it for so long, but it staggers me when I look at everything that has gone before me.

Matt Busby and his young players won five FA Youth Cups in a row in the 1950s, and they set the benchmark for this club and made Manchester United what it is today. Everyone who follows the club, or is associated with it, owes everything to them.

Ever since, we have tried to follow in their footsteps. Winning league titles, FA Cups and European Cups is, to me, just following in a tradition that they set. Fortunately, we've been able to do so over the last two decades or so. It's remarkable to think that the club managed to find another Matt Busby, but in Sir Alex Ferguson they have.

Thirty or 40 years from now, people will look back on this period as one of the most successful in the club's history, and it's incredible to think what Sir Alex has achieved here. Aside from everything else, he has won 12 league titles! So has Ryan Giggs, who has taken the club's appearances record from another legend, Sir Bobby Charlton, and I feel privileged to have known and worked with these people.

Being a part of Manchester United is such an enormous privilege. I always say that you can't have a bad day when you're a part of this club. You might be having a bad day in football terms, but when you look down at that badge on your shirt you realise that really, it's a good day after all.

That's because this is a club of such rich history that, in my eyes at least, no other comes close – which is why I'm sure you will enjoy reading all about it.

Gary Neville
Manchester, June 2011

Introduction

IN THE EARLY 19th century, things began to change; even those who had traditionally toiled from dawn to dusk every day of the week, saw a glimpse of a new and more leisured society in the making. By the middle of the century, the practice of early Saturday closing had spread to the mills and factories of the north, and with time and a little money the working man could now indulge in organised pastimes. Soon football would become the British national game.

The rules had been formalised by 1859, the Football Association began in 1863 and by the mid-1870s the game belonged to public schoolboys, trade unions and working men's associations (who formed many of the early clubs), which is how the story of Manchester United begins.

Once a team of hardly-known railway workers, their modern-day descendants are world-famous superstars, watched and loved by millions. In the intervening 130 years there have been many stories, and what stories they are! Some are mundane and on other occasions glorious; there are tales of near-bankruptcy (twice), and an interlude when unimaginable tragedy struck the club.

The cast of characters is unforgettable: the men with the money and influence, including John Henry Davies, the club's first financial saviour, who helped fund the construction of Old Trafford; the triumvirate of great managers: Ernest Mangnall, Sir Matt Busby and Sir Alex Ferguson, all of whom built championship-winning teams, the latter two conquering Europe in the process. And then there are the players, from the loyal tradesmen working for the team and the railway company, to the giants of every era.

English historian C.V. Wedgwood once wrote, 'it has been said that without passion there might be no errors, but without passion there would certainly be no history'. Manchester United's remarkable story is unarguably rooted in passion, which is why it is so rich in history, and has a future that promises so many future triumphs and new, fascinating stories.

Ross Biddiscombe
Jonathan Hayden
June 2011

1

The Origins

Above: An 1868 engraving entitled "Winter Amusements – Football."

1878-83 | One of the club's inaugural vice-presidents is local Manchester East MP Arthur Balfour, who would go one to become Prime Minister from 1902-05.

1878-1883: Newton Heath Lancashire & Yorkshire Railway Football Club is born

The first five years in the life of Newton Heath Lancashire & Yorkshire Railway Football Club, the forerunners of Manchester United, are shrouded in mystery. This was a time when any kind of competitive club football in Great Britain was still in its infancy; organised football was less than a decade old. Of course, the sport itself had been played in some form or other for centuries, but now it was finally developing a coherent structure, with organising bodies, annual competitions, formal playing rules and recognised teams.

In fact, national teams of amateur players from England, Wales and Scotland had only begun playing international matches against each other in 1872, while the oldest football competition in the world – the Football Association (FA) Cup – had been created in 1871. That first FA Cup was won by a team of public schoolboys, Wanderers, and in Newton

Heath's first season, 1878-79, it would be won by another team of amateurs, Old Etonians.

Despite the game being an amateur occupation at the time, the main growth of the organised game had been among working men, especially those in the industrial north and Midlands. The Lancashire & Yorkshire Railway Company had been formed in 1847, at a time when the notion of organised sport was yet to feature on the social landscape (the Football Association came into existence only in 1863). By the mid-1860s, many in the company's workforce were already fans of the game. Men from the coach-building section of the railway company had been paying a few pennies to play games for several years before a formal team was set up, and by the late 1870s they wanted to arrange themselves into a club and needed a ground to play on.

The team that would be known as Newton Heath for the next 24 years can thank Liverpudlian Frederick Attock for its birth. Attock was a superintendent engineer at the railway company, and he spoke for the men of the carriage and wagon works at the Lancashire & Yorkshire Railway Company who wanted funds to form a football team.

Attock helped arrange the money – an early form of sponsorship for kit and equipment – and permission to play that would come from the company's Dining Room Committee. The committee was told how the men wanted to play organised football on their Saturday afternoons, particularly against other teams of railwaymen and, with the committee's support, the men began to arrange their first matches in 1878. For his role in the club's formation, Attock became its first president.

The formation of Newton Heath LYR FC was of little significance other than to the workers of the local railway company in the north of Manchester; they were just one of many teams being formed at that time.

The name Newton Heath LYR was chosen because Newton Heath was the area of Manchester that just happened to be at one end of the LYRC railway line (the other end was in Leeds), and it was the base for the carriage and wagon works. By using the LYR initials, the team were distinguished from another group of railway workers in the Motive Power Division who formed Newton Heath Loco.

No records exist of who played for Newton Heath LYR that year or which teams they faced, but it can be assumed that other groups of railway workers were their first opposition along with local clubs in and around their part of Manchester. These earliest games would be have been friendly matches rather than within organised competitions or played for specific trophies. Although little is known of the club in these years, the men were determined to move the club forward.

The original base of the club was the Shears Hotel on Oldham Road and The Heathens (as the team soon became known) did have a ground, a simple field near to the railway yard in North Road that was leased by the railway company. The pitch was often a bog in the winter and cement-hard in the summer, but it served as home to the club for 15 years. Records say that the team was made up of "tough, diligent men who formed a powerful side" and, within a few

seasons, the management at the LYR works would note that the Newton Heath LYR matches could bring cachet to the company.

And, as Newton Heath LYR grew, so did the rest of the football network elsewhere; competitiveness was increasingly important and teams were already fighting to secure the best players. It would become a period in the early development of English football when players were known as 'shamateurs'. The FA, as the ruling body, enforced a ban on players being paid, but a club like Newton Heath was largely protected because while it was being supported by the railway company, the club was able to offer talented players a job in the railway works in return for turning out for the company's football team.

1883-84: An era of friendly matches plus a meeting with mighty Blackburn Olympic

Informal networks of regional teams playing regular friendly matches had been cropping up all over England for several years and Manchester was among the forerunners, along with many other towns and cities in the north and Midlands.

Newton Heath was a relatively well-established team by now, playing games against other teams in

1883-84 Records state that spectators paid 3d (about 1p) to watch the Newton Heath against Blackburn Olympic match.

Left: November 1872, A hand-coloured engraving recording the historic first match between Scotland and England. The game was played on the West of Scotland Cricket Ground and watched by a crowd of just 4,000. A photographer was arranged, but left without taking any pictures because the players would not guarantee to buy any.

1884-85 The first match against Eccles in the Manchester Cup is replayed because the opposition protests that Newton Heath's third and winning goal is offside. The successful protest does not help because the Heathens win the replay 3-0.

1885-86 There is controversy surrounding Newton Heath's second goal in the final of the Manchester Cup because of a possible offside decision, but despite protests, the goal stands.

1886-87 Jack Powell is not the only coveted player to join the Heathens this season; brothers John and Roger Doughty, who both previously worked as coal miners, also sign up.

Above: "Good old Sam! Very few as enthusiastic as he." So said the Newton Heath Bazaar Programme (1901) of full back Sam Black, here photographed in 1885. He was a player at Newton Heath before the Football League was founded or the club entered the FA Cup so there are no official appearances listed, but he made lots of appearances for the club in local competitions and friendlies.

the Manchester district and east Lancashire. Seventeen such matches are recorded for the season with eight wins, five draws and just four defeats.

However, the Heathens did try to step up in class and played in the Lancashire Cup for the first time this season, only to lose 7-2 in their opening match to Blackburn Olympic Reserves. Newton Heath were level at 2-2 just after half-time, but superior fitness almost certainly took its toll as the more experienced team then scored five unanswered goals. Played on 27 October 1883, it was the club's first match in an official competition and, given that Blackburn Olympic's first XI had won the FA Cup the previous

season and were regarded as one of the top professional teams in the country, this match helped the Heathens understand what it would take for them to rise to the top of English football's ladder.

1884-85: A first taste of cup success is denied

Seven years after their formation, there were now two important tournaments for Newton Heath LYR to take part in. The first competition of the season was the Lancashire Cup, although the Heathens managed to progress through only one round before losing 1-0 to Baxenden.

A few months later, the team entered the inaugural Manchester Cup (also known as the Manchester and District Senior Cup or Challenge Cup) for the first time and went on to make the final.

The opening round was against Eccles and the Heathens won after a replay. They then beat Manchester FC, followed by Dalton Hall Owens College in the semi-final. However, Newton Heath's run was ended when they were beaten 3-2 by Hurst FC in the final in front of 3,500 spectators.

Nevertheless, it was a first taste of success that helped the club to grow. Managers at the railway company were now recognising the growing social significance of the team and consequently, allowed players to have time off work to prepare for games. Players at the club were already talking about full professionalism.

1885-86: The club's first ever trophy is won – the Manchester Cup

The main focus of the club now was on the Manchester Cup and, just one season after being runners-up in the competition, Newton Heath returned to the final, this time proving victorious. The journey to the final included four knockout matches, the most convincing of which being a 10-0 win over Thornham in the third round.

The Heathens then beat Manchester FC 2-1 on 3 April to win the trophy in front of 6,000 fans, with goals by Black and Watkins. The game was played in a strong wind that favoured Newton Heath in a first half, after which they led 2-0 and never looked back. It would be the club's first recorded trophy in their long history.

By now, professionalism in English football had begun in earnest, and the sport was about to take major steps forward. The informal regional groups of teams who played against each other in various competitions that had been forming over the last few years would soon lead to more organised leagues containing teams from many different parts of the country. Newton Heath certainly had ambitions to be a part of these developments.

1886-87: A decade old with a new breed of players

By now almost ten years old, Newton Heath was still making progress as a club and would begin signing established players from different teams around the country. Welsh international Jack Powell joined the club this season from Bolton Wanderers and, like many before him, the reason was money; he was also offered a job with the railway company (as a fitter) as part of his transfer.

The club entered the FA Cup to test the club's mettle. Their first round match was against fellow Lancastrians, Fleetwood Rangers at Fleetwood Park in front of a crowd of around 2,000 people. When the game ended in a 2-2 draw, the referee asked both teams to play a period of extra time, but the Heathens refused and Fleetwood were awarded the victory. The club protested unsuccessfully to the FA and then boycotted the competition until 1889. However, there was better news in the Manchester Cup as Newton Heath made the final only to lose 2-1 to West Manchester.

1887-88: League football must wait but another cup is won

Newton Heath were now itching to play league football. The club was signing the best players they could find – from outside the railway fraternity and from outside the district – but playing in a formal league would have to wait another year.

Instead, another round of friendly matches was supplemented by a fourth campaign in the Manchester Cup. A 7-0 win against Hooley Hill was the Heathens' opening game (actually in the second round) and enough to set up a semi-final against Hurst FC, the team that beat the Heathens in their first Manchester Cup final appearance. This time, however, Newton

Heath were the victors, winning 2-0 with goals each from the Doughty brothers, Roger and Jack.

In the final at the neutral Whalley Range ground, the Heathens then walloped Denton 7-1 in front of a crowd estimated to be 8,000, to take the cup for the second time after reaching the final for the fourth consecutive year. Jack Doughty scored a hat-trick and brother Roger scored two in a very easy win that clearly indicated the team had out-grown the local opposition and was in need of new challenges.

1887-88 | Both Doughty brothers were born in Staffordshire, but both play international football for Wales via their Welsh mother.

Below: One of the earliest known football programmes in existence. Everton v Newton Heath from the game played in 1889.

1888-89: A one-off season in a one-off league

The Football League was formed this year, but Newton Heath were judged not strong enough to be one of the 12 founding teams. The Heathens' application to join drew just a single vote, so the club joined a rival organisation, The Combination, instead. Also newly formed, The Combination was a group of 20 northern and Midlands teams. However, teams were told to make their own fixtures rather than answer to a central organisation and, not surprisingly, chaos quickly followed; many teams failed to play out a full season and often could not decide if matches were league games or mere friendlies.

The Heathens won eight, drew two and lost two of their recorded games, but the league collapsed in April 1889. However, Newton Heath again won the Manchester Cup (beating Hooley Hill 7-0 in the final) and also entered the Lancashire Junior Cup.

In another first, this season saw the club's first international match when a touring Canadian football team were opponents in front of an estimated 3,000 people at North Road.

1889-90: The Heathens join the Alliance and meet The Invincibles

After the collapse of The Combination and with Football League entry still impossible, Newton Heath helped form the Football Alliance, a competition for clubs not yet strong enough for the elite league. Teams were drawn from as far afield as Sunderland, Birmingham, Grimsby, Nottingham and Long Eaton in Derbyshire. The Heathens finished eighth in the 12-team league, with Scot Willie Stewart top scorer with ten goals. The team performed well enough at home (seven wins and four losses), but won only twice on their travels.

Newton Heath also took part in the FA Cup again after their self-imposed boycott. Their opponents were Preston North End, known at that time as The Invincibles, and current holders of the Cup.

The game at Preston's Deepdale stadium ended in an emphatic 6-1 win for the Football League founders, and even scoring one goal against them was regarded by Newton Heath as something of a success. However, one trophy did not escape the Heathens,

who won the Manchester Cup for the third year running and the fourth time in five years.

1890-91: The 'LYR' disappears as independence is sought

Newton Heath and its players had been growing more independent from the railway company in the last few seasons and decided that now was the time to drop the connection from their name; Newton Heath LYR became simply Newton Heath.

It was a significant move and a risky one because the Lancashire & Yorkshire Railway company's money would not be easily replaced. However, the club was sufficiently well run to play for the second year running in the Alliance League, although results were no better.

Several heavy defeats – for example, an 8-2 loss at Nottingham Forest – were commonplace, and the team finished ninth, one place lower than last season. Nevertheless, there were indications of progress by the Heathens, who managed a first-ever victory in an FA Cup match, albeit in the first qualifying round rather than in the main competition. Newton Heath beat Higher Walton 2-0 on 4 October, but then lost to Bootle Reserves 1-0 in the next qualifying round.

The Heathens lost in the second round of the season's Lancashire Cup, but did make the final of the Manchester Cup only to lose 1-0 to West Manchester.

1891-92: Alliance runners-up and the Football League finally beckons

In their third and final season in the Alliance League, Newton Heath finally began to show their class on the field as well as developing off it. The club was now entirely independent of the railway company, although most players still worked there. The Heathens were also a limited company with £2,000 worth of share capital (all shares were £1 each) and operated by their first full-time official, A H 'Alf' Albut who was also the team manager.

League results were so impressive – including a 10-1 victory over Lincoln City and 4-2 at Sheffield Wednesday – that Newton Heath finished runners-up. In addition, the growing FA Cup competition proved more successful than ever this season. The Heathens beat cross-town rivals Ardwick (a club to be re-named Manchester City two seasons later) in

the first qualifying round before receiving a walkover against Heywood and then winning 2-0 against South Shore in the third qualifying round. However, Blackpool came to North Road in the next round and beat the Heathens 4-3.

In the close season, the Football League and the Alliance League agreed to join forces and form two divisions under the Football League banner. After finishing second in the Alliance's final season, Newton Heath were granted a place among English football's elite for their next campaign – in the Football League First Division.

1892-93: A tough first Football League season but survival is achieved

To take part in the Football League for the first time was a major step up in class for Newton Heath, and would be a serious call on the club's resources. A total of 30 competitive league games at a very high level, mostly against more experienced clubs, would always be a difficult task. And so it proved.

The historic opening-day match against mighty Blackburn Rovers (already five times FA Cup winners) in a heavy rainstorm brought a creditable result, albeit a 4-3 loss. An estimated crowd of 10,000 then turned up for the first game at North Road (a 1-1 draw against Burnley), but it took seven games before the Heathens managed a league victory, a remarkable 10-1 thrashing of Wolverhampton Wanderers.

The season, not surprisingly, was largely one of heavy defeats; in 13 of the 30 league matches, the Heathens conceded at least four goals. However, the win over Wolverhampton Wanderers in October plus the 7-1 defeat of Derby County in December

1892-93 | Scottish centre forward Bob Donaldson scores Newton Heath's first ever goal in the Football League in the match against Blackburn Rovers on 3 September, while the 10-1 victory over Wolverhampton Wanderers a month later is a club record win for over 60 years.

Above: Newton Heath Football Club in 1892, the year they join the Football League. Back row (l-r): Massey (trainer), J.Warner, J.Davies Middle row: T. Taylor (director), Alf Albut (secretary), T. Fairbrother (director), A. Mitchell, G. Perrins, W. Stewart, J. Brown, F. Erentz, J. Clements, J. Lateward (director). Front row: A.H. Farman, J. Coupar, R. Donaldson, A. Carson, W. Hood, W. Mathieson.

1893-94 | In an era of Test Match play-offs, where First Division teams could retain their status, Newton Heath's loss to Liverpool makes them the first club ever to suffer relegation to the Second Division.

1894-95 | The Heathens' Bank Street ground has a terrible reputation among other league teams. Walsall initially refuse to play on the pitch when they find tons of sand mixed with wet, brown soil. After losing 14-0, the visitors successfully protest, asking for the result to be voided. The protest is only partially successful as the replayed game ends in a 9-0 win for Newton Heath.

In March 1894, a costly lawsuit in which Newton Heath sued for damages against the Birmingham Gazette newspaper was settled. The judge gave the club only ¼d in compensation and told each side to pay their own costs. This financial burden would weigh heavily on the Heathens for several years.

were undoubted highlights. In January, Blackburn turned up again to knock Newton Heath out of the season's FA Cup in the first round and, by April, the club had finished bottom of the league, five points adrift of the next team, Accrington Stanley.

The good news, however, was that the Heathens faced Small Heath (later known as Birmingham City), the champions of the Second Division, in a so-called Test Match (effectively a modern-day play-off) to decide which team would play First Division football next season. The Lancashire team won 5-2 after a replay to secure their position. In addition, the Heathens won the Manchester Cup for the fourth time in nine years to confirm that they were the strongest team in the city.

1893-94: The ignominy of the first club to be relegated

Just like modern-day football, the game in the late 19th century was about big and little fish – both trying to survive in an increasingly competitive league, and Newton Heath would be considered something of a little fish as they set about their second season in the First Division. New players arrived like halfback Will Davidson and inside forwards Jack Peden and James McNaught, but the results were similar to the previous season's.

Support was still strong as the club moved to its new Bank Street ground in the eastern part of Manchester in the suburb of Clayton. The team's former home at North Road was not popular with opponents as the notorious pitch was either soggy or rock-strewn or both, while the changing rooms were in a pub a few minutes' walk away. However, Bank Street was little improvement, with an often over-sanded pitch and a stadium bedevilled by thick smoke from neighbouring factories.

Three victories in the first seven games of the season were unrepresentative of a campaign that would bring only three more wins in the other 23 games. In one three and a half month period, United lost 11 straight league matches.

During this period, the Heathens did win an FA Cup first round match 4-0 at home to Middlesbrough, but Blackburn Rovers – for the second consecutive season – knocked them out of the competition in the next round.

Above: 1895. A reward notice posted by the city of Birmingham police after the FA cup had been stolen from a shop window where it had been on display following Aston Villa's victory.

Worse was to come when Newton Heath finished last in the league, five points below newly promoted Darwen. This meant another play-off, this time against Liverpool, the top team in Division Two. The Heathens lost that game 2-0 and were relegated.

1894-95: Life is easier and results are better in the Second Division

The Second Division of the Football League was definitely a place more suited to Newton Heath's level of talent; the club was far more competitive throughout their third season of league football. Instead of a string of defeats, the club suddenly enjoyed plenty of wins, 15 in all during the season, including the first two Manchester derbies against City in the league.

The Heathens won both, 5-2 at City's ground in Hyde Road in front of 14,000 fans and then 4-1 at home in Bank Street with a crowd of 12,000. Bury were runaway winners of the league and Newton Heath missed out on the runners-up spot in a dramatic final match of the season against Notts County, who were their rivals for the second place.

The Heathens had already played Bury twice in the final four games of the season, which produced just one point out of a possible four and, in the match against County, they could only manage a 3-3 draw so that the Nottingham team finished a single point ahead. Nevertheless, Newton Heath played in another Test Match, this time for a chance to return to Division One. The match against Stoke City, however, was lost 3-0 and despite a season of success in a new division, the Heathens would stay put.

1895-96: Inconsistency is the problem in a mediocre season

There was no doubt that Newton Heath were now an established team in the Second Division of the Football League, but the competition for promotion was increasingly intense. The Heathens could – and did – beat the lesser teams in the league with aplomb; two of the first three games of the season were 5-0 thrashings of Crewe Alexandra and Burton Swifts.

But, the club was also prone to losing heavily: 7-1 against Liverpool (the eventual league champions). In fact, it was the Heathens' away form that cost them any chance of promotion; they won just three of 15 games away from their Bank Street home.

A fifth place league finish and a loss to First Division Derby County 5-1 in a replay in the second round of the FA Cup meant the season was at best mediocre, and they were also unsuccessful in both the Manchester Cup and Lancashire Cup.

1896-97: A chance of promotion goes begging in the test matches

Last season's disappointing lack of progress by the team was replaced by a campaign of thrilling wins in both league and cup. The signing of international centre half Caesar Jenkyns helped the Second Division campaign begin with six wins in the opening seven matches, and saw none of the heavy losses of the previous 12 months.

The team was more solid all round and also showed its class in the early qualifying rounds of the FA Cup when West Manchester were toppled 7-0. In fact, Newton Heath got through three qualifying rounds by January and then beat Kettering in the first round proper 5-1. A 6-0 win immediately followed in the league against Loughborough Town and Newton Heath's season was gathering pace.

1895-96 | The initial FA Cup tie against Derby County brings a crowd of around 20,000 to the Bank Street ground, a huge total considering average home attendances are just over 6,500 at the time.

1896-97 | Harry Stafford, who will take a key role in the club's survival in a few years' time, plays his first full season making 32 appearances.

ON HEATH F.C. IN 1894.

Left: 1894. Newton Heath competed in the newly formed Football Alliance in the 1889-90 season. The Heathens played in red and white quartered shirts with navy blue knickerbockers. Evidence of the red and white kit comes from a newspaper report of a game at Bolton Wanderers on 7 September 1889, which included a description of Newton Heath playing in "Their familiar red and white costumes."

1897-98 Rivalry with Manchester City is already intense. 20,000 fans turn up at Bank Street to see the Heathens win 3-0 and there is a 25,000 crowd for the return tie when City win 4-0.

1898-99 Newton Heath's conquerors in the FA Cup this year, South Shore, will cease to exist before the end of the season after amalgamating with Blackpool FC.

Despite mighty Derby County again – for the second successive season – putting the Heathens out of the FA Cup, confidence was high and the team lost just one of its last eight games, overhauling Grimsby Town to finish second in the league. Newton Heath then faced two rounds of play-offs, overcoming Burnley, but losing over two legs to Sunderland, which meant another season in the Second Division. The season also saw the team reach the semi-finals of the Manchester Cup, losing to Bury.

1897-98: Big wins and big losses as the City rivalry intensifies

This was Newton Heath's fourth successive season in the Second Division and a pattern had developed; the team continued to perform well against weak opposition, but were often put in their place by stronger teams.

The Heathens were naturally trying to improve all the time and forward Bob Donaldson – who had scored the club's first ever league goal – was transferred to fellow Second Division team Luton Town in December mainly because Harry Boyd was enjoying his one and only stand-out season for the club; his 22 goals were more than Donaldson had managed in any of the five previous seasons.

However, Newton Heath were inconsistent in the league for the first six months of the season; seven times they scored four or more goals, yet then conceded five against Woolwich Arsenal and six versus Burnley. The team could not stay unbeaten for a reasonable run of games.

1898-99: Trouble among the team and another fourth-place finish

Something was obviously missing from Newton Heath's make-up because each season they threatened to play their way out of the Second Division (which now expanded from 16 to 18 teams), but failed to do so. The board tried to find a solution in mid-season by responding to alleged indiscipline among the players and placed two forwards – Harry Boyd, who had top-scored last season, and John Cunningham – on the transfer list.

Drink was said to be at the core of the problem and the press and fans also complained of wages being too high. By now the 'normal' pattern had emerged, with

Right: 1899. By now football was attracting a huge following, as can be seen in this photograph of the FA Cup final between Sheffield United and Derby County at Crystal Palace. The match attracted a crowd of nearly 74,000 – a world record at the time. Sheffield United beat Derby 4-1.

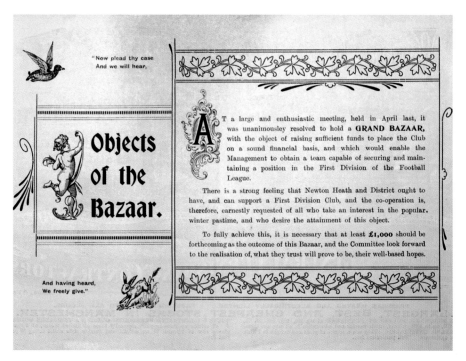

"Now plead thy case
And we will hear,

Objects of the Bazaar.

And having heard,
We freely give."

A T a large and enthusiastic meeting, held in April last, it was unanimousley resolved to hold a **GRAND BAZAAR**, with the object of raising sufficient funds to place the Club on a sound financial basis, and which would enable the Management to obtain a team capable of securing and maintaining a position in the First Division of the Football League.

There is a strong feeling that Newton Heath and District ought to have, and can support a First Division Club, and the co-operation is, therefore, earnestly requested of all who take an interest in the popular. winter pastime, and who desire the attainment of this object.

To fully achieve this, it is necessary that at least **£1,000** should be forthcoming as the outcome of this Bazaar, and the Committee look forward to the realisation of, what they trust will prove to be, their well-based hopes.

1899-00 | Newton Heath's first official secretary and team manager Alf Albut leaves the club at the end of the season after eight years in charge.

1900-01 | The state of the club at this point is reflected in the attendance at the final home match of the season against Chesterfield, just 1,000 turn up.

The 1901 fund-raising bazaar aimed to raise at least £1,000 to stave off bankruptcy even attracts a donation from rivals Manchester City.

Above: 27 February 1901. A page taken from the Bazaar Programme. "At a large and enthusiastic meeting held in April last year, it was unanimously resolved to hold a GRAND BAZAAR, with the object of raising sufficient funds to place the club on a sound financial basis, and which would enable the Management to obtain a team capable of securing and maintaining a position in the First Division of the Football League."

massive wins – 9-0 against Darwen and 6-1 versus both Loughborough Town and Gainsborough Trinity – mixed with awful away performances, 5-1 losses at Burton Swifts and Arsenal plus a 4-0 beating by Manchester City.

A first round exit in the FA Cup against Tottenham Hotspur left the Heathens with only the league to worry about from early February, but again a very late run of results – unbeaten in the last seven games – left the team in fourth place for the second season in a row.

1899-00: Stagnation on the field and financial problems off it

The stagnation of the team on the field was having an effect off the field as well; Newton Heath were slowly going out of business. Crowds had been steadily falling and proposed ground improvements at Bank Street stadium were costing too much money.

Loosening the ties to the railway company – which provided the club's original funds and leased its original ground in North Road – earlier in the decade had been a risk and now the gamble was starting to look like the wrong option, as the costs of signing good players (plus paying their wages) was taking a toll.

But despite these financial problems, the team continued to play decent football guaranteeing them status in the top half of the Second Division. For the second year running, a host of new players were

brought in and a remarkable number of players for the era – 27 – were used in league and cup games during the season. However, the many team changes seemed only to bring more inconsistency and a third successive fourth-place finish meant continuing frustration. At the end of the season, star forward Joe Cassidy was sold for £250 to Manchester City to help balance the books.

1900-01: Another Manchester Cup win but the financial game is almost lost

By now, Newton Heath were edging ever closer to the brink of financial ruin. A lost court case against the Manchester Evening News almost a decade ago was said to have been the start, but many people close to the club knew that the story was more complicated, with player wages and diminishing crowds also contributing.

On the field under new secretary/manager James West, the Heathens remained marooned in a group of clubs outside the Second Division promotion race. A tenth-place finish was not unexpected from a team that was now in its seventh straight season in the lower level.

Home form was solid as always, mostly because opponents disliked the Bank Street pitch so much, and the defence conceded just nine goals in 15 games there, fewer than the champions Grimsby Town gave up in their home matches.

However, Newton Heath goals were increasingly hard to come by, as the loss of the transferred Joe Cassidy was felt badly; the team failed to score in 12 of 34 league matches and that was not promotion form. Although a Manchester Cup final victory over Manchester City was most welcome, average gates were now down below 6,000 and the club needed funds fast.

1901-02: Manchester United is born and Newton Heath rests in peace

There was now no escaping Newton Heath's fall from grace; from First Division of the Football League to the lower reaches of the Second Division in eight years. And that was just the on-field decline. The issue of potential bankruptcy was now hurting the club to the extent that it was desperate for short-term money to help play its fixtures.

In February 1901, it was decided to stage a fund-raising bazaar over four days at St James's Hall in Oxford Street, Manchester. The team's right back and captain Harry Stafford brought along his giant St Bernard dog, named Major, and strapped a collection box to his back in the hope of increasing donations. The early days of the bazaar had not proved a great success, so Stafford's stunt seemed like just another crazy idea until it set up a chance meeting with the man who would eventually save Newton Heath and transform it into Manchester United.

The exact details of how Stafford met Manchester businessman John Henry Davies and how the funds were secured are now entrenched in club mythology, and various versions of the story exist. One of the most common versions says that on an evening after the day's fund-raising was over, Major the St Bernard went wandering out of the hall and got lost. He was eventually found by a friend of Davies (James Taylor who would later join Davies in his football venture). Legend then has it that the dog-loving Davies wanted to buy Major for his daughter, but had to track down the St Bernard's original owner in order to do so. When Davies met with Stafford, the two men struck up a conversation about the plight of Newton Heath. Stafford initially suggested a donation to the club rather than buying Major, but the wealthy businessman shrewdly could see the potential in the club.

Some time later, in 1902, Newton Heath's president, William Heath, went to court applying for a winding up in order to recover £240 that was owed to him. In fact, the club's debts were some £2,670 – a huge sum then – and a creditors' meeting was held, after which the official receivers padlocked the gates of the Bank Street ground shut.

Home fixtures now had to be played at a temporary venue and an immediate cash injection of £2,000 was required. After an existence of almost a quarter of a century, the Heathens were declared bankrupt and staring at extinction because of poor financial management, the fate of many football clubs at this time, including former Football League counterparts such as Bootle, Burton Swifts and New Brighton Tower.

Harry Stafford led a fightback. The club captain had already been central in borrowing money and begging favours in order to facilitate travelling expenses to games. And after he kept the team playing football, Stafford told creditors that four businessmen he had met through the fund-raiser last year would put up £500 each. Led by Davies, who was managing director of Manchester Breweries and one of the leading businessmen in the city, the future of Newton Heath was saved. Although Davies and his colleagues wanted control of the club in exchange for their investment, this seemed like a small price to pay and the current board had no alternative but to agree.

The next piece of good news was that Stafford and his team were able to complete all 30 games in the league season and the Heathens even won three of their last five games to finish 15th, thus avoiding having to apply to the league for re-election. So, within days of the final game of the 1901-02 season, the changes began.

The first and biggest change was that Newton Heath would become Manchester United Football Club; in addition, the new club colours would be red shirts and white shorts. Davies's involvement immediately galvanised the whole club and he became president. With money to support them, a new name and a football-mad city to play in, Manchester United's future seemed suddenly bright.

1901-02 | When John Henry Davies decides to change the name of the team, alternatives included Manchester Central and Manchester Celtic.

The name of Manchester United is apparently the suggestion of club director Louis Rocca, an Italian immigrant who would play a significant role in United's future.

The three other new directors besides John Henry Davies are his friend James Taylor plus associates J. Brown and W. Deakin.

Harry Stafford is made a club director for bringing in Davies and his colleagues to save the club.

The Grand Bazaar took place between 27 February and 2 March 1902 and aimed to raise at least £1,000. Visitors found the hall split into various geographic areas such as Mediterranean, Eastern, Indian and Egypt & the Nile.

Left: John Davies who rescued Newton Heath financially, would be instrumental in renaming the club Manchester United and orchestrated their move to Old Trafford in 1910.

Overleaf: Newton Heath 1900-01 season. Back row (l-r): unknown (trainer), Mr Anderson (director), Mr Palmer (director), Harry Stafford, (possibly) Mr Deakin (director), Jimmy Whitehouse, Fred Erentz, Mr West (Secretary) Middle row (l-r): Billy Morgan, Billy Griffiths, Walter Cartwright. Front row (l-r): (possibly) Richard Smith, Hugh Morgan, Tom Leigh, unknown, James Fisher.

2

The Seasons

The Seasons

AFTER OVER 120 years of organised league football in England, there is one team that stands out as the most remarkable and the reasons are many. Achieving the status as England's best ever team is not just a question of how many championships and trophies, although Manchester United have won more league titles, more FA Cups and more major trophies in total than any other English professional football club. Neither is it about the number of glamorous players, although again United can top any rival, while in terms of longevity the Red Devils have been winning trophies throughout their history, from 1908 to 2011. And, if 19th century trophies like the Manchester Cup are counted, then significant silverware was in the club cabinet back in the days of Newton Heath LYR. In short, Manchester United is one of the few football clubs in the country that has consistently – and even occasionally tragically – touched the nation's consciousness.

There were the early financial crises of 1902 and 1931; the role of Billy Meredith and Charlie Roberts in setting up a players' union; the emergence of George Best as fifth Beatle, the first indication of footballers as social superstars, like David Beckham a generation later. But most of all, of course, the Munich air crash was an incident that not only took lives but also changed lives; it shocked the whole of the sport and millions beyond; and it imbued the club with a sense of destiny that it was above and beyond football.

The first 24 seasons of United's origins were under the name Newton Heath, a club formed by workers of the Lancashire & Yorkshire Railway Company hungry to play football and with a vision to create a strong and lasting team in the sports-mad city of Manchester. But by 1902, heavy debts caused the club to struggle in the Second Division of the Football League; new investment was required and Manchester United Football Club came into existence.

The new club owners saw the Reds promoted after just four seasons and then secure their inaugural First Division championship in 1907-08, followed by a second three years later with an FA Cup triumph in between. Throw in a couple of Charity Shields and United – with a brand new state-of-the-art stadium in Old Trafford – had become one of the leading clubs in the land, with star names like Billy Meredith revered throughout the game. But World War I came along and the Reds declined again. Second Division football returned for three seasons between 1922 and 1925, and even a return to the top flight could not forestall a second financial crisis.

The club had to be saved from extinction again after another relegation in 1932 and the Reds spent six of the next seven seasons stuck in the Second Division, once only missing relegation to the Third Division North by a single point. Then in 1939, another world war shut down professional sport and, this time, the stoppage worked in United's favour because they emerged with a manager who would become a legend.

Matt Busby was an Army physical training instructor and former Manchester City player when he

took over as the Reds' manager in 1945 and began constructing a team mostly of local young men who had come through the team's youth structure. United won their second FA Cup trophy in 1948 and another league title in 1952 before 'The Busby Babes' became the heartbeat of United's historical story. This was a team in the manager's image that played with an astonishing flair and an unquenchable enthusiasm to attack. Duncan Edwards was the outstanding star among many and these Reds won two First Division championships and became the first British team to reach the European Cup semi-finals. But instead of years of domination, eight Babes including Edwards fell foul of the tragedy of the Munich air crash and the world mourned. The remarkable Busby recovered from near-fatal injuries to create a third winning team and, after another FA Cup and two league trophies were won, the manager finally captured the European Cup in 1968, a victory that seemed to honour the Munich dead as much as it celebrated the new team inspired by Best and led by crash survivor Bobby Charlton.

Busby's departure a year after the club's first triumph in Europe led to seven years in the wilderness and even one season in the Second Division. Various managers tried and failed to live up to the newly knighted Sir Matt's reputation until Alex Ferguson arrived as manager during the 1986-87 season. By now United had won seven First Division titles, six FA Cups and one European Cup, yet the next 24 years under the former Rangers striker and Aberdeen boss, the trophy cabinet would be overflowing.

Starting with an FA Cup win in 1990, the boss would see the trophy cabinet full to overflowing: 12 Premiership titles, five FA Cups, four League Cups, one Cup-Winners' Cup, one Super Cup, one Intercontinental Cup, one Club World Cup, nine Community Shields and, most important of all to the Scot, two Champions League titles.

United, during the Alex Ferguson years, have enjoyed seasons of doubles and even trebles and have been fabulously successful because of the manager's dedication to the legacy of United's attacking principles as well as his incessant desire to continually renew and improve the best team in English football. His own version of the Busby Babes – Fergie's Fledglings with Ryan Giggs, David Beckham Paul Scholes and Gary Neville as the obvious stars – have helped create continuity with a sprinkling of foreign flair from the likes of Eric Cantona, Peter Schmeichel and Cristiano Ronaldo.

There have been off-the-field dramas during these years as well: Cantona's incendiary disciplinary problems; shocking transfers both in and out of the club; and even another new set of owners. But nothing has disturbed the United juggernaut that has driven the Red Devils to a position as perhaps the top football club brand in the world and, with the 19th league title secured in 2011, Liverpool's total of 18 now lies in second place much to the delight of all Reds fans. Manchester United, the top team in history of English football – there are no longer any arguments and long may it continue so.

Top Left: 26 May 1999. Sir Alex Ferguson, United's and possibly football's greatest manager of the modern age, celebrates with the cup in the dressing room in the Nou Camp stadium after the Champions League final.

Top Right: 19 February 1946. Stan Pearson returns to Manchester United after war service and is photographed shaking hands with United's first managerial colossus, Matt Busby.

1902/03

Year one for Manchester United FC means changes galore

- Newly signed centre forward Jack Peddie comes from Newcastle United and scores 15 goals in 36 league and cup games this season.

- Alexander "Alex" Bell arrives from Ayr Parkhouse for a record fee. (The previous highest transfer amount was just £40).

IF MANCHESTER UNITED FC (newly renamed) wanted a sign that the recent changes were all for the good, then it happened on the opening two days of the season: firstly, the team in new red kit beat Gainsborough Trinity 1-0 away and, when they began their home campaign at Bank Street, a good crowd of 15,000 came to watch.

In the spirit of the moment, thankfully, United won their home opener 1-0 against Burton United and the financial impetus from John Henry Davies had found its way onto the field. Although United were not the finished product on the field

just yet, there were certainly more wins than losses this season.

Even in the FA Cup, there was more success than recently; United got through four pre-qualifying rounds (including a 7-0 drubbing of Accrington Stanley) to make the competition proper and then beat Liverpool of the First Division 2-1. A 3-1 defeat at Everton in the second round was no disgrace.

At the end of Manchester United's first season, a fifth place finish in the Second Division was a return to those places just outside the promotion spots, where Newton Heath had hit a glass ceiling. Davies' job was to move the new United past that hurdle.

Final League Table Division Two

		P	W	D	L	F	A	Pt
1	Manchester City	34	25	4	5	95	29	54
2	Birmingham City	34	24	3	7	74	36	51
3	Arsenal	34	20	8	6	66	30	48
4	Bristol City	34	17	8	9	59	38	42
5	**MANCHESTER UNITED**	**34**	**15**	**8**	**11**	**53**	**38**	**38**
6	Chesterfield	34	14	9	11	67	40	37
7	Preston North End	34	13	10	11	56	40	36
8	Barnsley	34	13	8	13	55	51	34
9	Port Vale	34	13	8	13	57	62	34
10	Lincoln City	34	12	6	16	46	53	30
11	Glossop	34	11	7	16	43	58	29
12	Gainsborough Trinity	34	11	7	16	41	59	29
13	Burton United	34	11	7	16	39	59	29
14	Blackpool	34	9	10	15	44	59	28
15	Leicester City	34	10	8	16	41	65	28
16	Doncaster Rovers	34	9	7	18	35	72	25
17	Stockport County	34	7	6	21	39	74	20
18	Burnley	34	6	8	20	30	77	20

Appearances

PLAYER	LGE	FAC	TOT
Peddie	30	6	36
Pegg	28	7	35
Read	27	6	33
Griffiths	25	7	32
Birchenough	25	5	30
Rothwell	22	6	28
Downie	22	5	27
Cartwright	22	4	26
Hurst	16	5	21
Morrison	20	-	20
Schofield	16	4	20
Banks	13	3	16
Morgan	12	2	14
Beadsworth	9	3	12
Stafford	10	2	12
Richards	8	3	11
Smith	8	2	10
Williams	8	2	10

PLAYER	LGE	FAC	TOT
Arkesden	9	-	9
Whitehouse	7	1	8
Marshall	6	-	6
Bell	5	-	5
Fitchett	5	-	5
L'appin	5	-	5
Ball	4	-	4
Preston	4	-	4
Street	1	2	3
Bunce	2	-	2
Hayes	2	-	2
Saunders	1	1	2
Christie	1	-	1
Cleaver	1	-	1
Turner	-	1	1

Goalscorers

PLAYER	LGE	FAC	TOT
Peddie	11	4	15
Pegg	7	6	13
Morrison	7	-	7
Griffiths	4	2	6
Downie	5	-	5
Hurst	4	-	4
Schofield	3	1	4
Williams	-	4	4
Preston	3	-	3
Arkesden	2	-	2
Beadsworth	1	1	2
Richards	1	1	2
Bell	1	-	1
Fitchett	1	-	1
Lappin	1	-	1
Smith	1	-	1
Banks	-	1	1
Morgan	-	1	1
own goal	1	-	1

FOOTBALL LEAGUE DIVISION TWO: FIFTH POSITION

FA CUP: LOSE TO EVERTON (1-3) IN 2ND ROUND.

1903/04

Ernest Mangnall becomes manager amid controversy

- In the intermediate round of the FA Cup, United draw 1-1 with Birmingham City three times before winning the fourth game 3-1.

- The Reds go out of the cup to First Division Sheffield Wednesday 6-0.

BEFORE THE FIRST month of the season was over, United had a new manager. This change happened after another off-field controversy when current secretary James West and club captain Harry Stafford were suspended by the Football Association over alleged illegal payments to players. West resigned in late September, but Stafford defended his actions by saying: "Everything I have done has been in the interests of the club." However, despite those words and the debt that the club owed him for finding John Henry Davies and his money, Stafford never played for United again.

The new secretary-manager was Ernest Mangnall who was brought in from nearby Burnley where he had enjoyed relatively little success. Despite misgivings of some fans, the team continued to build on last season's progress as Mangnall tried out a large group of players – 28 in total – in search of his best team.

The new manager lifted United to third in the league, just a single point from a promotion spot after a run of seven points out of a possible eight in their final four games.

The Bank Street ground again proved difficult for opponents; only champions-to-be Preston North End won there.

Final League Table Division Two

		P	W	D	L	F	A	Pt
1	Preston North End	34	20	10	4	62	24	50
2	Arsenal	34	21	7	6	91	22	49
3	**MANCHESTER UNITED**	**34**	**20**	**8**	**6**	**65**	**33**	**48**
4	Bristol City	34	18	6	10	73	41	42
5	Burnley	34	15	9	10	50	55	39
6	Grimsby Town	34	14	8	12	50	49	36
7	Bolton Wanderers	34	12	10	12	59	41	34
8	Barnsley	34	11	10	13	38	57	32
9	Gainsborough Trinity	34	14	3	17	53	60	31
10	Bradford City	34	12	7	15	45	59	31
11	Chesterfield	34	11	8	15	37	45	30
12	Lincoln City	34	11	8	15	41	58	30
13	Port Vale	34	10	9	15	54	52	29
14	Burton United	34	11	7	16	45	61	29
15	Blackpool	34	11	5	18	40	67	27
16	Stockport County	34	8	11	15	40	72	27
17	Glossop	34	10	6	18	57	64	26
18	Leicester City	34	6	10	18	42	82	22

Appearances

PLAYER	LGE	FAC	TOT
Bonthron	33	7	40
Griffiths	30	7	37
Downie	29	6	35
Schofield A	26	7	33
Arkesden	26	6	32
Robertson A	27	5	32
Grassam	23	5	28
Sutcliffe	21	7	28
Robertson S	24	2	26
Hayes	21	3	24
Morrison	9	7	16
Pegg	13	3	16
Cartwright	9	6	15
McCartney	13	-	13
Moger	13	-	13
Blackstock	7	3	10
Read	8	1	9
Wilkinson	8	1	9

PLAYER	LGE	FAC	TOT
Gaudie	7	1	8
Hall	8	-	8
Bell	6	-	6
Robertson T	3	-	3
Kerr	2	-	2
Lyons	2	-	2
Roberts	2	-	2
Schofield J	2	-	2
Duckworth	1	-	1
Hartwell	1	-	1

New manager Ernest Mangnall was recruited from local rivals Burnley. He was hired as the third manager of United and the second after the club changed its name from Newton Heath.

Goalscorers

PLAYER	LGE	FAC	TOT
Arkesden	11	4	15
Grassam	11	1	12
Griffiths	11	-	11
Robertson A	10	-	10
Schofield A	6	3	9
Pegg	6	1	7
Downie	4	1	5
Hall	2	-	2
Bell	1	-	1
Bonthron	1	-	1
Duckworth	1	-	1
McCartney	1	-	1
Morrison	-	1	1

FOOTBALL LEAGUE DIVISION TWO: THIRD POSITION

FA CUP: LOSE TO SHEFFIELD WEDNESDAY (0-6) IN 2ND ROUND.

Mangnall's men threaten promotion once again

AFTER TRYING A host of players last season, secretary-manager Ernest Mangnall decided instead to acquire talent rather than develop his team from within. The key man was Charlie Roberts, a centre half signed for the considerable amount of £600 from Grimsby Town at the very end of the previous season.

Roberts was a man apart who led United on the field while also helping the move to unionise his footballing colleagues. This was his first season as Mangnall's on-field general and United again chased promotion hard. An opening series of games that featured a 4-1 win over Bristol City as well as a loss and a draw was followed by a run of 18 unbeaten games including a phenomenal 16 wins.

However, four losses during the run-in in April left United three points short of second place while scoring 81 goals, the most for many a year. The Reds scored four or more goals on nine occasions.

Unsurprisingly with so much exciting football being played by United, attendances at Bank Street held up well compared to the euphoria of the inaugural season of the new club.

- During the 18-game unbeaten run, United put six past Port Vale and Doncaster Rovers.

- Jack Peddie returns to Manchester United after a season with Plymouth Argyle and is again top scorer.

Final League Table Division Two

		P	W	D	L	F	A	Pt
1	Liverpool	34	27	4	3	93	25	58
2	Bolton Wanderers	34	27	2	5	87	32	56
3	**MANCHESTER UNITED**	**34**	**24**	**5**	**5**	**81**	**30**	**53**
4	Bristol City	34	19	4	11	66	45	42
5	Chesterfield	34	14	11	9	44	35	39
6	Gainsborough Trinity	34	14	8	12	61	58	36
7	Barnsley	34	14	5	15	38	56	33
8	Bradford City	34	12	8	14	45	49	32
9	Lincoln City	34	12	7	15	42	40	31
10	West Bromwich Albion	34	13	4	17	56	48	30
11	Burnley	34	12	6	16	43	52	30
12	Glossop	34	10	10	14	37	46	30
13	Grimsby Town	34	11	8	15	33	46	30
14	Leicester City	34	11	7	16	40	55	29
15	Blackpool	34	9	10	15	36	48	28
16	Port Vale	34	10	7	17	47	72	27
17	Burton United	34	8	4	22	30	84	20
18	Doncaster Rovers	34	3	2	29	23	81	8

Appearances

PLAYER	LGE	FAC	TOT
Bonthron	32	3	35
Downie	32	3	35
Moger	32	3	35
Bell	29	3	32
Peddie	32	-	32
Arkesden	28	3	31
Roberts	28	-	28
Allan	27	-	27
Schofield	24	3	27
Hayes	22	3	25
Williams	22	2	24
Fitchett	11	2	13
Beddow	9	-	9
Grassam	6	3	9
Duckworth	8	-	8
Robertson S	8	-	8
Wombwell	8	-	8
Mackie	5	2	7

PLAYER	LGE	FAC	TOT
Blackstock	3	-	3
Hartwell	2	1	3
Griffiths	2	-	2
Robertson A	1	1	2
Valentine	2	-	2
Holden	1	-	1
Lyons	-	1	1

The FA Cup match against Fulham played on 14 January 1905 finishes in a 2-2 draw.

Goalscorers

PLAYER	LGE	FAC	TOT
Peddie	17	-	17
Allan	16	-	16
Arkesden	15	1	16
Duckworth	6	-	6
Williams	6	-	6
Roberts	5	-	5
Schofield	4	-	4
Mackie	3	1	4
Grassam	2	-	2
Beddow	1	-	1
Bell	1	-	1
Downie	1	-	1
Hayes	1	-	1
Robertson S	1	-	1
Wombwell	1	-	1
own goal	1	-	1

FOOTBALL LEAGUE DIVISION TWO: THIRD POSITION

FA CUP: LOSE TO FULHAM (0-1) IN INTERMEDIATE ROUND 2ND REPLAY

Promotion at last and a hint of the good times to come

WITH ERNEST MANGNALL now in his third season at the club, United were not to be denied promotion, even with the Second Division expanding from 18 to 20 teams. The campaign could hardly have started better, with six straight wins to begin with, including a 5-1 victory over Bristol City, who would be United's main rivals at the top of the league during the season.

The Reds never stumbled seriously during the league and their run-in of games featured eight wins and a draw in the final ten. Promotion was confirmed with two games to spare, although Bristol were champions by four points. United finished runners-up nine points ahead of Chelsea.

But it was the FA Cup run to the quarter-finals (United's best performance in the competition to date) that caught the fans' imagination. Easy wins over non-league teams Staple Hill and Norwich City brought mighty Aston Villa of the First Division to Bank Street. When they were dispatched 5-1, United's progress under Mangnall was put into better context.

- Billy Meredith is signed 12 October 1906 by the astute United secretary-manager Ernest Mangnall after a bribery scandal at Manchester City, although suspension means he cannot play for the Reds until January 1907.

Final League Table Division Two

		P	W	D	L	F	A	Pt
1	Bristol City	38	30	6	2	83	28	66
2	**MANCHESTER UNITED**	**38**	**28**	**6**	**4**	**90**	**28**	**62**
3	Chelsea	38	22	9	7	90	37	53
4	West Bromwich Albion	38	22	8	8	79	36	52
5	Hull City	38	19	6	13	67	54	44
6	Leeds United	38	17	9	12	59	47	43
7	Leicester City	38	15	12	11	53	48	42
8	Grimsby Town	38	15	10	13	46	46	40
9	Burnley	38	15	8	15	42	53	38
10	Stockport County	38	13	9	16	44	56	35
11	Bradford City	38	13	8	17	46	60	34
12	Barnsley	38	12	9	17	60	62	33
13	Lincoln City	38	12	6	20	69	72	30
14	Blackpool	38	10	9	19	37	62	29
15	Gainsborough Trinity	38	12	4	22	44	57	28
16	Glossop	38	10	8	20	49	71	28
17	Port Vale	38	12	4	22	49	82	28
18	Chesterfield	38	10	8	20	40	72	28
19	Burton United	38	10	6	22	34	67	26
20	Leyton Orient	38	7	7	24	35	78	21

Appearances

PLAYER	LGE	FAC	TOT
Bell	36	4	40
Downie	34	4	38
Roberts	34	4	38
Peddie	34	3	37
Picken	33	4	37
Holden	27	4	31
Moger	27	4	31
Bonthron	26	4	30
Schofield	23	4	27
Wombwell	25	2	27
Sagar	20	3	23
Beddow	21	1	22
Blackstock	21	-	21
Williams	10	2	12
Duckworth	10	-	10
Valentine	8	-	8
Arkesden	7	-	7
Allan	5	1	6
Wall	6	-	6
Donaghy	3	-	3

PLAYER	LGE	FAC	TOT
Montgomery	3	-	3
Lyons	2	-	2
Blew	1	-	1
Dyer	1	-	1
Robertson	1	-	1

Goalscorers

PLAYER	LGE	FAC	TOT
Picken	20	5	25
Peddie	18	2	20
Sagar	16	4	20
Beddow	11	3	14
Allan	5	1	6
Roberts	4	-	4
Schofield	4	-	4
Wall	3	-	3
Bell	2	-	2
Bonthron	2	-	2
Wombwell	2	-	2
Williams	1	1	2
Downie	-	1	1
own goals	2	-	2

Left: The 1905-06 team: Back row (l-r) A. Downie, H. Moger (goalkeeper), R. Bonthron. Middle row (l-r) J. E. Mangnall (Secretary), J. Picken, C. Sagar, T. Blackstock, J. Peddie, F. Bacon (Trainer). Front row J. Beddow, C. Roberts, A. Bell, T. Arkesden.

FOOTBALL LEAGUE DIVISION TWO: RUNNERS-UP (PROMOTED)

FA CUP: LOSE TO WOOLWICH ARSENAL (2-3) IN 4TH ROUND

1906/07

United enjoy First Division return and unexpected help from City

- An estimated 40,000 fans turn up to see the four ex-City men make their debuts in a 1-0 win against Aston Villa.

- Before Meredith & Co begin playing for United in January, the Reds are only 15th in the league.

MANAGER ERNEST MANGNALL always seemed to have a plan and, with United into the First Division, he already had better players in the wings. They came from rivals Manchester City, who had been much more successful at this time. But City had a major problem after an FA investigation had uncovered illegal player payments within the club that caused 17 player suspensions, with some men banned from turning out in City colours ever again.

Many months earlier, Mangnall had signed his first City star, Billy Meredith who joined United because of fallout from a different scandal and now three more players crossed over: Herbert Burgess, Sandy Turnbull and Jimmy Bannister.

All four ex-Sky Blue players started for the Reds in the same match, a 1-0 win against Aston Villa (Turnbull scored from a Meredith cross) and a team that had won only six early season games and could well have been relegated suddenly put 11 wins together in the last 17 games. United finished a comfortable eighth in the league and nine places above City.

Final League Table Division One

		P	W	D	L	F	A	Pt
1	Newcastle United	38	22	7	9	74	46	51
2	Bristol City	38	20	8	10	66	47	48
3	Everton	38	20	5	13	70	46	45
4	Sheffield United	38	17	11	10	57	55	45
5	Aston Villa	38	19	6	13	78	52	44
6	Bolton Wanderers	38	18	8	12	59	47	44
7	Arsenal	38	20	4	14	66	59	44
8	**MANCHESTER UNITED**	**38**	**17**	**8**	**13**	**53**	**56**	**42**
9	Birmingham City	38	15	8	15	52	52	38
10	Sunderland	38	14	9	15	65	66	37
11	Middlesbrough	38	15	6	17	56	63	36
12	Blackburn Rovers	38	14	7	17	56	59	35
13	Sheffield Wednesday	38	12	11	15	49	60	35
14	Preston North End	38	14	7	17	44	57	35
15	Liverpool	38	13	7	18	64	65	33
16	Bury	38	13	6	19	58	68	32
17	Manchester City	38	10	12	16	53	77	32
18	Notts County	38	8	15	15	46	50	31
19	Derby County	38	9	9	20	41	59	27
20	Stoke City	38	8	10	20	41	64	26

Appearances

PLAYER	LGE	FAC	TOT
Moger	38	2	40
Wall	38	2	40
Bell	35	2	37
Roberts	31	1	32
Duckworth	28	2	30
Bonthron	28	1	29
Holden	27	2	29
Picken	26	2	28
Downie	19	1	20
Menzies	17	2	19
Meredith	16	2	18
Burgess	17	-	17
Peddie	16	-	16
Wombwell	14	2	16
Turnbull	15	-	15
Sagar	10	-	10
Schofield	10	-	10
Berry	9	-	9
Bannister	4	-	4
Blackstock	3	1	4

PLAYER	LGE	FAC	TOT
Allan	3	-	3
Beddow	3	-	3
Buckley	3	-	3
Williams	3	-	3
Yates	3	-	3
Young	2	-	2

Goalscorers

PLAYER	LGE	FAC	TOT
Wall	11	2	13
Peddie	6	-	6
Turnbull	6	-	6
Meredith	5	-	5
Picken	4	1	5
Menzies	4	-	4
Sagar	4	-	4
Bell	2	-	2
Downie	2	-	2
Duckworth	2	-	2
Roberts	2	-	2
Schofield	2	-	2
Bannister	1	-	1
Williams	1	-	1
own goal	1	-	1

Left: Season tickets were an object of beauty at this time; this is a photograph of the cover of this season's booklet.

FOOTBALL LEAGUE DIVISION ONE: EIGHTH POSITION

FA CUP: LOSE TO PORTSMOUTH (1-2) IN 1ST ROUND REPLAY.

1907/08

A league championship is captured in style

- Among Sandy Turnbull's 25 league goals this season are a hat-trick against Liverpool in a 4-0 win and all four in a 4-2 victory over Arsenal.

- On 21 December, Sandy Turnbull becomes the first United player to be sent off in a 3-1 win over Manchester City.

The rise of the team had been constant since the financial recovery under John Henry Davies just five short years ago. There was no question that the players brought over from Manchester City by the astute United secretary-manager Ernest Mangnall were quality additions to a team that was already on the move. Three of the former Sky Blues – Billy Meredith, Sandy Turnbull and Jimmy Bannister – scored 40 of the team's 81 league goals this season, but Mangnall's magic was not limited to these players. He had also brought in another goalscorer in

the off-season, Jimmy Turnbull (no relation to Sandy), from Leyton Orient who grabbed 10 goals in 26 league games.

It was the start-of-season surge that set up United's championship, with only two draws and two losses in the 20 games before the end of December. Runners-up Aston Villa may have beaten United towards the end of the season, but the title was bound for Manchester by then. Winning the inaugural Charity Shield at the end of the season against Southern League champions Queens Park Rangers was a bonus.

Final League Table Division One

		P	W	D	L	F	A	Pt
1	**MANCHESTER UNITED**	**38**	**23**	**6**	**9**	**81**	**48**	**52**
2	Aston Villa	38	17	9	12	77	59	43
3	Manchester City	38	16	11	11	62	54	43
4	Newcastle United	38	15	12	11	65	54	42
5	Sheffield Wednesday	38	19	4	15	73	64	42
6	Middlesbrough	38	17	7	14	54	45	41
7	Bury	38	14	11	13	58	61	39
8	Liverpool	38	16	6	16	68	61	38
9	Nottingham Forest	38	13	11	14	59	62	37
10	Bristol City	38	12	12	14	58	61	36
11	Everton	38	15	6	17	58	64	36
12	Preston North End	38	12	12	14	47	53	36
13	Chelsea	38	14	8	16	53	62	36
14	Blackburn Rovers	38	12	12	14	51	63	36
15	Arsenal	38	12	12	14	51	63	36
16	Sunderland	38	16	3	19	78	75	35
17	Sheffield United	38	12	11	15	52	58	35
18	Notts County	38	13	8	17	39	51	34
19	Bolton Wanderers	38	14	5	19	52	58	33
20	Birmingham City	38	9	12	17	40	60	30

Appearances

PLAYER	LGE	FAC	TOT
Meredith	37	4	41
Bannister	36	4	40
Wall	36	4	40
Bell	35	4	39
Duckworth	35	3	38
Roberts	32	3	35
Turnbull A	30	4	34
Moger	29	4	33
Burgess	27	3	30
Holden	26	3	29
Turnbull J	26	3	29
Stacey	18	3	21
Downie	10	-	10
Broomfield	9	-	9
Picken	8	-	8
Halse	6	-	6
Menzies	6	-	6
Berry	3	1	4
Thomson	3	-	3
McGillivray	1	1	2

PLAYER	LGE	FAC	TOT
Dalton	1	-	1
Hulme	1	-	1
Whiteside	1	-	1
Williams	1	-	1
Wilson	1	-	1

Goalscorers

PLAYER	LGE	FAC	TOT
Turnbull A	25	2	27
Wall	19	3	22
Turnbull J	10	1	11
Meredith	10	-	10
Bannister	5	1	6
Halse	4	-	4
Roberts	2	-	2
Bell	1	-	1
Berry	1	-	1
Picken	1	-	1
Stacey	1	-	1
own goals	2	-	2

Left: The inaugural Charity Shield match between United, the First Division champions, and the winners of the Southern League, Queens Park Rangers, is watched by a crowd of 6,000 paying record receipts of £1,054.

FOOTBALL LEAGUE DIVISION ONE: CHAMPIONS

FA CUP: LOSE TO FULHAM (1-2) IN 4TH ROUND

FA CHARITY SHIELD: WINNERS. 29 APRIL 1908. STAMFORD BRIDGE, LONDON.
BEAT QUEENS PARK RANGERS 4-0 J. TURNBULL (3), WALL

A first FA Cup trophy is won but a league title defence fails

THE CLUB WAS now buzzing after winning its first major trophy. This mood was enhanced by plans for a new stadium and a group of talented players that delivered a highly entertaining brand of football. When the champions began the defence of their title on 5 September with a 3-0 win against Preston North End and followed that by reeling off five more wins in the next six games, including a 2-1 victory at Hyde Road against Manchester City, another league title looked highly likely.

However, injuries and poor form followed and the Reds fell foul of an old problem: inconsistency. They suffered a 6-1 loss at Sunderland at the end of October and on 9 January they lost 5-0 at Middlesbrough; this was already the team's seventh defeat, one more than in the whole of last season.

It seemed the longer the cup run lasted the more the league title slipped away. The Red Devils reached their first FA Cup final and beat Bristol City at Crystal Palace, but five days later lost to Bradford City to end their title defence.

■ Owing to injury, Herbert Burgess, one of the four ex-City stars, plays only four games this season and leaves the Reds. At one point he becomes a pub licensee before moving abroad to take up coaching appointments.

Final League Table Division One

		P	W	D	L	F	A	Pt
1	Newcastle United	38	24	5	9	65	41	53
2	Everton	38	18	10	10	82	57	46
3	Sunderland	38	21	2	15	78	63	44
4	Blackburn Rovers	38	14	13	11	61	50	41
5	Sheffield Wednesday	38	17	6	15	67	61	40
6	Arsenal	38	14	10	14	52	49	38
7	Aston Villa	38	14	10	14	58	56	38
8	Bristol City	38	13	12	13	45	58	38
9	Middlesbrough	38	14	9	15	59	53	37
10	Preston North End	38	13	11	14	48	44	37
11	Chelsea	38	14	9	15	56	61	37
12	Sheffield United	38	14	9	15	51	59	37
13	**MANCHESTER UNITED**	38	15	7	16	58	68	37
14	Nottingham Forest	38	14	8	16	66	57	36
15	Notts County	38	14	8	16	51	48	36
16	Liverpool	38	15	6	17	57	65	36
17	Bury	38	14	8	16	63	77	36
18	Bradford City	38	12	10	16	47	47	34
19	Manchester City	38	15	4	19	67	69	34
20	Leicester City	38	8	9	21	54	102	25

Appearances

PLAYER	LGE	FAC	TOT
Moger	36	6	42
Wall	34	6	40
Duckworth	33	6	39
Meredith	34	4	38
Stacey	32	6	38
Halse	29	6	35
Roberts	27	6	33
Hayes	22	6	28
Turnbull J	22	6	28
Bell	20	6	26
Turnbull A	19	6	25
Downie	23	-	23
Bannister	16	-	16
Livingstone	11	2	13
Picken	13	-	13
Linkson	10	-	10
Curry	8	-	8
Burgess	4	-	4
Ford	4	-	4
Hardman	4	-	4

PLAYER	LGE	FAC	TOT
Hulme	3	-	3
Christie	2	-	2
Holden	2	-	2
McGillivray	2	-	2
Payne	2	-	2
Wilcox	2	-	2
Berry	1	-	1
Donnelly	1	-	1
Quinn	1	-	1
Thomson	1	-	1

Goalscorers

PLAYER	LGE	FAC	TOT
Turnbull J	17	5	22
Halse	14	4	18
Wall	11	-	11
Turnbull A	5	4	9
Livingstone	3	-	3
Picken	3	-	3
Bell	2	-	2
Bannister	1	-	1
Payne	1	-	1
Roberts	1	-	1

The FA Cup winning side of 1909. Back row (l-r): A. Downie, H. Burgess. Standing (l-r): J. Taylor (Director), J. Nuttall (Assistant Trainer), H. Stafford (Director), H. Broomfield, G. Stacey, D. Duckworth, R.Holden, A.Bell, H. Moger, F. Bacon (Trainer), J.E. Mangall (Secretary and Manager). Seated (l-r): J. Picken, J. Bannister, J.Turnbull, C. Roberts (Captain), H. Halse, A. Turnbull. Front row (l-r): W. Meredith, G. Wall, and the trophies (l-r): FA Charity Shield, Championship Cup and Manchester Cup.

Old Trafford is opened after the union dispute is settled

THE BATTLE BETWEEN the football authorities and the Association of Football Players' and Trainers Union (known more colloquially as The Players' Union) reached a climax as the season approached.

As the dispute escalated, the Football Association threatened life bans on union members playing for Football League teams after the players threatened to strike over the union's attempts to join the Federation of Trades Unions. With Billy Meredith and Charlie Roberts to the fore, United players were the most solidly in favour of union policies and even undertook pre-season games under the name Outcasts FC.

On the eve of the league season the football authorities backed down and United's outcasts played on as normal. While all this was happening off the field, United were putting the finishing touches to their new stadium, Old Trafford. On 19 February, it opened with a game against Liverpool. The new stadium – initially called United Football Ground – attracted an estimated 45,000 supporters in a mass celebration.

■ Old Trafford is one of the most modern stadiums of that era with fold-up seats and even a plunge bath for the players.

■ The Reds lose their first game in the new stadium, but go on to win all seven remaining matches at home in the league.

Final League Table Division One

		P	W	D	L	F	A	Pt
1	Aston Villa	38	23	7	8	84	42	53
2	Liverpool	38	21	6	11	78	57	48
3	Blackburn Rovers	38	18	9	11	73	55	45
4	Newcastle United	38	19	7	12	70	56	45
5	**MANCHESTER UNITED**	38	19	7	12	69	61	45
6	Sheffield United	38	16	10	12	62	41	42
7	Bradford City	38	17	8	13	64	47	42
8	Sunderland	38	18	5	15	66	51	41
9	Notts County	38	15	10	13	67	59	40
10	Everton	38	16	8	14	51	56	40
11	Sheffield Wednesday	38	15	9	14	60	63	39
12	Preston North End	38	15	5	18	52	58	35
13	Bury	38	12	9	17	62	66	33
14	Nottingham Forest	38	11	11	16	54	72	33
15	Tottenham Hotspur	38	11	10	17	53	69	32
16	Bristol City	38	12	8	18	45	60	32
17	Middlesbrough	38	11	9	18	56	73	31
18	Arsenal	38	11	9	18	37	67	31
19	Chelsea	38	11	7	20	47	70	29
20	Bolton Wanderers	38	9	6	23	44	71	24

Appearances

PLAYER	LGE	FAC	TOT
Moger	36	1	37
Stacey	32	1	33
Wall	32	1	33
Meredith	31	1	32
Hayes	30	1	31
Duckworth	29	1	30
Roberts	28	1	29
Halse	27	1	28
Bell	27	-	27
Turnbull A	26	1	27
Picken	19	1	20
Turnbull J	19	-	19
Homer	17	-	17
Livingstone	16	-	16
Blott	10	-	10
Whalley	9	-	9
Connor	8	-	8
Holden	7	-	7
Donnelly	4	-	4
Downie	3	-	3

PLAYER	LGE	FAC	TOT
Hooper	2	-	2
Round	2	-	2
Bannister	1	-	1
Burgess	1	-	1
Curry	-	1	1
Ford	1	-	1
Quinn	1	-	1

Goalscorers

PLAYER	LGE	FAC	TOT
Wall	14	-	14
Turnbull A	13	-	13
Turnbull J	9	-	9
Homer	8	-	8
Picken	7	-	7
Halse	6	-	6
Meredith	5	-	5
Roberts	4	-	4
Blott	1	-	1
Connor	1	-	1
Hooper	1	-	1

Billy Meredith continued to be the star of the team playing 32 games, scoring five times and creating many more goals for his teammates.

1910/11

A dramatic second league championship is won

- Over 65,000 fans turn up at Old Trafford for the clash-of-the-titans third round FA Cup clash with Aston Villa. United win 2-1.

THE DISRUPTION OF the players' union dispute and changing stadiums were over. The season began with the same storming start as when the Reds had won the title two years ago; seven wins in the first eight games.

A glut of goals from a new forward signed immediately after the end of last season from Nottingham Forest, Enoch 'Knocker' West, was sparking the team. United's main rivals for the title were reigning champions Aston Villa, but the Reds beat the Birmingham team 2-0 in December to at least gain

psychological advantage. However, as the season reached the final stages, Villa looked the favourites. Then came the crucial return match between the two teams at Villa Park in April; it was United's penultimate game and a 4-2 win for Villa seemed to count the Reds out. However, the Birmingham side failed to win either of their own last two games meaning victory for United in their final match against Sunderland would bring a second league championship in four years. A 5-1 win was duly secured and United had another league championship.

Final League Table Division One

		P	W	D	L	F	A	Pt
1	MANCHESTER UNITED	38	22	8	8	72	40	52
2	Aston Villa	38	22	7	9	69	41	51
3	Sunderland	38	15	15	8	67	48	45
4	Everton	38	19	7	12	50	36	45
5	Bradford City	38	20	5	13	51	42	45
6	Sheffield Wednesday	38	17	8	13	47	48	42
7	Oldham Athletic	38	16	9	13	44	41	41
8	Newcastle United	38	15	10	13	61	43	40
9	Sheffield United	38	15	8	15	49	43	38
10	Arsenal	38	13	12	13	41	49	38
11	Notts County	38	14	10	14	37	45	38
12	Blackburn Rovers	38	13	11	14	62	54	37
13	Liverpool	38	15	7	16	53	53	37
14	Preston North End	38	12	11	15	40	49	35
15	Tottenham Hotspur	38	13	6	19	52	63	32
16	Middlesbrough	38	11	10	17	49	63	32
17	Manchester City	38	9	13	16	43	58	31
18	Bury	38	9	11	18	43	71	29
19	Bristol City	38	11	5	22	43	66	27
20	Nottingham Forest	38	9	7	22	55	75	25

Appearances

PLAYER	LGE	FAC	TOT
Stacey	36	3	39
Meredith	35	3	38
Turnbull	35	3	38
West	35	3	38
Roberts	33	3	36
Bell	27	3	30
Wall	26	3	29
Moger	25	2	27
Duckworth	22	3	25
Halse	23	2	25
Donnelly	15	3	18
Picken	14	1	15
Whalley	15	-	15
Edmonds	13	1	14
Livingstone	10	-	10
Hofton	9	-	9
Holden	8	-	8
Connor	7	-	7
Homer	7	-	7
Linkson	7	-	7

PLAYER	LGE	FAC	TOT
Curry	5	-	5
Sheldon	5	-	5
Hodge	2	-	2
Hooper	2	-	2
Blott	1	-	1
Hayes	1	-	1

Goalscorers

PLAYER	LGE	FAC	TOT
West	19	1	20
Turnbull	18	1	19
Halse	9	1	10
Homer	6	-	6
Wall	5	1	6
Meredith	5	-	5
Picken	4	1	5
Duckworth	2	-	2
Connor	1	-	1
Roberts	1	-	1
own goals	2	-	2

Left: George Stacey (right) was United's left back and played more games than any other player this season. Here he is seen during pre-season training wearing very English headgear.

FOOTBALL LEAGUE DIVISION ONE: CHAMPIONS

FA CUP: LOSE TO WEST HAM UNITED (1-2) IN 3RD ROUND

1911/12

The reigning league champions again let themselves down

- The season's only highlight is that United win the FA Charity Shield for the second time, beating Southern League champions Swindon Town 8-4.

- United finish the season in 13th place, but just four points safe from relegation.

THESE WERE VOLATILE times in English football. The players' union dispute and the heavy-handed nature of the football authorities' decisions had left scars on the game and teams that ruled the game a few years ago were just as likely to drift into mediocrity as not.

In the last few years, United had become a team of surprises: a league title one year, mid-table the next. And so it was again. Billy Meredith and Charlie Roberts still led the reigning champions, but something was missing. There was no rocket-like

start and although the first half of the season was reasonable (just five losses before January), the second half was awful.

Not only did United lose nine games in this period, but there were very heavy defeats, all away from Old Trafford. A 4-0 loss to Everton on 6 January was followed by 5-0 at Sunderland, 6-0 at Aston Villa and 6-1 at Sheffield United.

The Red Devils made a brave stab at the FA Cup – losing in the quarter-finals – but only a burst of five points out of six in the last three games took them out of relegation worries.

Final League Table Division One

		P	W	D	L	F	A	Pt
1	Blackburn Rovers	38	20	9	9	60	43	49
2	Everton	38	20	6	12	46	42	46
3	Newcastle United	38	18	8	12	64	50	44
4	Bolton Wanderers	38	20	3	15	54	43	43
5	Sheffield Wednesday	38	16	9	13	69	49	41
6	Aston Villa	38	17	7	14	76	63	41
7	Middlesbrough	38	16	8	14	56	45	40
8	Sunderland	38	14	11	13	58	51	39
9	West Bromwich Albion	38	15	9	14	43	47	39
10	Arsenal	38	15	8	15	55	59	38
11	Bradford City	38	15	8	15	46	50	38
12	Tottenham Hotspur	38	14	9	15	53	53	37
13	MANCHESTER UNITED	38	13	11	14	45	60	37
14	Sheffield United	38	13	10	15	63	56	36
15	Manchester City	38	13	9	16	56	58	35
16	Notts County	38	14	7	17	46	63	35
17	Liverpool	38	12	10	16	49	55	34
18	Oldham Athletic	38	12	10	16	46	54	34
19	Preston North End	38	13	7	18	40	57	33
20	Bury	38	6	9	23	32	59	21

Appearances

PLAYER	LGE	FAC	TOT
Meredith	35	6	41
Wall	33	6	39
Bell	32	6	38
West	32	6	38
Roberts	32	5	37
Edmonds	30	6	36
Turnbull	30	6	36
Stacey	29	6	35
Duckworth	26	6	32
Halse	24	6	30
Linkson	21	4	25
Hamill	16	-	16
Donnelly	13	-	13
Hodge	10	-	10
Holden	6	2	8
Hofton	7	-	7
Knowles	7	-	7
Blott	6	-	6
Moger	6	-	6
Nuttall	6	-	6

PLAYER	LGE	FAC	TOT
Whalley	5	1	6
Sheldon	5	-	5
Royals	2	-	2
Anderson	1	-	1
Capper	1	-	1
Homer	1	-	1
Livingstone	1	-	1
McCarthy	1	-	1

Arsenal forwards give United keeper Hugh Edmonds (with cap) a hard time during a match at Plumstead. The Reds lost 2-1.

Goalscorers

PLAYER	LGE	FAC	TOT
West	17	6	23
Halse	8	4	12
Turnbull	7	3	10
Wall	3	1	4
Meredith	3	-	3
Nuttall	2	-	2
Roberts	2	-	2
Stacey	2	-	2
Hamill	1	-	1
own goal	-	1	1

United's George Wall who won seven England international caps from 1907-1913.

FOOTBALL LEAGUE DIVISION ONE: THIRTEENTH POSITION

FA CUP: LOSE TO BLACKBURN ROVERS (2-4) IN 4TH ROUND REPLAY

FA CHARITY SHIELD: WINNERS, 25 SEPTEMBER 1911. STAMFORD BRIDGE, LONDON. BEAT SWINDON TOWN 8-4 HALSE (6), TURNBULL, WALL.

Ernest Mangnall leaves for Manchester City and a decline begins

1912/13

JUST DAYS BEFORE Ernest Mangnall was about to start his tenth year as United manager, he exited the club. Obviously, the timing of the move was highly damaging to United, but that fact paled into insignificance when fans learned that Mangnall – the man who had brought two league titles and an FA Cup win to the Red Devils – was heading for Manchester City, the very club whose players had formed the backbone of his title-winning team.

However, despite the loss of their off-field leader, the likes of long-time stars Charlie Roberts and Billy Meredith were still leading the team on the field. Mangnall's ex-charges fought hard in both league and cup for new manager John 'JJ' Bentley and even beat eventual runners-up Aston Villa 4-0 in March.

A fourth place finish – two places above City and only four points out of second place – was something of a surprise, but the team of champions that Mangnall had built was starting to break up and United no longer had the finances to counter the decline that was coming.

- In the pre-season, regular goalscorer Harry Halse is sold to Aston Villa for £1,200 as United begin to struggle financially.

- A hat-trick on 14 December against Newcastle United by Enoch West wins the game 3-1 for the Reds.

Final League Table Division One

		P	W	D	L	F	A	Pt
1	Sunderland	38	25	4	9	86	43	54
2	Aston Villa	38	19	12	7	86	52	50
3	Sheffield Wednesday	38	21	7	10	75	55	49
4	MANCHESTER UNITED	38	19	8	11	69	43	46
5	Blackburn Rovers	38	16	13	9	79	43	45
6	Manchester City	38	18	8	12	53	37	44
7	Derby County	38	17	8	13	69	66	42
8	Bolton Wanderers	38	16	10	12	62	63	42
9	Oldham Athletic	38	14	14	10	50	55	42
10	West Bromwich Albion	38	13	12	13	57	50	38
11	Everton	38	15	7	16	48	54	37
12	Liverpool	38	16	5	17	61	71	37
13	Bradford City	38	12	11	15	50	60	35
14	Newcastle United	38	13	8	17	47	47	34
15	Sheffield United	38	14	6	18	56	70	34
16	Middlesbrough	38	11	10	17	55	69	32
17	Tottenham Hotspur	38	12	6	20	45	72	30
18	Chelsea	38	11	6	21	51	73	28
19	Notts County	38	7	9	22	28	56	23
20	Arsenal	38	3	12	23	26	74	18

Appearances

PLAYER	LGE	FAC	TOT
Beale	37	5	42
Stacey	36	5	41
Wall	36	5	41
West	36	4	40
Turnbull	35	4	39
Whalley	26	5	31
Anderson	24	5	29
Duckworth	24	5	29
Roberts	24	5	29
Meredith	22	5	27
Bell	26	-	26
Hodge	19	5	24
Hamill	15	2	17
Linkson	17	-	17
Sheldon	16	-	16
Nuttall	10	-	10
Hunter	3	-	3
Blott	2	-	2
Gipps	2	-	2
Holden	2	-	2

PLAYER	LGE	FAC	TOT
Knowles	2	-	2
Livingstone	2	-	2
Donnelly	1	-	1
Mew	1	-	1

Goalscorers

PLAYER	LGE	FAC	TOT
West	21	1	22
Anderson	12	2	14
Wall	10	2	12
Turnbull	10	-	10
Whalley	4	-	4
Hunter	2	-	2
Meredith	2	-	2
Nuttall	2	-	2
Roberts	1	1	2
Blott	1	-	1
Hamill	1	-	1
Livingstone	1	-	1
Sheldon	1	-	1
Stacey	1	-	1

On 2 December 1907 Charlie Roberts and Billy Meredith convened the organisation of the Association of Football Players' and Trainers' union at the Imperial Hotel, Manchester. The Union was formed because the Football League had ratified a maximum wage for footballers in 1901 of just £4. This is the union badge.

FOOTBALL LEAGUE DIVISION ONE: FOURTH POSITION

FA CUP: LOSE TO OLDHAM ATHLETIC (1-2) IN 3RD ROUND REPLAY.

The debt burden of Old Trafford takes a heavy toll

1913/14

JUST FOUR SEASONS after the opening of Old Trafford, the debt on the new stadium was becoming a millstone. Other leading clubs saw what was happening and immediately started signing United's best players. With their finances so stretched, the Reds were forced to sell. The most notable casualty was club captain Charlie Roberts who was shipped to Oldham Athletic just before the season began.

After that loss, United were definitely short of leaders and talent. There were still just enough good players to keep the Reds in the First Division, but the signs were ominous, the club had slipped off its lofty perch. Two away losses – 5-0 at Everton in December and then 6-1 at Bolton Wanderers a month later – were not good news, but things got worse when Aston Villa came to Old Trafford in March; a poor United side were comprehensively thumped 6-0.

United finished a sorry 14th in the league, just six points above the relegation zone, and even lost their opening FA Cup match to Swindon Town of the Southern League.

- Despite a poor season, United pick up three out of four points against champions Blackburn Rovers, winning 1-0 at Ewood Park and drawing 0-0 at Old Trafford.

Final League Table Division One

		P	W	D	L	F	A	Pt
1	Blackburn Rovers	38	20	11	7	78	42	51
2	Aston Villa	38	19	6	13	65	50	44
3	Middlesbrough	38	19	5	14	77	60	43
4	Oldham Athletic	38	17	9	12	55	45	43
5	West Bromwich Albion	38	15	13	10	46	42	43
6	Bolton Wanderers	38	16	10	12	65	52	42
7	Sunderland	38	17	6	15	63	52	40
8	Chelsea	38	16	7	15	46	55	39
9	Bradford City	38	12	14	12	40	40	38
10	Sheffield United	38	16	5	17	63	60	37
11	Newcastle United	38	13	11	14	39	48	37
12	Burnley	38	12	12	14	61	53	36
13	Manchester City	38	14	8	16	51	53	36
14	MANCHESTER UNITED	38	15	6	17	52	62	36
15	Everton	38	12	11	15	46	55	35
16	Liverpool	38	14	7	17	46	62	35
17	Tottenham Hotspur	38	12	10	16	50	62	34
18	Sheffield Wednesday	38	13	8	17	53	70	34
19	Preston North End	38	12	6	20	52	69	30
20	Derby County	38	8	11	19	55	71	27

Appearances

PLAYER	LGE	FAC	TOT
Meredith	34	1	35
Stacey	34	1	35
Anderson	32	-	32
Beale	31	1	32
West	30	1	31
Wall	29	1	30
Hodge, James	28	1	29
Hamill	26	-	26
Knowles	18	1	19
Whalley	18	1	19
Turnbull	17	1	18
Haywood	14	-	14
Travers	13	-	13
Woodcock	11	1	12
Gipps	11	-	11
Duckworth	9	-	9
Hudson	9	-	9
Norton	8	-	8
Hunter	7	-	7
Potts	6	-	6

PLAYER	LGE	FAC	TOT
Thomson	6	-	6
Royals	5	-	5
Chorlton	4	-	4
Hodge, John	4	-	4
Livingstone	3	1	4
Cashmore	3	-	3
Hooper	3	-	3
Mew	2	-	2
Roberts	2	-	2
Rowe	1	-	1

Goalscorers

PLAYER	LGE	FAC	TOT
Anderson	15	-	15
Wall	11	-	11
West	6	-	6
Travers	4	-	4
Turnbull	4	-	4
Meredith	2	-	2
Whalley	2	-	2
Woodcock	2	-	2
Knowles	1	-	1
Potts	1	-	1
Stacey	1	-	1
Thomson	1	-	1
own goals	2	-	2

Left: Tottenham Hotspur's goalkeeper makes a save during a league match against United at Old Trafford.

FOOTBALL LEAGUE DIVISION ONE: FOURTEENTH POSITION

FA CUP: LOSE TO SWINDON TOWN (0-1) IN 1ST ROUND.

1914/15

Three United players are banned as World War One begins

- Jack Robson comes to manage United after three jobs as club secretary and manager at Middlesbrough, Crystal Palace and Brighton & Hove Albion.

ALTHOUGH WORLD WAR I began in the summer of 1914, it did not stop the First Division league fixtures starting on 2 September. With the war predicted to be over by Christmas, football continued as normal for a whole season.

However, the slump that United were now in continued and another new manager, John 'Jack' Robson was not going to stop it. With relegation looming, another forgettable season looked likely until 2 April – Good Friday – when United beat Liverpool 2-0. Within days a betting scandal erupted. Both

clubs were accused and in the end, three players from United, four from Liverpool and one from Chester were banned for life. United's disgraced three were Sandy Turnbull, Enoch West, and Arthur Whalley. The effect on United's form was devastating and only a win against strugglers Chelsea in their penultimate game helped save them from relegation.

Only regional football would be played during the war years, in which all disgraced United players served. The authorities would slowly rescind the bans - 1945 in the case of West.

Final League Table Division One

		P	W	D	L	F	A	Pt
1	Everton	38	19	8	11	76	47	46
2	Oldham Athletic	38	17	11	10	70	56	45
3	Blackburn Rovers	38	18	7	13	83	61	43
4	Burnley	38	18	7	13	61	47	43
5	Manchester City	38	15	13	10	49	39	43
6	Sheffield United	38	15	13	10	49	41	43
7	Sheffield Wednesday	38	15	13	10	61	54	43
8	Sunderland	38	18	5	15	81	72	41
9	Bradford Park Avenue	38	17	7	14	69	65	41
10	West Bromwich Albion	38	15	10	13	49	43	40
11	Bradford City	38	13	14	11	55	49	40
12	Middlesbrough	38	13	12	13	62	74	38
13	Liverpool	38	14	9	15	65	75	37
14	Aston Villa	38	13	11	14	62	72	37
15	Newcastle United	38	11	10	17	46	48	32
16	Notts County	38	9	13	16	41	57	31
17	Bolton Wanderers	38	11	8	19	68	84	30
18	**MANCHESTER UNITED**	38	9	12	17	46	62	30
19	Chelsea	38	8	13	17	51	65	29
20	Tottenham Hotspur	38	8	12	18	57	90	28

Appearances

PLAYER	LGE	FAC	TOT
Beale	37	1	38
O'Connell	34	1	35
West	33	1	34
Norton	29	-	29
Meredith	26	1	27
Hodge, John	26	-	26
Stacey	24	1	25
Anderson	23	1	24
Knowles	19	-	19
Woodcock	19	-	19
Wall	17	1	18
Potts	17	-	17
Hunter	15	1	16
Cookson	12	1	13
Turnbull	13	-	13
Allman	12	-	12
Haywood	12	-	12
Spratt	12	-	12
Montgomery	11	-	11
Gipps	10	-	10

PLAYER	LGE	FAC	TOT
Travers	8	-	8
Hodge, James	4	1	5
Hudson	2	-	2
Fox	-	1	1
Mew	1	-	1
Prince	1	-	1
Whalley	1	-	1

Goalscorers

PLAYER	LGE	FAC	TOT
Anderson	10	-	10
West	9	-	9
Woodcock	7	-	7
Potts	4	-	4
Stacey	4	-	4
Norton	3	-	3
Hunter	2	-	2
O'Connell	2	-	2
Turnbull	2	-	2
Wall	2	-	2
own goal	1	-	1

Left: 24 April 1915. Wounded soldiers watch the FA Cup final at Old Trafford between Sheffield United and Chelsea. Staged in Manchester rather than at Crystal Palace to avoid travel disruption in London, it was almost the last match before competitive football was abandoned because of the war.

FOOTBALL LEAGUE DIVISION ONE: EIGHTEENTH POSITION

FA CUP: LOSE TO SHEFFIELD WEDNESDAY (0-1) IN 1ST ROUND.

1919/20

After war ends, a new team emerges under Jack Robson

- This season sees the First Division expand from 20 teams to 22 with two teams relegated; United finish just four points off 21st place.

- Joe Spence debuts and finishes top scorer with 14 goals.

AFTER THE DEVASTATION of World War I, there were few football clubs in good shape either commercially or in terms of playing staff. United were no exception. Some players, like goal-scoring forward Sandy Turnbull, had been killed in the conflict while many others had left the club or were ageing. In addition, the Old Trafford ground was proving a financial albatross and the winning years of Ernest Mangnall's pre-war team seemed long gone.

Jack Robson, now aged 59 and who had been appointed before the war, remained in charge and led the team to 12th place in the First Division while United lost in the second round of the FA Cup to eventual winners Aston Villa. The only player of note to return to United was the remarkable Billy Meredith, although the shortage of money at the club in particular and within football in general made the star forward reluctant to renew his playing career.

Final League Table Division One

		P	W	D	L	F	A	Pt
1	West Bromwich Albion	42	28	4	10	104	47	60
2	Burnley	42	21	9	12	65	59	51
3	Chelsea	42	22	5	15	56	51	49
4	Liverpool	42	19	10	13	59	44	48
5	Sunderland	42	22	4	16	72	59	48
6	Bolton Wanderers	42	19	9	14	72	65	47
7	Manchester City	42	18	9	15	71	62	45
8	Newcastle United	42	17	9	16	44	39	43
9	Aston Villa	42	18	6	18	75	73	42
10	Arsenal	42	15	12	15	56	58	42
11	Bradford Park Avenue	42	15	12	15	60	63	42
12	**MANCHESTER UNITED**	42	13	14	15	54	50	40
13	Middlesbrough	42	15	10	17	61	65	40
14	Sheffield United	42	16	8	18	59	69	40
15	Bradford City	42	14	11	17	54	63	39
16	Everton	42	12	14	16	69	68	38
17	Oldham Athletic	42	15	8	19	49	52	38
18	Derby County	42	13	12	17	47	57	38
19	Preston North End	42	14	10	18	57	73	38
20	Blackburn Rovers	42	13	11	18	64	77	37
21	Notts County	42	12	12	18	56	74	36
22	Sheffield Wednesday	42	7	9	26	28	64	23

Appearances

PLAYER	LGE	FAC	TOT
Mew	42	2	44
Hopkin	39	2	41
Silcock	40	1	41
Meehan	36	2	38
Moore	36	2	38
Hilditch	32	2	34
Spence	32	1	33
Woodcock	28	2	30
Whalley	23	2	25
Grimwood	22	2	24
Bissett	22	-	22
Meredith	19	2	21
Hodges	18	-	18
Hodge	16	-	16
Montgomery	14	-	14
Toms	12	1	13
Barlow	7	-	7
Harris	7	-	7
Forster	5	-	5
Potts	4	1	5
Robinson	2	-	2
Sapsford	2	-	2

PLAYER	LGE	FAC	TOT
Williamson	2	-	2
Prentice	1	-	1
Spratt	1	-	1

Goalscorers

PLAYER	LGE	FAC	TOT
Spence	14	-	14
Woodcock	11	1	12
Bissett	6	-	6
Hopkin	5	-	5
Hodges	4	-	4
Toms	3	1	4
Hilditch	2	-	2
Hodge	2	-	2
Meehan	2	-	2
Meredith	2	-	2
Grimwood	1	-	1
Harris	1	-	1
Montgomery	1	-	1

Tommy Meehan played for Rochdale during the First World War before moving to United in 1919 and made 53 appearances, scoring six goals. He signed for Chelsea in 1920 for £3,300. At the time of his move south, Meehan was rated one of the best half-backs in England, making his debut for the national side in October 1923.

FOOTBALL LEAGUE DIVISION ONE: TWELFTH POSITION

FA CUP: LOSE TO ASTON VILLA (1-2) IN 2ND ROUND.

Billy Meredith leaves after 15 years to work with arch-rivals City

1920/21

UNITED BEGAN THIS season in average form and manager Jack Robson could do little to change that. The good news was that fans were returning to football grounds – including Old Trafford – in huge numbers by now and crowds of 40,000-plus were commonplace. In fact, this season's average home gate was 37,000, more than 10,000 per game higher than the previous season.

However, United was still a mid-table team almost from start to finish, and 13th was just about what they deserved. Even the FA Cup was disappointing as Liverpool put United out after a first round replay. The Reds needed a goalscorer, but no player stepped forward as four men, including Joe Spence, top-scored with only seven league goals each.

Billy Meredith played only 14 league games and contributed just one goal. Meredith left Old Trafford at the end of the season to become player/coach at arch-rivals Manchester City.

- Billy Meredith joins Manchester City aged 46 and plays only one more full season after this one, making just a handful of appearances for two more.

Final League Table Division One

		P	W	D	L	F	A	Pt
1	Burnley	42	23	13	6	79	36	59
2	Manchester City	42	24	6	12	70	50	54
3	Bolton Wanderers	42	19	14	9	77	53	52
4	Liverpool	42	18	15	9	63	35	51
5	Newcastle United	42	20	10	12	66	45	50
6	Tottenham Hotspur	42	19	9	14	70	48	47
7	Everton	42	17	13	12	66	55	47
8	Middlesbrough	42	17	12	13	53	53	46
9	Arsenal	42	15	14	13	59	63	44
10	Aston Villa	42	18	7	17	63	70	43
11	Blackburn Rovers	42	13	15	14	57	59	41
12	Sunderland	42	14	13	15	57	60	41
13	**MANCHESTER UNITED**	**42**	**15**	**10**	**17**	**64**	**68**	**40**
14	West Bromwich Albion	42	13	14	15	54	58	40
15	Bradford City	42	12	15	15	61	63	39
16	Preston North End	42	15	9	18	61	65	39
17	Huddersfield Town	42	15	9	18	42	49	39
18	Chelsea	42	13	13	16	48	58	39
19	Oldham Athletic	42	9	15	18	49	86	33
20	Sheffield United	42	6	18	18	42	68	30
21	Derby County	42	5	16	21	32	58	26
22	Bradford Park Avenue	42	8	8	26	43	76	24

Appearances

PLAYER	LGE	FAC	TOT
Mew	40	2	42
Silcock	37	2	39
Hilditch	34	-	34
Hopkin	31	2	33
Partridge	28	2	30
Harris	26	2	28
Forster	26	1	27
Grimwood	25	2	27
Miller	25	2	27
Moore	26	-	26
Harrison	23	2	25
Sapsford	21	-	21
Barlow	19	1	20
Meehan	15	-	15
Spence	15	-	15
Bissett	12	2	14
Meredith	14	-	14
Myerscough	13	-	13
Leonard	10	-	10
Robinson	7	-	7
Goodwin	5	-	5
Hodges	2	-	2

PLAYER	LGE	FAC	TOT
Hofton	1	1	2
Montgomery	2	-	2
Steward	2	-	2
Albinson	-	1	1
Radford	1	-	1
Schofield	1	-	1
Toms	1	-	1

Goalscorers

PLAYER	LGE	FAC	TOT
Miller	7	1	8
Partridge	7	1	8
Sapsford	7	-	7
Spence	7	-	7
Leonard	5	-	5
Myerscough	5	-	5
Bissett	4	-	4
Grimwood	4	-	4
Meehan	4	-	4
Harrison	3	-	3
Hopkin	3	-	3
Robinson	2	-	2
Goodwin	1	-	1
Harris	1	-	1
Hilditch	1	-	1
Meredith	1	-	1
Silcock	1	-	1
own goal	1	-	1

Left: John Mew (back row, middle) and Jack Silcock (to his left) in the North England team at Burnley, Lancashire.

FOOTBALL LEAGUE DIVISION ONE: THIRTEENTH POSITION

FA CUP: LOSE TO LIVERPOOL (1-2) IN 1ST ROUND REPLAY.

A dismal season featuring managerial change ends in relegation

1921/22

JACK ROBSON'S REIGN as United manager was to end in October of this season. Ill-health was affecting him badly and the team was under-performing, so he was replaced after being in charge for less than four seasons. In his place Scot John Chapman, who had previously managed only one club (Airdrieonians) in the Scottish leagues, took charge.

But the change of manager could not halt the downturn in form and John Chapman's term in office would begin disappointingly when his first 14 league games resulted in just a single victory. During this poor run, United were also dumped out of the FA Cup by Cardiff City, who beat them 4-1 at Old Trafford.

The slide to relegation was almost inevitable and four wins before the end of the season were not enough to prevent Manchester United finishing 22nd and last in the First Division, eight points from safety.

- United win just one game away from home this season, a 1-0 victory against Birmingham City on 8 February.

- United's former secretary Ernest Mangnall, who had moved to Manchester City almost a decade earlier, opens the new Maine Road stadium to much fanfare.

Final League Table Division One

		P	W	D	L	F	A	Pt
1	Liverpool	42	22	13	7	63	36	57
2	Tottenham Hotspur	42	21	9	12	65	39	51
3	Burnley	42	22	5	15	72	54	49
4	Cardiff City	42	19	10	13	61	53	48
5	Aston Villa	42	22	3	17	74	55	47
6	Bolton Wanderers	42	20	7	15	68	59	47
7	Newcastle United	42	18	10	14	59	45	46
8	Middlesbrough	42	16	14	12	79	69	46
9	Chelsea	42	17	12	13	40	43	46
10	Manchester City	42	18	9	15	65	70	45
11	Sheffield United	42	15	10	17	59	54	40
12	Sunderland	42	16	8	18	60	62	40
13	West Bromwich Albion	42	15	10	17	51	63	40
14	Huddersfield Town	42	15	9	18	53	54	39
15	Blackburn Rovers	42	13	12	17	54	57	38
16	Preston North End	42	13	12	17	42	65	38
17	Arsenal	42	15	7	20	47	56	37
18	Birmingham City	42	15	7	20	48	60	37
19	Oldham Athletic	42	13	11	18	38	50	37
20	Everton	42	12	12	18	57	55	36
21	Bradford City	42	11	10	21	48	72	32
22	**MANCHESTER UNITED**	**42**	**8**	**12**	**22**	**41**	**73**	**28**

Appearances

PLAYER	LGE	FAC	TOT
Mew	41	1	42
Partridge	37	1	38
Silcock	36	-	36
Spence	35	1	36
Lochhead	31	1	32
Hilditch	29	1	30
Sapsford	29	1	30
Grimwood	28	-	28
Radford	26	1	27
Scott	23	1	24
McBain	21	1	22
Harrison	21	-	21
Bennion	15	-	15
Harris	13	1	14
Gibson	11	1	12
Robinson	12	-	12
Brett	10	-	10
Henderson	10	-	10
Myerscough	7	-	7
Bissett	6	-	6
Forster	4	-	4
Howarth	4	-	4

PLAYER	LGE	FAC	TOT
Barlow	3	-	3
Thomas	3	-	3
Goodwin	2	-	2
Haslam	1	-	1
Pugh	1	-	1
Schofield	1	-	1
Steward	1	-	1
Taylor	1	-	1

Goalscorers

PLAYER	LGE	FAC	TOT
Spence	15	-	15
Sapsford	9	1	10
Lochhead	8	-	8
Partridge	4	-	4
Harrison	2	-	2
Henderson	2	-	2
Robinson	1	-	1

John Mew made the most appearances for the Red Devils in the 1921/22 season and will win one England international cap.

FOOTBALL LEAGUE DIVISION ONE: TWENTY SECOND POSITION (RELEGATED)

FA CUP: LOSE TO CARDIFF CITY (1-4) IN 1ST ROUND.

1922/23

The new manager brings in new blood yet still misses promotion

- United beat all the three teams who finish ahead of them in the league including champions Notts County 6-1 away from home.

THIS WAS UNITED'S first season in the Second Division for 16 years and, although most of the players from last season returned, manager John Chapman also brought in new blood in half back Frank Barson from Aston Villa for a massive £5,000 transfer fee in pre-season and goal-scorer Ernie Goldthorpe from Leeds United in November.

There was an early inkling of better times ahead when the team opened with six wins and two losses in its first eight games, yet a poor run then followed of 13 games and just two victories. With Goldthorpe's 13 league goals and Barson in a defence that let in just 36 goals in 42 games, United staged a late run for promotion. But just four points from the last four games was not enough to challenge for the top two spots and United took fourth place, just three points short of a First Division return.

Final League Table Division Two

		P	W	D	L	F	A	Pt
1	Notts County	42	23	7	12	46	34	53
2	West Ham United	42	20	11	11	63	38	51
3	Leicester City	42	21	9	12	65	44	51
4	MANCHESTER UNITED	42	17	14	11	51	36	48
5	Blackpool	42	18	11	13	60	43	47
6	Bury	42	18	11	13	55	46	47
7	Leeds United	42	18	11	13	43	36	47
8	Sheffield Wednesday	42	17	12	13	54	47	46
9	Barnsley	42	17	11	14	62	51	45
10	Fulham	42	16	12	14	43	32	44
11	Southampton	42	14	14	14	40	40	42
12	Hull City	42	14	14	14	43	45	42
13	South Shields	42	15	10	17	35	44	40
14	Derby County	42	14	11	17	46	50	39
15	Bradford City	42	12	13	17	41	45	37
16	Crystal Palace	42	13	11	18	54	62	37
17	Port Vale	42	14	9	19	39	51	37
18	Coventry City	42	15	7	20	46	63	37
19	Leyton Orient	42	12	12	18	40	50	36
20	Stockport County	42	14	8	20	43	58	36
21	Rotherham United	42	13	9	20	44	63	35
22	Wolverhampton Wanderers	42	9	9	24	42	77	27

Appearances

PLAYER	LGE	FAC	TOT
Mew	41	3	44
Silcock	37	3	40
Grimwood	36	3	39
Lochhead	34	3	37
Radford	34	3	37
Spence	35	2	37
Hilditch	32	3	35
Barson	31	3	34
Partridge	30	3	33
Goldthorpe	22	3	25
McBain	21	-	21
Thomas	18	-	18
Wood	15	1	16
Bennion	14	-	14
Myerscough	13	1	14
Moore	12	-	12
Mann	10	-	10
Williams	5	-	5
Bain	4	-	4
Barber	2	1	3
Cartman	3	-	3
Lievesley	2	1	3
Lyner	3	-	3
Henderson	2	-	2
MacDonald	2	-	2
Broome	1	-	1
Pugh	1	-	1
Sarvis	1	-	1
Steward	1	-	1

A colour illustration presented with Football Favourite in October 1922, shows Jack Silcock of United and England. Silcock played for the Reds at full back from 1919 to 1934 and gained three England caps 1921-23.

Goalscorers

PLAYER	LGE	FAC	TOT
Goldthorpe	13	1	14
Lochhead	13	-	13
Spence	11	-	11
Myerscough	3	-	3
McBain	2	-	2
Williams	2	-	2
Bain	1	-	1
Henderson	1	-	1
Hilditch	1	-	1
MacDonald	1	-	1
Radford	1	-	1
Wood	1	-	1
Barber	-	1	1
Partridge	-	1	1
own goal	1	-	1

1923/24

United settle for mid-table again in the Second Division

- United take three points out of a possible four from champions-to-be Leeds United when they play the Yorkshire team twice in December.

ANY SUPPORTERS WHO believed that United's spirited previous season meant they were now ready for promotion back to the First Division were going to be sadly disappointed. Although three wins began this campaign, it was about as close as United would get to the Second Division promotion race. Star forward Ernie Goldthorpe was suffering from a severe knee injury and could manage only four league games, so the team's goal scoring was not up to standard; the Reds failed to score in 16 of their 42 league games.

In addition, United were poor away from Old Trafford (just three wins and 15 goals in 21 games) and also lacked consistency. A run of just one win in ten games around the turn of the year put paid to any thoughts of promotion and United settled for 14th place in a hard-fought league. And there was no consolation of a long FA Cup run as Huddersfield Town beat United 3-0 at Old Trafford in the second round.

Final League Table Division Two

		P	W	D	L	F	A	Pt
1	Leeds United	42	21	12	9	61	35	54
2	Bury	42	21	9	12	63	35	51
3	Derby County	42	21	9	12	75	42	51
4	Blackpool	42	18	13	11	72	47	49
5	Southampton	42	17	14	11	52	31	48
6	Stoke City	42	14	18	10	44	42	46
7	Oldham Athletic	42	14	17	11	45	52	45
8	Sheffield Wednesday	42	16	12	14	54	51	44
9	South Shields	42	17	10	15	49	50	44
10	Leyton Orient	42	14	15	13	40	36	43
11	Barnsley	42	16	11	15	57	61	43
12	Leicester City	42	17	8	17	64	54	42
13	Stockport County	42	13	16	13	44	52	42
14	MANCHESTER UNITED	42	13	14	15	52	44	40
15	Crystal Palace	42	13	13	16	53	65	39
16	Port Vale	42	13	12	17	50	66	38
17	Hull City	42	10	17	15	46	51	37
18	Bradford City	42	11	15	16	35	48	37
19	Coventry City	42	11	13	18	52	68	35
20	Fulham	42	10	14	18	45	56	34
21	Nelson	42	10	13	19	40	74	33
22	Bristol City	42	7	15	20	32	65	29

Appearances

PLAYER	LGE	FAC	TOT
Moore	42	2	44
Hilditch	41	2	43
Lochhead	40	2	42
Spence	36	2	38
Bennion	34	2	36
McPherson	34	2	36
Steward	30	2	32
Radford	30	1	31
Mann	25	2	27
Grimwood	22	-	22
Bain	18	1	19
Barson	17	2	19
Mew	12	-	12
Smith	12	-	12
Ellis	11	-	11
Silcock	8	1	9
Haslam	7	-	7
MacDonald	7	-	7
Evans	6	-	6
Kennedy	6	-	6
Thomas	6	-	6
Partridge	5	-	5

PLAYER	LGE	FAC	TOT
Goldthorpe	4	-	4
Miller	4	-	4
Dennis	3	-	3
Barber	1	-	1
Henderson	-	1	1
Tyler	1	-	1

Play and Players

Goalscorers

PLAYER	LGE	FAC	TOT
Lochhead	14	-	14
Spence	10	-	10
Bain	8	-	8
Smith	4	-	4
Mann	3	-	3
Evans	2	-	2
Grimwood	2	-	2
McPherson	1	1	2
Barber	1	-	1
Goldthorpe	1	-	1
Kennedy	1	-	1
MacDonald	1	-	1
Miller	1	-	1
own goals	3	-	3

Left: Pages from the 15 September 1923 programme. The writer is bemoaning the previous week's loss to Bury (2-0) when spectator trouble marred the spectacle. A quirk of the fixture list meant United played Bury at Old Trafford a week later; they lost again (1-0).

Joyful fans celebrate promotion thanks to startling Joe Spence

OGDEN'S CIGARETTES.

F. BARSON,
MANCHESTER UNITED.

STARTING A THIRD season in the Second Division, United needed to open their points account fast and eight wins before the end of October sent the team charging into the promotion race. Their strength was the defence: Alf Steward in goal, full backs Charlie Moore and Jack Silcock and Frank Barson at centre half. The defence conceded a Second Division league record 23 goals in 42 games.

Meanwhile, Joe Spence on the right wing was at his startling best and he found a counterpart on the left wing in young Frank McPherson who scored seven goals (two more than Spence himself). A 16-game unbeaten run during the autumn set up a thrilling finale as United - along with Leicester City and Derby County - fought for the two promotion places.

Another first round FA Cup exit in January against Sheffield Wednesday was probably a blessing in disguise and, although Derby beat United 1-0 in a crucial game in early April, the Manchester boys remained undefeated for the rest of the season's seven games while County struggled.

Level on points with four games left, United had two crucial wins. Promotion for the Reds was actually secured with a 4-0 victory over Port Vale in front of 33,500 fans and with one game to go.

■ To keep a promise if the team won promotion, club chairman John Henry Davies presents Frank Barson with a pub in Ardwick Green.

Above: A 1925 illustration of Frank Barson, United's long-time centre half, who won one England international cap in 1920.

Far Left: In his sixth season at Old Trafford, Jack Silcock will go on to make 449 appearances, scoring two goals, in 15 seasons.

Left: This is the front page of the programme for the match against Port Vale on 25 April 1925; United won 4-0.

Final League Table Division Two

		P	W	D	L	F	A	Pts
1	Leicester City	42	24	11	7	90	32	59
2	**MANCHESTER UNITED**	42	23	11	8	57	23	57
3	Derby County	42	22	11	9	71	36	55
4	Portsmouth	42	15	18	9	58	50	48
5	Chelsea	42	16	15	11	51	37	47
6	Wolverhampton Wanderers	42	20	6	16	55	51	46
7	Southampton	42	13	18	11	40	36	44
8	Port Vale	42	17	8	17	48	56	42
9	South Shields	42	12	17	13	42	38	41
10	Hull City	42	15	11	16	50	49	41
11	Leyton Orient	42	14	12	16	42	42	40
12	Fulham	42	15	10	17	41	56	40
13	Middlesbrough	42	10	19	13	36	44	39
14	Sheffield Wednesday	42	15	8	19	50	56	38
15	Barnsley	42	13	12	17	46	59	38
16	Bradford City	42	13	12	17	37	50	38
17	Blackpool	42	14	9	19	65	61	37
18	Oldham Athletic	42	13	11	18	35	51	37
19	Stockport County	42	13	11	18	37	57	37
20	Stoke City	42	12	11	19	34	46	35
21	Crystal Palace	42	12	10	20	38	54	34
22	Coventry City	42	11	9	22	45	84	31

Appearances

PLAYER	LGE	FAC	TOT
Spence	42	1	43
Steward	42	1	43
Moore	40	1	41
Grimwood	39	1	40
McPherson	38	1	39
Lochhead	37	-	37
Mann	32	1	33
Barson	32	-	32
Smith	31	1	32
Silcock	29	-	29
Henderson	22	1	23
Bennion	17	-	17
Jones	15	1	16
Pape	16	-	16
Kennedy	11	1	12
Hilditch	4	1	5
Rennox	4	-	4
Hanson	3	-	3
Thomas	3	-	3
Bain	1	-	1
Goldthorpe	1	-	1
Haslam	1	-	1

PLAYER	LGE	FAC	TOT
Partridge	1	-	1
Taylor	1	-	1

Goalscorers

PLAYER	LGE	FAC	TOT
Henderson	14	-	14
Lochhead	13	-	13
McPherson	7	-	7
Pape	5	-	5
Smith	5	-	5
Spence	5	-	5
Hanson	3	-	3
Kennedy	3	-	3
Goldthorpe	1	-	1
Grimwood	1	-	1

QUALITY CIGARETTES SERIES F.B.1 - 96.

Jack Grimwood joined United in May 1919, and made his debut for the club in the first Manchester derby on 11 October 1919. Capable of playing in all three half-back positions, he was considered a utility player for the club.

GRIMWOOD, MANCHESTER UNITED. F.B.83

1925/26

- Frank Barson is suspended for eight weeks by the FA for an alleged punch in the cup semi-final which results in a City player being knocked unconscious.

- Johnny Berry is born in Aldershot on 1 June and will play 273 times for the Reds and survive the Munich air crash.

- Scotsman Charlie Rennox's real first name is Clatworthy.

- Manchester City's first goal in their 3-0 win over United in the FA Cup semi-final is hotly disputed, firstly for a foul and also it was questioned whether the ball actually crossed the line.

Above: United goalkeeper John Mew cannot stop Fulham scoring a goal in a sixth round FA Cup match at Craven Cottage in March. The Red Devils still won 2-1

Right: The United and Arsenal captains Lal Hilditch and Charles Buchan search for the coin tossed by the referee onto a snow-covered football pitch before their match at Highbury.

Consolidation in the First Division is achieved but the semi-final loss to rivals City hurts

THE RETURN TO the First Division after three seasons tested a solid team, but they were up to the task. Goals were not as easy to score as in the Second Division and the much-vaunted defence would leak 73 goals, 50 more than last year. And while the higher league brought out the inconsistency in the team (a 5-0 loss at Liverpool in September was immediately followed by a 6-1 win at home to Burnley), it was the FA Cup that saw United's best form. A trip to the semi-finals was good, but the subsequent loss to Manchester City was hard to swallow.

The emergence of inside forward Charlie Rennox was a key this year. After just four appearances in his debut season in the Second Division, Rennox was United's top scorer this season in the First Division with 17 goals in 34 games. Former winger Frank McPherson, who moved to the centre forward position towards the end of the season, would also have his best ever year – 16 goals from 29 appearances.

Soon after the FA Cup campaign ended, United's league form showed signs of a reaction; there was a five-game losing streak including a 7-0 blasting from Blackburn, but three wins in the last four games brought respectability to their final position of ninth.

Final League Table Division One

		P	W	D	L	F	A	Pts
1	Huddersfield Town	42	23	11	8	92	60	57
2	Arsenal	42	22	8	12	87	63	52
3	Sunderland	42	21	6	15	96	80	48
4	Bury	42	20	7	15	85	77	47
5	Sheffield United	42	19	8	15	102	82	46
6	Aston Villa	42	16	12	14	86	76	44
7	Liverpool	42	14	16	12	70	63	44
8	Bolton Wanderers	42	17	10	15	75	76	44
9	**MANCHESTER UNITED**	42	19	6	17	66	73	44
10	Newcastle United	42	16	10	16	84	75	42
11	Everton	42	12	18	12	72	70	42
12	Blackburn Rovers	42	15	11	16	91	80	41
13	West Bromwich Albion	42	16	8	18	79	78	40
14	Birmingham City	42	16	8	18	66	81	40
15	Tottenham Hotspur	42	15	9	18	66	79	39
16	Cardiff City	42	16	7	19	61	76	39
17	Leicester City	42	14	10	18	70	80	38
18	West Ham United	42	15	7	20	63	76	37
19	Leeds United	42	14	8	20	64	76	36
20	Burnley	42	13	10	19	85	108	36
21	Manchester City	42	12	11	19	89	100	35
22	Notts County	42	13	7	22	54	74	33

Appearances

PLAYER	LGE	FAC	TOT
Spence	39	7	46
Mann	34	7	41
Rennox	34	7	41
Moore	33	7	40
Silcock	33	7	40
Steward	35	2	37
McPherson	29	7	36
Smith	30	5	35
Thomas	29	6	35
Barson	28	4	32
Hilditch	28	3	31
Hanson	24	2	26
McCrae	9	4	13
Haslam	9	2	11
Mew	6	5	11
Jones	10	-	10
Grimwood	7	1	8
Bennion	7	-	7
Inglis	7	-	7
Taylor	6	-	6
Hannaford	4	1	5
Lochhead	5	-	5

PLAYER	LGE	FAC	TOT
Hall	3	-	3
Partridge	3	-	3
Sweeney	3	-	3
Bain	2	-	2
Pape	2	-	2
Astley	1	-	1

United's defence concedes a goal from Roberto of Manchester City from a corner kick in the FA Cup semi-final. The Reds lose 3-0 to the Sky Blues.

Goalscorers

PLAYER	LGE	FAC	TOT
McPherson	16	4	20
Rennox	17	1	18
Spence	7	4	11
Smith	3	4	7
Taylor	6	-	6
Thomas	5	1	6
Hanson	5	-	5
Barson	2	-	2
Lochhead	2	-	2
Hilditch	1	-	1
Inglis	1	-	1
Sweeney	1	-	1

A huge crowd of happy supporters at Craven Cottage, London for a Fulham vs Manchester United football match in the sixth round of the FA Cup.

Mysterious scandal costs John Chapman his job while the team responds to a player/manager

1926/27

THERE WERE DARK goings-on behind the scenes at United at this time that would eventually impact the team. Manager John Chapman's five-year reign in charge came to an undistinguished end in October 1926 when the Football Association suspended him amid rumours of financial improprieties. "Improper conduct" officially ended the reign of United's sixth manager, but the FA gave no further details or reasons.

Chapman's team was mediocre at best when he left and half back Lal Hilditch became player/manager for the rest of the season (he is still the first and only United player to take on the joint role). The Reds responded to their much-respected new boss and, despite drawing a third of their league games (14 in total), the team finished ten points clear of the relegation places in 15th place.

Star forward Joe Spence had his best season so far with the club, scoring 18 goals in 40 league appearances, while on the other wing Frank McPherson enjoyed another fine year with 15 goals from just 32 games. After such a good FA Cup run last season, a loss in the third round to Reading from the Third Division South was embarrassing.

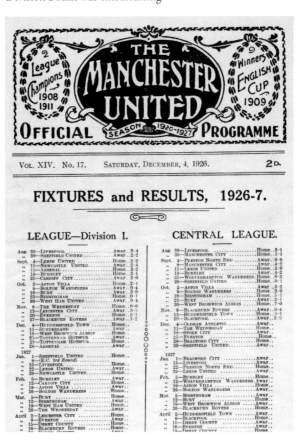

■ When Lal Hilditch takes on the role as manager he is reluctant to select himself to play, much to the detriment of the team's results.

Above: Charlie Moore originally joined United in May 1919. After two seasons, a recurring injury forced him to stop playing football, but in September 1922 he returned to play for United for a further eight years, making a total of 328 appearances for the club before retiring at the end of the 1929–1930 season.

Far Left: Joe Spence was one of United's few true stars between the wars.

Left: The United programmes of the 1920s consisted of a few flimsy pieces of paper, but were relatively cheap costing 2d.

Final League Table Division One

		P	W	D	L	F	A	Pts
1	Newcastle United	42	25	6	11	96	58	56
2	Huddersfield Town	42	17	17	8	76	60	51
3	Sunderland	42	21	7	14	98	70	49
4	Bolton Wanderers	42	19	10	13	84	62	48
5	Burnley	42	19	9	14	91	80	47
6	West Ham United	42	19	8	15	86	70	46
7	Leicester City	42	17	12	13	85	70	46
8	Sheffield United	42	17	10	15	74	86	44
9	Liverpool	42	18	7	17	69	61	43
10	Aston Villa	42	18	7	17	81	83	43
11	Arsenal	42	17	9	16	77	86	43
12	Derby County	42	17	7	18	86	73	41
13	Tottenham Hotspur	42	16	9	17	76	78	41
14	Cardiff City	42	16	9	17	55	65	41
15	MANCHESTER UNITED	42	13	14	15	52	64	40
16	Sheffield Wednesday	42	15	9	18	75	92	39
17	Birmingham City	42	17	4	21	64	73	38
18	Blackburn Rovers	42	15	8	19	77	96	38
19	Bury	42	12	12	18	68	77	36
20	Everton	42	12	10	20	64	90	34
21	Leeds United	42	11	8	23	69	88	30
22	West Bromwich Albion	42	11	8	23	65	86	30

Appearances

PLAYER	LGE	FAC	TOT
Steward	42	3	45
Spence	40	3	43
Bennion	37	3	40
McPherson	32	3	35
Moore	30	3	33
Silcock	26	3	29
Barson	21	3	24
Rennox	22	1	23
Hanson	21	1	22
Jones	21		21
Wilson	21	-	21
Hilditch	16	3	19
Partridge	16	3	19
Chapman	17		17
Grimwood	17		17
Sweeney	13	3	16
Thomas	16		16
Mann	14		14
Smith T	10	1	11
Hannaford	7		7
Inglis	6		6
Smith A	5		5

PLAYER	LGE	FAC	TOT
Harris	4		4
Haslam	4		4
Haworth	2	-	2
Astley	1	-	1
Iddon	1	-	1

Goalscorers

PLAYER	LGE	FAC	TOT
Spence	18	1	19
McPherson	15	1	16
Rennox	7		7
Hanson	5	-	5
Sweeney	3	1	4
Barson	2	-	2
Harris	1	-	1
Smith A	1	-	1
Bennion	-	1	1

Clarence 'Lal' George Hilditch, also known as Clarrie, is the only person ever to have been simultaneously a player and the manager at United. He retired in 1932 without winning any medals with the club.

1927/28

QUALITY CIGARETTES SERIES F.B. 1 - 96.

STEWARD. MANCHESTER UNITED. F.B.71.

- Joe Spence's 24 goals this season is set to be the best in his long career at Old Trafford.

- In July just before this season began, an exhibition tennis match is played on the Old Trafford pitch between two Wimbledon champions, Suzanne Lenglen and Bill Tilden.

Above: Alfred Steward joined United as cover for first-choice keeper Jack Mew as an unpaid amateur in 1919. A year later, he turned professional and became a regular in the side in the 1923-24 season. Between April 1924 and September 1927, he missed only seven league games out of a possible 139.

Another new manager and another real relegation scare

THE APPOINTMENT OF former referee Herbert Bamlett to the post of manager in time for the start of this season (interim player/manager Lal Hilditch returned to his on-pitch-only duties) brought another new style to the team. Bamlett had enjoyed considerable success at all three previous clubs he managed – Oldham Athletic, Wigan Borough and Middlesbrough – where his forte was the revival of struggling teams. However, there was little immediate impact, save for a couple of spirited opening wins.

Then in October, the sad news came that chairman John Henry Davies, the man who had saved the club from extinction, had died. While all at United mourned, the team's league position was becoming increasingly perilous due to inconsistent play; two straight wins would often be followed by a longer string of defeats.

With three league games to go, United were bottom of the table and three points from safety. However, a 2-1 win at home to Sunderland gave them renewed hope and then an unexpected win away at Arsenal 1-0 in the penultimate game left United needing a convincing victory at home to Liverpool in the final match of the season to avoid relegation. Joe Spence decided to take centre stage and scored a hat-trick in a remarkable 6-1 win. United finished just one point ahead of relegated Tottenham Hotspur.

PRESENTED FREE WITH BOYS' MAGAZINE

MANCHESTER UNITED F.C., 1928
BACK ROW : Jones, Hilditch, Silcock, Steward, Bennion, Moore, Mr. Bamlett, Wilson.
FRONT ROW : Chapman, Hanson, Spence, Partridge, McPherson, Barson (Captain).

Final League Table Division One

		P	W	D	L	F	A	Pts
1	Everton	42	20	13	9	102	66	53
2	Huddersfield Town	42	22	7	13	91	68	51
3	Leicester City	42	18	12	12	96	72	48
4	Derby County	42	17	10	15	96	83	44
5	Bury	42	20	4	18	80	80	44
6	Cardiff City	42	17	10	15	70	80	44
7	Bolton Wanderers	42	16	11	15	81	66	43
8	Aston Villa	42	17	9	16	78	73	43
9	Newcastle United	42	15	13	14	79	81	43
10	Arsenal	42	13	15	14	82	86	41
11	Birmingham City	42	13	15	14	70	75	41
12	Blackburn Rovers	42	16	9	17	66	78	41
13	Sheffield United	42	15	10	17	79	86	40
14	Sheffield Wednesday	42	13	13	16	81	78	39
15	Sunderland	42	15	9	18	74	76	39
16	Liverpool	42	13	13	16	84	87	39
17	West Ham United	42	14	11	17	81	88	39
18	**MANCHESTER UNITED**	**42**	**16**	**7**	**19**	**72**	**80**	**39**
19	Burnley	42	16	7	19	82	98	39
20	Portsmouth	42	16	7	19	66	90	39
21	Tottenham Hotspur	42	15	8	19	74	86	38
22	Middlesbrough	42	11	15	16	81	88	37

Appearances

PLAYER	LGE	FAC	TOT
Spence	38	5	43
Bennion	36	5	41
Jones	33	5	38
Wilson	33	5	38
Johnston	31	5	36
Richardson	32	4	36
Hanson	30	5	35
Mann	26	5	31
Silcock	26	4	30
McPherson	26	3	29
Moore	25	1	26
Partridge	23	3	26
Williams	13	3	16
Thomas	13	-	13
Rawlings	12	-	12
Barson	11	-	11
Steward	10	1	11
McLenahan	10	-	10
Chapman	9	-	9
Hilditch	5	-	5
Nicol	4	1	5
Ferguson	4	-	4

PLAYER	LGE	FAC	TOT
Sweeney	4	-	4
Haslam	3	-	3
Ramsden	2	-	2
Taylor	2	-	2
Bain	1	-	1

Goalscorers

PLAYER	LGE	FAC	TOT
Spence	22	2	24
Hanson	10	4	14
Johnston	8	3	11
Rawlings	10	-	10
McPherson	6	1	7
Partridge	5	-	5
Nicol	2	-	2
Thomas	2	-	2
Williams	2	-	2
Bennion	1	-	1
McLenahan	1	-	1
Sweeney	1	-	1
own goals	2	-	2

Herbert Bamlett was only 32 when he refereed the 1914 FA Cup final between Liverpool and Burnley. He started in football management in the same year at Oldham Athletic before moving to Wigan (1921–23), Middlesbrough (1923–26), and then to United in April 1927.

End-of-season run of wins hoists United up to mid-table safety

1928/29

THIS WAS ANOTHER season in which United started off poorly. During a period from November to January, the team failed to win a single league game in 14 attempts and scored only 13 goals while conceding 35. An ignominious loss in the FA Cup fourth round to Bury was followed by two more defeats at the start of February (including a 5-0 drubbing at Newcastle United) that seemed to indicate relegation for United.

However, in the final third of the season, forwards Tom Reid and Jimmy Hanson began finding the net on a more regular basis and wins came thick and fast. Scotsman Reid was the real star after coming to Old Trafford in early February in a transfer from Oldham Athletic (manager Herbert Bamlett's former club). He scored on his debut and bagged 14 goals in just 17 appearances. Although Hanson's total of 19 goals was bigger and easily his best ever in six seasons at Old Trafford, it took him 42 appearances.

In the last 15 games, United won ten times and lost just once; it was a sequence of results that hoisted them to a 12th place finish. Bamlett, with assistant Louis Rocca – a remnant of the Newton Heath days and a former team scout – were now bringing out the best in the team.

■ United's crucial 15-game end-of-season streak towards safety contains just one loss – a stunning 6-1 defeat away to Derby County, strangely, with almost exactly the same team as managed all the other results.

MANCHESTER UNITED.F.C.1928-9

Above: Before Football League titles and FA Cups took precedence, the Lancashire Cup was a major trophy for United who first took this trophy as Newton Heath in 1897-98 season and this year won it again for the fifth time.

Left: A confident early season team picture. United players seem to be early fans of Brylcreem, the hair product created this year and soon to become popular with sportsmen.

Final League Table Division One

		P	W	D	L	F	A	Pts
1	Sheffield Wednesday	42	21	10	11	86	62	52
2	Leicester City	42	21	9	12	96	67	51
3	Aston Villa	42	23	4	15	98	81	50
4	Sunderland	42	20	7	15	93	75	47
5	Liverpool	42	17	12	13	90	64	46
6	Derby County	42	18	10	14	86	71	46
7	Blackburn Rovers	42	17	11	14	72	63	45
8	Manchester City	42	18	9	15	95	86	45
9	Arsenal	42	16	13	13	77	72	45
10	Newcastle United	42	19	6	17	70	72	44
11	Sheffield United	42	15	11	16	86	85	41
12	**MANCHESTER UNITED**	**42**	**14**	**13**	**15**	**66**	**76**	**41**
13	Leeds United	42	16	9	17	71	84	41
14	Bolton Wanderers	42	14	12	16	73	80	40
15	Birmingham City	42	15	10	17	68	77	40
16	Huddersfield Town	42	14	11	17	70	61	39
17	West Ham United	42	15	9	18	86	96	39
18	Everton	42	17	4	21	63	75	38
19	Burnley	42	15	8	19	81	103	38
20	Portsmouth	42	15	6	21	56	80	36
21	Bury	42	12	7	23	62	99	31
22	Cardiff City	42	8	13	21	43	59	29

Appearances

PLAYER	LGE	FAC	TOT
Hanson	42	1	43
Moore	37	2	39
Steward	37	2	39
Spence	36	2	38
Spencer	36	2	38
Bennion	34	-	34
Silcock	27	2	29
Mann	25	2	27
Rowley	25	-	25
Wilson	19	2	21
Rawlings	19	1	20
Thomas	19	1	20
Dale	19	-	19
Williams	18	1	19
Reid	17	-	17
Johnston	12	-	12
Hilditch	11	-	11
Sweeney	6	2	8
Partridge	5	-	5
Ramsden	5	-	5
Richardson	5	-	5
Taylor	3	1	4

PLAYER	LGE	FAC	TOT
Nicol	2	-	2
Boyle	1	-	1
Inglis	1	-	1
McLenahan	1	-	1
Thomson	-	1	1

Goalscorers

PLAYER	LGE	FAC	TOT
Hanson	19	1	20
Reid	14	-	14
Rawlings	6	-	6
Spence	5	1	6
Johnston	5	-	5
Rowley	5	-	5
Thomas	4	-	4
Ramsden	3	-	3
Hilditch	1	-	1
Mann	1	-	1
Silcock	1	-	1
Sweeney	1	-	1
Wilson	1	-	1
Taylor	-	1	1

An official programme for the 17 November 1928 home match against Derby County. United lost 1-0.

1929/30

Herbert Bamlett's third season sees little improvement in either league or cup performances

YET ANOTHER SLUGGISH sequence of games started the season and, by the end of October, United had just eight league points and a defence that was again leaking too many goals. But just as signs of improvement were noted as the New Year approached, centre forward Jimmy Hanson broke his leg.

With Tom Reid unable to repeat the form of last season due to injury, the team had to rely on stalwart Joe Spence to score at a time when his career was starting to wind down. When 1930 began with four straight defeats (including a 2-0 FA Cup third round loss at home to Swindon), another relegation looked odds on. However, luckily for United, there were at least half a dozen teams also on losing streaks and, by scrambling to 38 points by the end of the season, the Old Trafford crowd were guaranteed First Division football for another year.

This was Herbert Bamlett's third season in charge without significant improvement and the club's poor finances hung over the whole club; supporters lost faith and the Great Depression caused average attendances to drop from over 23,500 per game the previous season to 18,500 this season.

■ United's Old Trafford ground remains an asset; they even hold champions Sheffield Wednesday to a draw at home after losing 7-2 away at Hillsborough.

■ There is growing unrest among the supporters this season as the team finish just two points above the relegation zone; next season, a group of fans will print leaflets demanding changes.

Above: An illustration from the 1930s of Jack Silcock.

Right: Circa. 1930. An aerial view of Old Trafford stadium showing the surrounding houses, railway tracks and factory units.

Final League Table Division One

		P	W	D	L	F	A	Pts
1	Sheffield Wednesday	42	26	8	8	105	57	60
2	Derby County	42	21	8	13	90	82	50
3	Manchester City	42	19	9	14	91	81	47
4	Aston Villa	42	21	5	16	92	83	47
5	Leeds United	42	20	6	16	79	63	46
6	Blackburn Rovers	42	19	7	16	99	93	45
7	West Ham United	42	19	5	18	86	79	43
8	Leicester City	42	17	9	16	86	90	43
9	Sunderland	42	18	7	17	76	80	43
10	Huddersfield Town	42	17	9	16	63	69	43
11	Birmingham City	42	16	9	17	67	62	41
12	Liverpool	42	16	9	17	63	79	41
13	Portsmouth	42	15	10	17	66	62	40
14	Arsenal	42	14	11	17	78	66	39
15	Bolton Wanderers	42	15	9	18	74	74	39
16	Middlesbrough	42	16	6	20	82	84	38
17	**MANCHESTER UNITED**	**42**	**15**	**8**	**19**	**67**	**88**	**38**
18	Grimsby Town	42	15	7	20	73	89	37
19	Newcastle United	42	15	7	20	71	92	37
20	Sheffield United	42	15	6	21	91	96	36
21	Burnley	42	14	8	20	79	97	36
22	Everton	42	12	11	19	80	92	35

Appearances

PLAYER	LGE	FAC	TOT
Spence	42	1	43
Rowley	40	1	41
Steward	39	1	40
Moore	28	1	29
Wilson	28	1	29
Bennion	28	-	28
Hilditch	27	1	28
Ball	23	1	24
McLachlan	23	1	24
Silcock	21	-	21
Thomas	21	-	21
Dale	19	-	19
Hanson	18	-	18
Jones	16	1	17
Taylor	16	1	17
Boyle	15	1	16
Mann	14	-	14
Reid	13	-	13
McLenahan	10	-	10
Spencer	10	-	10
Rawlings	4	-	4
Chesters	3	-	3

PLAYER	LGE	FAC	TOT
Warburton	2	-	2
Sweeney	1	-	1
Thomson	1	-	1

Goalscorers

PLAYER	LGE	FAC	TOT
Rowley	12	-	12
Spence	12	-	12
Ball	11	-	11
Boyle	6	-	6
McLenahan	6	-	6
Hanson	5	-	5
Reid	5	-	5
Rawlings	3	-	3
McLachlan	2	-	2
Hilditch	1	-	1
Mann	1	-	1
Thomas	1	-	1
Warburton	1	-	1
Wilson	1	-	1

M.U. F.C. LTD.
1930   1931.
GRAND STAND
GENTS'
CHAIRS.

More club financial problems, fan protests, a sacked manager and almost inevitable relegation

THERE ARE FEW seasons in United's history that are as awful as this one; while the team slumped badly, the club's finances were in even worse shape and supporters were up in arms. The team had been avoiding relegation by fractions for several seasons and when the first 12 games were all losses - including 6-0 to Huddersfield Town and 7-4 to Newcastle United, both matches at home – the club was officially in crisis.

Supporter protests reached a peak in October when a public meeting called for a boycott of the home game against Arsenal. Almost inevitably manager Herbert Bamlett was removed from his post before the season finished and replaced by current club

secretary Walter Crickmer. They had only two wins before the end of 1930 and the New Year brought little change.

An exit from the FA Cup in the fourth round (losing 1-0 at Grimsby Town) was no respite from the slide to the Second Division which slowly gained pace and relegation came in March with over half a dozen games still to play.

The only player to enhance his reputation was forward Tom Reid, whose 17 goals in 30 league games stood out against a team of under-performers. Long-suffering supporters were now openly protesting at the way their club was run and a pitiful 3,969 turned up for the final home match of the season.

1930/31

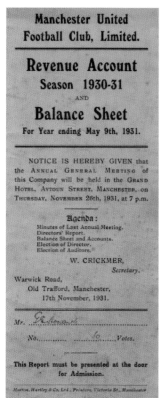

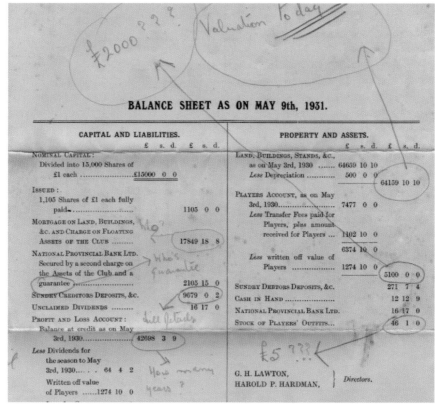

BALANCE SHEET AS ON MAY 9th, 1931.

- While losing 27 of their 42 games this season, United concede an astounding 115 goals and score just 53.

- In the first ten games of the season the Reds concede an astonishing 43 goals.

- The relegation season is full of unwanted statistics - the nine home defeats and 18 away are both club records.

Above: 1 November 1930. Programme for the match against Birmingham City showing 12 consecutive losses. United won this match 2-0 in front of just 11,479 fans.

Left: 9 May 1931. With the club facing financial meltdown for the second time, Herbert Davies – brother of original United benefactor John Henry Davies (d. 1927) – makes notes on the company's financial report querying items of expenditure.

Final League Table Division One

	P	W	D	L	F	A	Pts
1 Arsenal	42	28	10	4	127	59	66
2 Aston Villa	42	25	9	8	128	78	59
3 Sheffield Wednesday	42	22	8	12	102	75	52
4 Portsmouth	42	18	13	11	84	67	49
5 Huddersfield Town	42	18	12	12	81	65	48
6 Derby County	42	18	10	14	94	79	46
7 Middlesbrough	42	19	8	15	98	90	46
8 Manchester City	42	18	10	14	75	70	46
9 Liverpool	42	15	12	15	86	85	42
10 Blackburn Rovers	42	17	8	17	83	84	42
11 Sunderland	42	16	9	17	89	85	41
12 Chelsea	42	15	10	17	64	67	40
13 Grimsby Town	42	17	5	20	82	87	39
14 Bolton Wanderers	42	15	9	18	68	81	39
15 Sheffield United	42	14	10	18	78	84	38
16 Leicester City	42	16	6	20	80	95	38
17 Newcastle United	42	15	6	21	78	87	36
18 West Ham United	42	14	8	20	79	94	36
19 Birmingham City	42	13	10	19	55	70	36
20 Blackpool	42	11	10	21	71	125	32
21 Leeds United	42	12	7	23	68	81	31
22 MANCHESTER UNITED	**42**	**7**	**8**	**27**	**53**	**115**	**22**

Appearances

PLAYER	LGE	FAC	TOT
McLachlan	42	4	46
Steward	38	4	42
Bennion	36	4	40
Mellor	35	4	39
Spence	35	2	37
Reid	30	3	33
Gallimore	28	4	32
Hilditch	25	4	29
Rowley	29	-	29
Dale	22	4	26
Silcock	25	-	25
Warburton	18	4	22
Wilson	20	2	22
McLenahan	21	-	21
Hopkinson	17	2	19
Bullock	10	-	10
Parker	9	-	9
Ramsden	7	2	9
Jones	5	-	5
Chesters	4	-	4
Thomson	2	1	3
Williams	3	-	3

PLAYER	LGE	FAC	TOT
Lydon	1	-	1

Goalscorers

PLAYER	LGE	FAC	TOT
Reid	17	3	20
Rowley	7	-	7
Spence	6	1	7
Gallimore	5	1	6
Hopkinson	4	2	6
Warburton	5	-	5
Bullock	3	-	3
McLachlan	2	-	2
Bennion	1	-	1
McLenahan	1	-	1
Thomson	1	-	1
Wilson	1	-	1

1931/32

Admit one person

Mʳˢ Amy Davies
Bramhall Hall
Cheadle Hulme
Stockport

to all Matches played by
the M.U.F.C. Ltd. (except
Cup Ties & Charity Matches)

This Ticket must be shown
on all occasions.

NOT TRANSFERABLE.

W. CRICKMER, Sec.

- Stalwart star winger Joe Spence (actually in his penultimate year with United) and centre forward Tom Reid are the standout players scoring 19 and 17 goals respectively.

- 12th place in the Second Division was the club's second worst finish in its history. Only the 15th place in 1901-02, the time of its previous financial crisis, was worse.

- Despite using so many players during the season (34), nine men racked up more than 25 appearances topped by Joe Spence on 38.

Above: A season ticket for the 1931-32 campaign belonging to Amy Davies, wife of the club's 1902 financial saviour, the late John Henry Davies.

Opposite: The financial accounts of United showing the club made a loss of £5,036 18s 0d at the end of the 1931-32 season.

James W. Gibson's investment saves the club from bankruptcy as the team responds to Walter Crickmer

THE CRISIS THAT had been looming off the field for several years was still in evidence as the season began: crowds were thin (3,507 for the Old Trafford opener against Southampton) and there was no money to pay off loans on stadium building work or amounts owed for new players. These were also difficult times on the field, with Walter Crickmer in his first full season in charge and with the team back in the Second Division following another relegation. In fact, United had finished ten points from safety last season and could easily be candidates to drop into the Third Division North if they faltered badly during this campaign.

Unsurprisingly, the Reds did start badly with only three wins in their first 14 games. Then by Christmas, with the team already looking at the possibility of a disastrous second relegation in two seasons, the financial problems came to a head as player salaries were not paid.

But, just when it was needed, another source of money for the club emerged, although without some of the apparent luck of 30 years earlier. Sports writer Stacey Lintott approached local garment manufacturer James W Gibson about United's financial plight, and the businessman – who manufactured uniforms for the police – responded by offering to take on the financial responsibilities of the club in return for becoming chairman and choosing his own directors. The amount Gibson was prepared to underwrite was less than the sum Davies had provided for the construction of Old Trafford, but nonetheless it was a substantial commitment.

Before this, bankruptcy had once again been a distinct possibility, so, just as John Henry Davies had done at the start of the century, Gibson took on the mantle of club saviour.

So now, with the financial backing in place, the team was able to focus on playing as Walter Crickmer and his influential assistant Louis Rocca wanted. Rocca had been with the club since its days as Newton Heath. Crickmer, originally club secretary, and had been put in control of the team only at the end of the previous season as the club was slipping into its

latest crisis. His term in the manager's chair would be brief (he would leave the post following this season), but his steady hand was to prove vital this season.

Crickmer's team had managed a modest resurgence of form during December. Just as Gibson's rescue package was going through, Crickmer's team managed three wins and six defeats (including a 7-0 thrashing at Wolverhampton Wanderers) in nine league games in December and January. Hopes that the FA Cup might provide a distraction were quickly shattered as United lost 4-1 at Plymouth Argyle. Despite the cash injection, the club was facing relegation and the fans had little to cheer.

In fact, one problem Crickmer had was that of too many players – with all the off-field problems, and the need to find the best players for a crisis situation, there was an unprecedented total of 34 men who wore United colours during the season. The lack of a stable team had not helped Crickmer or United's cause.

However, United eventually managed to put their troubles behind them and won ten games of the remaining 17 to finish a creditable 12th in the league. There was a huge sigh of relief among the supporters who had been so vociferous and genuinely feared the nightmare scenario of dropping into the third level of English football for the first time. The supporters' club had printed leaflets calling for massive changes: new management and directors as well as a better scouting system. The pleas may have fallen on deaf ears as the pre-Gibson board did little to halt the slide, but the fans began to turn up again in larger numbers at Old Trafford in the spring. Over 37,000 came to the Good Friday fixture against Charlton Athletic, although the Reds would lose 2-0.

But as the final league games were played out, it was clear that the club had been given a second fresh start within three decades. Gibson's investment would give a new manager money to spend (Crickmer went back to being secretary at the end of the season) and the chairman had paid off all outstanding debts, including those to the Inland Revenue and the local council for maintenance to roads around Old Trafford.

Final League Table Division Two

		P	W	D	L	F	A	Pts
1	Wolverhampton Wanderers	42	24	8	10	115	49	56
2	Leeds United	42	22	10	10	78	54	54
3	Stoke City	42	19	14	9	69	48	52
4	Plymouth Argyle	42	20	9	13	100	66	49
5	Bury	42	21	7	14	70	58	49
6	Bradford Park Avenue	42	21	7	14	72	63	49
7	Bradford City	42	16	13	13	80	61	45
8	Tottenham Hotspur	42	16	11	15	87	78	43
9	Millwall	42	17	9	16	61	61	43
10	Charlton Athletic	42	17	9	16	61	66	43
11	Nottingham Forest	42	16	10	16	77	72	42
12	MANCHESTER UNITED	42	17	8	17	71	72	42
13	Preston North End	42	16	10	16	75	77	42
14	Southampton	42	17	7	18	66	77	41
15	Swansea City	42	16	7	19	73	75	39
16	Notts County	42	13	12	17	75	75	38
17	Chesterfield	42	13	11	18	64	86	37
18	Oldham Athletic	42	13	10	19	62	84	36
19	Burnley	42	13	9	20	59	87	35
20	Port Vale	42	13	7	22	58	89	33
21	Barnsley	42	12	9	21	55	91	33
22	Bristol City	42	6	11	25	39	78	23

Appearances

PLAYER	LGE	FAC	TOT
Spence	37	1	38
Silcock	35	1	36
Mellor	33	1	34
Steward	32	1	33
Bennion	28	1	29
Johnston	28	1	29
McLachlan	28	1	29
Reid	25	1	26
Gallimore	25	-	25
Hopkinson	19	-	19
Hilditch	17	1	18
Vincent	16	-	16
Ridding	14	1	15
Mann	13	-	13
Jones	12	-	12
McLenahan	11	1	12
Robinson	10	-	10
Page	9	-	9
Wilson	9	-	9
Ferguson	8	-	8
Fitton	8	-	8
Moody	8	-	8

PLAYER	LGE	FAC	TOT
Parker	8	-	8
Warburton	7	-	7
Dale	4	-	4
Black	3	-	3
Manley	3	-	3
Chesters	2	-	2
Dean	2	-	2
Lievesley	2	-	2
Lydon	2	-	2
McDonald	2	-	2
Rowley	1	-	1
Whittle	1	-	1

Goalscorers

PLAYER	LGE	FAC	TOT
Spence	19	-	19
Reid	17	1	18
Johnston	11	-	11
Gallimore	6	-	6
Hopkinson	5	-	5
Ridding	3	-	3
Warburton	3	-	3
Black	2	-	2
Fitton	2	-	2
Mann	2	-	2
Ferguson	1	-	1

Manchester United Football Club, Limited.

Dr.   **REVENUE ACCOUNT for the Season 1931-32, ended May 7th, 1932.**   **Cr.**

	£	s.	d.	£	s.	d.		£	s.	d.	£	s.	d.
To PLAYERS' WAGES, &C. :—							By Gate Receipts (First Team)	14847	12	6			
Wages : Players	9463	10	0				,, Share of Gate Receipts from away matches	1931	8	7			
,, Bonuses	991	10	0					16779	1	1			
Trainers	786	0	0										
Office	709	10	0				*Less* Share of Visiting Teams 2004 18 6						
Groundsmen	767	15	0				*Less* Share payable to Football League 116 9 8	2121	8	2			
Special Training Expenses	21	16	9								14657	12	11
Players Outfits	164	18	11				,, Central League Matches				1251	6	0
Medical Fees	96	10	8				,, Northern Mid Week League Matches				50	16	9
Travelling and Hotel Expenses	1842	7	9				,, Charity Matches (per contra)				87	12	9
Insurance	60	7	2				,, Cup Ties, *less* share paid to League, etc.				990	18	0
,, Health and Unemployment	150	10	4				,, Season Tickets				409	16	6
				15054	16	7	,, Advertising Rents, etc.				473	15	0
,, ADVERTISING, ETC. :							,, Sale of Programmes, Net				260	14	7
Band	60	18	0				,, Rent Receivable, Net				61	0	7
Gatemen and Checkers	363	19	7				,, Balance—Net Loss				5036	18	0
Police	171	8	6										
Referee and Linesmen	291	1	1										
Advertising, Printing and Billposting	467	12	4										
				1354	19	6							
,, TAXATION :													
Income Tax	20	8	1										
Entertainment Tax	2743	5	10										
				2763	13	11							
,, DONATIONS & SUBSCRIPTIONS :													
Subscriptions to Charity (per contra)	87	12	9										
Other Donations and Subscriptions	20	5	0										
				107	17	9							
,, LEAGUE & ASSOCIATION EXPENSES :													
Subscriptions to Association and Leagues				55	11	0							
,, ESTABLISHMENT CHARGES, &C. :													
Ground Expenses	59	7	4										
Coal, Gas, Water, and Electricity	112	0	10										
Rates	466	5	10										
Chief Rent	94	0	0										
Depreciation	500	0	0										
				1231	14	0							
,, INTEREST, &C. :													
Bank Interest and Commission	391	2	8										
Loan and Mortgage Interest	1730	13	0										
				2121	15	8							
,, SUNDRY EXPENSES :													
Postages	34	14	6										
Telephones	66	19	11										
Washing and Cleaning	9	15	7										
Sundry Expenses	176	6	9										
Repairs and Renewals	302	5	11										
				590	2	8							
				£23280	11	1					£23280	11	1

1932/33

With finances intact, Scott Duncan arrives from Scotland to take over in the manager's chair

THE IMMEDIATE FINANCIAL woes of the club were firmly put behind them, when the board decided it was time for a new manager to lift the team for this season. Scotsman Scott Duncan (who was a player for both Rangers and Celtic) moved down from a job at Cowdenbeath to Old Trafford to take over from Walter Crickmer.

Duncan even had money to spend on players and brought several down from his native land. However, a number of early, heavy defeats (including a 6-1 thrashing by Tottenham Hotspur) left United near the bottom of the table by the end of

September. Duncan's work on the team began to bear fruit the following month, with three wins and two draws in five games. Defence was proving the team's Achilles' heel as they would keep only six clean sheets all season.

United steadily climbed the table after that and, despite yet another poor FA Cup campaign (a 4-1 home loss to Middlesbrough in the third round), the team finished a creditable sixth in the league. This was also the end of an era: forward Joe Spence, after 510 appearances and 168 goals (both records that lasted for decades) spanning 14 seasons, moved to Bradford.

- Appointing an ex-player as manager is still a rarity in this era of the game, so Scott Duncan is seen as something of a gamble by the new board.

- Winger Joe Spence becomes the first player in either the Newton Heath or Manchester United eras to play 500 games for the club; his landmark game is a 7-1 win over Millwall on 22 October although he does not score.

Above: Scott Duncan joined United as manager on 1 August 1932.

Right: This programme from the opening home game of the season against Stoke City actually once belonged to Scott Duncan who kept it as a souvenir of his first game in charge. He wrote the two phone numbers on the front cover.

Opposite: Managers in the 1930s were altogether more accessible. From this rare United Supporters' Club magazine, Scott Duncan proves the point on a trip to Scotland.

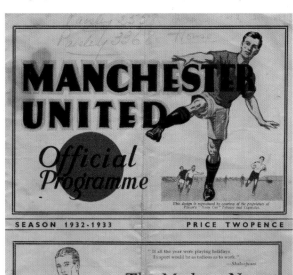

Final League Table Division Two

		P	W	D	L	F	A	Pts
1	Stoke City	42	25	6	11	78	39	56
2	Tottenham Hotspur	42	20	15	7	96	51	55
3	Fulham	42	20	10	12	78	65	50
4	Bury	42	20	9	13	84	59	49
5	Nottingham Forest	42	17	15	10	67	59	49
6	**MANCHESTER UNITED**	42	15	13	14	71	68	43
7	Millwall	42	16	11	15	59	57	43
8	Bradford Park Avenue	42	17	8	17	77	71	42
9	Preston North End	42	16	10	16	74	70	42
10	Swansea City	42	19	4	19	50	54	42
11	Bradford City	42	14	13	15	65	61	41
12	Southampton	42	18	5	19	66	66	41
13	Grimsby Town	42	14	13	15	79	84	41
14	Plymouth Argyle	42	16	9	17	63	67	41
15	Notts County	42	15	10	17	67	78	40
16	Oldham Athletic	42	15	8	19	67	80	38
17	Port Vale	42	14	10	18	66	79	38
18	Lincoln City	42	12	13	17	72	87	37
19	Burnley	42	11	14	17	67	79	36
20	West Ham United	42	13	9	20	75	93	35
21	Chesterfield	42	12	10	20	61	84	34
22	Charlton Athletic	42	12	7	23	60	91	31

Appearances

PLAYER	LGE	FAC	TOT
Moody	42	1	43
Mellor	40	1	41
Vincent	40	1	41
Frame	33	1	34
Silcock	27	1	28
Brown	25	-	25
McLenahan	24	1	25
Ridding	23	1	24
Chalmers	22	1	23
Stewart	21	1	22
McDonald	21	-	21
Spence	19	1	20
Manley	19	-	19
McLachlan	17	-	17
Dewar	15	-	15
Hine	14	-	14
Gallimore	12	-	12
Reid	11	1	12
Jones	10	-	10
Hopkinson	6	-	6
Warburton	6	-	6
Topping	5	-	5

PLAYER	LGE	FAC	TOT
Fitton	4	-	4
Page	3	-	3
Black	1	-	1
Heywood	1	-	1
Mitchell	1	-	1

Goalscorers

PLAYER	LGE	FAC	TOT
Ridding	11	-	11
Brown	10	-	10
Reid	10	-	10
Spence	7	1	8
Dewar	6	-	6
Gallimore	5	-	5
Hine	5	-	5
McDonald	4	-	4
Stewart	3	-	3
Frame	2	-	2
McLenahan	2	-	2
Chalmers	1	-	1
Hopkinson	1	-	1
Vincent	1	-	1
Warburton	1	-	1
own goals	2	-	2

ANNUAL OUTING OF THE SUPPORTERS' CLUB

A six-days' tour through one of the loveliest parts of Scotland was thoroughly enjoyed by a large party of Supporters. From July 19th to July 24th there was hardly a break, except for rest and food. Setting off from Salford, decked out in United colours, and coaching north-west via Dumfries to Dumbarton, where the company met the Manager of the Football Club (Mr. Scott-Duncan). The latter arranged many delightful trips from his home town. His kindness was much appreciated. Afterwards the tour was resumed through the Trossachs, returning via Stirling and the east coast to Edinburgh; then travelling through Berwick-on-Tweed and via the West Riding to Harrogate, and so back to Salford again, covering a distance of 850 miles.

A HAPPY GATHERING WITH MR. SCOTT-DUNCAN AT LUSS, LOCH LOMOND.

1933/34

Dramatic last game win avoids a drop to Third Division North

WITH SCOTT DUNCAN now settled into his job and his team beginning to gel, hopes for this season were high. But instead of making a push for promotion, the team slid down the table. Two heavy losses in the first two weeks of the season (4-1 at Plymouth and 5-1 at home to Bolton Wanderers) set a doom-laden tone and, though the team rallied, the defence was still shipping far too many goals (five against Lincoln City, six against Bradford Park Avenue and seven against Grimsby Town).

When Portsmouth beat United 4-1 in an FA Cup third round replay, injuries and poor form left the team unsettled – an incredible 38 players donned a United shirt during the season. Finally, after just five wins since the start of 1934, United had one game left to salvage a terrible season; they were in the relegation zone (21st position in the table), their lowest ever league position and needed a dramatic win against fellow strugglers Millwall to escape the drop.

The Londoners were one place and one point above United, whose trip south to The Den ended in a glorious 2-0 victory. United had avoided being relegated to the Third Division North for the first time in their history and a small crowd greeted them off the train on their return to Manchester.

- In the same week that United beat Millwall to avoid relegation, Matt Busby plays in the Manchester City team that wins the FA Cup.

- Jack Cape joins in January from Newcastle United and scores four vital goals in the last seven games to help his new team avoid relegation.

- Crucially, United are unbeaten in their final five games – two wins and three draws – to escape relegation to the Third Division North.

Above: Front cover of the Millwall programme for the vital last game of the season.

Right: The back page of the above programme showing Millwall's first and second team fixtures and results, but with 0-2 inserted neatly by hand for the final match result.

Far Right: 25 December 1933. With James W. Gibson now in control, this Christmas Day match against Grimsby Town was a time of hope. But the game was lost 3-1 and the season nearly ended in disaster.

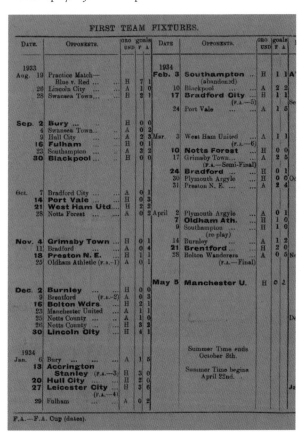

Final League Table Division Two

		P	W	D	L	F	A	Pts
1	Grimsby Town	42	27	5	10	103	59	59
2	Preston North End	42	23	6	13	71	52	52
3	Bolton Wanderers	42	21	9	12	79	55	51
4	Brentford	42	22	7	13	85	60	51
5	Bradford Park Avenue	42	23	3	16	86	67	49
6	Bradford City	42	20	6	16	73	67	46
7	West Ham United	42	17	11	14	78	70	45
8	Port Vale	42	19	7	16	60	55	45
9	Oldham Athletic	42	17	10	15	72	60	44
10	Plymouth Argyle	42	15	13	14	69	70	43
11	Blackpool	42	15	13	14	62	64	43
12	Bury	42	17	9	16	70	73	43
13	Burnley	42	18	6	18	60	72	42
14	Southampton	42	15	8	19	54	58	38
15	Hull City	42	13	12	17	52	68	38
16	Fulham	42	15	7	20	48	67	37
17	Nottingham Forest	42	13	9	20	73	74	35
18	Notts County	42	12	11	19	53	62	35
19	Swansea City	42	10	15	17	51	60	35
20	**MANCHESTER UNITED**	**42**	**14**	**6**	**22**	**59**	**85**	**34**
21	Millwall	42	11	11	20	39	68	33
22	Lincoln City	42	9	8	25	44	75	26

Appearances

PLAYER	LGE	FAC	TOT
Jones	39	2	41
Hine	33	2	35
Manley	30	2	32
Stewart	25	2	27
Hall	23	2	25
McMillen	23	2	25
McLenahan	22	2	24
Dewar	21	-	21
Ball	18	2	20
Vose	17	2	19
Frame	18	-	18
Cape	17	-	17
Silcock	16	1	17
Brown	15	1	16
Chalmers	12	-	12
Griffiths	10	-	10
Hacking	10	-	10
McKay	10	-	10
Robertson	10	-	10
Green	9	-	9
Hopkinson	9	-	9
McGillivray	8	1	9

PLAYER	LGE	FAC	TOT
Hillam	8	-	8
Vincent	8	-	8
Gallimore	7	-	7
Topping	6	-	6
Mellor	5	-	5
Nevin	4	1	5
Ridding	5	-	5
Black	4	-	4
Byrne	4	-	4
McDonald	4	-	4
Heywood	3	-	3
Ainsworth	2	-	2
Manns	2	-	2
Newton	2	-	2
Warburton	2	-	2
Behan	1	-	1

Goalscorers

PLAYER	LGE	FAC	TOT
Dewar	8	-	8
Brown	7	-	7
Cape	7	-	7
Hine	6	-	6
Ball	5	1	6
Green	4	-	4
Stewart	4	-	4
Byrne	3	-	3
Gallimore	3	-	3
Frame	2	-	2
Heywood	2	-	2
Manley	2	-	2
Black	1	-	1
McMillen	1	-	1
Topping	1	-	1
Vose	1	-	1
McLenahan	-	1	1
own goals	2	-	2

Scott Duncan's team surge back up the Second Division table as fans return to Old Trafford

1934/35

AFTER SUCH A close shave with disaster the previous season, Scott Duncan's men defied last year's poor showing to surge back up the table. Duncan's changes since he took the manager's job in 1932 were now significant; this was a team without any of its most recent stars – Joe Spence, Jack Silcock, Charlie Moore, Alf Steward and Lal Hilditch had all left the club by now.

Inside forward George Mutch made his debut at the beginning of this season and was the lynchpin with 18 league goals in 40 games. An eight-game winning streak during the autumn set up the team for a solid year, although the second half of the season was not as successful and included a frustrating 3-0 FA Cup loss at home in a replay to Nottingham Forest.

A final league placing of 5th in the Second Division was commendable, only six points away from a promotion place, but for some fans it was consolidation at best and definitely not what new owner James Gibson or the board were hoping for in the longer term. The attendance average of almost 23,000 at Old Trafford, however, was a sign of hopeful times ahead, and quite a contrast to the crisis days of just four seasons ago.

■ United's improving defence is proved by the fact that they concede just 55 goals this season compared to 85 a year ago.

■ Tommy Bamford scores the winning goal on his debut against Newcastle United in a 1-0 win in October.

Above: Just after this improved season finished, James Brown arrived from Burnley for £1,800.

Left: Scott Duncan's magic was beginning to work and after this campaign, here is the team that the canny Scot compiled for the push towards promotion in 1936. Back row (l-r): Bamford, Griffiths, Porter, Breedon, Manley, Vose, McKay. Front row (l-r): Bryant, Mutch, Brown, Rowley, Chester.

Final League Table Division Two

		P	W	D	L	F	A	Pts
1	Brentford	42	26	9	7	93	48	61
2	Bolton Wanderers	42	26	4	12	96	48	56
3	West Ham United	42	26	4	12	80	63	56
4	Blackpool	42	21	11	10	79	57	53
5	**MANCHESTER UNITED**	**42**	**23**	**4**	**15**	**76**	**55**	**50**
6	Newcastle United	42	22	4	16	89	68	48
7	Fulham	42	17	12	13	76	56	46
8	Plymouth Argyle	42	19	8	15	75	64	46
9	Nottingham Forest	42	17	8	17	76	70	42
10	Bury	42	19	4	19	62	73	42
11	Sheffield United	42	16	9	17	79	70	41
12	Burnley	42	16	9	17	63	73	41
13	Hull City	42	16	8	18	63	74	40
14	Norwich City	42	14	11	17	71	61	39
15	Bradford Park Avenue	42	11	16	15	55	63	38
16	Barnsley	42	13	12	17	60	83	38
17	Swansea City	42	14	8	20	56	67	36
18	Port Vale	42	11	12	19	55	74	34
19	Southampton	42	11	12	19	46	75	34
20	Bradford City	42	12	8	22	50	68	32
21	Oldham Athletic	42	10	6	26	56	95	26
22	Notts County	42	9	7	26	46	97	25

Appearances

PLAYER	LGE	FAC	TOT
Griffiths	40	3	43
Mutch	40	3	43
Vose	39	3	42
McKay	38	3	41
Robertson	36	3	39
Manley	30	1	31
Jones, Tom	27	2	29
Rowley	24	3	27
Bryant	24	2	26
Hacking	22	2	24
Bamford	19	3	22
Cape	21	1	22
Jones, Tommy	20	2	22
Porter	15	1	16
Owen	15		15
Langford	12	-	12
McLenahan	10	-	10
Hall	8	1	9
Boyd	6	-	6
Hine	4	-	4
McMillen	4	-	4

PLAYER	LGE	FAC	TOT
Mellor	1	-	1
Topping	1	-	1

Goalscorers

PLAYER	LGE	FAC	TOT
Mutch	18	1	19
Bamford	9	2	11
Manley	9	-	9
Cape	8	-	8
Rowley	8	-	8
Bryant	6	-	6
Boyd	4	-	4
Jones, Tommy	4	-	4
McKay	3	-	3
Ball	1	-	1
Hine	1	-	1
McLenahan	1	-	1
McMillen	1	-	1
Owen	1	-	1
Robertson	1	-	1
own goal	1	-	1

Left: In additon to his contract, every player was issued with his own Training Rules and Players' Instructions booklet.

1935/36

A Second Division championship is gallantly secured with just a game to spare

I T WAS PROBABLY now-or-never for Scott Duncan's team to return to the First Division. The previous season had been closer to the club's expectations and Duncan's team of hard workers had settled into a successful pattern. However, the early season offered little indication of what was to come.

United were uninspiring up until December, a month that began with a 4-1 defeat at Blackpool. However, the Reds then turned the corner and were defeated just once in the next 24 games (including a run of 19 games without a loss to end the season).

The team was still only in fourth place in the league in March because of their slow start to the season, yet the Reds' surge allowed them to clinch promotion with a game to spare, while still needing a point in their final match to take the title from Charlton Athletic. Sure enough, against bottom-of-the-table Hull, United managed a 1-1 draw to return to the First Division in style by taking the Second Division championship.

George Mutch and Harry Rowley made a formidable goalscoring partnership (21 and 19 in the league respectively) while the defence did not concede a goal in eight of that stretch of 24 games.

- During the 19-game unbeaten run, United win 11 and draw eight matches while George Mutch scores 11 goals.

- Fifties winger Albert Scanlon is born on 10 October; he is the nephew of famous United forward Charlie Mitten.

- Stan Pearson, a 16-year-old Salford schoolboy, is signed by United scout Louis Rocca on 1 December 1935. Pearson will score 148 goals in 343 appearances.

Above: Full back William 'Billy' Porter played in every game this season, 45 in total.

Right: United's top scorer George Mutch and a West Ham United defender compete for the ball in the air as the Londoners take on the Reds in a Second Divison promotion battle at Upton Park. United won the match 2-1.

Final League Table Division Two

		P	W	D	L	F	A	Pts
1	**MANCHESTER UNITED**	**42**	**22**	**12**	**8**	**85**	**43**	**56**
2	Charlton Athletic	42	22	11	9	85	58	55
3	Sheffield United	42	20	12	10	79	50	52
4	West Ham United	42	22	8	12	90	68	52
5	Tottenham Hotspur	42	18	13	11	91	55	49
6	Leicester City	42	19	10	13	79	57	48
7	Plymouth Argyle	42	20	8	14	71	57	48
8	Newcastle United	42	20	6	16	88	79	46
9	Fulham	42	15	14	13	76	52	44
10	Blackpool	42	18	7	17	93	72	43
11	Norwich City	42	17	9	16	72	65	43
12	Bradford City	42	15	13	14	55	65	43
13	Swansea City	42	15	9	18	67	76	39
14	Bury	42	13	12	17	66	84	38
15	Burnley	42	12	13	17	50	59	37
16	Bradford Park Avenue	42	14	9	19	62	84	37
17	Southampton	42	14	9	19	47	65	37
18	Doncaster Rovers	42	14	9	19	51	71	37
19	Nottingham Forest	42	12	11	19	69	76	35
20	Barnsley	42	12	9	21	54	80	33
21	Port Vale	42	12	8	22	56	106	32
22	Hull City	42	5	10	27	47	111	20

Appearances

PLAYER	LGE	FAC	TOT
Mutch	42	3	45
Porter	42	3	45
Griffiths	41	3	44
Vose	41	3	44
Brown	40	3	43
Rowley	37	3	40
Hall	36	3	39
McKay	35	3	38
Manley	31	3	34
Bamford	27	2	29
Bryant	21	1	22
Cape	17	-	17
Gardner	12	2	14
Chester	13	-	13
Ferrier	7	1	8
Lang	4	-	4
Breedon	3	-	3
Langford	3	-	3
Owen	2	-	2
Wassall	2	-	2
Whalley	2	-	2
Morton	1	-	1

PLAYER	LGE	FAC	TOT
Redwood	1	-	1
Robbie	1	-	1
Robertson	1	-	1

Goalscorers

PLAYER	LGE	FAC	TOT
Mutch	21	2	23
Rowley	19	-	19
Bamford	16	-	16
Manley	14	1	15
Bryant	8	-	8
Cape	2	-	2
Chester	1	-	1
Gardner	1	-	1
Griffiths	1	-	1
Lang	1	-	1
own goal	1	-	1

Left: Players and officials at the Midland Hotel in Manchester for a celebration dinner after winning the the 1935 - 1936 Second Division championship.

The yo-yo years continue as a disappointed United suffer another season of relegation

1936/37

ONCE AGAIN, A season began at Old Trafford with great expectations: Scott Duncan had performed well as manager to gain promotion; his team contained proven goalscorers and a steady defence; and there was the renewed confidence a title under their belts could give. United now wanted to consolidate on their return to the First Division after a five-year absence, and everything looked on course after eight games which included three wins and two draws.

But suddenly the goals dried up and United went 11 games without a win. Even two consecutive victories just after Christmas proved to be a short-term fix and soon another poor streak (one win in 11 games) followed.

Duncan's team now looked weak in all areas against better opposition. There was still a chance of avoiding relegation in the final month of the season, but United could muster only a single win in April, and were eventually left two points adrift of safety in 21st position; it meant an immediate return to the Second Division.

The Reds would score only 55 goals in 42 games (compared to 85 the previous season, albeit in the Second Division) as forwards George Mutch and Harry Rowley were out of action for much of the season and managed just 11 goals between them. United also had defensive issues, conceding 78 goals as opposed to just 43 a year earlier.

■ Among the disappointing United team this season is Walter Winterbottom, who will go on to manage England's national team and receive a knighthood.

■ Duncan Edwards is born on 1 October in Dudley, West Midlands. While a month later Eddie Colman is born in Salford.

■ In the very first minute of goalkeeper Tommy Breen's debut against Leeds United on 28 November, the player is picking the ball out of his own net. United lose 2-1.

Above: United supporters arrive at Euston Station in London enroute to Highbury, where the Reds would meet Arsenal in a fourth round FA Cup match. United would lose 5-0

Left: A frozen, wintry scene from the match between United and Arsenal.

Final League Table Division One

		P	W	D	L	F	A	Pts
1	Manchester City	42	22	13	7	107	61	57
2	Charlton Athletic	42	21	12	9	58	49	54
3	Arsenal	42	18	16	8	80	49	52
4	Derby County	42	21	7	14	96	90	49
5	Wolverhampton Wanderers	42	21	5	16	84	67	47
6	Brentford	42	18	10	14	82	78	46
7	Middlesbrough	42	19	8	15	74	71	46
8	Sunderland	42	19	6	17	89	87	44
9	Portsmouth	42	17	10	15	62	66	44
10	Stoke City	42	15	12	15	72	57	42
11	Birmingham City	42	13	15	14	64	60	41
12	Grimsby Town	42	17	7	18	86	81	41
13	Chelsea	42	14	13	15	52	55	41
14	Preston North End	42	14	13	15	56	67	41
15	Huddersfield Town	42	12	15	15	62	64	39
16	West Bromwich Albion	42	16	6	20	77	98	38
17	Everton	42	14	9	19	81	78	37
18	Liverpool	42	12	11	19	62	84	35
19	Leeds United	42	15	4	23	60	80	34
20	Bolton Wanderers	42	10	14	18	43	66	34
21	**MANCHESTER UNITED**	**42**	**10**	**12**	**20**	**55**	**78**	**32**
22	Sheffield Wednesday	42	9	12	21	53	69	30

Appearances

PLAYER	LGE	FAC	TOT
Bryant	37	2	39
Roughton	33	2	35
Brown	31	2	33
Bamford	29	2	31
Manley	31	-	31
McKay	29	2	31
Mutch	28	2	30
Breen	26	2	28
Vose	26	1	27
Winterbottom	21	2	23
Redwood	21	1	22
Griffiths	21	-	21
Whalley	19	2	21
Rowley	17	-	17
John	15	-	15
Baird	14	-	14
Lang	8	1	9
Gladwin	8	-	8
Wrigglesworth	7	1	8
Wassall	7	-	7
Ferrier	6	-	6
McClelland	5	-	5

PLAYER	LGE	FAC	TOT
Cape	4	-	4
Gardner	4	-	4
Halton	4	-	4
McLenahan	3	-	3
Mellor	2	-	2
Porter	2	-	2
Thompson	2	-	2
Breedon	1	-	1
Jones	1	-	1

Goalscorers

PLAYER	LGE	FAC	TOT
Bamford	14	1	15
Bryant	10	-	10
Mutch	7	-	7
Manley	5	-	5
McKay	4	-	4
Rowley	4	-	4
Baird	3	-	3
Cape	1	-	1
Ferrier	1	-	1
Gladwin	1	-	1
Halton	1	-	1
McClelland	1	-	1
Thompson	1	-	1
Wassall	1	-	1
Wrigglesworth	1	-	1

Left: Cartoonist George Butterworth, who signed his work GEEBEE, was a regular contributor to programmes in the 1930s. Here he is celebrating United's return to the First Division.

1937/38

- As United are promoted to the First Division, cross-town rivals Manchester City are relegated to the Second Division.

- Walter Crickmer makes several key changes when he takes charge of the team, including bringing in Jack Breedon in goal, Bert Redwood at right back and Stan Pearson at inside left.

Above: Centre forward Jack Smith arrived from Newcastle United in February 1938 for a £6,500 fee and scored eight goals this season in just 17 games.

Right: 26 January 1938. The official programme for the FA Cup fourth round, against Barnsley.

Instant promotion back to First Division under Walter Crickmer's steady guidance

UNITED'S STAY IN the Second Division proved to be the briefest possible and yet the season began very unconvincingly. Scott Duncan – who had been in charge since 1932 – resigned in early November when it became clear that a medical condition his wife was suffering from was not being helped by the polluted atmosphere in Manchester. He would go to manage Ipswich Town of the Southern League.

After five managers in just 11 seasons, the club's directors wanted a familiar face in charge of the team and they immediately re-appointed Walter Crickmer as caretaker manager for the second time. Crickmer's experienced head on the shoulders of a struggling team caused an improvement in results and cheered the supporters. In his first game in charge, United handed out a 7-1 thrashing to Chesterfield away from home. Tthe tide seemed to be turning.

Not only was the Old Trafford team galvanised by a new manager, but also there was a new star in the making: Irishman Johnny Carey, who had made his debut (originally at inside forward) just a few weeks into the season.

United became one of the division's form teams, giving chase to champions-to-be Aston Villa. With one game to play, the second promotion place was still available, and a 2-0 win against Bury confirmed the Red Devils' immediate return to the First Division on goal average from Sheffield United.

Final League Table Division Two

		P	W	D	L	F	A	Pts
1	Aston Villa	42	25	7	10	73	35	57
2	**MANCHESTER UNITED**	42	22	9	11	82	50	53
3	Sheffield United	42	22	9	11	73	56	53
4	Coventry City	42	20	12	10	66	45	52
5	Tottenham Hotspur	42	19	6	17	76	54	44
6	Burnley	42	17	10	15	54	54	44
7	Bradford Park Avenue	42	17	9	16	69	56	43
8	Fulham	42	16	11	15	61	57	43
9	West Ham United	42	14	14	14	53	52	42
10	Bury	42	18	5	19	63	60	41
11	Chesterfield	42	16	9	17	63	63	41
12	Luton Town	42	15	10	17	89	86	40
13	Plymouth Argyle	42	14	12	16	57	65	40
14	Norwich City	42	14	11	17	56	75	39
15	Southampton	42	15	9	18	55	77	39
16	Blackburn Rovers	42	14	10	18	71	80	38
17	Sheffield Wednesday	42	14	10	18	49	56	38
18	Swansea City	42	13	12	17	45	73	38
19	Newcastle United	42	14	8	20	51	58	36
20	Nottingham Forest	42	14	8	20	47	60	36
21	Barnsley	42	11	14	17	50	64	36
22	Stockport County	42	11	9	22	43	70	31

Appearances

PLAYER	LGE	FAC	TOT
Bryant	39	4	43
Roughton	39	4	43
McKay	37	3	40
Baird	35	4	39
Breen	33	4	37
Vose	33	4	37
Redwood	29	4	33
Brown	28	3	31
Rowley	25	4	29
Bamford	23	4	27
Manley	21	1	22
Carey	16	3	19
Griffiths	18	-	18
Smith	17	-	17
Pearson	11	1	12
Breedon	9	-	9
Wassall	9	-	9
Gladwin	7	-	7
Whalley	6	-	6
Ferrier	5	-	5
Savage	4	1	5
Murray	4	-	4

PLAYER	LGE	FAC	TOT
Winterbottom	4	-	4
Wrigglesworth	4	-	4
Mutch	2	-	2
Porter	2	-	2
Jones	1	-	1
Thompson	1	-	1

Goalscorers

PLAYER	LGE	FAC	TOT
Bamford	14	1	15
Baird	12	3	15
Bryant	12	-	12
Rowley	9	-	9
Smith	8	-	8
Manley	7	-	7
McKay	7	-	7
Carey	3	1	4
Ferrier	3	-	3
Pearson	2	1	3
Redwood	2	-	2
Brown	1	-	1
Wassall	1	-	1
Wrigglesworth	1	-	1

A season of consolidation in the First Division but war is looming on the horizon

A S THE DARK DAYS of the Second World War loomed ahead, United were focused on their own troubles, attempting to keep their new place in the First Division. Two pieces of good news helped their cause: firstly, Walter Crickmer remained as the team's manager for the season and, secondly, Johnny Carey was able to blossom as a star inside forward. The Dubliner repaid much of the £200 transfer fee United paid for him with a series of impressive performances. Apart from Carey, another star of the season was John Hanlon who had signed as an amateur in 1934 and was finally given his chance in the first team. The young forward – only 5ft 7in tall and weighing just ten stones – had not played for the first team before this season, but would score 12 goals in just 27 league appearances.

However, the team was basically the same as the one that won promotion and was not really strong enough for the First Division. It did not help that last season's two top scorers were transferred – Thomas Bamford went to Swansea and Harry Baird to Huddersfield Town – and when the Reds began with only one win in their first six games, leaving them 18th in the table out of 22 teams, the fans naturally feared the worst.

But a 5-1 win in their next home fixture against Chelsea boosted their confidence and, when Hanlon made his debut in November, there were more wins to enjoy. By the end of December, the Reds were up to 13th place.

However, United were never able to put a decent run of results together and so move very far up the table. The team's form was hit and miss throughout the season; a 7-1 crushing at Charlton Athletic was immediately followed by a 5-3 win at Blackpool, with Hanlon scoring a hat-trick.

This was a season of consolidation, but there were compensations in that Carey played almost a full season and the crowds returned to Old Trafford. A mid-table finish – 14th with 38 points, but just six points above the relegation zone – was acceptable and only just below the other newly promoted club Aston Villa who were 12th.

1938/39

- Future European Cup winner Paddy Crerand is born on 19 February 1939 in Glasgow. The Scottish international will make 397 appearances for United between 1963 and 1971.

- The Manchester United Junior Athletic Club was formed in time for the start of this season to give the club a much stronger scouting and youth set-up, paving the way for the Busby Babes.

Above: United full back Jack Griffiths (left) fights for the ball with Arsenal player Alf Kirchen during a match at Highbury.

Left: Back row (l-r): Brown, Roughton, Breedon, Manley, Breen, McKay, Baird. Middle row (l-r): Inglis (Assistant Trainer), Bryant, Craven, Smith, Griffiths, Vose, Curry (Trainer). Front row (l-r): Redwood, Gladwin, Pearson.

Final League Table

		P	W	D	L	F	A	Pts
1	Everton	42	27	5	10	88	52	59
2	Wolverhampton Wanderers	42	22	11	9	88	39	55
3	Charlton Athletic	42	22	6	14	75	59	50
4	Middlesbrough	42	20	9	13	93	74	49
5	Arsenal	42	19	9	14	55	41	47
6	Derby County	42	19	8	15	66	55	46
7	Stoke City	42	17	12	13	71	68	46
8	Bolton Wanderers	42	15	15	12	67	58	45
9	Preston North End	42	16	12	14	63	59	44
10	Grimsby Town	42	16	11	15	61	69	43
11	Liverpool	42	14	14	14	62	63	42
12	Aston Villa	42	15	11	16	71	60	41
13	Leeds United	42	16	9	17	59	67	41
14	**MANCHESTER UNITED**	**42**	**11**	**16**	**15**	**57**	**65**	**38**
15	Blackpool	42	12	14	16	56	68	38
16	Sunderland	42	13	12	17	54	67	38
17	Portsmouth	42	12	13	17	47	70	37
18	Brentford	42	14	8	20	53	74	36
19	Huddersfield Town	42	12	11	19	58	64	35
20	Chelsea	42	12	9	21	64	80	33
21	Birmingham City	42	12	8	22	62	84	32
22	Leicester City	42	9	11	22	48	82	29

Appearances

PLAYER	LGE	FAC	TOT
Vose	39	1	40
Rowley	38	1	39
Griffiths	35	2	37
Redwood	35	2	37
Carey	32	2	34
Warner	29	2	31
Hanlon	27	2	29
Wassall	27	2	29
Bryant	27	-	27
Manley	23	-	23
Breedon	22	-	22
McKay	20	2	22
Smith	19	1	20
Tapken	14	2	16
Roughton	14	-	14
Wrigglesworth	12	2	14
Gladwin	12	1	13
Craven	11	-	11
Pearson	9	-	9
Breen	6	-	6
Dougan	4	-	4
Brown	3	-	3

PLAYER	LGE	FAC	TOT
Bradbury	2	-	2
Whalley	2	-	2

Goalscorers

PLAYER	LGE	FAC	TOT
Hanlon	12	-	12
Rowley	10	-	10
Bryant	6	-	6
Carey	6	-	6
Smith	6	-	6
Wassall	4	-	4
Manley	3	-	3
Wrigglesworth	3	-	3
Craven	2	-	2
Redwood	1	1	2
Bradbury	1	-	1
McKay	1	-	1
Pearson	1	-	1
own goal	1	-	1

Left: 6 May 1939. Team details in the United against Liverpool programme. It will be the last official game for both teams before war breaks out. Matt Busby lined up for the Merseysiders at right half.

1939/45

Official football stops but the war leagues and cups carry on

ALTHOUGH THE FIRST few games of the 1939-40 season were played, the Second World War eventually stopped the Football League in early September 1939. United actually played three games in this abandoned season, winning 4-0 on the opening weekend against Grimsby Town at Old Trafford in front of more than 22,000 fans; drawing away at Chelsea 1-1 and losing at Charlton Athletic 2-0 on 2 September. The Reds were ninth in the league after the three games.

Many players throughout the league, including those from United, then went to war and, for those who remained and also in an effort to maintain morale, the Football League organised a War League to replace its normal league format and also a War League Cup to take the place of the FA Cup. The first season of the league was split into ten regional divisions with a 50-mile travel limit for players and fans so they would not waste too much time (or even much-needed petrol resources) on attending matches. United were placed in the Western Division and finished fourth; they were beaten by Blackburn Rovers in the second round of the new cup competition.

The following season, the ten divisions were replaced by a more simple structure of a Northern League and a Southern League. A United team played in the Northern League through-out the rest of the war and made the Northern League cup final

in 1944-45. Also during this time, United won the Lancashire Cup in 1941, but none of the war-time appearances or goals scored during this period count in the club's official records.

Of the players that went to war, Hubert Redwood, a full back who made 93 appearances from 1935 to 1939, joined the army and died in 1943 of tuberculosis after being invalided out of the forces; George Curless, a youth team player, was killed while serving in bomber command; and Ben Carpenter, a member of the reserves, died during the retreat from Dunkirk.

The other casualty was the Old Trafford stadium which suffered severe bomb damage in March 1941 when the main stand, a large part of the terraces and the pitch itself all took direct hits.

Above: 9 February 1944. As the war drags on, Matt Busby captains the Scotland team playing England at Wembley. Here seen introducing his team to King George VI.

Right: Future manager Busby spent the war in the army and is seen opposite (far left) in 1940 with Liverpool keeper Arthur Riley showing him how to use a rifle.

1945/46

Post-war football returns and Matt Busby becomes manager

■ Matt Busby originally signs a five-year manager's contract after serving in the war in the Ninth Battalion of the King's Liverpool Regiment.

ONE OF THE most significant moments in United's history happened before any football was even played this season. The Second World War was slowly drawing to a close as 1945 dawned, but there was no professional football being played. However, in February that year, United appointed a new manager. A young Scottish physical training instructor named Alexander Matthew Busby was still in the army when he got the job at a club whose stadium had been all but destroyed by German bombs.

When the war ended in May, sport in Great Britain was in no shape to return to normal immediately, and the Football League calendar was empty throughout 1945. Matt Busby was de-mobilised in October, by which time the Football Association had decided to stage an FA Cup competition that would begin in January 1946 with each tie taking place over two legs.

Four players from the last pre-war game in 1939 actually

returned to the team for the first post-war match – Jack Rowley, Johnny Carey, Jack Warner and Jimmy Hanlon. But, although Busby's United won their opening tie against Accrington Stanley 7-3 on aggregate, they fell to Preston North End in round two 3-2.

Opposite: Matt Busby would end the war as Company Sergeant Major Busby at the Sandhurst Military Academy. Here he lines up (3rd from the left) for a United Services team in a match played in Belfast in 1945. Stanley Matthews is front row left.

Appearances

PLAYER	LGE	FAC	TOT
Carey	-	4	4
Cockburn	-	4	4
Crompton	-	4	4
Hanlon	-	4	4
Rowley	-	4	4
Smith	-	4	4
Warner	-	4	4

PLAYER	LGE	FAC	TOT
Whalley	-	4	4
Wrigglesworth	-	4	4
Chilton	-	3	3
Roach	-	2	2
Walton	-	2	2
Bainbridge	-	1	1

Goalscorers

PLAYER	LGE	FAC	TOT
Hanlon	-	2	2
Rowley	-	2	2
Wrigglesworth	-	2	2
Bainbridge	-	1	1
Smith	-	1	1
own goal	-	1	1

FA CUP: LOSE TO PRESTON NORTH END (2-3 ON AGGREGATE) IN 4TH ROUND.

'Homeless' United still manage to battle hard for the league championship

IN THEIR FIRST full season of post-war league action, United left behind years of mediocrity and graduated to the elite level. Matt Busby and his new coaching partner Jimmy Murphy assembled a strong squad of players despite the club being £15,000 in debt and Old Trafford still out of use owing to bomb damage.

Busby rejected interference from the club's directors (something of a tradition in football up until this time) and was ruthless in team selection. Led by the developing Johnny Carey and including new stars-of-the-future, and short-term fix Jimmy Delaney signed for a £4,000 transfer fee from Celtic,

United began the season with five straight wins. Busby's team never let up and scored hats full of goals in the process of a concerted title challenge – 95 by the end of the season, with Jack Rowley top scorer with 26.

Playing at their neighbour's home stadium Maine Road, crowds of over 50,000 were typical and United lost only one of their 'home' fixtures as they battled with Liverpool, Wolverhampton Wanderers and Stoke City for the First Division championship. Perhaps the most decisive game was late in the season in May at Anfield, where Liverpool won 1-0; the Merseysiders would take the title by a single point.

- Matt Busby's team already includes all the members of the Famous Five forward line: Jimmy Delaney, Jack Rowley, Johnny Morris, Charlie Mitten and Stan Pearson.

- Charlie Mitten and Jimmy Delaney make their full league debuts for United in the season opener, a 2-1 home win over Grimsby Town on 31 August. Delaney was manager Matt Busby's first signing while Mitten signed as a Red before World War II and played for the club in the unofficial War League.

Above: Johnny Carey (dark shirt) of United and Ireland tackles a Brentford player during a league match at Brentford's ground, Griffin Park. The game ended goalless.

Left: United's goalkeeper, Bill Fielding (wearing gloves) is out of position and stranded as John Aston attempts in vain to stop the ball from going over the snow covered goal line for an Arsenal score at Highbury. The Red Devils lost 6-2.

Final League Table Division One

		P	W	D	L	F	A	Pt
1	Liverpool	42	25	7	10	84	52	57
2	**MANCHESTER UNITED**	**42**	**22**	**12**	**8**	**95**	**54**	**56**
3	Wolverhampton Wanderers	42	25	6	11	98	56	56
4	Stoke City	42	24	7	11	90	53	55
5	Blackpool	42	22	6	14	71	70	50
6	Sheffield United	42	21	7	14	89	75	49
7	Preston North End	42	18	11	13	76	74	47
8	Aston Villa	42	18	9	15	67	53	45
9	Sunderland	42	18	8	16	65	66	44
10	Everton	42	17	9	16	62	67	43
11	Middlesbrough	42	17	8	17	73	68	42
12	Portsmouth	42	16	9	17	66	60	41
13	Arsenal	42	16	9	17	72	70	41
14	Derby County	42	18	5	19	73	79	41
15	Chelsea	42	16	7	19	69	84	39
16	Grimsby Town	42	13	12	17	61	82	38
17	Blackburn Rovers	42	14	8	20	45	53	36
18	Bolton Wanderers	42	13	8	21	57	69	34
19	Charlton Athletic	42	11	12	19	57	71	34
20	Huddersfield Town	42	13	7	22	53	79	33
21	Brentford	42	9	7	26	45	88	25
22	Leeds United	42	6	6	30	45	90	18

Appearances

PLAYER	LGE	FAC	TOT
Pearson	42	2	44
Chilton	41	2	43
Delaney	37	2	39
Rowley	37	2	39
Warner	34	2	36
McGlen	33	2	35
Carey	31	2	33
Cockburn	32	-	32
Crompton	29	1	30
Hanlon	27	-	27
Morris	24	2	26
Aston	21	2	23
Mitten	20	-	20
Walton	15	-	15
Burke	13	-	13
Buckle	5	2	7
Collinson	7	-	7
Fielding	6	1	7
Wrigglesworth	4	-	4
Whalley	3	-	3
Worrall	1	-	1

Goalscorers

PLAYER	LGE	FAC	TOT
Rowley	26	2	28
Pearson	19	-	19
Burke	9	-	9
Delaney	8	-	8
Mitten	8	-	8
Morris	8	-	8
Hanlon	7	-	7
Buckle	3	1	4
Wrigglesworth	2	-	2
Chilton	1	-	1
McGlen	1	-	1
Warner	1	-	1
own goals	2	-	2

Right: Old Trafford suffered extensive damage when it was bombed on the night of 11 March 1941. This is a map given to the Luftwaffe navigator who was present on the raid that night.

1947/48

- United's second FA Cup victory is achieved 39 years to the day from the first in 1909.

- United's home match at Maine Road against champions-elect Arsenal caught the fans' imagination. The attendance was the largest ever for a league match involving the Reds.

- All six opponents in this season's FA Cup camapign came from the First Division and United beat them all without a replay.

Above: John Aston Snr moves away from Portsmouth's Peter Harris.

Right: The United team that took the cup this season. Back row (l-r): Warner, Anderson, Chilton, Crompton, Rowley, Aston, Cockburn, Curry (Trainer). Front row (l-r): Delaney, Morris, Busby (Manager), Carey, Crickmer (Secretary), Pearson, Mitten.

A second FA Cup win, a second consecutive runners-up league spot and the fans return in huge numbers

THE FIRST GREAT team under manager Matt Busby was now assembled and his players were becoming noted for their attack-minded tactics and high scoring. Johnny Aston established himself as yet another United star during this campaign, playing every league match and helping shore up a defence that had leaked a few too many goals the previous season (54) compared to this year (48).

But a slight tightening up in defence led to fewer goals scored (just 81 this season) and fewer points. Some observers argued that league form suffered because of the FA Cup winning campaign, but in the end, Arsenal were easy winners of the First Division title with United seven points adrift.

During this season United broke their own record for attendance at one of their games when Arsenal visited Maine Road in January; 81,962 fans watched a 1-1 draw between the league's top two teams. In fact, more than one million fans came to watch United's home games and significantly helped ease the debt that the Red Devils had been living under.

Another highlight for the fans was the first Manchester derby games for over a decade against City, although neither were classics (two draws, 0-0 and 1-1). The effectiveness of Jack Rowley (23 goals) was not quite enough to win the title and United finished runners-up for the second consecutive season.

Final League Table Division One

		P	W	D	L	F	A	Pt
1	Arsenal	42	23	13	6	81	32	59
2	MANCHESTER UNITED	42	19	14	9	81	48	52
3	Burnley	42	20	12	10	56	43	52
4	Derby County	42	19	12	11	77	57	50
5	Wolverhampton Wanderers	42	19	9	14	83	70	47
6	Aston Villa	42	19	9	14	65	57	47
7	Preston North End	42	20	7	15	67	68	47
8	Portsmouth	42	19	7	16	68	50	45
9	Blackpool	42	17	10	15	57	41	44
10	Manchester City	42	15	12	15	52	47	42
11	Liverpool	42	16	10	16	65	61	42
12	Sheffield United	42	16	10	16	65	70	42
13	Charlton Athletic	42	17	6	19	57	66	40
14	Everton	42	17	6	19	52	66	40
15	Stoke City	42	14	10	18	41	55	38
16	Middlesbrough	42	14	9	19	71	73	37
17	Bolton Wanderers	42	16	5	21	46	58	37
18	Chelsea	42	14	9	19	53	71	37
19	Huddersfield Town	42	12	12	18	51	60	36
20	Sunderland	42	13	10	19	56	67	36
21	Blackburn Rovers	42	11	10	21	54	72	32
22	Grimsby Town	42	8	6	28	45	111	22

FOOTBALL LEAGUE DIVISION ONE: RUNNERS-UP

Appearances

PLAYER	LGE	FAC	TOT
Aston	42	6	48
Chilton	41	6	47
Pearson	40	6	46
Rowley	39	6	45
Mitten	38	6	44
Morris	38	6	44
Carey	37	6	43
Crompton	37	6	43
Delaney	36	6	42
Cockburn	26	6	32
Anderson	18	5	23
Warner	15	1	16
McGlen	13	-	13
Hanlon	8	-	8
Burke	6	-	6
Walton	6	-	6
Worrall	5	-	5
Brown	3	-	3
Buckle	3	-	3
Lynn	3	-	3
Dale	2	-	2
Lowrie	2	-	2

PLAYER	LGE	FAC	TOT
Pegg	2	-	2
Ball	1	-	1
Cassidy	1	-	1

Left: United's Stan Pearson (white shorts) competes with the Preston North End goalkeeper and a defender in the sixth round FA Cup match at Maine Road. Pearson scores twice in a 4-2 win.

Goalscorers

PLAYER	LGE	FAC	TOT
Rowley	23	5	28
Pearson	18	8	26
Morris	18	3	21
Mitten	8	3	11
Delaney	8	1	9
Anderson	1	1	2
Buckle	1	-	1
Burke	1	-	1
Carey	1	-	1
Cockburn	1	-	1
Hanlon	1	-	1
Warner	-	1	1

FA CUP: WINNERS. 24 APRIL 1948. WEMBLEY, LONDON. BEAT BLACKPOOL 4-2 ROWLEY 28', ROWLEY 70', PEARSON 80', ANDERSON 82'

Charlie Mitten is the star but fixture congestion slows down United's twin trophy dreams

1948/49

THERE WAS NO doubting the quality of Matt Busby's team in the league, but near misses were not good enough for the tough Scot. Again, United battled on both fronts – the league and the FA Cup. However, five league defeats before the end of October was not championship-winning form and, despite a run of 13 games unbeaten towards Christmas and into the New Year, United were always chasing the other contenders for the title.

Goalscoring was no problem, with Jack Rowley and Charlie Mitten both having their best ever campaigns while United's other strength this season was their away form – they won 10 games away from Old Trafford, two more than any other team. Yet once again a long run in the FA Cup – this time coupled with postponements due to bad weather – left United with too much to do at the end of the season.

A remarkable 12 league games needed to be played in 31 days from the beginning of April and although United won their last four in a row, they crucially lost three earlier on. A win against Portsmouth on the season's last day after the Hampshire team had already secured the title was no compensation for United as they finished in the runners-up spot for the third successive year.

There had also been other distractions: the Reds lost 4-3 to Arsenal in the FA Charity Shield game at Highbury in October and the run in the FA Cup to the semi-finals also failed to bring home a trophy despite big wins over Bournemouth (6-0), Bradford Park Avenue (5-0) and Yeovil Town (8-0). Rowley scored nine goals during the eight cup games, but eventually Wolverhampton Wanderers outlasted the Reds in the semi-final, winning the replay 1-0.

- In United's FA Cup games, Jack Rowley's strike rate is nine goals in eight games, even better than his 20 in 39 league matches.

- In a fifth round FA Cup tie against Yeovil Town, Jack Rowley nets five times in an 8-0 win in front of 81,565 at Maine Road.

- Harry Halse who scored 56 goals in just 125 United appearances dies on 25 March aged 63.

- On his debut, John Downie scores in a 3-2 win over Charlton Athletic on 5 March.

Above: Jimmy Delaney sends over a cross during a match against Arsenal at Highbury in August 1948. The Reds won 1-0.

Left: United forward Charlie Mitten scores despite the best efforts of Wolverhampton Wanderers and England goalkeeper, Bert Williams.

Final League Table Division One

	P	W	D	L	F	A	Pt
1 Portsmouth	42	25	8	9	84	42	58
2 MANCHESTER UNITED	42	21	11	10	77	44	53
3 Derby County	42	22	9	11	74	55	53
4 Newcastle United	42	20	12	10	70	56	52
5 Arsenal	42	18	13	11	74	44	49
6 Wolverhampton Wanderers	42	17	12	13	79	66	46
7 Manchester City	42	15	15	12	47	51	45
8 Sunderland	42	13	17	12	49	58	43
9 Charlton Athletic	42	15	12	15	63	67	42
10 Aston Villa	42	16	10	16	60	76	42
11 Stoke City	42	16	9	17	66	68	41
12 Liverpool	42	13	14	15	53	43	40
13 Chelsea	42	12	14	16	69	68	38
14 Bolton Wanderers	42	14	10	18	59	68	38
15 Burnley	42	12	14	16	43	50	38
16 Blackpool	42	11	16	15	54	67	38
17 Birmingham City	42	11	15	16	36	38	37
18 Everton	42	13	11	18	41	63	37
19 Middlesbrough	42	11	12	19	46	57	34
20 Huddersfield Town	42	12	10	20	40	69	34
21 Preston North End	42	11	11	20	62	75	33
22 Sheffield United	42	11	11	20	57	78	33

Appearances

PLAYER	LGE	FAC	TOT
Chilton	42	8	50
Mitten	42	8	50
Crompton	41	8	49
Carey	41	7	48
Aston	39	8	47
Pearson	39	8	47
Rowley	39	8	47
Cockburn	36	8	44
Delaney	36	6	42
McGlen	23	8	31
Morris	21	1	22
Anderson	15	1	16
Burke	9	6	15
Downie	12	-	12
Ball	8	1	9
Lowrie	8	-	8
Buckle	5	2	7
Warner	3	-	3
Brown	1	-	1
Cassidy	1	-	1
Hanlon	1	-	1

Goalscorers

PLAYER	LGE	FAC	TOT
Rowley	20	9	29
Mitten	18	5	23
Pearson	14	3	17
Burke	6	6	12
Morris	6	-	6
Downie	5	-	5
Delaney	4	-	4
Buckle	2	-	2
Carey	1	-	1
McGlen	1	-	1

Forwards Johnny Aston (l) and Stan Pearson were two of the stars of this season.

Goalkeeper Jack Crompton (dark shirt, right foreground) in action during a match against Hull City. United won the match 1-0.

FOOTBALL LEAGUE DIVISION ONE: RUNNERS-UP

FA CUP: LOSE TO WOLVERHAMPTON WANDERERS (0-1) IN SEMI-FINAL REPLAY

FA CHARITY SHIELD: RUNNERS-UP. 6 OCTOBER 1948. HIGHBURY, LONDON. LOST TO ARSENAL 3-4
ROWLEY, BURKE, MITTEN.

1949/50

Although the team returns to Old Trafford it fails to prompt a return to winning major trophies

THIS WOULD PROVE to be a frustrating league season for many fans, but it was a year that marked a different kind of victory – a return to home matches at Old Trafford just two days short of 10 years since the last match at the famous stadium. The return to their real home meant no more £5,000-a-year rent and no sharing of gate receipts with landlords Manchester City from the Reds' games at their temporary home of Maine Road. The re-opening on 24 August was another triumph – a 3-0 win over Bolton Wanderers.

There was still work to be done (the main stand was roofless) and the capacity was smaller than their long-time temporary home of Maine Road, but the team was happy to return to home territory. They even managed two exceptionally big wins in front of their fans: 6-0 against Huddersfield Town in November and 7-0 vs Aston Villa in March.

Another season of challenging for the First Division championship was by now almost taken for granted by Matt Busby's United. Busby's attacking style still bought lots of goals – Jack Rowley again led the attack (20 goals in 39 games) while Charlie Mitten chipped in with 16 – yet once again the team fell short. United never put a long unbeaten run together to threaten the leaders, so Portsmouth won their second consecutive title and were three points ahead at season's end with United finishing 4th.

■ Portsmouth are tipped by many to win the league and cup double until meeting United in the FA Cup fifth round and being beaten 3-1 on their home ground after forcing a 3-3 draw at Old Trafford.

■ Three of Charlie Mitten's four goals in a 7-0 thrashing of Aston Villa in March are from the penalty spot.

■ The Reds pay Queens Park Rangers £11,000 for goalkeeper Reg Allen, a record amount for a keeper at the time.

Above: 9 January 1950. United forward Jack Rowley (left) near the Weymouth goalmouth during their third round FA Cup tie at Old Trafford. United won the match 4-0.

Right: 9 January 1950. Weymouth defenders cannot stop a shot from Jack Rowley, after their keeper had been drawn from goal. Rowley's score was United's second in a comfortable victory.

Final League Table Division One

		P	W	D	L	F	A	Pt
1	Portsmouth	42	22	9	11	74	38	53
2	Wolverhampton Wanderers	42	20	13	9	76	49	53
3	Sunderland	42	21	10	11	83	62	52
4	MANCHESTER UNITED	42	18	14	10	69	44	50
5	Newcastle United	42	19	12	11	77	55	50
6	Arsenal	42	19	11	12	79	55	49
7	Blackpool	42	17	15	10	46	35	49
8	Liverpool	42	17	14	11	64	54	48
9	Middlesbrough	42	20	7	15	59	48	47
10	Burnley	42	16	13	13	40	40	45
11	Derby County	42	17	10	15	69	61	44
12	Aston Villa	42	15	12	15	61	61	42
13	Chelsea	42	12	16	14	58	65	40
14	West Bromwich Albion	42	14	12	16	47	53	40
15	Huddersfield Town	42	14	9	19	52	73	37
16	Bolton Wanderers	42	10	14	18	45	59	34
17	Fulham	42	10	14	18	41	54	34
18	Everton	42	10	14	18	42	66	34
19	Stoke City	42	11	12	19	45	75	34
20	Charlton Athletic	42	13	6	23	53	65	32
21	Manchester City	42	8	13	21	36	68	29
22	Birmingham City	42	7	14	21	31	67	28

Appearances

PLAYER	LGE	FAC	TOT
Delaney	42	5	47
Mitten	42	5	47
Aston	40	5	45
Pearson	41	4	45
Rowley	39	5	44
Carey	38	5	43
Chilton	35	5	40
Cockburn	35	5	40
Crompton	27	1	28
Warner	21	4	25
Bogan	18	4	22
Downie	18	2	20
Feehan	12	2	14
McGlen	13	1	14
Ball	13	-	13
Lynn	10	-	10
Buckle	7	-	7
Lancaster	2	2	4
Lowrie	3	-	3
McNulty	2	-	2
Birch	1	-	1
Clempson	1	-	1

PLAYER	LGE	FAC	TOT
Whitefoot	1	-	1
Wood	1	-	1

Johnny Carey, the United captain, leads his team out.

Goalscorers

PLAYER	LGE	FAC	TOT
Rowley	20	3	23
Mitten	16	3	19
Pearson	15	2	17
Downie	6	1	7
Delaney	4	2	6
Bogan	4	-	4
Carey	1	-	1
Chilton	1	-	1
Cockburn	1	-	1
own goal	1	-	1

United outside left Charlie Mitten scored 19 goals in 47 appearances in this his final season at the club.

Controversy among the players over wages as another First Division title is denied at the death

THIRTY YEARS AFTER United star Billy Meredith led player unrest over low wages, the same situation arose again, this time partly because of Matt Busby's reluctance to follow rival clubs and find under-the-counter ways to remunerate his players. So, this development along with the emergence of talented youth team players and a couple of key transfer acquisitions, meant it was a time of change.

In the dog house was star winger Charlie Mitten, who fled to Colombia chasing the promise of a huge salary, while one of the leaders of dressing room dissent is said to be Johnny Morris and he is transferred to Derby County.

Meanwhile, in came Reg Allen in goal from QPR and Eddie McIlvenny (captain of the USA's recent World Cup win against England) joined at half back from the Philadelphia Nationals. However, yet another season in which United won praise for great attacking football ended in severe disappointment.

The problem was nine defeats before the New Year, although when United beat high-flying Tottenham Hotspur 2-1 at Old Trafford in their first league match of 1951, a long-awaited title still appeared possible. That victory began a fabulous run of 14 wins and only one defeat until the end of the season.

But Spurs held on and United were runners-up again, for the fourth time in five seasons, four points short of the title. The prolific Stan Pearson was top scorer, this season with 18 goals in 39 games, while Johnny Aston contributed a remarkable 15 goals after switching from left back to the No 9 shirt in December.

■ Star forward of the 1940s Jimmy Delaney is transferred to Aberdeen in November for £3,500 at the age of 36.

■ United lose in the sixth round of the FA Cup for the second successive season, this time to Birmingham City 1-0.

Above: Jeff Whitefoot started his career as a trainee with Manchester United in 1949. When he made his debut against Portsmouth in April 1950 he was, at the time, the youngest player to start in a league match for United at just 16 years and 105 days.

Left: The team were runners-up to Tottenham Hotspur for the First Division championship. Back row (l-r): Curry, (Trainer) Carey, Redman, Chilton, Allen, McGlen, Aston. Front row (l-r): Delaney, Downie, Rowley, Pearson, McShane.

Final League Table Division One

		P	W	D	L	F	A	Pts
1	Tottenham Hotspur	42	25	10	7	82	44	60
2	**MANCHESTER UNITED**	42	24	8	10	74	40	56
3	Blackpool	42	20	10	12	79	53	50
4	Newcastle United	42	18	13	11	62	53	49
5	Arsenal	42	19	9	14	73	56	47
6	Middlesbrough	42	18	11	13	76	65	47
7	Portsmouth	42	16	15	11	71	68	47
8	Bolton Wanderers	42	19	7	16	64	61	45
9	Liverpool	42	16	11	15	53	59	43
10	Burnley	42	14	14	14	48	43	42
11	Derby County	42	16	8	18	81	75	40
12	Sunderland	42	12	16	14	63	73	40
13	Stoke City	42	13	14	15	50	59	40
14	Wolverhampton Wanderers	42	15	8	19	74	61	38
15	Aston Villa	42	12	13	17	66	68	37
16	West Bromwich Albion	42	13	11	18	53	61	37
17	Charlton Athletic	42	14	9	19	63	80	37
18	Fulham	42	13	11	18	52	68	37
19	Huddersfield Town	42	15	6	21	64	92	36
20	Chelsea	42	12	8	22	53	65	32
21	Sheffield Wednesday	42	12	8	22	64	83	32
22	Everton	42	12	8	22	48	86	32

Appearances

PLAYER	LGE	FAC	TOT
Aston	41	4	45
Allen	40	4	44
Carey	39	4	43
Pearson	39	4	43
Chilton	38	4	42
Rowley	39	3	42
Cockburn	35	4	39
Gibson	32	3	35
McShane	30	1	31
Downie	29	-	29
McGlen	26	1	27
Redman	16	2	18
Birkett	9	4	13
Delaney	13	-	13
Birch	8	4	12
Bogan	11	-	11
McNulty	4	1	5
Jones	4	-	4
Clempson	2	-	2
Crompton	2	-	2
McIlvenny	2	-	2
Whitefoot	2	-	2

PLAYER	LGE	FAC	TOT
Cassidy	1	-	1
Lowrie	-	1	1

Striker Jack Rowley in action in November 1950.

Goalscorers

PLAYER	LGE	FAC	TOT
Pearson	18	5	23
Aston	15	1	16
Rowley	14	1	15
Downie	10	-	10
McShane	7	-	7
Birch	4	1	5
Bogan	3	-	3
Birkett	2	-	2
Delaney	1	-	1
own goal	-	1	1

Stan Pearson is the season's top goal scorer with 23 goals.

1951/52

Reporter Tom Jackson, who coined the phrase 'The Busby Babes' this season, will tragically die in the Munich air disaster six years later.

Among the debutants during this campaign are Jackie Blanchflower and Roger Byrne, who both start their first games on 24 November in a 0-0 draw against Liverpool inspiring Jackson's new term.

Above: Official programme for the last game of the season. United walloped Arsenal 6-1. Jack Rowley scored a hat-trick.

Right: United forward Frank Clempson (foreground) enjoyed his best spell in the first team in the championship winning team of 1951-1952.

The birth of the Busby Babes and a dramatic league title win after a managerial masterstroke

THE LEVEL OF frustration at Old Trafford had risen with every league championship near-miss of the last few seasons, but Matt Busby declined to panic and kept making only minor changes to what was already a gifted team. For this season, Busby brought in two more key players: Johnny Berry at outside right from Birmingham and Roger Byrne at left back from the junior ranks.

Once again, United set off among the title contenders; powerful wins against Aston Villa (5-2 away) and West Bromwich Albion (5-1 at home) were among the highlights. As the New Year dawned, three of the powerhouse teams of the post-war period – United, Arsenal and Portsmouth – were all level at the top of the league. But there was no FA Cup glory this year for the Reds; for the first time since proper professional football began after the Second World War, the team was knocked out in their opening match of the competition, a surprise 2-0 defeat against Second Division strugglers Hull City.

However, solid league form through into February – including a 2-0 home win against last year's champions Tottenham Hotspur – put United ahead of their rivals. But nervousness seemed to grab the team as the run-in began and United suffered consecutive losses to lowly Huddersfield (who would ultimately be relegated) and contenders Portsmouth in March.

So to win the championship would require something special from both manager and players. Busby was inspirational and, once again, devoid of panic. The manager's masterstroke was to switch the reliable Johnny Aston and his new young full back Byrne. Immediately after those two consecutive defeats and for all the final six games of the season, Aston returned to his old left back position and the younger man was tried on the left wing. Byrne was a revelation and scored six goals in the next four games – two wins and two draws – to effectively put one hand on the trophy that was last won in the 1907-08 season.

Two home matches remained and, in the penultimate game of the season, United all but wrapped up the championship with a convincing 3-0 win against Chelsea. A 6-1 thumping of Arsenal in the last game confirmed the championship, the first

in 41 years. Rowley's season haul of 30 was his best ever total (and a club record), but Byrne (who scored his seventh in six games against Arsenal) could probably argue that his total was just as important. And to mark an exceptional season, *Manchester Evening News* reporter Tom Jackson wrote about 'The Busby Babes' for the first time.

Final League Table Division One

		P	W	D	L	F	A	Pts
1	**MANCHESTER UNITED**	42	23	11	8	95	52	57
2	Tottenham Hotspur	42	22	9	11	76	51	53
3	Arsenal	42	21	11	10	80	61	53
4	Portsmouth	42	20	8	14	68	58	48
5	Bolton Wanderers	42	19	10	13	65	61	48
6	Aston Villa	42	19	9	14	79	70	47
7	Preston North End	42	17	12	13	74	54	46
8	Newcastle United	42	18	9	15	98	73	45
9	Blackpool	42	18	9	15	64	64	45
10	Charlton Athletic	42	17	10	15	68	63	44
11	Liverpool	42	12	19	11	57	61	43
12	Sunderland	42	15	12	15	70	61	42
13	West Bromwich Albion	42	14	13	15	74	77	41
14	Burnley	42	15	10	17	56	63	40
15	Manchester City	42	13	13	16	58	61	39
16	Wolverhampton Wanderers	42	12	14	16	73	73	38
17	Derby County	42	15	7	20	63	80	37
18	Middlesbrough	42	15	6	21	64	88	36
19	Chelsea	42	14	8	20	52	72	36
20	Stoke City	42	12	7	23	49	88	31
21	Huddersfield Town	42	10	8	24	49	82	28
22	Fulham	42	8	11	23	58	77	27

Appearances

PLAYER	LGE	FAC	TOT
Chilton	42	1	43
Pearson	41	1	42
Rowley	40	1	41
Carey	38	1	39
Cockburn	38	1	39
Berry	36	1	37
Allen	33	1	34
Downie	31	1	32
Byrne	24	1	25
McNulty	24	1	25
Bond	19	1	20
Aston	18	-	18
Redman	18	-	18
Gibson	17	-	17
McShane	12	-	12
Crompton	9	-	9
Clempson	8	-	8
Jones	3	-	3
Whitefoot	3	-	3
Birch	2	-	2
McGlen	2	-	2
Walton	2	-	2

PLAYER	LGE	FAC	TOT
Blanchflower	1	-	1
Cassidy	1	-	1

John Downie, centre, stretches for the ball as a Hull City player tries to clear in the 2-0 FA Cup defeat.

Goalscorers

PLAYER	LGE	FAC	TOT
Rowley	30	-	30
Pearson	22	-	22
Downie	11	-	11
Byrne	7	-	7
Berry	6	-	6
Aston	4	-	4
Bond	4	-	4
Carey	3	-	3
Clempson	2	-	2
Cockburn	2	-	2
McShane	1	-	1
own goals	3	-	3

Full back John Aston pictured at home playing blow football with his family.

Busby Babes including Duncan Edwards make their debuts as legend Johnny Carey retires

1952/53

IN CELEBRATION OF the First Division championship, this pre-season was different to normal; United played commercially successful exhibition matches in America and were watched by large crowds. However, the games themselves were the friendliest of friendlies and did little for the club's league campaign.

Three games were lost in the first five matches as the champions started the defence of their title unimpressively. Matt Busby's team seemed to be suffering a post-title hangover and were losing to the likes of strugglers Stoke City and neighbours Manchester City during the first three months of the season. After the euphoria of winning the title, Busby's team suddenly looked past its best.

Yes, there was the compensation of a 4-2 FA Charity Shield win over Newcastle United at Old Trafford, so the Reds did pick up another piece of silverware, but this was merely a sideshow to the league defence.

Four wins and a draw in December lifted United up the table, but the New Year brought a return to mediocrity and too many sluggish defeats as goals dried up (Stan Pearson's 16 goals was the team leader, while Jack Rowley could only manage 11) and the defence leaked goals (72 compared to 52 in the championship-winning year). A finishing position of eighth and eight points behind league winners Arsenal was a poor showing after so much expectation.

Even the FA Cup was a disappointment. After United stumbled past Millwall and non-league Walthamstow Avenue (only after a replay), a 2-1 defeat to Everton in the fifth round was no surprise.

However, Busby had not let the season slip aimlessly away. In March, he signed another star of the future: centre forward Tommy Taylor from Second Division Barnsley for £29,999 (deliberately £1 short of making him a £30,000 player which Busby felt might be a burden). Seven goals in his first 11 games quickly cemented Taylor's reputation. This would eventually be seen as the season when many key members of the Busby Babes would emerge: Bill Foulkes, David Pegg, Dennis Viollet

and Duncan Edwards who all made their debuts, while Jackie Blanchflower made only his second appearance in two seasons.

In fact, Busby tried 30 players in his first team this year, looking unsuccessfully for the championship form of last season and he also made a concerted effort to scout more impressive young players (a strategy that would bear fruit later in the decade).

The final game of the season – an ignominious 5-0 thrashing by Middlesbrough – would prove to be the last for Johnny Carey, club captain and a star of the team since before World War II. His exit at the age of 34 after 344 first team appearances was another pointer to the entry of new blood into the United team.

- The great Duncan Edwards makes his first team debut on 4 April in a 4-1 defeat at home to Cardiff City; he is just 16 and a half years old.

- United win the inaugural FA Youth Cup with a 9-3, two-leg victory over Wolverhampton Wanderers; the Reds would also win the next four of these competitions in succession.

- FA Cup opponents Walthamstow Avenue from the Isthmian League stage the fourth round replay against United at Arsenal's Highbury ground and attract over 49,000 fans.

Above: Bobby Charlton, aged 15, a schoolboy football prospect, helps with the washing at the family home at Ashington, Northumberland. He signed as a United trainee in January 1953.

Left: Players compete in the United penalty area as Millwall play the Reds at The Den in the FA Cup.

Final League Table Division One

		P	W	D	L	F	A	Pts
1	Arsenal	42	21	12	9	97	64	54
2	Preston North End	42	21	12	9	85	60	54
3	Wolverhampton Wanderers	42	19	13	10	86	63	51
4	West Bromwich Albion	42	21	8	13	66	60	50
5	Charlton Athletic	42	19	11	12	77	63	49
6	Burnley	42	18	12	12	67	52	48
7	Blackpool	42	19	9	14	71	70	47
8	**MANCHESTER UNITED**	**42**	**18**	**10**	**14**	**69**	**72**	**46**
9	Sunderland	42	15	13	14	68	82	43
10	Tottenham Hotspur	42	15	11	16	78	69	41
11	Aston Villa	42	14	13	15	63	61	41
12	Cardiff City	42	14	12	16	54	46	40
13	Middlesbrough	42	14	11	17	70	77	39
14	Bolton Wanderers	42	15	9	18	61	69	39
15	Portsmouth	42	14	10	18	74	83	38
16	Newcastle United	42	14	9	19	59	70	37
17	Liverpool	42	14	8	20	61	82	36
18	Sheffield Wednesday	42	12	11	19	62	72	35
19	Chelsea	42	12	11	19	56	66	35
20	Manchester City	42	14	7	21	72	87	35
21	Stoke City	42	12	10	20	53	66	34
22	Derby County	42	11	10	21	59	74	32

Appearances

PLAYER	LGE	FAC	TOT
Chilton	42	4	46
Aston	40	4	44
Berry	40	4	44
Byrne	40	4	44
Pearson	39	4	43
Carey	32	4	36
Rowley	26	4	30
Cockburn	22	4	26
Crompton	25	-	25
McNulty	23	-	23
Downie	20	2	22
Pegg	19	2	21
Gibson	20	-	20
Wood	12	4	16
Lewis	10	4	14
Taylor	11	-	11
Whitefoot	10	-	10
Doherty	5	-	5
McShane	5	-	5
Clempson	4	-	4
Viollet	3	-	3
Allen	2	-	2

PLAYER	LGE	FAC	TOT
Foulkes	2	-	2
Jones	2	-	2
Olive	2	-	2
Scott	2	-	2
Blanchflower	1	-	1
Bond	1	-	1
Edwards	1	-	1
Redman	1	-	1

Left: United played non-league Walthamstow Avenue in a fourth round FA Cup replay at Highbury. The Avenue number 9 crashes to the ground after a tussle with United goalkeeper Ray Wood.

Goalscorers

PLAYER	LGE	FAC	TOT
Pearson	16	2	18
Rowley	11	3	14
Lewis	7	2	9
Aston	8	-	8
Berry	7	-	7
Taylor	7	-	7
Pegg	4	-	4
Downie	3	-	3
Byrne	2	1	3
Doherty	2	-	2
Carey	1	-	1
Viollet	1	-	1

FOOTBALL LEAGUE DIVISION ONE: EIGHTH POSITION

FA CUP: LOSE TO EVERTON (1-2) IN 5TH ROUND.

FA CHARITY SHIELD: WINNERS. 24 SEPTEMBER 1952. OLD TRAFFORD, MANCHESTER. BEAT NEWCASTLE UNITED 4-2 ROWLEY (2), BYRNE, DOWNIE.

1953/54

Matt Busby's young and talented team is on the rise, but not yet ready for ultimate glory

ROGER BYRNE WAS the new captain of Matt Busby's team and, at 24 (fully ten years younger than one of his predecessor in the job, the retired Johnny Carey) and in only his second full season, it was quite a statement by the manager. When United failed to win any of their first eight games of the season as Busby chopped and changed the starting line-up, neither captain nor manager was looking overjoyed as the young team were taught harsh lessons by more experienced opponents.

However, a 4-1 home win against Middlesbrough in mid-September sparked a mini revival and, just at the time when Duncan Edwards, Dennis Viollet and Jackie Blanchflower became regulars, United went through November and December with just one defeat and a clutch of exciting, high-scoring displays that was becoming a mark of the latest Busby era: a 6-1 win at Cardiff City and home victories against Liverpool and Sheffield Wednesday by 5-1 and 5-2 respectively.

As the season wore on, United's youngsters were still prone to occasional poor performances, such as a 5-1 loss at Old Trafford to Bolton Wanderers, but overall Busby was pleased with his Babes who won three of their last four games to finish a respectable fourth, well behind a Wolverhampton Wanderers team that was touted among the best of the post-war period.

However, the fact that United beat Wolves 1-0 at home in March was a mark of how much potential the team was showing, at least on one-off occasions. The two teams also played in very different styles: Wolves a physical, direct game; United a more elegant, passing method.

United were also now becoming a team of younger men. Tommy Taylor was establishing himself as a top-line centre forward after his big money transfer last season and his 22 goals in 35 matches would set a high standard. Yet, 13 goals from Jackie Blanchflower at inside right from only 27 appearances were also significant. In fact, this was the first time since the war that neither Jack Rowley nor Stan Pearson had finished top scorer.

This would also be the end for stalwarts like Rowley and Pearson as well as centre half Allenby Chilton and the adaptable John Aston. Rowley, Pearson and Chilton had played for United before the war and Pearson was the first to go, transferred in February 1954 to Bury for £4,500. It would be the penultimate season for Rowley and Chilton. Rowley would no longer be regular starter, but Chilton would set a record for consecutive appearances that only ended when he left.

Chilton played 43 games in all, while Rowley totalled 37, but both would be transferred to new clubs during the next year. Aston actually retired from the game at the end of the season at the age of 32. There was no turning back from Busby's decision to go with younger (and often local) players.

- Burnley are United's bogey team of the year beating the Reds twice in the league and 5-3 at Turf Moor in the third round of the FA Cup.

- Allenby Chilton actually guested for six other teams during football's war years and played in the War Cup South final for Charlton Athletic.

- Although Stan Pearson had already been transferred, John Aston would play his final games for United in the last match of the season, a 1-1 draw at Sheffield United.

Above: Jack Rowley (left) duels with Alf Ramsey of Tottenham Hotspur during their match at White Hart Lane.

Right: United goalkeeper Ray Wood and right back Bill Foulkes make a concerted effort to clear a corner kick from Tottenham Hotspur during a match at White Hart Lane. The game ended in a 1-1 draw.

Final League Table Division One

		P	W	D	L	F	A	Pts
1	Wolverhampton Wanderers	42	25	7	10	96	56	57
2	West Bromwich Albion	42	22	9	11	86	63	53
3	Huddersfield Town	42	20	11	11	78	61	51
4	**MANCHESTER UNITED**	42	18	12	12	73	58	48
5	Bolton Wanderers	42	18	12	12	75	60	48
6	Blackpool	42	19	10	13	80	69	48
7	Burnley	42	21	4	17	78	67	46
8	Chelsea	42	16	12	14	74	68	44
9	Charlton Athletic	42	19	6	17	75	77	44
10	Cardiff City	42	18	8	16	51	71	44
11	Preston North End	42	19	5	18	87	58	43
12	Arsenal	42	15	13	14	75	73	43
13	Aston Villa	42	16	9	17	70	68	41
14	Portsmouth	42	14	11	17	81	89	39
15	Newcastle United	42	14	10	18	72	77	38
16	Tottenham Hotspur	42	16	5	21	65	76	37
17	Manchester City	42	14	9	19	62	77	37
18	Sunderland	42	14	8	20	81	89	36
19	Sheffield Wednesday	42	15	6	21	70	91	36
20	Sheffield United	42	11	11	20	69	90	33
21	Middlesbrough	42	10	10	22	60	91	30
22	Liverpool	42	9	10	23	68	97	28

Appearances

PLAYER	LGE	FAC	TOT
Chilton	42	1	43
Byrne	41	1	42
Whitefoot	38	1	39
Berry	37	1	38
Rowley	36	1	37
Taylor	35	1	36
Foulkes	32	1	33
Viollet	29	1	30
Blanchflower	27	1	28
Wood	27	1	28
Edwards	24	1	25
Cockburn	18	-	18
Crompton	15	-	15
Aston	12	-	12
Pearson	11	-	11
McShane	9	-	9
Pegg	9	-	9
Gibson	7	-	7
Lewis	6	-	6
McNulty	4	-	4
McFarlane	1	-	1
Redman	1	-	1

PLAYER	LGE	FAC	TOT
Webster		1	-	1

United's youth team in Bangor, Northern Ireland at the Hotel Pickie.

Goalscorers

PLAYER	LGE	FAC	TOT
Taylor	22	1	23
Blanchflower	13	1	14
Rowley	12	-	12
Viollet	11	1	12
Berry	5	-	5
Byrne	3	-	3
Aston	2	-	2
Pearson	2	-	2
Chilton	1	-	1
Foulkes	1	-	1
Lewis	1	-	1

Duncan Edwards training after being selected for England's Under 23 team at the age of 17 years.

Youth comes of age in a major way as the Babes show their mettle

IT WAS CLEAR that United were still not the finished article three seasons after a league win, but were in the middle of reconstruction work undertaken by Matt Busby. The Reds were without a necessary spark to make another run for the league title for which the manager continually yearned. However, this season began more favourably than the last: five wins in a row after an opening weekend loss.

So, although the famous Busby Babes line-up was all but assembled by now, they were still without the last couple of missing pieces in the jigsaw and not able to dominate the rival clubs. But if this United side lacked consistency, there were plenty of outstanding, goal-filled games that labelled Busby's young men as the most exciting team in the First Division.

A string of four autumn matches summed up the reasons why the Reds were so highly thought of: firstly, a classic derby against Manchester City was lost 3-2 at Maine Road; then the high-flying Wolverhampton Wanderers were worried by the dashing Reds, although the Molineux side prevailed 4-2; yet the two defeats were forgotten in next game at Old Trafford which was a 5-2 win against Cardiff City; and all that was topped off with an amazing 6-5 win at Stamford Bridge.

This was a season when the goals flowed in at either end; United scored 84 goals (only nine fewer than their championship-winning season in 1951-52), but conceded a disappointing 74 (16 more than the previous season).

Allenby Chilton was now 36-years-old and starting to show his age. He asked Busby for a rest and, in February, played his last three games at centre half when United lost 5-0 and 2-0 to Manchester City (latterly in the FA Cup) and 4-2 to Wolverhampton Wanderers. Busby made young Mark Jones his new No 5. Jones had come through the junior ranks and had made his debut aged 17 in 1950 and although he needed a game to settle into the team (he could not help a 3-0 loss at Cardiff City in his season debut), things slowly improved and United's defence kept four clean sheets in its final 12 games.

Meanwhile, the partnership between Tommy Taylor and Dennis Viollet (both scored 20 league goals) continued to

blossom. In the final game of the season, United completed a second league win over the champions-elect Chelsea 2-1 at Old Trafford, a victory that would augur well for the future. United finished just five points behind Chelsea in the league in fifth place and actually won as many games and scored three more goals (84 compared to 81). However, ten away defeats in the league, as many as 20th-placed Cardiff City, proved an Achilles' heel.

- Duncan Edwards makes his England international debut on 2 April in a 7-2 win against Scotland in the British Home Championship.

- Manchester City win all three games against United this season including the fourth round FA Cup tie in front of 75,000 at Maine Road.

- In the same game Allenby Chilton becomes the second player to be sent off in a Manchester derby. The Red Devils lose the FA Cup tie 2-0.

Above: United goalkeeper Ray Wood clears his lines during a match against Reading.

Left: Allenby Chilton, a stalwart half back since 1939, leaves United this season, transferred to Grimsby Town.

Final League Table Division One

		P	W	D	L	F	A	Pts
1	Chelsea	42	20	12	10	81	57	52
2	Wolverhampton Wanderers	42	19	10	13	89	70	48
3	Portsmouth	42	18	12	12	74	62	48
4	Sunderland	42	15	18	9	64	54	48
5	**MANCHESTER UNITED**	42	20	7	15	84	74	47
6	Aston Villa	42	20	7	15	72	73	47
7	Manchester City	42	18	10	14	76	69	46
8	Newcastle United	42	17	9	16	89	77	43
9	Arsenal	42	17	9	16	69	63	43
10	Burnley	42	17	9	16	51	48	43
11	Everton	42	16	10	16	62	68	42
12	Huddersfield Town	42	14	13	15	63	68	41
13	Sheffield United	42	17	7	18	70	86	41
14	Preston North End	42	16	8	18	83	64	40
15	Charlton Athletic	42	15	10	17	76	75	40
16	Tottenham Hotspur	42	16	8	18	72	73	40
17	West Bromwich Albion	42	16	8	18	76	96	40
18	Bolton Wanderers	42	13	13	16	62	69	39
19	Blackpool	42	14	10	18	60	64	38
20	Cardiff City	42	13	11	18	62	76	37
21	Leicester City	42	12	11	19	74	86	35
22	Sheffield Wednesday	42	8	10	24	63	100	26

Appearances

PLAYER	LGE	FAC	TOT
Foulkes	41	3	44
Berry	40	3	43
Byrne	39	3	42
Wood	37	3	40
Viollet	34	3	37
Edwards	33	3	36
Gibson	32	3	35
Blanchflower	29	3	32
Chilton	29	3	32
Taylor	30	1	31
Rowley	22	3	25
Whitefoot	24	-	24
Webster	17	2	19
Scanlon	14	-	14
Jones	13	-	13
Whelan	7	-	7
Pegg	6	-	6
Crompton	5	-	5
Goodwin	5	-	5
Bent	2	-	2
Cockburn	1	-	1
Greaves	1	-	1

PLAYER	LGE	FAC	TOT
Kennedy	1	-	1

United tour America in 1952. Comedian Jerry Lewis inevitably hams it up for the cameras.

Goalscorers

PLAYER	LGE	FAC	TOT
Viollet	20	1	21
Taylor	20	-	20
Webster	8	3	11
Blanchflower	10	-	10
Rowley	7	1	8
Edwards	6	-	6
Scanlon	4	-	4
Berry	3	-	3
Byrne	2	-	2
Pegg	1	-	1
Whelan	1	-	1
own goals	2	-	2

Ray Wood guards the United goal in a third round FA Cup tie vs Reading.

1955/56

With players averaging just 22 years of age, United win the league title in impressive style for the fourth time

SINCE UNITED'S LEAGUE title win four years ago, Matt Busby had been making constant adjustments to his team, replacing older, established stars with new, younger talent, much of it from either Manchester, Lancashire, Yorkshire and the West Midlands. But the manager now had a fair number of critics of this strategy because although the team was mesmerising at times, it was also thought to be losing too many winnable games.

With an average age of just 22, this season's Busby Babes were thought to be too raw to sustain their bursts of great form over a whole season. For this season, the only members of the previous championship winning team were Roger Byrne and Johnny Berry, who were aged 26 and 29 respectively. The last remaining senior players from previously successful seasons, like Allenby Chilton, John Aston and Jack Rowley (who were all stars, but over 30-years-old), had been gone for a whole season and in had come inexperienced replacements like half back Eddie Colman, the latest recruit from United's youth team, who would make his debut in November, just over a week after his 19th birthday.

So when the season opened with a typical United run of inconsistent results, no one was surprised and any expectations of silverware were kept to a minimum. In the early months, no team seemed to dominate the First Division table and this allowed United to stay in touch with the league leaders as the New Year began.

There was a hint of things to come when United played arch rivals Manchester City on New Year's Eve in front of a huge crowd of 60,956 inside Old Trafford and an estimated 20,000 locked out. The Reds came back from 1-0 down to win 2-1 and secure their first Manchester derby victory since September 1951. Then came perhaps a blessing in disguise because when Second Division Bristol Rovers performed a giant killing act in the third round of the FA Cup by beating a full strength United team 4-0, the league became the team's sole focus.

At first, nothing seemed to have changed as Busby's young men beat Sheffield United at home 3-1 immediately after the

cup defeat and then lost by the same score away to Preston North End. However, United then began a run for the title that would leave all challengers in their wake: 10 of the final 14 games were victories and the other four matches drawn. A fabulous unbeaten run, gaining 24 points from a possible 28, proved decisive, as United scored 26 goals and conceded just nine.

The title was actually secured with two games to spare when closest rivals Blackpool were beaten 2-1 at Old Trafford in front of over 62,000 fans. United eventually won the league by an astonishing 11 points (the largest winning margin so far in the 20th century) and was born out of a consistent team selection; eight of Busby's first-choice XI played more than three quarters of the league games. The Reds were powerful up front, with Tommy Taylor scoring 25 goals and Dennis Viollet 20 out of United's impressive tally of 83, but it was in defence where the team had the best record, conceding just 51 goals. Perhaps most important of all, Duncan Edwards was now in his pomp and still not 20 years old. Roger Byrne summed up the team spirit and the understanding among the Babes. He commented: "Nearly all of us grew up together as boy footballers and the Manchester United way is the only way we know."

If more evidence was needed of how Busby, along with his trusted assistant Jimmy Murphy, was thinking long term: the Central League (for First Division reserve teams) and the Youth Cup (for the fourth successive time) were both won this season. Busby's comments at the time showed how important the reserves and youth team were: "From the start, I had envisaged making my own players, having a kind of nursery so that they could be trained in the kind of pattern I was trying to create for Manchester United." It might have been an open secret that a team of good, young players was a successful strategy, but the rest of the football world could not stop the Busby Babes juggernaut this season and the future looked bright for a vibrant United era that could last a decade.

- Among the squad this year are two men who would go on to be successful First Division managers in the sixties and seventies, Freddie Goodwin and Ian Greaves.

- Other teams try to copy the Busby Babes soubriquet; Chelsea named their title winners of last season Drake's Ducklings after manager Ted Drake.

- United's incredible home form – 18 wins and three draws – is the key to the league title; lowly Cardiff City and Tottenham Hotspur manage two of the three draws.

Above: Left wing David Pegg was a stalwart this season. Here he is during training at Old Trafford.

Opposite: Centre forward Tommy Taylor scores his team's first goal against Chelsea in a 3-0 home win in November.

Final League Table Division One

		P	W	D	L	F	A	Pts
1	**MANCHESTER UNITED**	42	25	10	7	83	51	60
2	Blackpool	42	20	9	13	86	62	49
3	Wolverhampton Wanderers	42	20	9	13	89	65	49
4	Manchester City	42	18	10	14	82	69	46
5	Arsenal	42	18	10	14	60	61	46
6	Birmingham City	42	18	9	15	75	57	45
7	Burnley	42	18	8	16	64	54	44
8	Bolton Wanderers	42	18	7	17	71	58	43
9	Sunderland	42	17	9	16	80	95	43
10	Luton Town	42	17	8	17	66	64	42
11	Newcastle United	42	17	7	18	85	70	41
12	Portsmouth	42	16	9	17	78	85	41
13	West Bromwich Albion	42	18	5	19	58	70	41
14	Charlton Athletic	42	17	6	19	75	81	40
15	Everton	42	15	10	17	55	69	40
16	Chelsea	42	14	11	17	64	77	39
17	Cardiff City	42	15	9	18	55	69	39
18	Tottenham Hotspur	42	15	7	20	61	71	37
19	Preston North End	42	14	8	20	73	72	36
20	Aston Villa	42	11	13	18	52	69	35
21	Huddersfield Town	42	14	7	21	54	83	35
22	Sheffield United	42	12	9	21	63	77	33

Appearances

PLAYER	LGE	FAC	TOT
Jones	42	1	43
Wood	41	1	42
Byrne	39	1	40
Pegg	35	1	36
Berry	34	1	35
Viollet	34	1	35
Taylor	33	1	34
Edwards	33	-	33
Foulkes	26	1	27
Colman	25	1	26
Blanchflower	18	-	18
Doherty	16	1	17
Whitefoot	15	1	16
Greaves	15	-	15
Webster	15	-	15
Whelan	13	-	13
Goodwin	8	-	8
Scanlon	6	-	6
Bent	4	-	4
Lewis	4	-	4
McGuinness	3	-	3
Crompton	1	-	1

PLAYER	LGE	FAC	TOT
Scott	1	-	1
Whitehurst	1	-	1

Captain Roger Byrne holds the First Division championship trophy above his head after the presentation at Old Trafford.

Goalscorers

PLAYER	LGE	FAC	TOT
Taylor	25	-	25
Viollet	20	-	20
Pegg	9	-	9
Berry	4	-	4
Doherty	4	-	4
Webster	4	-	4
Whelan	4	-	4
Blanchflower	3	-	3
Byrne	3	-	3
Edwards	3	-	3
Jones	1	-	1
Lewis	1	-	1
McGuinness	1	-	1
Scanlon	1	-	1

Centre half Mark Jones (right) and Dennis Viollet. The two Busby Babes were key to winning the league, especially Viollet's 20 goals.

1956/57

- There are three Manchester derbies again this year: two league wins for United and also a 1-0 victory at Maine Road in the FA Charity Shield.

- Dennis Viollet plays in only six European matches this season, but scores nine goals including five in the two games against Anderlecht.

- Once again, Matt Busby enjoys consistency of selection in the league campaign with nine men playing at least 30 games.

- The 2-2 draw on 25 April against Real Madrid in the European Cup is the first European tie at Old Trafford under floodlights. The four-tower lighting system cost £40,000.

Above: Billy Whelan takes a corner during a game.

Right: Goalkeeper Ray Wood is stretchered off the Wembley pitch after breaking his jaw in an eighth minute collision with Aston Villa forward Peter McParland. The incident cost United the FA Cup trophy.

A great team, a great championship win and many great performances plus a century of goals

THE UNITED TEAM that began this season was becoming legendary. Busby's tinkering was complete, the understanding of so many players developed via the youth system was producing immaculate results and a core of 14 players (now including 18-year-old Bobby Charlton) would bestride the league and the FA Cup this year. Plus, at the same time, the United youngsters would face European Cup opposition for the first time.

Battling on three fronts seemed to only inspire greater feats from the Reds, despite a heavy workload on their young bodies; seven players (Bill Foulkes, Johnny Berry, Liam "Billy" Whelan, Ray Wood, David Pegg, Roger Byrne and Eddie Colman) turned out for the team at least 51 competitive times in a 57-game season, unheard of numbers in those days. The inconsistent performances that had been United's weakness in so many previous seasons were now a thing of the past.

There were no defeats in any of the first 12 league games of the season running into mid-October as United raced to the top of the table. But what was even more remarkable was the number of goals being scored throughout the whole team. Only once in the opening unbeaten run did United score fewer than two goals in a league game and they totalled a massive 57 league goals before the end of December. Not only that, but United were crushing European opposition: 10-0 in the home leg alone against Anderlecht of Belgium; and a 3-2 aggregate victory over Borussia Dortmund of Germany before November was out.

Back home, United's form in the First Division was also outstanding. Into the New Year there were huge wins over Newcastle United (6-1), Arsenal (6-2) and Charlton Athletic (5-1). It was as much the manner of the victories – overwhelming attacking football – as the results themselves that fascinated the crowds. The European Cup quarter-final against Athletic Bilbao of Spain was more of a tester; the Reds lost 5-3 in Spain, but staged a fantastic comeback at Maine Road to win that match 3-0 and take the tie 6-5 on aggregate.

This year, the league title was safely returned to Old Trafford with three games to spare; a 4-0 win at home to Sunderland earned the championship-clinching points. This was Busby's sixth trophy in eleven seasons, effectively with two different teams. Nine days before the title was clinched, United ran out of European steam. They played Real Madrid in the European Cup semi-final and lost in Spain 3-1.

A second consecutive escape against Spanish opposition, however, proved elusive and a 2-2 draw at Old Trafford put United out of the competition. An unlikely 2-1 loss to Aston Villa in May, when goalkeeper Ray Wood suffered a bad injury during the game, curtailed the possibility of a league and cup double (a feat not achieved since Aston Villa in 1897), but such an accomplishment seemed within reach very soon.

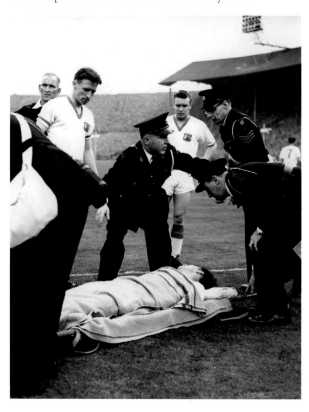

Final League Table Division One

		P	W	D	L	F	A	Pts
1	**MANCHESTER UNITED**	42	28	8	6	103	54	64
2	Tottenham Hotspur	42	22	12	8	104	56	56
3	Preston North End	42	23	10	9	84	56	56
4	Blackpool	42	22	9	11	93	65	53
5	Arsenal	42	21	8	13	85	69	50
6	Wolverhampton Wanderers	42	20	8	14	94	70	48
7	Burnley	42	18	10	14	56	50	46
8	Leeds United	42	15	14	13	72	63	44
9	Bolton Wanderers	42	16	12	14	65	65	44
10	Aston Villa	42	14	15	13	65	55	43
11	West Bromwich Albion	42	14	14	14	59	61	42
12	Birmingham City	42	15	9	18	69	69	39
13	Chelsea	42	13	13	16	73	73	39
14	Sheffield Wednesday	42	16	6	20	82	88	38
15	Everton	42	14	10	18	61	79	38
16	Luton Town	42	14	9	19	58	76	37
17	Newcastle United	42	14	8	20	67	87	36
18	Manchester City	42	13	9	20	78	88	35
19	Portsmouth	42	10	13	19	62	92	33
20	Sunderland	42	12	8	22	67	88	32
21	Cardiff City	42	10	9	23	53	88	29
22	Charlton Athletic	42	9	4	29	62	120	22

Appearances

PLAYER	LGE	FAC	EC	TOT
Berry	40	5	8	53
Foulkes	39	6	8	53
Whelan	39	6	8	53
Wood	39	6	8	53
Pegg	37	6	8	51
Byrne	36	6	8	50
Colman	36	6	8	50
Edwards	34	6	7	47
Taylor	32	4	8	44
Jones	29	4	6	39
Viollet	27	5	6	38
Charlton	14	2	1	17
Blanchflower	11	2	3	16
McGuinness	13	1	1	15
Bent	6	-	-	6
Goodwin	6	-	-	6
Webster	5	1	-	6
Scanlon	5	-	-	5
Dawson	3	-	-	3
Doherty	3	-	-	3
Greaves	3	-	-	3
Clayton	2	-	-	2

PLAYER	LGE	FAC	EC	TOT
Cope	2	-	-	2
Hawksworth	1	-	-	1

Fitness was a strength of United's team in the fifties thanks to coach Bert Whalley, here seen putting four players (l-r) David Gaskell, unidentified player, Alex Dawson and Reg Holland, through a workout.

Goalscorers

PLAYER	LGE	FAC	EC	TOT
Taylor	22	4	8	34
Whelan	26	4	3	33
Viollet	16	-	9	25
Berry	8	4	2	14
Charlton	10	1	1	12
Pegg	6	-	1	7
Edwards	5	1	-	6
Dawson	3	-	-	3
Webster	3	-	-	3
Scanlon	2	-	-	2
Colman	1	-	-	1
Byrne	-	1	-	1
own goal	1	-	-	1

David Pegg (left) and Eddie Colman were among the stars of United's league-winning team.

FOOTBALL LEAGUE DIVISION ONE: CHAMPIONS

FA CUP: RUNNERS-UP. 4 MAY 1957. WEMBLEY, LONDON.
LOST TO ASTON VILLA 1-2 TAYLOR 83'

EUROPEAN CUP: LOSE TO REAL MADRID (3-5 ON AGGREGATE)
IN SEMI-FINAL.

FA CHARITY SHIELD: WINNERS. 24 OCTOBER 1956. MAINE ROAD,
MANCHESTER. BEAT MANCHESTER CITY 1-0 VIOLLET.

Young lives are taken and other lives changed forever in the tragedy on a snowy runway in Munich

THE WORD 'TRAGEDY' hardly seems to encompass the Munich plane crash when eight players from Matt Busby's remarkable team lost their lives. Before that snowy Thursday afternoon, 6 February 1958, this was almost certainly going to be a season memorable for more trophy wins. United were the team of the moment, with unquestionably the most talent of any in English football and, possibly, also in Europe. The same flamboyant, goalscoring style that won the title last year was even more in evidence at the start of this league season.

Another fast start brought five wins in the first six matches and 22 goals. A third championship in a row looked possible even though there were a few too many sloppy defeats (seven before year's end, which was one more than the whole of the previous season).

Another FA Cup campaign then began in January and the European Cup quarter-final first leg against Red Star Belgrade at Old Trafford was won 2-1, while in the league, Bolton Wanderers (something of a recent bogey team up until now) were thumped 7-2 at home and Arsenal beaten 5-4 at Highbury. Then came the fateful trip to Belgrade for the second leg.

1957/58

21 DEAD
7 MANCHESTER UTD PLAYERS PERISH
HERO! IN AIR CRASH

■ Roger Byrne did not know that his wife was pregnant at the time of his death, while Geoff Bent's daughter Karen was just a small baby at the time.

■ Duncan Edwards sends a telegram to his landlady in Manchester saying all flights are cancelled and he will return home the next day. Soon after the pilot decides to try once again to take off. The telegram arrives two hours after the crash.

Above: The early edition of the front page of the *Daily Sketch* reports only 21 dead from the Munich air crash. Eventually, 23 people would lose their lives, including eight United players.

Left: British European Airways flight 609 lies stricken after the fateful crash.

Final League Table Division One

		P	W	D	L	F	A	Pts
1	Wolverhampton Wanderers	42	28	8	6	103	47	64
2	Preston North End	42	26	7	9	100	51	59
3	Tottenham Hotspur	42	21	9	12	93	77	51
4	West Bromwich Albion	42	18	14	10	92	70	50
5	Manchester City	42	22	5	15	104	100	49
6	Burnley	42	21	5	16	80	74	47
7	Blackpool	42	19	6	17	80	67	44
8	Luton Town	42	19	6	17	69	63	44
9	**MANCHESTER UNITED**	42	16	11	15	85	75	43
10	Nottingham Forest	42	16	10	16	69	63	42
11	Chelsea	42	15	12	15	83	79	42
12	Arsenal	42	16	7	19	73	85	39
13	Birmingham City	42	14	11	17	76	89	39
14	Aston Villa	42	16	7	19	73	86	39
15	Bolton Wanderers	42	14	10	18	65	87	38
16	Everton	42	13	11	18	65	75	37
17	Leeds United	42	14	9	19	51	63	37
18	Leicester City	42	14	5	23	91	112	33
19	Newcastle United	42	12	8	22	73	81	32
20	Portsmouth	42	12	8	22	73	88	32
21	Sunderland	42	10	12	20	54	97	32
22	Sheffield Wednesday	42	12	7	23	69	92	31

Appearances

PLAYER	LGE	FAC	EC	TOT
Foulkes	42	8	8	58
Byrne	26	2	6	34
Edwards	26	2	5	33
Taylor T	25	2	6	33
Colman	24	2	5	31
Gregg	19	8	4	31
Viollet	22	3	6	31
Webster	20	6	5	31
Charlton	21	7	2	30
Goodwin	16	6	3	25
Pegg	21	-	4	25
Wood	20	-	4	24
Berry	20	-	3	23
Whelan	20	-	3	23
Cope	13	6	2	21
Blanchflower	18	-	2	20
Greaves	12	6	2	20
Morgans	13	2	4	19
Taylor E	11	6	2	19
Crowther	11	5	2	18
Dawson	12	6	-	18
Jones	10	2	4	16

PLAYER	LGE	FAC	EC	TOT
Pearson	8	4	2	14
Scanlon	9	2	3	14
McGuinness	7	-	1	8
Brennan	5	2	-	7
Harrop	5	1	-	6
Gaskell	3	-	-	3
Doherty	1	-	-	1
Heron	1	-	-	1
Jones	1	-	-	1

Left: Matt Busby photographed with his wife Jean, daughter Sheena and nursing sisters recovering in a Munich hospital after the tragic air crash.

Goalscorers

PLAYER	LGE	FAC	EC	TOT
Viollet	16	3	4	23
Taylor T	16	-	3	19
Charlton	8	5	3	16
Whelan	12	-	2	14
Dawson	5	5	-	10
Webster	6	1	1	8
Pegg	4	-	3	7
Edwards	6	-	-	6
Berry	4	-	1	5
Taylor E	2	1	1	4
Scanlon	3	-	-	3
Brennan	-	3	-	3
Doherty	1	-	-	1
Colman	-	-	1	1
own goals	2	-	-	2

■ Yugoslav writer Miro Rado-
jcic is planning to be on
the flight, but misses the
plane when he realises he
has forgotten his passport.

■ Along with the nine players
and manager, eleven others
survive: four crew, two photographers, one journalist,
the travel agent's wife, a
Yugoslav diplomat and a
mother and child.

■ Goalkeeper Harry Gregg is
dubbed the hero of Munich
after pulling several people
from the wreckage includ-
ing Busby, Charlton, Viollet
and Blanchflower plus the
mother and her child.

■ Both Duncan Edwards and
Tommy Taylor are engaged
to be married, while Eddie
Colman had celebrated his
21st birthday just three
months earlier.

Above: This ticket from this season's
FA Cup final is extremely rare.

Right: Dennis Viollet with his wife
Barbara and children at home
following the Munich air crash.

Far Right: Nurses at the Rechts
der Isar Hospital in Munich tend to
Matt Busby in his oxygen tent.

The match itself was hard-fought and finished 3-3, with United racing to a 3-0 lead only to be pulled back in the second half and be forced to hang on for the draw for the final five minutes. Afterwards, players from both sides joined each other for a meal in a local restaurant. The mood was joyful for the Babes because the result meant another European Cup semi-final.

The next morning there were a few sore heads from the cele-brations, but everything else was normal. The plane carrying players, officials and journalists would stop off at Munich to re-fuel. Two take-off attempts were aborted and the pilot reported the plane's engines over-accelerating. The passengers went back to the airport lounge for coffee. It was just after four o' clock in the afternoon local time on Thursday 6 February when the BEA Elizabethan airliner tried to take off from the main runway for the third time in bitterly cold and snowy conditions. The slushy conditions meant the plane failed to reach take-off speed and crashed through a fence at the end of the runway into a house, a tree and a hut containing a truck full of fuel. An explo-sion ripped through the plane as one wing and part of the tail were torn off. The crash would eventually take the lives of 23 people: eight players, three other members of United's staff, nine journalists, the plane's pilot, a United supporter and the travel agent who had arranged the flight.

Twenty one people actually died on the day of the crash and two – the co-pilot Capt Kenneth Rayment and United's great-est player of the time, Duncan Edwards – were both taken to hospital with critical injuries; Edwards died just over a fort-night later. Twenty people survived including nine players: Johnny Berry, Jackie Blanchflower, Bobby Charlton, Bill Foulkes, Harry Gregg, Ken Morgans, Albert Scanlon, Dennis Viollet and Ray Wood, although two (Berry and Blanchflower) never played professional football again. Meanwhile, Matt Busby recovered only after a long and painful period in hospital and was at one time even read the last rites by a local priest. It was a loss of such devastating proportions, that it still resonates to this day.

So with no manager and the whole club grieving, Busby's assistant Jimmy Murphy was forced into the spotlight. "Keep the flag flying," Busby told him from his hospital bed and Murphy – who had only missed the Belgrade trip by chance while he travelled with the Welsh national team – did just that.

Thirteen days after the crash and with a team made up of two survivors – goalkeeper Gregg and stalwart defender Foulkes – plus reserves and a few new signings, United won an FA Cup tie against Sheffield Wednesday at Old Trafford before nearly 60,000 still-grieving fans.

Then on 22 February the club returned to league action with a 1-1 draw at home to Nottingham Forest. The heartbreak of the whole United community would take many years to

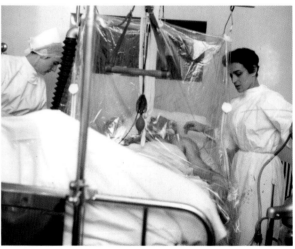

ROGER BYRNE, FULL BACK AND CAPTAIN	LIAM WHELAN, FORWARD	GEORGE FOLLOWS, JOURNALIST	ERIC THOMPSON, JOURNALIST
GEOFF BENT, FULL BACK	WALTER CRICKMER, CLUB SECRETARY	TOM JACKSON, JOURNALIST	BELA MIKLOS, TRAVEL AGENT
EDDIE COLMAN, HALF BACK	TOM CURRY, CLUB TRAINER	ARCHIE LEDBROKE, JOURNALIST	
DAVID PEGG, FORWARD	BERT WHALLEY, CLUB COACH	HENRY ROSE, JOURNALIST	WILLIE SATINOFF, SUPPORTER AND CLOSE FRIEND OF MATT BUSBY
MARK JONES, HALF BACK			
TOMMY TAYLOR, FORWARD	ALF CLARKE, JOURNALIST	FRANK SWIFT, FORMER MANCHESTER CITY AND ENGLAND GOALKEEPER AND JOURNALIST	CAPT KENNETH RAYMENT, CO-PILOT
DUNCAN EDWARDS, HALF BACK	DONNY DAVIES, JOURNALIST		TOM CABLE, AIR STEWARD

Dear Mr and Mrs Taylor

I don't know what to say
to you, we are heartbroken,
and we know how you must
be feeling.

Poor darling Tommy,
I didn't think for one
moment anything like
this would happen when I
waved them off on Monday
morning, (Tommy, Duncan
and Kenny Morgan (sic))
my heart aches for you,
your family.

Tommy was just like
one of our own, you are
welcome here any time. I
won't let anybody touch
anything belonging to him
until I hear from you, or
see you.

God bless you both also
Mrs English & your family.

mend, and United would win only one more league match all
season and finish ninth. Some more survivors, including
Charlton and Viollet, would return before the end of the
season, but simply completing the remaining fixtures was a
remarkable job in itself.

Somehow the patched-up team reached its second consecutive FA Cup final while the last games of the season were the
much-delayed two legs of the European Cup semi-final in
mid-May. United, with Busby watching from the sidelines but
still needing to use two walking sticks, beat AC Milan at Old
Trafford 2-1, but lost the away leg 4-0. However, the loss of
matches and a league title were of little overall importance as
the club needed to mourn its dead and begin to re-build.

Above: A poignant letter
written by Tommy Taylor's
landlady to the player's mother
shortly after the disaster.

Top Left: The memorial window at
a church in Dudley, the town where
Duncan Edwards was born.

Left: 12 February 1958. The
first hearse to leave Old Trafford
contains the remains of
Eddie Colman.

1958/59

- The opening home league game is not the largest attendance at Old Trafford this season, that comes in the third match against Blackburn Rovers when 65,187 fans turn up.

- Albert Quixall's record transfer to United is not an overwhelming success as the inside forward scores only four goals in 34 games.

- United's total of 103 league goals was only bettered by champions Wolverhampton Wanderers with 110.

Above: New United captain and forward Dennis Viollet takes to the pitch with his post-Munich team.

Right: United youngsters Ronnie Cope and Freddie Goodwin were among the players who stepped up from the reserves after Munich.

The first post-Munich season produces a remarkable and emotional runners-up finish in the league

WHEN THIS SEASON began, the Munich air crash was just six months ago and the event was still sharp in the minds of everyone involved with United. Some survivors were still recovering, including Matt Busby, whose trusted assistant Jimmy Murphy had been given the task of leading the re-building of the team. Busby attended games at the very end of last year and while the manager slowly grew healthier in the off-season, Murphy filled his considerable shoes. But by the start of this season, Busby was back at his desk and ready to resume the full-time rigours of his job.

A number of new faces would be brought in to bolster the Reds, but there was no helter-skelter rush to sign players. The £45,000 paid for Albert Quixall from Sheffield Wednesday (a record amount between two British clubs) in September was the standout acquisition. United relied mainly on reserves and other young players from the junior conveyor belt in order to continue to play in the United way, a fast, open style.

Survivors of the Munich crash such as Dennis Viollet, Bobby Charlton, Albert Scanlon and Bill Foulkes all played in the opening match, a 5-2 victory at Old Trafford against Chelsea. Busby's team was still instructed to play in the exciting way that he taught, but, not surprisingly, the Reds were a little inconsistent in the first half of the season and lost four out of five games in October. For example during this period, United beat Blackburn Rovers 6-1, but then immediately lost the next game 3-2 at West Ham United only to play the Hammers again nine days later and win 4-1.

But after Bolton Wanderers knocked the young United over at Burnden Park with a 6-3 win, the Red Devils found their balance. A run of 11 wins and one draw in 12 league games from the end of November until late February sent United soaring into contention for the championship. During this period, a 3-0 loss at Norwich City put United out of the FA Cup and, perhaps thankfully, there were no trips to Europe to de-stabilise the re-building programme and remind the players and officials of the tragedy that had so recently happened. And, as the season wore on, so even some of the emergency signings after Munich – like inside forward Ernie Taylor and wing half Stan Crowther, both experienced players – were released as a new generation of Busby Babes was being groomed.

The race for the title, however, pitted United and their free-flowing, attacking style against a formidable Wolverhampton Wanderers team who were the reigning champions. United beat Wolves at Old Trafford 2-1 in the final match of their 12-game unbeaten run in February, to actually reach the top of the table. However, the Midlands team then went on to the end of the season without losing another match after their defeat. It was enough to give them the title as the Reds lost three more times and finished a creditable second, with more than 100 goals scored including 29 from Charlton, 21 from Viollet and 16 from Scanlon.

Final League Table Division One

		P	W	D	L	F	A	Pts
1	Wolverhampton Wanderers	42	28	5	9	110	49	61
2	**MANCHESTER UNITED**	42	24	7	11	103	66	55
3	Arsenal	42	21	8	13	88	68	50
4	Bolton Wanderers	42	20	10	12	79	66	50
5	West Bromwich Albion	42	18	13	11	88	68	49
6	West Ham United	42	21	6	15	85	70	48
7	Burnley	42	19	10	13	81	70	48
8	Blackpool	42	18	11	13	66	49	47
9	Birmingham City	42	20	6	16	84	68	46
10	Blackburn Rovers	42	17	10	15	76	70	44
11	Newcastle United	42	17	7	18	80	80	41
12	Preston North End	42	17	7	18	70	77	41
13	Nottingham Forest	42	17	6	19	71	74	40
14	Chelsea	42	18	4	20	77	98	40
15	Leeds United	42	15	9	18	57	74	39
16	Everton	42	17	4	21	71	87	38
17	Luton Town	42	12	13	17	68	71	37
18	Tottenham Hotspur	42	13	10	19	85	95	36
19	Leicester City	42	11	10	21	67	98	32
20	Manchester City	42	11	9	22	64	95	31
21	Aston Villa	42	11	8	23	58	87	30
22	Portsmouth	42	6	9	27	64	112	21

Appearances

PLAYER	LGE	FAC	TOT
Goodwin	42	1	43
Scanlon	42	1	43
Gregg	41	1	42
McGuinness	39	1	40
Charlton	38	1	39
Viollet	37	1	38
Greaves	34	–	34
Cope	33	1	34
Foulkes	32	1	33
Bradley	24	1	25
Carolan	23	1	24
Dawson	11	–	11
Taylor	11	–	11
Webster	7	–	7
Harrop	5	–	5
Pearson	4	–	4
Crowther	2	–	2
Morgans	2	–	2
Brennan	1	–	1
Hunter	1	–	1
Wood	1	–	1

Goalscorers

PLAYER	LGE	FAC	TOT
Charlton	29	–	29
Viollet	21	–	21
Scanlon	16	–	16
Bradley	12	–	12
Goodwin	6	–	6
Webster	5	–	5
Dawson	4	–	4
Quixall	4	–	4
Cope	2	–	2
McGuinness	1	–	1
Pearson	1	–	1
own goals	2	–	2

Right: Bobby Charlton (left) and Wilf McGuinness are players for the Red Devils this season, but just over a decade later McGuinness will be Charlton's manager.

Time for Matt Busby to look to the future again and start building another great team

1959/60

WITH THE MUNICH disaster still so fresh in the minds of everyone involved with United, the previous season's runners-up finish in the league had given a huge boost to the club and its supporters. Matt Busby was now determined to build another great team as there were still outstanding young players emerging and the style of football played at Old Trafford was as exciting as anything in the country.

However, this season proved to be something of a return to earth with a bump. It was as if there had to be an end to the emotional momentum that Munich was responsible for and a return to the harsh realities of life in the First Division. United lost their opening two matches of the season and, in the first two months, were as likely to win heavily (6-3 at Chelsea and 6-0 against Leeds United at Old Trafford) as lose by almost as many goals (a 5-1 drubbing at home to Tottenham Hotspur and 4-0 at Preston North End).

All season, the Red Devils were in a quixotic mood. So, although United would score almost as many goals as last season (102 compared to 103, a total only beaten this season by league runners-up Wolverhampton Wanderers with 106), the defence was much more porous (80 goals conceded this year and only 66 last year).

Nevertheless, Busby was addressing the defensive frailties slowly by introducing players like Maurice Setters at wing half (a mid-season signing for £30,000 from West Bromwich Albion) and young Shay Brennan (who had been thrown into the team in the initial post-Munich matches from the reserves, but then played just one game last season) who began on the wing and would eventually move to full back.

But this season would be all about the forwards, and Dennis Viollet's 32 goals in just 36 games made him the First Division top scorer and also the record goalscorer for United in a single league season. In addition, Bobby Charlton's 18 league goals plus 15 from Alex Dawson and 13 from Albert Quixall were all healthy contributions.

In fact, United scored four or more goals in 11 League matches, but then countered that good form by conceding three or more in 13 games, including a horrid 7-3 thrashing at Newcastle United in January.

With such haywire results, the FA Cup was a possible solution for success, but after strong away wins over Derby County (4-2) and Liverpool (3-1), United lost 1-0 at home to Sheffield Wednesday in the fifth round. A seventh place finish in the league – ten points behind champions Burnley – was the result of too many goals conceded, but the fans were still showing outstanding support; attendances were still high, with an average of more than 48,000. Indeed, the long-suffering fans standing in the Stretford End had a memorable season because a roof was built over the terrace to give them some protection from the Manchester weather for the first time.

■ Johnny Giles makes his debut on 12 September against Tottenham Hotspur and plays ten league games this season.

■ Of all the strange results this season, the 7-3 loss at Newcastle United stands out; goalkeeper that day, David Gaskell, did not play for the first team again for another three months.

■ United played champions-to-be Burnley twice in the space of three days over Christmas, losing at home 2-1 and then winning 4-1 at Turf Moor.

■ Stalwart fullback of the eighties, Mike Duxbury, is born in Accrington, Lancashire on 1 September.

Above: Bill Foulkes was now the heartbeat of the team and a commanding presence in the dressing room.

Left: Bobby Charlton pictured during a training session.

Final League Table Division One

		P	W	D	L	F	A	Pts
1	Burnley	42	24	7	11	85	61	55
2	Wolverhampton Wanderers	42	24	6	12	106	67	54
3	Tottenham Hotspur	42	21	11	10	86	50	53
4	West Bromwich Albion	42	19	11	12	83	57	49
5	Sheffield Wednesday	42	19	11	12	80	59	49
6	Bolton Wanderers	42	20	8	14	59	51	48
7	**MANCHESTER UNITED**	42	19	7	16	102	80	45
8	Newcastle United	42	18	8	16	82	78	44
9	Preston North End	42	16	12	14	79	76	44
10	Fulham	42	17	10	15	73	80	44
11	Blackpool	42	15	10	17	59	71	40
12	Leicester City	42	13	13	16	66	75	39
13	Arsenal	42	15	9	18	68	80	39
14	West Ham United	42	16	6	20	75	91	38
15	Everton	42	13	11	18	73	78	37
16	Manchester City	42	17	3	22	78	84	37
17	Blackburn Rovers	42	16	5	21	60	70	37
18	Chelsea	42	14	9	19	76	91	37
19	Birmingham City	42	13	10	19	63	80	36
20	Nottingham Forest	42	13	9	20	50	74	35
21	Leeds United	42	12	10	20	65	92	34
22	Luton Town	42	9	12	21	50	73	30

Appearances

PLAYER	LGE	FAC	TOT
Foulkes	42	3	45
Carolan	41	3	44
Cope	40	3	43
Charlton	37	3	40
Viollet	36	3	39
Gregg	33	3	36
Quixall	33	3	36
Scanlon	31	3	34
Brennan	29	3	32
Bradley	29	2	31
Dawson	22	1	23
Goodwin	18	1	19
McGuinness	19	–	19
Setters	17	2	19
Giles	10	–	10
Pearson	10	–	10
Gaskell	9	–	9
Lawton	3	–	3
Greaves	2	–	2
Heron	1	–	1

Goalscorers

PLAYER	LGE	FAC	TOT
Viollet	32	–	32
Charlton	18	3	21
Dawson	15	–	15
Quixall	13	–	13
Bradley	8	1	9
Scanlon	7	1	8
Pearson	3	–	3
Giles	2	–	2
Goodwin	1	1	2
own goals	3	1	4

Bobby Charlton has his pulse checked by Jack Crompton after training.

United players and officials at Munich airport after playing two pre-season friendlies in Germany 18 months after the fateful crash.

1960/61

NOBBY STILES
(Manchester United and England)

- On 26 December Alex Dawson scores a hat-trick against Chelsea and then repeats the feat against Manchester City three days later before scoring two more a week later, against Middlesbrough in the FA Cup; all the games are at Old Trafford.

- In the fifities, United had been close to winning the first league and cup double of the 20th century, but this season Tottenham Hotspur finally achieve it.

- Munich survivor Kenny Morgans is transferred to Swansea City in March for £3,000.

Above: Capped five times for England Schools, Nobby Stiles joined United in 1957 and made his first team debut in 1961. He is seen here with the compliments of Typhoo Tea.

Right: 31 December 1960. United's Alex Dawson (centre in the dark shirt) stretches for a high ball as Manchester City's Denis Law (far right and soon to play for United) watches. United win 5-1.

New arrivals at Old Trafford and many debutants cannot prevent an inconsistent season

THE SADNESS OF the post-Munich period was starting to abate as the new decade began, and it became obvious that Matt Busby's re-building programme would take time. A runners-up place in the first season after the disaster had proved a false dawn. This season would see Busby try as many as 27 players in league games as he continued to look for his future stars.

Among those that debuted in 1960-61 were right half Nobby Stiles, while inside forward Johnny Giles more than doubled his appearances this season. A pair of Irish full backs were signed – Noel Cantwell from West Ham for £29,500 and Tony Dunne from Shelbourne for £5,000 – to help shore up the leaky defence.

The league season began with a strange series of games; only two wins in the first nine between August and the end of September, including a 6-1 win over West Ham United. The Reds lost six of the other seven and could not score more than one goal in the process. There was just no guessing what United would do from game to game. In fact, the win over Everton came just seven days after the Reds lost 4-0 themselves to the same team at Goodison Park. Then there was trouble up

front when scoring machine Dennis Viollet was injured in December and did not return until April.

In fact, with all Busby's tweaking of the team, the same inconsistency emerged as last season and prevented any real progress. Even in the season's fifth month, December, United would begin a run of five consecutive wins, including a 6-0 thumping of Chelsea, but then let the sequence end by losing 6-0 themselves, this time to Leicester City. The Red Devils were also beaten 2-1 by Bradford City in the second round of a new competition, the League Cup, in November and another strange defeat – 7-2 in a replay against Sheffield Wednesday – knocked United out of the FA Cup in February, so there was no cup glory this year either.

Instead, fans enjoyed the goals that Bobby Charlton (21), Alex Dawson (16) and Viollet (15) were scoring, although the team's total of 88 was under 100 for the first time in three seasons. A second consecutive seventh place finish proved to Busby that he still had work to do to find the right blend of players but, although attendances suffered (an average of 38,500 at Old Trafford this season), he believed that some of the pieces were already in place.

Final League Table Division One

		P	W	D	L	F	A	Pts
1	Tottenham Hotspur	42	31	4	7	115	55	66
2	Sheffield Wednesday	42	23	12	7	78	47	58
3	Wolverhampton Wanderers	42	25	7	10	103	75	57
4	Burnley	42	22	7	13	102	77	51
5	Everton	42	22	6	14	87	69	50
6	Leicester City	42	18	9	15	87	70	45
7	**MANCHESTER UNITED**	42	18	9	15	88	76	45
8	Blackburn Rovers	42	15	13	14	77	76	43
9	Aston Villa	42	17	9	16	78	77	43
10	West Bromwich Albion	42	18	5	19	67	71	41
11	Arsenal	42	15	11	16	77	85	41
12	Chelsea	42	15	7	20	98	100	37
13	Manchester City	42	13	11	18	79	90	37
14	Nottingham Forest	42	14	9	19	62	78	37
15	Cardiff City	42	13	11	18	60	85	37
16	West Ham United	42	13	10	19	77	88	36
17	Fulham	42	14	8	20	72	95	36
18	Bolton Wanderers	42	12	11	19	58	73	35
19	Birmingham City	42	14	6	22	62	84	34
20	Blackpool	42	12	9	21	68	73	33
21	Newcastle United	42	11	10	21	86	109	32
22	Preston North End	42	10	10	22	43	71	30

Appearances

PLAYER	LGE	FAC	LC	TOT
Brennan	41	3	2	46
Foulkes	40	3	2	45
Setters	40	3	2	45
Charlton	39	3	–	42
Quixall	38	2	1	41
Nicholson	31	3	3	37
Dawson	28	3	3	34
Pearson	27	3	3	33
Stiles	26	3	2	31
Gregg	27	1	2	30
Cantwell	24	3	–	27
Viollet	24	1	2	27
Giles	23	–	2	25
Gaskell	10	–	1	11
Scanlon	8	–	3	11
Moir	8	–	–	8
Cope	6	–	1	7
Bradley	4	–	–	4
Dunne	3	–	1	4
Haydock	4	–	–	4
Pinner	4	–	–	4
Briggs	1	2	–	3

PLAYER	LGE	FAC	LC	TOT
Carolan	2	–	1	3
Lawton	1	–	1	2
Morgans	2	–	–	2
Bratt	–	–	1	1
Heron	1	–	–	1

Goalscorers

PLAYER	LGE	FAC	LC	TOT
Charlton	21	–	–	21
Dawson	16	3	1	20
Viollet	15	–	1	16
Quixall	13	–	2	15
Pearson	7	1	1	9
Nicholson	5	–	–	5
Setters	4	–	–	4
Giles	2	–	1	3
Stiles	2	–	–	2
Cantwell	–	2	–	2
Moir	1	–	–	1
Scanlon	1	–	–	1
own goal	1	–	–	1

More team re-building and one of the poorest seasons for Matt Busby in many years

1961/62

THE RE-BUILDING OF the team was now becoming a regular pre-season discussion topic. Matt Busby was torn between buying talent to provide a short-term solution and allowing the next generation to progress from the youth team. The most significant signing for this season was David Herd, a forward from Arsenal, costing £35,000 and already a Scottish international. Herd became one of 23 players who would be involved in either the league or FA Cup games this season, including a few youth teamers who Busby knew needed to either take their chance or move aside.

Herd started the season in the No 9 shirt as part of another exciting forward line alongside Bobby Charlton, Dennis Viollet, Mark 'Pancho' Pearson and Albert Quixall. The season opened with some bright results – a 6-1 home win against Blackburn Rovers – and only one defeat in the opening nine games. However, there then followed a ten-match run without a single win and only two draws, so any hopes of a return to the heady days of challenging for the league were over. In that stretch of games, United conceded 31 goals and scored just eight; in one three-game streak they lost 4-1, 4-1 and 5-1 to Ipswich Town, Burnley and Everton.

It was a low point for Busby who was rarely able to field the same 11 players in two consecutive games. After Christmas, the team's form continued to bounce from good to bad: they celebrated Boxing Day with a 6-3 thrashing of Nottingham Forest, Nobby Lawton scoring a hat-trick. Fortunately for the fans, they were able to begin a good run in the FA Cup. A third round win at Old Trafford against Bolton Wanderers was followed by victories over Arsenal, Sheffield Wednesday (the third season in succession that the two teams had met in the competition) and Preston North End after a replay. On the final day of March, United faced the previous season's winners of the league and FA Cup double Tottenham Hotspur, and fell to a 3-1 defeat at Hillsborough.

Despite the FA Cup glamour, United stumbled to 15th place in the league, the club's worst season in the First Division for more than 20 years. They finished only seven points above the relegation zone. The oddest thing of all, though, was that the surprising champions of this season, Ipswich Town managed by Alf Ramsey, were thrashed 5-0 at Old Trafford in early April, mainly thanks to an Albert Quixall hat-trick. It was easily the champions' worst defeat of the season. One good thing to happen, however, was that David Herd had settled in quickly at the club after his move from Arsenal and he was top scorer with 14 goals, but the team only scored a total of 72 goals while conceding 75.

- After beating United in the semi-final, Tottenham Hotspur go on to retain the FA Cup with a 3-1 win against Burnley.

- Alex Dawson plays only four games for United this season and is then transferred to Preston North End where he becomes known as The Black Prince of Deepdale.

- Nobby Stiles scores a remarkable seven goals this season out of a total of 19 during his whole 11-year career with United.

- David Herd ends his first season at United as top scorer with 17 goals in 32 games.

Above: Scottish international David Herd, who was frustrated at Arsenal by their lack of success, moved to United in July 1961 and would become the Reds top scorer this season.

Left: Half back Nobby Lawton is beaten to the ball by Preston North End goalkeeper Alan Kelly.

Final League Table Division One

		P	W	D	L	F	A	Pts
1	Ipswich Town	42	24	8	10	93	67	56
2	Burnley	42	21	11	10	101	67	53
3	Tottenham Hotspur	42	21	10	11	88	69	52
4	Everton	42	20	11	11	88	54	51
5	Sheffield United	42	19	9	14	61	69	47
6	Sheffield Wednesday	42	20	6	16	72	58	46
7	Aston Villa	42	18	8	16	65	56	44
8	West Ham United	42	17	10	15	76	82	44
9	West Bromwich Albion	42	15	13	14	83	67	43
10	Arsenal	42	16	11	15	71	72	43
11	Bolton Wanderers	42	16	10	16	62	66	42
12	Manchester City	42	17	7	18	78	81	41
13	Blackpool	42	15	11	16	70	75	41
14	Leicester City	42	17	6	19	72	71	40
15	**MANCHESTER UNITED**	42	15	9	18	72	75	39
16	Blackburn Rovers	42	14	11	17	50	58	39
17	Birmingham City	42	14	10	18	65	81	38
18	Wolverhampton Wanderers	42	13	10	19	73	86	36
19	Nottingham Forest	42	13	10	19	63	79	36
20	Fulham	42	13	7	22	66	74	33
21	Cardiff City	42	9	14	19	50	81	32
22	Chelsea	42	9	10	23	63	94	28

Appearances

PLAYER	LGE	FAC	TOT
Brennan	41	6	47
Foulkes	40	7	47
Setters	38	7	45
Charlton	37	6	43
Stiles	34	4	38
Giles	30	7	37
Dunne	28	7	35
Herd	27	5	32
Gaskell	21	7	28
Lawton	20	7	27
Quixall	21	3	24
Nicholson	17	4	21
Cantwell	17	2	19
Pearson	17	–	17
Chisnall	9	4	13
Gregg	13	–	13
Viollet	13	–	13
McMillan	11	–	11
Moir	9	–	9
Briggs	8	–	8
Bradley	6	1	7
Dawson	4	–	4

PLAYER	LGE	FAC	TOT
Haydock	1	–	1

Left: (l-r) Johnny Giles, Shay Brennan and Noel Cantwell watch teammate Bill Foulkes drive from the tee during a golf day.

Goalscorers

PLAYER	LGE	FAC	TOT
Herd	14	3	17
Quixall	10	–	10
Charlton	8	2	10
Stiles	7	–	7
Viollet	7	–	7
Lawton	6	–	6
McMillan	6	–	6
Setters	3	1	4
Giles	2	1	3
Brennan	2	–	2
Cantwell	2	–	2
Dawson	2	–	2
Chisnall	1	–	1
Pearson	1	–	1
Nicholson	–	1	1
own goal	1	–	1

1962/63

- Dennis Viollet had played almost 300 games for United and scored 179 goals before being transferred to Stoke City.

- This season's league finish of nineteenth is the worst under Matt Busby in his 24 seasons as manager.

- Former United player Walter Winterbottom is replaced as England national team manager in April by Alf Ramsey, former manager of Ipswich Town.

- The Red Devils lose nine of 21 home games this season to equal a club record set in 1930-31.

- Denis Law scores a hat-trick against Leicester City at Filbert Street on 16 April, but United still lose 4-3.

Above: A congratulatory telegram from Irish friends of Paddy Crerand on making his United debut against Blackpool on 23 February 1963. Although Irish-born, Crerand played international football for Scotland.

Right: 25 May 1963. United captain Noel Cantwell and his teammates celebrate their 3-1 win against Leicester City in the FA Cup at Wembley.

A first trophy since the Munich air crash hides a desperate fight against relegation

LAST SEASON'S LEAGUE performances were just not good enough and everyone, including Matt Busby, knew it. Busby's actions, however, were somewhat surprising in that Alex Dawson and, more particularly, Dennis Viollet were dispatched during the off-season. His solution was to make a couple of big signings, firstly with Denis Law being bought from Torino for the remarkable sum of £115,000 during the pre-season.

This was making a statement to both the team and the fans that enough was enough and Busby would follow up by bringing in stout-hearted midfielder Paddy Crerand from Celtic in February. Nevertheless, another year of struggle in the league ensued. Up to Christmas, United won just seven matches and lost 10. Then as December was ending, one of the coldest and snowiest winters on record brought football fixtures to a halt for almost two months.

By now Crerand had arrived, but the mid-winter break did not help United's league form; they did not win a league match in 1963 until 9 April when they beat Aston Villa 2-1 away from home. Yet despite no league wins in March, United managed to progress from the third round of the FA Cup all the way to the semi-finals. Four cup victories – against Huddersfield (5-0), Villa (1-0), Chelsea (2-1) and Coventry City (3-1) in the sixth round showed that United could raise themselves for the big game.

Then in April as league results continued to vary wildly, United secured a trip to Wembley by beating Southampton 1-0 in the FA Cup semi-final. The joy of this victory was muted by the fact that relegation from the league was now a real possibility. Two defeats in three games after the semi-final plummeted United towards the Second Division and, with four games remaining, there would be a battle between them, Birmingham City and cross-town rivals Manchester City for the one remaining relegation place.

Fate meant United played both City teams and already relegated Leyton Orient in the next three games in May. A loss to Birmingham seemed fatal, but a scruffy draw at Maine Road was followed by an easy 3-1 home win against Orient. Yes, a Manchester club would play in the Second Division next season, but it would be City, not United who had done enough to finish 19th, three points clear of the drop.

All that was left for United was to face Leicester City in the FA Cup final, a 3-1 victory at least regained some pride for the club.

Herd and Law both scored in the final and totalled 21 and 29 goals each during the season. This was not the kind of United campaign that Busby had envisaged, but it did bring the club's third FA Cup win and also, perhaps more significantly, United's first trophy since the Munich disaster.

Final League Table Division One

		P	W	D	L	F	A	Pts
1	Everton	42	25	11	6	84	42	61
2	Tottenham Hotspur	42	23	9	10	111	62	55
3	Burnley	42	22	10	10	78	57	54
4	Leicester City	42	20	12	10	79	53	52
5	Wolverhampton Wanderers	42	20	10	12	93	65	50
6	Sheffield Wednesday	42	19	10	13	77	63	48
7	Arsenal	42	18	10	14	86	77	46
8	Liverpool	42	17	10	15	71	59	44
9	Nottingham Forest	42	17	10	15	67	69	44
10	Sheffield United	42	16	12	14	58	60	44
11	Blackburn Rovers	42	15	12	15	79	71	42
12	West Ham United	42	14	12	16	73	69	40
13	Blackpool	42	13	14	15	58	64	40
14	West Bromwich Albion	42	16	7	19	71	79	39
15	Aston Villa	42	15	8	19	62	68	38
16	Fulham	42	14	10	18	50	71	38
17	Ipswich Town	42	12	11	19	59	78	35
18	Bolton Wanderers	42	15	5	22	55	75	35
19	**MANCHESTER UNITED**	**42**	**12**	**10**	**20**	**67**	**81**	**34**
20	Birmingham City	42	10	13	19	63	90	33
21	Manchester City	42	10	11	21	58	102	31
22	Leyton Orient	42	6	9	27	37	81	21

Appearances

PLAYER	LGE	FAC	TOT
Foulkes	41	6	47
Law	38	6	44
Herd	37	6	43
Giles	36	6	42
Brennan	37	4	41
Quixall	31	5	36
Stiles	31	4	35
Charlton	28	6	34
Setters	27	6	33
Cantwell	25	5	30
Dunne	25	3	28
Gregg	24	4	28
Crerand	19	3	22
Gaskell	18	2	20
Lawton	12	-	12
Nicholson	10	-	10
Moir	9	-	9
Chisnall	6	-	6
McMillan	4	-	4
Pearson	2	-	2
Haydock	1	-	1
Walker	1	-	1

Goalscorers

PLAYER	LGE	FAC	TOT
Law	23	6	29
Herd	19	2	21
Quixall	7	4	11
Charlton	7	2	9
Giles	4	1	5
Stiles	2	-	2

PLAYER	LGE	FAC	TOT
Cantwell	1	-	1
Chisnall	1	-	1
Moir	1	-	1
Setters	1	-	1
own goal	1	-	1

Denis Law fires a shot at the Tottenham Hotspur goalkeeper Bill Brown.

The United trinity of Charlton, Best & Law take the field together for the first time

1963/64

WITH ANOTHER TROPHY to celebrate from last season, Matt Busby now had a platform for his new generation of Busby Babes. The confidence and consistency that was previously lacking could now be sensed around Old Trafford even though the Charity Shield was lost 4-0 to a spirited Everton team at the start of the campaign.

Despite this loss, the United of old – full of attacking verve – was soon on display; a 5-1 revenge win against Everton at the end of August was followed by a 7-2 dismantling of Ipswich Town in the very next game. In September, the Reds returned to European club competition for the first time since the Munich air disaster season of 1957-58 in the European Cup-Winners' Cup; it was actually their first entry into this competition. United swamped Willem II of the Netherlands 7-2 in the opening round and then took out the cup holders Tottenham Hotspur 4-3 on aggregate in the next round to prove their new-found status.

As New Year celebrations came and went, United were still apt to wild swings in form (defeats of 4-0 and 6-1 in December to Everton and Burnley were then followed by a 5-1 win in a return match against Burnley), but at least another FA Cup run was started. United eased through to the sixth round after easy wins over Southampton, Bristol Rovers and Barnsley.

Once in the last eight, the Reds faced a tough Sunderland team who would go on to gain promotion from the Second Division by the end of this season. The Wearsiders took United to a second replay before United triumphed 5-1, but the three games took their toll. Just five days later, United lost the FA Cup semi-final to West Ham 3-1 and a further four days after that they flew to Sporting Lisbon in Portugal for the second leg of the Cup-Winners' Cup quarter final. United were overwhelmed 5-0 and lost 6-4 on aggregate.

A total of ten games in the month of March was too much for a brittle United team and their league challenge also faded, although they did manage the runners-up spot, four points behind Liverpool. Denis Law with 46 goals in all competitions was the star of this season's show; he scored the remarkable total in just 42 appearances and included 30 goals in the league, one for each of his 30 appearances. David Herd's 27 were also not insignificant, perhaps more memorable was that George Best was also given his chance this season and played 26 games, scoring six goals.

In fact, this season was the first time the holy trinity of Best, Charlton and Law took to the field together; it was at West Bromwich Albion on 18 January 1964. United won 4-1 and all three men scored, Law twice and the other two once each. Best had actually made his debut against the same club on 14 September four months earlier, but injuries and the fact that this was Best's debut season meant the three players did not all play together for over four months. Nevertheless, this season was where the three United legends finally joined forces.

■ Apart from George Best, another debutant in 1963-64 and product of the youth system is David Sadler who can play in both the forward line and the defence.

■ United win the FA Youth Cup for the first time in seven years with a 5-2 win against Swindon Town over two legs. The Red Devils had won the first five of these youth trophies in succession in the fifties.

■ In a ceremonial game to mark the 100th anniversary of the Football Association, England play a Rest of the World team at Wembley and win 2-1. Denis Law scores for the visitors.

■ Denis Law is crowned European Footballer of the Year, the first – and so far only - Scottish player to win the award.

Above: Defender Shay Brennan (right) hooks the ball away from Liverpool's Ian St.John.

Left: A young George Best signs autographs for even younger fans.

Final League Table Division One

		P	W	D	L	F	A	Pts
1	Liverpool	42	26	5	11	92	45	57
2	**MANCHESTER UNITED**	**42**	**23**	**7**	**12**	**90**	**62**	**53**
3	Everton	42	21	10	11	84	64	52
4	Tottenham Hotspur	42	22	7	13	97	81	51
5	Chelsea	42	20	10	12	72	56	50
6	Sheffield Wednesday	42	19	11	12	84	67	49
7	Blackburn Rovers	42	18	10	14	89	65	46
8	Arsenal	42	17	11	14	90	82	45
9	Burnley	42	17	10	15	71	64	44
10	West Bromwich Albion	42	16	11	15	70	61	43
11	Leicester City	42	16	11	15	61	58	43
12	Sheffield United	42	16	11	15	61	64	43
13	Nottingham Forest	42	16	9	17	64	68	41
14	West Ham United	42	14	12	16	69	74	40
15	Fulham	42	13	13	16	58	65	39
16	Wolverhampton Wanderers	42	12	15	15	70	80	39
17	Stoke City	42	14	10	18	77	78	38
18	Blackpool	42	13	9	20	52	73	35
19	Aston Villa	42	11	12	19	62	71	34
20	Birmingham City	42	11	7	24	54	92	29
21	Bolton Wanderers	42	10	8	24	48	80	28
22	Ipswich Town	42	9	7	26	56	121	25

FOOTBALL LEAGUE DIVISION ONE: RUNNERS-UP

Appearances

PLAYER	LGE	FAC	ECWC	TOT
Crerand	41	7	6	54
Foulkes	41	7	6	54
Charlton	40	7	6	53
Dunne	40	7	6	53
Setters	32	7	6	45
Herd	30	7	6	43
Law	30	6	5	41
Cantwell	28	2	4	34
Chisnall	20	4	4	28
Gaskell	17	7	4	28
Gregg	25	-	2	27
Best	17	7	2	26
Brennan	17	5	2	24
Sadler	19	-	2	21
Stiles	17	2	2	21
Moore	18	1	-	19
Moir	18	-	-	18
Quixall	9	-	3	12
Anderson	2	1	-	3
Tranter	1	-	-	1

FA CUP: LOSE TO WEST HAM UNITED (1-3) IN SEMI-FINAL

Goalscorers

PLAYER	LGE	FAC	ECWC	TOT
Law	30	10	6	46
Herd	20	4	3	27
Charlton	9	2	4	15
Chisnall	6	1	1	8
Best	4	2	-	6
Sadler	5	-	-	5
Moore	4	1	-	5
Setters	4	-	1	5
Moir	3	-	-	3
Quixall	3	-	-	3
Crerand	1	1	-	2
Foulkes	1	-	-	1
own goal	-	1	-	1

Reserve team coaches and former United players John Aston, left, and Henry Cockburn

EUROPEAN CUP WINNERS CUP: LOSE TO SPORTING LISBON (4-6 ON AGGREGATE) IN QUARTER-FINAL

Chased by autograph hunters, this season's new signing John Connelly arrives at Old Trafford.

FA CHARITY SHIELD: RUNNERS-UP 17 AUGUST 1963.
GOODISON PARK, LIVERPOOL: LOST TO EVERTON 0-4

1964/65

- The league title is the sixth in United's history but easily the most closely fought and the first they had won with the benefit of goal difference.

- In another great season, Denis Law scores 39 goals in all competitions to make his two-season total a remarkable 85.

- When Aston Villa beat United in the final game of the season, it is a huge shock because the Reds had won the earlier match between the two teams in October 7-0.

- John Aston Jnr makes his debut in a home match against Leicester City eleven years after his father John Snr played his last game for the Red Devils.

Above: In his second season playing in the United first team, George Best relaxes at home playing music.

Right: Star forward Denis Law seems to guide home United's only goal during a 2-1 loss against Fulham, but the scorer is actually John Connelly who can be seen in the background.

A league title is won by the slenderest of margins but a coin toss helps put United out of Europe

NOW WAS THE time for Matt Busby to push forward once again with a key addition to the team and also use the momentum from the FA Cup win in 1963. Busby had already bought John Connelly from Burnley for £60,000 and now made George Best a regular starter. In addition, he brought in a new goalkeeper, Pat Dunne from Shamrock Rovers, while using Shay Brennan as his permanent right back.

The Reds were now becoming a more formidable outfit week-in, week-out and it meant much improved league results. Despite a nervous start (only two points from the opening three games) and just one win in the first six games, United's team began to settle, especially when Dunne was given his chance in early September, a selection that sparked a stretch of 15 unbeaten games. Not only were the Reds winning, but also they were again scoring plenty of league goals – four each against Tottenham Hotspur and Wolverhampton Wanderers and seven against Aston Villa.

European opposition were also easily dealt with, first Djurgardens of Sweden 7-2 on aggregate in the Inter-Cities' Fairs Cup and then Borussia Dortmund 10-1 in the second round. This colossal effort seemed to stall United's league form and they won just one of their next eight league games.

However, another FA Cup run was beginning; Chester City, Stoke City, Burnley and Wolves were all beaten on the path to another semi-final, this time against a Leeds United team fresh from promotion to the First Division. United had returned to winning ways in the league before the semi, but on poor pitches, firstly at Hillsborough where the teams drew 0-0 and then at the City Ground in a replay, Leeds eventually muscled past the Red Devils 1-0.

Nevertheless, FA Cup disappointment was forgotten as the same two teams sprinted head-on for the league title. United managed a seven-game streak of wins before unexpectedly losing the final game of the season at Aston Villa. However, this time after many runners-up disappointments over the years, United squeaked the prize on goal average, by just 0.686 of a goal.

With the league championship secured, the rather tortuous European competition took over the Reds' schedule. United had beaten Everton in the Fairs Cup third round in February and now, in mid-May, Strasbourg were given a 5-0 hiding in France in the first leg of the quarter-final. A goalless draw at Old Trafford then set up a semi-final against Hungarian powerhouse Ferencvaros.

When the two sides were tied 3-3 after two legs and without the away goals system or penalties to decide who would play in the final, United lost the toss of a coin and were forced to head back to Hungary for a playoff. Ten days later in mid-June, it was an exhausted United team that lost 2-1. The 1964-65 season had lasted nearly 11 months, but winning the league title again made it a memorable one.

Final League Table Division One

		P	W	D	L	F	A	Pts
1	**MANCHESTER UNITED**	**42**	**26**	**9**	**7**	**89**	**39**	**61**
2	Leeds United	42	26	9	7	83	52	61
3	Chelsea	42	24	8	10	89	54	56
4	Everton	42	17	15	10	69	60	49
5	Nottingham Forest	42	17	13	12	71	67	47
6	Tottenham Hotspur	42	19	7	16	87	71	45
7	Liverpool	42	17	10	15	67	73	44
8	Sheffield Wednesday	42	16	11	15	57	55	43
9	West Ham United	42	19	4	19	82	71	42
10	Blackburn Rovers	42	16	10	16	83	79	42
11	Stoke City	42	16	10	16	67	66	42
12	Burnley	42	16	10	16	70	70	42
13	Arsenal	42	17	7	18	69	75	41
14	West Bromwich Albion	42	13	13	16	70	65	39
15	Sunderland	42	14	9	19	64	74	37
16	Aston Villa	42	16	5	21	57	82	37
17	Blackpool	42	12	11	19	67	78	35
18	Leicester City	42	11	13	18	69	85	35
19	Sheffield United	42	12	11	19	50	64	35
20	Fulham	42	11	12	19	60	78	34
21	Wolverhampton Wanderers	42	13	4	25	59	89	30
22	Birmingham City	42	8	11	23	64	96	27

Appearances

PLAYER	LGE	FAC	LC	TOT
Brennan	42	7	11	60
Connelly	42	7	11	60
Dunne A	42	7	11	60
Foulkes	42	7	11	60
Best	41	7	11	59
Charlton	41	7	11	59
Stiles	41	7	11	59
Crerand	39	7	11	57
Dunne P	37	7	11	55
Herd	37	7	11	55
Law	36	6	10	52
Sadler	6	–	–	6
Setters	5	–	1	6
Gaskell	5	–	–	5
Cantwell	2	–	–	2
Fitzpatrick	2	–	–	2
Aston	1	–	–	1
Kinsey	–	1	–	1
Moir	1	–	–	1

Goalscorers

PLAYER	LGE	FAC	LC	TOT
Law	28	3	8	39
Herd	20	2	6	28
Connelly	15	–	5	20
Charlton	10	–	8	18
Best	10	2	2	14
Crerand	3	2	–	5
Cantwell	1	–	–	1
Sadler	1	–	–	1
Kinsey	–	1	–	1
own goal	1	–	–	1

Bobby Charlton sails past Sheffield Wednesday's Colin Dobson

Two for the future: John Fitzpatrick (left) and John Aston are tipped for stardom. Fitzpatrick got his first start this season and Aston played his debut game in April.

A consistent team and plenty of chances to win yet nothing new to put in the trophy room

1965/66

MANAGER MATT BUSBY was by now happy and confident with his first XI selection and those players had now experienced enough games together to be working competently as a team (Shay Brennan, John Connelly, Tony Dunne and Bill Foulkes played all 60 matches the previous season). However, if that was the good news, then the bad news was that injuries after such a long season were inevitable and because the 1965-66 campaign began just 59 days after the last one ended, there was little chance for Busby's favourite XI to play the same number of games this time around.

Yet the excitement of a return to the European Cup kept early season hopes high and provided players with plenty of adrenaline. United began the league season unconvincingly; early losses to Nottingham Forest and Burnley were unexpected, while early forays into Europe (easy two-leg wins over HJK Helsinki of Finland and ASK Vorwaerts of East Germany) took energy from the team. Then league inconsistency crept in again, for example a 5-1 loss to Tottenham Hotspur was immediately followed by a 4-1 win over Fulham.

In the New Year United were fighting on three fronts as another FA Cup campaign started with a 5-2 win over Derby County in the opening round. By the end of March Benfica of Portugal had been defeated 8-3 to put United into the European Cup semi-finals. The second leg of this quarter-final battle against the Portuguese is still regarded as one of the club's best ever performances in Europe.

After a 3-2 home win against a team that had reached the final of the competition in four of the last five seasons, United pulverised a full-strength Benfica team - which included the legendary Eusebio – 5-1 in Lisbon in the return. George Best in particular looked irresistible throughout and scored twice.

Manager Matt Busby said his plan was for his team to soak up early pressure, but Best ignored the advice and helped put United 2-0 up before Benfica could catch their breath.

Two weeks later, a 3-1 win in the sixth round of the FA Cup over Preston North End meant the Reds had lined up another semi-final contest. However, the run-in for all three trophies would end in disappointment as tired United players faltered during a spate of 13 games in just over six weeks. The European Cup semi was lost to Partizan Belgrade of Yugoslavia, the same city United had visited before stopping off at Munich where the air disaster occurred. United seemed out of sorts and lost the away leg 2-0. In the second leg at Old Trafford, a single goal from Stiles was not enough and left Busby devastated.

Three days later, another semi-final was lost when Everton slipped past a jaded United 1-0 at Burnden Park in front of 60,000 fans. The Reds were without George Best, who had a knee injury, while much was made in the press about the fact that Everton had played a near-reserve team in their previous game to rest their best players. At the same time in the title run-in, the Reds dropped five valuable points in seven games and finished fourth, some ten points behind Liverpool.

- United share the FA Charity Shield with Liverpool after a 2-2 draw at Old Trafford in the now traditional season opening game.

- Bobby Charlton, Nobby Stiles and John Connelly all make the England squad for the World Cup that followed this season; Charlton and Stiles star in the final itself.

- Everton's cunning team selection before the FA Cup semi-final is noted by the Football League who later fine them £2,000 for playing an under-strength team.

- In the famous George Best-inspired 5-1 win over Benfica in the European Cup, Shay Brennan is the only mildly unhappy United player – he puts through his own net to score the Portuguese team's goal.

Above: A cheeky George Best offers Chelsea's Terry Venables the ball in his hands after the midfielder failed to get it with his feet.

Left: Bobby Charlton in full flow.

Final League Table Division One

		P	W	D	L	F	A	Pts
1	Liverpool	42	26	9	7	79	34	61
2	Leeds United	42	23	9	10	79	38	55
3	Burnley	42	24	7	11	79	47	55
4	**MANCHESTER UNITED**	**42**	**18**	**15**	**9**	**84**	**59**	**51**
5	Chelsea	42	22	7	13	65	53	51
6	West Bromwich Albion	42	19	12	11	91	69	50
7	Leicester City	42	21	7	14	80	65	49
8	Tottenham Hotspur	42	16	12	14	75	66	44
9	Sheffield United	42	16	11	15	56	59	43
10	Stoke City	42	15	12	15	65	64	42
11	Everton	42	15	11	16	56	62	41
12	West Ham United	42	15	9	18	70	83	39
13	Blackpool	42	14	9	19	55	65	37
14	Arsenal	42	12	13	17	62	75	37
15	Newcastle United	42	14	9	19	50	63	37
16	Aston Villa	42	15	6	21	69	80	36
17	Sheffield Wednesday	42	14	8	20	56	66	36
18	Nottingham Forest	42	14	8	20	56	72	36
19	Sunderland	42	14	8	20	51	72	36
20	Fulham	42	14	7	21	67	85	35
21	Northampton Town	42	10	13	19	55	92	33
22	Blackburn Rovers	42	8	4	30	57	88	20

Appearances

PLAYER	LGE	FAC	EC	TOT
Crerand	41	7	7	55
Dunne A	40	7	8	55
Stiles	39	7	8	54
Charlton	38	7	8	53
Herd	36 (1)	7	7	50 (1)
Foulkes	33	7	8	48
Law	33	7	8	48
Connelly	31 (1)	6	8	45 (1)
Best	31	5	6	42
Brennan	28	5	5	38
Gregg	26	7	5	38
Cantwell	23	2	3	28
Aston	23	2	2	27
Dunne P	8	–	2	10
Sadler	10	–	–	10
Gaskell	8	–	1	9
Anderson	5 (1)	1	1	7 (1)
Fitzpatrick	3 (1)	–	1	4 (1)
Ryan	4	–	–	4
Noble	2	–	–	2

Goalkeeper Pat Dunne screams in frustration after letting in Tottenham Hotspur's fourth goal during a 5-1 loss at White Hart Lane.

Goalscorers

PLAYER	LGE	FAC	EC	TOT
Herd	24	3	5	32
Law	15	6	3	24
Charlton	16	–	2	18
Best	9	3	4	16
Connelly	5	2	6	13
Aston	4	–	–	4
Sadler	4	–	–	4
Stiles	2	–	1	3
Cantwell	2	–	–	2
Dunne A	1	–	–	1
Ryan	1	–	–	1
Crerand	–	–	1	1
Foulkes	–	–	1	1
own goals	1	–	–	1

The usual suspects: the United team and manager line up in front of the Discoveries Monument in Lisbon before their European Cup tie against Benfica.

1966/67

MANCHESTER UNITED FOOTBALL CLUB • OFFICIAL PROGRAMME

UNITED REVIEW

UNITED v LIVERPOOL, 10th December, 1966.

■ Goalkeeper Harry Gregg plays his last games for United this season before being transferred to Stoke City where he played just two matches before retiring.

■ John Connelly is transferred to Blackburn Rovers of the Second Division during the early part of the season for a fee of £40,000.

■ The league title marks Matt Busby's tenth trophy as United manager: five league championships, two FA Cups and three Charity Shields.

Above: The programme for the home match against Sheffield United. United won 2-0 with goals from Paddy Crerand and David Herd.

Right: 10 September 1966. Denis Law scores in a game against Tottenham Hotspur at White Hart Lane.

A triumphant league title returns to Old Trafford to satisfy the manager's desire

MATT BUSBY WAS said to have contemplated retirement after the disappointments of last season, especially the European Cup semi-final loss that brought back so many memories of Munich. However, his team was becoming ever stronger and this season he could ask for regular contributions from more former youth team players like winger John Aston (son of the former United great of the same name) and full back Bobby Noble. Plus, Bobby Charlton, Nobby Stiles and John Connelly were returning as world champions after the England World Cup win, so another season of success beckoned.

Yet perhaps the most important addition to the team was Alex Stepney in goal, signed for £50,000 from Chelsea during the close season. The league campaign then started rather sloppily as good wins were matched with bad losses, particularly away from home where Stoke City and Nottingham Forest both won by three clear goals 3-0 and 4-1. When a full-strength team lost 5-1 to Blackpool (a club set to be relegated this season from the First Division) in the opening round of the League Cup in September, the prospects for the year were not bright.

Nevertheless, the Red Devils won nine of the next 11 games and then beat two of their closest rivals – Tottenham Hotspur and Nottingham Forest – in the first few weeks of the New Year. At the same time, a fourth round FA Cup loss to Norwich City meant United had only the league to worry about because they had failed to qualify for any European competition the previous season. In fact, from the time of the FA Cup exit to the end of the season, United did not lose a league game; a sharp contrast to the over-worked team of 12 months previous that struggled during the spring.

Not only that, but goalkeeper Stepney's form and his support for the defence had also proved crucial. After a Boxing Day loss 2-1 to Sheffield United, Stepney kept eleven clean sheets in the next 20 games and never conceded more than two goals in any single game.

The First Division championship was secured with a spectacular 6-1 win at West Ham United and a game remaining;

Forest and Spurs finished four points back. More than 61,000 fans turned out for the crowning of the champions in the last match of the season at Old Trafford, even though a 0-0 draw against Stoke City provided a rather dull ending to a title-winning season.

George Best played every game – 45 in all competitions compared to 56 last season – and scored ten goals. However, Denis Law with 25 goals (23 in the league) and David Herd (who scored 16 league goals before breaking his leg in March) did most of the damage in attack, while Charlton managed 12 goals himself.

Final League Table Division One

		P	W	D	L	F	A	Pts
1	**MANCHESTER UNITED**	**42**	**24**	**12**	**6**	**84**	**45**	**60**
2	Nottingham Forest	42	23	10	9	64	41	56
3	Tottenham Hotspur	42	24	8	10	71	48	56
4	Leeds United	42	22	11	9	62	42	55
5	Liverpool	42	19	13	10	64	47	51
6	Everton	42	19	10	13	65	46	48
7	Arsenal	42	16	14	12	58	47	46
8	Leicester City	42	18	8	16	78	71	44
9	Chelsea	42	15	14	13	67	62	44
10	Sheffield United	42	16	10	16	52	59	42
11	Sheffield Wednesday	42	14	13	15	56	47	41
12	Stoke City	42	17	7	18	63	58	41
13	West Bromwich Albion	42	16	7	19	77	73	39
14	Burnley	42	15	9	18	66	76	39
15	Manchester City	42	12	15	15	43	52	39
16	West Ham United	42	14	8	20	80	84	36
17	Sunderland	42	14	8	20	58	72	36
18	Fulham	42	11	12	19	71	83	34
19	Southampton	42	14	6	22	74	92	34
20	Newcastle United	42	12	9	21	39	81	33
21	Aston Villa	42	11	7	24	54	85	29
22	Blackpool	42	6	9	27	41	76	21

Appearances

PLAYER	LGE	FAC	LC	TOT
Best	42	2	1	45
Charlton	42	2	-	44
Dunne A	40	2	1	43
Crerand	39	2	1	42
Stiles	37	2	1	40
Sadler	35 (1)	2	1	38 (1)
Law	36	2	-	38
Stepney	35	2	-	37
Foulkes	33	1	1	35
Herd	28	2	1	31
Noble	29	2	-	31
Aston	26 (4)	-	1	27 (4)
Brennan	16	-	1	17
Connelly	6	-	1	7
Ryan	4 (1)	1	-	5 (1)
Gaskell	5	-	-	5
Cantwell	4	-	-	4
Fitzpatrick	3	-	-	3
Gregg	2	-	-	2
Dunne P	-	-	1	1
Anderson	- (1)	-	-	- (1)

Goalscorers

PLAYER	LGE	FAC	LC	TOT
Law	23	2	-	25
Herd	16	1	1	18
Charlton	12	-	-	12
Best	10	-	-	10
Aston	5	-	-	5
Sadler	5	-	-	5
Foulkes	4	-	-	4
Crerand	3	-	-	3
Stiles	3	-	-	3
Connelly	2	-	-	2
own goal	1	-	-	1

Bobby Charlton fires a fierce shot at goal.

David Herd receives care after breaking his left leg in a game against Leicester City in March.

A season of dreams as United finally win the European Cup in memory of absent friends

MATT BUSBY'S SIDE was now a superb blend of youth and experience and they feared no team in any competition. Young players were still emerging through the club's youth system and he continued to unearth talent (this season's key debutants were two 18-year-olds: Brian Kidd in the forward line and Francis Burns at full back). For manager Matt Busby, this was another season in which winning the European Cup and defending their league title would be the main goals.

In the league, in fact, United started in August with a defeat at Everton 3-1, but would not lose another game until the end of October. By the end of the following month, the Reds had won through to the quarter-finals of the European Cup and were again challenging for the league with a five-point lead at one stage. The difference in the league title battle this year was that there was a new team involved, Manchester City.

By mid-February, United's league form turned sour and at one time they lost five out of eight games, including a 3-1 defeat at home to their now main rivals City. The Red Devils also lost in the third round of the FA Cup to Tottenham Hotspur after a replay, although this proved to be a blessing in disguise for the European campaign as it reduced the number of end-of-season matches.

Gornik Zabrze of Poland were the European quarter-final opponents and were beaten in a hard-fought tie 2-1 on aggregate, to set up a classic semi-final with Real Madrid. At the same time as the championship was still at stake, United beat the Spanish giants 1-0 in the first leg. So with three league matches to play before the second leg, United really needed three wins, but instead lost twice, including the last match of the season at home to Sunderland just four days before the Real return when they were without an injured Denis Law.

City took advantage and won their own final league match to take the title by two points and leave United as runners-up. However, in one of the all-time great European matches in Madrid before a crowd of 125,000, United came back from a 3-1 deficit at half-time to draw 3-3 and win 4-3 on aggregate.

Fittingly, the crucial third goal was scored by Munich survivor Bill Foulkes.

Two weeks later at Wembley Stadium – again without Law – United reached the pinnacle of their recent achievements with a 4-1 win over Benfica after extra time in the European Cup final. Amid tears of joy, Busby, Bobby Charlton and Foulkes – the last three Munich survivors still at United – celebrated the fulfilment of a long-held dream for the Reds to be crowned the best team in Europe for the first time.

- In the Manchester derby game in March as the title is being decided, City win 3-1 at Old Trafford to offset a 2-1 United victory at Maine Road back in September.

- The United XI that lose the crucial last league game at home to Sunderland is exactly the same as the one that wins the European Cup 18 days later.

- Brian Kidd makes his debut in the very first match of the season, the 3-3 draw against Tottenham Hotspur in the Charity Shield. He goes on to play 50 first team games and score 17 goals including one in the European Cup final against Benfica on the day of his 19th birthday.

Above: Bobby Charlton and Nobby Stiles on the train to London to play Benfica in the 1968 European Cup final.

Left: 30 May 1968. Matt Busby holds the ultimate European prize.

Final League Table Division One

		P	W	D	L	F	A	Pts
1	Manchester City	42	26	6	10	86	43	58
2	**MANCHESTER UNITED**	**42**	**24**	**8**	**10**	**89**	**55**	**56**
3	Liverpool	42	22	11	9	71	40	55
4	Leeds United	42	22	9	11	71	41	53
5	Everton	42	23	6	13	67	40	52
6	Chelsea	42	18	12	12	62	68	48
7	Tottenham Hotspur	42	19	9	14	70	59	47
8	West Bromwich Albion	42	17	12	13	75	62	46
9	Arsenal	42	17	10	15	60	56	44
10	Newcastle United	42	13	15	14	54	67	41
11	Nottingham Forest	42	14	11	17	52	64	39
12	West Ham United	42	14	10	18	73	69	38
13	Leicester City	42	13	12	17	64	69	38
14	Burnley	42	14	10	18	64	71	38
15	Sunderland	42	13	11	18	51	61	37
16	Southampton	42	13	11	18	66	83	37
17	Wolverhampton Wanderers	42	14	8	20	66	75	36
18	Stoke City	42	14	7	21	50	73	35
19	Sheffield Wednesday	42	11	12	19	51	63	34
20	Coventry City	42	9	15	18	51	71	33
21	Sheffield United	42	11	10	21	49	70	32
22	Fulham	42	10	7	25	56	98	27

Appearances

PLAYER	LGE	FAC	EC	TOT
Best	41	2	9	52
Charlton	41	2	9	52
Crerand	41	2	9	52
Stepney	41	2	9	52
Sadler	40 (1)	2	9	51 (1)
Kidd	38	2	9	49
Dunne	37	2	9	48
Burns	36	2	7	45
Aston	34 (3)	2	6	42 (3)
Foulkes	24	-	6	30
Law	23	1	3	27
Stiles	20	-	7	27
Fitzpatrick	14 (3)	2	2	18 (3)
Brennan	13	-	3	16
Ryan	7 (1)	-	1	8 (1)
Herd	6	1	1	8
Gowling	4 (1)	-	-	4 (1)
Kopel	1 (1)	-	-	1 (1)
Rimmer	1	-	-	1

Goalscorers

PLAYER	LGE	FAC	EC	TOT
Best	28	1	3	32
Charlton	15	1	2	18
Kidd	15	-	2	17
Aston	10	-	1	11
Law	7	-	2	9
Sadler	3	-	3	6
Burns	2	-	-	2
Ryan	2	-	-	2
Foulkes	1	-	1	2
Brennan	1	-	-	1
Crerand	1	-	-	1
Dunne	1	-	-	1
Gowling	1	-	-	1
Herd	1	-	-	1
own goals	1	-	2	3

Right: George Best sinks to his knees during the 2-2 FA Cup tie in January against Tottenham Hotspur at Old Trafford. United lose the replay 1-0.

FOOTBALL LEAGUE DIVISION ONE: RUNNERS-UP

FA CUP: LOSE TO TOTTENHAM HOTSPUR (0-1) IN 3RD ROUND REPLAY.

EUROPEAN CUP: WINNERS. 29 MAY 1968. WEMBLEY, LONDON. BEAT BENFICA 4-1 CHARLTON 53', BEST 93', KIDD 94', CHARLTON 99'

FA CHARITY SHIELD: SHARED. 12 AUGUST 1967. OLD TRAFFORD, MANCHESTER. DREW WITH TOTTENHAM HOTSPUR 3-3 CHARLTON (2), LAW.

1968/69

- Although United had not won the league last season, they were allowed to defend their European Cup title as champions.

- The 59-year-old Matt Busby is knighted in May 1968 and tells a news conference: "It's time to make way for a younger man, a track-suited manager."

- After 24 managing the club, Sir Matt Busby takes on the role of general manager.

- In a bad-tempered two-leg Inter-Continental Cup against Estudiantes of Argentina, one United player is sent off in each game, both for retaliating - Nobby Stiles in the first and George Best in the second.

Above: George Best is reduced to pedal power after receiving a six month driving ban from a Manchester court.

Right: There were many outstanding performances by United goalkeeper Alex Stepney this season including, this match against Liverpool at Anfield.

A post-European Cup hangover produces a poor season as Sir Matt Busby bows out as manager

THE EUPHORIA THAT gripped Manchester United the club as well as Manchester the city after the European Cup victory was immense. The manager and players celebrated in an open-top bus ride through the city streets and were lauded at every turn. But the emotional energy expended during the European Cup and the eventual win in the final was to take its toll, especially for Matt Busby.

That Wembley victory had come just as some of the older players were reaching the end of their careers and another influx of new blood was needed. Stalwart Bill Foulkes would play only 18 games this season and another key defender Shay Brennan managed only 16, while others such as Bobby Charlton and Denis Law were suffering more injuries. Busby had now built three highly successful teams, but was he ready to construct another?

The manager did bring in talented winger Willie Morgan from Burnley for £110,000, but it was a lacklustre United that started this season in the league and won just three of their first nine games. By mid-September, another European Cup campaign had begun with Waterford of the Irish Republic dispatched 10-2 on aggregate and, as European champions, United would represent the continent in a two-leg Inter-Continental Cup against the champions of South America, Estudiantes de la Plata of Argentina.

The matches were unpleasant affairs with outrageous fouls against United players and gross intimidation. The Reds were defeated 1-0 away and drew 1-1 at Old Trafford to lose 2-1 on aggregate. The whole season suddenly seemed tainted and United's league form fizzled out, so that by the end of 1968 – just seven months after the European Cup triumph – United had won just seven First Division matches and were in the lower half of the table.

Although Anderlecht of Belgium had been beaten in the second round of the European Cup, the newly knighted Sir Matt decided it was time to announce his intention to retire at the end of the season; the strain of over 20 years in charge was beginning to show. There were a few sparkling games in Busby's last league campaign, like an 8-1 win at home to Queens Park Rangers, but the league title was never really an option this year. The Red Devils finished in 11th place.

In the FA Cup, United reached the sixth round, but then lost 1-0 at home to a strong Everton team. The European Cup remained in their sights and Rapid Vienna of Austria were beaten 3-0 in the quarter-finals. That set up another semi-final classic, this time against AC Milan who won the first leg in Italy 2-0 in front of 80,000 fans at the San Siro.

AC then put on a highly impressive defensive display and, with the help of some questionable refereeing decisions, they limited United to just one goal at Old Trafford. United, without the verve of last season and in the knowledge of Busby's imminent departure, were not the unstoppable force of 12 months earlier and so lost 2-1 on aggregate. A season without a trophy was a rather inappropriate send-off for Busby.

Final League Table Division One

		P	W	D	L	F	A	Pts
1	Leeds United	42	27	13	2	66	26	67
2	Liverpool	42	25	11	6	63	24	61
3	Everton	42	21	15	6	77	36	57
4	Arsenal	42	22	12	8	56	27	56
5	Chelsea	42	20	10	12	73	53	50
6	Tottenham Hotspur	42	14	17	11	61	51	45
7	Southampton	42	16	13	13	57	48	45
8	West Ham United	42	13	18	11	66	50	44
9	Newcastle United	42	15	14	13	61	55	44
10	West Bromwich Albion	42	16	11	15	64	67	43
11	**MANCHESTER UNITED**	**42**	**15**	**12**	**15**	**57**	**53**	**42**
12	Ipswich Town	42	15	11	16	59	60	41
13	Manchester City	42	15	10	17	64	55	40
14	Burnley	42	15	9	18	55	82	39
15	Sheffield Wednesday	42	10	16	16	41	54	36
16	Wolverhampton Wanderers	42	10	15	17	41	58	35
17	Sunderland	42	11	12	19	43	67	34
18	Nottingham Forest	42	10	13	19	45	57	33
19	Stoke City	42	9	15	18	40	63	33
20	Coventry City	42	10	11	21	46	64	31
21	Leicester City	42	9	12	21	39	68	30
22	Queens Park Rangers	42	4	10	28	39	95	18

Appearances

PLAYER	LGE	FAC	EC	TOT
Stiles	41	6	8	55
Best	41	6	6	53
Stepney	38	5	6	49
Crerand	35	4	8	47
Charlton	32	6	8	46
Dunne	33	6	6	45
Law	30	6	7	43
Kidd	28 (1)	5	7	40 (1)
Fitzpatrick	28 (2)	6	4	38 (2)
Morgan	29	5	4	38
Sadler	26 (3)	- (1)	5	31 (4)
James	21	6	2	29
Burns	14 (2)	1	3 (1)	18 (3)
Brennan	13	-	3	16
Foulkes	10 (3)	-	5	15 (3)
Sartori	11 (2)	2	2	15 (2)
Aston	13	-	-	13
Kopel	7 (1)	1	1	9 (1)
Rimmer	4	1	2 (1)	7 (1)
Ryan	6	-	1	7
Gowling	2	-	-	2

Goalscorers

PLAYER	LGE	FAC	EC	TOT
Law	14	7	9	30
Best	19	1	2	22
Morgan	6	1	1	8
Charlton	5	-	2	7
Fitzpatrick	3	1	-	4
Kidd	1	2	1	4
Aston	2	-	-	2
Crerand	1	1	-	2
Stiles	1	-	1	2
James	1	-	-	1
Ryan	1	-	-	1
Burns	-	-	1	1
Sartori	-	-	1	1
own goals	3	1	-	4

Right: In United's 7-1 win over Waterford in the European Cup, Denis Law nets four times and here he celebrates one of the goals.

FOOTBALL LEAGUE DIVISION ONE: ELEVENTH POSITION   FA CUP: LOSE TO EVERTON (0-1) IN QUARTER-FINAL.   EUROPEAN CUP: LOSE TO MILAN (1-2 ON AGGREGATE) IN SEMI-FINAL.   INTERCONTINENTAL CUP: LOSE TO CLUB ESTUDIANTES DE LA PLATA (1-2 ON AGGREGATE) IN FINAL.

A tough first season for new manager Wilf McGuinness despite receiving Sir Matt's blessing

AFTER MORE THAN six months of speculation, Wilf McGuinness was announced as Sir Matt Busby's replacement in June. McGuinness, a former United player himself, was already one of the coaching staff at the club and was chosen by Sir Matt himself, who continued to work at the club as general manager. The new man in charge had been a key man in Sir Alf Ramsey's coaching team that helped win the World Cup for England in 1966 and also the national side's youth team coach.

Yet United's board decided to give McGuinness only the title of head coach rather than manager. Manchester-born McGuinness was just 31 – younger than his star player Bobby Charlton – and a popular appointment both with players and fans, but he took over a team in transition as well as one that had been managed by a legend. His would be a difficult task.

The new head coach's start in the job was less than auspicious – just three points from the first six games and only three goals scored – and this with most of the same players who had starred for the last few seasons. The new head coach's only significant signing had been tough centre half Ian Ure from Arsenal to replace the near-retiring Bill Foulkes. The big Scot made a powerful impression on the defence, which began to gel after the early stutter and the next ten league games produced six wins to move United well up the table.

A League Cup campaign also began at this time; it was the first time United had entered the competition since 1966-67 season, but with no European matches, it made sense. And as the Reds' league form improved towards the end of 1969, so they made progress in this new cup competition, all the way to a semi-final meeting with Manchester City over two legs in December.

McGuinness had utilised a few new players in this competition, including Carlo Sartori and Paul Edwards, but City won 2-1 at Maine Road and then held on at Old Trafford for a 2-2 draw to put United out 4-3 on aggregate. The inconsistencies of earlier times had now returned to the Red Devils and, as the new decade of the seventies began, their league form remained

mercurial. They were now heading for mid-table and while they could lose badly in one game, such as 5-1 at Newcastle United in April, the same basic team could then thrash West Bromwich Albion at home 7-0 in the next match.

The lack of consistency did not stop United making a bid for the FA Cup and by May, they had reached another semi-final where they again played a strong Leeds United team. After two 0-0 draws, a second replay was lost 1-0, with David Sadler playing at centre half for the injured Ure and Denis Law only fit enough to be a substitute. United's season was again one of disappointment, especially for McGuinness. Two semi-finals and eighth in the league were not up to expectations just two years after the ultimate European Cup triumph.

- This season's FA Cup run includes a George Best performance out of the top drawer when the Northern Irishman scores six goals in the FA Cup against Northampton Town

- George Best's disciplinary problems begin with clashes with the new manager as well as being banned by the Football Association at one stage this season.

- Bill Foulkes finally retires aged 37 after playing just 21 games in the last two seasons. He remained at Old Trafford as youth team coach.

- Bobby Charlton plays his last game for England in the famous 3-2 defeat to West Germany in the 1970 World Cup. He was substituted with his team 2-0 ahead.

Above: George Best with former England winger Tom Finney who admires the Best beard.

Left: The inimitable Nobby Stiles played just 13 games for the Red Devils this season.

Final League Table Division One

		P	W	D	L	F	A	Pts
1	Everton	42	29	8	5	72	34	66
2	Leeds United	42	21	15	6	84	49	57
3	Chelsea	42	21	13	8	70	50	55
4	Derby County	42	22	9	11	64	37	53
5	Liverpool	42	20	11	11	65	42	51
6	Coventry City	42	19	11	12	58	48	49
7	Newcastle United	42	17	13	12	57	35	47
8	**MANCHESTER UNITED**	42	14	17	11	66	61	45
9	Stoke City	42	15	15	12	56	52	45
10	Manchester City	42	16	11	15	55	48	43
11	Tottenham Hotspur	42	17	9	16	54	55	43
12	Arsenal	42	12	18	12	51	49	42
13	Wolverhampton Wanderers	42	12	16	14	55	57	40
14	Burnley	42	12	15	15	56	61	39
15	Nottingham Forest	42	10	18	14	50	71	38
16	West Bromwich Albion	42	14	9	19	58	66	37
17	West Ham United	42	12	12	18	51	60	36
18	Ipswich Town	42	10	11	21	40	63	31
19	Southampton	42	6	17	19	46	67	29
20	Crystal Palace	42	6	15	21	34	68	27
21	Sunderland	42	6	14	22	30	68	26
22	Sheffield United	42	8	9	25	40	71	25

Appearances

PLAYER	LGE	FAC	LC	TOT
Charlton	40	9	8	57
Sadler	40	9	8	57
Stepney	37	9	8	54
Best	37	8	8	53
Morgan	35	9	5	49
Kidd	33 (1)	9	6	48 (1)
Dunne	33	7	8	48
Ure	34	7	7	48
Burns	30 (2)	3 (1)	6	39 (3)
Crerand	25	9	2	36
Aston	21 (1)	1 (1)	6	28 (2)
Edwards	18 (1)	7	2	27 (1)
Fitzpatrick	20	1	5	26
Sartori	13 (4)	7	1 (2)	21 (6)
Law	10 (1)	- (2)	3	13 (3)
Stiles	8	3	2	13
Brennan	8 (1)	1	1	10 (1)
Gowling	6 (1)	-	- (1)	6 (2)
Givens	4 (4)	-	1	5 (4)
Rimmer	5	-	-	5
Foulkes	3	-	-	3
James	2	-	1	3

PLAYER	LGE	FAC	LC	TOT
Ryan	- (1)	-	-	- (1)

Left: Wilf McGuinness discusses tactics with one of his most senior players, Bobby Charlton.

Goalscorers

PLAYER	LGE	FAC	LC	TOT
Best	15	6	2	23
Kidd	12	6	2	20
Charlton	12	1	1	14
Morgan	7	2	-	9
Burns	3	-	-	3
Fitzpatrick	3	-	-	3
Gowling	3	-	-	3
Law	2	-	1	3
Sadler	2	-	1	3
Sartori	2	1	-	3
Aston	1	-	-	1
Crerand	1	-	-	1
Givens	1	-	-	1
Ure	1	-	-	1
Edwards	-	-	1	1
own goals	1	1	-	2

FOOTBALL LEAGUE DIVISION ONE: EIGHTH POSITION.

FA CUP: LOSE TO LEEDS UNITED (0-1) IN SEMI-FINAL SECOND REPLAY.

LEAGUE CUP: LOSE TO MANCHESTER CITY (3-4 ON AGGREGATE) IN SEMI-FINAL.

1970/71

- After being relieved of the job as manager, Wilf McGuinness leaves the club altogether in February 1971.

- There is some consolation in the last match of the season in which United managed a 4-3 win at Maine Road over Manchester City with Best, Law and Charlton all on the scoresheet.

- A knife thrown onto the Old Trafford pitch in a match against Newcastle United in February causes an FA investigation and United have to play their opening two home games next season at neutral grounds.

Above: Bobby Charlton stretches during training exercises.

Right: George Best pictured with British actor Hywel Bennett and Penny Brahms during the filming of *Percy* in which Bennett starred and Best had a small role as a footballer.

Manager Wilf McGuinness is shown the door and a tortuous season for George Best

IN AUGUST AS the season began, Wilf McGuinness was given the title of manager, the delay in upgrading his title from coach had already possibly damaged his command of the team, some of whom perhaps saw him as an equal rather than a leader because of his age.

Although this was the start of his second season in charge, McGuinness had done little to change a team that seemed to be ageing. The opening match, for example, featured eight of the players who won the European Cup in 1968, but this Red Devils team had lost its sparkle and lost the opener 1-0 at home to Leeds United.

A run of mediocre league performances followed, including 4-0 losses at Arsenal and Ipswich, although McGuinness managed to inspire a second consecutive League Cup campaign to the semi-final stage by December. Aston Villa of the Second Division were this year's opponents and the Reds were the obvious favourites, but the outcome was the same as the previous season – United could only draw at home and lost the away leg by a single goal.

Another trip to Wembley had gone begging and then after a Boxing Day 4-4 draw at Derby County, the board decided that McGuinness should be replaced immediately. Rather than sack him, he was demoted to reserve team manager and, in his place, Sir Matt Busby returned until the end of the season.

Although Sir Matt's first game in charge saw United exit in the third round of the FA Cup to Middlesbrough after a replay, the legendary manager immediately set about freshening up the way things were done: Nobby Stiles was transferred and Alan Gowling was given a regular chance in the forward line. Busby stabilised the team's form, but another mid-table league finish was inevitable after a poor start; United ended the season in eighth position.

While United looked for a new manager, the other concern was to satisfy their best player, George Best. Still only 24-years-old and at the peak of his powers, Best had scored 80 League goals in the last four years including 18 this season, but there was no sense of a return to European glory and he spoke out about the team's relative decline. His Beatles-style life off the field and a poor disciplinary record – with both United and the Football Association fining him at different times – proved a major distraction this season.

The most prominent disciplinary problem had come on Christmas Day under McGuinness's watch when Best failed to turn up for training, despite a game against Derby County being played the next day. When he reported for work on Boxing Day, McGuinness originally decided to send him home, but then had second thoughts, fined him £50 and played him in the team. United staged a dramatic comeback in the game to 4-4 and Best scored.

Best's mentor Sir Matt could not offer a long-term answer to the player and while United clearly needed their best player to stay, the club also needed a new manager who could handle him.

Final League Table Division One

		P	W	D	L	F	A	Pts
1	Arsenal	42	29	7	6	71	29	65
2	Leeds United	42	27	10	5	72	30	64
3	Tottenham Hotspur	42	19	14	9	54	33	52
4	Wolverhampton Wanderers	42	22	8	12	64	54	52
5	Liverpool	42	17	17	8	42	24	51
6	Chelsea	42	18	15	9	52	42	51
7	Southampton	42	17	12	13	56	44	46
8	**MANCHESTER UNITED**	**42**	**16**	**11**	**15**	**65**	**66**	**43**
9	Derby County	42	16	10	16	56	54	42
10	Coventry City	42	16	10	16	37	38	42
11	Manchester City	42	12	17	13	47	42	41
12	Newcastle United	42	14	13	15	44	46	41
13	Stoke City	42	12	13	17	44	48	37
14	Everton	42	12	13	17	54	60	37
15	Huddersfield Town	42	11	14	17	40	49	36
16	Nottingham Forest	42	14	8	20	42	61	36
17	West Bromwich Albion	42	10	15	17	58	75	35
18	Crystal Palace	42	12	11	19	39	57	35
19	Ipswich Town	42	12	10	20	42	48	34
20	West Ham United	42	10	14	18	47	60	34
21	Burnley	42	7	13	22	29	63	27
22	Blackpool	42	4	15	23	34	66	23

Appearances

PLAYER	LGE	FAC	LC	TOT
Charlton	42	2	6	50
Best	40	2	6	48
Fitzpatrick	35	2	6	43
Dunne	35	2	5	42
Sadler	32	2	5	39
Law	28	2	4	34
Edwards	29 (1)	1	2	32 (1)
Kidd	24 (1)	2	6	32 (1)
Morgan	25	2	2	29
Rimmer	20	2	6	28
Crerand	24	2	1	27
Aston	19 (1)	-	3 (1)	22 (2)
Stepney	22	-	-	22
Stiles	17	-	2	19
Gowling	17 (3)	- (1)	1	18 (4)
Burns	16 (4)	-	1 (1)	17 (5)
Ure	13	1	3	17
James	13	-	3 (1)	16 (1)
Watson	8	-	2	10
Sartori	2 (5)	-	1	3 (5)
Donald	-	-	1	1
O'Neil	1	-	-	1

PLAYER	LGE	FAC	LC	TOT
Young	-	- (1)	-	- (1)

17 October 1970. Ian Ure (right) leads the protests with the referee in a 2-2 draw against Leeds United.

Goalscorers

PLAYER	LGE	FAC	LC	TOT
Best	18	1	2	21
Law	15	-	1	16
Kidd	8	-	5	13
Gowling	8	-	-	8
Charlton	5	-	3	8
Aston	3	-	-	3
Morgan	3	-	-	3
Fitzpatrick	2	-	1	3
Sartori	2	-	-	2
Sadler	1	-	-	1

First team new boy Alan Gowling challenges Ipswich Town goalkeeper David Best in a league match in September.

Irishman Frank O'Farrell brings charm to Old Trafford's managerial hot seat

1971/72

AFTER TALKS WITH the likes of Jock Stein at Celtic and Dave Sexton at Chelsea, the United board – led by Sir Matt Busby's recommendations – finally appointed the genial Frank O'Farrell as the club's new manager. The Irishman had previously enjoyed great success winning the Second Division title with Leicester City and accepted the challenge of re-building a United team that had signed just three significant players – Alex Stepney, Willie Morgan and Ian Ure – in the last six seasons and whose famed youth team had, for once, failed to deliver enough quality replacements.

O'Farrell – with head coach Malcolm Musgrove who followed him from Leicester – decided to open the season with largely the same squad of players and the early signs were good. By the end of October, the Red Devils had lost only twice in the league – 1-0 to both Everton and then to Leeds United. George Best, Denis Law and Bobby Charlton were all scoring goals and there were flashes of the glamorous play of seasons past, like a 4-2 win at home to West Ham United in which Best scored a hat-trick.

Meanwhile, two rounds of the League Cup were negotiated and during November and December, United's league form continued to give great pleasure to fans – one run of five games produced four wins and 17 goals – and moved them to the top of the table by New Year. A fourth-round League Cup exit to Stoke City after a second replay seemed like a blip as O'Farrell's men seemed to be hitting their stride, but then there was a turnaround in form from January into the beginning of March that was both staggering and unfathomable – seven straight losses and just three league goals.

Although United kept themselves in the FA Cup during this period – Southampton, Preston North End and Middlesbrough were all dispatched to put the Reds into the sixth round – O'Farrell had seen enough and acted decisively. In March, he brought in defender Martin Buchan from Aberdeen for £125,000 and winger Ian Storey-Moore from Nottingham Forest for £180,000, but the slide was only marginally slowed and a third consecutive eighth place finish in the league was the result.

Buchan could not inspire a way past Stoke City in the sixth round of the FA Cup (Storey-Moore was cup-tied); the Staffordshire team won a replay 2-1 at their Victoria Ground and so had now dumped the Reds out of both cups.

Best put his shoulder to the wheel by leading the team with most appearances – 53, the same number as Charlton – and goals, with 26. But the Northern Irish legend was increasingly unhappy at United; he still wanted the team to refresh itself with new players and he also desired the captaincy from Charlton.

By May 1972, after a number of unexplained absences from training sessions, he finally admitted that he had a drinking problem. At the end of the season, Best left for a holiday in Spain and said he was retiring from football at the age of 26. He would actually remain on United's books for two more seasons, but played only 35 more games for the Reds.

- Sammy McIlroy makes a stunning debut at just 17-years-old when he scores in a 3-3 thriller of a derby game at Maine Road in November.

- John Aston, star of the European Cup win four years ago, is transferred to Luton Town at the end of this season along with full back Francis Burns, who leaves for Southampton.

- Defence is a problem as United's 61 goals conceded is the fifth worst in the division.

- Just before the season starts, Jack Crompton – a long-time star goalkeeper and now member of the coaching staff – leaves to coach Barrow after 27 years at the club.

Above: Denis Law tries his hand at taking photos rather than being the subject of them.

Left: United's Willie Morgan (right) enjoys a drink with Manchester City's Francis Lee (left) and Everton's Alan Ball (seated).

Final League Table Division One

		P	W	D	L	F	A	Pts
1	Derby County	42	24	10	8	69	33	58
2	Leeds United	42	24	9	9	73	31	57
3	Liverpool	42	24	9	9	64	30	57
4	Manchester City	42	23	11	8	77	45	57
5	Arsenal	42	22	8	12	58	40	52
6	Tottenham Hotspur	42	19	13	10	63	42	51
7	Chelsea	42	18	12	12	58	49	48
8	**MANCHESTER UNITED**	42	19	10	13	69	61	48
9	Wolverhampton Wanderers	42	18	11	13	65	57	47
10	Sheffield United	42	17	12	13	61	60	46
11	Newcastle United	42	15	11	16	49	52	41
12	Leicester City	42	13	13	16	41	46	39
13	Ipswich Town	42	11	16	15	39	53	38
14	West Ham United	42	12	12	18	47	51	36
15	Everton	42	9	18	15	37	48	36
16	West Bromwich Albion	42	12	11	19	42	54	35
17	Stoke City	42	10	15	17	39	56	35
18	Coventry City	42	9	15	18	44	67	33
19	Southampton	42	12	7	23	52	80	31
20	Crystal Palace	42	8	13	21	39	65	29
21	Nottingham Forest	42	8	9	25	47	81	25
22	Huddersfield Town	42	6	13	23	27	59	25

Appearances

PLAYER	LGE	FAC	LC	TOT
Best	40	7	6	53
Charlton	40	7	6	53
Stepney	39	7	6	52
O'Neil	37	7	6	50
Sadler	37	6	6	49
James	37	5	6	48
Morgan	35	7	6	48
Gowling	35 (2)	6 (1)	6	47 (3)
Kidd	34	4	5	43
Law	32 (1)	7	2	41 (1)
Dunne	34	4	3	41
Burns	15 (2)	5	3	23 (2)
Buchan	13	2	-	15
McIlroy	8 (8)	1 (2)	2	11(10)
Storey-Moore	11	-	-	11
Edwards	4	2	-	6
Young	5 (2)	-	-	5 (2)
Aston	2 (7)	- (1)	2 (2)	4(10)
Connaughton	3	-	-	3
Sartori	- (2)	-	1	1 (2)
Fitzpatrick	1	-	-	1

Goalscorers

PLAYER	LGE	FAC	LC	TOT
Best	18	5	3	26
Law	13	-	-	13
Charlton	8	2	2	12
Kidd	10	-	-	10
Gowling	6	2	1	9
Storey-Moore	5	-	-	5
McIlroy	4	-	-	4
Morgan	1	1	1	3
Sadler	1	1	-	2
Buchan	1	-	-	1
Burns	1	-	-	1
James	1	-	-	1
Aston	-	1	-	1

Frank O'Farrell (left) and assistant Malcolm Musgrove were given the difficult task of following directly in the footsteps of the great Sir Matt Busby.

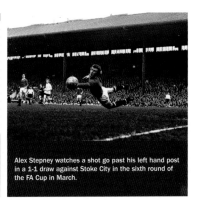

Alex Stepney watches a shot go past his left hand post in a 1-1 draw against Stoke City in the sixth round of the FA Cup in March.

FOOTBALL LEAGUE DIVISION ONE: EIGHTH POSITION | FA CUP: LOSE TO STOKE (1-2) IN 6TH ROUND REPLAY | LEAGUE CUP: LOSE TO STOKE (1-2) IN 4TH ROUND 2ND REPLAY

1972/73

- Although no one realises it at the time, the home match against Norwich City on 8 April is Denis Law's final game for United.

- Bobby Charlton's last season probably sees him playing in the worst United team of his career; he finishes top scorer, but with only six league goals.

- Tommy Docherty is not just bringing new players to Old Trafford, but also new coaches, most notably Tommy Cavanagh from Hull City.

- Cavanagh, who played with Tommy Docherty at Preston North End, is the new manager's first appointment at United in December 1972.

Above: Manager Tommy Docherty is chased by an autograph hunter.

Right: Chelsea chairman Brian Mears presents Bobby Charlton with a silver cigarette box prior to the Red legend playing his last league match for United.

Frank O'Farrell's stay is over and Tommy Docherty arrives while Bobby Charlton waves farewell

THE OFF-SEASON of turmoil in the life of United's leading player George Best – he originally announced his retirement, but later returned in time for the start of the season – was not the only problem for the team.

Manager Frank O'Farrell's early confidence was now beginning to evaporate and he started with the squad of players who finished the previous season so disappointingly, not adding to his two signings from late last season – Martin Buchan and Ian Storey-Moore. So it was of little surprise when United failed to win a league match until 23 September, the tenth in their campaign, a 3-0 victory over Derby County at home. This game marked the debut of O'Farrell's latest signing, striker Wyn Davies from Manchester City, who scored a goal in that win. In the same month, Ted MacDougall, a veritable scoring machine from Bournemouth in the Third Division, was also snapped up and he scored in his second match for the club in October.

But respite was in short supply for O'Farrell. The fans and the board were already unhappy when lowly Bristol Rovers eliminated United from the League Cup with a 2-1 win at Old Trafford in a replay in October; the manager's position was becoming untenable.

When United's form continued to show few signs of improvement culminating in a 5-0 defeat to Crystal Palace in mid-December, O'Farrell was fired with three and a half years left on his contract. His self-effacing and mild-mannered demeanour had failed to calm a discontented dressing room and his relationship with senior players like Best had never developed as much as might have been hoped.

The manager also failed to live happily under the shadow of Sir Matt Busby and later blamed him for a lack of support. It was not a period that the club can remember with any great pride, as it struggled to come to terms with the post-Busby era. However, a new man in charge was required in a hurry and the board plumped for another Scot, the former Chelsea boss Tommy Docherty, who was actually in charge of the Scotland national team at the time.

In terms of personality, Docherty was the polar opposite of O'Farrell: charismatic and confrontational. The Doc's initial effect on results was minimal. He made experienced midfielder George Graham from Arsenal his first signing, but it took five games before the manager celebrated victory and during that time United slumped to the bottom of the league.

However, Docherty made it clear that the new broom would sweep clean. His team lost in the third round of the FA Cup to Wolverhampton Wanderers, finished 18th in the league (just seven points above the relegation zone) and won only seven games in total for him that season. So at a time of turmoil, the retirement of Bobby Charlton, the last surviving United player with a link to the Munich air disaster and a star for 17 seasons and a record 758 appearances, seemed somehow fitting because not even this Red Devils legend could avert the club's slide.

Final League Table Division One

		P	W	D	L	F	A	Pts
1	Liverpool	42	25	10	7	72	42	60
2	Arsenal	42	23	11	8	57	43	57
3	Leeds United	42	21	11	10	71	45	53
4	Ipswich Town	42	17	14	11	55	45	48
5	Wolverhampton Wanderers	42	18	11	13	66	54	47
6	West Ham United	42	17	12	13	67	53	46
7	Derby County	42	19	8	15	56	54	46
8	Tottenham Hotspur	42	16	13	13	58	48	45
9	Newcastle United	42	16	13	13	60	51	45
10	Birmingham City	42	15	12	15	53	54	42
11	Manchester City	42	15	11	16	57	60	41
12	Chelsea	42	13	14	15	49	51	40
13	Southampton	42	11	18	13	47	52	40
14	Sheffield United	42	15	10	17	51	59	40
15	Stoke City	42	14	10	18	61	56	38
16	Leicester City	42	10	17	15	40	46	37
17	Everton	42	13	11	18	41	49	37
18	**MANCHESTER UNITED**	42	12	13	17	44	60	37
19	Coventry City	42	13	9	20	40	55	35
20	Norwich City	42	11	10	21	36	63	32
21	Crystal Palace	42	9	12	21	41	58	30
22	West Bromwich Albion	42	9	10	23	38	62	28

Appearances

PLAYER	LGE	FAC	LC	TOT
Buchan	42	1	4	47
Morgan	39	1	4	44
Stepney	38	1	4	43
Charlton	34 (2)	1	4	39 (2)
Young	28 (2)	1	3	32 (2)
Storey-Moore	26	-	4	30
Dunne	24	- (1)	3	27 (1)
James	22	-	4	26
Best	19	-	4	23
Sadler	19	1	2	22
Kidd	17 (5)	1	2	20 (5)
Graham	18	1	-	19
MacDougall	18	-	-	18
O'Neil	16	-	1	17
Davies	15 (1)	1	-	16 (1)
Macari	16	-	-	16
Holton	15	-	-	15
Martin	14 (2)	-	-	14 (2)
Law	9 (2)	1	2	12 (2)
Forsyth	8	1	-	9
Fitzpatrick	5	-	1	6
Donald	4	-	1	5

PLAYER	LGE	FAC	LC	TOT
McIlroy	4 (6)	-	- (3)	4 (9)
Rimmer	4	-	-	4
Watson	3	-	1	4
Anderson	2 (5)	-	-	2 (5)
Sidebottom	2	-	-	2
Edwards	1	-	-	1
Fletcher	- (2)	-	-	- (2)

Goalscorers

PLAYER	LGE	FAC	LC	TOT
Charlton	6	-	1	7
Storey-Moore	5	-	1	6
Best	4	-	2	6
Macari	5	-	-	5
MacDougall	5	-	-	5
Davies	4	-	-	4
Kidd	4	-	-	4
Morgan	3	-	1	4
Holton	3	-	-	3
Martin	2	-	-	2
Law	1	-	1	2
Anderson	1	-	-	1
Graham	1	-	-	1
McIlroy	-	-	1	1

Left: Brian Kidd sends a spectacular header towards goal in a 1-1 draw against Tottenham Hotspur in March. Kidd scored four goals this season.

The long decline is unstoppable and relegation comes for the first time in nearly four decades

WITH TOMMY DOCHERTY starting his first full season in charge and following the retirement of the legendary Bobby Charlton, this would be a season of transition for the team. Docherty sent Denis Law to Manchester City and Tony Dunne to Bolton Wanderers while in came a string of new names: Jim Holton, Lou Macari, Mick Martin and Gerry Daly had already joined the club before the end of the previous campaign. During the season, others would arrive like Stewart Houston, a full back from Brentford, and Jim McCalliog from Wolverhampton Wanderers, while the youth squad produced Brian Greenhoff as good enough for the first team.

Meanwhile, other famous names would also leave including Brian Kidd (transferred to Arsenal), Ian Storey-Moore (retired due to injury) and David Sadler (who moved to Preston North End to join Charlton who had become the team's manager). There had never been such a revolving door of player movement in the team's history and 25 players wore a United shirt during the season compared to just 19 in the European Cup winning year.

But the biggest casualty of the changes was to be George Best, who saw no future at Old Trafford and who Docherty wanted to leave anyway. Best played his last game on 1 January 1974 at Queens Park Rangers in a 1-0 loss; it was only his 12th appearance that season and he had scored just two goals.

By mid-season, Docherty's strategy was looking anything but successful: United were relegation material in the league; they had exited the League Cup in their opening fixture in that competition; and lasted only two rounds of the FA Cup before losing 1-0 at home to Ipswich Town.

All that was left was to save their status in the First Division and, as the final month of games approached, United were in deep trouble having won just three of their last 22 league games. Their problem was goal-scoring, a fact indicated by goalkeeper Alex Stepney at one point in mid-season being leading scorer with two goals, both from penalties. April began with three wins from five games, but the trapdoor

was still wide open and the Red Devils were falling fast.

With two games remaining, United needed to win both and hope relegation rivals Birmingham City lost their ultimate game. On 27 April, ironically against a Manchester City team with ex-United star Denis Law in their forward line, the fate of the Reds was settled. Law scored the only goal in a 1-0 win by the Sky Blues when he famously back-heeled the ball into the net, but showed no signs of joy in scoring a goal that seemed symbolically to be the final act in United's relegation woes. The Scot's goal was not the final nail in his former team's coffin; in fact, even a win would not have been enough for United that day as relegation rivals Birmingham City won on the same Saturday when the Reds needed them to lose.

So United finished 21st in the First Division and would play in the Second Division for the first time in nearly 40 years. Relegation came just six years after Charlton, Best and co had lifted the European Cup and the club was thrown into a state of shock.

- Almost 57,000 fans see the United-City game at the end of the season, but the average attendance at Old Trafford had fallen to 42,000 because of the Red Devils' struggles at the bottom of the league.

- United's defence lets in only 48 goals, better than 13 other sides in the First Division, but they can score only 38, the second worst total.

- George Buchan, brother of captain Martin, makes four substitute appearances in his only season at Old Trafford. He never starts a single game.

- United's Lou Macari and Mike Doyle of City are sent off in a 0-0 draw in the Manchester derby in March at Maine Road.

Above: Winger Willie Morgan was the toast of the Old Trafford terraces for a while post-George Best, but he scored just two goals this year and would leave the club after the following season.

Left: The Manchester derby ends in chaos as rival fans invade the pitch. The fans hoped to force a replay if officials abandoned the match.

Final League Table Division One

		P	W	D	L	F	A	Pts
1	Leeds United	42	24	14	4	66	31	62
2	Liverpool	42	22	13	7	52	31	57
3	Derby County	42	17	14	11	52	42	48
4	Ipswich Town	42	18	11	13	67	58	47
5	Stoke City	42	15	16	11	54	42	46
6	Burnley	42	16	14	12	56	53	46
7	Everton	42	16	12	14	50	48	44
8	Queens Park Rangers	42	13	17	12	56	52	43
9	Leicester City	42	13	16	13	51	41	42
10	Arsenal	42	14	14	14	49	51	42
11	Tottenham Hotspur	42	14	14	14	45	50	42
12	Wolverhampton Wanderers	42	13	15	14	49	49	41
13	Sheffield United	42	14	12	16	44	49	40
14	Manchester City	42	14	12	16	39	46	40
15	Newcastle United	42	13	12	17	49	48	38
16	Coventry City	42	14	10	18	43	54	38
17	Chelsea	42	12	13	17	56	60	37
18	West Ham United	42	11	15	16	55	60	37
19	Birmingham City	42	12	13	17	52	64	37
20	Southampton	42	11	14	17	47	68	36
21	**MANCHESTER UNITED**	**42**	**10**	**12**	**20**	**38**	**48**	**32**
22	Norwich City	42	7	15	20	37	62	29

Appearances

PLAYER	LGE	FAC	LC	TOT
Buchan M	42	2	1	45
Stepney	42	2	1	45
Morgan	41	2	1	44
Greenhoff	36	2	1	39
Macari	34 (1)	2	1	37 (1)
Holton	34	2	1	37
Young	29	2	1	32
McIlroy	24 (5)	1 (1)	-	25 (6)
Graham	23 (1)	1	1	25 (1)
Kidd	21	1 (1)	1	23 (1)
James	21	1	1	23
Forsyth	18 (1)	2	-	20 (1)
Houston	20	-	-	20
Daly	14 (2)	-	1	15 (2)
Martin	12 (4)	2	-	14 (4)
Best	12	-	-	12
Anderson	11 (1)	-	-	11 (1)
McCalliog	11	-	-	11
Griffiths	7	-	-	7
Fletcher	2 (3)	-	-	2 (3)
Bielby	2 (2)	-	-	2 (2)
Sadler	2 (1)	-	-	2 (1)

PLAYER	LGE	FAC	LC	TOT
Sidebottom	2	-	-	2
Storey-Moore	2	-	-	2
Buchan G	- (3)	-	- (1)	- (4)

Goalscorers

PLAYER	LGE	FAC	LC	TOT
McIlroy	6	-	-	6
Macari	5	1	-	6
McCalliog	4	-	-	4
Greenhoff	3	-	-	3
Best	2	-	-	2
Holton	2	-	-	2
Houston	2	-	-	2
James	2	-	-	2
Kidd	2	-	-	2
Morgan	2	-	-	2
Stepney	2	-	-	2
Anderson	1	-	-	1
Daly	1	-	-	1
Forsyth	1	-	-	1
Graham	1	-	-	1
Storey-Moore	1	-	-	1
Young	1	-	-	1

Left: 13 April 1974. United midfielder Jim McCalliog celebrates after scoring the winning goal. United beat Newcastle United 1-0.

1974/75

A swift return to the top flight as Tommy Docherty finds inspiration with new recruits

DESPITE RELEGATION, MANAGER Tommy Docherty remained ever optimistic that he had constructed a good United team and they only needed time together. For sure, the squad for this season was unrecognisable from the glory days, and perhaps the final key addition had been centre forward Stuart Pearson from Hull City for £222,222. But however much Docherty declared his team favourites for a quick return to the First Division, history showed that supporters in the thirties had to be patient last time the team was in this position when promotion had proved very difficult. Forty years later, it was clear that the fans of the seventies would not suffer a similar delay.

The good news came quickly to all at Old Trafford when the Second Division season started and United roared out of the blocks winning their first four games and heading straight to the top of the table. In fact, relegation had actually helped turn around the pattern of dwindling attendances. The end of the season average had been just 42,721, but by November in a home match against second-placed Sunderland, more than 60,500 fans turned up, a record for a Second Division game. By the end-of-season average attendance at Old Trafford was over 48,000, up almost 6,000 from the previous season.

Amid all the extra fan interest came plenty of goals where they had been so scarce before: a 4-0 win at home to Millwall in the opening fixture at Old Trafford and a 5-1 League Cup win against Charlton Athletic, a victory that started a run deep into this competition. Meanwhile, Docherty was still ringing the changes and 24 players were used during the campaign.

In mid-season, while United were ahead of a chasing pack, Docherty kept giving a chance to more young more talent, including youth team players Jimmy Nicholl, David McCreery and Arthur Albiston plus young winger Steve Coppell signed from Tranmere Rovers. Meanwhile out-of-favour Jim McCalliog would soon be sold to Southampton.

In January, United's League Cup quest ended with a two-leg semi-final defeat to Norwich City, while the team also went out of the FA Cup with a disappointing 3-2 replay loss to lowly

Walsall. But winning promotion was paramount and although league form also suffered a dip in February, with three losses in four games, United still looked the classiest team in the Second Division. This was proved from 1 March (Coppell's debut as a substitute) until the final game at home to Blackpool on 26 April, a period during which United won eight of their last 11 games. In fact, they clinched promotion with three games remaining and were eventually crowned Second Division champions.

With the Docherty era well and truly under way, he continued to ring the changes. Experienced winger Willie Morgan lost his position in the side and was eventually sold to Burnley in the close season.

Above: TV icon Michael Parkinson (right) with his footballing hero at the launch of the Parkinson-penned George Best biography.

Right: Police struggle to hold back an enthusiastic crowd at Old Trafford celebrating United's return to the First Division.

Final League Table Division Two

		P	W	D	L	F	A	Pts
1	MANCHESTER UNITED	42	26	9	7	66	30	61
2	Aston Villa	42	25	8	9	79	32	58
3	Norwich City	42	20	13	9	58	37	53
4	Sunderland	42	19	13	10	65	35	51
5	Bristol City	42	21	8	13	47	33	50
6	West Bromwich Albion	42	18	9	15	54	42	45
7	Blackpool	42	14	17	11	38	33	45
8	Hull City	42	15	14	13	40	53	44
9	Fulham	42	13	16	13	44	39	42
10	Bolton Wanderers	42	15	12	15	45	41	42
11	Oxford United	42	15	12	15	41	51	42
12	Leyton Orient	42	11	20	11	28	39	42
13	Southampton	42	15	11	16	53	54	41
14	Notts County	42	12	16	14	49	59	40
15	York City	42	14	10	18	51	55	38
16	Nottingham Forest	42	12	14	16	43	55	38
17	Portsmouth	42	12	13	17	44	54	37
18	Oldham Athletic	42	10	15	17	40	48	35
19	Bristol Rovers	42	12	11	19	42	64	35
20	Millwall	42	10	12	20	44	56	32
21	Cardiff City	42	9	14	19	36	62	32
22	Sheffield Wednesday	42	5	11	26	29	64	21

Appearances

PLAYER	LGE	FAC	LC	TOT
McIlroy	41 (1)	2	7	50 (1)
Buchan	41	2	7	50
Stepney	40	2	7	49
Houston	40	2	6	48
Greenhoff	39 (2)	2	6	47 (2)
Daly	36 (1)	2	7	45 (1)
Forsyth	39	-	6	45
Macari	36 (2)	2	6 (1)	44 (3)
Morgan	32 (2)	1	6 (1)	39 (3)
Pearson	30 (1)	2	4	36 (1)
McCalliog	20	1	5 (1)	26 (1)
Holton	14	-	3	17
Sidebottom	12	2	2	16
James	13	-	2	15
Young	7 (8)	2	1 (4)	10(12)
Coppell	9 (1)	-	-	9 (1)
Martin	7 (1)	-	1	8 (1)
Albiston	2	-	1	3
Baldwin	2	-	-	2
Roche	2	-	-	2
Davies	- (8)	- (2)	-	-(10)
McCreery	- (2)	-	-	- (2)

PLAYER	LGE	FAC	LC	TOT
Graham	- (1)	-	-	- (1)
Nicholl	- (1)	-	-	- (1)

Stuart Pearson poses for a picture at Old Trafford, as (l-r) Brian Greenhoff, Stewart Houston, Jim Holton, Gerry Daly and Lou Macari await their turn.

Goalscorers

PLAYER	LGE	FAC	LC	TOT
Pearson	17	-	1	18
Macari	11	-	7	18
Daly	11	1	1	13
McIlroy	7	1	2	10
Houston	6	-	1	7
Greenhoff	4	-	-	4
Morgan	3	-	1	4
McCalliog	3	-	-	3
Coppell	1	-	-	1
Forsyth	1	-	-	1
own goals	2	-	1	3

Brian Greenhoff is chased by excited United fans after the team had clinched the Second Division championship

FOOTBALL LEAGUE DIVISION TWO: CHAMPIONS

FA CUP: LOSE TO WALSALL (2-3) IN 3RD ROUND REPLAY

LEAGUE CUP: LOSE TO NORWICH CITY (2-3 ON AGGREGATE) IN SEMI-FINAL

A strong championship challenge and an FA Cup final appearance both end painfully

1975/76

THE BUZZ OF anticipation was back at Old Trafford for the start of the team's returning season to the First Division. Manager Tommy Docherty had constructed a bright, young team and the hangover from the European Cup triumph was confined to United's history. Docherty added midfielder Tommy Jackson to his squad on a free transfer and kept faith with the rest of the team that won promotion. That faith was rewarded in the early weeks of the season as United won five of their first six games and drew the other; it was enough to send them to the top of the table.

Goals were coming for all areas of the team and a 2-1 win over Brentford in their first League Cup game of the season was more confirmation of a team on the rise. A couple of league defeats in September plus a League Cup loss to Manchester City by 4-0 stopped the juggernaut and by mid-November United dropped to fifth in the league. Docherty was not slow to see a need for yet more new blood and signed left winger Gordon Hill from Millwall for £80,000. The transfer did the trick and United embarked on a 14-game unbeaten run including three FA Cup victories against Oxford United, Peterborough United and Leicester City.

The Reds were now up with the leaders of the First Division

and also into the sixth round of the FA Cup; the good old days appeared to have returned. A 4-0 home league win at Old Trafford against West Ham United to end the month of February was a further indication of a title fight and the perfect start to March was victory in the sixth round of the FA Cup, 3-2 against Wolverhampton Wanderers in a replay at Molineux. Three wins and a draw in the rest of the month set up a thrilling season finale.

A 2-0 FA Cup semi-final win against Derby County, thanks to two goals by Hill, meant a return to Wembley, but that prospect seemed to undermine United's league title challenge. Three of the six league games before the FA Cup final were lost, and both Liverpool and Queens Park Rangers sprinted ahead to leave United to finish third. Then there was more disappointment as Second Division Southampton beat the Red Devils 1-0 in the FA Cup final in one of the biggest shocks in this celebrated match in recent years.

By most teams' standards this was a highly successful season – third in the league and FA Cup finalists – and it was certainly the best the Old Trafford faithful had seen since the 1968 European Cup win. However, losing to Southampton at Wembley left a bad taste in the mouth and Docherty's team were determined to put it right next year.

- The Southampton team that beat United in the FA Cup final includes Jim McCalliog, one of many former Old Trafford favourites sold by Tommy Docherty.

- United score 68 goals this season, 30 more than their relegation season in the First Division two years earlier.

- Small consolation for the FA Cup final loss is a 2-0 win over Manchester City at Old Trafford three days later.

- The pop song 'Manchester United' is released on Decca Records in time for the FA Cup final. It charts at number 50 for one week.

Above: Gordon Hill is ecstatic after scoring in the 2-0 FA Cup semi-final win over Derby County.

Left: The players pose for photographers at the traditional pre-season photocall.

Final League Table Division One

		P	W	D	L	F	A	Pts
1	Liverpool	42	23	14	5	66	31	60
2	Queens Park Rangers	42	24	11	7	67	33	59
3	**MANCHESTER UNITED**	**42**	**23**	**10**	**9**	**68**	**42**	**56**
4	Derby County	42	21	11	10	75	58	53
5	Leeds United	42	21	9	12	65	46	51
6	Ipswich Town	42	16	14	12	54	48	46
7	Leicester City	42	13	19	10	48	51	45
8	Manchester City	42	16	11	15	64	46	43
9	Tottenham Hotspur	42	14	15	13	63	63	43
10	Norwich City	42	16	10	16	58	58	42
11	Everton	42	15	12	15	60	66	42
12	Stoke City	42	15	11	16	48	50	41
13	Middlesbrough	42	15	10	17	46	45	40
14	Coventry City	42	13	14	15	47	57	40
15	Newcastle United	42	15	9	18	71	62	39
16	Aston Villa	42	11	17	14	51	59	39
17	Arsenal	42	13	10	19	47	53	36
18	West Ham United	42	13	10	19	48	71	36
19	Birmingham City	42	13	7	22	57	75	33
20	Wolverhampton Wanderers	42	10	10	22	51	68	30
21	Burnley	42	9	10	23	43	66	28
22	Sheffield United	42	6	10	26	33	82	22

Appearances

PLAYER	LGE	FAC	LC	TOT
Buchan	42	7	3	52
Houston	42	7	3	52
Daly	41	7	3	51
McIlroy	41	7	3	51
Greenhoff	40	7	3	50
Coppell	39	7	3	49
Pearson	39	7	3	49
Stepney	38	7	2	47
Macari	36	6	3	45
Forsyth	28	7	-	35
Hill	26	7	-	33
Jackson	16 (1)	-	3	19 (1)
Nicholl	15 (5)	- (2)	3	18 (7)
McCreery	12(16)	1 (2)	- (1)	13(19)
Roche	4	-	1	5
Albiston	2 (1)	-	-	2 (1)
Coyne	1 (1)	-	-	1 (1)
Grimshaw	- (1)	-	- (1)	- (2)
Kelly	- (1)	-	-	- (1)
Young	- (1)	-	-	- (1)

Goalscorers

PLAYER	LGE	FAC	LC	TOT
Macari	12	1	2	15
Pearson	13	1	-	14
McIlroy	10	2	1	13
Daly	7	4	-	11
Hill	7	3	-	10
Coppell	4	-	1	5
McCreery	4	-	-	4
Forsyth	2	1	-	3
Houston	2	-	-	2
Coyne	1	-	-	1
Greenhoff	-	1	-	1
own goals	6	-	-	6

Lou Macari celebrates one of his two goals on the opening day of the season.

Steve Coppell was key in United's first season back in the top flight and takes on Aston Villa's John Gidman in a 2-1 league loss in February. Gidman would join the Reds in 1981.

FOOTBALL LEAGUE DIVISION ONE: THIRD POSITION

FA CUP: RUNNERS-UP. 1 MAY 1976 WEMBLEY, LONDON. LOST TO SOUTHAMPTON 0-1 STOKES 82'

LEAGUE CUP: LOSE TO MANCHESTER CITY (0-4) IN 4TH ROUND

1976/77

- Gordon Hill is top goalscorer with 22 goals including 15 in the league. Stuart Pearson also scored 15 League goals plus four in other competitions.

- Brian Greenhoff and Alex Stepney each play the most games of any player this season – 57 including 40 in the league and 17 in all the cup competitions.

- Eighteen days before beating Liverpool in the FA Cup final, United lose to the Merseysiders 1-0 in a league match at Anfield.

Above: 21 May 1977. Gordon Hill wears the FA Cup trophy lid during the celebrations.

Right: An over-enthusiastic United fan celebrates the Wembley triumph.

Opposite: Stuart Pearson (left) flies high for a header in the FA Cup final with Liverpool's Tommy Smith in attendance.

The Doc's personality is truly stamped on his team that wins the FA Cup for the first time in over a decade

DESPITE A SLIGHTLY disappointing end to the previous season, United had moved back to a position among the First Division elite and could also welcome back European football to Old Trafford for the first time since 1969. Manager Tommy Docherty had just three players left from the Busby/McGuinness/O'Farrell years, Alex Stepney in goal, central defender and club captain Martin Buchan and Sammy McIlroy, while his band of new players were growing ever more confident. Docherty lost one of his assistants when stalwart of the European Cup winning team Pat Crerand went to manage Northampton Town, but nothing seemed to stop the team who started brightly again, despite a rash of games in three competitions: the league, the League Cup and the UEFA Cup.

A thrilling two-leg win over Ajax of Amsterdam in the first round of the European competition was a highlight and United also reached the fifth round of the League Cup shortly afterwards thanks to a second replay win over Sunderland and a 7-2 thrashing of Newcastle United. By the time the second leg of the next round of the UEFA Cup took place – a match away to Juventus with United holding a 1-0 lead – the Red Devils had already played 20 games in the first 10 1/2 weeks of the season. When the Italians thumped United 3-0 to send them out of Europe, there was a definite stumble, as the early-season exertions perhaps began to affect players. By the end of the campaign, nine of the squad would have played more than 50 games.

Four winless league matches were soon followed by a 3-0 League Cup exit at home to Everton. Bad weather then shut down English football for two weeks and allowed Docherty to help his latest new signing settle in. Jimmy Greenhoff was Brian's older brother and had come to join him at Old Trafford from Stoke City in mid November as a fillip for the team. After a short period of acclimatisation, the incoming Greenhoff seemed to spark his teammates, who would lose one game from Christmas to the end of March.

While trying to maintain a nip and tuck battle with Liverpool in the league, United benefited most from this run of good form in the FA Cup. Walsall were beaten in the third round and

Queens Park Rangers in the next. Then fate decided to pair United with Southampton in the fifth round and revenge proved sweet as the Reds won a replay 2-1 at home against their conquerors in last year's final. Next came a sixth round tie at home to Aston Villa which was won by the same score.

The pick of a glut of nine games in April was another 2-1 win, this time in the FA Cup semi-final against old rivals Leeds United at Hillsborough in front of a crowd of 55,000. Yet for the second consecutive season, the prospect of a Wembley appearance disrupted league form and United won two games out of seven that followed the semi. The FA Cup final was a tense affair as United reached for their first trophy in almost a decade and their opponents Liverpool were attempting a league, cup and European Cup treble. After a scoreless first half, the two teams exchanged goals before a rather fortunate deflection off Jimmy Greenhoff's chest looped into the net for the winning goal to deny Liverpool a third trophy this season.

The significance of United's new piece of silverware was that it was the first in the post-Busby years and also the club's first FA Cup win for 14 years. But the happy smiling face of Docherty and his team was removed almost immediately. Soon afterwards, the manager announced in a tabloid newspaper that he was leaving his own wife Agnes, who he had married in 1949, and his four children to live with the wife of the club's physiotherapist, Laurie Brown. The scandal brought unwelcome headlines and rocked the club. The board decided it had no alternative but to sack Docherty in early July, believing he had broken the club's moral code.

Final League Table Division One

		P	W	D	L	F	A	Pts
1	Liverpool	42	23	11	8	62	33	57
2	Manchester City	42	21	14	7	60	34	56
3	Ipswich Town	42	22	8	12	66	39	52
4	Aston Villa	42	22	7	13	76	50	51
5	Newcastle United	42	18	13	11	64	49	49
6	MANCHESTER UNITED	42	18	11	13	71	62	47
7	West Bromwich Albion	42	16	13	13	62	56	45
8	Arsenal	42	16	11	15	64	59	43
9	Everton	42	14	14	14	62	64	42
10	Leeds United	42	15	12	15	48	51	42
11	Leicester City	42	12	18	12	47	60	42
12	Middlesbrough	42	14	13	15	40	45	41
13	Birmingham City	42	13	12	17	63	61	38
14	Queens Park Rangers	42	13	12	17	47	52	38
15	Derby County	42	9	19	14	50	55	37
16	Norwich City	42	14	9	19	47	64	37
17	West Ham United	42	11	14	17	46	65	36
18	Bristol City	42	11	13	18	38	48	35
19	Coventry City	42	10	15	17	48	59	35
20	Sunderland	42	11	12	19	46	54	34
21	Stoke City	42	10	14	18	28	51	34
22	Tottenham Hotspur	42	12	9	21	48	72	33

Appearances

PLAYER	LGE	FAC	LC	UC	TOT
Greenhoff B	40	7	6	4	57
Stepney	40	7	6	4	57
McIlroy	39 (1)	7	6	4	56 (1)
Coppell	40	7	5	4	56
Hill	38 (1)	7	6	4	55 (1)
Nicholl	39	7	5	4	55
Macari	38	7	4	4	53
Pearson	39	7	4	3	53
Houston	36	6	5	4	51
Buchan	33	7	4	2	46
Greenhoff J	27	7	-	-	34
Daly	16 (1)	- (1)	6	4	26 (2)
Albiston	14 (3)	1	2 (2)	2 (1)	19 (6)
McCreery	9 (16)	- (3)	3 (2)	1 (3)	13 (24)
Forsyth	3 (1)	-	1	-	4 (1)
Waldron	3	-	1	-	4
Paterson	2	-	1	- (2)	3 (2)
Jackson	2	-	1	-	3
McGrath	2 (4)	-	- (1)	-	2 (5)
Roche	2	-	-	-	2
Foggon	- (3)	-	-	-	- (3)
Clark	- (1)	-	-	-	- (1)

Goalscorers

PLAYER	LGE	FAC	LC	UC	TOT
Hill	15	2	4	1	22
Pearson	15	1	3	-	19
Macari	9	3	1	1	14
Greenhoff J	8	4	-	-	12
Coppell	6	1	1	-	8
Daly	4	-	3	-	7
Greenhoff B	3	-	2	-	5
Houston	3	1	1	-	5
McIlroy	2	-	-	1	3
McCreery	2	-	-	-	2
Nicholl	-	-	1	-	1
own goals	4	-	1	-	5

Right: Lou Macari and Jimmy Nicholl congratulate Gordon Hill for his goal in a 3-1 win over Tottenham in February.

FOOTBALL LEAGUE DIVISION ONE: SIXTH POSITION

FA CUP: WINNERS. 21 MAY 1977. WEMBLEY, LONDON. BEAT LIVERPOOL 2-1 PEARSON 52', J. GREENHOFF 55'

LEAGUE CUP: LOSE TO EVERTON (0-3) IN 5TH ROUND

UEFA CUP: LOSE TO JUVENTUS (1-3 ON AGGREGATE) IN 2ND ROUND

1977/78

■ New manager Dave Sexton had been given his first job in football at Chelsea as an assistant coach by the very man he was replacing at United – Tommy Docherty.

■ The signing of Gordon McQueen from Leeds United for £450,000 breaks the British transfer record.

■ Alex Stepney retires at the end of the season aged 35 after 12 years at Old Trafford; he is the last remaining player from the European Cup victory in 1968.

Above: A pensive looking Dave Sexton.

Right: 15 March 1978. United centre forward Joe Jordan in classic toothless pose.

In the wake of the scandal over Tommy Docherty's love affair, Dave Sexton is appointed as manager

THE DRAMA OF this off-season had begun early when the scandal over Tommy Docherty's dismissal unfolded in early summer. Not surprisingly, Dave Sexton, the new manager, was scandal-free and did not court press attention, but came with a first-class reputation as a coach. The contrast between the characters of the two men could hardly have been more sharp. In fact, Sexton had been on United's radar when they appointed Docherty and, in the last couple of seasons, had performed wonders with Queens Park Rangers, almost winning the league title.

Although the Sexton era began with a 0-0 draw in the FA Charity Shield in August (the trophy was shared with Liverpool), the first league match was a 4-1 win at Birmingham City with a Lou Macari hat-trick. Then 55,000 fans turned up for the home opener, a 2-1 victory over Coventry City. Though different characters, the fans thought that the results of the two managers might be the same, although it was clear that Sexton wanted to take a more cautious approach, which meant unsettling Docherty's winning formula predicated on attack.

A quick exit from the League Cup (a 3-2 defeat to Arsenal) and then a loss to Manchester City 3-1 at Maine Road in the league, both in September, were less auspicious. But problems then came off the field in the opening Cup-Winners' Cup match at St Etienne, when fans of both teams started fighting inside the French stadium. Riot police were sent in to quell the trouble and UEFA decided United should be punished.

Initially, the English team was expelled from the competition, but this punishment was reduced shortly afterwards to an order for United to play the second leg at least 300 kilometres from Old Trafford. After all the fuss and a 1-1 draw in France, United won the second leg at Plymouth Argyle's ground 2-0. United then lost 4-0 to Porto of Portugal in the next round's first leg and even a 5-2 Old Trafford win was not enough to save them.

With league form now flagging, United's first season under Sexton was unravelling as the new manager began to change Docherty's team. Goalkeeper Alex Stepney was replaced while other favourites were pushed out of the team. Then Sexton made a bold move, a double dip into the transfer market early in 1978 for Leeds United players Joe Jordan and Gordon McQueen who would cost £450,000.

These arrivals would definitely strengthen the team, but they could not stop United from exiting the FA Cup in the fourth round (after a replay against West Bromwich Albion) and remaining a mid-table club for the moment. United finished tenth in the league, but perhaps more importantly to the fans, the team seemed to have lost much of the flair that had been such a part of the previous manager's system. When Gordon Hill moved to Derby County (now managed by Docherty) in April, then the Doc's era was definitely over.

Final League Table Division One

		P	W	D	L	F	A	Pts
1	Nottingham Forest	42	25	14	3	69	24	64
2	Liverpool	42	24	9	9	65	34	57
3	Everton	42	22	11	9	76	45	55
4	Manchester City	42	20	12	10	74	51	52
5	Arsenal	42	21	10	11	60	37	52
6	West Bromwich Albion	42	18	14	10	62	53	50
7	Coventry City	42	18	12	12	75	62	48
8	Aston Villa	42	18	10	14	57	42	46
9	Leeds United	42	18	10	14	63	53	46
10	**MANCHESTER UNITED**	**42**	**16**	**10**	**16**	**67**	**63**	**42**
11	Birmingham City	42	16	9	17	55	60	41
12	Derby County	42	14	13	15	54	59	41
13	Norwich City	42	11	18	13	52	66	40
14	Middlesbrough	42	12	15	15	42	54	39
15	Wolverhampton Wanderers	42	12	12	18	51	64	36
16	Chelsea	42	11	14	17	46	69	36
17	Bristol City	42	11	13	18	49	53	35
18	Ipswich Town	42	11	13	18	47	61	35
19	Queens Park Rangers	42	9	15	18	47	64	33
20	West Ham United	42	12	8	22	52	69	32
21	Newcastle United	42	6	10	26	42	78	22
22	Leicester City	42	5	12	25	26	70	22

Appearances

PLAYER	LGE	FAC	LC	ECWC	TOT
Coppell	42	4	1	4	51
McIlroy	39	4	-	4	47
Nicholl	37	4	1	4	46
Hill	36	3	1	4	44
Macari	32	4	1	2	39
Pearson	30	4	1	3	38
Buchan	28	4	1	4	37
Albiston	27 (1)	4	1	4	36 (1)
Houston	31	3	-	2 (1)	36 (1)
Greenhoff B	31	1	1	2	35
Stepney	23	-	1	4	28
Greenhoff J	22 (1)	2 (1)	-	1	25 (2)
Roche	19	4	-	-	23
McCreery	13 (4)	- (1)	1	3	17 (5)
Jordan	14	2	-	-	16
McQueen	14	-	-	-	14
McGrath	9 (9)	-	- (1)	3 (1)	12 (11)
Grimes	7 (6)	1	1	- (2)	9 (8)
Ritchie	4	-	-	-	4
Forsyth	3	-	-	- (1)	3 (1)
Rogers	1	-	-	-	1

Goalscorers

PLAYER	LGE	FAC	LC	ECWC	TOT
Hill	17	1	-	1	19
Pearson	10	3	1	1	15
Macari	8	3	-	-	11
McIlroy	9	-	-	-	9
Coppell	5	1	-	3	9
Greenhoff J	6	-	-	-	6
Jordan	3	-	-	-	3
Nicholl	2	-	-	1	3
Grimes	2	-	-	-	2
McCreery	1	-	1	-	2
Buchan	1	-	-	-	1
Greenhoff B	1	-	-	-	1
McGrath	1	-	-	-	1
McQueen	1	-	-	-	1
own goals	-	-	-	2	2

Right: 5 November 1977. Gordon Hill celebrates after scoring against Arsenal during their match at Old Trafford. United lost 2-1.

FOOTBALL LEAGUE DIVISION ONE: TENTH POSITION

FA CUP: LOSE TO WEST BROMWICH ALBION (2-3) IN 4TH ROUND REPLAY

LEAGUE CUP: LOSE TO ARSENAL (2-3) IN 2ND ROUND

EUROPEAN CUP WINNERS CUP: LOSE TO PORTO (6-5 ON AGGREGATE) IN 2ND ROUND

FA CHARITY SHIELD: 13 AUGUST 1977, WEMBLEY, LONDON, DRAW WITH LIVERPOOL 0-0

A cruel late defeat in the FA Cup final typifies the bad luck of the team under Sexton

IN THE OPENING two league games of Dave Sexton's second campaign as manager, United again claimed victories, just as they had done last season. The wins – including an away win at Leeds United – settled the nerves of Reds fans, some of whom were still prone to nostalgia over Tommy Docherty.

But unfortunately that promising start was followed by a five-game run of one defeat and four consecutive 1-1 draws. The mood at Old Trafford immediately darkened and it did not improve when Watford then knocked United out of the League Cup at home in front of a crowd of 40,000 in early October.

It was true that Sexton had made changes this season: the selection of Gary Bailey as first choice goalkeeper; the acquisition of Mickey Thomas on the left wing (as replacement for Gordon Hill); giving young striker Andy Ritchie a run of games; and dispensing with an injured Stuart Pearson (eventually sold to West Ham United). However, United looked unconvincing and in late December lost three straight games including home losses to Liverpool 3-0 and West Bromwich Albion 5-3.

Bad weather then brought the season to a near complete halt and United played only two matches in the entire month of January. Strangely, both games were in the FA Cup – 3-0 at home to Chelsea and then a 1-1 draw at Fulham. The weather break worked wonders for United and from February and into the first week of April, the Reds lost just two league games and progressed to the semi-final of the FA Cup.

However, once the semi-final had been won against old rivals Liverpool, United's league form never recovered; they would win only two more games while drawing seven. Finishing ninth was a disappointing result for Sexton, particularly as home form was below par; it was not just the lack of wins (only nine), but also the lack of goals (just 29 at Old Trafford while, for example, even Coventry City in tenth scored 41).

Nevertheless, when Sexton led out his team at Wembley it was United's third appearance in the final in four years and league form was forgotten. For the vast majority of the match

against Arsenal, the Londoners dominated and were even ahead 2-0 as late as the 85th minute. A scrambled United goal by Gordon McQueen gave United fans hope and then an equaliser from Sammy McIlroy almost immediately after the re-start sent Red Devils fans into paroxysms of joy; this change of momentum would surely see the Reds win in extra time. However, more drama still had time to play itself out and it was Arsenal who scored the decisive goal – the third in just four minutes – in the final minute of normal time to win the trophy.

"To lose after that was like winning the pools only to find you'd forgotten to post the coupon," said a dejected McIlroy afterwards. Defeat also meant there would again be no European football next season to look forward to at Old Trafford, for the second year running.

- For the second season in a row, Steve Coppell plays in every game of the campaign.

- Centre back Kevin Moran makes his debut this season in a 1-1 draw against Southampton in April.

- After Jimmy Greenhoff's 17 goals this season that make him United's top scorer, the striker scores only one more goal in a United career that ended in December 1980.

Above: Brian Greenhoff's seven seasons at Old Trafford came to an end after this campaign. He was transferred to Leeds United for £350,000.

Left: Goalkeeper Gary Bailey leaps acrobatically to push a powerful Tottenham Hotspur shot just over the bar.

Final League Table Division One

		P	W	D	L	F	A	Pts
1	Liverpool	42	30	8	4	85	16	68
2	Nottingham Forest	42	21	18	3	61	26	60
3	West Bromwich Albion	42	24	11	7	72	35	59
4	Everton	42	17	17	8	52	40	51
5	Leeds United	42	18	14	10	70	52	50
6	Ipswich Town	42	20	9	13	63	49	49
7	Arsenal	42	17	14	11	61	48	48
8	Aston Villa	42	15	16	11	59	49	46
9	**MANCHESTER UNITED**	42	15	15	12	60	63	45
10	Coventry City	42	14	16	12	58	68	44
11	Tottenham Hotspur	42	13	15	14	48	61	41
12	Middlesbrough	42	15	10	17	57	50	40
13	Bristol City	42	15	10	17	47	51	40
14	Southampton	42	12	16	14	47	53	40
15	Manchester City	42	13	13	16	58	56	39
16	Norwich City	42	7	23	12	51	57	37
17	Bolton Wanderers	42	12	11	19	54	75	35
18	Wolverhampton Wanderers	42	13	8	21	44	68	34
19	Derby County	42	10	11	21	44	71	31
20	Queens Park Rangers	42	6	13	23	45	73	25
21	Birmingham City	42	6	10	26	37	64	22
22	Chelsea	42	5	10	27	44	92	20

Appearances

PLAYER	LGE	FAC	LC	TOT
Coppell	42	9	2	53
McIlroy	40	9	2	51
Buchan	37	9	2	48
McQueen	36	9	2	47
Greenhoff J	33	9	-	44
Albiston	32 (1)	7	2	41 (1)
Greenhoff B	32 (1)	5	2	39 (1)
Macari	31 (1)	5	1	37 (1)
Bailey	28	9	-	37
Jordan	30	4 (1)	2	36 (1)
Thomas	25	8	-	33
Nicholl	19 (2)	6 (2)	-	25 (4)
Houston	21 (1)	2	1	24 (1)
Ritchie	16 (1)	3 (1)	-	19 (2)
Roche	14	-	2	16
McCreery	14 (1)	-	- (1)	14 (2)
Grimes	5 (11)	3	2	10 (11)
Sloan	3 (1)	-	-	3 (1)
Connell	2	-	-	2
Pearson	-	2	-	2
Paterson	1 (2)	-	-	1 (2)
Moran	1	-	-	1

PLAYER	LGE	FAC	LC	TOT
McGrath	- (2)	-	-	- (2)

Goalscorers

PLAYER	LGE	FAC	LC	TOT
Greenhoff J	11	5	1	17
Coppell	11	1	-	12
Ritchie	10	-	-	10
Jordan	6	2	2	10
McIlroy	5	2	1	8
McQueen	6	1	-	7
Macari	6	-	-	6
Greenhoff B	2	1	-	3
Buchan	2	-	-	2
Thomas	1	1	-	2
Grimes	-	1	-	1

Steve Coppell adapted well to the slightly more withdrawn role he played under Sexton and still scored 12 goals, his best return.

FOOTBALL LEAGUE DIVISION ONE: NINETH POSITION

FA CUP: RUNNERS-UP. 12 MAY 1979. WEMBLEY, LONDON. MANCHESTER UNITED 2-3 ARSENAL. MCQUEEN 86', MCILROY 88'.

LEAGUE CUP: LOSE TO WATFORD (1-2) IN 3RD ROUND

1979/80

- A disputed penalty given for handball against Gordon McQueen is the second goal in a 2-0 defeat against Leeds United in the final league match of the season that presents Liverpool with the title.

- Ex-United player Brian Greenhoff is in the Leeds United team that beat the Reds on the final Saturday of the season and plays a part in the decisive second goal.

- Martin Edwards becomes chairman almost exactly ten years after he had joined the United board at the age of just 25.

Above: Long-time chairman Louis Edwards is replaced by his son Martin this season.

Right: 22 March 1980. Gordon McQueen celebrates a goal in the Manchester derby at Old Trafford.

A strong league finish and key player signings bring hope of good times to come

THE PRESSURE TO bring silverware to Old Trafford was just one reason behind manager Dave Sexton's move into the transfer market in the summer of 1979. He paid a club record fee of £777,777 to Chelsea for midfielder Ray Wilkins (a player Sexton had mentored as a teenager), while selling Brian Greenhoff to Leeds United. Wilkins was brought in to add even more of the Sexton playing method to United and also to fill a creative midfield void that appeared the previous season.

Early season form showed improvement as United lost just once in their opening nine league games. But whereas Docherty's team had played with brio and less regard for defence, Sexton was a more cautious tactician who saw the value of a clean sheet. Despite a loss to Norwich City in the League Cup in late September, United's new signing helped inspire another good run – from mid-October until Christmas Day there were six wins and only one defeat in 11 matches.

Then on Boxing Day with United in the slipstream of Liverpool at the top of the League, the two teams met at Anfield; a 2-0 win for the Merseysiders would eventually prove significant.

But the title race was not on United minds in January after a third round FA Cup replay defeat against Tottenham Hotspur and then more off-the-pitch problems when a wall collapsed at Ayresome Park, Middlesbrough, after United's game in the north east. Two people were left dead in the accident and Reds fans were said to be involved.

However, these latest unwanted headlines soon disappeared when others emerged: a *World In Action* television documentary accused club chairman Louis Edwards of corruption as well as irregular payments to prospective young players. Edwards died of a heart attack a month after the programme was screened and, although there were inquiries staged by the Football League and Football Association, the allegations died with him. Martin Edwards, Louis's son, took over as chairman and would watch United take the title race to the wire.

Back in the race for the league, United actually beat Liverpool at Old Trafford in early April with goals from Mickey Thomas and Jimmy Greenhoff. The Red Devils then won their next five games and played Leeds United on the last day of the season with the title still to be decided. However, United lost that game and eventually finished as runners-up, two points behind the Merseyside team, though even a victory would not have brought the title to United because of Liverpool's much better goal difference. In the era of just two points for a win, that earlier loss at Anfield had proved vital.

Home form had been solid all season – only five points out of a possible 42 were dropped at Old Trafford – but United were disappointing on their travels with only seven wins. And, although this was a determined challenge for the league and United's best finish for just over a decade, the style of Sexton's team still did not fully capture all the fans' imagination; the last year of the Docherty era (when United finished sixth in the league) saw average league crowds of 53,700, two thousand more per game than watched this runners-up campaign.

Final League Table Division One

		P	W	D	L	F	A	Pts
1	Liverpool	42	25	10	7	81	30	60
2	**MANCHESTER UNITED**	42	24	10	8	65	35	58
3	Ipswich Town	42	22	9	11	68	39	53
4	Arsenal	42	18	16	8	52	36	52
5	Nottingham Forest	42	20	8	14	63	43	48
6	Wolverhampton Wanderers	42	19	9	14	58	47	47
7	Aston Villa	42	16	14	12	51	50	46
8	Southampton	42	18	9	15	65	53	45
9	Middlesbrough	42	16	12	14	50	44	44
10	West Bromwich Albion	42	11	19	12	54	50	41
11	Leeds United	42	13	14	15	46	50	40
12	Norwich City	42	13	14	15	58	66	40
13	Crystal Palace	42	12	16	14	41	50	40
14	Tottenham Hotspur	42	15	10	17	52	62	40
15	Coventry City	42	16	7	19	56	66	39
16	Brighton & Hove Albion	42	11	15	16	47	57	37
17	Manchester City	42	12	13	17	43	66	37
18	Stoke City	42	13	10	19	44	58	36
19	Everton	42	9	17	16	43	51	35
20	Bristol City	42	9	13	20	37	66	31
21	Derby County	42	11	8	23	47	67	30
22	Bolton Wanderers	42	5	15	22	38	73	25

Appearances

PLAYER	LGE	FAC	LC	TOT
Bailey	42	2	3	47
Buchan	42	2	3	47
Nicholl	42	2	3	47
Coppell	42	2	2	46
McIlroy	41	2	2	45
Macari	39	2	3	44
Wilkins	37	2	3	42
Thomas	35	2	3	40
McQueen	33	2	2	37
Jordan	32	2	2	36
Albiston	25	-	3	28
Grimes	20 (6)	-	1	21 (6)
Houston	14	2	1	17
Moran	9	-	-	9
Ritchie	3 (5)	-	1 (2)	4 (7)
Greenhoff	4 (1)	-	-	4 (1)
Sloan	1 (4)	-	-	1 (4)
Jovanovic	1 (1)	-	-	1 (1)
Paterson	- (1)	-	1	1 (1)
McGrath	- (1)	-	-	- (1)

Goalscorers

PLAYER	LGE	FAC	LC	TOT
Jordan	13	-	-	13
Thomas	8	-	2	10
Macari	9	-	-	9
McQueen	9	-	-	9
Coppell	8	-	1	9
McIlroy	6	1	1	8
Grimes	3	-	-	3
Ritchie	3	-	-	3
Wilkins	2	-	-	2
Greenhoff	1	-	-	1
Moran	1	-	-	1
own goals	2	-	1	3

Right: 22 September 1979. Steve Coppell hurdles the tackle of George Berry during a 3-1 loss to Wolverhampton Wanderers at Molineux.

Another season of disappointing results and performances leave Dave Sexton sacked after four trophyless years

1980/81

DAVE SEXTON AND his team knew that they must now build on last season's runners-up finish and a few new faces were emerging, such as defenders Kevin Moran and Mike Duxbury, while the manager tried to find some European know-how and was hopeful about Nikki Jovanovic, a defender from Yugoslavia signed late the previous season.

However, a long-term injury to Ray Wilkins from the start of the season seemed to hinder United and by the start of October, there were problems on all fronts. Coventry City knocked the Reds out of the League Cup; Widzew Lodz of Poland achieved the same feat in the UEFA Cup first round; and, at the same time, league form was lacklustre. Including the European game in which United went out on away goals after draws of 1-1 at home and 0-0 in Poland, the Red Devils drew seven of their first 12 matches.

By the end of October, Sexton brought out the cheque book once again and, for the second time in two years, shattered the club transfer fee. This time it was Nottingham Forest striker Garry Birtles who came to Old Trafford for £1.25 million to partner Joe Jordan. At the same time, Sexton surprisingly sold promising ex-youth team player Andy Ritchie, who had even scored 13 goals himself in just 42 appearances in the first team.

Sexton was choosing experience for his front line and Birtles' debut saw United win 2-1 at Stoke City; then in his first game in front of home fans, there was a 2-0 win over Everton. However, the new signing struggled to spark the team and also failed to score himself. In fact, United were destined to draw their way out of contention for the league title race; the Reds would eventually draw 18 of their 42 league matches – more than any other team that season.

The high pre-season expectations were now beginning to haunt Sexton in particular, but it was not just the team that was suffering, but one man in particular became a symbol of the manager's problem: Birtles. Sexton's big signing looked increasingly forlorn and in fact went goalless in all of his 25 league appearances and his only goal of the season was in a 2-0

win over lowly Brighton & Hove Albion in a third round FA Cup replay in January.

When United lost their fourth round tie – ironically to Birtles' former club, Forest – a few weeks later, the season was as good as over. Wilkins returned in February and United did win their last seven games on the trot, but an eighth place league finish was flattering. Supporters were disgruntled and had stayed away; only just over 40,000 attended the final home game, 12,000 less than the corresponding fixture the year before. The board had witnessed four seasons under Sexton, too many dour team performances, no silverware and too little excitement; the manager was fired within a week of the season's end.

- After a win and a loss in their two opening games, United then go 12 games unbeaten in the league, although that included only four wins.

- The league title is won by Aston Villa whose manager Ron Saunders is a man United would unsuccessfully chase to be their replacement for Sexton.

- Despite turmoil at neighbouring Manchester City – Malcolm Allison is sacked and replaced by John Bond – Dave Sexton cannot even win against the Sky Blues this season, suffering a 2-2 draw and a 1-0 defeat.

Above: The steadiness of captain Martin Buchan will be essential during the transition to a another new manager.

Left: Crowd favourite Arthur Albiston scored his first goal for the Red Devils this season in the derby game in September.

Final League Table Division One

		P	W	D	L	F	A	Pts
1	Aston Villa	42	26	8	8	72	40	60
2	Ipswich Town	42	23	10	9	77	43	56
3	Arsenal	42	19	15	8	61	45	53
4	West Bromwich Albion	42	20	12	10	60	42	52
5	Liverpool	42	17	17	8	62	42	51
6	Southampton	42	20	10	12	76	56	50
7	Nottingham Forest	42	19	12	11	62	44	50
8	**MANCHESTER UNITED**	**42**	**15**	**18**	**9**	**51**	**36**	**48**
9	Leeds United	42	17	10	15	39	47	44
10	Tottenham Hotspur	42	14	15	13	70	68	43
11	Stoke City	42	12	18	12	51	60	42
12	Manchester City	42	14	11	17	56	59	39
13	Birmingham City	42	13	12	17	50	61	38
14	Middlesbrough	42	16	5	21	53	61	37
15	Everton	42	13	10	19	55	58	36
16	Coventry City	42	13	10	19	48	68	36
17	Sunderland	42	14	7	21	52	53	35
18	Wolverhampton Wanderers	42	13	9	20	43	55	35
19	Brighton & Hove Albion	42	14	7	21	54	67	35
20	Norwich City	42	13	7	22	49	73	33
21	Leicester City	42	13	6	23	40	67	32
22	Crystal Palace	42	6	7	29	47	83	19

Appearances

PLAYER	LGE	FAC	LC	UC	TOT
Albiston	42	3	2	2	49
Coppell	42	3	2	2	49
Bailey	40	3	2	2	47
Macari	37 (1)	3	2	1	43 (1)
Nicholl	36	3	2	2	43
Jordan	33	3	-	1	37
Thomas	30	3	2	2	37
McIlroy	31 (1)	1	2	2	36 (1)
Moran	32	1	-	- (1)	33 (1)
Buchan	26	2	2	2	32
Duxbury	27 (6)	- (2)	-	1 (1)	28 (9)
Birtles	25	3	-	-	28
Jovanovic	19	1	2	2	24
Wilkins	11 (2)	2	-	-	13 (2)
McQueen	11	2	-	-	13
Greenhoff	8 (1)	-	2	1	11 (1)
Grimes	6 (2)	-	-	2	8 (2)
Ritchie	3 (1)	-	2	-	5 (1)
Roche	2	-	-	-	2
McGrath	1	-	-	-	1
Sloan	- (2)	-	- (1)	-	- (3)
McGarvey	- (2)	-	-	-	- (2)

PLAYER	LGE	FAC	LC	UC	TOT
Whelan	- (1)	-	-	-	- (1)

New signing Garry Birtles mans the United souvenir shop.

Goalscorers

PLAYER	LGE	FAC	LC	UC	TOT
Jordan	15	-	-	-	15
Macari	9	-	-	-	9
Coppell	6	-	-	-	6
McIlroy	5	-	-	1	6
Jovanovic	4	-	-	-	4
Duxbury	2	1	-	-	3
Thomas	2	1	-	-	3
Grimes	2	-	-	-	2
McQueen	2	-	-	-	2
Nicholl	1	1	-	-	2
Albiston	1	-	-	-	1
Birtles	-	1	-	-	1
own goals	2	-	-	-	2

Despite much hoopla, Nikki Jovanovic disappointed with only four goals this season.

FOOTBALL LEAGUE DIVISION ONE: EIGHTH POSITION

FA CUP: LOSE TO NOTTINGHAM FOREST (0-1) IN 4TH ROUND

LEAGUE CUP: LOSE TO COVENTRY CITY (0-2 ON AGGREGATE) IN 2ND ROUND

UEFA CUP: LOSE TO WIDZEW LODZ (1-1 ON AWAY GOALS) IN 1ST ROUND

1981/82

■ Norman Whiteside is given his United debut 13 days before his 17th birthday in a 1-0 win away at Brighton & Hove Albion.

■ After failing to score a league goal in 25 attempts last season, Garry Birtles opens his account in the fifth game of the season, a 1-0 win against Swansea City.

■ Just before the season ends, United agree to pay St Patrick's Athletic of the Republic of Ireland £30,000 for 22-year-old defender Paul McGrath.

Above: Norman Whiteside congratulates goalscoring Bryan Robson.

Right: New signing Bryan Robson waves to the crowd as he completes his £1.5 million transfer to Old Trafford from West Bromwich Albion.

Ron Atkinson takes over the reins and a new era begins with a large-scale clearout

REPLACING DAVE SEXTON as manager proved a rather longer task than the United board had originally planned. Several top class managers reportedly decided against a move to Old Trafford including Lawrie McMenemy, Bobby Robson and Ron Saunders. When Ron Atkinson signed his contract, the personality of the man meant a return to the days of The Doc. Atkinson had built a talented team at West Bromwich Albion and was not frightened to tell the world about it; he not only wanted United to play attractive football, but he also wanted to entertain the press and the fans with his version of the manager as showman.

The larger-than-life Atkinson made plenty of changes: back room staff including coaches Harry Gregg and Jack Crompton, who had returned under Docherty, plus youth coach Syd Owen were all dismissed and Mick Brown came from Albion to be the assistant coach. Players who would arrive included centre forward Frank Stapleton from Arsenal, full back John Gidman from Everton and two signings from his former club – Bryan Robson and Remi Moses. Stapleton replaced Joe Jordan who had signed for AC Milan while the likes of Lou Macari and Sammy McIlroy were eased out.

Robson – bought at the same time as Moses in October in a combined transfer deal worth £2 million – was soon to be Atkinson's kingpin and captain. In fact, the £1.5 million valuation of Robson within the deal was a British transfer record. And, after a stuttering start, United began to justify Atkinson's confident approach as two five-goal performances in the autumn – 5-0 at home to Wolverhampton Wanderers and 5-1 away to Sunderland – harked back to past days of glory (Sexton's teams scored five goals or more in league games only three times in four whole seasons).

Indeed, by the end of October, United sat at the top of the league table as Atkinson impressed both the fans and the media. An early exit in the League Cup to Tottenham Hotspur over two legs, earlier in October, did not dent the hopes of a league title for the first time since 1968 and when the New Year dawned with United holding their lofty position in the league

and no sign of arch rivals Liverpool, the Old Trafford faithful dared to dream.

Defeat in the third round of the FA Cup to a dangerous Watford team from the Second Division was then taken in stride and the push for the title began. United lost just four of 24 matches from January to May, but Liverpool staged an almighty resurgence during this period and took another league title, leaving United in third place also behind Ipswich Town.

Although the team was still not scoring huge numbers of goals (just 59 in the league compared, for example, to champions Liverpool's 80), there were plenty of goalscorers: 14 players hit the net in the league, including Frank Stapleton with 13 and Garry Birtles with 11.

Final League Table Division One

		P	W	D	L	F	A	Pts
1	Liverpool	42	26	9	7	80	32	87
2	Ipswich Town	42	26	5	11	75	53	83
3	**MANCHESTER UNITED**	42	22	12	8	59	29	78
4	Tottenham Hotspur	42	20	11	11	67	48	71
5	Arsenal	42	20	11	11	48	37	71
6	Swansea City	42	21	6	15	58	51	69
7	Southampton	42	19	9	14	72	67	66
8	Everton	42	17	13	12	56	50	64
9	West Ham United	42	14	16	12	66	57	58
10	Manchester City	42	15	13	14	49	50	58
11	Aston Villa	42	15	12	15	55	53	57
12	Nottingham Forest	42	15	12	15	42	48	57
13	Brighton & Hove Albion	42	13	13	16	43	52	52
14	Coventry City	42	13	11	18	56	62	50
15	Notts County	42	13	8	21	61	69	47
16	Birmingham City	42	10	14	18	53	61	44
17	West Bromwich Albion	42	11	11	20	46	57	44
18	Stoke City	42	12	8	22	44	63	44
19	Sunderland	42	11	11	20	38	58	44
20	Leeds United	42	10	12	20	39	61	42
21	Wolverhampton Wanderers	42	10	10	22	32	63	40
22	Middlesbrough	42	8	15	19	34	52	39

Appearances

PLAYER	LGE	FAC	LC	TOT
Albiston	42	1	2	45
Wilkins	42	1	2	45
Stapleton	41	1	2	44
Bailey	39	1	2	42
Gidman	36 (1)	1	2	39 (1)
Coppell	35 (1)	-	2	37 (1)
Birtles	32 (1)	1	2	35 (1)
Robson	32	1	2	35
Moran	30	1	2	33
Buchan	27	1	2	30
Moses	20 (1)	1	1	22 (1)
McQueen	21	-	-	21
Duxbury	19 (5)	-	- (1)	19 (6)
McIlroy	12	1	1	14
McGarvey	10 (6)	-	-	10 (6)
Macari	10 (1)	- (1)	-	10 (2)
Grimes	9 (2)	-	-	9 (2)
Roche	3	-	-	3
Whiteside	1 (1)	-	-	1 (1)
Davies	1	-	-	1
Nicholl	- (1)	-	-	- (1)

Goalscorers

PLAYER	LGE	FAC	LC	TOT
Stapleton	13	-	-	13
Birtles	11	-	-	11
Coppell	9	-	-	9
Moran	7	-	-	7
Robson	5	-	-	5
McIlroy	3	-	-	3
Macari	2	-	-	2
McGarvey	2	-	-	2
Moses	2	-	-	2
Albiston	1	-	-	1
Grimes	1	-	-	1
Gidman	1	-	-	1
Whiteside	1	-	-	1
Wilkins	1	-	-	1

Right: 17 April 1982. Gordon McQueen challenges Tottenham's Garth Crooks during the Reds' 2-0 win. Crooks would join United in November 1983.

A first trophy in six seasons brings a smile to the face of both manager and club

1982/83

WITH ONE SEASON under his belt, manager Ron Atkinson needed to push for trophies and he signed Arnold Muhren from Ipswich Town on a free transfer to add one of the most cultured talents in the league to his midfield. Along with the signing of little known centre half Paul McGrath from St Patrick's Athletic in Ireland earlier in the year, Atkinson was now ready for his team to deliver.

The early league form – five wins in the first six matches – showed United's intent and even a 2-1 aggregate loss in the first round of the UEFA Cup could not dilute a great start to the season. By the end of September, the Reds were already slotted behind Liverpool in second place and a run in the League Cup was underway in October, with wins over Bournemouth, Bradford City and Southampton before the end of the year.

As 1983 was greeted, United were well set in third place in the league and also ready for an FA Cup campaign which began with two 2-0 wins in January over West Ham United and Luton Town. Now fighting on three fronts, Atkinson was in his element and by the end of February, United had beaten Arsenal 6-3 over two legs of the League Cup semi-final and also Derby County 1-0 away from home to book a place in the FA Cup sixth round. At the same time, league title favourites Liverpool were held to a 1-1 draw at Old Trafford. Soon after came Everton in the FA Cup and a Frank Stapleton goal settled the game and sent United into the semi-finals.

Atkinson's first Wembley visit then came in the League Cup, but Liverpool, their continual tormentors at this time, proved too strong and won 2-1 in extra time. The missed opportunity of Atkinson's first silverware for United was not mourned too much because United still had two more trophies to chase and when the FA Cup semi against Arsenal was won with second half goals by Robson and Whiteside, optimism returned.

League form, however, then dipped and four late season defeats left United third behind Liverpool and Watford in the final league table, a position that did not reflect their potential or the team's quality compared to the two above them. United were actually unbeaten in four league games against Liverpool

and Watford: two wins over the surprise team from Hertfordshire and two draws against the Merseysiders.

But despite the disappointment of the league finish, there was still the climax of a second Wembley appearance in late May. Brighton & Hove Albion were the FA Cup final opponents and United led 2-1 with just 16 minutes to go. Then the drama began as a Brighton goal against the run of play gave the south coast team hope and only a brave save from Gary Bailey in the dying moments prevented a United defeat. However, in the replay five days later, United's class told and a 4-0 victory was secured along with the trophy for the fifth time in the club's history.

- This is the final season for Martin Buchan who makes six appearances; he totalled 456 games in 12 seasons.

- Peter Beardsley – a £250,000 signing from Vancouver Whitecaps – makes his one United appearance in the League Cup tie against Bournemouth before returning to the Whitecaps at the end of the season.

- United's arch rivals Manchester City are relegated after a huge spending spree of over £5 million over the last four years.

Above: The cultured left foot of Arnold Muhren helped bring another trophy to Old Trafford.

Left: Striker Frank Stapleton celebrates after scoring the first goal against Brighton & Hove Albion during the FA Cup final.

Final League Table Division One

		P	W	D	L	F	A	Pts
1	Liverpool	42	24	10	8	87	37	82
2	Watford	42	22	5	15	74	57	71
3	**MANCHESTER UNITED**	**42**	**19**	**13**	**10**	**56**	**38**	**70**
4	Tottenham Hotspur	42	20	9	13	65	50	69
5	Nottingham Forest	42	20	9	13	62	50	69
6	Aston Villa	42	21	5	16	62	50	68
7	Everton	42	18	10	14	66	48	64
8	West Ham United	42	20	4	18	68	62	64
9	Ipswich Town	42	15	13	14	64	50	58
10	Arsenal	42	16	10	16	58	56	58
11	West Bromwich Albion	42	15	12	15	51	49	57
12	Southampton	42	15	12	15	54	58	57
13	Stoke City	42	16	9	17	53	64	57
14	Norwich City	42	14	12	16	52	58	54
15	Notts County	42	15	7	20	55	71	52
16	Sunderland	42	12	14	16	48	61	50
17	Birmingham City	42	12	14	16	40	55	50
18	Luton Town	42	12	13	17	65	84	49
19	Coventry City	42	13	9	20	48	59	48
20	Manchester City	42	13	8	21	47	70	47
21	Swansea City	42	10	11	21	51	69	41
22	Brighton & Hove Albion	42	9	13	20	38	68	40

Appearances

PLAYER	LGE	FAC	LC	UC	TOT
Duxbury	42	7	9	2	60
Stapleton	41	7	9	2	59
Albiston	38	7	9	2	56
Whiteside	39	7	7 (2)	2	55 (2)
Bailey	37	7	9	2	55
McQueen	37	7	8	1	53
Robson	33	6	8	2	49
Muhren	32	6	8	-	46
Moran	29	7	7	1	44
Moses	29	5	8	1	43
Coppell	29	4	8	1 (1)	42 (1)
Wilkins	26	4	3 (1)	2	35 (1)
Grimes	15 (1)	1	2	2	20 (1)
McGrath	14	- (1)	1	-	15 (1)
Buchan	3	-	1	2	6
Wealands	5	-	-	-	5
Davies	2 (1)	2	-	-	4 (1)
Macari	2 (7)	- (1)	1 (2)	- (1)	3 (11)
McGarvey	3 (4)	-	-	-	3 (4)
Cunningham	3 (2)	-	-	-	3 (2)
Gidman	3	-	-	-	3
Beardsley	-	-	1	-	1

Goalscorers

PLAYER	LGE	FAC	LC	UC	TOT
Stapleton	14	3	2	-	19
Robson	10	3	1	1	15
Whiteside	8	3	3	-	14
Coppell	4	1	6	-	11
Muhren	5	1	1	-	7
Moran	2	1	2	-	5
McGrath	3	-	-	-	3
McQueen	-	-	3	-	3
Grimes	2	-	-	-	2
Macari	2	-	-	-	2
Albiston	1	-	1	-	2
Wilkins	1	1	-	-	2
Moses	-	1	1	-	2
Cunningham	1	-	-	-	1
Duxbury	1	-	-	-	1
McGarvey	1	-	-	-	1
own goals	1	-	1	-	2

Right: Remi Moses scored only two goals this season, one in each of the cup campaigns, and both were vital.

FOOTBALL LEAGUE DIVISION ONE: THIRD POSITION

FA CUP: WINNERS. REPLAY - 26 MAY 1983. WEMBLEY, LONDON.
BEAT BRIGHTON 4-0 ROBSON 25' & 44', WHITESIDE 30', MUHREN 62'.

LEAGUE CUP: RUNNERS-UP. 26 MARCH 1983. WEMBLEY, LONDON.
LOST TO LIVERPOOL 1-2 WHITESIDE 12', WHELAN 98'.

UEFA CUP: LOSE TO VALENCIA (1-2 ON AGGREGATE) IN 1ST ROUND

1983/84

- The Barcelona team beaten in the European Cup-Winners' Cup quarter-final includes stars such as Argentina's Diego Maradona and Bernd Schuster of Germany.

- After Robert Maxwell fails to take over United in February 1984, the tycoon moves to the Midlands and buys Derby County instead three years later.

- Before the final two league games are played, Ray Wilkins agrees to join AC Milan next season for £1.5 million. He plays in 56 of the 58 games this season.

Above: Bryan Robson is congratulated by teammate Kevin Moran after scoring the first goal in their Cup-Winners' Cup quarter-final 2nd leg match against Barcelona.

Right: Two-goal hero against Barca Bryan Robson is carried shoulder high by jubilant supporters.

A failed takeover bid and more memorable nights in Europe but no more silverware

WITH A TROPHY under their belt for the first time in six seasons, United were in confident mood with an ultra-confident manager in Ron Atkinson and were looking forward to an even more successful season. When Liverpool were beaten 2-0 in the Charity Shield at Wembley in August, with two goals from Bryan Robson, the predictions of a glorious year looked accurate. Four wins in the opening five league games also augured well.

Atkinson had signed Scottish winger Arthur Graham from Leeds United for £45,000 to replace the injured Steve Coppell and give further attacking options. So it was no surprise that United were sticking close to Liverpool in the early weeks of the league season and were top of the table by the end of October. Meanwhile, the opening rounds of the European Cup-Winners' Cup in the autumn brought victories against Czech side Dukla Prague and Spartak Varna from Bulgaria. The League Cup campaign also began with wins over Port Vale and Colchester United.

However, United were still prone to annoying lapses such as a 3-0 loss at Southampton in September and then a League Cup fourth round defeat to the Third Division's top side Oxford United in December. Ironically, a few weeks later, the media tycoon Robert Maxwell, the Oxford owner, would make noises about a takeover bid for the Old Trafford club and reportedly made a £10 million offer which was turned down.

Before the takeover drama unfolded, United were just three points behind Liverpool as 1983 closed, but then another annoyingly poor performance in the FA Cup campaign in January allowed Third Division team AFC Bournemouth to trip up the Red Devils unexpectedly. The south coast team won 2-0 at their home ground which left some United supporters chanting anti-Atkinson songs and clearly meant his team was not living up to everyone's high expectations.

Nevertheless, the FA Cup loss spurred on the Reds in the league with 10 games undefeated up to mid-March. At the same time, the quarter-finals of the European competition pitched United against mighty Barcelona, who dominated the first leg in the Nou Camp and won easily 2-0. The return leg turned out to be one of the most memorable European nights for decades as Bryan Robson starred in a 3-0 win that put United into the semi-finals.

The joy was short lived, though, as Juventus of Italy denied the Reds another European final winning 3-2 on aggregate. So this left just the league title to fight for and at the end of April it looked like a two-horse race between United and Liverpool. But after returning from Italy, the Reds failed to win another game that season and finished six points behind Liverpool.

The Reds did not even make the runners-up spot as first Southampton raced past them and then United were pushed into fourth place by Nottingham Forest, who won 2-0 at Old Trafford in their final league game. There was consolation of a UEFA Cup place for the following season, but too many draws away from home (11 in all, the most by any Division One team that season) was the Reds' undoing.

Final League Table Division One

		P	W	D	L	F	A	Pts
1	Liverpool	42	22	14	6	73	32	80
2	Southampton	42	22	11	9	66	38	77
3	Nottingham Forest	42	22	8	12	76	45	74
4	**MANCHESTER UNITED**	**42**	**20**	**14**	**8**	**71**	**41**	**74**
5	Queens Park Rangers	42	22	7	13	67	37	73
6	Arsenal	42	18	9	15	74	60	63
7	Everton	42	16	14	12	44	42	62
8	Tottenham Hotspur	42	17	10	15	64	65	61
9	West Ham United	42	17	9	16	60	55	60
10	Aston Villa	42	17	9	16	59	61	60
11	Watford	42	16	9	17	68	77	57
12	Ipswich Town	42	15	8	19	55	57	53
13	Sunderland	42	13	13	16	42	53	52
14	Norwich City	42	12	15	15	48	49	51
15	Leicester City	42	13	12	17	65	68	51
16	Luton Town	42	14	9	19	53	66	51
17	West Bromwich Albion	42	14	9	19	48	62	51
18	Stoke City	42	13	11	18	44	63	50
19	Coventry City	42	13	11	18	57	77	50
20	Birmingham City	42	12	12	18	39	50	48
21	Notts County	42	10	11	21	50	72	41
22	Wolverhampton Wanderers	42	6	11	25	27	80	29

Appearances

PLAYER	LGE	FAC	LC	ECWC	TOT
Stapleton	42	1	6	8	57
Albiston	40	1	6	8	55
Wilkins	42	1	6	6	55
Bailey	40	1	5	8	54
Duxbury	39	1	6	8	54
Moran	38	-	5	8	51
Robson	33	1	6	6	46
Graham	33 (4)	1	5	6 (1)	45 (5)
Whiteside	30 (7)	1	6	5 (1)	42 (8)
Moses	31 (4)	1	5 (1)	5 (1)	42 (6)
Muhren	26	1	2	5	34
McQueen	20	-	4	4	28
Hogg	16	1	-	4	21
McGrath	9	-	1	2	12
Hughes	7 (4)	-	1 (1)	2 (2)	10 (7)
Crooks	6 (1)	-	-	-	6 (1)
Gidman	4	-	1	1 (1)	6 (1)
Davies	3	-	-	- (1)	3 (1)
Wealands	2	-	1	-	3
Macari	- (5)	- (1)	- (2)	2	2 (8)
Blackmore	1	-	-	-	1
Dempsey	-	-	-	- (1)	- (1)

Goalscorers

PLAYER	LGE	FAC	LC	ECWC	TOT
Stapleton	13	-	2	4	19
Robson	12	-	4	-	16
Whiteside	10	-	1	1	12
Muhren	8	-	-	-	8
Moran	7	-	-	-	7
Graham	5	-	1	1	7
Hughes	4	-	1	-	5
Wilkins	3	-	1	1	5
Moses	2	-	1	-	3
Albiston	2	-	-	-	2
Crooks	2	-	-	-	2
McQueen	1	-	1	-	2
Hogg	1	-	-	-	1
McGrath	1	-	-	-	1
Davies	-	-	-	1	1

Right: Frank Stapleton has just felt the full might of Juventus hard man Claudio Gentile as he leaves the scene in the Cup-Winners' Cup semi-final.

United win the FA Cup to deny rivals a double yet tragedies in English football leave a blemish on the season

THIS WOULD BE a pivotal season for English football, but before tragic events stepped in to change the lives of everyone involved in the sport in this country, United manager Ron Atkinson decided he was not about to let the status quo at the club remain. He had agreed to sell Ray Wilkins to AC Milan before the previous season ended and also allowed Lou Macari to leave to manage Swindon Town.

The manager brought in a several significant new faces and again the emphasis was on attack. Alan Brazil moved in from Tottenham; Gordon Strachan arrived from Aberdeen; Jesper Olsen was signed from Ajax of Amsterdam and Mark Hughes was ready for a regular place up front. The only defensive news was the continued emergence of Paul McGrath, who had signed two years earlier.

As the league season opened, United's recent penchant for the draw seemed to extend into this campaign – all four opening games ended in draws as the new players settled in. However, a 5-0 thrashing of Newcastle United in the fifth league game got Atkinson's team into a more positive mood, and the goals began to flow. Hughes was in the starting line-up along with Brazil and goals started to flow. September saw the UEFA Cup and League Cup campaigns begin successfully, although there was also a first league defeat, 3-0 to Aston Villa at the beginning of October.

Bur it was the second league defeat of the season later that month – 5-0 to Everton – that proved to be more of a shock and highlighted the team's continued erratic form. Three days later, Everton also knocked United out of the League Cup, a 2-1 win for the Merseysiders at their Goodison Park ground.

In the UEFA Cup, opponents Raba Vasas of Hungary, PSV Eindhoven of the Netherlands and Scotland's Dundee United were all dispatched during the first half of the season, although not without some difficulty. United beat the Dutch just 1-0 on aggregate and had to win 3-2 in Dundee to beat the Scots 5-4 over the two legs.

In early January, United were drawn against AFC Bournemouth in the FA Cup third round for the second season running, but the Reds this time gained revenge with a 3-0 win. Coventry City, Blackburn Rovers and West Ham United were then beaten in the next three rounds to put the Reds into the semi-final. However, the news was not so good in the UEFA Cup where a surprisingly strong Videoton of Hungary put United out in the quarter-finals on penalties.

A spark of four straight wins after the UEFA exit gave United hope of a league title challenge, but the FA Cup semi-final against Liverpool, which was settled only after a replay, took the wind out of the Reds' sails. Everton clinched the title with three games to go and United finished fourth. However, United beat the Toffees 1-0 in the FA Cup final to deny them the league and cup double.

But memories of the 1984-85 season would be forever tainted by two horror stories in May: first, on the final day of the league season, 56 fans were killed in the Bradford City stadium fire disaster and later 39 spectators at the European Cup final between Liverpool and Juventus were crushed to death in Heysel Stadium in Brussels.

- Ron Atkinson gave former youth team striker Mark Hughes a few starts in the last campaign, something that is soon to pay dividends in this one.

- Legend George Best is convicted of drinking and driving, assaulting a policeman and failing to surrender to bail. He is sentenced to 12 weeks in jail and spends Christmas 1984 behind bars.

- Eighteen-year-old midfielder David Platt is given a free transfer in February and signs for Crewe Alexandra.

- The 1-0 FA Cup final win against Everton foils the Merseyside team's attempt to be the first English club to complete a unique treble: the domestic league and cup double plus a European trophy in the same season. This treble is achieved by the Reds in 1999.

Above: Scottish international Alan Brazil was one of three key pre-season signings.

Left: Gary Bailey would make 375 United appearances in nine years.

Final League Table Division

		P	W	D	L	F	A	Pts
1	Everton	42	28	6	8	88	43	90
2	Liverpool	42	22	11	9	68	35	77
3	Tottenham Hotspur	42	23	8	11	78	51	77
4	**MANCHESTER UNITED**	42	22	10	10	77	47	76
5	Southampton	42	19	11	12	56	47	68
6	Chelsea	42	18	12	12	63	48	66
7	Arsenal	42	19	9	14	61	49	66
8	Sheffield Wednesday	42	17	14	11	58	45	65
9	Nottingham Forest	42	19	7	16	56	48	64
10	Aston Villa	42	15	11	16	60	60	56
11	Watford	42	14	13	15	81	71	55
12	West Bromwich Albion	42	16	7	19	58	62	55
13	Luton Town	42	15	9	18	57	61	54
14	Newcastle United	42	13	13	16	55	70	52
15	Leicester City	42	15	6	21	65	73	51
16	West Ham United	42	13	12	17	51	68	51
17	Ipswich Town	42	13	11	18	46	57	50
18	Coventry City	42	15	5	22	47	64	50
19	Queens Park Rangers	42	13	11	18	53	72	50
20	Norwich City	42	13	10	19	46	64	49
21	Sunderland	42	10	10	22	40	62	40
22	Stoke City	42	3	8	31	24	91	17

Appearances

PLAYER	LGE	FAC	LC	UC	TOT
Albiston	39	7	3	8	57
Strachan	41	7	2	6	56
Bailey	38	6	3	8	55
Hughes	38	7	2	8	55
Olsen	36	6	2	6 (1)	50 (1)
Robson	32 (1)	4	2	7	45 (1)
Hogg	29	5	3	6	43
Gidman	27	6	1	6 (1)	40 (1)
Moses	26	3	3	6	38
Duxbury	27 (3)	2 (1)	2	6	37 (4)
Whiteside	23 (4)	6	1	4 (1)	34 (5)
McGrath	23	7	-	2	32
Stapleton	21 (3)	5	1 (1)	4 (1)	31 (5)
Moran	19	3	2	4	28
Brazil	17 (3)	- (1)	2 (1)	2	21 (5)
McQueen	12	1	-	2	15
Muhren	7 (5)	1	1	3	12 (5)
Pears	4	1	-	-	5
Garton	2	-	1	- (1)	3 (1)
Blackmore	1	-	1	-	2
Graham	-	-	1	-	1

Goalscorers

PLAYER	LGE	FAC	LC	UC	TOT
Hughes	16	3	3	2	24
Strachan	15	2	-	2	19
Robson	9	2	1	2	14
Whiteside	9	4	-	-	13
Stapleton	6	2	-	1	9
Brazil	5	-	3	1	9
Olsen	5	-	1	-	6
Moran	4	-	-	-	4
Gidman	3	-	-	-	3
Moses	3	-	-	-	3
Muhren	-	-	-	3	3
McQueen	1	1	-	-	2
McGrath	-	2	-	-	2
Duxbury	1	-	-	-	1
own goal	-	-	-	1	1

Right: 8 September 1984. Gordon Strachan (left) and Jesper Olsen were brought in to score goals. The Scot has just converted a penalty against Newcastle United in a 5-0 win.

FOOTBALL LEAGUE DIVISION ONE: FOURTH POSITION

FA CUP: WINNERS. 18 MAY 1985. WEMBLEY, LONDON.
BEAT EVERTON 1-0 WHITESIDE 110'

LEAGUE CUP: LOSE TO EVERTON (1-2) IN 3RD ROUND

UEFA CUP: LOSE TO VIDEOTON (1-1 ON AGGREGATE, 4-5 ON PENALTIES) IN QUARTER-FINAL

1985/86

The manager is under pressure as the team fails to click after plenty of early-season promise

■ United's 10-game winning streak to open the season ends on 5 October with a 1-1 draw at Luton Town and was one game short of the league record of 11 set 25 years earlier by Tottenham Hotspur.

■ United shareholder and rock star Phil Lynott dies in a Salisbury hospital in January 1986 at the age of 36. He had suffered multiple organ failure as a result of alcoholism and drug abuse.

■ A 2-0 defeat against Everton in the Charity Shield means the season got off to a disappointing start.

Above: 13 April 1986. Ron Atkinson agonises during the league match against Sheffield Wednesday at Old Trafford. The Reds lose 2-0.

Right: 21 September 1985. After scoring the second goal in a 5-1 win over West Bromwich Albion, Gordon Strachan dislocated his shoulder. Frank Stapleton sympathises.

THE INDEFINITE BAN imposed on English teams taking part in European competition meant United were denied a place in the UEFA Cup, but there were also other changes at Old Trafford: Gordon McQueen moved on to a coaching position in Hong Kong while Arnold Muhren returned to the Netherlands to play for Ajax of Amsterdam.

Ron Atkinson's supreme confidence in the ability of his side to win the league wasn't fully shared by the Old Trafford faithful. His only summer signing was England international Peter Barnes from Coventry, but some fans felt the Manchester-born winger's best days were behind him, even if he was just 28. Nevertheless, United's early league form was astonishing: a run of 10 wins to start the season sent the Reds to the top of the table with goals galore from no less than 12 different players including Barnes who had started brightly. United put four past Aston Villa in the opening match and scored five at The Hawthorns against WBA, Atkinson's former club. Not only that, but the defence conceded just three goals in this stretch.

By the end of October, the Red Devils were 10 points clear of their rivals, while their first league defeat was not until early November, a 1-0 loss at Sheffield Wednesday. Liverpool would then put United out of the League Cup before the end of November and the Merseyside club also moved within two points of the Reds in the league itself.

United suffered an end-of-year wobble: only two wins in December and two more defeats, while January was mostly taken up by FA Cup wins against Rochdale and Sunderland after a replay. Then, in the opening league game of February, United lost 2-1 at West Ham United and Everton overtook them at the top of the league. A season that had league and cup double possibilities was now in danger of becoming a severe disappointment.

Captain Bryan Robson had begun suffering a string of injuries (he would play just 21 league games) while an announcement that Mark Hughes would leave for Barcelona at the end of the season did little to calm the nerves of players or

supporters. When West Ham then put the Reds out of the FA Cup in early March, there was much wringing of hands.

Atkinson had wheeled and dealed for new players all season, including the likes of Colin Gibson from Aston Villa, Terry Gibson from Coventry City, Johnny Sivebaek from Vejle BK in Denmark and, latterly in March, Peter Davenport from Nottingham Forest. But none of the new signings could stop United's downward spiral in the second half of the season.

By the end of March, United were down to third place as Everton, Liverpool and even West Ham showed better form. United would go on to lose two of their final six games in the run-in and finish fourth in the league race, won again by Liverpool. Just under 39,000 fans watched the final game at Old Trafford, a 4-0 win against Leicester City, which was 10,000 down on the season opener. Manager Atkinson was now under pressure from all sides.

Left: 7 September 1985. Bryan Robson in action for the Red Devils against Oxford United at Old Trafford.

Final League Table Division One

		P	W	D	L	F	A	Pts
1	Liverpool	42	26	10	6	89	37	88
2	Everton	42	26	8	8	87	41	86
3	West Ham United	42	26	6	10	74	40	84
4	**MANCHESTER UNITED**	**42**	**22**	**10**	**10**	**70**	**36**	**76**
5	Sheffield Wednesday	42	21	10	11	63	54	73
6	Chelsea	42	20	11	11	57	56	71
7	Arsenal	42	20	9	13	49	47	69
8	Nottingham Forest	42	19	11	12	69	53	68
9	Luton Town	42	18	12	12	61	44	66
10	Tottenham Hotspur	42	19	8	15	74	52	65
11	Newcastle United	42	17	12	13	67	72	63
12	Watford	42	16	11	15	69	62	59
13	Queens Park Rangers	42	15	7	20	53	64	52
14	Southampton	42	12	10	20	51	62	46
15	Manchester City	42	11	12	19	43	57	45
16	Aston Villa	42	10	14	18	51	67	44
17	Coventry City	42	11	10	21	48	71	43
18	Oxford United	42	10	12	20	62	80	42
19	Leicester City	42	10	12	20	54	76	42
20	Ipswich Town	42	11	8	23	32	55	41
21	Birmingham City	42	8	5	29	30	73	29
22	West Bromwich Albion	42	4	12	26	35	89	24

Appearances

PLAYER	LGE	FAC	LC	TOT
McGrath	40	4	4	48
Whiteside	37	5	4	46
Albiston	37	5	3	45
Hughes	40	3	2	45
Stapleton	34 (7)	5	4	43 (7)
Strachan	27 (1)	5	1	33 (1)
Olsen	25 (3)	3 (2)	3	31 (5)
Bailey	25	2	4	31
Duxbury	21 (2)	3	3	27 (2)
Gidman	24	2	1	27
Robson	21	3	2	26
Moran	18 (1)	3	4	25 (1)
Gibson C	18	4	-	22
Turner	17	3	-	20
Hogg	17	-	2	19
Blackmore	12	2 (2)	2	16 (2)
Barnes	12 (1)	-	3	15 (1)
Davenport	11	-	-	11
Garton	10	1	-	11
Higgins	6	2	-	8
Brazil	1(10)	-	2 (2)	3(12)
Moses	4	-	-	4

PLAYER	LGE	FAC	LC	TOT
Gibson T	2 (5)	-	-	2 (5)
Sivebaek	2 (1)	-	-	2 (1)
Dempsey	1	-	-	1
Wood	- (1)	-	-	- (1)

Goalscorers

PLAYER	LGE	FAC	LC	TOT
Hughes	17	1	-	18
Olsen	11	2	-	13
Stapleton	7	2	-	9
Robson	7	-	-	7
Whiteside	4	1	2	7
Gibson C	5	-	-	5
Strachan	5	-	-	5
McGrath	3	-	1	4
Blackmore	3	-	-	3
Brazil	3	-	-	3
Barnes	2	-	1	3
Albiston	1	-	-	1
Davenport	1	-	-	1
Duxbury	1	-	-	1

Ron Atkinson is sacked by mid-season and the highly regarded Alex Ferguson moves in from Aberdeen

1986/87

AFTER SUCH A disappointing previous season, Ron Atkinson needed his team to start fast again, especially because the iconic Mark Hughes had left for Barcelona and a strike force of Frank Stapleton and Peter Davenport appeared less daunting to defences. However much Atkinson sounded confident as the first ball was kicked, the worst proceeded to happen.

The first three league games, all against London opposition – Arsenal, West Ham United and Charlton Athletic – were all lost. A 5-1 romp against Southampton in the fifth match – a game in which Bryan Robson returned from a long-term shoulder injury – was nothing but a false dawn and the next three league games were also lost.

By 1 November, the Red Devils were 19th in the league with just three wins. On that day, Atkinson's team drew 1-1 with Coventry City at home and then lost 4-1 in the League Cup three days later to the very Southampton team that they had trounced six weeks earlier. "I thought we could get a result at Southampton, but things didn't work out," said Atkinson after the match. The day after the defeat, Atkinson was sacked and the rumours about his replacement being Alex Ferguson, who had brought such success in Scotland and in Europe to Aberdeen, proved to be true.

Within a day of firing one manager, the United board appointed another: Ferguson took over with the stated task of bringing a league title to Old Trafford. However, at the start of his reign, the new manager was merely concerned with United remaining in the First Division.

An opening 2-0 defeat at Oxford United was an inauspicious start for Ferguson, but United's resilience soon sharpened up and by the end of January, the team was back on track having notched up wins against opposition including reigning league champions Liverpool at Anfield, Manchester City in the FA Cup third round and Arsenal at Old Trafford, all within the space of a month. Despite losing 1-0 to Coventry City in the next round of the cup, Ferguson's methods were working and United were climbing the league table.

Wanting to see what his players could do, Ferguson relied on improved tactics and attitude to rectify the decline. Eight players in the final match – a 3-1 win at home to Aston Villa – also played in the opening game defeat at Arsenal; the biggest change was obviously the manager. Ferguson also stressed a solid defence and United kept 12 clean sheets in the 31 games under the new manager this season.

The Reds finished 11th in the league and Ferguson had won over the fans very quickly; the win at Anfield (United's first away win of the season and Liverpool's first home defeat) plus the victory over City in the cup ensured a pleasant honeymoon period. Ferguson then ramped up his expected clear out of players by putting goalkeeper Chris Turner and defender Graeme Hogg on the transfer list immediately after the season ended.

- This final season for Ron Atkinson and the arrival of Alex Ferguson also marks the 20th anniversary since United last won the league title.

- Former United favourite Gordon Hill, now 32-years-old is signed by GM Vauxhall Conference team Northwich Victoria, managed by another ex-Reds player Stuart Pearson.

- In March, Alex Ferguson announces that he wants Mark Hughes to return to Old Trafford, although tax issues mean the transfer will not happen before April 1988.

- One of Alex Ferguson's first moves is to bring his assistant from Aberdeen, Archie Knox, to Old Trafford and the team's fitness improves immediately.

Above: Chris Turner, the United goalkeeper, in one of his 23 league starts against West Ham United.

Left: The start of an era. Alex Ferguson signs autographs for success-hungry fans.

Final League Table Division One

		P	W	D	L	F	A	Pts
1	Everton	42	26	8	8	76	31	86
2	Liverpool	42	23	8	11	72	42	77
3	Tottenham Hotspur	42	21	8	13	68	43	71
4	Arsenal	42	20	10	12	58	35	70
5	Norwich City	42	17	17	8	53	51	68
6	Wimbledon	42	19	9	14	57	50	66
7	Luton Town	42	18	12	12	47	45	66
8	Nottingham Forest	42	18	11	13	64	51	65
9	Watford	42	18	9	15	67	54	63
10	Coventry City	42	17	12	13	50	45	63
11	**MANCHESTER UNITED**	42	14	14	14	52	45	56
12	Southampton	42	14	10	18	69	68	52
13	Sheffield Wednesday	42	13	13	16	58	59	52
14	Chelsea	42	13	13	16	53	64	52
15	West Ham United	42	14	10	18	52	67	52
16	Queens Park Rangers	42	13	11	18	48	64	50
17	Newcastle United	42	12	11	19	47	65	47
18	Oxford United	42	11	13	18	44	69	46
19	Charlton Athletic	42	11	11	20	45	55	44
20	Leicester City	42	11	9	22	54	76	42
21	Manchester City	42	8	15	19	36	57	39
22	Aston Villa	42	8	12	22	45	79	36

Appearances

PLAYER	LGE	FAC	LC	TOT
Davenport	34 (5)	1 (1)	4	39 (6)
McGrath	34 (1)	- (1)	4	38 (2)
Strachan	33 (1)	2	2	37 (1)
Duxbury	32	2	3	37
Moran	32 (1)	2	2 (1)	36 (2)
Whiteside	31	2	3 (1)	36 (1)
Robson	29 (1)	-	3	32 (1)
Stapleton	25 (9)	2	4	31 (9)
Sivebaek	27 (1)	2	1	30 (1)
Turner	23	2	4	29
Gibson C	24	1	1	26
Olsen	22 (6)	2	1 (1)	25 (7)
Albiston	19 (3)	-	4	23 (3)
Moses	17 (1)	-	4	21 (1)
Walsh	14	-	-	14
Gibson T	12 (4)	1 (1)	- (2)	13 (7)
Hogg	11	-	2	13
Blackmore	10 (2)	1	-	11 (2)
Garton	9	2	-	11
O'Brien	9 (2)	-	-	9 (2)
Barnes	7	-	2	9
Bailey	5	-	-	5

PLAYER	LGE	FAC	LC	TOT
Wood	2	-	- (1)	2 (1)
Gill	1	-	-	1

Goalscorers

PLAYER	LGE	FAC	LC	TOT
Davenport	14	-	2	16
Whiteside	8	1	1	10
Stapleton	7	-	2	9
Robson	7	-	-	7
Strachan	4	-	-	4
Olsen	3	-	-	3
McGrath	2	-	-	2
Moses	-	-	2	2
Blackmore	1	-	-	1
Duxbury	1	-	-	1
Gibson C	1	-	-	1
Gibson T	1	-	-	1
Sivebaek	1	-	-	1
Barnes	-	-	1	1
own goals	2	-	-	2

Left: Centre half powerhouse Paul McGrath enjoys a spell as goalkeeper during a training session.

1987/88

- The transfer of Steve Bruce from Norwich City is only undertaken after United pull out of signing Terry Butcher from Glasgow Rangers at the last minute. Butcher breaks his leg 24 hours before the deal is due to be announced and Bruce is signed instead.

- In April 1988 as the season closes, winger Lee Sharpe is signed for £180,000 from Torquay; he is a month short of his 17th birthday.

- Full back Arthur Albiston is given a free transfer and a testimonial match at the end of the season after 11 years with the club.

Above: Gordon Strachan is at the height of his powers in the Red Devils midfield.

Right: 2 April 1988. Colin Gibson celebrates after scoring a rare goal against Derby County in a 4-1 win.

Ferguson sets the tone in his first full season in charge but cannot bring instant success

ALEX FERGUSON'S FIRST full season in charge was evidence that his strategy was evolution without revolution. There was no forced mass exodus of players or complementary influx of replacements from his former club, but just the more normal number of comings and goings. Among those who did leave Old Trafford were Gary Bailey (due to injury) and Terry Gibson, Johnny Sivebaek and Frank Stapleton (via transfers).

The incoming players, however, did prove to be significant. Scottish player of the year Brian McClair arrived from Celtic and Viv Anderson was acquired from Arsenal. These two would start the season and, by December, a third new face would come to United who also epitomised the new era: Steve Bruce came from Norwich City for £825,000 just before Christmas and these three would form part of the nucleus of Ferguson's new team.

Even before Bruce's arrival, United were obviously an improved team from a year ago; after the first five games of the season, they were unbeaten with three wins and two draws. However, the First Division was extremely competitive this campaign and even though Ferguson's team suffered only three defeats before the end of the year, Liverpool had overtaken them at the top, with Nottingham Forest second.

By now, Bruce had arrived to command the defence (a transfer partly caused by an injury to Paul McGrath) and McClair was scoring plenty of goals. Also, United had successfully beaten Hull City, Crystal Palace and Bury to progress to the fifth round of the League Cup. Ferguson's New Year was mixed: league form was solid and two rounds of the FA Cup were successfully navigated by beating Ipswich Town and Chelsea, but Oxford United (who would end the year relegated from Division One) beat his team 2-0 in the League Cup.

Ferguson was coming to a definite conclusion that runaway league leaders Liverpool (17 points clear of United at the end of January) were the benchmark for his team. Then when Arsenal beat the Reds 2-1 at Highbury in the FA Cup fifth round, there was little more than pride to fight for this season;

this was not what Ferguson or expectant fans had in mind, especially when two favourites, Norman Whiteside and Paul McGrath, both made transfer requests.

By now it was a somewhat embattled Ferguson who drove on his team to chase hard in the league; in their final 16 games, the Red Devils won 12 matches and lost only once. But for the club's and the manager's futures, the most significant game was against champions-elect Liverpool at Anfield. Despite trailing 3-1 and having Colin Gibson sent off after an hour, United snatched a 3-3 draw. After the match, Ferguson railed against the officials for alleged bias in favour of the Merseysiders. United had now been set a clear target to topple Liverpool and the rivalry between the two clubs was set to reach even greater levels.

The fine end-of-season run still left United as league runners-up, nine points short of the title, but McClair's 31 goals were the most by any Old Trafford player since George Best 20 years ago scored 32.

Final League Table Division One

		P	W	D	L	F	A	Pts
1	Liverpool	40	26	12	2	87	24	90
2	**MANCHESTER UNITED**	40	23	12	5	71	38	81
3	Nottingham Forest	40	20	13	7	67	39	73
4	Everton	40	19	13	8	53	27	70
5	Queens Park Rangers	40	19	10	11	48	38	67
6	Arsenal	40	18	12	10	58	39	66
7	Wimbledon	40	14	15	11	58	47	57
8	Newcastle United	40	14	14	12	55	53	56
9	Luton Town	40	14	11	15	57	58	53
10	Coventry City	40	13	14	13	46	53	53
11	Sheffield Wednesday	40	15	8	17	52	66	53
12	Southampton	40	12	14	14	49	53	50
13	Tottenham Hotspur	40	12	11	17	38	48	47
14	Norwich City	40	12	9	19	40	52	45
15	Derby County	40	10	13	17	35	45	43
16	West Ham United	40	9	15	16	40	52	42
17	Charlton Athletic	40	9	15	16	38	52	42
18	Chelsea	40	9	15	16	50	68	42
19	Portsmouth	40	7	14	19	36	66	35
20	Watford	40	7	11	22	27	51	32
21	Oxford United	40	6	13	21	44	80	31

Appearances

PLAYER	LGE	FAC	LC	TOT
McClair	40	3	5	48
Duxbury	39	3	5	47
Robson	36	2	5	43
Strachan	33 (3)	3	5	41 (3)
Anderson	30 (1)	3	4	37 (1)
Olsen	30 (7)	2 (1)	3 (1)	35 (9)
Whiteside	26 (1)	3	5	34 (1)
Gibson	26 (3)	2	5	33 (3)
Turner	24	3	3	30
Davenport	21 (13)	1 (1)	3 (1)	25 (15)
Bruce	21	3	-	24
McGrath	21 (1)	-	2	23 (1)
Moran	20 (1)	1	2	23 (1)
Blackmore	15 (7)	1 (1)	3 (1)	19 (9)
Moses	16 (1)	1	1 (1)	18 (2)
Walsh	16	-	2	18
Hogg	9 (1)	2	-	11 (2)
O'Brien	6 (11)	- (2)	- (2)	6 (15)
Garton	5 (1)	-	2 (1)	7 (2)
Albiston	5 (6)	-	-	5 (6)
Graham	1	-	- (1)	1 (1)

PLAYER	LGE	FAC	LC	TOT
Martin	- (1)	-	-	- (1)

Left: 2 January 1988. Defender Mike Duxbury at Vicarage Road. United beat Watford 1-0.

Goalscorers

PLAYER	LGE	FAC	LC	TOT
McClair	24	2	5	31
Robson	11	-	-	11
Whiteside	7	1	2	10
Strachan	8	-	1	9
Davenport	5	-	1	6
Blackmore	3	-	-	3
Anderson	2	1	-	3
McGrath	2	-	1	3
Bruce	2	-	-	2
Gibson	2	-	-	2
O'Brien	2	-	-	2
Olsen	2	-	-	2
own goals	1	1	-	2

A mid-table league finish and two tough cup exits shoot down the fans' high expectations

1988/89

IF THERE WAS one thing that United supporters had learned during the post-Busby era, it was to expect the unexpected. Several times in the last 20 years, United's managers had looked on the edge of a breakthrough in consistent winning form – especially in the league – and each time the fans had been disappointed. This was another season where hopes in some quarters were high after Alex Ferguson's team changes had started to bed in. A runners-up finish in the league had been deemed a success for his first full season in charge, but people now wanted more.

Ferguson's signings seemed to make sense to most pundits as he sought parity with Liverpool, who were dominating the First Division at this time, but there were still dissenting voices. He went back to his former club, Aberdeen, to solve his goalkeeping problems by signing Jim Leighton for £750,000 and Mark Hughes returned in triumph from Barcelona for £1.8 million. The exit door at Old Trafford was open wide this year: Remi Moses retired through injury while Graeme Hogg and Kevin Moran were transferred before the season started; goalkeeper Chris Turner left in September; and during the season Jesper Olsen, Peter Davenport and Gordon Strachan would all follow.

Yet instead of pushing on and challenging even harder for the league and cup competitions, Ferguson's team slumped into an unforeseen mediocrity. Goals proved harder to come by. While McClair and Hughes each scored a very respectable 16, there was much less threat from the rest of the team, where Bryan Robson was the only other player to chip in with more than five. Ferguson tried plenty of players this season – a whopping 27 in all – but results were inconclusive as Ferguson even tried youth teamers (he was by now re-vamping the youth squad and the scouting system).

The team was becoming draw specialists; at one time during the autumn they drew eight out of nine consecutive league games. By the end of December, United were not even in the chasing pack for the league and had exited the League Cup to Wimbledon in the third round.

The New Year did bring a deep run in the FA Cup, however. Queens Park Rangers were dismissed after two replays in the third round while Oxford United were then dispatched 4-0 followed by Bournemouth in the fifth round. By the end of February, United had also put a run of wins together in the league and had pushed into the top five.

Yet the last 10 weeks of the season saw an unsatisfactory stumble; Nottingham Forest knocked the Red Devils out of the FA Cup 1-0 at Old Trafford in the sixth round and the team managed just three wins after that in 12 matches. The finishing league position of 11th left many fans stunned after the previous season's second place. Inevitably, pressure mounted on Ferguson in whom some fans were losing faith; average home league attendances were just under 36,500, over 10,000 fewer than in 1985-86, which was Ron Atkinson's last full season in charge.

- Ferguson dips into the transfer market in October for full back Mal Donaghy from Luton Town for £650,000.

- On 6 May, Norman Whiteside plays his last game for United; he is transferred to Everton before the start of the next season.

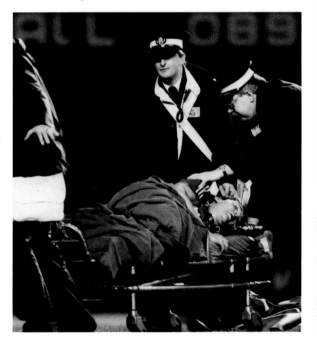

Above: Brian 'Choccy' McClair formed a deadly partnership with Mark Hughes this season.

Left: 7 January 1989. Bryan Robson is stretchered off after a clash of heads in a third round FA Cup match against QPR. He swallowed his tongue, but his life was saved by the club's quick-thinking physio Jim McGregor.

Final League Table Division One

		P	W	D	L	F	A	Pts
1	Arsenal	38	22	10	6	73	36	76
2	Liverpool	38	22	10	6	65	28	76
3	Nottingham Forest	38	17	13	8	64	43	64
4	Norwich City	38	17	11	10	48	45	62
5	Derby County	38	17	7	14	40	38	58
6	Tottenham Hotspur	38	15	12	11	60	46	57
7	Coventry City	38	14	13	11	47	42	55
8	Everton	38	14	12	12	50	45	54
9	Queens Park Rangers	38	14	11	13	43	37	53
10	Millwall	38	14	11	13	47	52	53
11	**MANCHESTER UNITED**	38	13	12	13	45	35	51
12	Wimbledon	38	14	9	15	50	46	51
13	Southampton	38	10	15	13	52	66	45
14	Charlton Athletic	38	10	12	16	44	58	42
15	Sheffield Wednesday	38	10	12	16	34	51	42
16	Luton Town	38	10	11	17	42	52	41
17	Aston Villa	38	9	13	16	45	56	40
18	Middlesbrough	38	9	12	17	44	61	39
19	West Ham United	38	10	8	20	37	62	38
20	Newcastle United	38	7	10	21	32	63	31

Appearances

PLAYER	LGE	FAC	LC	TOT
Bruce	38	7	3	48
Hughes	38	7	3	48
Leighton	38	7	3	48
McClair	38	7	3	48
Robson	34	6	3	43
Donaghy	30	7	-	37
Blackmore	26 (2)	5 (1)	3	34 (3)
Strachan	21	5	2 (1)	28 (1)
Sharpe	19 (3)	5 (1)	2	26 (4)
Milne	19 (3)	7	-	26 (3)
Martin	20 (4)	4 (1)	-	24 (5)
McGrath	18 (2)	4 (1)	1	23 (3)
Beardsmore	17 (6)	3 (2)	1 (1)	21 (9)
Duxbury	16 (2)	-	3	19 (2)
Garton	13 (1)	-	2	15 (1)
Davenport	7 (1)	-	1 (1)	8 (2)
Olsen	6 (4)	-	1 (1)	7 (5)
Gill	4 (5)	2 (2)	-	6 (7)
Whiteside	6	-	-	6
Anderson	5 (1)	-	- (1)	5 (2)

PLAYER	LGE	FAC	LC	TOT
Robins	1 (9)	1	- (1)	2(10)
Maiorana	2 (4)	-	-	2 (4)
O'Brien	1 (2)	-	1	2 (2)
Gibson	1 (1)	-	1	2 (1)
Wilson	- (4)	- (2)	-	- (6)
Brazil	- (1)	-	-	- (1)
Graham	-	- (1)	-	- (1)

Left: 23 June 1988. The press conference to announce the re-signing of Mark Hughes.

Goalscorers

PLAYER	LGE	FAC	LC	TOT
Hughes	14	2	-	16
McClair	10	3	3	16
Robson	4	2	2	8
Bruce	2	1	1	4
Blackmore	3	-	-	3
Milne	3	-	-	3
Davenport	2	-	1	3
Beardsmore	2	-	-	2
Gill	1	1	-	2
Martin	1	-	-	1
McGrath	1	-	-	1
Strachan	1	-	-	1
Graham	-	1	-	1
own goals	1	1	-	2

1989/90

- The 5-1 loss to Manchester City in October is United's worst in a Manchester derby for 34 years.

- Gary Pallister becomes Britain's most expensive defender when he joins United for £2 million.

- Despite a crucial third round FA Cup win over Forest, a league loss to Norwich City on 21 January leaves United just one point and one place outside a relegation spot.

- United's FA Cup final opponents Crystal Palace are managed by ex-Old Trafford favourite Steve Coppell.

- Laurie Cunningham, one of Ron Atkinson's favourite players who played for United during a loan spell in 1982-83, dies in a car crash aged 33.

- Jimmy Murphy, long-time assistant manager to Matt Busby, dies aged 81.

Above: Alex Ferguson with Michael Knighton, whose attempt to buy the club eventually fell through.

Opposite: 12 May 1990. Jim Leighton during the FA Cup final.

A slew of new signings help win a first trophy for Ferguson after a dramatic FA Cup run

THIS OFF-SEASON WAS marked by Alex Ferguson flashing the cheque book like never before, making £8 million worth of major signings. In came midfielder Paul Ince from West Ham United for £1.8 million, Gary Pallister from Middlesbrough for £2.3 million, Neil Webb from Nottingham Forest for £1.5 million, Danny Wallace from Southampton for £1.3 million and Mike Phelan from Norwich City for £750,000. One key transfer out of Old Trafford was Paul McGrath who left for Aston Villa for £450,000.

The transfer activity was a significant statement by the manager, but it failed to spark an early season run of form. Two convincing home wins – 4-1 against Arsenal and 5-1 over Millwall – could only part-disguise a team that was still trying to gel; four league defeats by the end of September were capped by a 5-1 loss to Manchester City. When United were knocked out of the League Cup by Tottenham Hotspur in October, Ferguson's back was against the wall.

Meanwhile, there was the disruption of a failed takeover bid in the summer and autumn – it centred on property tycoon Michael Knighton, who had even donned Reds kit and displayed his soccer skills at Old Trafford to show his passion for the club.

From the end of November until early February, United would undergo a disastrous winless run in the league that would last a total of 11 games. Ferguson's heavy spending over the last three seasons was now becoming a rod with which to beat the manager by elements of the media and, with two competitions now lost, Ferguson's hopes rested with the FA Cup and the third round tie at a tough Division One rival, Nottingham Forest.

Some segments of the Old Trafford fans were openly demanding Ferguson be fired at this time and home attendances were falling fast, so the Forest cup game was seen by many pundits as a make-or-break match for Ferguson, The manager duly got a 1-0 win, ironically thanks to a goal from ex-youth team player Mark Robins rather than one of his new signings.

So while their league form remained patchy, United surged through the FA Cup with away wins against three other

Uniteds: Hereford, Newcastle and Sheffield. All three fixtures being away from Old Trafford seemed to help the team who would finish the season with only eight wins in all competitions at their home ground. By early April and in mid-table in the league, only Oldham Athletic of the Second Division stood between Ferguson and a Wembley final.

The first semi-final between the two Lancashire teams was a pulsating 3-3 draw and it took another Mark Robins goal to win the replay 2-1. Although Ferguson had to settle for an ugly 13th place finish in the league, it was the FA Cup flourish that helped begin to win over those doubting fans. Ferguson's first trophy as United manager was secured with a win over Crystal Palace in an FA Cup final replay. The original game ended in a dramatic 3-3 draw, but another Fergie Fledgling (his version of the Busby Babes) Lee Martin scored the only goal of the replay and the manager's potential season of disaster had brought United their seventh FA Cup victory.

Some commentators look back on the win over Nottingham Forest in the FA Cup on 7 January 1990 as being the moment Ferguson actually saved himself from the sack. In fact, just a few weeks earlier, one disgruntled fan had unfurled a banner that summed up the feelings of many: "No more excuses. Three years and we're still crap. Ta ra Fergie!" Forest were in their pomp under manager Brian Clough at the time and with the game at the City Ground, United were certainly not favourites to win.

Although chairman at the time Martin Edwards and board member Bobby Charlton both later insisted that Ferguson's job was not on the line at this time, the myth about the Mark Robins goal and its significance has grown with time.

Suffice to say that earlier managers in the post-Busby era were sacked under similar circumstances, so press speculation was entirely understandable at that stage. But, over 20 years and dozens of trophies later, with Ferguson himself remaining tight-lipped about this critical moment in his managerial history, everyone at Old Trafford is now glad that the manager's mythical possible sacking this season remained just that – a myth.

Final League Table Division One

		P	W	D	L	F	A	Pts
1	Liverpool	38	23	10	5	78	37	79
2	Aston Villa	38	21	7	10	57	38	70
3	Tottenham Hotspur	38	19	6	13	59	47	63
4	Arsenal	38	18	8	12	54	38	62
5	Chelsea	38	16	12	10	58	50	60
6	Everton	38	17	8	13	57	46	59
7	Southampton	38	15	10	13	71	63	55
8	Wimbledon	38	13	16	9	47	40	55
9	Nottingham Forest	38	15	9	14	55	47	54
10	Norwich City	38	13	14	11	44	42	53
11	Queens Park Rangers	38	13	11	14	45	44	50
12	Coventry City	38	14	7	17	39	59	49
13	**MANCHESTER UNITED**	**38**	**13**	**9**	**16**	**46**	**47**	**48**
14	Manchester City	38	12	12	14	43	52	48
15	Crystal Palace	38	13	9	16	42	66	48
16	Derby County	38	13	7	18	43	40	46
17	Luton Town	38	10	13	15	43	57	43
18	Sheffield Wednesday	38	11	10	17	35	51	43
19	Charlton Athletic	38	7	9	22	31	57	30
20	Millwall	38	5	11	22	39	65	26

Appearances

PLAYER	LGE	FAC	LC	TOT
McClair	37	8	3	48
Phelan	38	7	3	48
Hughes	36 (1)	8	3	47 (1)
Pallister	35	8	3	46
Leighton	35	7	3	45
Bruce	34	7	2	43
Martin	28 (4)	8	1	37 (4)
Ince	25 (1)	6 (1)	3	34 (2)
Wallace	23 (3)	6 (1)	2	31 (4)
Robson	20	4	3	27
Blackmore	19 (9)	2 (1)	-	21(10)
Anderson	14 (2)	4	1	19 (2)
Donaghy	13 (1)	1	3	17 (1)
Duxbury	12 (7)	2 (2)	1 (1)	15(10)
Sharpe	13 (5)	-	1 (1)	14 (6)
Webb	10 (1)	4	-	14 (1)
Robins	10 (7)	3 (3)	-	13(10)
Beardsmore	8(13)	1 (2)	1	10(15)
Gibson	5 (1)	1 (1)	-	6 (2)
Sealey	2	1	-	3

PLAYER	LGE	FAC	LC	TOT
Bosnich	1	-	-	1
Maiorana	- (1)	-	- (1)	- (2)
Brazil	- (1)	-	-	- (1)
Graham	- (1)	-	-	- (1)
Milne	- (1)	-	-	- (1)

Goalscorers

PLAYER	LGE	FAC	LC	TOT
Hughes	13	2	-	15
Robins	7	3	-	10
McClair	5	3	-	8
Wallace	3	2	1	6
Robson	2	2	-	4
Bruce	3	-	-	3
Pallister	3	-	-	3
Blackmore	2	1	-	3
Webb	2	1	-	3
Beardsmore	2	-	-	2
Ince	-	-	2	2
Gibson	1	-	-	1
Phelan	1	-	-	1
Sharpe	1	-	-	1
Martin	-	1	-	1
own goal	1	-	-	1

Left: 15 June 1989. New signings Mike Phelan (left) and Neil Webb (centre) with their manager Alex Ferguson at Old Trafford.

FOOTBALL LEAGUE DIVISION ONE: THIRTEENTH POSITION | FA CUP: WINNERS. REPLAY - 17 MAY 1990. WEMBLEY, LONDON. | LEAGUE CUP: LOSE TO TOTTENHAM HOTSPUR (0-3) IN 3RD ROUND

BEAT CRYSTAL PALACE MARTIN 59'

1990/91

- ■ Mark Hughes is voted Professional Footballers' Association Player of the Year for his 21 goals and overall outstanding contribution to United's season.

- ■ Centre back Steve Bruce is joint top scorer in the league with Brian McClair on 13 goals and totalled 19 in all competitions.

- ■ United are deducted one league point (and Arsenal two) after a 21-player brawl in a 1-0 loss at Old Trafford on 20 October.

- ■ This is Alex Ferguson's second European Cup-Winners' Cup triumph – he won the same trophy with Aberdeen seven years earlier.

- ■ Viv Anderson joins Sheffield Wednesday on a free transfer in January although he does not play in the League Cup final three months later when his new club beat United.

Above: Legendary former United manager Sir Matt Busby (right) with the current boss Alex Ferguson.

Right: Two-goal hero Mark Hughes wrestles with Barcelona's Alberto Ferrer in the Cup-Winners' Cup final.

European glory returns after 13 years as Ferguson continues to build for the future

FERGUSON'S FIRST TROPHY with United last season did not mean his team building would end. Denis Irwin – so impressive for Oldham Athletic against United in the FA Cup – was signed for £625,000, while young players were continually given a chance; even the manager's son Darren started two league games.

This season saw a return of English clubs to European football competitions for the first time since the Heysel disaster in 1985; United would contest the European Cup-Winners' Cup. But before their opening match in Europe, the Charity Shield was shared with Liverpool after a 1-1 draw at Wembley and the league campaign opened inconclusively with some good wins as well as some horrible defeats (like the 4-0 loss at Anfield to Liverpool in mid September).

Nevertheless, United's cup form was good – two rounds of their European competition were successfully completed and, despite only being among the chasing pack in the league behind Liverpool, the Reds beat the Merseysiders in the third round of the League Cup. Then a stunning 6-2 win at Highbury against a strong Arsenal team in the next round at the end of November galvanised United's season.

The Reds went undefeated in the league until the end of February, while at the same time reached the final of the League Cup, thanks to wins over Southampton and Leeds United. The only blemish was a fifth round FA Cup loss to Norwich City.

Arsenal were clear league favourites by now, so United could focus on Europe and a League Cup final against Sheffield Wednesday. The quarter-final opponents in Europe were Montpellier Herault who would provide United's first real test in the competition (lowly Welsh club Wrexham and Hungarians Pecsi Munkas had already been dispatched with ease). When the French side forced a 1-1 draw at Old Trafford, Ferguson's team was under pressure, but goals from Clayton Blackmore and Steve Bruce in the return leg put United through 3-1 on aggregate. Poland's Legia Warsaw proved less tricky semi-final opponents thanks to a 3-1 win in the opening away leg.

However, reaching another European final was tempered by a frustrating display in the League Cup final that had been billed as a contest between a current United manager (Ferguson) and his predecessor (Ron Atkinson). Wednesday, who were about to be promoted from the Second Division, won 1-0 and rumours about Ferguson's assistant Archie Knox leaving to join Glasgow Rangers did not help.

Now the season's success rested on the European Cup-Winners' Cup final against Barcelona and, with constant questions about playing against his former team, Mark Hughes fittingly scored both goals in a 2-1 win. By now, Knox had indeed left and Brian Kidd had been appointed as the new assistant to Ferguson, who had now won two trophies in as many seasons; this one being United's first European title since the glory days of 1968 and Sir Matt Busby. Ferguson's methods were clearly beginning to bear fruit, as United finished in a decent sixth position in the league; the future was looking very bright, with a young winger named Ryan Giggs having made his debut.

Final League Table Division One

		P	W	D	L	F	A	Pts
1	Arsenal **	38	24	13	1	74	18	83
2	Liverpool	38	23	7	8	77	40	76
3	Crystal Palace	38	20	9	9	50	41	69
4	Leeds United	38	19	7	12	65	47	64
5	Manchester City	38	17	11	10	64	53	62
6	MANCHESTER UNITED *	38	16	12	10	58	45	59
7	Wimbledon	38	14	14	10	53	46	56
8	Nottingham Forest	38	14	12	12	65	50	54
9	Everton	38	13	12	13	50	46	51
10	Tottenham Hotspur	38	11	16	11	51	50	49
11	Chelsea	38	13	10	15	58	69	49
12	Queens Park Rangers	38	12	10	16	44	53	46
13	Sheffield United	38	13	7	18	36	55	46
14	Southampton	38	12	9	17	58	69	45
15	Norwich City	38	13	6	19	41	64	45
16	Coventry City	38	11	11	16	42	49	44
17	Aston Villa	38	9	14	15	46	58	41
18	Luton Town	38	10	7	21	42	61	37
19	Sunderland	38	8	10	20	38	60	34
20	Derby County	38	5	9	24	37	75	24

* deducted 1 point for disciplinary reasons
** deducted 2 points for disciplinary reasons

Appearances

PLAYER	LGE	FAC	LC	ECWC	TOT
Pallister	36	3	9	9	57
Blackmore	35	3	9	9	56
McClair	34 (2)	3	9	9	55 (2)
Sealey	31	3	8	8	50
Irwin	33 (1)	3	7 (1)	6	49 (2)
Bruce	31	3	7	8	49
Hughes	29 (2)	3	9	7 (1)	48 (3)
Phelan	30 (3)	1	7 (1)	8	46 (4)
Webb	31 (1)	2	7	6	46 (1)
Ince	31	2	6	7	46
Sharpe	20 (3)	3	7	6 (2)	36 (5)
Robson	15 (2)	3	5	4	27 (2)
Donaghy	17 (8)	-	3 (4)	2 (3)	22 (15)
Wallace	13 (6)	- (1)	1 (3)	2 (1)	16 (11)
Martin	7 (7)	1	2 (2)	3 (2)	13 (11)
Robins	7 (12)	- (1)	- (3)	2 (1)	9 (17)
Beardsmore	5 (7)	-	1	1 (1)	7 (8)
Walsh	5	-	-	1	6
Anderson	1	-	1	1	3
Ferguson	2 (3)	-	-	-	2 (3)

PLAYER	LGE	FAC	LC	ECWC	TOT
Bosnich	2	-	-	-	2
Giggs	1 (1)	-	-	-	1 (1)
Kanchelskis	1	-	-	-	1
Leighton	-	-	1	-	1
Whitworth	1	-	-	-	1
Wrattan	- (2)	-	-	-	- (2)

Goalscorers

PLAYER	LGE	FAC	LC	ECWC	TOT
McClair	13	2	2	4	21
Hughes	10	2	6	3	21
Bruce	13	-	2	4	19
Sharpe	2	-	6	1	9
Blackmore	4	-	2	2	8
Robins	4	-	-	1	5
Webb	3	-	1	1	5
Wallace	3	-	1	-	4
Ince	3	-	-	-	3
Giggs	1	-	-	-	1
Phelan	1	-	-	-	1
Robson	1	-	-	-	1
Anderson	-	-	1	-	1
Pallister	-	-	1	-	1

Left: 16 September 1990. Despite the result, Denis Irwin denies Liverpool's John Barnes during a loss 4-0 at Anfield.

A League Cup win cannot outweigh late defeats that mean another missed championship

DURING THE OFF-SEASON there was more news from the boardroom than the training ground as the continual speculation of takeovers at United ended when chairman Martin Edwards announced the club would be floated as a public company and also spend £7 million of its new funds on redeveloping the Stretford End of the Old Trafford ground.

Alex Ferguson did make two key signings, however, both to strengthen his defence: goalkeeper Peter Schmeichel from Brondby in Denmark for £500,000 and Paul Parker, an England international right back from Queens Park Rangers. The effect was immediate as United conceded just three goals in their opening 14 matches in three different competitions.

Andrei Kanchelskis, who had made his debut in the penultimate league game of last season after signing from Shakhtar Donetsk in April was now a regular on the wing along with Ryan Giggs. United's attack looked more exciting than many a year and the chances of a first league championship in almost 25 years were real as United went undefeated in all competitions until mid-October.

Then the Red Devils suffered a 3-0 defeat in Spain against Atletico Madrid and also their first league defeat of the season – after 13 games – three days later at Sheffield Wednesday. The league loss meant United were replaced at the top of the table by Leeds United as October drew to a close and that first leg deficit against Atletico could not be recovered in the home leg, meaning the Reds had made a rather poor defence of their European trophy.

In mid-November, League Cup progress had been made, but it was the league that Ferguson wanted and Leeds were surprisingly the main challengers, as perennial giants like Liverpool and Arsenal had poor seasons.

Having drawn 1-1 against the Yorkshire team at home in August, the two teams managed the same score in the return in December, but United had now re-gained the league leadership. When United then beat Leeds 3-1 at Elland Road in the League Cup fifth round in January and again 1-0 in the third

round of the FA Cup a week later, it seemed that the Reds were too good for all their rivals. Even a loss on penalties to Southampton in the FA Cup fourth round in February did not seem to derail United, who still led the league by two points at the end of this month.

In early March, Middlesbrough were overcome 2-1 on aggregate in the League Cup semi-final, but Leeds refused to let United build up a significant lead in the league and, as April arrived, United were just one point ahead. Nottingham Forest were then defeated 1-0 in the League Cup final with a goal from Brian McClair and the final six games of the league season would decide the title.

After a win and a draw, Ferguson's team lost the next three matches; firstly, a 2-1 home loss to Forest, then 1-0 away to already-relegated West Ham United and then the final indignity of a defeat at Anfield to Liverpool 2-0, which handed the initiative to Leeds United, who duly won their next game and the league.

■ This is the last season of four English divisions operated by the Football League; the FA Premier League will come into existence next season.

■ The League Cup win is United's first in their history in their third appearance in the final.

■ Ryan Giggs collects the FA Youth Cup final trophy after a 6-3 aggregate win over Crystal Palace. Also in the team are David Beckham, Gary Neville, Nicky Butt and Keith Gillespie.

Above: Ukrainian winger Andrei Kanchelskis signed for £650,000 from Shakhtar Donetsk and played his first full season scoring eight goals.

Left: Scorer of the winning goal, Brian McClair with the League Cup trophy and team-mates Ryan Giggs (left) and Denis Irwin (right).

Final League Table Division One

		P	W	D	L	F	A	Pts
1	Leeds United	42	22	16	4	74	37	82
2	**MANCHESTER UNITED**	**42**	**21**	**15**	**6**	**63**	**33**	**78**
3	Sheffield Wednesday	42	21	12	9	62	49	75
4	Arsenal	42	19	15	8	81	46	72
5	Manchester City	42	20	10	12	61	48	70
6	Liverpool	42	16	16	10	47	40	64
7	Aston Villa	42	17	9	16	48	44	60
8	Nottingham Forest	42	16	11	15	60	58	59
9	Sheffield United	42	16	9	17	65	63	57
10	Crystal Palace	42	14	15	13	53	61	57
11	Queens Park Rangers	42	12	18	12	48	47	54
12	Everton	42	13	14	15	52	51	53
13	Wimbledon	42	13	14	15	53	53	53
14	Chelsea	42	13	14	15	50	60	53
15	Tottenham Hotspur	42	15	7	20	58	63	52
16	Southampton	42	14	10	18	39	55	52
17	Oldham Athletic	42	14	9	19	63	67	51
18	Norwich City	42	11	12	19	47	63	45
19	Coventry City	42	11	11	20	35	44	44
20	Luton Town	42	10	12	20	38	71	42
21	Notts County	42	10	10	22	40	62	40
22	West Ham United	42	9	11	22	37	59	38

Appearances

PLAYER	LGE	FAC	LC	ECWC	TOT
McClair	41 (1)	3	8	4	56 (1)
Schmeichel	40	3	6	3	52
Pallister	37 (3)	3	8	3 (1)	51 (4)
Hughes	38 (1)	2 (1)	6	4	50 (2)
Irwin	37 (1)	3	7	2	49 (1)
Bruce	37	1	7	4	49
Ince	31 (2)	3	6 (1)	3	43 (3)
Giggs	32 (6)	2 (1)	6 (2)	1	41 (9)
Webb	29 (2)	3	6	3	41 (2)
Robson	26 (1)	2	5 (1)	3	36 (2)
Parker	24 (2)	3	6	2	35 (2)
Kanchelskis	28 (6)	2	4	1	35 (6)
Blackmore	19 (14)	1	4 (1)	1	25 (15)
Donaghy	16 (4)	2	3 (1)	-	21 (5)
Phelan	14 (4)	-	2 (1)	4	20 (5)
Sharpe	8 (6)	- (1)	1 (3)	-	9 (10)
Walsh	2	-	1	1	4
Robins	1 (1)	-	- (3)	2 (1)	3 (5)
Martin	- (1)	-	1	1 (2)	2 (3)
Ferguson	2 (2)	-	-	-	2 (2)
Beardsmore	-	-	-	1 (2)	1 (2)
Wallace	-	-	-	1 (1)	1 (1)

PLAYER	LGE	FAC	LC	ECWC	TOT
Wilkinson	-	-	1	-	1

Goalscorers

PLAYER	LGE	FAC	LC	ECWC	TOT
McClair	18	1	4	1	24
Hughes	11	1	-	2	14
Kanchelskis	5	1	2	-	8
Giggs	4	-	3	-	7
Bruce	5	-	1	-	6
Robson	4	-	1	-	5
Irwin	4	-	-	-	4
Blackmore	3	-	1	-	4
Ince	3	-	-	-	3
Webb	3	-	-	-	3
Sharpe	1	-	1	-	2
Robins	-	-	2	-	2
Pallister	1	-	-	-	1
own goal	1	-	-	-	1

Left: 12 April 1992. Alex Ferguson congratulates Ryan Giggs and Gary Pallister at the Professional Footballers' Association Awards dinner.

FOOTBALL LEAGUE DIVISION ONE: RUNNERS-UP

FA CUP: LOSE TO SOUTHAMPTON (2-2 AET; 2-4 ON PENALTY KICKS) IN 4TH ROUND REPLAY

LEAGUE CUP: WINNERS. 12 APRIL 1992. WEMBLEY, LONDON. BEAT NOTTINGHAM FOREST 1-0 McCLAIR 14'

EUROPEAN CUP-WINNERS CUP: LOSE TO ATLETICO MADRID (1-4 ON AGGREGATE) IN 2ND ROUND

EUROPEAN SUPER CUP: WINNERS. 19 NOVEMBER 1991. OLD TRAFFORD, MANCHESTER. BEAT RED STAR BELGRADE 1-0 McCLAIR 67'

1992/93

The 26-year wait for another league title is finally over in the first English Premiership season

AT THE END of last season, United had passed the milestone of a quarter of a century since the club's previous league title, however, this inaugural season of the FA Premiership would provide unprecedented glamour and money for English league football, something the Reds fans would only care about if it would also provide them with the new championship trophy. Capturing this prize was becoming all-important to Alex Ferguson and his team, but nothing looked more unlikely as United started the league season in topsy-turvy style: they lost their two opening games, then were held at home by Ipswich Town before winning their next five and drawing the five after that.

This was basically the same team that had all-but won the league last year, however this inconsistency was in danger of damaging their title prospects. Then in September in the opening round of the UEFA Cup, Torpedo Moscow eliminated United on penalties after two goalless draws, and in October Aston Villa beat the Red Devils 1-0 in the League Cup third round. Two league defeats immediately after that latest cup exit and Ferguson's team was well behind league leaders Blackburn Rovers, now managed by old adversary Kenny Dalglish.

Then in late November, with his team still looking lacklustre, Ferguson took an innocuous phone call from Leeds United enquiring about signing Denis Irwin. The Reds manager dismissed the request and, almost as an afterthought asked about the availability of Eric Cantona, the mercurial French forward who had helped Leeds win the league title last season.

When Ferguson was told Cantona was available, he immediately made a deal to bring the player to Old Trafford for just £1 million. The inclusion of Cantona in an already-fine United team changed the course of this season and, some would argue, many others to come. The Frenchman came on at half-time in the Manchester derby at Old Trafford for his debut appearance on 6 December and helped the Reds win 2-1. He then sparked a run that saw the team lose only twice for the rest of the season including a seven-game winning streak to finish off the campaign.

It was April before United reached the top of the table, leaving Aston Villa, Norwich City and Blackburn Rovers in their wake, but it was a position that they never relinquished and eventually they took the title by a 10-point margin with two games to play.

United were not playing on the day Villa lost to hand them the title and Ferguson was told of his triumph in a rather unglamorous way, after coming off the golf course. Nevertheless, United won English football's top accolade after waiting 26 years; it would be the eighth league championship in the club's history; and Ferguson had fulfilled the club's wishes after his seventh season. It had been an ordinary season in other competitions (losing a fifth round FA Cup match at Sheffield United was the team's best cup showing this year) and yet securing the elusive league title meant so much more.

- Gary Neville and David Beckham both make their debuts for United within a week of each other in September, against Torpedo Moscow and Brighton and Hove Albion respectively. Keith Gillespie and Nicky Butt would also play their first United games this season.

- The only significant pre-season signing is 23-year-old Dion Dublin from Cambridge United for £1 million in early August.

- Eric Cantona scores his first goal for United on 19 December in a 1-1 draw against Chelsea at Stamford Bridge.

Above: 3 May 1993. Title winners but fashion losers? A proud moment for Paul Ince and Ryan Giggs.

Right: 3 May 1993. With the title already won, Mark Hughes shoots at the Blackburn Rovers goal during United's penultimate league fixture, which they won 3-1.

Final League Table Premiership

		P	W	D	L	F	A	Pts
1	**MANCHESTER UNITED**	**42**	**24**	**12**	**6**	**67**	**31**	**84**
2	Aston Villa	42	21	11	10	57	40	74
3	Norwich City	42	21	9	12	61	65	72
4	Blackburn Rovers	42	20	11	11	68	46	71
5	Queens Park Rangers	42	17	12	13	63	55	63
6	Liverpool	42	16	11	15	62	55	59
7	Sheffield Wednesday	42	15	14	13	55	51	59
8	Tottenham Hotspur	42	16	11	15	60	66	59
9	Manchester City	42	15	12	15	56	51	57
10	Arsenal	42	15	11	16	40	38	56
11	Chelsea	42	14	14	14	51	54	56
12	Wimbledon	42	14	12	16	56	55	54
13	Everton	42	15	8	19	53	55	53
14	Sheffield United	42	14	10	18	54	53	52
15	Coventry City	42	13	13	16	52	57	52
16	Ipswich Town	42	12	16	14	50	55	52
17	Leeds United	42	12	15	15	57	62	51
18	Southampton	42	13	11	18	54	61	50
19	Oldham Athletic	42	13	10	19	63	74	49
20	Crystal Palace	42	11	16	15	48	61	49
21	Middlesbrough	42	11	11	20	54	75	44
22	Nottingham Forest	42	10	10	22	41	62	40

Appearances

PLAYER	PREM	FAC	LC	UC	TOT
Bruce	42	3	3	2	50
Pallister	42	3	3	2	50
McClair	41 (1)	3	3	2	49 (1)
Hughes	41	2	3	2	48
Irwin	40	3	3	2	48
Schmeichel	42	3	2	1	48
Ince	41	2	3	1	47
Giggs	40 (1)	2	2	1	45 (1)
Parker	31	3	2	- (1)	36 (1)
Sharpe	27	3	-	-	30
Cantona	21 (1)	1	-	-	22 (1)
Kanchelskis	14 (13)	1	2 (1)	1	18 (14)
Ferguson	15	-	1	-	16
Blackmore	12 (2)	- (1)	1	1	14 (3)
Phelan	5 (6)	2	-	1	8 (6)
Robson	5 (9)	- (1)	1	- (1)	6 (11)
Wallace	- (2)	1	1	2	4 (2)
Dublin	3 (4)	-	-	-	3 (4)
Webb	- (1)	-	1	2	3 (1)
Martin	-	-	1	1	2
Walsh	-	-	1	1	2
Gillespie	-	1 (1)	-	-	1 (1)

PLAYER	PREM	FAC	LC	UC	TOT
Beckham	-	-	- (1)	-	- (1)
Butt	- (1)	-	-	-	- (1)
Neville	-	-	- (1)	- (1)	- (1)

Goalscorers

PLAYER	PREM	FAC	LC	UC	TOT
Hughes	15	-	1	-	16
Giggs	9	2	-	-	11
Cantona	9	-	-	-	9
McClair	9	-	-	-	9
Ince	6	-	-	-	6
Bruce	5	-	-	-	5
Irwin	5	-	-	-	5
Kanchelskis	3	-	-	-	3
Dublin	1	-	-	-	1
Pallister	1	-	-	-	1
Parker	1	-	-	-	1
Robson	1	-	-	-	1
Sharpe	1	-	-	-	1
Gillespie	-	1	-	-	1
Phelan	-	1	-	-	1
Wallace	-	-	1	-	1
own goal	1	-	-	-	1

Left: Captain Steve Bruce leads out his team as champions for the first time in 26 years.

United win their first league and cup double, but the club grieves at Busby's death

1993/94

ALEX FERGUSON WAS now in a position of strength at the club and was not about to allow complacency to slip in just because a single league title had been won on his watch. Instead, he bought midfielder Roy Keane from Nottingham Forest and told his team to kick on and win more trophies. That was achieved in the opening match, the FA Charity Shield, which United won on penalties.

The Red Devils then roared out of the blocks in an attempt to retain their league title. Plenty of wins and plenty of goals were coming in the league right from the start of the campaign and it took United just four matches to climb to the top of the table, after a 2-1 win at Aston Villa. The squad now looked formidable, with a host of natural leaders of the team even though club captain Bryan Robson would play only the occasional match because of injury.

So it was a huge surprise when, after beating Honved of Hungary in the opening round of the European Cup, United slipped up against Turkish outsiders Galatasaray. A 3-3 draw at Old Trafford sounded the alarm bells. Then in the return leg, with Galatasaray fans raising banners stating "Welcome to hell" and with United players suffering physical abuse from local policemen in the tunnel, the Turkish champions held on to a 0-0 draw in their home stadium to put out one of the tournament favourites before the financially lucrative group stage of the competition. To make matters worse, Eric Cantona was even sent off during the chaotic scenes at the end of the ill-tempered game.

United, however, were more than a match for the rest of England as all-comers were sent to defeat and everything remained rosy in all three domestic competitions well into the New Year. In fact, by the end of 1993, United were 14 points clear in the race for a second successive league title. But on 20 January, the season took on a different hue when legendary former manager Sir Matt Busby died aged 84.

Nevertheless, United marched forward on all fronts. At the end of March, United reached the League Cup final and again ex-manager Ron Atkinson surprisingly got the better of the Reds; his Aston Villa team won 3-1. However, this match marked a low point in terms of club discipline as Andrei Kanchelskis was the latest to be dismissed. Cantona's sending off in the European game had prompted close press scrutiny and in January Ferguson began a row with BBC football pundit Jimmy Hill over accusations of vicious play by the Frenchman in a match against Norwich. Then in March Cantona was sent off again, this time for a stamp on the chest of a Swindon Town player and a crisis seemed to be looming.

But the team rallied after the League Cup disappointment and overcame a stubborn Oldham Athletic in the FA Cup semi-final to offer a chance of a very rare league and FA Cup double. The league championship was wrapped up with three games to go and then Chelsea were easily beaten 4-0 in the FA Cup final.

- United's league championship and FA Cup final victory makes them only the fourth club in the 20th century to win the double after Tottenham Hotspur, Arsenal and Liverpool.

- Eric Cantona wins the Professional Footballers' Association Player of the Year trophy and Alex Ferguson is presented with the Premier League Manager of the Year award.

- Club captain Bryan Robson leaves United at the end of the season to become player-manager of Middlesbrough. He has made 461 appearances and scored 99 goals.

Above: The all-action style of Roy Keane who joined this season was perfect for the Red Devils' midfield.

Left: The trophy belongs to talisman Eric Cantona who scored two goals in the FA Cup final.

Left: A view of the tributes to Sir Matt Busby at the entrance to Old Trafford. The former manager died on 20 January 1994 aged 84.

Final League Table Premiership

		P	W	D	L	F	A	Pts
1	MANCHESTER UNITED	42	27	11	4	80	38	92
2	Blackburn Rovers	42	25	9	8	63	36	84
3	Newcastle United	42	23	8	11	82	41	77
4	Arsenal	42	18	17	7	53	28	71
5	Leeds United	42	18	16	8	65	39	70
6	Wimbledon	42	18	11	13	56	53	65
7	Sheffield Wednesday	42	16	16	10	76	54	64
8	Liverpool	42	17	9	16	59	55	60
9	Queens Park Rangers	42	16	12	14	62	61	60
10	Aston Villa	42	15	12	15	46	50	57
11	Coventry City	42	14	14	14	43	45	56
12	Norwich City	42	12	17	13	65	61	53
13	West Ham United	42	13	13	16	47	58	52
14	Chelsea	42	13	12	17	49	53	51
15	Tottenham Hotspur	42	11	12	19	54	59	45
16	Manchester City	42	9	18	15	38	49	45
17	Everton	42	12	8	22	42	63	44
18	Southampton	42	12	7	23	49	66	43
19	Ipswich Town	42	9	16	17	35	58	43
20	Sheffield United	42	8	18	16	42	60	42
21	Oldham Athletic	42	9	13	20	42	68	40
22	Swindon Town	42	5	15	22	47	100	30

Appearances

PLAYER	PREM	FAC	LC	CL	TOT
Bruce	41	7	8 (1)	4	60 (1)
Irwin	42	7	8 (1)	3	60 (1)
Pallister	41	7	9	3	60
Schmeichel	40	7	8	4	59
Parker	39 (1)	7	6	3	55 (1)
Ince	39	7	5	4	55
Hughes	36	7	8	2	53
Giggs	32 (6)	7	6 (2)	4	49 (8)
Keane	34 (3)	6	6 (1)	3	49 (4)
Cantona	34	5	5	4	48
Kanchelskis	28 (3)	6	9	-	43 (3)
Sharpe	26 (4)	1 (2)	2 (2)	4	33 (8)
McClair	12 (14)	1 (4)	6 (1)	-	19 (19)
Robson	10 (5)	1 (1)	5	4	20 (6)
Martin	1	-	3	1 (1)	5 (1)
Phelan	1 (1)	-	2	1 (3)	4 (4)
Dublin	1 (4)	1 (1)	1 (1)	- (1)	3 (7)
Ferguson	1 (2)	-	1 (1)	-	2 (3)
Walsh	2 (1)	-	-	-	2 (1)
Neville	1	-	-	- (1)	1 (1)
Sealey	-	- (1)	1	-	1 (1)
McKee	1	-	-	-	1

PLAYER	PREM	FAC	LC	CL	TOT
Butt	- (1)	- (1)	-	-	- (2)
Thornley	- (1)	-	-	-	- (1)

Goalscorers

PLAYER	PREM	FAC	LC	CL	TOT
Cantona	18	4	1	2	25
Hughes	12	4	5	-	21
Giggs	13	1	3	-	17
Sharpe	9	-	2	-	11
Kanchelskis	6	3	1	-	10
Ince	8	1	-	-	9
Keane	5	1	-	2	8
Bruce	3	-	2	2	7
McClair	1	1	4	-	6
Irwin	2	2	-	-	4
Robson	1	1	-	1	3
Dublin	-	-	1	-	2
Pallister	1	-	-	-	1
own goal	-	-	-	1	1

PREMIERSHIP: CHAMPIONS	FA CUP: WINNERS. 14 MAY 1994. WEMBLEY, LONDON. BEAT CHELSEA 4-0 CANTONA 60' & 66', HUGHES 69', McCLAIR 90'
	LEAGUE CUP: RUNNERS-UP. 27 MARCH 1994. WEMBLEY, LONDON. LOST TO ASTON VILLA 1-3 ATKINSON 25', SAUNDERS 75' & 90', HUGHES 82'
	UEFA EUROPEAN CUP: LOSE TO GALATASARAY (3-3 ON AWAY GOALS) IN 2ND ROUND
	FA CHARITY SHIELD: WINNERS. 7 AUGUST 1993. WEMBLEY, LONDON. BEAT ARSENAL 1-1 (A.E.T) UNITED WON 5-4 ON PENALTY KICKS

1994/95

- Striker Dion Dublin is sold to Coventry City in September for £2 million after starting just six games in two seasons with United.

- Eric Cantona's sending off against Crystal Palace is his fifth dismissal while wearing a United shirt.

- Eric Cantona's press conference following the Crystal Palace kung fu kick is when he delivers his most famous quote: "When the seagulls follow the trawler it's because they think sardines will be thrown into the sea."

- Although Blackburn Rovers pip United to the title, the champions are beaten in both their games against the Reds, 4-2 at Ewood Park and then 1-0 at Old Trafford.

Above: A United fan shows her support for Eric Cantona.

Right: 20 May 1995. Ryan Giggs in despair on the Wembley pitch after the FA Cup final 1-0 loss.

Opposite: 17 December 1994. Eric Cantona catches the referee's attention during a 2-1 loss against Nottingham Forest.

Cantona in disgrace and United suffer the consequences of his actions both on and off the field

THIS SEASON BEGAN with Premier League referees being told to clamp down on violent tackles and dissent from players and, ironically, it would be a season for United that was dominated by a violent incident that no one could have predicted.

Alex Ferguson's team had another new addition – David May joined from Blackburn Rovers in July for £1.2 million and then played against his former team in the Charity Shield game at Wembley in August. United won 2-0.

The league season began just as promisingly, with three wins in the first four games, although Newcastle United managed by Kevin Keegan and Blackburn Rovers led by Kenny Dalglish emerged as early leaders. In Europe, United were placed directly into the group stage of the newly re-named Champions League this season without any pre-qualifying games and faced old rivals Barcelona of Spain and Turkey's Galatasaray plus Gothenburg of Sweden. The Reds began brightly with a 4-2 win at home to the Swedes, but then drew against Galatasaray and Barcelona before the Spanish champions beat them 4-0 in the Nou Camp. Another loss, this one to Gothenburg three weeks later in December, meant United failed to progress to the knockout stage of the competition.

By this time the Red Devils had also been knocked out of the League Cup after a 2-0 defeat at Newcastle and, while they had led the league at one time in November, they ended the year three points behind Blackburn. The prospects of more silverware were not looking very rosy.

An FA Cup run began innocently in early January with a 2-0 win over Sheffield United and then Alex Ferguson made another shock raid into the transfer market by signing Newcastle's star striker Andy Cole in a deal valued at £7 million. It seemed like a move guaranteed to turn United's season around, but in an away league match at Crystal Palace on 25 January, United's season was sent into a different direction and it was another Eric Cantona incident that caused the change.

The Frenchman had just been sent off at Selhurst Park in a rather angry match against the London team and he was leaving the pitch as normal when a Palace fan rushed down the aisle of the stand to hurl abuse at the player. This, on its own, was not an unusual occurrence for a player shown the red card, but what then happened shocked the football world.

Instead of ignoring the fan's finger pointing and his foul language, Cantona jumped into the crowd and landed a kung fu-style kick on the chest of the Palace supporter. The incident was caught by the TV cameras and the press, who not surprisingly, went into overdrive the next day calling for Cantona to be banned from football for life.

Eventually, the police charged the Frenchman with common assault and, after pleading guilty, Cantona was sentenced by magistrates to two weeks in prison. The sentence was another shock for both player and club and an immediate appeal was instigated. The matter calmed down slightly when Cantona was released on bail and later his sentence was reduced to 120 hours' community service.

Football punishment was stern as the FA suspended the player until 30 September 1995, more than a month into the following season. Under such a media spotlight, United's attempt to win a third consecutive title failed when they could only draw 1-1 with West Ham United on the final day of the season. To make the season utterly forgettable for Reds fans, the team without Cantona and the cup-tied Cole then lost 1-0 to Everton in the FA Cup final.

Final League Table Premiership

		P	W	D	L	F	A	Pts
1	Blackburn Rovers	42	27	8	7	80	39	89
2	MANCHESTER UNITED	42	26	10	6	77	28	88
3	Nottingham Forest	42	22	11	9	72	43	77
4	Liverpool	42	21	11	10	65	37	74
5	Leeds United	42	20	13	9	59	38	73
6	Newcastle United	42	20	12	10	67	47	72
7	Tottenham Hotspur	42	16	14	12	66	58	62
8	Queens Park Rangers	42	17	9	16	61	59	60
9	Wimbledon	42	15	11	16	48	65	56
10	Southampton	42	12	18	12	61	63	54
11	Chelsea	42	13	15	14	50	55	54
12	Arsenal	42	13	12	17	52	49	51
13	Sheffield Wednesday	42	13	12	17	49	57	51
14	West Ham United	42	13	11	18	44	48	50
15	Everton	42	11	17	14	44	51	50
16	Coventry City	42	12	14	16	44	62	50
17	Manchester City	42	12	13	17	53	64	49
18	Aston Villa	42	11	15	16	51	56	48
19	Crystal Palace	42	11	12	19	34	49	45
20	Norwich City	42	10	13	19	37	54	43
21	Leicester City	42	6	11	25	45	80	29
22	Ipswich Town	42	7	6	29	36	93	27

Appearances

PLAYER	PREM	FAC	LC	CL	TOT
Pallister	42	7	2	6	57
Irwin	40	7	2	5	54
Ince	36	6	-	5	47
McClair	35 (5)	6 (1)	3	2	46 (6)
Bruce	35	5	1	5 (1)	46 (1)
Hughes	33 (1)	6	-	5	44 (1)
Schmeichel	32	7	-	3	42
Giggs	29	6 (1)	-	3	38 (1)
Sharpe	26 (2)	6 (1)	- (2)	3	35 (5)
Keane	23 (2)	6 (1)	1	4	34 (3)
Kanchelskis	25 (5)	2 (1)	-	5	32 (6)
Cantona	21	1	-	2	24
Neville G	16 (2)	4	2 (1)	1 (1)	23 (4)
Butt	11 (11)	3 (1)	3	5 (1)	22 (13)
May	15 (4)	1	2	4	22 (4)
Cole	17 (1)	-	-	-	17 (1)
Walsh	10	-	3	3	16
Scholes	6 (11)	1 (2)	3	- (2)	10 (15)
Davies	3 (2)	-	3	2	8 (2)
Beckham	2 (2)	1 (1)	3	1	7 (3)
Gillespie	3 (6)	-	3	-	6 (6)
Parker	1 (1)	-	-	2 (1)	3 (2)

PLAYER	PREM	FAC	LC	CL	TOT
Neville P	1 (1)	1	-	-	2 (1)
O'Kane	-	1	1 (1)	-	2 (1)
Casper	-	-	1	-	1
Tomlinson	-	-	- (2)	-	- (2)
Pilkington	- (1)	-	-	-	- (1)

2 April 1995. Andy Cole bursts through the Leeds United defence in a 0-0 draw.

Goalscorers

PLAYER	PREM	FAC	LC	CL	TOT
Kanchelskis	14	-	-	1	15
Cantona	12	1	-	-	13
Cole	12	-	-	-	12
Hughes	8	2	-	2	12
McClair	5	2	1	-	8
Scholes	5	-	2	-	7
Sharpe	3	1	-	2	6
Irwin	2	4	-	-	6
Ince	5	-	-	-	5
Bruce	2	2	-	-	4
Pallister	2	2	-	-	4
Giggs	1	1	-	2	4
Keane	2	-	-	1	3
May	2	-	1	-	3
Butt	1	-	-	-	1
Gillespie	1	-	-	-	1
Beckham	-	-	-	1	1
Davies	-	-	-	1	1
own goals	-	1	-	1	2

PREMIERSHIP: RUNNERS-UP	FA CUP: RUNNERS-UP. 20 MAY 1995. WEMBLEY, LONDON. LOST TO EVERTON 0-1 RIDEOUT 30'	LEAGUE CUP: LOSE TO NEWCASTLE UNITED (0-2) IN 3RD ROUND	UEFA CHAMPIONS LEAGUE: LOSE IN FIRST GROUP STAGE

FA CHARITY SHIELD: WINNERS. 14 AUGUST 1994. WEMBLEY, LONDON. BEAT BLACKBURN ROVERS 2-0 CANTONA 22', INCE 81'

1995/96

- Before the season begins, Eric Cantona announces he will leave English football and cancel his contract with United. Two days later he agrees to stay at Old Trafford.

- Eric Cantona wins the two major Player of the Year awards from the Professional Footballers' Association and the Football Writers' Association.

- United's tenth league title is won in the first season of the newly aligned 20-team Premiership; the number of clubs was reduced from 22 to match the other major European leagues.

Above: 13 April 1996. Peter Schmeichel played in 45 games this season, more than any United player. A 3-1 loss at Southampton in this match was a rare disappointment.

Right: 28 April 1996. Ferguson's reliance on youth would ultimately pay dividends, and no more so than in the burgeoning career of Paul Scholes, who would score in this 5-0 thumping of Nottingham Forest at Old Trafford.

Despite major player exits and a warning about United's "kids", a league and cup double is won again

THERE WAS NOTHING ordinary about the build-up to this season: if Eric Cantona's suspension until the end of September was not enough of a story, Alex Ferguson created more headlines during the summer by dispatching three star players to new clubs. Paul Ince was sold to Inter Milan, Andrei Kanchelskis went to Everton and Mark Hughes left United for the second time, on this occasion to Chelsea.

The £12.5 million in income did not placate the fanbase, who saw no incoming players and the possible transfer of Cantona as evidence that United were set for a season of decline. Not only that, but the North Stand building project that also got underway in the summer was going to cost £28 million and meant that Ferguson would probably have to rely for a couple of seasons on his younger, inexperienced players to fill the gap left by established stars.

An opening day 3-1 loss to Aston Villa – with five members of the successful 1992 youth team in the 13-man squad – simply confirmed the fans' worst thoughts and the BBC pundit Alan Hansen famously commented: "You'll never win anything with kids." Although United floundered to defeats in the opening rounds of both the UEFA Cup against Rotor Volgograd of Russia and then, more embarrassingly, to York City in the League Cup, Ferguson's young team grew in confidence quickly and their league form was excellent.

When Cantona returned on 1 October in a home game against Liverpool and set up the first goal and before scoring the second with a penalty in a 2-2 draw, the Reds suddenly looked like a well-balanced team mixing youth and experience. However, Newcastle United were even more impressive in the early months of the league season and continually kept United in second place.

As the Red Devils began an FA Cup run in January with a win over Sunderland after a replay, the team hit top form. Reading were beaten in the fourth round and then Manchester City in the fifth. United beat Southampton 2-0 in the next round in mid-March and confirmed their excellent form by climbing to the top of the league table five days later after a 1-1 draw against Queens Park Rangers.

An impressive semi-final win over Chelsea in the FA Cup followed at the end of the month and Newcastle began to falter in the league; another league and cup double now looked possible. Ferguson then got involved with some high profile mind games with his counterpart at Newcastle, Kevin Keegan. The Scot had mused about whether Newcastle's late-season opponents might not try 100% against them, which prompted Keegan to react emotionally on a live Sky Sports post-match interview after beating Leeds, with two more games left, saying: "You simply don't say things like that in this game...I would love it if we beat them now, absolutely love it."

Ferguson's young team went to Middlesbrough on the final day of the season and completed a 3-0 win to take the title and six days later silenced every critic in the land by beating Liverpool 1-0 in the FA Cup final to achieve a second league and cup double in three seasons.

Final League Table Premiership

		P	W	D	L	F	A	Pts
1	**MANCHESTER UNITED**	38	25	7	6	73	35	82
2	Newcastle United	38	24	6	8	66	37	78
3	Liverpool	38	20	11	7	70	34	71
4	Aston Villa	38	18	9	11	52	35	63
5	Arsenal	38	17	12	9	49	32	63
6	Everton	38	17	10	11	64	44	61
7	Blackburn Rovers	38	18	7	13	61	47	61
8	Tottenham Hotspur	38	16	13	9	50	38	61
9	Nottingham Forest	38	15	13	10	50	54	58
10	West Ham United	38	14	9	15	43	52	51
11	Chelsea	38	12	14	12	46	44	50
12	Middlesbrough	38	11	10	17	35	50	43
13	Leeds United	38	12	7	19	40	57	43
14	Wimbledon	38	10	11	17	55	70	41
15	Sheffield Wednesday	38	10	10	18	48	61	40
16	Coventry City	38	8	14	16	42	60	38
17	Southampton	38	9	11	18	34	52	38
18	Manchester City	38	9	11	18	33	58	38
19	Queens Park Rangers	38	9	6	23	38	57	33
20	Bolton Wanderers	38	8	5	25	39	71	29

Appearances

PLAYER	PREM	FAC	LC	UC	TOT
Schmeichel	36	6	1	2	45
Giggs	30 (3)	7	2	2	41 (3)
Cole	32 (2)	7	1	1	41 (2)
Butt	31 (1)	7	-	2	40 (1)
Irwin	31	6	1	1	39
Bruce	30	5	1 (1)	2	38 (1)
Keane	29	7	- (1)	2	38 (1)
Cantona	30	7	1	-	38
Neville G	30 (1)	5 (1)	1	1	37 (2)
Beckham	26 (7)	3	2	2	33 (7)
Sharpe	21 (10)	4 (2)	2	2	29 (12)
Neville P	21 (3)	6 (1)	1 (1)	1	29 (5)
Pallister	21	3	2	2	28
Scholes	16 (10)	- (2)	1	1 (1)	18 (13)
McClair	12 (10)	-	1	-	13 (10)
May	11 (5)	2	-	-	13 (5)
Parker	5 (1)	1 (1)	1	- (1)	7 (3)
Pilkington	2 (1)	1	1	-	4 (1)
Davies	1 (5)	-	1	- (1)	2 (6)
Cooke	1 (3)	-	1 (1)	- (1)	2 (5)
Prunier	2	-	-	-	2
O'Kane	- (1)	-	-	1	1 (1)
McGibbon	-	-	1	-	1
Thornley	- (1)	-	-	-	- (1)

Top goalscorer and top manager - Eric Cantona and Alex Ferguson with the double trophies.

Goalscorers

PLAYER	PREM	FAC	LC	UC	TOT
Cantona	14	5	-	-	19
Scholes	10	1	2	1	14
Cole	11	2	-	-	13
Giggs	11	1	-	-	12
Beckham	7	1	-	-	8
Keane	6	-	-	-	6
Sharpe	4	2	-	-	6
McClair	3	-	-	-	3
Butt	2	1	-	-	3
Bruce	1	-	-	-	1
Irwin	1	-	-	-	1
May	1	-	-	-	1
Pallister	1	-	-	-	1
Cooke	-	-	1	-	1
Parker	-	1	-	-	1
Schmeichel	-	-	-	1	1
own goal	1	-	-	-	1

The youth policy bears more fruit with another championship but European glory is again thwarted

1996/97

THE TRANSFORMATION OF the United team over the past 18 months was now complete. Eric Cantona had experienced a remarkable redemption and players such as Ryan Giggs, David Beckham, Paul Scholes, Gary Neville and Nicky Butt had risen from youth team hopefuls to title winners and would all soon be regular internationals. Alex Ferguson was given a new, improved deal during the off-season after speculation that he was unhappy with his current contract.

The contract negotiations did not distract Ferguson from enriching his team with more transfer activity; he brought in Ole Gunnar Solskjaer from Norway and Czech star Karel Poborsky as well as Ronny Johnsen and Jordi Cruyff. However, his attempt to sign Alan Shearer from Blackburn Rovers for £12 million during the off-season was thwarted and the England striker eventually returned to his Geordie homeland to play for Newcastle United a few weeks later.

Still, the bright future of a new generation of 'Babes' was underlined when Newcastle United were thrashed 4-0 in the FA Charity Shield at Wembley and then Beckham scored an astounding goal from the halfway line in the opening league match against Wimbledon. There were some stumbles in the late autumn, firstly when an inspired Newcastle team won 5-0 at St James' Park in mid-October and then lowly Southampton managed a 6-3 victory at The Dell six days later and dropped United to fifth in the league table.

Immediately after those defeats, the Reds played their next four games at Old Trafford and lost three of them. Many pundits put the problems down to an already heavy fixture list: seven games in September and six more in October, including two tough Champions League games at Juventus in Italy and Fenerbahce in Turkey. A League Cup exit at Leicester City on 27 November added to a mood of despondency hanging over the team, but it proved to be a watershed moment.

The same opponents, Leicester, were beaten 3-1 at home three days later and progress to the knockout stages of the Champions League was then secured for the first time with an impressive 2-0 victory in Austria against Rapid Vienna.

The New Year started impressively with the Reds continuing a long unbeaten league run that culminated in United topping the table by the end of January; only an FA Cup replay loss to Wimbledon in the fourth round of the competition dampened the spirits in early February. In March, United beat Porto of Portugal 4-0 on aggregate to set up a Champions League semi-final against Borussia Dortmund.

Meanwhile, the charge towards a fourth league championship in five years continued unabated as United stayed in top spot into April. The first leg of the semi against Dortmund ended in a 1-0 defeat and, in the return leg a fortnight later, United were unimpressive in front of goal and lost again by the same 1-0 scoreline. With only the league title now to fight for, the FA and the Premier League forced United to play their final four games of the season in just eight days.

Despite this, the championship was won with two games remaining, although the eventual seven-point gap between United and second placed Newcastle United did not reflect the tension of another close-fought title race.

- Lee Sharpe, the scorer of several memorable goals in his eight seasons at Old Trafford, is transferred to Leeds United just before the start of the season for £4.5 million.

- Stan Pearson whose career spanned the 1930s, 40s and early 50s dies on 20 November aged 78; he scored 148 goals in 10 seasons.

- On 30 October, United are beaten at Old Trafford for the first time in 40 years of European competition when the Turkish side Fenerbahce win a Champions League group game 1-0.

- When Chelsea win 2-1 at Old Trafford on 2 November it broke a two-year unbeaten run at home for United in Premiership games.

Above: Steve Bruce and his fellow players protest to the referee during the Premiership match against Leeds United.

Left: 25 January 1997. Ryan Giggs in action during the FA Cup fourth round tie between United and Wimbledon.

Final League Table Premiership

		P	W	D	L	F	A	Pts
1	MANCHESTER UNITED	38	21	12	5	76	44	75
2	Newcastle United	38	19	11	8	73	40	68
3	Arsenal	38	19	11	8	62	32	68
4	Liverpool	38	19	11	8	62	37	68
5	Aston Villa	38	17	10	11	47	34	61
6	Chelsea	38	16	11	11	58	55	59
7	Sheffield Wednesday	38	14	15	9	50	51	57
8	Wimbledon	38	15	11	12	49	46	56
9	Leicester City	38	12	11	15	46	54	47
10	Tottenham Hotspur	38	13	7	18	44	51	46
11	Leeds United	38	11	13	14	28	38	46
12	Derby County	38	11	13	14	45	58	46
13	Blackburn Rovers	38	9	15	14	42	43	42
14	West Ham United	38	10	12	16	39	48	42
15	Everton	38	10	12	16	44	57	42
16	Southampton	38	10	11	17	50	56	41
17	Coventry City	38	9	14	15	38	54	41
18	Sunderland	38	10	10	18	35	53	40
19	Middlesbrough *	38	10	12	16	51	60	39
20	Nottingham Forest	38	6	16	16	31	59	34

* deducted 3 points for failure to fulfil fixture

Appearances

PLAYER	PREM	FAC	LC	CL	TOT
Cantona	36	3	-	10	49
Schmeichel	36	3	-	9	48
Beckham	33 (3)	2	-	10	45 (3)
Neville G	30 (1)	3	1	10	44 (1)
Irwin	29 (2)	3	-	8	40 (2)
May	28 (1)	1	2	7 (1)	38 (2)
Johnsen	26 (5)	2	-	9	37 (5)
Pallister	27	1	-	8	36
Giggs	25 (1)	3	-	6 (1)	34 (2)
Solskjaer	25 (8)	- (3)	-	8 (2)	33 (13)
Butt	24 (2)	-	-	8 (1)	32 (3)
Keane	21	3	2	6	32
Poborsky	15 (7)	2	-	3 (3)	22 (10)
Scholes	16 (8)	2	2	- (4)	20 (12)
Neville P	15 (3)	-	1	2 (2)	18 (5)
Cruyff	11 (5)	-	1	3 (1)	15 (6)
Cole	10 (10)	2 (1)	-	2 (3)	14 (14)
McClair	4 (15)	1 (2)	2	- (3)	7 (20)
Clegg	3 (1)	1	1	-	5 (1)
van der Gouw	2	-	2	1	5

PLAYER	PREM	FAC	LC	CL	TOT
Casper	- (2)	1	2	- (1)	3 (3)
Thornley	1 (1)	-	2	-	3 (1)
O'Kane	1	-	1	-	2
Appleton	-	-	1 (1)	-	1 (1)
Davies	-	-	- (2)	-	- (2)
Cooke	-	-	- (1)	-	- (1)

Left: 11 August 1996. David Beckham celebrates after scoring United's third goal during the FA Charity Shield.

Goalscorers

PLAYER	PREM	FAC	LC	CL	TOT
Solskjaer	18	-	-	1	19
Cantona	11	-	-	3	14
Beckham	8	1	-	2	11
Cole	6	-	-	1	7
Scholes	3	2	1	-	6
Butt	5	-	-	-	5
Giggs	3	-	-	2	5
May	3	-	-	1	4
Poborsky	3	-	1	-	4
Cruyff	3	-	-	-	3
Pallister	3	-	-	-	3
Keane	2	-	-	-	2
Irwin	1	-	-	-	1
Neville G	1	-	-	-	1
own goals	6	-	-	-	6

PREMIERSHIP: CHAMPIONS

FA CUP: LOSE TO WIMBLEDON (0-1) IN 4TH ROUND REPLAY

LEAGUE CUP: LOSE TO LEICESTER CITY (0-2) IN 4TH ROUND

UEFA CHAMPIONS LEAGUE: LOSE TO BORUSSIA DORTMUND (0-2 ON AGGREGATE) IN SEMI-FINAL

FA CHARITY SHIELD: WINNERS. 11 AUGUST 1996. WEMBLEY, LONDON. BEAT NEWCASTLE UNITED 4-0 CANTONA 24', BUTT 30', BECKHAM 85', KEANE 87'

1997/98

- Eric Cantona's retirement comes six days short of his 31st birthday; he won four league championships and two FA Cups during his four and a half years at Old Trafford.

- Teddy Sheringham's much-hyped debut against his old club Tottenham Hotspur in the first match of the season ends with a 2-0 win to United, but the new United star misses a penalty.

- Karel Poborsky is sold to Benfica in December after just 48 appearances and six goals over 18 months.

- Brazilian legend Pele opens United's three-floor, £4 million museum at Old Trafford.

Above: Gary Neville (left), David Beckham (centre) and Roy Keane (right) celebrate during the league match against West Ham.

Right: 18 March 1998. Despite Nicky Butt (left) and Ole Gunnar Solskjaer winning this battle with AS Monaco's Djibril Diawara, United are knocked out of the Champions League.

The post-Cantona era begins with a season of disappointment and only a Charity Shield for silverware

ERIC CANTONA'S ROLLERCOASTER career with United again dominated the off-season – on 18 May, the Frenchman announced his retirement from football. His four and a half years at the club had seen unprecedented success, but he left as surprisingly as he arrived, with a short statement wishing the club well in the future. Fans felt like there had been a death at the club, but Alex Ferguson moved swiftly and, after rumours of several foreign players coming to Old Trafford, the manager eventually bought Teddy Sheringham from Tottenham Hotspur in June.

There were then early season injury worries. Firstly, Ferguson's leading scorer from last season, Ole Gunnar Solskjaer, and key defender David May were not fit for the pre-season. Then the manager tried to solve his defensive problem by bringing in Henning Berg from Blackburn Rovers, only for another Norwegian centre back Ronnie Johnsen to find himself on the treatment room after the opening home league game.

Meanwhile, Ferguson had already decided to rest England stars including David Beckham and Gary Neville in the early games because of a tough international summer. So although an FA Charity Shield win (this time on penalties against Chelsea) was achieved in August, this was not the perfect start to the campaign.

The injury list was to grow in late September when club captain Roy Keane suffered a season-ending knee injury, but United showed the strength of their squad and suffered only two league defeats between the season opener in August and Christmas Day, while at the same time putting lowly opposition such as Barnsley (7-0), Sheffield Wednesday (6-1) and Wimbledon (5-2) to the sword; in late October they even took over from Arsenal at the top of the league.

The Reds did exit the League Cup in their opening round, losing 2-0 at Ipswich Town, yet progress through the group stage of the Champions League was smoother this season: five wins out of six and only the last game in Turin against Juventus was lost. As Christmas came and went, United still led the league, but dropped surprising points – losses at Coventry City and Southampton then at home to Leicester City – while two rounds of the FA Cup were negotiated against Chelsea (the cup holders) and Walsall. In February, despite a loss in a replay in the next round of the cup to Premiership new boys Barnsley, United's league form was sound and by the end of the month they had an 11-point lead on second-placed Blackburn Rovers and 12 points on Arsenal, although the Londoners had three games in hand.

Then in March, the Red Devils slightly stalled in the league and were knocked out of Europe; most disappointing was losing on away goals to Monaco in the Champions League quarter-finals over two legs. Between these two European matches United picked up just one point in three games, including a crucial loss to Arsenal 1-0 at Old Trafford.

The final seven games of the league season then produced five wins and two draws for the Reds, yet Arsenal still managed to overtake them with their games in hand and clinch the title by a single point. Living without Cantona had proved more difficult than the manager and the team imagined.

Final League Table Premiership

		P	W	D	L	F	A	Pts
1	Arsenal	38	23	9	6	68	33	78
2	MANCHESTER UNITED	38	23	8	7	73	26	77
3	Liverpool	38	18	11	9	68	42	65
4	Chelsea	38	20	3	15	71	43	63
5	Leeds United	38	17	8	13	57	46	59
6	Blackburn Rovers	38	16	10	12	57	52	58
7	Aston Villa	38	17	6	15	49	48	57
8	West Ham United	38	16	8	14	56	57	56
9	Derby County	38	16	7	15	52	49	55
10	Leicester City	38	13	14	11	51	41	53
11	Coventry City	38	12	16	10	46	44	52
12	Southampton	38	14	6	18	50	55	48
13	Newcastle United	38	11	11	16	35	44	44
14	Tottenham Hotspur	38	11	11	16	44	56	44
15	Wimbledon	38	10	14	14	34	46	44
16	Sheffield Wednesday	38	12	8	18	52	67	44
17	Everton	38	9	13	16	41	56	40
18	Bolton Wanderers	38	9	13	16	41	61	40
19	Barnsley	38	10	5	23	37	82	35
20	Crystal Palace	38	8	9	21	37	71	33

Appearances

PLAYER	PREM	FAC	LC	CL	TOT
Beckham	34 (3)	3 (1)	-	8	45 (4)
Neville G	34	2 (1)	-	8	44 (1)
Schmeichel	32	4	-	7	43
Pallister	33	3	-	6	42
Cole	31 (2)	3	1	6 (1)	41 (3)
Butt	31 (1)	1	-	7	39 (2)
Sheringham	28 (3)	2 (1)	-	7	37 (4)
Scholes	28 (3)	2	- (1)	6 (1)	36 (5)
Giggs	28 (1)	2	-	5	35 (1)
Neville P	24 (6)	3	1	5 (2)	33 (8)
Irwin	23 (1)	3 (1)	- (1)	6	32 (4)
Berg	23 (4)	2	-	5 (2)	30 (6)
Johnsen	18 (4)	3	1	5	27 (4)
Solskjaer	15 (7)	1 (1)	-	3 (3)	19 (11)
Keane	9	-	-	1	10
May	7 (2)	1	1	-	9 (2)
McClair	2 (11)	3	1	- (3)	6 (14)
Poborsky	3 (7)	-	1	2 (2)	6 (9)
van der Gouw	4 (1)	-	1	1	6 (1)
Curtis	3 (5)	-	1	-	4 (5)
Cruyff	3 (2)	- (1)	1	-	4 (3)
Thornley	- (5)	2	1	-	3 (5)
Clegg	1 (2)	2 (1)	-	- (1)	3 (4)
Nevland	- (1)	2 (1)	- (1)	-	2 (3)
Mulryne	1	- (1)	1	-	2 (1)
Pilkington	2	-	-	-	2
Brown	1 (1)	-	-	-	1 (1)
Higginbotham	- (1)	-	-	-	- (1)
Twiss	-	- (1)	-	-	- (1)
Wallwork	- (1)	-	-	-	- (1)

Goalscorers

PLAYER	PREM	FAC	LC	CL	TOT
Cole	15	5	-	5	25
Sheringham	9	3	-	2	14
Beckham	9	2	-	-	11
Scholes	8	-	-	2	10
Giggs	8	-	-	1	9
Solskjaer	6	2	-	1	9
Irwin	2	-	-	2	4
Butt	3	-	-	-	3
Johnsen	2	1	-	-	3
Keane	2	-	-	-	2
Poborsky	2	-	-	-	2
Berg	1	-	-	1	2
Neville P	1	-	-	-	1
own goals	5	-	-	1	6

Left: United players (l-r) David Beckham, Gary Neville, Nicky Butt and Paul Scholes relax while on England duty for the King Hassan II Cup in Morocco after the season finished.

PREMIERSHIP: RUNNERS-UP

FA CUP: LOSE TO BARNSLEY (2-3) IN 5TH ROUND REPLAY

LEAGUE CUP: LOSE TO IPSWICH TOWN (0-2) IN 3RD ROUND

UEFA CHAMPIONS LEAGUE: LOSE TO MONACO (1-1 ON AWAY GOALS) IN QUARTER-FINAL

FA CHARITY SHIELD: WINNERS. 3 AUGUST 1997. WEMBLEY, LONDON. BEAT CHELSEA 1-1 HUGHES 52', JOHNSON 58' (A.E.T) UNITED WON 4-2 ON PENALTY KICKS

Big spending, the unique, historic treble, mind-numbing match drama and a knighthood

1998/99

WITH ONLY THE FA Charity Shield to show for last season's efforts, Alex Ferguson was not about to let standards slip at Old Trafford and would spend a colossal £28 million on new talent before the end of August. Winger Jesper Blomqvist from the Italian team Parma and Jaap Stam from PSV Eindhoven in the Netherlands were the first to arrive in July and with skipper Roy Keane fully fit again after an injury, United looked stronger than ever.

No wonder there was plenty of optimism in the camp, but this year's Charity Shield rather deflated everyone at Old Trafford as Arsenal won convincingly 3-0. However, the league and Champions League campaigns began immediately afterwards and there were early signs of the new players blending together with the old. Then when Dwight Yorke was signed from Aston Villa on 20 August, the squad looked overflowing with ability. But again Arsenal burst the balloon of hope with another 3-0 beating of the Reds on 20 September.

Meanwhile, a very tough Champions League group pitted United with Barcelona and Bayern Munich. United drew all four games against the two European giants, including 3-3 draws both home and away against the Spanish team who would eventually fail to qualify, while the Reds and the German club moved into the knockout stage.

During this intensely busy period, Tottenham Hotspur took care of United's League Cup hopes with a 3-1 win at White Hart Lane and league form was somewhat hit-and-miss. However, there were extenuating circumstances as the team had played an astonishing 30 games before Christmas Day. But while that 30th game was lost (3-2 at home to Middlesbrough), the Boxing Day fixture against Nottingham Forest was a comfortable 3-0 win and Ferguson's team suddenly clicked.

Key results came thick and fast: revenge over Middlesbrough was achieved in early January with a 3-1 FA Cup third round win; and Liverpool were defeated 2-1 in the fourth round of the cup. Into March, the Red Devils beat Internazionale of Milan and Chelsea to progress to the semi-finals in the Champions League and the FA Cup respectively.

Then April saw six more key games that continued the run of success: four points from two league games and two semi-final triumphs: firstly, the victory over Arsenal in a replay; and then an incredible 4-3 aggregate success over Juventus of Italy in the Champions League. The word 'treble' now entered the conversations of United fans when discussing the rest of the season and indeed the first leg of that dream was secured on the final day of the league season with a 2-1 home win over Tottenham Hotspur.

With the Premiership title in the cabinet after an exhausting fight with Arsenal, the FA Cup final against Newcastle United just six days later proved an easier affair, with the Reds gaining a 2-0 win. That left the Champions League final in Barcelona against a Bayern Munich team that United had failed to beat twice in the group stages. The unique treble was finally achieved after a season that stretched to an astonishing 64 games with only five defeats.

- Two of club's all-time greats die this season: Jack Rowley was aged 78 and Dennis Viollet just 64.

- In November, Peter Schmeichel tells United that he will leave the club at the end of this season, his eighth at the club.

- On 17 March a proposed takeover of the club by BSkyB is vetoed by the Monopolies and Mergers Commission.

- In December, assistant manager Brian Kidd accepts the manager's post at Blackburn Rovers. Former United forward Brian McClair becomes his assistant.

Above: Goalscoring hero Ole Gunnar Solskjaer is mobbed by Ronny Johnsen, Dwight Yorke and Teddy Sheringham after scoring the winner against Bayern Munich in the Champions League final.

Left: Andy Cole's 17 league goals were a key to the Red Devils winning the Premiership once again.

Final League Table Premiership

		P	W	D	L	F	A	Pts
1	MANCHESTER UNITED	38	22	13	3	80	37	79
2	Arsenal	38	22	12	4	59	17	78
3	Chelsea	38	20	15	3	57	30	75
4	Leeds United	38	18	13	7	62	34	67
5	West Ham United	38	16	9	13	46	53	57
6	Aston Villa	38	15	10	13	51	46	55
7	Liverpool	38	15	9	14	68	49	54
8	Derby County	38	13	13	12	40	45	52
9	Middlesbrough	38	12	15	11	48	54	51
10	Leicester City	38	12	13	13	40	46	49
11	Tottenham Hotspur	38	11	14	13	47	50	47
12	Sheffield Wednesday	38	13	7	18	41	42	46
13	Newcastle United	38	11	13	14	48	54	46
14	Everton	38	11	10	17	42	47	43
15	Coventry City	38	11	9	18	39	51	42
16	Wimbledon	38	10	12	16	40	63	42
17	Southampton	38	11	8	19	37	64	41
18	Charlton Athletic	38	8	12	18	41	56	36
19	Blackburn Rovers	38	7	14	17	38	52	35
20	Nottingham Forest	38	7	9	22	35	69	30

Appearances

PLAYER	PREM	FAC	LC	CL	TOT
Schmeichel	34	8	-	13	55
Neville G	34	7	-	12	53
Beckham	33 (1)	7	- (1)	12	52 (2)
Keane	33 (2)	7	-	12	52 (2)
Stam	30	6 (1)	-	13	49 (1)
Yorke	32	5 (3)	-	11	48 (3)
Irwin	26 (3)	6	-	12	44 (3)
Cole	26 (6)	6 (1)	-	10	42 (7)
Scholes	24 (7)	3 (3)	- (1)	10 (2)	37 (13)
Giggs	20 (4)	5 (1)	1	9	35 (5)
Butt	22 (9)	5	2	4 (4)	33 (13)
Neville P	19 (9)	4 (3)	2	4 (2)	29 (14)
Blomqvist	20 (5)	3 (2)	- (1)	6 (1)	29 (9)
Johnsen	19 (3)	3 (2)	1	6 (2)	29 (7)
Berg	10 (6)	5	3	3 (1)	21 (7)
Solskjaer	9 (10)	4 (4)	3	1 (5)	17 (19)
Brown	11 (3)	2	- (1)	3 (1)	16 (5)
Sheringham	7 (10)	1 (3)	1	2 (2)	11 (15)
May	4 (2)	1	2	-	7 (2)
van der Gouw	4 (1)	-	3	-	7 (1)

PLAYER	PREM	FAC	LC	CL	TOT
Curtis	1 (3)	-	3	-	4 (3)
Greening	- (3)	- (1)	3	-	3 (4)
Clegg	-	-	3	-	3
Cruyff	- (5)	-	2	- (3)	2 (8)
Wilson	-	-	2	- (1)	2 (1)
Mulryne	-	-	2	-	2
Nevland	-	-	- (1)	-	- (1)
Notman	-	-	- (1)	-	- (1)
Wallwork	-	-	- (1)	-	- (1)

NOTTINGHAM FOREST 1
MANCHESTER UNITED 8

Goalscorers

PLAYER	PREM	FAC	LC	CL	TOT
Yorke	18	3	-	8	29
Cole	17	2	-	5	24
Solskjaer	12	1	3	2	18
Scholes	6	1	-	4	11
Giggs	3	2	-	5	10
Beckham	6	1	-	2	9
Keane	2	-	-	3	5
Sheringham	2	1	1	1	5
Johnsen	3	-	-	-	3
Irwin	2	1	-	-	3
Butt	2	-	-	-	2
Cruyff	2	-	-	-	2
Blomqvist	1	-	-	-	1
Neville G	1	-	-	-	1
Stam	1	-	-	-	1
Neville P	-	-	-	1	1
Nevland	-	-	1	-	1
own goals	2	-	-	-	2

1999/2000

- Club captain Roy Keane is voted Player of the Year by both the Professional Footballers' Association and the Football Writers' Association.

- This year's championship is United's sixth in eight years and the 18-point margin was a record.

- In terms of new outfield recruits, defender Mikael Silvestre comes in from Internazionale of Milan in September.

- In the Premiership, United lose just three games all season and win the title with four games to play.

- United's biggest win of the season – 7-1 over West Ham United – comes after they go a goal down. Paul Scholes hits a hat-trick.

Above: A giant poster welcoming United to their games at the Maracana Stadium for the Club World Championships in Rio de Janeiro, Brazil.

Right: It's another Premiership title. The players celebrate after the penultimate game of the season at home, following a win over Tottenham Hotspur.

Two more trophies in the post-treble season, as United rattle in the goals to win the Premier League by a mile

WITH THE UNIQUE treble achieved and the manager knighted, it would have been easy for United's off-season to be one of joyful reflection, but by the end of June the club was pitched into a new controversy. United withdrew from this season's FA Cup after accepting a place in a new competition, the Club World Championship to be staged in Brazil in January.

With the Football Association requesting United's presence to protect the integrity of England's 2006 World Cup bid the reason behind the withdrawal, it was a no-win situation for the club. The competition clashed with the FA Cup third round date and something had to give. Many at United would have preferred to defend their trophy, but instead they had to fly out to Brazil; in the end, it was all to no avail because it would eventually be Germany that hosted the World Cup seven years later.

Nevertheless, even without entering the FA Cup, United would be battling for no less than six trophies this season. Disappointingly, the first two were lost before August had ended; Arsenal beat the Reds 2-0 in the FA Charity Shield and Lazio of Rome won the Super Cup 1-0. Team-wise, United made several significant signings including two new goalkeepers in an attempt to replace Peter Schmeichel: in July, Mark Bosnich returned to the club for a second spell, this time from Aston Villa, then at the end of August, the club signed Massimo Taibi from Venezia in Italy. Meanwhile, United already had Schmeichel's deputy Raimond van der Gouw to consider for the position.

Despite losing the chance of two early trophies, United's league form was steady and after five wins and a draw in the opening month of the season, the club was top of the league once again. However, the goalkeeping situation was causing concern. All three keepers were given early chances, with Bosnich quickly establishing himself as the first choice. After their strong start in the league, things did not always go to plan over the following two months, with United suffering four defeats in five games in October, including an early exit from

the League Cup when Aston Villa knocked United out of the competition, although the team was made up almost entirely of reserves. However, progress was made in the Champions League to the second group stage, but not without a defeat on the way.

A trip to Tokyo for the Inter-Continental Cup final did end with a trophy as United beat Palmeiras of Brazil 1-0 and, despite the season's problems so far, the league performances were exceptional; only two defeats before Christmas.

The Club World Championship was a damp squib, as United did not even make the final of the competition and had David Beckham sent off in one game. However, their return from sunny South America sparked a return to top form and both league and European opponents were dismissed with a vengeance. In fact, United raced to the title in record time, winning by 18 points.

Having come through the second group stage as winners, United faced old rivals Real Madrid in the quarter-finals. A 0-0 draw in Spain seemed to make them favourites for the return at Old Trafford, but Madrid won through 3-2, despite a spirited late comeback from the Reds.

Final League Table Premiership

	P	W	D	L	F	A	Pts
1 MANCHESTER UNITED	38	28	7	3	97	45	91
2 Arsenal	38	22	7	9	73	43	73
3 Leeds United	38	21	6	11	58	43	69
4 Liverpool	38	19	10	9	51	30	67
5 Chelsea	38	18	11	9	53	34	65
6 Aston Villa	38	15	13	10	46	35	58
7 Sunderland	38	16	10	12	57	56	58
8 Leicester City	38	16	7	15	55	55	55
9 West Ham United	38	15	10	13	52	53	55
10 Tottenham Hotspur	38	15	8	15	57	49	53
11 Newcastle United	38	14	10	14	63	54	52
12 Middlesbrough	38	14	10	14	46	52	52
13 Everton	38	12	14	12	59	49	50
14 Coventry City	38	12	8	18	47	54	44
15 Southampton	38	12	8	18	45	62	44
16 Derby County	38	9	11	18	44	57	38
17 Bradford City	38	9	9	20	38	68	36
18 Wimbledon	38	7	12	19	46	74	33
19 Sheffield Wednesday	38	8	7	23	38	70	31
20 Watford	38	6	6	26	35	77	24

Appearances

PLAYER	PREM	FAC	LC	CL	TOT
Stam	33	-	-	13	46
Beckham	30 (1)	-	-	12	42 (1)
Giggs	30	-	-	11	41
Keane	28 (1)	-	-	12	40 (1)
Yorke	29 (3)	-	-	9 (2)	38 (5)
Scholes	27 (4)	-	-	11	38 (4)
Irwin	25	-	-	13	38
Cole	23 (5)	-	-	13	36 (5)
Silvestre	30 (1)	-	-	2 (2)	32 (3)
Neville P	25 (4)	-	-	6 (3)	31 (7)
Bosnich	23	-	1	7	31
Neville G	22	-	-	9	31
Berg	16 (6)	-	-	11 (1)	27 (7)
Butt	21 (11)	-	-	4 (2)	25 (13)
Solskjaer	15 (13)	-	1	4 (7)	20 (20)
Sheringham	15 (12)	-	-	3 (6)	18 (18)
van der Gouw	11 (3)	-	-	7	18 (3)
Fortune	4 (2)	-	-	1 (3)	5 (5)
Taibi	4	-	-	-	4
Cruyff	1 (7)	-	1	1 (3)	3 (10)

PLAYER	PREM	FAC	LC	CL	TOT
Greening	1 (3)	-	1	1 (1)	3 (4)
Wilson	1 (2)	-	-	2 (1)	3 (3)
Higginbotham	2 (1)	-	1	- (1)	3 (2)
Clegg	- (2)	-	1	1 (1)	2 (3)
Johnsen	2 (1)	-	-	-	2 (1)
Wallwork	- (5)	-	1	-	1 (5)
Curtis	- (1)	-	1	-	1 (1)
May	- (1)	-	-	1	1 (1)
Chadwick	-	-	1	-	1
O'Shea	-	-	1	-	1
Twiss	-	-	1	-	1
Culkin	- (1)	-	-	-	- (1)
Healy	-	-	- (1)	-	- (1)
Wellens	-	-	- (1)	-	- (1)

Goalscorers

PLAYER	PREM	FAC	LC	CL	TOT
Yorke	20	-	-	2	22
Cole	19	-	-	3	22
Solskjaer	12	-	-	3	15
Scholes	9	-	-	3	12
Keane	5	-	-	6	11
Beckham	6	-	-	2	8
Giggs	6	-	-	1	7
Sheringham	5	-	-	1	6
Butt	3	-	-	-	3
Cruyff	3	-	-	-	3
Irwin	3	-	-	-	3
Fortune	2	-	-	-	2
Berg	1	-	-	-	1
own goals	3	-	-	-	3

Left: During his one-year return to the Red Devils, Mark Bosnich lies exhausted during the friendly match against Australia played at the Melbourne Cricket Ground.

PREMIERSHIP: CHAMPIONS. LEAGUE CUP: LOSE TO ASTON VILLA (0-3) IN 3RD ROUND

UEFA CHAMPIONS LEAGUE: LOSE TO REAL MADRID (2-3 ON AGGREGATE) IN QUARTER-FINAL

EUROPEAN SUPER CUP: RUNNERS-UP 27 AUGUST 1999, STADE LOUIS II, MONACO. LOST TO LAZIO 0-1 SALAS 35'

INTERCONTINENTAL CUP: WINNERS. 30 NOVEMBER 1999. OLYMPIC STADIUM, TOKYO. BEAT PALMEIRAS 1-0 KEANE 35'

FA CHARITY SHIELD: RUNNERS-UP 1 AUGUST 1999, WEMBLEY, LONDON. LOST TO ARSENAL 1-2 YORKE 36', KANU 67', PARLOUR 78'

FIFA CLUB WORLD CHAMPIONSHIP: FINISH FIFTH

A third Premiership in a row proves United's dominant position in the English football landscape

2000/01

SIR ALEX FERGUSON made solving his goalkeeping problems a priority for this season by signing Fabien Barthez from AS Monaco in time from the beginning of a campaign in which United were under a strange kind of pressure – could they maintain their incredible standards. An FA Charity Shield loss to Chelsea did not exactly get the season off to a flying start.

However, United went top of the league in October, with Arsenal being their main rivals. A much-changed United side again went out of the League Cup early, while the Reds edged into the next stage of the Champions League only after a last-match victory against Dynamo Kiev on the same night that rivals PSV Eindhoven lost to group winners Anderlecht of Belgium.

This European performance was unconvincing and although United performed much more solidly in the second group stage against the likes of Valencia of Spain, Sturm Graz of Austria and Panathinaikos of Greece, they would face stern opposition in the first knockout round against old rivals Bayern Munich in April.

Before this, though, the Red Devils were on fire in the league. They had lost only two games up to the end of December and did not falter as the New Year was swept in; by the end of January they were 15 points ahead of Arsenal and in the middle of a 12-game unbeaten run. Only losing in the fourth round of the FA Cup at home to West Ham United spoiled a perfect few months.

But it was the Champions League quarter-final that caught the imagination of the fans, as Bayern wanted revenge for the final defeat two years ago. Things went the Germans' way in the opening leg at Old Trafford when a tight game looked like ending goalless until Bayern netted late on from a well-worked free kick move. This put the Reds under immense pressure to score at least twice in the heated atmosphere of Munich's Olympic Stadium. It was not to be; two first half Bayern scores made the tie all but safe and a Ryan Giggs second half goal could not prompt another late comeback like the Champions League final of 1999. United could take little consolation from being eliminated by the competition's eventual winners for a second season in a row.

United had wrapped up the league title before the disappointment in Europe. It was their third championship in a row and an incredible achievement, considering that only three other teams – Huddersfield Town, Arsenal and Liverpool – had ever managed it before in English football. The final 10-point gap rather flattered the Reds' rivals as the race had virtually ended when league runners-up Arsenal were beaten 6-1 at Old Trafford on 25 February, thanks to a stunning performance from Dwight Yorke, who scored a hat-trick inside 22 minutes. The Red Devils actually secured the title with five games still to play and used two of those matches to give extra experience to potential regular first teamers of the future like Luke Chadwick, Michael Stewart and Ronnie Wallwork.

- Teddy Sheringham is voted Professional Footballers' Association and Football Writers' Player of the Year.

- United's Charity Shield loss to Chelsea in August is the last club game ever played at the old Wembley stadium which is now closed for reconstruction.

- On 18 November, the first Manchester derby in five years ends with a 1-0 win to United thanks to a David Beckham goal.

Above: In Steve McClaren's second full season as coach, United win a third Premiership title in succession.

Left: 14 April 2001. Beckham, Scholes and Yorke celebrate Ryan Giggs' goal in a 4-2 win over Coventry City.

Final League Table Premiership

		P	W	D	L	F	A	Pts
1	MANCHESTER UNITED	38	24	8	6	79	31	80
2	Arsenal	38	20	10	8	63	38	70
3	Liverpool	38	20	9	9	71	39	69
4	Leeds United	38	20	8	10	64	43	68
5	Ipswich Town	38	20	6	12	57	42	66
6	Chelsea	38	17	10	11	68	45	61
7	Sunderland	38	15	12	11	46	41	57
8	Aston Villa	38	13	15	10	46	43	54
9	Charlton Athletic	38	14	10	14	50	57	52
10	Southampton	38	14	10	14	40	48	52
11	Newcastle United	38	14	9	15	44	50	51
12	Tottenham Hotspur	38	13	10	15	47	54	49
13	Leicester City	38	14	6	18	39	51	48
14	Middlesbrough	38	9	15	14	44	44	42
15	West Ham United	38	10	12	16	45	50	42
16	Everton	38	11	9	18	45	59	42
17	Derby County	38	10	12	16	37	59	42
18	Manchester City	38	8	10	20	41	65	34
19	Coventry City	38	8	10	20	36	63	34
20	Bradford City	38	5	11	22	30	70	26

Appearances

PLAYER	PREM	FAC	LC	CL	TOT
Neville G	32	2	-	14	48
Barthez	30	1	-	12	43
Keane	28	2	-	13	43
Beckham	29 (2)	2	-	11 (1)	42 (3)
Silvestre	25 (5)	2	-	13 (1)	40 (6)
Scholes	28 (4)	-	-	12	40 (4)
Brown	25 (3)	1	1	9 (2)	36 (5)
Giggs	24 (7)	2	-	9 (2)	35 (9)
Butt	24 (4)	2	-	8 (3)	34 (7)
Sheringham	23 (6)	1 (1)	-	8 (3)	32 (10)
Neville P	24 (5)	1	2	4 (2)	31 (7)
Irwin	20 (1)	1	-	7	28 (1)
Solskjaer	19 (12)	1 (1)	2	3 (8)	25 (21)
Cole	15 (4)	1	-	10	26 (4)
Yorke	15 (7)	1 (1)	2	7 (4)	25 (12)
Stam	15	1	-	6	22
Johnsen	11	-	1	4	16
van der Gouw	5 (5)	1	2	2	10 (5)
Chadwick	6 (10)	- (1)	2	1 (2)	9 (13)
Fortune	6 (1)	-	2	- (1)	8 (2)

PLAYER	PREM	FAC	LC	CL	TOT
Wallwork	4 (8)	- (1)	2	- (1)	6 (10)
Greening	3 (4)	-	2	1 (1)	6 (5)
Stewart	3	-	- (2)	-	3 (2)
Clegg	-	-	2	-	2
Goram	2	-	-	-	2
O'Shea	-	-	2	-	2
May	1 (1)	-	-	-	1 (1)
Rachubka	1	-	- (1)	-	1 (1)
Healy	- (1)	-	- (1)	-	- (2)
Berg	- (1)	-	-	-	- (1)
Djordjic	- (1)	-	-	-	- (1)
Webber	-	-	- (1)	-	- (1)

9 September 2000. Season's top scorer Teddy Sheringham celebrates a goal against Sunderland.

Goalscorers

PLAYER	PREM	FAC	LC	CL	TOT
Sheringham	15	1	-	5	21
Solskjaer	10	1	2	-	13
Cole	9	-	-	4	13
Yorke	9	-	2	1	12
Scholes	6	-	-	6	12
Beckham	9	-	-	-	9
Giggs	5	-	-	2	7
Butt	3	-	-	1	4
Keane	2	-	-	1	3
Chadwick	2	-	-	-	2
Fortune	2	-	-	-	2
Irwin	-	-	-	2	2
Johnsen	1	-	-	-	1
Neville G	1	-	-	-	1
Neville P	1	-	-	-	1
Silvestre	1	-	-	-	1
own goals	3	-	-	-	3

PREMIERSHIP: CHAMPIONS

FA CUP: LOSE TO WEST HAM (0-1) IN 4TH ROUND

LEAGUE CUP: LOSE TO SUNDERLAND (1-2) IN 4TH ROUND

UEFA CHAMPIONS LEAGUE: LOSE TO BAYERN MUNICH (1-3 ON AGGREGATE) IN QUARTER-FINAL

FA CHARITY SHIELD: RUNNERS-UP 13 AUGUST 2000. WEMBLEY, LONDON. LOST TO CHELSEA 0-2 HASSELBAINK 22', MELCHIOT 73'

2001/02

- United lose the Charity Shield to Liverpool 2-1 at the Millennium Stadium although Ruud van Nistelrooy did score his first goal for the club.

- Yet another goalkeeper arrives in time for this season – Roy Carroll from Wigan Athletic for £2.5 million.

Above: Fabien Barthez launches his own brand of goalkeeping gloves with a hand print in plaster.

Right: 23 October 2001. Man and ball arrive in the net after a Ruud van Nistelrooy goal in the Champions League Group G match against Olympiakos at Old Trafford.

Van Nistelrooy arrives and the manager stays but there is no United silverware for the first time in over a decade

HAVING ANNOUNCED HIS plans to step down from managing the club at the end of the previous campaign, Sir Alex Ferguson wasn't about to let things slip. Nevertheless, the level of expectation at the club was now so high that a season with just a league title to show for it was deemed by some to be a relative failure. And, certainly, Ferguson was not resting on any laurels for his swansong when he spent record amounts in the off-season transfer market.

In early July, Dutchman Ruud van Nistelrooy (who had been on the manager's shopping list a season earlier only to then suffer a serious knee injury) was bought for £19 million from PSV Eindhoven and three weeks later Juan Sebastian Veron was signed from Lazio in Italy for an English record amount, £28.1 million. However, there was also a very surprising change at the start of the season, when Jaap Stam was transferred to Lazio for £14.7 million shortly after some comments about the club appeared in his autobiography without United's permission. French World Cup hero of 1998 Laurent Blanc was brought in from Internazionale a few days later on a free transfer. Although this deal made financial sense, it was a shock to fans and media alike.

There was another key departure before the season began and it disrupted the backroom staff: assistant manager Steve McClaren left to become manager of Middlesbrough and would not therefore be taking over from his boss when the anticipated retirement of Ferguson took place at the end of the season.

Despite these latest team changes, the season opened brightly with van Nistelrooy in particular enjoying himself, scoring two goals on his league debut against Fulham in a 3-2 win in front of the Old Trafford faithful. However, there was a problem in defence because clean sheets were becoming a rarity and too many times United were conceding three or even more goals; the loss of Stam was seen as the reason by some experts.

In Phase One of the Champions League, the Reds were beaten twice by Deportivo La Coruna and were only runners-up in their group on goal difference, while the team was defeated six times in the league before Christmas and were, at one time, as low as ninth. At the start of December after a loss to Chelsea, Ferguson told the media his team would not win the league this season and then decided to upgrade his forward line: Andy Cole was sold to Blackburn Rovers in December and replaced three weeks later by Diego Forlan from Independiente of Argentina.

At the same time United climbed to the top of the league after eight successive wins. In the New Year, league form held up quite well, but Middlesbrough put the Reds out of the FA Cup in the fourth round when Ferguson rested a couple of players. There was better news in February when the manager announced he would not retire after all and began to plan for the long term. His team responded by sailing through into the Champions League knockout stage, where they beat Deportivo in both legs of the quarter-final less than six months after losing to them home and away in Phase One.

However, the Red Devils could not beat a determined Bayer Leverkusen, who went through to the final on away goals. This loss hurt, and the pain was increased when the battle for the league reached its denouement in early May. Arsenal won 1-0 at Old Trafford to clinch the league title and in the final week of the season the Reds were denied second place by Liverpool. This was United's first finish outside the top two in the league since 1991 and the Reds had failed to either win or finish runners-up in a major competition for the first time since 1989.

Final League Table Premiership

		P	W	D	L	F	A	Pts
1	Arsenal	38	26	9	3	79	36	87
2	Liverpool	38	24	8	6	67	30	80
3	**MANCHESTER UNITED**	38	24	5	9	87	45	77
4	Newcastle United	38	21	8	9	74	52	71
5	Leeds United	38	18	12	8	53	37	66
6	Chelsea	38	17	13	8	66	38	64
7	West Ham United	38	15	8	15	48	57	53
8	Aston Villa	38	12	14	12	46	47	50
9	Tottenham Hotspur	38	14	8	16	49	53	50
10	Blackburn Rovers	38	12	10	16	55	51	46
11	Southampton	38	12	9	17	46	54	45
12	Middlesbrough	38	12	9	17	35	47	45
13	Fulham	38	10	14	14	36	44	44
14	Charlton Athletic	38	10	14	14	38	49	44
15	Everton	38	11	10	17	45	57	43
16	Bolton Wanderers	38	9	13	16	44	62	40
17	Sunderland	38	10	10	18	29	51	40
18	Ipswich Town	38	9	9	20	41	64	36
19	Derby County	38	8	6	24	33	63	30
20	Leicester City	38	5	13	20	30	64	28

Appearances

PLAYER	PREM	FAC	LC	CL	TOT
Barthez	32	1	-	15	48
Neville G	31 (3)	2	-	14	47 (3)
Blanc	29	2	-	15	46
Scholes	30 (5)	2	-	13	45 (5)
Silvestre	31 (4)	2	-	10 (3)	43 (7)
van Nistelrooy	29 (3)	- (2)	-	14	43 (5)
Keane	28	2	-	11 (1)	41 (1)
Veron	24 (2)	1	-	13	38 (2)
Beckham	23 (5)	1	-	13	37 (5)
Giggs	18 (7)	- (1)	-	13	31 (8)
Solskjaer	23 (7)	2	-	5 (10)	30 (17)
Butt	20 (5)	2	-	8 (1)	30 (6)
Neville P	21 (7)	2	1	3 (4)	27 (11)
Brown	15 (2)	-	-	5 (2)	20 (4)
Irwin	10 (2)	-	-	8 (2)	18 (4)
Johnsen	9 (1)	-	-	8 (1)	17 (2)
Fortune	8 (6)	-	-	3 (2)	11 (8)
Carroll	6 (1)	1	1	1	9 (1)
Cole	7 (4)	-	-	1 (3)	8 (7)
Forlan	6 (7)	-	-	1 (4)	7 (11)

PLAYER	PREM	FAC	LC	CL	TOT
Chadwick	5 (3)	1 (1)	1	-	7 (4)
Yorke	4 (6)	- (1)	1	1 (2)	6 (9)
O'Shea	4 (5)	-	1	- (3)	5 (8)
Stewart	2 (1)	-	1	- (1)	3 (2)
May	2	-	-	1	3
Wallwork	- (1)	1	1	-	2 (1)
Davis	-	-	1	-	1
Djordjic	-	-	1	-	1
Roche	-	-	1	-	1
Stam	1	-	-	-	1
Webber	-	-	1	-	1
van der Gouw	- (1)	-	- (1)	-	- (2)
Clegg	-	-	- (1)	-	- (1)
Nardiello	-	-	- (1)	-	- (1)

Goalscorers

PLAYER	PREM	FAC	LC	CL	TOT
van Nistelrooy	23	2	-	10	35
Solskjaer	17	1	-	7	25
Beckham	11	-	-	5	16
Scholes	8	-	-	1	9
Giggs	7	-	-	2	9
Veron	5	-	-	-	5
Cole	4	-	-	1	5
Keane	3	-	-	1	4
Blanc	1	-	-	2	3
Neville P	2	-	-	-	2
Butt	1	-	-	-	1
Fortune	1	-	-	-	1
Johnsen	1	-	-	-	1
Yorke	1	-	-	-	1
Silvestre	-	-	-	1	1
own goals	2	-	-	1	3

PREMIERSHIP: THIRD POSITION
FA CUP: LOSE TO MIDDLESBROUGH (0-2) IN 4TH ROUND
LEAGUE CUP: LOSE TO ARSENAL (0-4) IN 3RD ROUND
UEFA CHAMPIONS LEAGUE: LOSE TO BAYER LEVERKUSEN (1-1 ON AWAY GOALS) IN SEMI-FINAL
FA CHARITY SHIELD: RUNNERS-UP 12 AUGUST 2001. WEMBLEY, LONDON. LOST TO LIVERPOOL 1-2 MCALLISTER 2', OWEN 16', VAN NISTELROOY 51'

Sir Alex brings home an eighth Premiership title in 11 years while record transfer Rio Ferdinand arrives

2002/03

RATHER THAN CARRY out his planned retirement, Sir Alex Ferguson signed a new three-year contract and did not waste time strengthening a team that had relatively little success last season – he broke the English transfer record by signing Rio Ferdinand from Leeds United for £30 million. Meanwhile, Dwight Yorke was transferred to Blackburn Rovers to renew his partnership with Andy Cole, who had left United for the same club late last year.

After a rare season without a major trophy, there were nerves at Old Trafford as the Premiership season started with United struggling both in defence and attack. By mid-September they were as low as ninth, while the likes of champions Arsenal and Liverpool looked stronger. United did clear the Champions League qualifying round hurdle with a 5-1 aggregate win over Zalaegerszeg of Hungary to make Phase One and had few problems there; they even beat Bayer Leverkusen (last season's European conquerors) twice.

From November, the League Cup wins over Leicester City, Burnley and Chelsea put United into the semi-finals before the end of 2002. Also in November, United lost 3-1 in the last Manchester derby game to be played at Maine Road – a ground that United called home for several years in the post-war period; it was also the first time the Reds had lost a competitive match to City since September 1989.

As January dawned, United were up to third in the league as their home form was impeccable (the Reds would actually lose only one league game at Old Trafford all season). Before the next batch of Champions League matches started in mid-February, United were through to the League Cup final after beating Blackburn Rovers 4-2 on aggregate in the semi, but they fell at home 2-0 to Arsenal in the FA Cup.

The pressure within the club was manifested after this game when David Beckham suffered a cut to his face in an alleged dressing room bust-up with his manager. The press had a field day and United suddenly looked less likely title candidates. The League Cup final gave little solace as old rivals Liverpool

beat a full-strength United 2-0 and on the same day Arsenal established an eight-point lead in the league.

However, in March Phase Two of the Champions League was completed successfully, with the highlights being home and away wins over Juventus of Turin. At the same time, United's league results hit a peak and, although the Red Devils had been held to draws by Bolton Wanderers and Manchester City, they then picked up 28 out of a possible 30 points in a run that left all-comers gasping.

A supposed title-decider at Highbury in mid-April finished 2-2 and it left United three points ahead of Arsenal, but with a slightly inferior goal difference. Yet, it was enough for the Reds to take the title with one game in hand. It was United's eighth Premiership win in 11 seasons. The surge in the league was not repeated in Europe as United left the competition in the quarter-finals, losing 6-5 to Real Madrid.

- There is extra incentive this year to make the Champions League final because Old Trafford is the venue. In the end, the Reds lose in the quarter-finals and AC Milan beat Juventus on penalties in Manchester in May after a 0-0 draw.

- Diego Forlan makes no fewer than 30 substitute appearances this season and starts only 15 games.

- After the season is over, fans learn that a relatively unknown teenage prospect from Portugal named Cristiano Ronaldo has signed from Sporting Lisbon for £12.2 million.

- On 7 July Munich air crash survivor, goalkeeper Ray Wood, dies aged 71.

Above: The commanding figure of Rio Ferdinand makes an immediate impact in the Red Devils defence.

Left: 26 October 2002. Diego Forlan is mobbed after scoring the equalising goal in the 1-1 draw against Aston Villa.

Final League Table Premiership

		P	W	D	L	F	A	Pts
1	MANCHESTER UNITED	38	25	8	5	74	34	83
2	Arsenal	38	23	9	6	85	42	78
3	Newcastle United	38	21	6	11	63	48	69
4	Chelsea	38	19	10	9	68	38	67
5	Liverpool	38	18	10	10	61	41	64
6	Blackburn Rovers	38	16	12	10	52	43	60
7	Everton	38	17	8	13	48	49	59
8	Southampton	38	13	13	12	43	46	52
9	Manchester City	38	15	6	17	47	54	51
10	Tottenham Hotspur	38	14	8	16	51	62	50
11	Middlesbrough	38	13	10	15	48	44	49
12	Charlton Athletic	38	14	7	17	45	56	49
13	Birmingham City	38	13	9	16	41	49	48
14	Fulham	38	13	9	16	41	50	48
15	Leeds United	38	14	5	19	58	57	47
16	Aston Villa	38	12	9	17	42	47	45
17	Bolton Wanderers	38	10	14	14	41	51	44
18	West Ham United	38	10	12	16	42	59	42
19	West Bromwich Albion	38	6	8	24	29	65	26
20	Sunderland	38	4	7	27	21	65	19

Appearances

PLAYER	PREM	FAC	LC	CL	TOT
Silvestre	34	2	5	13	54
Giggs	32 (4)	3	4 (1)	13 (2)	52 (7)
van Nistelrooy	33 (1)	3	4	10 (1)	50 (2)
Scholes	31 (2)	2 (1)	4 (2)	9 (1)	46 (6)
Barthez	30	2	4	10	46
Beckham	27 (4)	3	5	10 (3)	45 (7)
Ferdinand	27 (1)	3	4	11	45 (1)
O'Shea	26 (6)	1	3	12 (4)	42 (10)
Solskjaer	29 (8)	1 (1)	1 (3)	9 (5)	40 (17)
Veron	21 (4)	1	4 (1)	11	37 (5)
Neville G	19 (7)	3		8 (2)	35 (9)
Neville P	19 (6)	2	4	10 (2)	35 (8)
Brown	22	1 (1)	5	6	34 (1)
Keane	19 (2)	3	2	6	30 (2)
Blanc	15 (4)	1		9	25 (4)
Butt	14 (4)	– (2)	– (1)	8	22 (7)
Forlan	7 (18)	– (2)	3 (2)	5 (8)	15 (30)
Carroll	8 (2)	1	2	3	14 (2)
Fortune	5 (4)	–	1	3 (3)	9 (7)
Richardson	– (2)	1	– (1)	2 (3)	3 (6)

PLAYER	PREM	FAC	LC	CL	TOT
Ricardo	– (1)	–	–	3 (1)	3 (2)
Pugh	– (1)	3	1	1 (2)	2 (3)
May	– (1)	2	–	– (1)	2 (2)
Fletcher	–	–	–	2	2
Chadwick	– (1)	–	1	– (3)	1 (4)
Stewart	– (1)	– (1)	1	– (1)	1 (3)
Nardiello	–	–	1	– (1)	1 (1)
Roche	– (1)	–	–	1	1 (1)
Lynch	–	–	–	1	1
Timm	–	–	–	– (1)	– (1)
Webber	–	–	–	– (1)	– (1)

Goalscorers

PLAYER	PREM	FAC	LC	CL	TOT
van Nistelrooy	25	4	1	14	44
Scholes	14	1	3	2	20
Solskjaer	9	1	1	4	15
Giggs	8	2	–	5	15
Beckham	6	1	1	3	11
Forlan	6	–	2	1	9
Veron	2	–	–	4	6
Neville P	1	1	–	–	2
Silvestre	1	–	–	–	1
Blanc	–	–	–	1	1
Brown	–	–	–	1	1
Neville G	–	–	–	1	1
Richardson	–	–	1	–	1
own goals	2	–	–	1	3

PREMIERSHIP: CHAMPIONS

FA CUP: LOSE TO ARSENAL (0-2) IN 5TH ROUND

LEAGUE CUP: RUNNERS-UP, 2 MARCH 2003, MILLENNIUM STADIUM, CARDIFF. LOST TO LIVERPOOL 0-2 GERRARD 39', OWEN 86'

UEFA CHAMPIONS LEAGUE: LOSE TO REAL MADRID (5-6 ON AGGREGATE) IN QUARTER-FINAL

2003/04

■ The victory over Millwall at the Millennium Stadium in Cardiff brings the FA Cup to Old Trafford for the first time since 1999.

■ In mid-season, Sir Alex Ferguson dips into the transfer market again for another striker, Louis Saha from Fulham.

■ Despite Arsenal's unbeaten league season and ultimate championship, United are league leaders as late into the season as the end of January.

Above: 26 December 2003. American Tim Howard brought youth to the goalkeeping position. The Red Devils beat Everton 3-2.

Right: Sir Alex Ferguson welcomes his new signing to the United training ground. Cristiano Ronaldo will become one of the club's greatest stars.

FA Cup win No 11 elevates an otherwise disappointing post-Beckham season as Cristiano Ronaldo's star rises

IN PREVIOUS years, the biggest news at Old Trafford was of players being bought by United, this off-season the top headline was of a departing star. David Beckham joined Real Madrid on 17 June for £25 million after 12 years at the club. Beckham was not the only player to leave, however; Juan Sebastian Veron (a record signing just two seasons earlier) left for Chelsea.

Replacing these two were younger players, including Cristiano Ronaldo from Sporting Lisbon, who became the world's most expensive teenage signing at £12.24 million, and 20-year-old Frenchman David Bellion from Sunderland. It was an injection of youth into the squad that helped bring an early trophy: the Community Shield in a win over Arsenal on penalties. The youngsters may not have taken part in that match, but Ferguson was clearly looking to the future because the goalkeeping position was now given to Tim Howard, the young American replacing Fabien Barthez, who was sold on.

There was no suggestion in the early part of the season that United would not be contending for all the major trophies as they kept in touch at the top of the league and overcame most opposition in the Champions League Phase One. In fact, a Champions League format change meant only one group phase before an extended knockout competition this season; so fewer games for the Red Devils at the end of the season could only be an advantage. And while an inexperienced team exited the League Cup (a fourth round loss to West Bromwich Albion), by mid-December, United went top of the league for the first time in the season, giving hope they could retain the title.

However, controversy had been brewing around Rio Ferdinand since September when the high-priced defender in only his second season at the club had missed a mandatory drugs test. The player claimed to have simply forgotten, but the authorities took a dim view and on 19 December delivered an eight-month ban and £50,000 fine. Ferdinand appealed, but the ban was implemented a month later and took a huge toll on United's season.

In mid-January, United still led the league, but it was not for long as Arsenal were in the middle of an undefeated season in the league and would soon take over at the top before running out Premiership winners by the end of April. Yet perhaps the most obvious matches in which Ferdinand was missed were the two legs of the Champions League knockout matches against Porto.

The Portuguese side, managed by a then relatively unknown Jose Mourinho, won their home leg 2-1 and then scored a late goal in the second leg at Old Trafford to beat the more favoured and experienced United 3-2 on aggregate. When a 4-1 loss followed immediately afterwards in the Manchester derby, the Reds were suddenly focusing on only the FA Cup as a reward for another long season. Early opponents defeated in this cup competition had included Aston Villa and Manchester City, and a 1-0 semi-final win over Arsenal set up a final against non-Premiership opposition, Millwall from the First Division. A 3-0 win in the final for the Reds was no surprise.

Final League Table Premiership

		P	W	D	L	F	A	Pts
1	Arsenal	38	26	12	0	73	26	90
2	Chelsea	38	24	7	7	67	30	79
3	**MANCHESTER UNITED**	38	23	6	9	64	35	75
4	Liverpool	38	16	12	10	55	37	60
5	Newcastle United	38	13	17	8	52	40	56
6	Aston Villa	38	15	11	12	48	44	56
7	Charlton Athletic	38	14	11	13	51	51	53
8	Bolton Wanderers	38	14	11	13	48	56	53
9	Fulham	38	14	10	14	52	46	52
10	Birmingham City	38	12	14	12	43	48	50
11	Middlesbrough	38	13	9	16	44	52	48
12	Southampton	38	12	11	15	44	45	47
13	Portsmouth	38	12	9	17	47	54	45
14	Tottenham Hotspur	38	13	6	19	47	57	45
15	Blackburn Rovers	38	12	8	18	51	59	44
16	Manchester City	38	9	14	15	55	54	41
17	Everton	38	9	12	17	45	57	39
18	Leicester City	38	6	15	17	48	65	33
19	Leeds United	38	8	9	21	40	79	33
20	Wolverhampton Wanderers	38	7	12	19	38	77	33

Appearances

PLAYER	PREM	FAC	LC	CL	TOT
O'Shea	32 (1)	6	2	6 (1)	46 (2)
Silvestre	33 (1)	5	–	6	44 (1)
Howard	32	4	–	7	43
Giggs	29 (4)	5	–	8	42 (4)
Neville G	30	4	1	7	42
van Nistelrooy	31 (1)	3 (1)	–	7	41 (2)
Neville P	29 (2)	2 (1)	1	7	39 (3)
Scholes	24 (4)	6	–	5	35 (4)
Keane	25 (3)	4 (1)	–	4	33 (4)
Fortune	18 (5)	3	1	6 (1)	28 (6)
Fletcher	17 (5)	4 (1)	2	3 (3)	26 (9)
Ferdinand	20	–	–	6	26
Ronaldo	15 (14)	5	1	3 (2)	24 (16)
Brown	15 (2)	5 (1)	–	2	22 (3)
Butt	12 (9)	3 (2)	2	4 (1)	21 (12)
Forlan	10 (14)	2	1	2 (2)	15 (16)
Kleberson	10 (2)	1	1	1 (1)	13 (3)
Djemba-Djemba	10 (5)	– (1)	1	1 (3)	12 (9)
Carroll	6	2 (1)	2	1	11 (1)
Saha	9 (3)	–	–	1 (1)	10 (4)

PLAYER	PREM	FAC	LC	CL	TOT
Solskjaer	7 (6)	1 (2)	–	1 (1)	9 (9)
Bellion	4 (10)	1 (1)	2	– (4)	7 (15)
Richardson	–	– (1)	2	–	2 (1)
Bardsley	–	– (1)	1	–	1 (1)
Pugh	–	– (1)	1	–	1 (1)
Tierney	–	–	1	–	1
Eagles	–	–	– (2)	–	– (2)
Johnson	–	–	– (1)	–	– (1)
Nardiello	–	–	– (1)	–	– (1)

Goalscorers

PLAYER	PREM	FAC	LC	CL	TOT
van Nistelrooy	20	6	–	4	30
Scholes	9	4	–	1	14
Giggs	7	–	–	1	8
Forlan	4	1	1	2	8
Saha	7	–	–	–	7
Ronaldo	4	2	–	–	6
Keane	3	–	–	–	3
Bellion	2	–	1	–	3
Fortune	1	–	–	2	3
Kleberson	2	–	–	–	2
Neville G	2	–	–	–	2
O'Shea	2	–	–	–	2
Butt	1	–	–	1	2
Djemba-Djemba	–	–	1	1	2
Silvestre	–	1	–	1	2
Neville P	–	–	–	1	1
Solskjaer	–	–	–	1	1
own goal	–	1	–	–	1

Just before the season begins, David Beckham undergoes a medical before completing his transfer from United to Real Madrid.

FA CUP: WINNERS. 22 MAY 2004. MILLENNIUM STADIUM, CARDIFF. BEAT MILLWALL 3-0 RONALDO 44', VAN NISTELROOY 65' & 81'

PREMIERSHIP: THIRD POSITION

LEAGUE CUP: LOSE TO WEST BROMWICH ALBION (0-2) IN 4TH ROUND

UEFA CHAMPIONS LEAGUE: LOSE TO PORTO (2-3 ON AGGREGATE) IN 1ST KNOCKOUT STAGE

FA COMMUNITY SHIELD: WINNERS. 10 AUGUST 2003. MILLENNIUM STADIUM, CARDIFF. BEAT ARSENAL 1-1 SILVESTRE 15' (A.E.T) UNITED WON 4-3 ON PENALTY KICKS

A rare trophy-less season is endured as the takeover is completed and Wayne Rooney joins the Red Devils

2004/05

SIR ALEX FERGUSON NOW knew that his team faced double trouble from London when it came to honours for this season. Not only were Arsenal going to be full of confidence after an unbeaten league season, but Chelsea had owner Roman Abramovich's money to buy a team to challenge on all fronts.

New signing Louis Saha had made a promising start after his January transfer and scored seven goals in just 14 appearances, while the defence had been strengthened with the signing Argentine defender Gabriel Heinze from Paris St Germain in June and Alan Smith joined from Leeds. But, Ferguson also wanted a potential superstar in the making from Everton, Wayne Rooney; the 18-year-old had made only 67 appearances for the Merseysiders and was signed for £20 million on 31 August as United languished at ninth in the league table.

By now Chelsea had already beaten United in the league and the Red Devils suffered too many draws and unexpected losses to teams like Portsmouth. However, progress was made in both the pre-qualifying round and the group phase of the Champions League. Yet when Fenerbahce beat United 3-0 in Turkey, the Reds could only finish second in their group and faced a tough knockout opponent next year.

But, in the meantime, Arsenal were beaten in the League Cup quarter-final only for Chelsea to again beat United – this time over two legs – in the semi-final. These two London rivals were also dominating the league as the New Year arrived, with United in the chasing pack. The Reds then began their FA Cup campaign with a rather awkward draw at home to lowly Exeter City after fielding an inexperienced line-up. The replay was negotiated successfully 2-0, which coincided with a run of six consecutive league wins that would put a real challenge to Chelsea for the Premiership.

In early February, United made different kinds of headlines when American businessman Malcolm Glazer, owner of the Tampa Bay Buccaneers gridiron football team, made a £790 million bid for the team. Breathtaking as this was, Sir Alex Ferguson's February focus was the first leg of the Champions League knockout stage against AC Milan, but despite linking up Rooney with Cristiano Ronaldo in an exciting forward line, the Italians were far too savvy and won 1-0 in Manchester.

By early March, Chelsea's lead in the league had grown to eight points and when a few days later Milan engineered the same 1-0 scoreline in Milan to take the tie 2-0 on aggregate, United were out of Europe. By mid-April, the Reds had only the FA Cup to focus on after slip-ups in the league. Newcastle United were beaten 4-1 in the semi-final and that left Arsenal to face in the final at the Millennium Stadium.

In the meantime on 16 May just five days before the cup final, Glazer told the football world he had acquired 75% of the club's shares and announced he would de-list the club from the stock exchange. Back on the football field, nothing could separate United and Arsenal over 120 minutes, but the Londoners won the penalty shoot-out 5-4 to lift the cup. Ironically, just as United were being taken over they ended the season trophy-less.

■ Wayne Rooney's first team United debut brings him a hat-trick in the Champions League match against Fenerbahce of Turkey on 28 September.

■ Midfield stalwart Nicky Butt leaves before the season begins. He joins Newcastle United after making 387 appearances since 1992.

■ United lose the Community Shield and finish third in the league; it is the second time in four seasons the Reds have been left trophy-less.

Above: On his arrival, Wayne Rooney, meets the young fan who had held up a sign pleading for the club to bring the player to Old Trafford.

Left: 26 February 2005. Wayne Rooney scored twice in the 2-0 win against Portsmouth at Old Trafford.

Final League Table Premiership

		P	W	D	L	F	A	Pts
1	Chelsea	38	29	8	1	72	15	95
2	Arsenal	38	25	8	5	87	36	83
3	**MANCHESTER UNITED**	38	22	11	5	58	26	77
4	Everton	38	18	7	13	45	46	61
5	Liverpool	38	17	7	14	52	41	58
6	Bolton Wanderers	38	16	10	12	49	44	58
7	Middlesbrough	38	14	13	11	53	46	55
8	Manchester City	38	13	13	12	47	39	52
9	Tottenham Hotspur	38	14	10	14	47	41	52
10	Aston Villa	38	12	11	15	45	52	47
11	Charlton Athletic	38	12	10	16	42	58	46
12	Birmingham City	38	11	12	15	40	46	45
13	Fulham	38	12	8	18	52	60	44
14	Newcastle United	38	10	14	14	47	57	44
15	Blackburn Rovers	38	9	15	14	32	43	42
16	Portsmouth	38	10	9	19	43	59	39
17	West Bromwich Albion	38	6	16	16	36	61	34
18	Crystal Palace	38	7	12	19	41	62	33
19	Norwich City	38	7	12	19	42	77	33
20	Southampton	38	6	14	18	45	66	32

Appearances

PLAYER	PREM	FAC	LC	CL	TOT
Silvestre	33 (2)	2 (2)	2	7 (1)	44 (5)
Scholes	29 (4)	5 (1)	1 (1)	7	42 (6)
Ferdinand	31	5	1	5	42
Ronaldo	25 (8)	6 (1)	2	7 (1)	40 (10)
Keane	28 (3)	4	1	6	39 (3)
Heinze	26	4	2	7	39
Rooney	24 (5)	6	1 (1)	6	37 (6)
Giggs	26 (6)	2 (2)	1	6	35 (8)
Carroll	26	3	-	5	34
Neville G	22	4	1	7	34
Brown	18 (3)	6	3	6 (1)	33 (4)
O'Shea	16 (7)	3 (1)	4	5	28 (8)
Smith	22 (9)	- (3)	1 (1)	3 (2)	26 (15)
Howard	12	4	5	5	26
Fletcher	18	1 (2)	3	3 (2)	25 (4)
van Nistelrooy	16 (1)	3	-	6 (1)	25 (2)
Fortune	12 (5)	5 (1)	4	3 (2)	24 (8)
Neville P	12 (7)	4 (1)	3	1 (5)	20 (13)
Djemba-Djemba	3 (2)	2	4	5	14 (2)
Saha	7 (7)	- (2)	4	- (2)	11 (11)

PLAYER	PREM	FAC	LC	CL	TOT
Kleberson	6 (2)	-	3	2 (1)	11 (3)
Miller	3 (5)	2 (2)	2	3 (2)	10 (9)
Bellion	1 (9)	1	3	2 (1)	7 (10)
Richardson	- (2)	1	3	1 (1)	5 (3)
Spector	2 (1)	1	- (1)	1 (1)	4 (3)
Eagles	-	1	1 (2)	1 (1)	3 (3)
Pique	-	1	- (1)	- (1)	1 (2)
Jones	-	1	- (1)	-	1 (1)
Forlan	- (1)	-	-	- (1)	- (2)
Rossi	-	-	- (2)	-	- (2)
Ebanks-Blake	-	-	- (1)	-	- (1)

Goalscorers

PLAYER	PREM	FAC	LC	CL	TOT
Rooney	11	3	-	3	17
van Nistelrooy	6	2	-	8	16
Scholes	9	3	-	-	12
Smith	6	-	1	2	9
Ronaldo	5	4	-	-	9
Giggs	5	-	1	2	8
Bellion	2	-	1	2	5
Fletcher	3	-	-	-	3
O'Shea	2	1	-	-	3
Silvestre	2	-	-	-	2
Keane	1	1	-	-	2
Saha	1	-	1	-	2
Brown	1	-	-	-	1
Heinze	1	-	-	-	1
Fortune	-	1	-	-	1
Miller	-	-	1	-	1
Neville G	-	-	-	1	1
Richardson	-	-	1	-	1
own goals	3	-	1	1	5

PREMIERSHIP: THIRD POSITION

FA CUP: RUNNERS-UP. 21 MAY 2005. MILLENNIUM STADIUM, CARDIFF. LOST TO ARSENAL 0-0 (A.E.T.) UNITED LOST 4-5 ON PENALTY KICKS

LEAGUE CUP: LOSE TO CHELSEA (1-2 ON AGGREGATE) IN SEMI-FINAL

UEFA CHAMPIONS LEAGUE: LOSE TO MILAN (0-2 ON AGGREGATE) IN 1ST KNOCKOUT STAGE

FA COMMUNITY SHIELD: RUNNERS-UP. 8 AUGUST 2004. MILLENNIUM STADIUM, CARDIFF. LOST TO ARSENAL 1-3 SILVA 50', SMITH 55', REYES 58', SILVESTRE (OG) 79'

2005/06

- Noel Cantwell, captain of the 1963 FA Cup-winning team dies on 8 September of cancer aged 72.

- On 29 October in a 4-1 defeat away to Middlesbrough, the goal by Ronaldo is United's 1,000th in the Premiership; the Red Devils are the first team to reach this landmark.

- United legend George Best dies aged just 59 in a London hospital on 25 November 2005. The entire world of football mourns his passing.

Above: Stalwart Roy Keane leaves Old Trafford after a total of 480 appearances and 51 goals.

Right: 26 February 2006. Wayne Rooney celebrates scoring United's fourth goal during the Carling Cup final against Wigan Athletic.

Opposite: 30 November 2005. Fans pay tribute to the late George Best ahead of the League Cup match between United and West Bromwich Albion.

Concern in the stands, deaths of legends but a trophy suggests good times are just round the corner

UNITED WERE NOW owned by American businessman Malcolm Glazer just over two years after he first bought a 2.9% stake in the club. Glazer had begun his move to own the Reds in March 2003 and, by June the following year, his stake had grown to nearly 20%; four months later he made his first ownership approach as that stake had grown to nearly 30%. The negotiating then continued until Glazer secured the deal in May. During this time, some fans were concerned about what the new owners might do to the club, and even set up a new one – FC United of Manchester. The vast majority of fans put their faith in Ferguson and the rest of board and the staff that had brought United to this point. Season ticket sales maintained constant levels and, in a general atmosphere of cynicism about billionaire owners throughout top-flight English football, Malcolm Glazer and his sons, who were soon to play leading roles in the club's affairs, were going to be given a chance to prove their commitment to the Old Trafford cause.

Despite off-the-field headlines, Sir Alex Ferguson was trying to get his team back to trophy-winning ways. The only significant pre-season signings while the ownership issues were settling down were goalkeeper Edwin van der Sar and South Korean midfielder Ji-sung Park who came from PSV Eindhoven. Departures included Phil Neville to Everton, and Kleberson, after two seasons at Old Trafford, to Besiktas in Turkey.

Early season form was patchy; the pre-qualifying round of the Champions League against Debreceni of Hungary proved easy enough and United also won their opening three league games, but cracks soon began to show. While Chelsea were surging away in the league, United lost games to Blackburn Rovers and Middlesbrough. However, it was the Champions League form that angered fans and brought despair to Ferguson.

A group containing Lille of France, Benfica of Portugal and Villarreal of Spain never looked easy and the Reds began optimistically with a draw against the Spaniards and a win over Benfica. But two losses and two draws followed and United actually finished last in the group with just six points. It was the first time since the 1994-95 season that the Reds had failed to progress beyond the first stage of the competition.

Although Chelsea had been beaten 1-0 in the league during the Champions League debacle, United were a long way off the pace for another championship and in November club captain Roy Keane departed after several injuries; the Irishman eventually moved to Celtic.

Sir Alex Ferguson went to the transfer market to boost his team and club morale; he signed Patrice Evra from AS Monaco and centre back Nemanja Vidic from Spartak Moscow in January. By now, however, Chelsea were in control of the Premiership title, so United had only domestic cups to fight for. League Cup progress had been unhindered since a 4-1 win over Barnet in October, with the usual team of fringe players on show.

However, January's two-leg semi-final against Blackburn Rovers delivered a 3-2 aggregate victory. In the meantime, FA Cup progress was being made until Liverpool won a tight contest at Anfield 1-0 in the fifth round. This meant the League Cup final at Cardiff against the latest surprise team of the Premiership, Wigan Athletic, at the end of February would be hugely significant. United won easily enough at the Millennium Stadium by 4-0 to ensure a first trophy for the new owners. It sparked a nine-game unbeaten run in the Premier League, but the Reds never looked like catching Chelsea, who finished eight points clear of United. However, for those who wanted to see, there were very promising signs for the future.

Final League Table Premiership

		P	W	D	L	F	A	Pts
1	Chelsea	38	29	4	5	72	22	91
2	**MANCHESTER UNITED**	38	25	8	5	72	34	83
3	Liverpool	38	25	7	6	57	25	82
4	Arsenal	38	20	7	11	68	31	67
5	Tottenham Hotspur	38	18	11	9	53	38	65
6	Blackburn Rovers	38	19	6	13	51	42	63
7	Newcastle United	38	17	7	14	47	42	58
8	Bolton Wanderers	38	15	11	12	49	41	56
9	West Ham United	38	16	7	15	52	55	55
10	Wigan Athletic	38	15	6	17	45	52	51
11	Everton	38	14	8	16	34	49	50
12	Fulham	38	14	6	18	48	58	48
13	Charlton Athletic	38	13	8	17	41	55	47
14	Middlesbrough	38	12	9	17	48	58	45
15	Manchester City	38	13	4	21	43	48	43
16	Aston Villa	38	10	12	16	42	55	42
17	Portsmouth	38	10	8	20	37	62	38
18	Birmingham City	38	8	10	20	28	50	34
19	West Bromwich Albion	38	7	9	22	31	58	30
20	Sunderland	38	3	6	29	26	69	15

Appearances

PLAYER	PREM	FAC	LC	CL	TOT
van der Sar	38	2	3	8	51
Ferdinand	37	1 (1)	4 (1)	8	50 (2)
O'Shea	34	2	3 (1)	7	46 (1)
Rooney	34 (2)	2 (1)	3 (1)	5	44 (4)
Silvestre	30 (3)	4	4 (1)	6	44 (4)
van Nistelrooy	28 (7)	2	1 (1)	8	39 (8)
Ronaldo	24 (9)	1 (1)	4	8	37 (10)
Fletcher	23 (4)	2 (1)	4	7	36 (5)
Neville	24 (1)	2 (1)	5	3 (1)	34 (3)
Giggs	22 (5)	1 (1)	3	4 (1)	30 (7)
Brown	17 (2)	4	5	3	29 (2)
Park	23 (10)	1 (1)	3	- (6)	27 (17)
Scholes	18 (2)	-	-	7	25 (2)
Smith	15 (6)	- (2)	1	7 (1)	23 (10)
Richardson	12 (10)	4	4 (1)	2 (3)	22 (14)
Saha	12 (7)	3 (1)	5	- (2)	20 (10)
Vidic	9 (2)	2	- (2)	-	11 (4)
Bardsley	3 (5)	2	1 (1)	2 (1)	8 (7)
Evra	7 (4)	- (1)	1 (1)	-	8 (6)
Rossi	1 (4)	2	3	- (2)	6 (6)

PLAYER	PREM	FAC	LC	CL	TOT
Howard	- (1)	2	3	-	5 (1)
Keane	4 (1)	-	-	1	5 (1)
Pique	1 (2)	2	1 (1)	-	4 (3)
Heinze	2 (2)	-	-	2	4 (2)
Solskjaer	- (3)	2	-	-	2 (3)
Jones	-	1	1 (2)	-	2 (2)
Miller	- (1)	-	1	- (1)	1 (2)
Ebanks-Blake	-	-	1	-	1
Eckersley	-	-	1	-	1
Martin	-	-	1	-	1
Gibson	-	-	- (1)	-	- (1)

Goalscorers

PLAYER	PREM	FAC	LC	CL	TOT
van Nistelrooy	21	-	1	2	24
Rooney	16	-	2	1	19
Saha	7	2	6	-	15
Ronaldo	9	-	2	1	12
Richardson	1	3	1	1	6
Giggs	3	1	-	1	5
Rossi	1	2	1	-	4
Ferdinand	3	-	-	-	3
Scholes	2	-	-	1	3
O'Shea	1	-	1	-	2
Park	1	-	1	-	2
Heinze	-	-	-	2	2
Fletcher	1	-	-	-	1
Silvestre	1	-	-	-	1
Smith	1	-	-	-	1
Ebanks-Blake	-	-	1	-	1
Miller	-	-	1	-	1
own goals	4	-	-	-	4

PREMIERSHIP: RUNNERS-UP

FA CUP: LOSE TO LIVERPOOL (0-1) IN 5TH ROUND

LEAGUE CUP: WINNERS. 26 FEBRUARY 2006. MILLENNIUM STADIUM, CARDIFF. BEAT WIGAN 4-0 ROONEY 33' & 61', SAHA 55', RONALDO 59'

UEFA CHAMPIONS LEAGUE: LOSE IN GROUP PHASE

2006/07

- Alan Smith plays his last game for United this season after three years with the club and moves on to Newcastle United in the off-season.

- Tommy Cavanagh, assistant manager to Dave Sexton from 1977 to 1981, dies aged 78 on 14 March after a struggle with Alzheimer's disease.

Above: 13 May 2007. Alan Smith holds the Premiership trophy in front of the United faithful after the final game of the season against West Ham United.

Right: 13 January 2007. Cristiano Ronaldo wheels away in celebration after scoring United's third goal in a 3-1 win against Aston Villa.

The Red Devils may have started as outsiders but they still beat the Blues of Chelsea to the Premiership crown

IT WAS A somewhat strange off-season (one that featured the World Cup in Germany) and beginning to the new campaign. Sir Alex Ferguson dispatched leading scorer Ruud van Nistelrooy to Real Madrid in July, yet brought in only midfielder Michael Carrick from West Ham United. Meanwhile, Chelsea were the bookmakers' favourites to retain their league title, having topped the Premier League for the last two seasons under Jose Mourinho.

Nevertheless, four straight wins and 11 goals at the start of the league season was all that Ferguson could ask for and the manager was certainly using plenty of members of his squad, 17 in just the first four matches. The joy for Ferguson was that another group of former youth team players were again making substantial contributions: Scot Darren Fletcher had emerged last season in midfield; unsung heroes in defence Wes Brown and John O'Shea were playing extensively as was Kieran Richardson, another midfielder. But the best news of all was the relationship up front between Cristiano Ronaldo and Wayne Rooney that was delivering lots of goals.

The two had clashed in the World Cup when Ronaldo was accused of helping get Rooney sent off in the England-Portugal quarter-final, but the players were nothing but bosom buddies in United shirts. The pair helped United start with only one loss in 14 games in all competitions from August to the end of October.

In November, a re-jigged United side was knocked out of the League Cup by Southend and the Red Devils also lost two Champions League group games (although they still easily won the group by the following month), but the general form was still good. League wins continued to be racked up and a 1-1 draw against Chelsea at Old Trafford (also in November) meant United were three points ahead of the Londoners at the top of the table.

Then three wins over Christmas meant the gap lengthened to six points going into January. When Henrik Larsson joined United on loan in the January transfer window, the Reds started to look very impressive, while the defence remained very solid, with van der Sar, Ferdinand and Vidic at the heart of things. An FA Cup run was begun, Champions League knock-out games were negotiated successfully and league wins kept on coming. So by mid-March, United looked good in all three competitions, especially after a 7-1 thumping of Roma and in the FA Cup where a 4-1 semi-final win would mean a final against Chelsea in May. The next key games were also semi-finals, but this time over two legs against AC Milan in the Champions League.

By now Larsson had returned to Sweden and United may have missed his guile and, although a last-minute winner at Old Trafford by Rooney gave United a 3-2 first leg lead, the Brazilian Kaka was at this best in Milan to guide the Italian side to a relatively easy 3-0 second leg victory. A dream Champions League final against Liverpool was dashed.

A 1-0 win over Manchester City then wrapped up the ninth Premiership title in 15 years, but the FA Cup final with Chelsea for another double was a disappointingly scrappy match and a 1-0 defeat for the Reds.

Final League Table Premiership

		P	W	D	L	F	A	Pts
1	**MANCHESTER UNITED**	38	28	5	5	83	27	89
2	Chelsea	38	24	11	3	64	24	83
3	Liverpool	38	20	8	10	57	27	68
4	Arsenal	38	19	11	8	63	35	68
5	Tottenham Hotspur	38	17	9	12	57	54	60
6	Everton	38	15	13	10	52	36	58
7	Bolton Wanderers	38	16	8	14	47	52	56
8	Reading	38	16	7	15	52	47	55
9	Portsmouth	38	14	12	12	45	42	54
10	Blackburn Rovers	38	15	7	16	52	54	52
11	Aston Villa	38	11	17	10	43	41	50
12	Middlesbrough	38	12	10	16	44	49	46
13	Newcastle United	38	11	10	17	38	47	43
14	Manchester City	38	11	9	18	29	44	42
15	West Ham United	38	12	5	21	35	59	41
16	Fulham	38	8	15	15	38	60	39
17	Wigan Athletic	38	10	8	20	37	59	38
18	Sheffield United	38	10	8	20	32	55	38
19	Charlton Athletic	38	8	10	20	34	60	34
20	Watford	38	5	13	20	29	59	28

Appearances

PLAYER	PREM	FAC	LC	CL	TOT
Rooney	33 (2)	5 (2)	1	12	51 (4)
Ronaldo	31 (3)	6 (1)	1	11	49 (4)
Carrick	29 (4)	7	–	12	48 (4)
Ferdinand	33	7	–	8 (1)	48 (1)
van der Sar	32	3	–	12	47
Scholes	29 (1)	3 (1)	–	10 (1)	42 (3)
Giggs	25 (5)	6	–	8	39 (5)
Vidic	25	5	–	8	38
Neville	24	3	–	6	33
Brown	17 (5)	6	2	7	32 (5)
Heinze	17 (5)	6	2	7 (1)	32 (6)
Evra	22 (2)	3 (1)	– (1)	4 (3)	29 (7)
O'Shea	16 (16)	2 (3)	1	8 (3)	27 (22)
Fletcher	16 (8)	3 (3)	1	6 (3)	26 (14)
Saha	18 (6)	2	–	5 (3)	25 (9)
Solskjaer	9 (10)	3 (3)	1	2 (4)	15 (17)
Silvestre	6 (8)	2	2	3	13 (8)
Richardson	8 (7)	2 (1)	2	– (4)	12 (12)
Kuszczak	6	5	2	–	13
Park	8 (6)	4 (1)	–	– (1)	12 (8)

PLAYER	PREM	FAC	LC	CL	TOT
Smith	6 (3)	2 (1)	2	1 (3)	11 (7)
Larsson	5 (2)	3 (1)	–	2	10 (3)
Jones D	–	–	2	–	2
Lee	1	–	– (2)	–	1 (2)
Eagles	1 (1)	–	–	–	1 (1)
Dong	1	–	–	–	1
Gray	–	–	1	–	1
Jones R	–	–	1	–	1
Marsh	–	–	1	–	1
Shawcross	–	–	– (2)	–	– (2)
Barnes	–	–	– (1)	–	– (1)

Goalscorers

PLAYER	PREM	FAC	LC	CL	TOT
Ronaldo	17	3	–	3	23
Rooney	14	5	–	4	23
Saha	8	1	–	4	13
Solskjaer	7	2	1	1	11
Scholes	6	–	–	1	7
Giggs	4	–	–	2	6
Carrick	3	1	–	2	6
Park	5	–	–	–	5
O'Shea	4	–	–	1	5
Vidic	3	–	–	1	4
Fletcher	3	–	–	–	3
Larsson	1	1	–	1	3
Richardson	1	1	–	1	3
Evra	1	–	–	1	2
Eagles	1	–	–	–	1
Ferdinand	1	–	–	–	1
Silvestre	1	–	–	–	1
Heinze	–	1	–	–	1
Lee	–	–	1	–	1
Smith	–	–	–	1	1
own goals	3	–	–	–	3

PREMIERSHIP: CHAMPIONS

FA CUP: RUNNERS-UP. 19 MAY 2007. WEMBLEY, LONDON. LOST TO CHELSEA 0-1 DROGBA 118'

LEAGUE CUP: LOSE TO SOUTHEND UNITED (0-1) IN 4TH ROUND

UEFA CHAMPIONS LEAGUE: LOSE TO MILAN (3-5 ON AGGREGATE) IN SEMI-FINAL

A dramatic Champions League penalty shoot-out brings more glory in Europe while Munich is solemnly remembered

2007/08

SIR ALEX FERGUSON was still as determined as ever to keep re-energising his team, so it was no surprise that more transfer activity was the order of the off-season. West Ham's Argentinian star Carlos Tevez was signed on a two-year loan, while youngsters Nani and Anderson arrived from clubs in Portugal, and Owen Hargreaves was brought in from Bayern Munich. All in all, that was certainly enough new names to add to a squad already filled with international talent.

Yet, as is so often the case, the best-laid plans do not always work out immediately and so it seemed with unconvincing early season form. Surprisingly, with so many top attacking players in the squad, it was up front where the difficulties arose. United only once scored more than one goal in a match for the first dozen games. Fortunately, the exception came with a win over chief league rivals Chelsea, whose manager Jose Mourinho had resigned three days earlier.

Despite some ordinary early performances, results still put United on top of the league at the end of October after an eight-game winning streak. By this time another early exit in the League Cup had happened and the Champions League group stage had begun successfully (United would eventually top their group, by five points from Roma). The defence was the aspect of the team that Ferguson was most pleased with; Rio Ferdinand's partnership with Nemanja Vidic was proving highly successful. With Edwin van der Sar in imperious form in goal, United would actually progress through the entire season without ever conceding more than two goals in any match in any competition.

The New Year saw the forwards start to hit the back of the net with more regularity. Then in February in a home match against Manchester City, the 50th anniversary of the Munich air disaster was marked with United playing in fifties-style kit (no sponsors' logo on the chest) and wreathes being carried onto the pitch in tribute. United lost that game, but the entire city of Manchester ensured a fitting commemoration.

Next up was a 4-0 FA Cup win over Arsenal (one of the best performances of the season), while Olympique Lyonnais were then dispatched in the Champions League first knockout round. A loss at home to Portsmouth was a shock in the next round of the FA Cup, but both Roma and Barcelona (in the semi-final) were taken out in Europe.

With just two more league games to play, United had to win both to guarantee the Premiership and they did just that, beating West Ham United and Wigan Athletic to deny Chelsea. These two English giants then met in the final of the Champions League on 21 May in Moscow. The rivals could not stage a classic match and the title had to be settled on penalties, which United won 6-5 to become champions of Europe for the third time.

- United get revenge for last season's FA Cup loss by beating Chelsea on penalties in the FA Charity Shield after a 1-1 draw.

- Ryan Giggs' substitute appearance in the Champions League final is his 759th for the club, setting a new club record.

- United's squad system is in overdrive this season with John O'Shea actually making more substitute appearances (21) and than starts (17).

- The Red Devils' 17th league win now puts them just one behind the record of 18 set by Liverpool, who last won the title in 1989-90.

- The 1-0 win over Barcelona in the Champions League semi-final second leg is Sir Alex Ferguson's 700th win in 1204 games.

Above: 6 February 2008. Twenty three candles commemorate the victims of the Munich air crash. The memorial service was held at Old Trafford on the 50th anniversary of the tragedy.

Left: 1 September 2007. Carlos Tevez clashes with ex-United star Dwight Yorke (now at Sunderland) during United's 1-0 win at Old Trafford.

Final League Table Premiership

		P	W	D	L	F	A	Pts
1	MANCHESTER UNITED	38	27	6	5	80	22	87
2	Chelsea	38	25	10	3	65	26	85
3	Arsenal	38	24	11	3	74	31	83
4	Liverpool	38	21	13	4	67	28	76
5	Everton	38	19	8	11	55	33	65
6	Aston Villa	38	16	12	10	71	51	60
7	Blackburn Rovers	38	15	13	10	50	48	58
8	Portsmouth	38	16	9	13	48	40	57
9	Manchester City	38	15	10	13	45	53	55
10	West Ham United	38	13	10	15	42	50	49
11	Tottenham Hotspur	38	11	13	14	66	61	46
12	Newcastle United	38	11	10	17	45	65	43
13	Middlesbrough	38	10	12	16	43	53	42
14	Wigan Athletic	38	10	10	18	34	51	40
15	Sunderland	38	11	6	21	36	59	39
16	Bolton Wanderers	38	9	10	19	36	54	37
17	Fulham	38	8	12	18	38	60	36
18	Reading	38	10	6	22	41	66	36
19	Birmingham City	38	8	11	19	46	62	35
20	Derby County	38	1	8	29	20	89	11

Appearances

PLAYER	PREM	FAC	LC	CL	TOT
Ferdinand	35	4	–	11	50
Brown	34 (2)	4	– (1)	9 (1)	47 (4)
Evra	33	4	–	10	47
Ronaldo	31 (3)	3	–	11	45 (3)
Vidic	32	3	–	9	44
van der Sar	29	4	–	10	43
Tevez	31 (3)	2	–	6 (6)	39 (9)
Carrick	24 (7)	3 (1)	– (1)	11 (1)	38 (10)
Rooney	25 (2)	3 (1)	–	10 (1)	38 (4)
Giggs	26 (5)	2	–	4 (5)	32 (10)
Scholes	22 (2)	1 (2)	–	7	30 (4)
Nani	16 (10)	2	1	7 (4)	26 (14)
Anderson	16 (8)	2 (2)	1	6 (3)	25 (13)
Hargreaves	16 (7)	2 (1)	–	5 (3)	23 (11)
O'Shea	10 (18)	1 (1)	1	4 (2)	16 (21)
Park	8 (4)	2	–	4	14 (4)
Kuszczak	8 (1)	– (1)	1	3 (2)	12 (4)
Fletcher	5 (11)	1	–	5 (1)	11 (12)
Saha	6 (11)	1 (1)	–	3 (2)	10 (14)
Pique	5 (4)	–	1	3	9 (4)

PLAYER	PREM	FAC	LC	CL	TOT
Simpson	1 (2)	– (1)	1	2 (1)	4 (4)
Silvestre	3	–	–	1 (1)	4 (1)
Eagles	1 (3)	–	1	1	3 (3)
Evans	–	–	1	1 (1)	2 (1)
Dong	–	–	1	– (1)	1 (1)
Bardsley	–	–	1	–	1
Foster	1	–	–	–	1
Martin	–	–	1	–	1
Campbell	– (1)	–	– (1)	–	– (2)
Neville	–	–	–	– (1)	– (1)

Goalscorers

PLAYER	PREM	FAC	LC	CL	TOT
Ronaldo	31	3	–	8	42
Tevez	14	1	–	4	19
Rooney	12	2	–	4	18
Saha	5	–	–	–	5
Nani	3	1	–	–	4
Giggs	3	–	–	–	3
Ferdinand	2	–	–	1	3
Carrick	2	–	–	–	2
Hargreaves	2	–	–	–	2
Scholes	1	–	–	1	2
Fletcher	–	2	–	–	2
Pique	–	–	–	2	2
Brown	1	–	–	–	1
Park	1	–	–	–	1
Vidic	1	–	–	–	1
own goals	2	–	–	–	2

United hold aloft the trophy with the stadium clock showing 2am after winning the Champions League final against Chelsea.

PREMIERSHIP: CHAMPIONS

FA CUP: LOSE TO PORTSMOUTH (0-1) IN 6TH ROUND

LEAGUE CUP: LOSE TO COVENTRY CITY (0-2) IN 3RD ROUND

UEFA CHAMPIONS LEAGUE: WINNERS. 21 MAY 2008. LUZHNIKI STADIUM, MOSCOW. BEAT CHELSEA 1-1 RONALDO 26', LAMPARD 45' (A.E.T.) UNITED WON 6-5 ON PENALTY KICKS

FA COMMUNITY SHIELD: WINNERS. 5 AUGUST 2007. WEMBLEY, LONDON. BEAT CHELSEA 1-1 GIGGS 35', MALOUDA 45' (A.E.T.) UNITED WON 3-0 ON PENALTY KICKS

2008/09

- Danny Welbeck makes his United debut in the third round League Cup match against Middlesbrough and goes on to start in the final.

- United take part in three penalty shoot-outs, succeeding in the Community Shield and League Cup final but lose the FA Cup semi-final.

- A total of 36 players appear in United games this season while Nemanja Vidic plays in the most matches – starting 52 and a substitute in three others.

- Louis Saha is sold to Everton before the campaign starts after four and a half seasons at United.

Above: 1 March 2009. Ben Foster saves a penalty from Tottenham Hotspur's Jamie O'Hara during the dramatic League Cup final shootout.

Right: Captain Rio Ferdinand (centre) holds up a new trophy for the Old Trafford team after winning the FIFA Club World Cup 2008 in Yokohama, Japan.

An 18th league title plus more penalty kick dramas and European disappointment

AS HOLDERS OF the Champions League trophy as well as the Premiership title, the current United squad was now focused on confirming forecasts that this would be the greatest Old Trafford team ever. To add more class, Dimitar Berbatov was signed from Tottenham Hotspur as another attacking alternative.

A Community Shield victory by penalties over Portsmouth was a decent enough beginning, although the 0-0 scoreline for the match itself was an indication of a slow start to an extremely busy season. Losing 2-1 to Zenit St Petersburg in the European Super Cup in August was disappointing, but no more so than another 2-1 defeat in the league two weeks later, this time to Liverpool. That loss would spark United's league form and they would suffer just one defeat in 24 Premier League games running from the end of September until early March. After hovering near the top of the table in the autumn, this run took United to the top by January.

The League Cup and Champions League campaigns both began in September and would end with appearances in the respective finals. United beat Middlesbrough, Queens Park Rangers and Blackburn Rovers in the opening League Cup rounds using a mixture of experienced players and youngsters. At the same time, the Champions League group stage was negotiated and United topped their table with two wins and four draws.

By now it was December and the Club World Cup tournament in Japan was won for the first time; Liga de Quito of Ecuador were beaten 1-0 in the final with a goal by Wayne Rooney. As the year turned, Southampton became United's opening FA Cup victims while Derby County were defeated in the two-leg League Cup semi-final. The final in March against Tottenham Hotspur brought the third trophy of the season; staying faithful to the fringe players, Sir Alex Ferguson's team beat Tottenham Hotspur via penalties after a 0-0 score in normal time.

By now the Champions League knockout stages were underway and Internazionale of Italy and Porto of Portugal were both defeated; after a 2-2 draw at Old Trafford, it took an epic 1-0 away win in mid-April to defeat the Portuguese. Incredibly, United also managed to reach the FA Cup semi-final four days later, but a tough Everton team held on to a scoreless tie after 120 minutes of play and then beat a patched-up United team 4-2 on penalties.

This defeat merely spurred on United in both the league and Champions League. An earlier 11-game winning run was supplemented in the spring by another string of victories – seven in all – and after the very next game, which was a 0-0 draw at home to Arsenal, United were confirmed as league champions for the 18th time. All that remained was to take on Barcelona in the Champions League final (a game that was set up by United's defeat of Arsenal in an all-English semi-final). However, a dream season ended sourly when the Spanish champions scored an early goal against the run of play and ran out 2-0 winners. So, despite failing in the biggest game of the season, Ferguson's teams grabbed three more trophies and lost only eight games out of 66 in total.

Final League Table Premiership

		P	W	D	L	F	A	Pts
1	MANCHESTER UNITED	38	28	6	4	68	24	90
2	Liverpool	38	25	11	2	77	27	86
3	Chelsea	38	25	8	5	68	24	83
4	Arsenal	38	20	12	6	68	37	72
5	Everton	38	17	12	9	55	37	63
6	Aston Villa	38	17	11	10	54	48	62
7	Fulham	38	14	11	13	39	34	53
8	Tottenham Hotspur	38	14	9	15	45	45	51
9	West Ham United	38	14	9	15	42	45	51
10	Manchester City	38	15	5	18	58	50	50
11	Wigan Athletic	38	12	9	17	34	45	45
12	Stoke City	38	12	9	17	38	55	45
13	Bolton Wanderers	38	11	8	19	41	53	41
14	Portsmouth	38	10	11	17	38	57	41
15	Blackburn Rovers	38	10	11	17	40	60	41
16	Sunderland	38	9	9	20	34	54	36
17	Hull City	38	8	11	19	39	64	35
18	Newcastle United	38	7	13	18	40	59	34
19	Middlesbrough	38	7	11	20	28	57	32
20	West Bromwich Albion	38	8	8	22	36	67	32

Appearances

PLAYER	PREM	FAC	LC	CL	TOT
Vidic	33 (1)	4	2 (2)	9	48 (3)
Ronaldo	31 (2)	2	2 (2)	11 (1)	46 (5)
van der Sar	33	2	–	10	45
O'Shea	20 (10)	3 (1)	6	12	41 (11)
Evra	28	2 (1)	1 (1)	10 (1)	41 (3)
Ferdinand	24	3	1	11	39
Rooney	25 (5)	1 (1)	– (1)	11 (2)	37 (9)
Berbatov	29 (2)	2 (1)	–	5 (4)	36 (7)
Carrick	24 (4)	3	– (1)	9	36 (5)
Fletcher	25 (1)	2 (1)	– (1)	8	35 (3)
Tevez	18 (11)	3	5 (1)	4 (5)	30 (17)
Park	21 (4)	3	1	5 (4)	30 (8)
Evans	16 (1)	2 (1)	5	6 (1)	29 (3)
Giggs	15 (13)	2	3 (1)	6 (5)	26 (19)
Anderson	11 (6)	3	5 (1)	7 (2)	26 (9)
Nani	7 (6)	2	6	6 (1)	21 (7)
Rafael	12 (4)	2	5	2 (2)	21 (6)
Neville	13 (3)	2	3	3 (1)	21 (4)
Scholes	14 (7)	1 (1)	2 (1)	3 (3)	20 (12)
Gibson	1 (2)	2 (1)	5 (1)	1 (1)	9 (5)

PLAYER	PREM	FAC	LC	CL	TOT
Foster	2	3	3	1	9
Welbeck	1 (2)	3 (2)	4 (1)	–	8 (5)
Brown	6 (2)	–	1	– (2)	7 (4)
Kuszczak	3 (1)	–	2	2	7 (1)
Possebon	– (3)	– (2)	3	–	3 (5)
Macheda	2 (2)	1	–	–	3 (2)
Hargreaves	1 (1)	–	–	1	2 (1)
Fabio	–	2	–	–	2
Amos	–	–	1	–	1
Campbell	1	–	–	–	1
De Laet	1	–	–	–	1
Martin, Lee	1	–	–	–	1
Eckersley	– (2)	– (2)	–	–	– (4)
Manucho	– (1)	–	– (2)	–	– (3)
Tosic	– (2)	– (1)	–	–	– (3)
Chester	–	–	– (1)	–	– (1)

Goalscorers

PLAYER	PREM	FAC	LC	CL	TOT
Ronaldo	18	1	2	4	25
Rooney	12	1	–	4	17
Tevez	5	2	6	2	15
Berbatov	9	1	–	4	14
Nani	1	2	3	–	6
Vidic	4	–	–	1	5
Carrick	4	–	–	–	4
Giggs	2	–	1	1	4
Park	2	1	–	1	4
Fletcher	3	–	–	–	3
Scholes	2	1	–	–	3
Gibson	1	2	–	–	3
Welbeck	1	2	–	–	3
Macheda	2	–	–	–	2
O'Shea	–	–	1	1	2
Brown	1	–	–	–	1
Rafael	1	–	–	–	1

PREMIERSHIP: CHAMPIONS | FA CUP: LOSE TO EVERTON (1-1; 2-4 ON PENALTY KICKS) IN SEMI-FINAL | LEAGUE CUP: WINNERS. 1 MARCH 2009. WEMBLEY, LONDON. BEAT TOTTENHAM HOTSPUR 0-0 (A.E.T.) UNITED WON 4-1 ON PENALTY KICKS | UEFA CHAMPIONS LEAGUE: RUNNERS-UP. 27 MAY 2009. STADIO OLYMPICO, ROME. LOST TO BARCELONA 0-2 ETO'O 10', MESSI 70' | EUROPEAN SUPER CUP: RUNNERS-UP. 29 AUGUST 2008. STADE LOUIS II, MONACO. LOST TO ZENIT ST PETERSBURG 1-2 POGREBNIAK 44', DANNY 59', VIDIC 73' | FA COMMUNITY SHIELD: WINNERS. 10 AUGUST 2008. WEMBLEY, LONDON. BEAT PORTSMOUTH 0-0 (A.E.T.) UNITED WON 3-1 ON PENALTY KICKS.

Disappointment but not despair after Ronaldo and Tevez both pack their bags

2009/10

ONE OF THE biggest topics of conversation among Manchester football fans this off-season was how Carlos Tevez swapped the red of United for the blue of City after months of speculation in the media. Tevez was liked by the Old Trafford faithful who wanted him to stay, but his move to City was not something to be easily forgiven. Yet even the Tevez news was overshadowed by the departure of Cristiano Ronaldo to Real Madrid. The Portuguese winger had made no secret of his love of the Spanish giants, but to lose him now – even for a massive £80 million – was a blow to the club.

To compensate for losing two forwards, Sir Alex Ferguson signed two more: Michael Owen on a free transfer from Newcastle United and the lesser-known Antonio Valencia from Wigan Athletic. Some fans believed it would be much harder to achieve a record fourth successive league title, but the Reds found themselves fighting with Chelsea again at the top of the table all the way through to end of the season.

In the meantime, the League Cup games were all won to set up a two-leg semi-final in January, while the Champions League group stage ended with United in first place, ahead of CSKA Moscow. Then when Leeds United dumped the Reds out of the third round of the FA Cup at Old Trafford, it seemed to spark United into action: they would lose only one game in the next 12 in the league, while also beating neighbours City to reach the League Cup final against Aston Villa and win 2-1, despite going a goal down early on.

Perhaps the best two performances of the season were at this time in the Champions League quarter-final against an AC Milan side including ex-United favourite David Beckham. A 3-2 victory in Italy was followed by a 4-0 crushing of Milan at Old Trafford. This was Ferguson's young side at its best, playing the kind of free-flowing football that was part of the club's DNA. Three consecutive league wins then put pressure on Chelsea as the two clubs fought tooth and nail for the Premiership, but United's season suddenly came unstuck.

A 2-1 loss in the Champions League semi-final first leg against Bayern Munich seemed like a reasonable result, but four days later Chelsea beat the Red Devils by the same score in the league. The return against the German team seemed to be a stroll as United rocketed to a 3-0 lead. But the sending off of young full-back Rafael let the German team back in the tie and they scored two goals to finish the match 3-2 in arrears but won on away goals. All that was left was the league, yet despite four United wins and a draw in the last five games, Chelsea maintained their form and took the Premiership by a single point for their new manager Carlo Ancelotti.

- Wayne Rooney is named Footballer of the Year by the Professional Footballers' Association and the Football Writers' Association.

- For the third season in a row, United are involved in a FA Community Shield penalty shoot-out, this time losing to Chelsea.

- One of the most exciting derby games for years ends 4-3 to United at Old Trafford with a late winning goal from Michael Owen.

- The loss to Leeds United in the third round of the FA Cup is United's first defeat in this round of the competition in 26 years.

Above: Mascot Fred The Red greets ex-United favourite David Beckham who is back in Manchester with his new team AC Milan in the Champions League first knockout round second leg at Old Trafford.

Left: 20 September 2010. Michael Owen is the new hero of the Stretford End after scoring the 95th minute winner that beats Manchester City 4-3.

Final League Table Premiership

		P	W	D	L	F	A	Pts
1	Chelsea	38	27	5	6	103	32	86
2	**MANCHESTER UNITED**	38	27	4	7	86	28	85
3	Arsenal	38	23	6	9	83	41	75
4	Tottenham Hotspur	38	21	7	10	67	41	70
5	Manchester City	38	18	13	7	73	45	67
6	Aston Villa	38	17	13	8	52	39	64
7	Liverpool	38	18	9	11	61	35	63
8	Everton	38	16	13	9	60	49	61
9	Birmingham City	38	13	11	14	38	47	50
10	Blackburn Rovers	38	13	11	14	41	55	50
11	Stoke City	38	11	14	13	34	48	47
12	Fulham	38	12	10	16	39	46	46
13	Sunderland	38	11	11	16	48	56	44
14	Bolton Wanderers	38	10	9	19	42	67	39
15	Wolverhampton Wanderers	38	9	11	18	32	56	38
16	Wigan Athletic	38	9	9	20	37	79	36
17	West Ham United	38	8	11	19	47	66	35
18	Burnley	38	8	6	24	42	82	30
19	Hull City	38	6	12	20	34	75	30
20	Portsmouth *	38	7	7	24	34	66	19

* deducted 9 points for going into administration

Appearances

PLAYER	PREM	FAC	LC	CL	TOT
Evra	37 (1)	–	3	7 (2)	47 (3)
Rooney	32	1	2 (1)	6 (1)	41 (2)
Fletcher	29 (1)	–	3	6 (1)	38 (2)
Valencia	29 (5)	– (1)	2 (2)	6 (3)	37 (11)
Carrick	22 (8)	–	4 (1)	6 (2)	32 (11)
Vidic	24	–	2	7	33
Scholes	24 (4)	–	1 (1)	7	32 (5)
Nani	19 (4)	–	2	8	29 (4)
van der Sar	21	–	2	6	29
Evans	18	1	5	3	27
Brown	18 (1)	1	4 (1)	2 (2)	25 (4)
Neville	15 (2)	1	3 (1)	6	25 (3)
Giggs	20 (5)	– (1)	2	1 (2)	23 (8)
Anderson	10 (4)	1	3	5	19 (4)
Ferdinand	12 (1)	–	1	6	19 (1)
Park	10 (7)	–	2	5 (1)	17 (8)
Rafael	8	–	4	3 (1)	15 (1)
O'Shea	12 (3)	–	–	2 (1)	14 (4)
Kuszczak	8	1	3	2	14

PLAYER	PREM	FAC	LC	CL	TOT
Gibson	6 (9)	1	2 (1)	3 (1)	12 (11)
Owen	5 (14)	– (1)	3 (1)	3 (3)	11 (19)
Foster	9	–	1	2	12
Welbeck	1 (4)	1	3	2	7 (4)
Fabio	1 (4)	1	2	2	6 (4)
Obertan	1 (6)	1	2	1 (2)	5 (8)
Macheda	1 (4)	–	2 (1)	2	5 (5)
De Laet	2	–	1 (2)	–	3 (2)
Diouf	– (5)	–	– (1)	–	– (6)
Tosic	–	–	– (2)	–	– (2)
Hargreaves	– (1)	–	–	–	– (1)
King	–	–	– (1)	–	– (1)

Goalscorers

PLAYER	PREM	FAC	LC	CL	TOT
Rooney	26	–	2	5	33
Berbatov	12	–	–	–	12
Owen	3	–	2	4	9
Giggs	5	–	1	1	7
Valencia	5	–	–	2	7
Scholes	3	–	1	3	7
Nani	4	–	–	2	6
Fletcher	4	–	–	1	5
Carrick	3	–	1	1	5
Gibson	2	–	2	1	5
Park	3	–	–	1	4
Welbeck	–	–	2	–	2
Anderson	–	–	–	1	1
Diouf	1	–	–	–	1
Macheda	1	–	–	–	1
O'Shea	1	–	–	–	1
Rafael	1	–	–	–	1
Vidic	1	–	–	–	1
own goals	10	–	–	–	10

3 January 2010. Sometimes things don't go according to plan. Sir Alex watches as United exit the FA Cup in the third round with beaten by Leeds United.

PREMIERSHIP: RUNNERS-UP

FA CUP: LOSE TO LEEDS UNITED (0-1) IN 3RD ROUND

LEAGUE CUP: WINNERS. 28 FEBRUARY 2010. WEMBLEY, LONDON. BEAT ASTON VILLA 2-1 MILNER 5', OWEN 12', ROONEY 74'

UEFA CHAMPIONS LEAGUE: LOSE TO BAYERN MUNICH (4-4 ON AWAY GOALS) IN QUARTER-FINAL

FA COMMUNITY SHIELD: RUNNERS-UP. 9 AUGUST 2009. WEMBLEY, LONDON. LOSE TO CHELSEA 2-2 NANI 10', CARVALHO 52', LAMPARD 71', ROONEY 90+2' (A.E.T) UNITED LOST 1-4 ON PENALTY KICKS

2010/11

The critics grumbled about their style yet there was no doubt about the Reds' finish and a precious 19th championship

WINNING ONLY THE League Cup last season while also watching Chelsea achieve the league and FA Cup double, meant Sir Alex Ferguson demanded more from his team this term. His two main new recruits were Mexican World Cup star Javier Hernandez and young Fulham defender Chris Smalling, who would both go on to have excellent debut seasons for United. Both players were among the substitutes as United beat Chelsea in the Community Shield game at Wembley, with Hernandez actually scoring in the 3-1 victory.

However, it was Dimitar Berbatov who led the scoring for United in the early stages of the league season, including a hat-trick in the 3-2 home win over Liverpool in September. Chelsea and Arsenal, however, looked in better shape during the early part of the season while high-spending Manchester City were the latest team to threaten United's Premiership dominance.

The Reds were proving to be impressive at home, but rather workmanlike away; they were also showing their most dogged of qualities by scoring several crucial goals in the last few minutes of games to pick up extra points. But the team was disturbed in October by highly public contract negotiations with Wayne Rooney, who told the club he wanted to leave because of fears about their lack of cash for new players. There was even speculation that Rooney might sign for City. Just as fans became resigned to their star striker leaving Old Trafford, there was an abrupt turn-around a few days later when Rooney signed a new five-year contract.

By November United were grinding out points better than anyone and a 7-1 home win against Blackburn Rovers, with five goals from Berbatov, was enough to take the Reds to the top of the table. At the same time, progress was also completed from the group stage of the Champions League, but there would be no strong defence of their League Cup title; a weakened team lost embarrassingly 4-0 to West Ham United in the quarter-finals.

Into January and now fighting on just three fronts, United were still unbeaten in the league after 23 matches and top of the table. A 1-0 FA Cup third round win over Liverpool at home was achieved relatively comfortably (a Ryan Giggs goal), but the first league defeat of the season came next month, a surprising 2-1 loss to struggling Wolverhampton Wanderers at Molineux. Clearly, United would have to work hard for any trophies this season because the team was solid, but not dominating.

Consecutive league losses to Chelsea and Liverpool in March seemed to indicate a wobble, yet the Reds again steadied

- Wayne Rooney scores what many observers say is the goal of the season – a spectacular overhead kick – in a 2-1 win over Manchester City.

- Javier Hernandez – nick-named Chicharito or the Little Pea – is voted the United fans' player of the year in his first season at the club.

- To prove Sir Alex Ferguson's claims of his team's dogged determination, 15 of United's 78 league goals are scored in the 80th minute or later.

- A total of 21 players (a record number) win Premiership medals for having taken part in 10 league games or more.

Above: 28 May 2011. As Paul Scholes exits, Ryan Giggs will be the last of the 1992 class of Fergie's Fledglings to continue playing for the Red Devils.

Right: 26 October 2010. The sensational Chicharito gets a 90th minute winner to beat Wolves 3-2.

Final League Table Premiership

		Pld	W	D	L	F	A	Pts
1	**Manchester United**	38	23	11	4	78	37	80
2	Chelsea	38	21	8	9	69	33	71
3	Manchester City	38	21	8	9	60	33	71
4	Arsenal	38	19	11	8	72	43	68
5	Tottenham Hotspur	38	16	14	8	55	46	62
6	Liverpool	38	17	7	14	59	44	58
7	Everton	38	13	15	10	51	45	54
8	Fulham	38	11	16	11	49	43	49
9	Aston Villa	38	12	12	14	48	59	48
10	Sunderland	38	12	11	15	45	56	47
11	West Bromwich Albion	38	12	11	15	56	71	47
12	Newcastle United	38	11	13	14	56	57	46
13	Stoke City	38	13	7	18	46	48	46
14	Bolton Wanderers	38	12	10	16	52	56	46
15	Blackburn Rovers	38	11	10	17	46	59	43
16	Wigan Athletic	38	9	15	14	40	61	42
17	Wolverhampton Wanderers	38	11	7	20	46	66	40
18	Birmingham City	38	8	15	15	37	58	39
19	Blackpool	38	10	9	19	55	78	39
20	West Ham United	38	7	12	19	43	70	33

Appearances

PLAYER	PREM	FAC	LC	CL	TOT
Van der Saar	33	2	0	10	45
Neville	3	0	0 (1)	0	3 (1)
Evra	34 (1)	3	0	9 (1)	46 (2)
Hargreaves	1	0	0	0	1
Ferdinand	19	2	1	7	29
Brown	4 (3)	2 (1)	2 (1)	2	10 (5)
Owen	1 (10)	1 (1)	1	0 (2)	3 (13)
Anderson	14 (4)	2 (2)	2	4 (2)	22 (8)
Berbatov	24 (8)	2	0	6 (1)	32 (9)
Rooney	25 (3)	1 (1)	0	9	35 (4)
Giggs	19 (6)	1 (2)	1	6 (2)	27 (10)
Smalling	11 (5)	2 (2)	3	7 (2)	23 (9)
Park	13 (2)	1	2	8 (1)	24 (3)
Hernandez	15 (4)	4 (1)	2 (1)	6 (3)	27 (17)
Vidic	35	2	0	9	46
Carrick	23 (5)	3	1	11	37 (5)
Nani	30 (2)	2 (1)	0	9 (3)	41 (6)
Scholes	16 (6)	2 (1)	0	4 (3)	22 (10)
Fabio	5 (6)	4	2	5(2)	16 (8)
Rafael	15 (1)	3	1 (1)	6 (1)	25 (3)

PLAYER	PREM	FAC	LC	CL	TOT
O'Shea	18 (2)	4	1	5 (1)	28 (3)
Evans	10 (2)	2	2	2 (1)	16 (3)
Fletcher	23 (2)	1 (1)	1	5 (2)	30 (5)
Valencia	8 (2)	1 (1)	0	5 (2)	14 (5)
Obertan	3 (4)	2	2 (1)	1 (2)	8 (7)
Macheda	2 (5)	0	2 (1)	1 (1)	5 (7)
Gibson	6 (6)	3	2	3	14 (6)
Kuszczak	5	1	2	2	10
Bebe	0 (2)	1	2 (1)	0 (1)	3 (4)
Lindegaard	0	2	0	0	2
Amos	0	0	1	1	2
Morrison	0	0	0 (1)	0	0 (1)

Goalscorers

PLAYER	PREM	FAC	LC	CL	TOT
Berbatov	20	0	0	0	20
Hernandez	13	1	1	4	19
Rooney	11	1	0	4	16
Nani	9	0	0	1	10
Park	5	0	2	1	8
Vidic	5	0	0	0	5
Owen	2	1	2	0	5
Giggs	2	1	0	1	4
Anderson	1	0	0	3	4
Fletcher	2	0	0	1	3
Valencia	1	0	0	1	2
Bebe	0	0	1	1	2
Fabio	1	1	0	0	2
Gibson	0	0	1	1	2
Scholes	1	0	0	0	1
Smalling	0	0	1	0	1
Obertan	0	0	0	1	1
Macheda	1	0	0	0	1
Evra	1	0	0	0	1
Brown	0	1	0	0	1
Own Goals	3	0	0	0	3

The last few moments of Edwin van der Sar's career. He retires aged 40 after the Champions League final.

PREMIERSHIP: CHAMPIONS

FA CUP: LOSE TO MANCHESTER CITY (0-1) IN SEMI-FINAL

LEAGUE CUP: LOSE TO WEST HAM UNITED (0-4) IN QUARTER-FINAL

UEFA CHAMPIONS LEAGUE: RUNNERS-UP. 28 MAY 2011. WEMBLEY, LONDON. LOST TO BARCELONA 1-3 PEDRO 27', ROONEY 34', MESSI 54', VILLA 69'

FA COMMUNITY SHIELD: WINNERS. 8 AUGUST 2010. WEMBLEY, LONDON. BEAT CHELSEA 3-1 VALENCIA 41', HERNANDEZ 76', KALOU 83', BERBATOV 90'

Dimitar Berbatov equalled the Premiership goals-in-a-game record with five against Blackburn.

Paul Scholes retired at the end of the season after 676 appearances and 150 goals.

Javier Hernandez scored eight of his 20 goals after coming on as a substitute.

their ship by reaching the FA Cup semi-finals after a 2-0 win over Arsenal while also completing a 2-1 aggregate Champions League win against Olympique Marseille to reach the quarter-finals.

United entered the month of April still leading the league and promptly defeated a resurgent Chelsea in the Champions League quarter-finals. But the topsy-turvy nature of the season returned when arch-rivals Manchester City won a much-hyped FA Cup semi-final 1-0, a game that saw Paul Scholes sent off near the end. The month was not a total disaster as the Reds successfully returned to league business and stayed ahead of the chasing pack that was now led by Chelsea. After their last game in April, United were leading the Londoners by six points, but their next four games would be among the most crucial of the season.

Firstly, there was a very convincing 2-0 Champions League semi-final first leg win over Schalke 04 in Germany; then next up was Arsenal in the league, but United seemed lacklustre and dropped to a 1-0 defeat so the gap with Chelsea was cut to just three points. The second leg against Schalke 04, even with a deliberately depleted line-up, provided a confidence-boosting 4-1 win, so a Champions League final was assured and now the Reds could focus on the Premiership.

The home match with Chelsea four days later was billed as a championship decider and, with United's key players all

having enjoyed a short rest, Ferguson was right to be confident. When Hernandez scored in the very first minute of the game and Nemanja Vidic added a second after 23 minutes, the Reds looked home and dry. There was a minor scare when Chelsea pulled a goal back after 68 minutes through Frank Lampard, but the Reds would not be denied and ran out 2-1 winners. Their 19th English league title – one more than the previous record set by Liverpool – was secured a week later after one of the most drama-filled seasons for years.

The Champions League final at Wembley, though, was a disappointment as Barcelona dominated possession for long periods and ended as clear 3-1 winners. Ferguson admitted: "We were beaten by the best team in Europe and there is no shame in that."

"I think it's dangerous (to go for a draw) against a team like Chelsea, who can score goals against you. We have to go out and attack like Manchester United do at Old Trafford. The crowd wouldn't have it any other way."

Ryan Giggs on the day before the important match against their London rivals in early May.

"One of the great privileges of being a manager is playing a part in the development of young players, watching them grow in confidence and ability."

Sir Alex Ferguson prior to his youth team winning the Youth Cup for a record tenth time.

"I don't think we should be going there lacking confidence. Their form has been very good, we're playing a fantastic team, but there shouldn't be a sense of terror. We can't be frightened out of our skin. We've got to find a solution to playing against them."

Sir Alex Ferguson before the Champions League final against Barcelona.

"They are a great side and were the better team. Maybe we could have done better over a couple of their goals, but you have to give credit where credit is due."

Rio Ferdinand after the 3-1 Champions League final defeat against Barcelona.

"There was a match where he came to me in the dressing room and started to tell me off, but was calling me Rafael. He still gets us confused, but it doesn't matter."

Fabio da Silva talking about Sir Alex Ferguson mistaking him for his twin brother Rafael.

Above: Relaxing on the train journey down to London for the Champions League final against Barcelona are Edwin van der Sar, Ryan Giggs, Paul Scholes and Gary Neville, the former club captain who had announced his retirement on 2 February 2011.

Left: 12 February 2011. The much-acclaimed winning goal against arch-rivals Manchester City comes from a Wayne Rooney overhead kick.

3

The Players

At a club renowned for star players, Scotsman Arthur Albiston was the kind of down-to-earth, dependable player that managers love. With 485 United appearances over 14 seasons, Albiston made the full back slot his own during a career in which he picked up three FA Cup winner's medals and 14 caps for his country.

ALPHONSO 'ALF' AINSWORTH

Country: England
Born: 31 Jul 1913 **Died:** 25 May 1975
Debut: 3 Mar 1934 v Bury
Position: Inside forward
Appearances: 2 **Goals scored:** 0
Seasons: 1933/34
Clubs: Manchester United, New Brighton, Congleton

JOHN AITKEN

Country: Scotland
Born: 1870 **Died:** Unknown
Debut: 7 Sep 1895 v Crewe Alexndra
Position: Inside forward
Appearances: 2 **Goals scored:** 1
Seasons: 1895/96
Clubs: Newton Heath

GEORGE ALBINSON

Country: England
Born: 14 Feb 1897 **Died:** Apr 1975
Debut: 12 Jan 1921 v Liverpool
Position: Defender
Appearances: 1 **Goals scored:** 0
Seasons: 1920/21
Clubs: Manchester United, Manchester City, Crewe Alexandra

ARTHUR ALBISTON

Country: Scotland
Born: 14 Jul1957
Debut: 9 Oct 1974 v Manchester City
Position: Defender
Appearances: 467 (18) **Goals scored:** 7
Seasons: 1974/75 - 1987/1988
Clubs: Manchester United, West Bromwich Albion, Dundee, Chesterfield, Chester City

JACK ALLAN

Country: England
Born: 16 Jan 1883 **Died:** Unknown
Debut: 3 Sep 1904 v Port Vale
Position: Forward
Appearances: 36 **Goals scored:** 22
Seasons: 1904/05 - 1906/07
Clubs: Manchester United, Bishop Auckland

ARTHUR 'REG' ALLEN

Country: England
Born: 3 May 1919 **Died:** Apr 1976
Debut: 19 Aug 1950 v Fulham
Position: Goalkeeper
Appearances: 80 **Goals scored:** 0
Seasons: 1950/51 - 1952/53
Clubs: Queens Park Rangers, Manchester United, Altrincham

ARTHUR ALLMAN

Country: England
Born: 24 Dec 1890 **Died:** 22 Dec 1956
Debut: 13 Feb 1915 v Sheffield Wednesday
Position: Full back
Appearances: 12 **Goals scored:** 0
Seasons: 1914/15
Clubs: Shrewsbury Town, Wolverhampton Wanderers, Swansea Town, Stoke City, Manchester United, Millwall Athletic

ALFRED AMBLER

Country: England
Born: 1 Jul 1879 **Died:** Unknown
Debut: 2 Sep 1899 v Gainsborough Trinity
Position: Defender
Appearances: 10 **Goals scored:** 1
Seasons: 1899/1900 - 1900/01
Clubs: Hyde United, Newton Heath, Colne F.C.

BENJAMIN AMOS

Country: England
Born: 10 Apr 1990
Debut: 23 Sep 2008 v Middlesbrough
Position: Goalkeeper
Appearances: 3 **Goals scored:** 0
Seasons: 2009/09 - present
Clubs: Manchester United, Peterborough United (*loan*), Molde (*loan*), Oldham Athletic (*loan*)

GEORGE WALTER ANDERSON

Country: England
Born: Jan 1893 **Died:** Unknown
Debut: 9 Sep 1911 v Everton
Position: Forward
Appearances: 86 **Goals scored:** 39
Seasons: 1911/12 - 1914/15
Clubs: Bury, Manchester United

JOHN ANDERSON

Country: England
Born: 11 Oct 1921 **Died:** 8 Aug 2006
Debut: 20 Dec 1947 v Middlesbrough
Position: Defender
Appearances: 40 **Goals scored:** 2
Seasons: 1947/48 - 1948/49
Clubs: Plymouth Argyle, Manchester United, Nottingham Forest, Peterborough United

LUIS DE ABREU OLIVEIRA ANDERSON

Country: Brazil
Born: 13 Apr 1988

Above: Arthur Albiston, United's long-serving full back, who also won 14 Scotland international caps between 1982 and 1986.

Right: 24 April 1948. An FA Cup final souvenir from 1948 features both John Anderson and John Aston Snr.

Debit: 1 Sep 2007 v Sunderland
Position: Midfield
Appearances: 96 (34) **Goals scored:** 5
Seasons: 2007/08 – present
Clubs: Gremio, FC Porto, Manchester United

TREVOR ANDERSON
Country: Northern Ireland
Born: 3 Mar 1951
Debut: 31 Mar 1973 v Southampton
Position: Forward
Appearances: 13 (6) **Goals scored:** 2
Seasons: 1972/73 – 1973/74
Clubs: Portadown, Manchester United, Swindon Town, Peterborough, Linfield

VIVIAN 'VIV' ALEXANDER ANDERSON
Country: England
Born: 29 Aug 1956
Debut: 15 Aug 1987 v Southampton
Position: Defender
Appearances: 64 (5) **Goals scored:** 4
Seasons: 1987/88 – 1990/91
Clubs: Nottingham Forest, Arsenal, Manchester United, Sheffield Wednesday, Barnsley, Middlesbrough

Viv Anderson was Alex Ferguson's first signing when the the player arrived from Arsenal for £250,00 in 1987. Anderson would play for England 30 times and be awarded an MBE in 2000.

WILLIAM 'WILLIE' JOHN ANDERSON
Country: England
Born: 24 Jan 1947
Debut: 28 Dec 1963 v Burnley
Position: Forward
Appearances: 10 (2) **Goals scored:** 0
Seasons: 1963/64 – 1966/67
Clubs: Manchester United, Aston Villa, Cardiff City, Portland Timbers

MICHAEL APPLETON
Country: England
Born: 4 Dec 1975
Debut: 23 Oct 1996 v Swindon Town
Position: Midfield
Appearances: 1 (1) **Goals scored:** 0
Seasons: 1996/97
Clubs: Manchester United, Lincoln City (*loan*), Grimsby Town (*loan*), Preston North End, West Bromwich Albion

THOMAS 'TOMMY' ARTHUR ARKESDEN
Country: England
Born: tbc Jul 1878 **Died:** 25 Jun 1921
Debut: 14 Feb 1903 v Blackpool
Position: Forward
Appearances: 79 **Goals scored:** 33
Seasons: 1902/03 – 1905/06
Clubs: Burton Wanderers, Derby County, Burton United, Manchester United, Gainsborough Trinity

JOHN 'JOE' EMMANUEL ASTLEY
Country: England
Born: Apr 1889 **Died:** Oct 1967
Debut: 17 Mar 1926
Position: Defender
Appearances: 2 **Goals scored:** 0
Seasons: 1925/26 – 1926/27
Clubs: Cradley Heath, Manchester United, Notts County

JOHN ASTON JNR
Country: England
Born: 28 Jun 1947
Debut: 12 Apr 1965 v Leicester City
Position: Forward
Appearances: 166 (21) **Goals scored:** 27
Seasons: 1964/65 – 1971/72
Clubs: Manchester United, Luton Town, Mansfield Town, Blackburn Rovers

JOHN ASTON SNR
Country: England
Born: 3 Sep 1921 **Died:** 31 Jul 2003
Debut: 18 Sep 1946 v Chelsea
Position: Defender
Appearances: 284 **Goals scored:** 30
Seasons: 1946/47 – 1953/54
Clubs: Manchester United

Locally born and a product of the youth system, Aston was a fine player over nine seasons, either at left back or centre forward winning both a league and FA Cup medal. He was capped 17 times for England and his son (John Jnr) would also play for the Reds. After retiring from the game because he was suffering from tuberculosis, he served United as a coach and then as a scout.

GARY BAILEY
Country: England
Born: 9 Aug 1958
Debut: 18 Nov 1978 v Ipswich Town
Position: Goalkeeper
Appearances: 375 **Goals scored:** 0
Seasons: 1978/79 –1986/87
Clubs: Manchester United, Kaizer Chiefs

In a time before millionaire footballers, Bailey paid his own way from South Africa to Manchester for a trial in 1978. After joining the Reds, he established himself as the number one, helping United to FA Cup wins in 1983 and 1985. Following a knee injury he returned to South Africa where he finished his career with Kaizer Chiefs. Nowadays he is the face of Supersport Premier League

coverage. Gary is the son of former Ipswich goalkeepr Roy Bailey.

DAVID BAIN
Country: Scotland
Born: 5 Aug 1900 **Died:** Unknown
Debut: 14 Oct 1922 v Port Vale
Position: Forward
Appearances: 23 **Goals scored:** 9
Seasons: 1922/23 – 1923/24
Clubs: Rutherglen Glencairn, Manchester United, Everton

JAMES BAIN
Country: Scotland
Born: 1878 **Died:** Unknown
Debut: 16 Sep 1899 v Loughborough Town
Position: Forward
Appearances: 2 **Goals scored:** 0
Seasons: 1899/1900
Clubs: Dundee, Newton Heath

JIMMY BAIN
Country: Scotland
Born: 6 Feb 1891 **Died:** 22 Sep 1969
Debut: 7 Feb 1925 v Leyton Orient
Position: Defender
Appearances: 4 **Goals scored:** 0
Seasons: 1924/1925 – 1927/28
Clubs: Manchester United, Glasgow Strathclyde, Rutherglen Glencairn, Brentwood

Above: 19 August 1987. Viv Anderson in action against his old club Arsenal during the Division One match held at Old Trafford. The match ended in a 0-0 draw.

WILLIAM 'BILL' BAINBRIDGE
Country: England
Born: 9 Mar 1922
Debut: 9 Jan 1946 v Accrington Stanley
Position: Forward
Appearances: 1 **Goals scored:** 0
Seasons: 1945/46
Clubs: Ashington, Manchester
United, Bury, Tranmere Rovers

HENRY 'HARRY' BAIRD
Country: Northern Ireland
Born: 17 Aug 1913 **Died:** 22 May 1973
Debut: 23 Jan 1937 v Sheffield Wednesday
Position: Forward
Appearances: 53 **Goals scored:** 18
Seasons: 1936/37 – 1937/38
Clubs: Bangor F.C., Linfield, Windsor
Park Swifts, Manchester United,
Huddersfield Town, Ipswich Town

Harry Baird would score 15 goals in the
1937-1938 season (joint top scorer with
Tommy Bamford)and help secure
United's promotion back to the top flight.

TOMMY BALDWIN
Country: England
Born: 10 Jun 1945
Debut: 18 Jan 1975 v Sunderland
Position: Midfield
Appearances: 2 **Goals scored:** 0
Seasons: 1974/75
Clubs: Arsenal, Chelsea, Millwall,
Manchester United, Gravesend and
Northfleet, Seattle Sounders, Brentford

JOHN 'JACK' THOMAS BALL
Country: England
Born: 13 Sep 1907 **Died:** 2 Feb 1976
Debut: 11 Sep 1929 v Leicester City
Position: Forward
Appearances: 50 **Goals scored:** 18
Seasons: 1929/30 – 1934/35
Clubs: Southport, Manchester United, Sheffield
Wednesday, Huddersfield Town, Luton Town

JOHN BALL
Country: England
Born: 13 Mar 1925
Debut: 10 Apr 1948 v Everton
Position: Defender
Appearances: 23 **Goals scored:** 0
Seasons: 1947/48 – 1949/50
Clubs: Wigan Athletic, Gravesend,
Manchester United, Bolton Wanderers

WILLIAM 'BILLY' HENRY BALL
Country: England
Born: tbc Jun 1876 **Died:** Feb 1929
Debut: 8 Nov 1902 v Lincoln City
Position: Defender
Appearances: 4 **Goals scored:** 0
Seasons: 1902/03
Clubs: Blackburn Rovers,
Manchester United research

THOMAS 'TOMMY' BAMFORD
Country: Wales
Born: 2 Sep 1905 **Died:** 12 Dec 1967
Debut: 20 Oct 1934 v Newcastle United
Position: Forward
Appearances: 109 **Goals scored:** 57
Seasons: 1934/35 – 1937/38
Clubs: Wrexham, Manchester
United, Swansea Town

JOHN 'JACK' BANKS
Country: England
Born: 14 Jun 1871 **Died:** Jan 1947
Debut: 7 Sep 1901 v Gainsborough Trinity
Position: Defender
Appearances: 44 **Goals scored:** 1
Seasons: 1901/02 – 1902/03
Clubs: West Bromwich Albion, Manchester
United, Plymouth Argyle

Jack Banks straddled the Newton Heath
and Manchester United eras.

JAMES 'JIMMY' BANNISTER
Country: England
Born: 20 Sep 1880 **Died:** Unknown
Debut: 1 Jan 1907 v Aston Villa
Position: Forward
Appearances: 63 **Goals scored:** 8
Seasons: 1906/07 – 1909/10
Clubs: Leyland F.C., Chorley, Manchester
City, Manchester United, Preston
North End, Burslem Port Vale

JOHN 'JACK' BARBER
Country: England
Born: 8 Jan 1901 **Died:** 30 Mar 1961
Debut: 6 Jan 1923 v Hull City
Position: Forward
Appearances: 4 **Goals scored:** 2
Seasons: 1922/23 – 1923/24
Clubs: Chesterfield, Clayton,
Manchester United, Southport

PHILLIP 'PHIL' BARDSLEY
Country: Scotland
Born: 28 Jun 1985
Debut: 3 Dec 2003 v West Bromwich Albion
Position: Defender
Appearances: 10 (8) **Goals scored:** 0
Seasons: 2003/04 – 2007/08
Clubs: Royal Antwerp (loan), Burnley
(loan), Glasgow Rangers (loan), Aston Villa
(loan), Manchester United, Sunderland

CYRIL BARLOW
Country: England
Born: 22 Jan 1889 **Died:** Unknown
Debut: 7 Feb 1920 v Sunderland
Position: Defender
Appearances: 30 **Goals scored:** 0
Seasons: 1919/20 – 1921/22
Clubs: Northern Nomads, Manchester
United, New Cross F.C.

MICHAEL BARNES
Country: England

Born: 24 Jun 1988
Debut: 25 Oct 2006 v Crewe Alexandra
Position: Forward
Appearances: (1) **Goals scored:** 0
Seasons: 2006/07
Clubs: Manchester United, Chesterfield
(loan), Shrewsbury Town (loan)

PETER BARNES
Country: England
Born: 10 Jun 1957
Debut: 31 Aug 1985 v Nottingham Forest
Position: Forward
Appearances: 24 (1) **Goals scored:** 4
Seasons: 1985/86 – 1986/87
Clubs: Manchester City, West Bromwich
Albion, Leeds United, Real Betis, Coventry
City, Manchester United, Manchester City,
Hull City, S.C. Farense, Bolton Wanderers,
Sunderland, Bury, Drogheda United, Tampa
Bay Rowdies, Wrexham, Cliftonville

FRANK BARRETT
Country: Scotland
Born: 2 Aug 1872 **Died:** Aug 1907
Debut: 26 Sep 1896 v Newcastle United
Position: Goalkeeper
Appearances: 136 **Goals scored:** 0
Seasons: 1896/97 – 1899/1900
Clubs: Dundee, Newton Heath, New Brighton Tower,
Arbroath, Manchester City, Dundee, Aberdeen

FRANK BARSON
Country: England
Born: 10 Apr 1891 **Died:** 13 Sep 1968
Debut: 9 Sep 1922 v Wolverhampton Wanderers
Position: Half back
Appearances: 152 **Goals scored:** 4
Seasons: 1922/23 – 1927/28
Clubs: Barnsley, Aston Villa,
Manchester United, Watford

One of the toughest players in the
English game of his era, he was once
banned for seven months for his hard
tackling and on one occasion needed a
police guard to protect him from angry
opposition fans. Although injury-
plagued during his time at United, he
was known for his on-field leadership
and was given the captaincy of the club.
Bizarrely, for helping win promotion in
1924-25, he was given a pub as a prize
(he apparently gave it away on the opening night). He made one international
appearance.

FABIEN ALAIN BARTHEZ
Country: France
Born: 28 Jun 1971
Debut: 13 Aug 2000 v Chelsea
Position: Goalkeeper
Appearances: 139 **Goals scored:** 0
Seasons: 2000/01 – 2003/04

Clubs: Toulouse FC, Olympique Marseille, AS Monaco, Manchester United, Olympique Marseille (*loan*), Nantes

ARTHUR BEADSWORTH

Country: England
Born: Sep 1876 **Died:** 9 Oct 1917
Debut: 25 Oct 1902 v Arsenal
Position: Forward
Appearances: 12 **Goals scored:** 2
Seasons: 1902/03 - 1903/04
Clubs: Hinckley Town, Leicester Fosse, Preston North End, Manchester United, Swindon Town

ROBERT HUGHES BEALE

Country: England
Born: 8 Jan 1884 **Died:** 5 Oct 1950
Debut: 2 Sep 1912
Position: Goalkeeper
Appearances: 112 **Goals scored:** 0
Seasons: 1912/13 - 1914/15
Clubs: Maidstone United, Brighton & Hove Albion, Norwich City, Manchester United, Arsenal (WW1), Gillingham

PETER ANDREW BEARDSLEY

Country: England
Born: 10 Jan 1961
Debut: 6 Oct 1982 v AFC Bournemouth
Position: Forward
Appearances: 1 **Goals scored:** 0
Seasons: 1982/83
Clubs: Carlisle United, Vancouver White Caps, Manchester United, Vancouver White Caps, Newcastle United, Liverpool, Everton, Newcastle United, Bolton Wanderers, Manchester City (*loan*), Fulham, Hartlepool United, Melbourne Knights

RUSSELL PETER BEARDSMORE

Country: England
Born: 28 Sep 1968
Debut: 24 Sep 1988 v West Ham United
Position: Midfield
Appearances: 39 (34) **Goals scored:** 4
Seasons: 1988/89 - 1992/93
Clubs: Manchester United, Blackburn Rovers (*loan*), AFC Bournemouth

TIAGO MANUEL DIAS CORREIA 'BÉBÉ'

Country: Portugal
Born: 12 Jul 1990
Debut: 22 Sep 2010 v Scunthorpe United
Position: Forward
Appearances: 3 (4) **Goals scored:** 2
Seasons: 2010/11
Clubs: Estrela da Amadora Club, Vitória de Guimarães, Manchester United, Besiktas J.K. (*loan*)

R BECKETT

Country:
Born: Unknown **Died:** Unknown
Debut: 30 Oct 1886 Newton Heath v Fleetwood Rangers
Position: Goalkeeper
Appearances: 1 **Goals scored:** 0
Seasons: 1886/87
Clubs: Newton Heath

JOHN HARRY 'CLEM' BEDDOW

Country: England
Born: Oct 1885 **Died:** Unknown

Below: 23 November 2002. Fabien Barthez, perhaps United's most eccentric goakeeper. Brought in to replace Peter Schmeichel, he would both delight and infuriate the fans and Alex Ferguson alike. He won the World Cup in 1998 and Euro 2000 with France.

Debut: 25 Feb 1905 v Burnley
Position: Forward
Appearances: 34 **Goals scored:** 15
Seasons: 1905/06 – 1906/07
Clubs: Trent Rovers, Burton United, Manchester United, Burnley

WILLIAM 'BILLY' BEHAN
Country: Ireland
Born: 8 Aug 1911 **Died:** 12 Nov 1991
Debut: 3 Mar 1934 v Bury
Position: Goalkeeper
Appearances: 1 **Goals scored:** 0
Seasons: 1933/34
Clubs: Shamrock Rovers, Shelbourne, Manchester United, Shelbourne, Shamrock Rovers

ALEXANDER 'ALEX' BELL
Country: Scotland
Born: 1882 **Died:** 30 Nov 1934
Debut: 24 Jan 1903 v Glossop
Position: Half back
Appearances: 309 **Goals scored:** 10
Seasons: 1902/03 – 1912/13
Clubs: Ayr Springvale, Ayr Westerlea, Ayr Parkhouse, Manchester United, Blackburn Rovers

Bell's name was immortalised by former United team-mate Charlie Roberts, who became a tobacconist after retiring from football and named a brand of cigarettes "Ducrobel" after United's famous half back trio of Duckworth, Roberts and Bell.

DAVID BELLION
Country: France
Born: 27 Nov 1982
Debut: 27 Aug 2003 v Wolverhampton Wanderers
Position: Forward
Appearances: 15 (25) **Goals scored:** 8
Seasons: 2003/04 – 2004/05
Clubs: Cannes, Sunderland, Manchester United, West Ham United (*loan*), Nice (*loan*), Nice, Bordeaux, Nice (*loan*)

Above: 1956. Johnny Berry photographed in training at Old Trafford. Note the muddy pitch and the open stands behind. He was not only a highly skilful winger, he was extremely tough.

Right: 1957. United players relaxing while playing a game of snooker, Players include, Ray Wood, Mark Jones, Dennis Viollet and Geoff Bent.

SAMUEL RAYMOND BENNION
Country: Wales
Born: 1 Sep 1896 **Died:** 12 Mar 1958
Debut: 27 Aug 1921 v Everton
Position: Half back
Appearances: 301 **Goals scored:** 3
Seasons: 1921/22 – 1931/32
Clubs: Gwersylly School, Ragtimes FC, Chrichton's Athletic, Manchester United, Burnley

GEOFFREY 'GEOFF' BENT
Country: England
Born: 27 Sep 1932 **Died:** 6 Feb 1958
Debut: 11 Dec 1954 v Burnley
Position: Full back
Appearances: 12 **Goals scored:** 0
Seasons: 1954/55 – 1957/58
Clubs: Manchester United

DIMITAR IVANOV BERBATOV
Country: Bulgaria
Born: 30 Jan 1981
Debut: 13 Sep 2008 v Liverpool
Position: Forward
Appearances: 97 (32) **Goals scored:** 47
Seasons: 2008/09 - Present
Clubs: Pirin Blagoevgrad, CSKA Sofia, Bayer Leverkusen, Tottenham Hotspur, Manchester United

Signed from Tottenham Hotspur for a fee of around £30 million, the Bulgarian international is one of the most elegant strikers in the game, with superb vision and touch. In November 2010, he equalled the Premier League record when he scored five goals against Blackburn Rovers in United's 7-1 win.

HENNING STILLE BERG
Country: Norway
Born: 1 Sep 1969
Debut: 13 Aug 1997
Position: Defender
Appearances: 81 (22) **Goals scored:** 3
Seasons: 1997/98 – 2000/01

Clubs: Valarenga, Lillestrom, Blackburn Rovers, Manchester United, Blackburn Rovers (*loan*), Blackburn Rovers, Rangers

REGINALD JOHN 'JOHNNY' BERRY
Country: England
Born: 1 Jun 1926 **Died:** 16 Sep 1994
Debut: 1 Sep 1951 v Bolton Wanderers
Position: Winger
Appearances: 276 **Goals scored:** 45
Seasons: 1951/52 – 1957/58
Clubs: Birmingham City, Manchester United

The young winger came to Old Trafford after outstanding performances against United for Birmingham City. Two-footed, fast and tricky, Berry provided the crosses for hundreds of goals by his fellow Busby Babes. Severe injuries from the Munich air crash ended his career aged 28.

WILLIAM ALEXANDER 'BILL' BERRY
Country: England
Born: Jul 1884 **Died:** 1 Mar 1943
Debut: 17 Nov 1906 v Sheffield Wednesday
Position: Forward
Appearances: 14 **Goals scored:** 1
Seasons: 1906/07 – 1908/09
Clubs: Sunderland, Tottenham Hotspur, Manchester United, Stockport County

PAUL ANTHONY BIELBY
Country: England
Born: 24 Nov 1956
Debut: 13 Mar 1974 v Manchester City
Position: Midfield
Appearances: 2 (2) **Goals scored:** 0
Seasons: 1972/73 – 1975/76
Clubs: Manchester United, Hartlepool (*loan*), Hartlepool, Huddersfield Town

Paul Bielby was awarded a MBE in 2008 for services to young people through his coaching work in Darlington.

DAVID ROBERT JOSEPH BECKHAM

Country: England
Born: 2 May 1975
Debut: 23 Sep 1992 v Brighton & Hove Albion
Position: Midfield
Appearances: 356 (38) **Goals scored:** 85
Seasons: 1992/93 - 2002/03
Clubs: Manchester United, Preston North End (*loan*), Real Madrid, LA Galaxy, AC Milan (*loan*)

Asked in 1999 what set David Beckham apart from his peers, Alex Ferguson provided a simple explanation: "He practises with a relentless application that the vast majority of less gifted players wouldn't contemplate." This combination of work rate and ability propelled Beckham from United youth teamer to England captain and eventually worldwide sporting icon. As well as talent and dedication, Beckham epitomised the off-field glitz and glamour of being a modern-day footballer with what became 'The Beckham Brand'.

Born in Leytonstone, East London, to a United-supporting family, the young Beckham started out at the Tottenham Hotspur School of Excellence, but signed schoolboy forms with United on his fourteenth birthday. He quickly rose through the ranks and made his mark as part of a group of players including Ryan Giggs, Gary Neville and Nicky Butt who would win the FA Youth Cup in 1992. His professional debut followed in September of the next season and he was then loaned out to Preston North End for more first team experience. Beckham's breakthrough season came in 1995-96, when he helped United win a second Premiership and FA Cup double.

The following season a piece of improvised brilliance in the opening league match – an incredible chipped goal from 60-yards out – brought him to the attention of the nation. He gained a first England cap a few days later. By the 1998 World Cup, Beckham was an England regular, however, he was sent off infamously against Argentina for kicking out against an opponent and returned home to an initially unforgiving press and much public hostility.

Nevertheless, United supporters stuck by their player and redemption was to come as part of the glorious treble-winning team of 1998-99, scoring the equalising goal in the final league match of the season to clinch the title. Further glory followed in the Champions League final as two Beckham corners led to the injury-time goals that sealed an unforgettable victory.

Following his marriage to Spice Girls pop star Victoria Adams, the Beckham Brand was now taking off and the footballer was becoming a sponsor's dream.

But this new lifestyle caused some concern in case it distracted him from his football and eventually led to the end of his Old Trafford days. In 2003 a football boot kicked by Ferguson hit Beckham on the head and left the player with a cut above the eye.

A £25 million move to Real Madrid soon followed as Beckham continued to become a global football star. Then, as his on-field talents diminished due to age and injury, periods with LA Galaxy in America (where the whole league seemed to rely on his image to improve the awareness of 'soccer') and A.C. Milan brought fewer world-class performances.

It was as a Red with 394 appearances and 85 goals that Beckham the player peaked. His many individual achievements include twice being runner-up in the FIFA World Player of the Year, winning 115 England caps, receiving the OBE in 2003 and even fronting both the London Olympic bid and the English FA attempt to win the 2018 World Cup.

Left: 27 Aug 1997. A young David Beckham celebrates after scoring a goal against Everton played at Goodison Park.

Below: 15 May 1992. United Youth team, winners of the FA Youth Cup final. Back row (l-r) Ben Thornley, Nicky Butt, Gary Neville, Simon Davies, Chris Casper, Kevin Pilkington and Keith Gillespie; front row, (l-r)John O'Kane, Robbie Savage, George Switzer, Ryan Giggs and David Beckham.

GEORGE BEST

Country: Northern Ireland
Born: 22 May 1946 **Died:** 25 Nov 2005
Debut: 14 Sep 1963 v West Bromwich Albion
Position: Forward
Appearances: 470 **Goals scored:** 179
Seasons: 1963/64 - 1973/74
Clubs: Manchester United, Dunstable Town, Stockport County, Cork Celtic, LA Aztecs, Fulham, LA Aztecs, Fort Lauderdale Strikers, Motherwell, Hibernian, San Jose Earthquakes, See Bea, Hong Kong Rangers, Bournemouth, Brisbane Lions

United fans who saw him play feel privileged. United opponents who faced him often felt overwhelmed — by his skill, his imagination and a talent that was sublime and quite possibly unique. He is perhaps most perfectly summed up by the local saying in his native Northern Ireland: Maradona good, Pelé better, George Best. In due course, in 2004 the great Pelé would name him as one of the 125 best living footballers.

The Belfast Boy in a red shirt showing off his transcendent footballing skills defined much of Matt Busby's final great United team. Along with Bobby Charlton and Denis Law, Best captured not just trophies, but also captured hearts. This was the fifth Beatle, the first

British football celebrity with the mop of dark black hair and the smile that melted women's hearts; women fell in love with him, men wanted to be like him. His meteoric 11-year career is filled with magical moments that the YouTube generation can still appreciate — and it all began like a fairytale. The shy young Best was just one of many skinny teenagers kicking a ball around the tough Cregagh Estate in Belfast until a United scout, Bob Bishop, saw his potential. He sent a telegram to Matt Busby: "Boss, I think I've found a genius."

The teenager was plucked from obscurity and taken to Manchester, but soon suffered from homesickness and initially returned to Belfast. Busby coaxed him back, and the teenager eventually signed professional forms on his seventeenth birthday. His league debut came only four months later, on 14 September 1963 against West Bromwich Albion at Old Trafford. It was a run-of-the-mill 1-0 win for United, but the manager liked what he saw and the winger played 26 games that season, scoring six goals.

After that relatively quiet first season, Best's rise to superstardom really began in 1964-65. He played in 59 of United's 60 games that season and it ended with a

league championship trophy. Despite playing alongside the established players Charlton and Law, the Northern Irishman was far from overshadowed, in fact, he attracted considerable media coverage because he was younger and rather handsomer than his teammates. Best was simply dazzling. He had overcome his natural shyness and, while some of the glitz and glamour of sport started to invade his world, his performances on the field simply took the breath away.

In 1965-66, Best and United returned to European Cup competition for the first time since the Munich air crash and the bigger stage brought out the best in the young winger who was still not 20 years old. He was now winning games almost single-handed, including a 5-1 thrashing of Benfica in the European Cup quarter-final in Lisbon. It prompted the 'El Beatle' headlines and although there were no trophies to show for it at the end of the season, Best had won himself legendary status.

Winning another league championship in 1966-67 launched a second European Cup campaign for United the following season and, this time, Best would lead the charge. He was inspired by the team's ambition to bring the

Above: 1968. Best jumps to head a ball watched by a Chelsea player.

Right: 1964."The Fifth Beatle" makes adjustments to his fashionably styled haircut.

ultimate club trophy to Manchester for the first time. Best was superb throughout the whole tournament and particularly in the final against Benfica where he scored the second goal in the 4-1 win in extra-time with typical aplomb. In fact, he scored a remarkable 32 goals during the season in all competitions. He was simply untouchable, and it was no surprise that he was voted European Footballer of the Year in addition to Player of the Year by the English football writers.

At the time, few people would have believed that Best had now peaked. On the field he could score glorious goals, like his six in a single match against Northampton Town in a fifth round FA Cup tie in 1970, but off the field he was distracted by opening his own nightclub, countless pretty girls and the beginnings of his alcohol problems. His football decline was most likely linked to the retirement of the newly knighted and patrician Sir Matt Busby in 1969 who had been something of a father figure.

The replacement managers – Wilf McGuinness, Frank O'Farrell and then Tommy Docherty – clashed with Best, because of his indiscipline. The player threatened to quit after the 1971-72 season when he played 53 games and scored 26 goals. With the club not buying new players or even making him captain (a long-held wish), he famously vanished to Marbella, but was tempted to return. However, after two ordinary seasons and with the Reds heading for the Second Division, he exited Old Trafford for good on 2 January 1974 at the age of just 27.

United were relegated at the end of Best's final season in which he played just 12 league games and his football journey for the next decade was long and winding, from Dunstable Town and Fulham to Los Angeles Aztecs, Brisbane Lions and Hong Kong Rangers.

While Best's world tour was happening, his international career with Northern Ireland also fizzled out. His 37 caps and nine goals are very ordinary statistics for such an influential player, but his most memorable moment in the green shirt of his country remains as an example of a footballing brain that moved faster than any other. Against England in 1971 at Windsor Park, Belfast, Best stole the ball from the world's best goalkeeper Gordon Banks with his own outstretched leg as the keeper tried to kick the ball out of his hands. Best scored a goal that was wrongly disallowed simply because it was so outrageous.

It was a slow decline for Best, although even in his later years, awards came to him aplenty. He was given an honorary doctorate from Queens University, Belfast, in 2001 and was made a freeman of Castlereagh, his birthplace, a year later. But his long fight with alcoholism was a battle he could not win. After several marriages, some time in jail, drunken appearances on TV, a kidney transplant and despite the best wishes and sympathy of a nation, Best died just short of his 60th birthday.

Above: 29 May 1968. European Cup final at Wembley: Best scores United's second goal to give them the lead in extra time.

BRIAN BIRCH

Country: England
Born: 18 Nov 1931 **Died:** Unknown
Debut: 27 Aug 1949 v West Bromwich Albion
Position: Forward
Appearances: 15 **Goals scored:** 5
Seasons: 1949/50 - 1951/52
Clubs: Manchester United, Wolverhampton Wanderers, Lincoln City, Boston United, Barrow, Exeter City, Oldham Athletic, Rochdale

HERBERT BIRCHENOUGH

Country: England
Born: 21 Sep 1874 **Died:** 28 Feb 1942
Debut: 25 Oct 1902 v Arsenal
Position: Goalkeeper
Appearances: 30 **Goals scored:** 0
Seasons: 1902/03
Clubs: Haslington, Crewe Hornets, Nantwich, Sandbach St Mary's, Audley, Burslem Port Vale, Glossop, Manchester United, Crewe Alexandra

CLIFFORD BIRKETT

Country: England
Born: 17 Sep 1933 **Died:** 11 Jan 1997
Debut: 2 Dec 1950 v Newcastle United
Position: Forward
Appearances: 13 **Goals scored:** 2
Seasons: 1950/51 - 1955/56
Clubs: Manchester United, Southport

GARY BIRTLES

Country: England
Born: 27 Jul 1956
Debut: 22 Oct 1980 v Stoke City
Position: Forward
Appearances: 63 (1) **Goals scored:** 12
Seasons: 1980/81 - 1981/82
Clubs: Nottingham Forest, Manchester United, Nottingham Forest, Notts County, Grimsby Town

GEORGE BISSETT

Country: Scotland
Born: 25 Jan 1896 **Died:** 1946
Debut: 15 Nov 1919 v Burnley
Position: Forward
Appearances: 42 **Goals scored:** 10
Seasons: 1919/20 - 1921/22
Clubs: Glencraig Thistle, Third Lanark, Manchester United, Wolverhampton Wanderers, Pontypridd, Southend United

ARTHUR RICHARD 'DICK' BLACK

Country: Scotland
Born: 18 Feb 1907 **Died:** Unknown
Debut: 23 Apr 1932 v Bradford City
Position: Forward
Appearances: 8 **Goals scored:** 3
Seasons: 1931/32 - 1933/34
Clubs: Stenhousemuir, Blantyre Victoria, Greenock Morton, Manchester United, St Mirren

CLAYTON GRAHAM BLACKMORE

Country: Wales
Born: 23 Sep 1964
Debut: 16 May 1984 v Nottingham Forest
Position: Defender/Midfield
Appearances: 201 (44) **Goals scored:** 26
Seasons: 1983/84 - 1992/93
Clubs: Manchester United, Middlesbrough, Bristol City (loan), Barnsley, Notts County, Leigh RMI, Bangor City, Portmadog, Neath Athletic

Clayton Blackmore spent twelve seasons with Manchester United. He was an extraordinarily versatile player and, uniquely, wore every outfield shirt number (2-11) during his time with the club. He won cups in 1990, 1991 and 1992 and was part of the championship winning squad in 1993. He left United for Middlesbrough in 1994 and was capped 39 times by Wales.

PETER BLACKMORE

Country: England
Born: Jul 1879 **Died:** Unknown

Debut: 21 Oct 1899 v New Brighton Tower
Position: Forward
Appearances: 2 **Goals scored:** 0
Seasons: 1899/1900
Clubs: Newton Heath

THOMAS 'TOMMY' BLACKSTOCK

Country: Scotland
Born: 1882 **Died:** 8 Apr 1907
Debut: 3 Oct 1903 v Arsenal
Position: Full back
Appearances: 38 **Goals scored:** 0
Seasons: 1903/04 - 1906/07
Clubs: Dunniker Rovers, Blue Bell, Raith Rovers, Leith Athletic, Cowdenbeath, Manchester United

Tragically died on the pitch after heading the ball in a match for United against St. Helens.

LAURENT ROBERT BLANC

Country: France
Born: 19 Nov 1965
Debut: 8 Sep 2001 v Everton
Position: Centre back
Appearances: 71 (4) **Goals scored:** 4
Seasons: 2001/02 - 2002/03
Clubs: Montpellier, Napoli, Nimes, St Etienne, Auxerre, Barcelona, Marseille, Inter Milan, Manchester United

JOHN 'JACKIE' BLANCHFLOWER

Country: Northern Ireland
Born: 7 Mar 1933 **Died:** 2 Sep 1998
Debut: 24 Nov 1951 v Liverpool
Position: Half back
Appearances: 117 **Goals scored:** 27
Seasons: 1951/52 - 1957/58
Clubs: Manchester United

The younger brother of Danny Blanchflower. Jackie retired after career-ending injuries sustained in the Munich air crash.

HORACE ELFORD BLEW

Country: Wales
Born: Jan 1878 **Died:** 1 Feb 1957

Above: 19 Oct 1991. Clayton Blackmore in action for United against Arsenal. The Neath-born utility player had his best season in 1990-91, when he missed only three of United's 60 games.

Right: 1938/39. Back row (l-r): Brown, Roughton, Breedon, Manley, Breen, McKay, Baird, Sitting (l-r): Inglis, (Assistant Trainer), Bryant, Craven, Smith, J. Griffiths, Vose, T. Curry, (Trainer), On the ground (l-r): Redwood, Gladwin, Pearson.

Debut: 13 Apr 1906 v Chelsea
Position: Full back
Appearances: 1 **Goals scored:** 0
Seasons: 1905/06
Clubs: Grove Park School, Wrexham
Old Boys, Rhostyllen, Wrexham, Bury,
Manchester United, Manchester City

LARS JESPER BLOMQVIST
Country: Sweden
Born: 5 Feb 1974
Debut: 9 Sep 1998 v Charlton Athletic
Position: Left wing
Appearances: 29 (9) **Goals scored:** 1
Seasons: 1998/99 – 2000/01
Clubs: Umea, IFK Gothenburg, AC Milan, Parma,
Manchester United, Everton, Charlton Athletic,
Djurgarden, Enkoping, Hammarby, Peresbaya 1927

SAMUEL PRINCE BLOTT
Country: England
Born: 1 Jan 1886 **Died:** 1 Jan 1969
Debut: 1 Sep 1909 v Bradford City
Position: Forward
Appearances: 19 **Goals scored:** 2
Seasons: 1909/10 – 1912/13
Clubs: Bradford Park Avenue, Southend
United, Manchester United, Plymouth Argyle

THOMAS 'TOMMY' BOGAN
Country: Scotland
Born: 18 May 1920 **Died:** 23 Sep 1993
Debut: 8 Oct 1949
Position: Outside right
Appearances: 33 **Goals scored:** 7
Seasons: 1948/49 – 1951/52
Clubs: Strathclyde, Blantyre Celtic, Renfrew
Juniors, Hibernian, Glasgow Celtic, Preston
North End, Manchester United, Aberdeen,
Southampton, Blackburn Rovers

JAMES ERNEST 'ERNIE' BOND
Country: England
Born: 4 May 1929
Debut: 18 Aug 1951 v West Bromwich Albion
Position: Outside left
Appearances: 21 **Goals scored:** 4
Seasons: 1950/51 – 1952/53
Clubs: Leyland Motors FC, Manchester
United, Carlisle United, Queen of the South

ROBERT POLLOCK 'BOB' BONTHRON
Country: Scotland
Born: 1880 **Died:** Unknown
Debut: 5 Sep 1903 v Bristol City
Position: Right back
Appearances: 134 **Goals scored:** 3
Seasons: 1903/04 – 1906/07
Clubs: Raith Athletic, Raith Rovers, Dundee,
Manchester United, Sunderland, Northampton
Town, Birmingham, Airdrieonians, Leith Athletic

Bob Bonthron has the unfortunate reputation of closing the Valley Parade
ground. He was attacked by Bradford
City fans after a game after his alleged

rough treatment of an opposing winger.
The fans were prosecuted and the
ground temporarily closed.

WILLIAM BOOTH
Country: England
Born: Oct 1880 **Died:** Unknown
Debut: 26 Dec 1900 v Blackpool
Position: Forward
Appearances: 2 **Goals scored:** 0
Seasons: 1900/01
Clubs: Edge Lane, Newton Heath

MARK JOHN BOSNICH
Country: Australia
Born: 13 Jan 1972
Debut: 30 Apr 1990 v Wimbledon
Position: Goalkeeper
Appearances: 38 **Goals scored:** 0
Seasons: 1989/90 – 1990/91
& 1999/00 – 2000/01
Clubs: Sydney Croatia , Manchester United,
Aston Villa, Manchester United, Chelsea,
Central Coast Mariners, Sydney Olympic

HENRY BOYD
Country: Scotland
Born: 6 May 1868 **Died:** Jul 1935
Debut: 20 Jan 1897 v Blackpool
Position: Forward
Appearances: 62 **Goals scored:** 35
Seasons: 1896/97 – 1898/99
Clubs: Sunderland Albion, Burnley, West Bromwich
Albion, Woolwich Arsenal, Newton Heath, Falkirk

WILLIAM GILLESPIE 'BILLY' BOYD
Country: Scotland
Born: 27 Nov 1905 **Died:** 14 Dec 1967
Debut: 9 Feb 1935 v Swansea City
Position: Forward
Appearances: 6 **Goals scored:** 4
Seasons: 1934/35
Clubs: Regent Star, Royal Albert, Larkhill Thistle,
Clyde, Sheffield United, Manchester United,
Workington, Luton Town, Southampton, Weymouth

THOMAS WILKINSON BOYLE
Country: England
Born: 21 Jan 1897 **Died:** Unknown
Debut: 30 Mar 1929 v Derby County
Position: Forward
Appearances: 17 **Goals scored:** 6
Seasons: 1928/29 – 1929/30
Clubs: Sheffield United, Northampton
Town, Manchester United

LEONARD BRADBURY
Country: England
Born: Jul 1914 **Died:** 2007
Debut: 28 Jan 1939 v Chelsea
Position: Forward
Appearances: 2 **Goals scored:** 1
Seasons: 1938/39
Clubs: Manchester United, Northwich
Victoria, Manchester University,
Manchester United, Old Wittonians

WARREN BRADLEY
Country: England
Born: 20 Jun 1933 **Died:** 6 Jun 2007
Debut: 15 Nov 1958 v Bolton Wanderers
Position: Outside right
Appearances: 67 **Goals scored:** 21
Seasons: 1957/58 – 1961/62
Clubs: Durham City, Bolton Wanderers,
Bishop Auckland, Manchester United,
Bury, Northwich Victoria, Macclesfield
Town, Bangor City, Macclesfield Town

Became the first and only player to represent England at full and amateur level
in the same season in 1959.

Above: Munich survivor Jackie
Blanchflower was spotted playing
for Boyland in East Belfast
by one of United's team of
scouts in Northern Ireland.

HAROLD BRATT
Country: England
Born: 8 Oct 1939
Debut: 2 Nov 1960 v Bradford City
Position: Defender
Appearances: 1 **Goals scored:** 0
Seasons: 1960/61
Clubs: Manchester United, Doncaster Rovers

ALAN BERNARD BRAZIL
Country: Scotland
Born: 15 Jun 1959
Debut: 25 Aug 1984 v Watford
Position: Forward
Appearances: 24 (17) **Goals scored:** 12
Seasons: 1984/85 - 1985/86
Clubs: Ipswich Town, Detroit Express
(loan), Tottenham Hotspur, Manchester
United, Coventry City, Queens Park Rangers,
Witham Town, Wollongong City, FC Baden

DEREK MICHAEL BRAZIL
Country: Ireland
Born: 14 Dec 1968
Debut: 10 May 1989 v Everton
Position: Defender
Appearances: 0 (2) **Goals scored:** 0
Seasons: 1988/89 - 1989/90
Clubs: Manchester United, Oldham Athletic
(loan), Swansea City (loan), Cardiff City, Newport
County, Inter Cardiff, Haverfordwest County

JOHN 'JACK' NORMAN BREEDON
Country: England

Born: 29 Dec 1912 **Died:** 12 Dec 1967
Debut: 31 Aug 1935 v Plymouth Argyle
Position: Goalkeeper
Appearances: 35 **Goals scored:** 0
Seasons: 1935/36 - 1939/40
Clubs: Barnsley, Sheffield Wednesday,
Bolton Wanderers, Burnley, Manchester
City, Manchester United, Rochdale

THOMAS 'TOMMY' BREEN
Country: Ireland
Born: 15 Jun 1912 **Died:** 1 Mar 1988
Debut: 28 Nov 1936 v Leeds United
Position: Goalkeeper
Appearances: 71 **Goals scored:** 0
Seasons: 1936/37 - 1938/39
Clubs: Newry Town, Belfast Celtic,
Manchester United, Belfast Celtic, Linfield,
Shamrock Rovers, Glentoran

SEAMUS ANTHONY 'SHAY' BRENNAN
Country: Ireland
Born: 6 May 1937 **Died:** 9 Jun 2000
Debut: 19 Feb 1958 v Sheffield Wednesday
Position: Full back
Appearances: 358 (1) **Goals scored:** 6
Seasons: 1957/58 - 1969/70
Clubs: Manchester United, Waterford United

Shay Brennan made his debut, scoring twice, for United in an emotionally charged game on 19 February 1958; it was United's first match after the Munich air disaster and Brennan was playing in a position left vacant by the death of David Pegg and in the absence of Albert Scanlon who was suffering from what would be career-ending injuries. The cool-headed Brennan became the club's regular right back for seven seasons winning the European Cup and two league championship medals. He would also win 19 caps for the Republic of Ireland although born in Manchester. He died of a heart attack while playing golf and was the first member of the 1968 European Cup winning side to die.

FRANK BERNARD BRETT
Country: England
Born: 10 Mar 1899 **Died:** 21 Jul 1988
Debut: 27 Aug 1921 v Everton
Position: Full back
Appearances: 10 **Goals scored:** 0
Seasons: 1921/22
Clubs: Manchester United, Aston Villa,
Northampton Town, Brighton & Hove Albion,
Tunbridge Wells Rangers, Hove FC

WILLIAM RONALD 'RONNIE' BRIGGS
Country: Northern Ireland
Born: 29 Mar 1943 **Died:** 28 Aug 2008
Debut: 21 Jan 1961 v Leicester City
Position: Goalkeeper

Appearances: 11 **Goals scored:** 0
Seasons: 1960/61 - 1961/62
Clubs: Manchester United, Swansea
City, Bristol Rovers

Only eleven appearances, but is renowed for conceding six goals on his debut.

WILLIAM HENRY BROOKS
Country: England
Born: Jul 1873 **Died:** Unknown
Debut: 22 Oct 1898 v Loughborough Town
Position: Forward
Appearances: 3 **Goals scored:** 3
Seasons: 1898/99
Clubs: Newton Heath, Stalybridge Rovers

ALBERT HENRY BROOME
Country: England
Born: 30 May 1900 **Died:** Dec 1989
Debut: 28 Apr 1923 v Barnsley
Position: Forward
Appearances: 1 **Goals scored:** 0
Seasons: 1922/23
Clubs: Manchester United, Oldham Athletic

HERBERT BROOMFIELD
Country: England
Born: 11 Dec 1878 **Died:** Unknown
Debut: 21 Mar 1908 v Arsenal
Position: Goalkeeper
Appearances: 9 **Goals scored:** 0
Seasons: 1907/08
Clubs: Manchester City, Manchester United,
Northwich Victoria, Bolton Wanderers

JAMES BROWN
Country: Scotland
Born: Unknown **Died:** Unknown
Debut: 3 Sep 1892 v Blackburn Rovers
Position: Full back
Appearances: 7 **Goals scored:** 0
Seasons: 1892/93
Clubs: Dundee Old Boys, Newton Heath, Dundee

JAMES 'JIM' BROWN
Country: USA
Born: 31 Dec 1908 **Died:** 9 Nov 1994
Debut: 17 Sep 1932 v Grimsby Town
Position: Winger
Appearances: 41 **Goals scored:** 17
Seasons: 1932/33 - 1933/34
Clubs: New York Giants, New York Soccer
Club, Brooklyn Wanderers, Newark
Americans, Manchester United, Brentford,
Tottenham Hotspur, Guildford City, Clyde

Although he was born in Scotland, Brown moved to the USA in 1927 and played for his new country in the 1930 World Cup, scoring in the semi-final. When he sailed back to Britain in 1932, United manager Scott Duncan took a boat out to meet him and signed him up before he could dock, beating all his rivals to get his man.

MARTIN MCLEAN BUCHAN

Country: Scotland
Born: 6 Mar 1949
Debut: 4 Mar 1972 v Tottenham Hotspur
Position: Centre back
Appearances: 456 **Goals scored:** 4
Seasons: 1971/72 – 1982/83
Clubs: Aberdeen, Manchester United, Oldham Athletic

There was an elegance about Martin Buchan that few centre backs could match in the seventies. His cultured play during his 12 seasons at United, including six as captain, helped the club rebound from the Second Division and to win the FA Cup. These were difficult times to be a United player, but the Scot held the team together for much of the time when it was searching for a new personality in the post-Matt Busby era.

In 1949 Buchan was born in Aberdeen where his local team signed him as a professional 16 years later. The young Buchan was part of a footballing family dynasty: his father and brother also played for Aberdeen and his son would do so a generation later.

As a fast and intelligent defender, Buchan's career at Aberdeen was meteoric. In 1970, at just 21 years-of-age, he lifted the Scottish Cup trophy as captain of the Dons, becoming the youngest player ever to skipper a cup winning team in Scotland. Two years later Frank O'Farrell signed him for United for £125,000, expecting him to be a pivotal part of United's defence. The Reds also signed his brother George from the Dons, but he would be less successful and play only a handful of matches for United.

Although Buchan achieved his goal of anchoring the United defence, he could not prevent the club from slipping into the Second Division after his second season in Manchester. He started every United game in those first two seasons and this level of consistency, combined with his calmness under pressure and precision tackling were to mark him out as the club's outstanding player.

With O'Farrell replaced by new manager Tommy Docherty, Buchan stayed with the newly relegated side even though he had offers to leave. When United succeeded in securing instant promotion back to the First Division, the defence had played a phenomenal role, conceding just 30 goals. Under Docherty, things improved for Buchan; United won the FA Cup in 1977, although it would be the only other trophy Buchan lifted with the Reds. Again, he set a record as the first player to captain cup final-winning teams in both England and Scotland.

By now there were injuries to contend with as well as different managers to play for, as Docherty was followed by Dave Sexton and later Ron Atkinson. Towards the end of his career injuries took away some of his pace, but Buchan balanced that with even greater positional sense. His 456 appearances and four goals (the best of which was a screamer against Everton in September 1978) did not span United's greatest years, but Buchan was certainly one of the leading players of the seventies era and gained significant international recognition with 34 caps for Scotland between 1971 and 1978. He also played in two World Cups and captained his country on two occasions.

He left United in August 1983 to play two seasons with Oldham Athletic before spending a short time as manager of Burnley. Buchan now works for the Professional Footballers' Association (PFA).

Left: September 1980. In action during a Division One match against Leicester City at Old Trafford.

Below: May 1977. Martin Buchan and Kevin Keegan during the FA Cup final at Wembley. United beat Liverpool 2-1.

Appearances: 313 (49) **Goals scored:** 5
Seasons: 1997/98 - 2010/11
Clubs: Manchester United, Sunderland

After joining United's youth team in 1996 Wes Brown made 362 appearances at the club. He suffered a series of injuries that restricted his career somewhat. However, as a versatile defender he could play anywhere across the back four and was capped by England on 23 occasions. He won multiple honours while at Old Trafford and was voted into the 2001 PFA Team of the Year. In July 2011 he moved to Sunderland.

WILLIAM 'RIMMER' BROWN

Country: England
Born: Unknown **Died:** Unknown
Debut: 1 Sep 1896 Newton Heath v Gainsborough Trinity
Position: Forward
Appearances: 7 **Goals scored:** 2
Seasons: 1896/97 -
Clubs: Stalybridge Rovers, Chester, Newton Heath, Stockport County

STEPHEN ROGER 'STEVE' BRUCE

Country: England
Born: 31 Dec 1960
Debut: 21 Dec 1987 v Portsmouth
Position: Centre back
Appearances: 411 (3) **Goals scored:** 51
Seasons: 1987/88 - 1995/96
Clubs: Gillingham, Norwich City, Manchester United, Birmingham City, Sheffield United

Geordie-born Bruce joined United from Norwich City in 1987. He was a major reason why the Reds under Alex Ferguson began hoovering up trophies at the start of the nineties, winning the Premier League, FA Cup and the Football League Cup. He also became the first English player of the twentieth century to captain a team to the double. Aged almost 27 when he came to Old Trafford, his partnership with Gary Pallister shored up the defence for years. Bruce became a successful manager when he stopped playing in 1999 and is currently in charge of Premier League side Sunderland.

WILLIAM 'WILLIE' BRYANT

Country: England
Born: 1874 **Died:** 25 Oct 1918
Debut: 1 Sep 1896 v Gainsborough Trinity
Position: Forward
Appearances: 127 **Goals scored:** 33
Seasons: 1896/97 - 1899/1900
Clubs: Wath FC, Chesterfield FC, Rotherham Town, Newton Heath, Blackburn Rovers

JAMES BROWN

Country: Scotland
Born: 1907 **Died:** Unknown
Debut: 31 Aug 1935 v Plymouth Argyle
Position: Half back
Appearances: 110 **Goals scored:** 1
Seasons: 1935/36 - 1938/39
Clubs: East Fife, Burnley, Manchester United, Bradford City

ROBERT BERESFORD 'BERRY' BROWN

Country: England
Born: 6 Sep 1927 **Died:** Jul 2001
Debut: 31 Jan 1948 v Sheffield United
Position: Goalkeeper
Appearances: 4 **Goals scored:** 0
Seasons: 1946/47 - 1948/49
Clubs: Manchester United, Doncaster Rovers, Hartlepool United

WESLEY MICHAEL 'WES' BROWN

Country: England
Born: 13 Oct 1979
Debut: 4 May 1998 v Leeds United
Position: Defender

WILLIAM 'BILLY' BRYANT

Country: England
Born: 26 Nov 1913 **Died:** 25 Dec 1975
Debut: 3 Nov 1934 v Blackpool
Position: Outside right
Appearances: 157 **Goals scored:** 42
Seasons: 1934/35 - 1938/39
Clubs: Wolverhampton Wanderers, Wrexham, Manchester United, Chester (guest), Bradford City, Altrincham, Stalybridge Celtic

GEORGE BUCHAN

Country: Scotland
Born: 2 May 1950
Debut: 15 Sep 1973 v West Ham United
Position: Right wing
Appearances: 0 (4) **Goals scored:** 0
Seasons: 1973/74
Clubs: Aberdeen, Manchester United, Bury, Mossley

HERBERT EDWARD WILLIAM 'TED' BUCKLE

Country: England
Born: 28 Oct 1924 **Died:** 14 Jun 1990
Debut: 4 Jan 1947 v Charlton Athletic
Position: Outside forward
Appearances: 24 **Goals scored:** 7
Seasons: 1946/47 - 1949/50
Clubs: Manchester United, Everton, Exeter City, Prestatyn, Dolgellau

MAJOR FRANKLIN 'FRANK' CHARLES BUCKLEY

Country: England
Born: 3 Oct 1882 **Died:** 21 Dec 1964
Debut: 29 Sep 1906 v Derby County
Position: Defender
Appearances: 3 **Goals scored:** 0
Seasons: 1906/07
Clubs: Aston Villa, Brighton & Hove Albion, Manchester United, Manchester City, Birmingham City, Derby County, Bradford City, Norwich City

Commanded the 'Football Battalion' as part of the Middlesex Regiment during the First World War.

Above: 14 May 1994. Captain Steve Bruce with the FA Cup. United defeated Chelsea 4-0 to become only the sixth club in English history to capture both the FA Cup and league title in the same season.

Right: 25 Nov 2009. Wes Brown in Champions League action for United against Besiktas. Described by Sir Alex Ferguson as the best natural defender at the club, he gave 13 years of service to the Reds.

ROGER WILLIAM BYRNE
Country: England
Born: 8 Feb 1929 **Died:** 6 Feb 1958
Debut: 24 Nov 1951 v Liverpool
Position: Defender
Appearances: 280 **Goals scored:** 20
Seasons: 1951/52 – 1957/58
Clubs: Manchester United

Roger Byrne might not have been the most glamorous of the Busby Babes nor the most well known to fans of later eras, but this was the team's skipper during the key period of the fifties, and the player the rest of the Babes respected beyond question. He was the team's spokesman, their on-field general and one of the most effective left backs in the club's history.

Born in Gorton, Manchester in 1929, Byrne did his national service in the Air Force and then signed for United as a trainee at the age of 20. He actually boxed in the forces rather than play football, but it did not take long for him to make his mark with the Reds. Byrne was a highly talented player with tremendous positional awareness and a forthright personality, but probably his best quality was his intelligence – something he demonstrated both on and off the field.

Naturally right-footed, he usually played anywhere on the left side of the field and made his first team debut in November 1951 at left back. It was a tremendous first season because as Byrne was establishing himself opposite long-time club hero Johnny Carey

at right back, United were fighting for their first league title in over 40 years. The young Byrne played a key role in the championship win of that season. Matt Busby had been searching for inspiration in the forward line all season and when he moved Byrne to left wing for the final six games of the 1951-52 season, the looked-for spark was found as the rookie scored seven goals in an unbeaten run that took United to the title.

However, Byrne was not happy in the forward line and, as one of the few players with enough self-confidence to stand up to his manager, asked for a transfer in October 1952. Busby, who respected Byrne's opinions, immediately returned the player to left back and then made him the successor to Carey as captain the following year. He was just 24.

With his on-the-field general now firmly in place, Busby's Babes took shape as the manager went about creating almost an entirely new team. Byrne, along with right winger Johnny Berry, were the only two players to play significant roles in both the 1952 league title and the United successes that would follow.

Some of United's greatest players like Duncan Edwards, Bobby Charlton and Tommy Taylor all looked to Byrne for leadership during this outstanding period in the club's history. Winning two more league titles in 1956 and 1957, it seemed to be just the start of a period of continuing success for Byrne and the Babes. Not only was the club captain revered in Manchester, but he had become an England regular and would win a total of 33 caps after his international debut in 1954.

Instead on a snow-swept runway in February 1958, the Munich air crash took Byrne's life and that of seven other United players. He was two days short of his 29th birthday and died not knowing that he had left behind a pregnant wife who gave birth to Roger Byrne Jr nine months later.

Left: May 1957. Johnny Dixon (l) captain of Aston Villa and Roger Byrne (r) pose ahead of the FA Cup final.

Below: April 1957. European Cup semi-final first leg. United goalkeeper Ray Wood saves under pressure from Real Madrid's Alfredo Di Stefano as United players (l-r,) Duncan Edwards, Roger Byrne and Jackie Blanchflower look on.

JAMES 'JIMMY' BULLOCK
Country: England
Born: 25 Mar 1902 **Died:** 9 Mar 1977
Debut: 20 Sep 1930 v Sheffield Wednesday
Position: Forward
Appearances: 10 **Goals scored:** 3
Seasons: 1930/31
Clubs: Manchester City, Crewe Alexandra, Southampton, Chesterfield, Manchester United, Dundalk, Llanelli, Hyde United

WILLIAM BUNCE
Country: England
Born: Apr 1877 **Died:** Unknown
Debut: 4 Oct 1902 v Chesterfield
Position: Full back
Appearances: 2 **Goals scored:** 0
Seasons: 1902/03
Clubs: Manchester United, Rochdale Athletic, Stockport County

HERBERT LARRY BURGESS
Country: England
Born: 1 Jan 1883 **Died:** Jul 1954
Debut: 1 Jan 1907 v Aston Villa
Position: Left back
Appearances: 54 **Goals scored:** 0
Seasons: 1906/07 - 1909/10
Clubs: Gorton St Francis, Openshaw United, Edge Lane FC, Moss Side FC, Glossop, Manchester City, Manchester United, Kristiania FC, MTK Budapest

Burgess went on to manage teams both in Hungary and Italy.

RONALD STEWART 'RONNIE' BURKE
Country: England
Born: 13 Aug 1921 **Died:** Dec 2003
Debut: 26 Oct 1946 v Sunderland
Position: Forward

Appearances: 35 **Goals scored:** 23
Seasons: 1946/47 - 1948/49
Clubs: Liverpool, Manchester City, Rotherham United (all during WW1), Manchester United, Huddersfield Town, Rotherham United, Exeter City, Tunbridge Wells United, Biggleswade Town

THOMAS 'TOM' BURKE
Country: Wales
Born: 1862 **Died:** 1914
Debut: 30 Oct 1886 v Fleetwood Rangers
Position: Half back
Appearances: 1 **Goals scored:** 0
Seasons: 1886/87
Clubs: Wrexham Grosvenor, Wrexham Feb, Wrexham Olympic, Liverpool Cambrians, Newton Heath, Wrexham Victoria

FRANCIS BURNS
Country: Scotland
Born: 17 Oct 1948
Debut: 2 Sep 1967 v West Ham United
Position: Left back
Appearances: 143 (13) **Goals scored:** 7
Seasons: 1965/66 - 1971/72
Clubs: Manchester United, Southampton, Preston North End, Shamrock Rovers

Played in six European Cup games in the run to the final before he lost his place to Shay Brennan.

NICHOLAS 'NICKY' BUTT
Country: England
Born: 21 Jan 1975
Debut: 21 Nov 1992 v Oldham Athletic
Position: Midfield
Appearances: 307 (80) **Goals scored:** 26
Seasons: 1992/93 - 2003/04
Clubs: Manchester United, Preston North End (loan), Newcastle United, Birmingham City (loan), South China

During the FIFA World Cup of 2002, Pelé named Nicky Butt as one of his players of the tournament. He played a key role in United's 1999 Champions League final triumph in place of the suspended Roy Keane. While often unsung, Butt was an integral squad member during 12 seasons with United, picking up six championship medals and numerous other trophies. He moved to Newcastle United in 2004.

DAVID BYRNE
Country: Ireland
Born: 28 Apr 1905 **Died:** May 1990
Debut: 21 Oct 1933 v Bury
Position: Forward
Appearances: 4 **Goals scored:** 3
Seasons: 1933/34
Clubs: Shamrock Rovers, Bradford City, Shelbourne, Sheffield United, Manchester United, Coleraine, Glentoran, Larne

JAMES CAIRNS
Country: Unknown
Born: Unknown **Died:** Unknown
Debut: 15 Apr 1895 v Bury
Position: Full back
Appearances: 1 **Goals scored:** 0
Seasons: 1894/95
Clubs: Ardwick, Newton Heath

JAMES CAIRNS
Country: Unknown
Born: Unknown **Died:** Unknown
Debut: 8 Oct 1898 v Burslem Port Vale
Position: Inside right
Appearances: 1 **Goals scored:** 0
Seasons: 1898/99
Clubs: Stevenson Thistle, Glossop North End, Lincoln City, Newton Heath, Berry's Association

FRAIZER LEE CAMPBELL
Country: England
Born: 13 Sep 1987
Debut: 19 Aug 2007 v Manchester City
Position: Forward
Appearances: 1 (3) **Goals scored:** 0
Seasons: 2007/08 - 2008/09
Clubs: Manchester United, Royal Antwerp (loan), Hull City (loan), Tottenham Hotspur (loan), Sunderland

WILLIAM CECIL CAMPBELL
Country: Scotland
Born: 25 Oct 1865 **Died:** Unknown
Debut: 25 Nov 1893 v Sheffield United
Position: Forward
Appearances: 5 **Goals scored:** 1
Seasons: 1893/94
Clubs: Royal Arsenal, Preston North End, Middlesbrough, Darwen, Blackburn Rovers, Newton Heath, Notts County, Everton

NOEL EUCHARIA CORNELIUS CANTWELL
Country: Ireland
Born: 28 Feb 1932 **Died:** 8 Sep 2005
Debut: 26 Nov 1960 v Cardiff City
Position: Full back
Appearances: 146 **Goals scored:** 8
Seasons: 1960/61 - 1966/67
Clubs: Western Rovers, Cork Athletic, West Ham United, Manchester United

Signed from West Ham United for a then record fee for a full back of £29,500, while at Upton Park, Cantwell played alongside two future United managers in Frank O'Farrell and Dave Sexton. Appointed captain for 1962-63, he led United to FA Cup success that season, but hardly played in United's two title-winning campaigns of the 1960s.

JOHN 'JACK' PHILLIPS CAPE

Country: England
Born: 16 Nov 1911 **Died:** 6 Jun 1994
Debut: 27 Jan 1934 v Brentford
Position: Forward
Appearances: 60 **Goals scored:** 18
Seasons: 1933/34 – 1936/37
Clubs: Penrith, Carlisle United, Newcastle United, Manchester United, Queens Park Rangers, Scarborough

ALFRED 'FREDDY' CAPPER

Country: England
Born: Jul 1891 **Died:** 31 Oct 1955
Debut: 23 Mar 1912 v Liverpool
Position: Forward
Appearances: 1 **Goals scored:** 0
Seasons: 1911/12
Clubs: Northwich Victoria, Witton Albion, Manchester United

JAMES CARMAN

Country: England
Born: 1876 **Died:** Unknown
Debut: 25 Dec 1897 Newton Heath v Manchester City
Position: Forward
Appearances: 3 **Goals scored:** 1
Seasons: 1897/98
Clubs: Darwen, Oldham County, Newton Heath

JOSEPH 'JOE' FRANCIS CAROLAN

Country: Ireland
Born: 8 Sep 1937
Debut: 22 Nov 1958 v Luton Town
Position: Full back
Appearances: 71 **Goals scored:** 0
Seasons: 1955/56 – 1960/61
Clubs: Manchester United, Brighton & Hove Albion, Tonbridge, Canterbury City

MICHAEL CARRICK

Country: England
Born: 28 Jul 1981
Debut: 23 Aug 2006 v Charlton Athletic
Position: Midfield
Appearances: 197 (36) **Goals scored:** 17
Seasons: 2006/07 - present
Clubs: West Ham United, Swindon Town (*loan*), Birmingham City (*loan*), Tottenham Hotspur, Manchester United

A product of the West Ham United Youth Academy, Carrick was signed by United from Tottenham Hotspur in 2006. It would be 2009 before Michael Carrick finished a season as anything other than a Premier League winner. He is a classy passer of the ball and is known for his vision on the field. He scored one of the penalties that helped United to the 2008 Champions League title and has represented England on 22 occasions.

ROY ERIC CARROLL

Country: Northern Ireland
Born: 30 Sep 1977
Debut: 26 Aug 2001 v Aston Villa
Position: Goalkeeper
Appearances: 68 (4) **Goals scored:** 0
Seasons: 2001/02 – 2004/05
Clubs: Hull City, Wigan Athletic, Manchester United, West Ham United, Rangers, Derby County, Odense Boldklub

ADAM CARSON

Country: Scotland
Born: Unknown **Died:** Unknown
Debut: 3 Sep 1892 v Blackburn Rovers
Position: Forward
Appearances: 13 **Goals scored:** 3
Seasons: 1892/93
Clubs: Glasgow Thistle, Newton Heath, Ardwick, Liverpool

HERBERT REDVERS CARTMAN

Country: England
Born: 28 Feb 1900 **Died:** 5 Apr 1955
Debut: 16 Dec 1922 v Stockport County
Position: Forward
Appearances: 3 **Goals scored:** 0
Seasons: 1922/23
Clubs: Manchester United, Waterloo Temperance, Bolton Wanderers, Tranmere Rovers

WALTER CARTWRIGHT

Country: England
Born: Jan 1871 **Died:** Unknown
Debut: 7 Sep 1895 v Crewe Alexandra
Position: Half back
Appearances: 257 **Goals scored:** 8
Seasons: 1895/96 – 1903/04
Clubs: Nantwich, Heywood Central, Crewe Alexandra, Newton Heath/Manchester United

Walter Cartwright straddled both the Newton Heath and Manchester United eras as a versatile player whose best position was half back. He was unfortunate to play all his football for the club in the Second Division and retired just a couple of seasons before the Reds won promotion and began to win major honours.

ARTHUR CASHMORE

Country: England
Born: 30 Oct 1893 **Died:** 1969
Debut: 13 Sep 1913 v Bolton Wanderers
Position: Forward
Appearances: 3 **Goals scored:** 0
Seasons: 1913/14
Clubs: Manchester United, Oldham Athletic, Cardiff City, Notts County

CHRISTOPHER MARTIN 'CHRIS' CASPER

Country: England
Born: 28 Apr 1975
Debut: 5 Oct 1994 v Port Vale

Position: Defender
Appearances: 4 (3) **Goals scored:** 0
Seasons: 1993/94 – 1996/97
Clubs: Manchester United, Bournemouth (*loan*), Swindon Town (*loan*), Reading (*loan*), Reading

JOSEPH 'JOE' CASSIDY

Country: Scotland
Born: 30 Jul 1872 **Died:** Unknown
Debut: 31 Mar 1893 v Stoke City
Position: Forward
Appearances: 174 **Goals scored:** 100
Seasons: 1892/93 – 1899/00
Clubs: Motherwell, Blythe, Newton Heath, Celtic, Newton Heath, Manchester City, Middlesbrough, Workington

Joe Cassidy was the first player in United's history to score 100 goals for the club, scoring six hat-tricks in that time.

Above: 6 April 2011. Michael Carrick is pursued by Frank Lampard of Chelsea during the Champions League quarter-final first leg match.

Above: 14 January 2003. Luke Chadwick in action during a reserve team game against Sheffield Wednesday at Hillsborough.

Opposite: 25 May 1963. Captain Noel Cantwell on his way back to Manchester after United won the FA Cup final against Leicester City at Wembley.

LAURENCE CASSIDY
Country: England
Born: 10 Mar 1923 **Died:** Unknown
Debut: 10 Apr 1948 v Everton
Position: Forward
Appearances: 4 **Goals scored:** 0
Seasons: 1947/48 - 1951/56
Clubs: Manchester United, Oldham Athletic

LUKE HARRY CHADWICK
Country: England
Born: 18 Nov 1980
Debut: 13 Oct 1999 v Aston Villa
Position: Winger
Appearances: 18 (21) **Goals scored:** 2
Seasons: 1999/00 - 2002/03
Clubs: Manchester United, Royal Antwerp (loan), Reading (loan), Burnley (loan), West Ham United, Stoke City (loan), Norwich City (loan), Norwich City, Milton Keynes Dons (loan), Milton Keynes Dons

WILLIAM STEWART CHALMERS
Country: Scotland

Born: 5 Mar 1907 **Died:** Unknown
Debut: 1 Oct 1932 v Preston North End
Position: Inside forward
Appearances: 35 **Goals scored:** 1
Seasons: 1932/33 - 1933/34
Clubs: Queens Park, Heart of Midlothian, Manchester United, Dunfermline Athletic

WILLIAM 'BILLY' CHAPMAN
Country: England
Born: 21 Sep 1902 **Died:** 2 Dec 1967
Debut: 18 Sep 1926 v Burnley
Position: Outside right
Appearances: 26 **Goals scored:** 0
Seasons: 1926/27 - 1927/28
Clubs: Sheffield Wednesday, Manchester United, Burnley

JAMES GRANT CHESTER
Country: England
Born: 23 Jan 1989
Debut: 20 Jan 2009 v Derby County
Position: Centre back
Appearances: 0 (1) **Goals scored:** 0
Seasons: 2008/09
Clubs: Manchester United, Peterborough United (loan), Plymouth Argyle (loan), Carlisle United (loan), Hull City

REGINALD ALFRED 'REG' CHESTER
Country: England
Born: 21 Nov 1904 **Died:** 24 Apr 1977
Debut: 31 Aug 1935 v Plymouth Argyle
Position: Forward
Appearances: 13 **Goals scored:** 1
Seasons: 1935/36
Clubs: Aston Villa, Manchester United, Huddersfield Town, Darlington

ARTHUR CHESTERS
Country: England
Born: 14 Feb 1910 **Died:** 23 Mar 1963
Debut: 28 Dec 1929 v Newcastle United
Position: Goalkeeper
Appearances: 9 **Goals scored:** 0
Seasons: 1929/30 - 1931/32
Clubs: Manchester United, Exeter City

ALLENBY CHILTON
Country: England
Born: 16 Sep 1918 **Died:** 15 Jun 1996
Debut: 5 Jan 1946 v Accrington Stanley
Position: Centre back
Appearances: 391 **Goals scored:** 3
Seasons: 1945/46 - 1954/55
Clubs: Liverpool, Manchester United, Grimsby Town

One of a rare breed of player to make the move from Liverpool to Manchester, Allenby Chilton appeared 391 times in a United shirt. After his career was interrupted by the Second World War, Chilton was part of Matt Busby's team that lifted the 1948 FA Cup. He was also a member of the 1952 championship winning side and went on to become

captain for two seasons. He left United for Grimsby in 1955.

JOHN PHILIP 'PHIL' CHISNALL
Country: England
Born: 27 Oct 1942
Debut: 2 Dec 1961 v Everton
Position: Inside forward
Appearances: 47 **Goals scored:** 10
Seasons: 1961/62 - 1963/64
Clubs: Manchester United, Liverpool, Southend United, Stockport County

Chisnall was the last player to be transferred directly between United and Liverpool.

TOM CHORLTON
Country: England
Born: 1882 **Died:** 1952
Debut: 11 Oct 1913 v Burnley
Position: Full back
Appearances: 4 **Goals scored:** 0
Seasons: 1913/14
Clubs: Stockport County, Accrington Stanley, Liverpool, Manchester United, Stalybridge Celtic

Another of the select few who transferred directly between Liverpool and United.

DAVID CHRISTIE
Country: Scotland
Born: 1885 **Died:** Unknown
Debut: 7 Sep 1908 v Bury
Position: Inside left
Appearances: 2 **Goals scored:** 0
Seasons: 1908/09
Clubs: Hurlford, Manchester United

JOHN CHRISTIE
Country; England
Born: 1883 **Died:** Unknown
Debut: 28 Feb 1903 v Doncaster Rovers
Position: Full back
Appearances: 1 **Goals scored:** 0
Seasons: 1902/03
Clubs: Sale Homefield, Manchester United, Manchester City

JONATHAN CLARK
Country: Wales
Born: 12 Nov 1958
Debut: 10 Nov 1976 v Sunderland
Position: Midfield
Appearances: 0 (1) **Goals scored:** 0
Seasons: 1976/77
Clubs: Manchester United, Derby County, Preston North End, Bury, Carlisle United

JOSEPH CLARK
Country: Scotland
Born: 1874 **Died:** Unknown
Debut: 30 Sep 1899 v Sheffield Wednesday
Position: Forward
Appearances: 9 **Goals scored:** 0
Seasons: 1899/00
Clubs: Dundee, Newton Heath

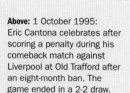

Above: 1 October 1995: Eric Cantona celebrates after scoring a penalty during his comeback match against Liverpool at Old Trafford after an eight-month ban. The game ended in a 2-2 draw.

Right: 31 March 1996. FA Cup semi-final at Villa Park. Alex Ferguson celebrates the victory with his captain after Manchester United beat Chelsea 2-1.

ERIC DANIEL PIERRE CANTONA

Country: France
Born: 24 May 1966
Debut: 6 Dec 1992 v Manchester City
Position: Forward
Appearances: 184 (1) **Goals scored:** 82
Seasons: 1992/93 – 1996/97
Clubs: Auxerre, Martigues (*loan*), Marseille, Bordeaux (*loan*), Montpellier (*loan*), Nimes, Leeds United, Manchester United

Of all the signings made during Sir Alex Ferguson's time as United manager, for many fans one transfer stands out above all others, arguably changing the course of Red Devil history. It took place on 27 November 1992 when Frenchman Eric Daniel Pierre Cantona joined the Reds from previous year's league champions Leeds United for £1 million. Cantona would go on to win four league titles in five seasons at Old Trafford, including two league and cup doubles in an exhilarating and at times controversial career.

Eric Cantona was born in Marseille, France in 1966 and started his football career as an amateur with SO Caillolais, but signed professionally with Auxerre. His talent was obvious, yet he would spend a tumultuous and often peripatetic eight years in France as coach after coach failed to manage his volatile temperament. The first signs of disciplinary problems came in the 1986-87 season when he was fined for punching teammate Bruno Martini.

In 1988 he transferred to Marseille and, at the same time, was part of the successful French U21 side that won the 1988 European Championship. However, trouble arose once again as he received an indefinite ban from international football soon after for calling coach Henri Michel 'a bag of shit' on live TV. Cantona failed to settle at Marseille and was loaned first to Bordeaux then to Montpellier where he was banned for throwing his boots in a teammate's face. Despite calls for him to be sacked, senior players backed him and he played a key role in Montpellier's 1990 French Cup win.

He returned to Marseille and helped them to the Ligue 1 title in 1991, yet the very next season he was moved on to Nimes. Then in December 1991 during a league match, Cantona took exception at a referee's decision and threw the ball at the official. He was banned for a month and responded by calling the each member of the hearing committee an 'idiot'. His ban was immediately increased by two months and Cantona promptly retired from football.

Fortunately for the player (and United), Cantona was persuaded by new French coach Michel Platini to restart his career, but away from France. His psychoanalyst suggested England and so Cantona found himself in January 1992 on a week's trial at Sheffield Wednesday. He rejected the offer of a second week's trial and instead joined Yorkshire rivals Leeds United where he played 15 games and was instrumental in them pipping the Reds to the First Division title.

After hat-tricks the following summer in a 4-3 Community Shield win over Liverpool and a 5-0 league thumping of Tottenham, Cantona appeared settled at Leeds. Yet manager Howard Wilkinson still had reservations about his temperament and in November a chance enquiry by the United manager about the Frenchman's availability led to a surprise transfer.

United were still in search of the first league championship in a quarter of a century, and Cantona's finesse as a striker and unpredictability was just what Ferguson was looking for. Cantona made his United debut as a substitute in a 2-1 win over Manchester City on 6 December 1992. Nine league goals then helped the Reds to a first league title in 26 years. Cantona was naturally seen as the catalyst for the success and had become the first player to win back-to-back top division titles in England with different clubs.

In 1993-94 Cantona was handed the iconic number 7 shirt, drawing inevitable comparisons with George Best. His response was to raise his game to new levels as United secured their first ever league and cup double. Cantona contributed a total of 22 goals, including two penalties in the 4-0 final thrashing of Chelsea. In recognition of his efforts he was voted Professional Footballers' Association Player of the Year, yet in true Cantona fashion the season was not without controversy. He was sent off following a stand up row with the referee as United exited the Champions League against Galatasaray S.K., and received red cards in successive games against Arsenal and Swindon, the latter for a stamp in full view of officials.

The following year's title defence started promisingly, but 25 January 1995 was a day to change everything and live in football infamy. After a red card at Crystal Palace, Cantona launched a kung-fu style attack on an abusive fan, following it up with a flurry of punches. The FA, backed by FIFA, handed out a massive eight-month worldwide ban and a £10,000 fine, Graham Kelly describing the attack as 'a stain on our game'. Cantona, in typical fashion, responded at a press conference shortly afterwards with football's most enigmatic quote: "When the seagulls follow the trawler, it's because they think sardines will be thrown into the sea."

After selling several senior players in the summer, United's 'kids' struggled at the start of the next season. However, Cantona's return against Liverpool provided an immediate impact – with an assist and a penalty earning a 2-2 draw. His winner at West Ham in January sparked a run of 13 wins in 15 games (Cantona scoring in nine of them) as United overhauled Newcastle United to win the Premiership. Scoring the winner in the FA Cup final saw Cantona help United seal their second double. He was voted the Football Writers' Footballer of the Year.

In 1996-97, Ferguson made Cantona club captain and he led United to their fourth title in five seasons. Then at the age of 30, Cantona promptly announced his retirement. While a shock to many fans, it was entirely in keeping with his enigmatic persona. He ended his Old Trafford career with 82 goals from 185 appearances.

Following his retirement Cantona moved into acting and became captain of the French beach football team. He retains a love for United and Old Trafford, stating in 2004: "I'm so proud the fans still sing my name." An outstanding showman and a maverick talent in true United fashion, he is remembered for his outrageous skills and known to the United faithful simply as 'King Eric'.

Above: 10 February 1996. A Cantona throw-in during a league match against Blackburn Rovers at Old Trafford.

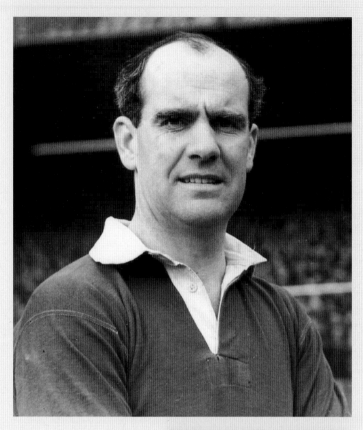

Above: 1950. United and Ireland footballer Johnny Carey.

Right: 24 April 1948. In action during the FA Cup final against Blackpool at Wembley. United won 4-2.

JOHN JOSEPH 'JOHNNY' CAREY

Country: Ireland/Northern Ireland
Born: 23 Feb 1919 **Died:** 22 Aug 1995
Debut: 25 Sep 1937 v Southampton
Position: Full back
Appearances: 344 **Goals scored:** 17
Seasons: 1937/38 – 1952/53
Clubs: St James' Gate, Manchester United

Johnny "Gentleman John" Carey was a thoroughbred footballer and one of the few United stars who straddled the pre- and post-World War II eras. The inside forward-turned-full back led the Reds to two key trophies, the first under manager Matt Busby's charge, and helped set the standard for the great players and teams to come. His career would have been even more stellar, but he, along with so many young men, lost six prime years to the conflict. Still, he emerges as one of United's most important players.

Carey was born in Dublin in 1919 and, naturally for an Irish youngster of the day, was as interested in Gaelic football as he was in the association version. He eventually chose association football and signed for the League of Ireland team St James' Gate in 1936. He was spotted by former United player Billy Behan, and recommended to chief scout Louis Rocca. The 17-year-old Carey, with his skilful elegance – allegedly playing only his third full game of football – caught their eye. United signed him in November 1937 for £200, a record for an Irish league player.

The Red Devils were still in the Second Division at the time, but with Carey added to the team at inside left, his first season at Old Trafford saw United gain promotion. The new boy had played 16 league games and scored three goals. The following season, 1938-39, Carey established himself firmly in the team and the future looked bright, both for him and United. The onset of war meant Carey had to decide if he wanted to return to Dublin to live in a war-neutral country for the duration or join the British Army and fight for the country that was offering him a living. A highly principled young man, he chose the latter course.

Carey continued to learn his football craft in the wartime leagues, but these were not fully-recognised games, with guest players on many teams. He played over 100 games for United from 1939 to 1943 and scored 47 goals as well as guesting for several other clubs and playing for the League of Ireland in representative matches. Then after 1943, he spent time with the army in both North Africa and Italy where he continued to play football. In fact, Cario as he was nicknamed in Italy, was offered contracts by several Italian teams at the end of the war.

In 1945 with the war over, Carey, now aged 26, returned to Old Trafford to meet new manager Matt Busby. The player was at the height of his powers and Busby recognised the qualities in him that would make him the key man for his new team and on-field lieutenant. When league football returned in August 1946, Carey was made team captain and converted to full back. Busby particularly admired his calmness under pressure. "Don't panic," the new skipper once told his teammate. "Keep playing football the way we have all season. The way the boss wants us to play."

Busby was clearly building a good team and Carey was at the heart of it in those early post-war years along with Jack Rowley, Stan Pearson, Charlie Mitten, John Aston and Allenby Chilton. These were all mature men in their mid-twenties busy making up for lost time. During the 1946-47 season, Carey and his team missed the league title by a single point and were runners-up again the following year. There was some consolation because Carey lifted the 1948 FA Cup. It was an impressive, attacking performance that brought a 4-2 win in the final against Blackpool, a team containing the two great Stans – Matthews and Mortensen. It was Carey's calm manner when the team was 2-1 down at half-time that played a significant role in United winning the trophy for only the second time.

Two more second place league finishes over the next three seasons – in 1948-49 and 1950-51 – were galling, but Carey would not be denied. The following season he missed just four league games, scored three goals and finally lifted the championship trophy. It would be the pinnacle of his playing career, while getting his hands on the Charity Shield at the start of next season proved to be his last club honour.

As a player, the pipe-smoking Carey was a soft-spoken, selfless and genial man who led by example. On the field it was his incredible versatility that was a huge asset. He played in every position except on the wing for the Reds, and even started one match in goal on 18

February 1953 when regular keeper Ray Wood was injured. Carey stood between the posts and helped his team to a 2-2 draw.

In the international arena, he held the distinction of being one of the few players to wear the shirt of both Northern Ireland and the Republic of Ireland and totalled 36 representative caps. He captained a Rest of Europe XI against a Great Britain team, and was voted Player of the Year by the Footballer Writers'

Association in 1949, only the second man to win the award. It is notable that Carey succeeded Stanley Matthews for the honour and that no other United player was to be similarly lauded by the prestigious FWA until Bobby Charlton in 1966 demonstrates the high esteem in which Carey was held.

By the early fifties, Busby already had his eyes on younger players coming through the youth team. After the 1952-53 season at the age of 33, Carey retired

from the game. Immediately on retirement, Carey took to management. First with Blackburn Rovers for five years and then for the Republic of Ireland national team until 1967. A few other club appointments followed, but he left football management in 1971 after a one-season return to Rovers and was a part-time scout for United for a few years while also working for Trafford Borough Council in the treasurer's office. He died in August 1995 aged 76.

Above: 14 April 1947. Carey is actually posing in this pre-match photograph.

SIR ROBERT 'BOBBY' CHARLTON CBE

Country: England
Born: 11 Oct 1937
Debut: 6 Oct 1956 v Charlton Athletic
Position: Midfield/Forward
Appearances: 756 (2) **Goals scored:** 249
Seasons: 1956/57 - 1972/73
Clubs: Manchester United, Preston North End

Above: The 1970s. Bobby Charlton controls the ball during a training session.

Right: 23 April 1973. A massage before his final appearance for United at Old Trafford.

Opposite Top: 13 April 1968. A beautiful strike at the Dell where United beat Southampton 2-1.

Opposite Bottom: 4 February 1958. Bobby Charlton leads out United for practice at the Yugoslav Army Stadium where they would play Red Star Belgrade in a European Cup-tie the following evening.

as player manager at Preston North End, Charlton has been a symbol of United's story across a 60-year period and his dedication to football brought him a knighthood in 1994, the freedom of the city of Manchester in 2009 and, in 1966, the thanks of a nation for helping England win the World Cup.

He was born in the north east of England in 1937, the younger brother of Jack. The two boys were related to the famous Milburn family of footballers who included Newcastle United and England's Jackie Milburn, his mother's cousin. Shorter and faster than his older brother, Bobby played for England schoolboys and was spotted by United who beat a clutch of rival clubs to the teenager's signature. However, the uncertainty of professional sports meant that his mother insisted he also take on an apprenticeship as an electrical engineer, something he did until October 1954 when he signed professional forms on his seventeenth birthday.

Charlton's senior football apprenticeship now began; he played youth team and reserve team football along with the Duncan Edwards (with whom he did his national service) and Wilf McGuinness (who would manage him at Old Trafford 15 years later). Then in October 1956, five days short of his nineteenth birthday and after many impressive performances in the reserves, Charlton got his chance in the first team – and what a debut it was. Against Charlton Athletic in front of over 41,000 fans at Old Trafford, the teenager (who later admitted to playing with a slightly sprained ankle) scored twice in a 4-2 win. Charlton played another 16 games that season, scoring a remarkable 12 goals and won himself a league championship medal. He was now a member of the Busby Babes, a team of young men highly skilled and with a determination to play attacking football.

However, this United team was so good that even Charlton could not command a regular place in the first team. When the 1957-58 season began, he was left out of the side for the first ten matches and would only get a run of games towards the end of 1957, while at

the same time getting some European Cup experience when he played in both legs of the quarter-final against Red Star Belgrade. In fact, Charlton scored twice in the 3-3 draw against the Yugoslavs on 5 February 1958 and was looking forward to a season of more medals and accolades.

The following day the plane taking the team home made a refuelling stop at Munich Airport. When the passengers re-boarded the aircraft for a third take-off attempt Charlton and teammate Dennis Viollet swapped seats with Tommy Taylor and David Pegg who felt they would be safer at the back of the plane. The plane never left the ground, crashing at the end of the runway killing, eight players (including Taylor and Pegg) and 15 others. Miraculously, Charlton – who was thrown 40 yards clear of the wreckage – suffered just a few cuts, bruises and a minor head wound and left hospital just eight days later.

Still only 20, Charlton then became one of the key figures in the post-Munich United team that Matt Busby would go on to build. That great sixties side, led by captain Charlton as its heartbeat and with George Best and Denis Law at his side, won its first trophy, the

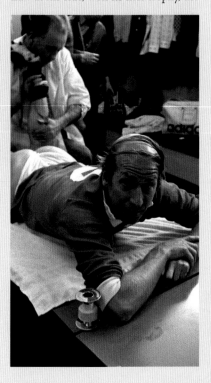

"There has never been a more popular footballer… he was as near perfection as man and player as it's possible to be." Those words from Sir Matt Busby sum up perfectly one of Manchester United's greatest ever players, Bobby Charlton. The man famous for his thunderous shooting with either foot is still a fixture at Old Trafford 40 years after his remarkable playing career ended. He has served the club, man and boy, for much of that time since he signed as a trainee in January 1953. Despite a brief period

FA Cup, in 1963 (actually without Best) and two league titles in 1965 and 1967.

By now Charlton's powers were peaking. His shooting prowess, his ability to come from deep, his awareness of teammates and his graciousness on and off the field all served to make him a truly great player. Busby used him first as an inside-forward, then as a left-winger and centre-forward and later in midfield. Before United won the 1967 championship, Charlton (along with brother Jack who was a centre half at Leeds United) had played a vital role in winning the World Cup with England and had also been named both European Footballer of the Year and English Football Writers' Association Player of the Year. But his career needed a European Cup triumph to top it off and to also honour his dead teammates. In 1968, he achieved this feat with Busby and another Munich survivor, Bill Foulkes, all elevated to hero status at the club after the 4-1 win over Benfica. The tears flowed unashamedly from all three after Charlton (who scored two goals in the final) lifted the gigantic trophy, but a mark of the man is that he chose to avoid the post-match celebrations and quietly remember the Babes who could not be there.

After that match, United fell into decline, despite Charlton's best efforts. He eventually left the club after the 1972-73 season having made 758 appearances and scored 249 goals and headed for Preston North End where he was manager and also player-manager for a time. A brief period playing for Waterford in Ireland was the final on-field activity for a player who had won a then-record 106 caps for England. His complete retirement from playing led to a place on the board at Wigan Athletic and later a caretaker manager's role in 1982-83. But his heart never left Old Trafford. In June 1984, Charlton – already awarded an OBE and CBE – enjoyed a proud moment by being made a director at United and since then he has acted as both ambassador for the club and its spiritual figurehead. Finally, the nation honoured him in 1994 when he was knighted for his services to football.

Above: 4 November 2000. Andy Cole, striking partner of Dwight Yorke, is challenged by Richard Shaw of Coventry during a Premier League match. Cole scored in the 2-1 win.

Opposite: Eddie Colman was just 21 when he died in the Munich disaster. During his brief career, he made 108 appearances scoring two goals, the second of which came in the first leg of the fateful European Cup quarter-final tie against Red Star Belgrade.

JOHN CLARKIN

Country: Scotland
Born: 1872 **Died:** Unknown
Debut: 13 Jan 1894 v Sheffield Wednesday
Position: Forward
Appearances: 74 **Goals scored:** 23
Seasons: 1893/94 - 1895/96
Clubs: Bootle, Glasgow Thistle, Newton Heath, Blackpool

GORDON CLAYTON

Country: England
Born: 3 Nov 1936 **Died:** 29 Sep 1991
Debut: 16 Mar 1957 v Wolverhampton Wanderers
Position: Goalkeeper
Appearances: 2 **Goals scored:** 0
Seasons: 1956/57
Clubs: Manchester United, Tranmere Rovers

HARRY CLEAVER

Country: England
Born: 1880 **Died:** Unknown
Debut: 4 Apr 1903 v Burnley
Position: Forward
Appearances: 1 **Goals scored:** 0
Seasons: 1902/03
Clubs: Desborough Town, Manchester United

MICHAEL JAMIE CLEGG

Country: England
Born: 3 Jul 1977

Debut: 23 Nov 1996 v Middlesbrough
Position: Defender
Appearances: 15 (9) **Goals scored:** 0
Seasons: 1996/97 - 2001/02
Clubs: Manchester United, Ipswich Town (*loan*), Wigan Athletic (*loan*), Oldham Athletic

JOHN ERNEST CLEMENTS

Country; England
Born: 1867 **Died:** Unknown
Debut: 3 Oct 1891 v Manchester City
Position: Full back
Appearances: 42 **Goals scored:** 0
Seasons: 1891/92 - 1893/94
Clubs: Notts County, Newton Heath, Rotherham Town

FRANK CLEMPSON

Country: England
Born: 27 May 1930 **Died:** 24 Dec 1970
Debut: 18 Feb 1950 v Sunderland
Position: Wing half
Appearances: 15 **Goals scored:** 2
Seasons: 1949/50 - 1952/53
Clubs: Manchester United, Stockport County, Chester, Hyde United

HENRY 'HARRY' COCKBURN

Country: England
Born: 14 Sep 1921 **Died:** 2 Feb 2004
Debut: 5 Jan 1946 v Accrington Stanley
Position: Left half
Appearances: 275 **Goals scored:** 4
Seasons: 1946/47 - 1954/55
Clubs: Manchester United, Bury, Peterborough United, Corby

At 5ft 4ins, Cockburn was a small but consistent member of the post-war team at left half. Then an injury in the 1953-54 season let in Duncan Edwards who took his position for good. Transferred to nearby Bury in October of the following season. Was also a fine club cricketer in Lancashire.

ANDREW 'ANDY' ALEXANDER COLE

Country: England
Born: 15 Oct 1971
Debut: 22 Jan 1995 v Blackburn Rovers
Position: Forward
Appearances: 231 (44) **Goals scored:** 121
Seasons: 1994/95 - 2001/02
Clubs: Arsenal, Fulham (*loan*), Bristol City, Newcastle United, Manchester United, Blackburn Rovers, Fulham, Manchester City, Portsmouth, Birmingham City (*loan*), Sunderland, Burnley (*loan*), Nottingham Forest

Cole was one half of a deadly strike partnership with Dwight Yorke that contributed 53 goals in the 1998-99 treble winning season. In his first year at Old Trafford he set a Premier League record, scoring five goals in a game against Ipswich Town. With 189 goals he is second only to Alan Shearer in the all-time Premier League scoring charts.

CLIFFORD 'CLIFF' COLLINSON

Country: England
Born: 3 Mar 1920 **Died:** Sep 1990
Debut: 2 Nov 1946 v Aston Villa
Position: Goalkeeper
Appearances: 7 **Goals scored:** 0
Seasons: 1946/47
Clubs: Manchester United

JIMMY COLLINSON

Country: England
Born: 1876 **Died:** Unknown
Debut: 16 Nov 1895 v Lincoln City
Position: Forward
Appearances: 71 **Goals scored:** 17
Seasons: 1895/96 - 1900/01
Clubs: Newton Heath

EDWARD 'EDDIE' COLMAN

Country: England
Born: 1 Nov 1936 **Died:** 6 Feb 1958
Debut: 12 Nov 1955 v Bolton Wanderers
Position: Half back
Appearances: 108 **Goals scored:** 2
Seasons: 1955/56 - 1957/58
Clubs: Manchester United

At 21 and 3 months, Eddie Colman was the youngest of the eight players to die in the Munich disaster.

JAMES COLVILLE

Country: Scotland
Born: Unknown **Died:** Unknown
Debut: 12 Nov 1892 v Notts County
Position: Forward
Appearances: 10 **Goals scored:** 1
Seasons: 1892/93
Clubs: Newton Heath, Anne Bank, Fairfield Athletic

JAMES CONNACHAN

Country: Scotland
Born: 29 Aug 1874 **Died:** Unknown
Debut: 5 Nov 1898 Newton Heath v Grimsby Town
Position: Forward
Appearances: 4 **Goals scored:** 0
Seasons: 1898/99
Clubs: Glasgow Perthshire, Duntocher Hibernian, Celtic, Airdrieonians, Glossop North End, Newton Heath

PATRICK JOHN CONNAUGHTON

Country: England
Born: 23 Sep 1949
Debut: 4 Apr 1972 v Sheffield United
Position: Goalkeeper
Appearances: 3 **Goals scored:** 0
Seasons: 1971/72 - 1972/73
Clubs: Manchester United, Halifax Town (*loan*), Torquay United (*loan*), Sheffield United, Port Vale, Altrincham

THOMAS EUGENE CONNELL
Country: Northern Ireland
Born: 25 Nov 1957
Debut: 22 Dec 1978 v Bolton Wanderers
Position: Full back
Appearances: 2 **Goals scored:** 0
Seasons: 1978/79 – 1981/82
Clubs: Newry Town, Coleraine, Manchester United, Glentoran

JOHN MICHAEL CONNELLY
Country: England
Born: 18 Jul 1938
Debut: 22 Aug 1964 v West Bromwich Albion
Position: Winger
Appearances: 112 (1) **Goals scored:** 35
Seasons: 1964/65 – 1966/67
Clubs: Burnley, Manchester United, Blackburn Rovers, Bury

Connelly was the third United player to play in England's 1966 World Cup campaign, alongside Bobby Charlton and Nobby Stiles, but appeared in only the first game.

EDWARD 'TED' CONNOR
Country: England
Born: 1884 **Died:** 1955
Debut: 27 Dec 1909 v Sheffield Wednesday
Position: Forward
Appearances: 15 **Goals scored:** 2
Seasons: 1909/10 – 1910/11
Clubs: Manchester United, Sheffield United, Exeter City, Rochdale, Chesterfield

TERENCE JOHN 'TERRY' COOKE
Country: England
Born: 5 Aug 1976
Debut: 16 Sep 1995 v Bolton Wanderers
Position: Midfield
Appearances: 2 (6) **Goals scored:** 1
Seasons: 1995/96 – 1996/97
Clubs: Manchester United, Sunderland (loan), Birmingham City (loan), Wrexham (loan), Manchester City (loan), Manchester City, Wigan Athletic (loan), Sheffield Wednesday (loan), Grimsby Town (loan), Sheffield Wednesday, Colorado Rapids, North Queensland Fury, Gabala

SAMUEL PERCY COOKSON
Country: Wales
Born: 1891 **Died:** Unknown
Debut: 26 Dec 1914 v Liverpool
Position: Half back
Appearances: 13 **Goals scored:** 0
Seasons: 1914/15
Clubs: Bargoed Town, Manchester United

RONALD 'RONNIE' COPE
Country: England
Born: 5 Oct 1934
Debut: 29 Sep 1956 v Arsenal
Position: Centre back
Appearances: 106 **Goals scored:** 2
Seasons: 1956/57 – 1960/61
Clubs: Manchester United, Luton Town

STEPHEN JAMES 'STEVE' COPPELL
Country: England
Born: 9 Jul 1955
Debut: 1 Mar 1975 v Cardiff City

Position: Right midfield
Appearances: 393 (3) **Goals scored:** 70
Seasons: 1974/75 – 1982/83
Clubs: Tranmere Rovers, Manchester United

Coppell gained a degree in Economics from Liverpool University while playing for Manchester United. A knee injury forced him to retire from the game at the early age of 28. Before then he had been a pacey winger, known for his quick feet and crossing ability. He was remarkably consistent, appearing in a record 206 consecutive league matches between January 1977 and November 1981. For United he won the FA Cup in 1977 as well as earning 42 caps and scoring seven goals for England.

JAMES 'JIMMY' COUPAR
Country: Scotland
Born: 1869 **Died:** Jan 1953
Debut: 3 Sep 1892 v Blackburn Rovers
Position: Forward
Appearances: 34 **Goals scored:** 10
Seasons: 1892/93 – 1901/02
Clubs: Dundee Our Boys, Newton Heath, St Johnstone, Rotherham Town, Luton Town, Swindon Town, Linfield

PETER DAVID COYNE
Country: England
Born: 13 Nov 1958
Debut: 21 Feb 1976 v Aston Villa
Position: Forward
Appearances: 1 (1) **Goals scored:** 1
Seasons: 1975/76 – 1976/77
Clubs: Manchester United, Crewe Alexandra, Los Angeles Aztecs, Hyde United, Swindon Town, Aldershot Town, Colne Dynamoes, Glossop North End

T CRAIG
Country: Unknown
Born: Unknown **Died:** Unknown
Debut: 18 Jan 1890 v Preston North End
Position: Forward
Appearances: 2 **Goals scored:** 1
Seasons: 1889/90 – 1890/91
Clubs: Newton Heath

CHARLES 'CHARLIE' CRAVEN
Country: England
Born: 2 Dec 1909 **Died:** 30 Mar 1972
Debut: 27 Aug 1938 v Middlesbrough
Position: Inside left
Appearances: 11 **Goals scored:** 2
Seasons: 1938/39
Clubs: Grimsby Town, Manchester United, Birmingham City

PATRICK TIMOTHY 'PADDY' CRERAND
Country: Scotland
Born: 19 Feb 1939
Debut: 23 Feb 1963 v Blackpool

Below: Winger Steve Coppell was one of United's all-time greats in that position, helping the Reds to FA Cup success in 1977.

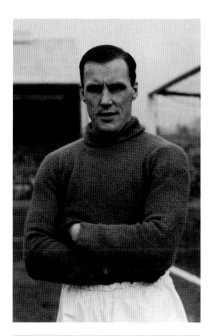

Position: Midfield
Appearances: 397 **Goals scored:** 15
Seasons: 1962/63 - 1970/71
Clubs: Celtic, Manchester United

In a side containing the mercurial talents of George Best and Bobby Charlton, Paddy Crerand provided the hard-tackling heartbeat of a successful United team. Born in Scotland of Irish descent, he spent six years at Celtic before he moved to United. He won the league championship in 1965 and 1967 and helped United to the 1963 FA Cup and the European Cup in 1968. Crerand was capped 16 times by Scotland. In 1971 he retired from playing, taking a coaching job with United before he spent one season managing Northampton Town. He then embarked on a successful media career and is well known today by younger United fans as he presents his own show on MUTV.

JOHN 'JACK' CROMPTON
Country: England
Born: 18 Dec 1921
Debut: 5 Jan 1946 v Accrington Stanley
Position: Goalkeeper
Appearances: 212 **Goals scored:** 0
Seasons: 1945/46 - 1955/56
Clubs: Manchester United

A local lad, Crompton was the popular goalkeeper in the United team that won the 1948 FA Cup. Two years after retiring in 1956 he became the club trainer and clocked up over a decade of service in the role during two different periods.

He was also interim United manager after Dave Sexton was fired. Jack Crompton was briefly Bobby Charlton's assistant at Preston North End in 1973-74. He is the only surviving member of either team that played in the 1948 FA Cup final.

GARTH ANTHONY CROOKS
Country: England
Born: 10 Mar 1958
Debut: 19 Nov 1983 v Watford
Position: Forward
Appearances: 6 (1) **Goals scored:** 2
Seasons: 1983/84
Clubs: Stoke City, Tottenham Hotspur, Manchester United (*loan*), West Bromwich Albion, Charlton Athletic

Garth Crooks was the first black player to be elected chairman of the PFA. Now a succesful media personality.

STANLEY 'STAN' CROWTHER
Country: England
Born: 3 Sep 1935
Debut: 19 Feb 1958 v Sheffield Wednesday
Position: Wing half
Appearances: 20 **Goals scored:** 0
Seasons: 1957/58 - 1958/59
Clubs: Aston Villa, Manchester United, Chelsea, Brighton & Hove Albion

Stanley Crowther retired at 27 citing his disillusionment with the game. He had signed for United hours before their first post-Munich fixture.

JOHAN JORDI CRUYFF
Country: Netherlands

Born: 9 Feb 1974
Debut: 17 Aug 1996 v Wimbledon
Position: Forward
Appearances: 26 (32) **Goals scored:** 8
Seasons: 1996/97 - 1999/2000
Clubs: Barcelona, Manchester United, Celta Vigo (*loan*), Alaves, Espanyol, Metalurh Donetsk, Valletta

NICHOLAS JAMES 'NICK' CULKIN
Country: England
Born: 6 Jul 1978
Debut: 22 Aug 1999 v Arsenal
Position: Goalkeeper
Appearances: 0 (1) **Goals scored:** 0
Seasons: 1999/2000
Clubs: Manchester United, Hull City (*loan*), Bristol Rovers (*loan*), Livingstone (*loan*), Queens Park Rangers, Radcliffe Borough

Nick Culkin holds the record for the shortest debut (and only United appearance) in Premier League history, having just 80 seconds of action over seven years at the club, after replacing Raimond van der Gouw in stoppage time against Arsenal at Highbury on 22 Aug 1999.

JOHN CUNNINGHAM
Country: Scotland
Born: 1868 **Died:** Unknown
Debut: 5 Nov 1898 v Grimsby Town
Position: Forward
Appearances: 17 **Goals scored:** 2
Seasons: 1898/99
Clubs: Celtic, Partick Thistle, Heart of Midlothian, Rangers, Glasgow Thistle, Preston North End, Sheffield United, Aston Villa, Wigan County, Newton Heath

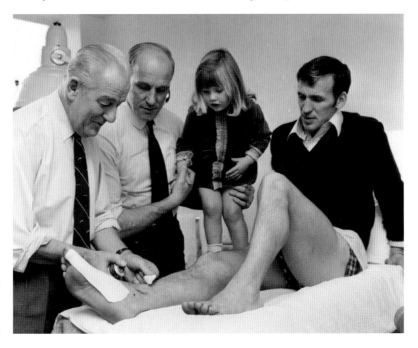

Above: 1950. United goalkeeper Jack Crompton. He would return to the club in the aftermath of the Munich disaster.

Left: 17 October 1968. Pat Crerand is treated for an injury to his foot as his daughter looks on. He sustained the injury during a bad tempered Inter-Continental Cup match against the Argentinian side Estudiantes.

LAWRENCE 'LAURIE' CUNNINGHAM
Country: England
Born: 8 Mar 1956 **Died:** 15 Jul 1989
Debut: 19 Apr 1983 v Everton
Position: Forward
Appearances: 3 (2) **Goals scored:** 1
Seasons: 1982/83
Clubs: Leyton Orient, West Bromwich Albion, Real Madrid, Manchester United (*loan*), Sporting Gijon (*loan*), Marseille, Leicester City, Rayo Vallecano, Charleroi, Wimbledon, Rayo Vallecano

Laurie Cunningham was the first black player to represent England at any level (U21) and first to play in a full competitive fixture. He died in a car crash in Madrid aged 33.

JOSEPH 'JOE' CURRY
Country: England
Born: 1887 **Died:** 1 Apr 1936
Debut: 21 Nov 1908 v Bradford City
Position: Defender
Appearances: 14 **Goals scored:** 0
Seasons: 1908/09 - 1910/11
Clubs: Scotswood, Manchester United, Southampton

JOHN CHARLES KEYWORTH CURTIS
Country: England
Born: 3 Sep 1978
Debut: 14 Oct 1997 v Ipswich Town
Position: Full back
Appearances: 9 (10) **Goals scored:** 0
Seasons: 1997/98 - 1999/2000
Clubs: Manchester United, Barnsley (*loan*), Blackburn Rovers, Sheffield United (*loan*), Leicester City, Portsmouth, Preston North End (*loan*), Nottingham Forest, Queens Park Rangers, Worcester City, Wrexham, Northampton Town, Gold Coast United

FABIO DA SILVA
Country: Brazil
Born: 9 Jul 1990
Debut: 24 Jan 2009 v Tottenham Hotspur
Position: Fullback
Appearances: 24 (14) **Goals scored:** 2
Seasons: 2008/09 - present
Clubs: Fluminense, Manchester United

RAFAEL PEREIRA DA SILVA
Country: Brazil
Born: 9 Jul 1990
Debut: 17 Aug 2008 v Newcastle United
Position: Fullback
Appearances: 62 (11) **Goals scored:** 2
Seasons: 2008/09 - present
Clubs: Fluminense, Manchester United

HERBERT DALE
Country: England
Born: Jan 1867 **Died:** Dec 1925
Debut: 25 Oct 1890 v Bootle Reserves
Position: Forward
Appearances: 1 **Goals scored:** 0
Seasons: 1889/90
Clubs: Manchester FA, Newton Heath

JOSEPH DALE
Country: England
Born: 3 Jul 1921 **Died:** 11 Sep 2000
Debut: 27 Sep 1947 v Preston North End
Position: Outside right
Appearances: 2 **Goals scored:** 2
Seasons: 1947/48
Clubs: Witton Albion, Manchester United, Port Vale, Witton Albion

WILLIAM 'BILLY' DALE
Country: England
Born: 17 Feb 1905 **Died:** 30 May 1987
Debut: 25 Aug 1928 v Leicester City
Position: Full back
Appearances: 68 **Goals scored:** 0
Seasons: 1928/29 - 1931/32
Clubs: Manchester United, Manchester City, Ipswich Town, Norwich City

EDWARD 'TED' DALTON
Country: England
Born: Apr 1882 **Died:** Unknown
Debut: 25 Mar 1908 v Liverpool
Position: Full back
Appearances: 1 **Goals scored:** 0
Seasons: 1907/08
Clubs: Manchester United, Pendlebury FC

GERALD 'GERRY' ANTHONY DALY
Country: Ireland
Born: 30 Apr 1954
Debut: 25 Aug 1973 v Arsenal
Position: Midfield
Appearances: 137 (5) **Goals scored:** 32
Seasons: 1973/74 - 1976/77
Clubs: Bohemians, Manchester United, Derby

Right: 28 July 2010. Rafael (l) and twin Fabio Da Silva (r) pose with the Allstar Trophy at the Reliant Stadium in Houston, Texas, during the pre-season tour of the USA.

County, New England Tea Men (*loan*), Coventry City, Leicester City (*loan*), Birmingham City, Shrewsbury Town, Stoke City, Doncaster Rovers, Telford United

PETER DAVENPORT

Country: England
Born: 24 Mar 1961
Debut: 15 Mar 1986 v Queens Park Rangers
Position: Forward
Appearances: 83 (23) **Goals scored:** 26
Seasons: 1985/86 - 1988/89
Clubs: Cammell Laird, Nottingham Forest, Manchester United, Middlesbrough, Sunderland, Airdrieonians, St Johnstone, Stockport County, Southport, Macclesfield Town

WILLIAM R DAVIDSON

Country: Unknown
Born: Unknown **Died:** Unknown
Debut: 2 Sep 1893 v Burnley
Position: Half back
Appearances: 44 **Goals scored:** 2
Seasons: 1893/94 - 1894/95
Clubs: Annbank, Newton Heath

ALAN DAVIES

Country: Wales
Born: 5 Dec 1961 **Died:** 4 Feb 1992
Debut: 1 May 1982 v Southampton
Position: Winger
Appearances: 8 (2) **Goals scored:** 1
Seasons: 1981/82 - 1983/84
Clubs: Trainee, Manchester United, Newcastle United, Charlton Athletic (*loan*), Carlisle United (*loan*), Swansea City, Bradford City, Swansea City

JOHN DAVIES

Country: Unknown
Born: Unknown **Died:** Unknown
Debut: 14 Jan 1893 Newton Heath v Nottingham Forest
Position: Goalkeeper
Appearances: 10 **Goals scored:** 0
Seasons: 1892/93 - 1893/94
Clubs: Hurst, Burslem Port Vale, Newton Heath

JOSEPH DAVIES

Country: Wales
Born: 12 Jul 1864 **Died:** 7 Oct 1943
Debut: 30 Oct 1886 v Fleetwood Rangers
Position: Half back
Appearances: 2 **Goals scored:** 0
Seasons: 1886/87 - 1889/90
Clubs: Druids, Newton Heath, Wolverhampton Wanderers, Druids

L DAVIES

Country: Unknown
Born: Unknown **Died:** Unknown
Debut: 30 Oct 1886 v Fleetwood Rangers
Position: Forward
Appearances: 1 **Goals scored:** 0
Seasons: 1886/87
Clubs: Newton Heath

RONALD TUDOR DAVIES

Country: Wales

Born: 25 May 1942
Debut: 30 Nov 1974 v Sunderland
Position: Forward
Appearances: 0 (10) **Goals scored:** 0
Seasons: 1974/75
Clubs: Chester, Luton Town, Norwich City, Southampton, Portsmouth, Manchester United, Millwall (*loan*), Arcadia Shephards

RONALD WYN DAVIES

Country: Wales
Born: 20 Mar 1942
Debut: 23 Sep 1972 v Derby County
Position: Forward
Appearances: 16 (1) **Goals scored:** 4
Seasons: 1972/73
Clubs: Locomotive Llanberis, Caernarfon Town, Wrexham, Bolton Wanderers, Newcastle United, Manchester City, Manchester United, Blackpool, Crystal Palace (*loan*), Stockport County, Crewe Alexandra, Bangor City

SIMON ITHEL DAVIES

Country: Wales
Born: 23 Apr 1974
Debut: 21 Sep 1994 v Port Vale
Position: Midfield
Appearances: 10 (10) **Goals scored:** 1
Seasons: 1995/95 - 1996/97
Clubs: Manchester United, Exeter City (*loan*), Huddersfield Town (*loan*), Luton Town, Macclesfield Town, Rochdale, Bangor City, Total Network Solutions, Bangor City, Rhyl, Chester City, Airbus UK

JAMES 'JIMMY' DAVIS

Country: England
Born: 6 Feb 1982 **Died:** 9 Aug 2003
Debut: 5 Nov 2001 v Arsenal
Position: Winger
Appearances: 1 **Goals scored:** 0
Seasons: 2001/02
Clubs: Manchester United, Royal Antwerp (*loan*), Swindon Town (*loan*), Watford (*loan*)

Died agecd just 21 in car accident.

ALEXANDER 'ALEX' DOWNIE DAWSON

Country: Scotland
Born: 21 Feb 1940
Debut: 22 Apr 1957 v Burnley
Position: Forward
Appearances: 93 **Goals scored:** 54
Seasons: 1956/57 – 1961/62
Clubs: Manchester United, Preston North End, Bury, Brighton & Hove Albion, Brentford (*loan*), Corby Town

DAVID DE GEA QUINTANA

Country: Spain
Born: 7 Nov 1990
Debut: 7 Aug 2011 v Manchester City
Position: Goalkeeper
Appearances: 1 **Goals scored:** 0
Seasons: 2011/12
Clubs: Atlético Madrid, Manchester United

RITCHIE RIA ALFONS DE LAET

Country: Belgium
Born: 28 Nov 1988
Debut: 24 May 2009 v Hull City
Position: Defender
Appearances: 4 (2) **Goals scored:** 0
Seasons: 2008/09 - present
Clubs: Royal Antwerp, Stoke City, Wrexham (*loan*), Manchester United, Sheffield United (*loan*), Preston North End (*loan*), Portsmouth (*loan*)

HAROLD DEAN

Country: England
Born: 1910 **Died:** Unknown
Debut: 26 Sep 1931 v Chesterfield
Position: Forward
Appearances: 2 **Goals scored:** 0
Seasons: 1931/32
Clubs: Old Trafford FC, Manchester United, Mossley

Above: 4 August 1960. Alex Dawson – a bustling centre forward who scored a goal in United's first game after Munich, and later in that FA Cup run became the last player to score a hat-trick at the semi-final stage of the competition.

Above: Circa 1950. John 'Jack' Doherty playing for Manchester Boys. He signed for Manchester United in 1950 but his career was injury plagued and first team football was limited.

JAMES 'JIMMY' DELANEY

Country: Scotland
Born: 3 Sep 1914 **Died:** 26 Sep 1989
Debut: 31 Aug 1946 v Grimsby Town
Position: Outside right
Appearances: 184 **Goals scored:** 28
Seasons: 1946/47 - 1950/51
Clubs: Celtic, Manchester United, Aberdeen, Falkirk, Derry City, Cork Athletic, Elgin City

Matt Busby's first signing as manager of United, Delaney cost £4,000 from Celtic and was part of the 1948 FA Cup-winning side.

MARK JAMES DEMPSEY

Country: England
Born: 14 Jan 1964
Debut: 2 Nov 1983 v Spartak Varna
Position: Midfield
Appearances: 1 (1) **Goals scored:** 0
Seasons: 1983/84 - 1985/86
Clubs: Manchester United, Swindon Town (loan), Sheffield United, Chesterfield (loan), Rotherham United, Macclesfield Town

In 2010 the former United youth coach joined Ole Gunnar Solskjaer's coaching team at Molde.

J DENMAN

Country: Unknown
Born: Unknown **Died:** Unknown
Debut: 5 Dec 1891 v Blackpool
Position: Full back
Appearances: 1 **Goals scored:** 0
Seasons: 1891/92
Clubs: South Bank, Newton Heath

WILLIAM 'BILLY' DENNIS

Country: England
Born: 21 Sep 1896 **Died:** Unknown
Debut: 13 Oct 1923 v Oldham Athletic
Position: Full back
Appearances: 3 **Goals scored:** 0
Seasons: 1923/24
Clubs: Ashton PSA, Denton, Birkenhead Comets, (WW1), Linfield, (WW1), Tranmere Rovers, (WW1), Stalybridge Celtic, Blackburn Rovers, Stalybridge Celtic, Manchester United, Chesterfield, Wigan Borough, Macclesfield Town, Hurst, Mossley

NEIL HAMILTON DEWAR

Country: Scotland
Born: 11 Nov 1908 **Died:** Unknown
Debut: 11 Feb 1933 v Preston North End
Position: Forward
Appearances: 36 **Goals scored:** 14
Seasons: 1932/33 - 1933/34
Clubs: Third Lanark, Manchester United, Sheffield Wednesday, Third Lanark

MAME BIRAM DIOUF

Country: Senegal
Born: 16 Dec 1987
Debut: 9 Jan 2010 v Birmingham City
Position: Forward
Appearances: 0 (6) **Goals scored:** 1
Seasons: 2009/10 - present
Clubs: ASC Diaraf, Molde, Manchester United, Molde (loan), Blackburn Rovers (loan)

ERIC DANIEL DJEMBA-DJEMBA

Country: Cameroon
Born: 4 May 1981
Debut: 10 Aug 2003 v Arsenal
Position: Midfield
Appearances: 27 (12) **Goals scored:** 2
Seasons: 2003/04 - 2004/05
Clubs: Brasseries Du Cameroun, Kadji Sport Academie De Douala, Nantes, Manchester United, Aston Villa, Burnley (loan), Quatar SC, Odense Boldklub

BOJAN DJORDJIC

Country: Sweden
Born: 6 Feb 1982
Debut: 19 May 2001 v Tottenham
Position: Midfield
Appearances: 1 (1) **Goals scored:** 0
Seasons: 2000/01 - 2001/02
Clubs: Brommapojkarna, Manchester United, Sheffield Wednesday (loan), Arthus Gymnastyk Forening (loan), Red Star Belgrade (loan), Glasgow Rangers, Plymouth Argyle, AIK Athens, Videoton

JOHN PETER DOHERTY

Country: England
Born: 12 Mar 1935 **Died:** 13 Nov 2007
Debut: 6 Dec 1952 v Middlesbrough
Position: Inside right
Appearances: 26 **Goals scored:** 7
Seasons: 1952/53 - 1957/58
Clubs: Manchester United, Leicester City

Chaired the Former Manchester United Players' Association before his death in 2007.

BERNARD DONAGHY

Country: Ireland
Born: 3 Dec 1882 **Died:** 1 Jul 1916
Debut: 4 Nov 1905 v Lincoln City
Position: Inside forward
Appearances: 3 **Goals scored:** 0
Seasons: 1905/06
Clubs: Derry Celtic, Glentoran, Derry Celtic, Manchester United, Derry Celtic, Burnley

Died on the first day of fighting at The Battle of the Somme, 1 July 1916.

MALACHY MARTIN 'MAL' DONAGHY

Country: Northern Ireland
Born: 13 Sep 1957
Debut: 30 Oct 1988 v Everton
Position: Defender
Appearances: 98 (21) **Goals scored:** 0
Seasons: 1988/89 - 1991/92
Clubs: Cromac Albion, Larne, Luton Town, Manchester United, Luton Town (loan), Chelsea

IAN RICHARD DONALD

Country: Scotland
Born: 28 Nov 1951
Debut: 7 Oct 1970 v Portsmouth
Position: Full back
Appearances: 6 **Goals scored:** 0
Seasons: 1970/71 - 1972/73
Clubs: Manchester United, Partick Thistle, Arbroath

ROBERT 'BOB' DONALDSON

Country: Scotland
Born: 27 Aug 1871 **Died:** 28 Apr 1947
Debut: 3 Sep 1892 v Blackburn Rovers
Position: Forward
Appearances: 155 **Goals scored:** 66
Seasons: 1892/93 - 1897/98
Clubs: Aidrieonians, Blackburn Rovers, Newton Heath, Luton Town, Glossop North End, Ashford Town

His debut goal was Newton Heath's first ever league goal.

DONG FANGZHUO

Country: China
Born: 23 Jan 1985
Debut: 9 May 2007 v Chelsea
Position: Forward
Appearances: 2 (1) **Goals scored:** 0
Seasons: 2006/07 - 2007/08
Clubs: Dalian Saidelong, Dalian Shide, Manchester United, Royal Antwerp (loan), Dalian Shide, Legia Warsaw, Portimonense, Mika

Dong Fangzhuo was the first Chinese player to sign for United.

DONNELLY

Country: Unknown
Born: Unknown **Died:** Unknown
Debut: 25 Oct 1890 v Bootle Reserves
Position: Forward
Appearances: 1 **Goals scored:** 0
Seasons: 1890/91
Clubs: Newton Heath

ANTHONY DONNELLY

Country: England
Born: Apr 1886 **Died:** Apr 1947
Debut: 15 Mar 1909 v Sunderland
Position: Full back
Appearances: 37 **Goals scored:** 0
Seasons: 1908/09 - 1912/13
Clubs: Tongue FC, Heywood United, Manchester United, Glentoran, Heywood United, Chester, Southampton, Middleton Borough

THOMAS 'TOMMY' DOUGAN

Country: Scotland
Born: 22 Nov 1915 **Died:** Unknown
Debut: 29 Mar 1939 v Everton
Position: Forward
Appearances: 4 **Goals scored:** 0
Seasons: 1938/39 - 1939/40
Clubs: Alloa Athletic, Tunbridge Wells Rangers, Plymouth Argyle, Manchester United, Heart of Midlothian

JOHN 'JACK' DOUGHTY

Country: Wales
Born: Oct 1865 **Died:** Apr 1937
Debut: 30 Oct 1886 v Fleetwood Rangers
Position: Forward
Appearances: 3 **Goals scored:** 3
Seasons: 1886/87 and 1891/92
Clubs: Druids, Newton Heath, Hyde, Fairfield

The elder brother of Roger Doughty, Jack Doughty scored Newton Heath's first competitive goal in FA Cup.

ROGER DOUGHTY

Country: Wales
Born: Oct 1865 **Died:** 19 Dec 1914
Debut: 18 Jan 1890 v Preston North End
Position: Half back
Appearances: 8 **Goals scored:** 1
Seasons: 1889/90 - 1891/92 and 1896/97
Clubs: Druids, Newton Heath, Fairfield FC, West Manchester, Newton Heath

WILLIAM 'HUGH' DOUGLAS

Country: Scotland
Born: Unknown **Died:** Unknown
Debut: 3 Feb 1894 v Aston Villa
Position: Goalkeeper
Appearances: 57 **Goals scored:** 0
Seasons: 1893/94 - 1895/96

Clubs: Dundee Old Boys, Ardwick, Newton Heath, Derby County

JOHN MACDIARMID DOW

Country: Scotland
Born: 1873 **Died:** Unknown
Debut: 24 Mar 1894 v Bolton Wanderers
Position: Defender
Appearances: 50 **Goals scored:** 6
Seasons: 1893/94 - 1896/97
Clubs: Dundee, Dundee Our Boys, Newton Heath, Fairfield FC

ALEXANDER LEEK BROWN 'ALEX' DOWNIE

Country: Scotland
Born: 1876 **Died:** 9 Dec 1953
Debut: 22 Nov 1902 v Leicester City
Position: Half back
Appearances: 191 **Goals scored:** 14
Seasons: 1902/03 - 1909/10
Clubs: Glasgow Perthshire, Third Lanark, Manchester United, Oldham Athletic, Crewe Alexandra

Downie learned his trade in Scotland, but made a big impact when he arrived as one of the first signings by the new owners in 1902. He could play all three half back positions and helped the club win promotion and then their first major trophy, the First Division title, in the 1907-08 season.

Above: 3 March 2004. Dong Fangzhuo, United's first signing from China, was unable to establish himself in the Reds' team.

JOHN DENIS DOWNIE

Country: Scotland
Born: 19 Jul 1925
Debut: 5 Mar 1949 v Charlton Athletic
Position: Forward
Appearances: 116 **Goals scored:** 37
Seasons: 1948/49 – 1952/53
Clubs: Bradford Park Avenue, Manchester United, Luton Town, Hull City, Mansfield Town

LEVI WILLIAM 'BILL' DRAYCOTT

Country: England
Born: 15 Feb 1869 **Died:** Unknown
Debut: 1 Sep 1896 v Gainsborough Trinity
Position: Half back
Appearances: 95 **Goals scored:** 6
Seasons: 1896/97 – 1899/1900
Clubs: Burslem Port Vale, Stoke, Burton Wanderers, Newton Heath, Bedminster, Bristol Rovers, Wellingborough, Luton Town

DION DUBLIN

Country: England
Born: 22 Apr 1969
Debut: 15 Aug 1992 v Sheffield United
Position: Forward
Appearances: 6 (11) **Goals scored:** 3
Seasons: 1992/93 – 1994/95
Clubs: Norwich City (trainee), Cambridge City, Barnet (*loan*), Manchester United, Coventry City, Aston Villa, Millwall (*loan*), Leicester City, Celtic, Norwich City

Away from football, Dublin is also an amateur percussionist. He invented a percussion instrument, which he called "The Dube", and in 2011 accompanied Ocean Colour Scene during a gig at the University of East Anglia.

RICHARD 'DICK' DUCKWORTH

Country: England
Born: 14 Sep 1882 **Died:** Unknown
Debut: 19 Dec 1903 v Gainsborough Trinity
Position: Half back
Appearances: 254 **Goals scored:** 11
Seasons: 1903/04 – 1913/14
Clubs: Manchester United

Enjoyed seven significant seasons in the early 1900s after coming through the United youth system. He played a key role in two league titles and an FA Cup win, taking over as the leading half back from Alex Downie. He suffered a severe knee injury in December 1913 and was forced to retire.

WILLIAM DUNN

Country: England
Born: Jul 1877 **Died:** Unknown
Debut: 4 Sep 1897 v Lincoln City
Position: Forward
Appearances: 12 **Goals scored:** 0
Seasons: 1896/97 – 1898/99
Clubs: South Bank, Newton Heath

PATRICK 'PAT' DUNNE

Country: Ireland
Born: 9 Feb 1943
Debut: 8 Sep 1964 v Everton
Position: Goalkeeper
Appearances: 67 **Goals scored:** 0
Seasons: 1964/65 – 1966/67
Clubs: Shamrock Rovers, Everton, Manchester United, Plymouth Argyle, Shamrock Rovers, Thurles Town, Shelbourne

ANTHONY 'TONY' PETER DUNNE

Country: Ireland
Born: 24 Jul 1941
Debut: 15 Oct 1960 v Burnley
Position: Left back
Appearances: 534 (1) **Goals scored:** 2
Seasons: 1960/61 – 1972/73
Clubs: Shelbourne FC, Manchester United, Bolton Wanderers, Detroit Express

Anthony Peter Dunne is seventh in the all-time appearances list for Manchester United. With 534 starts at left-back he had a highly successful career winning the 1963 FA Cup and First Division Championships in 1965 and 1967. He was also a member of the victorious 1968 European Cup side and played 33 times for the Republic of Ireland, captaining his country on four occasions.

MICHAEL DUXBURY

Country: England
Born: 1 Sep 1959
Debut: 23 Aug 1980 v Birmingham City
Position: Full back
Appearances: 345 (33) **Goals scored:** 7
Seasons: 1980/81 – 1989/90
Clubs: Manchester United, Blackburn Rovers, Bradford City, Golden FC

Mike Duxbury joined Manchester United as a schoolboy in 1975. As a steady right back he spent 14 seasons at the club, during which he won two FA Cup winners medals, in 1983 and 1985. In 1990 he transferred to Blackburn Rovers and after a spell at Bradford finished his career in Hong Kong.

JAMES ARTHUR 'JIMMY' DYER

Country: England
Born: 24 Aug 1883 **Died:** Unknown
Debut: 14 Oct 1905 v West Bromwich Albion
Position: Forward
Appearances: 1 **Goals scored:** 0
Seasons: 1905/06
Clubs: Wombwell FC, Barnsley, Doncaster Rovers, Ashton Town, Manchester United, West Ham United

CHRISTOPHER MARK 'CHRIS' EAGLES

Country: England
Born: 19 Nov 1985
Debut: 28 Oct 2003 v Leeds United
Position: Midfield
Appearances: 7 (10) **Goals scored:** 1
Seasons: 2003/04 – 2007/08
Clubs: Manchester United, Watford (*loan*), Sheffield Wednesday (*loan*), Watford (*loan*), NEC Nijmegen (*loan*), Burnley, Bolton

JOHN EARP

Country: England
Born: 1860 **Died:** Unknown
Debut: 30 Oct 1886 v Fleetwood Rangers
Position: Forward
Appearances: 1 **Goals scored:** 0
Seasons: 1886/87
Clubs: Newton Heath

SYLVAN AUGUS EBANKS-BLAKE

Country: England
Born: 29 Mar 1986
Debut: 27 Oct 2004 v Crewe Alexandra
Position: Forward
Appearances: 1 (1) **Goals scored:** 1
Seasons: 2004/05 – 2005/06
Clubs: Manchester United, Royal Antwerp (*loan*), Plymouth Argyle, Wolverhampton Wanderers

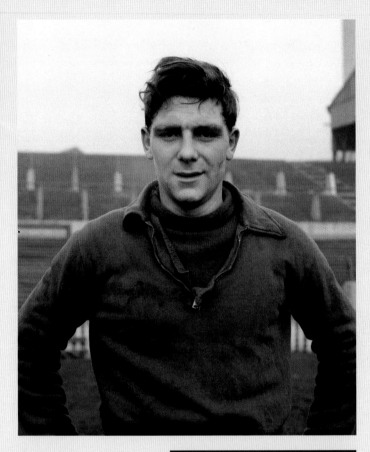

DUNCAN EDWARDS

Country: England
Born: 1 Oct 1936 **Died:** 21 Feb 1958
Debut: 4 Apr 1953 v Cardiff City
Position: Half back
Appearances: 177 **Goals scored:** 21
Seasons: 1952/53 - 1957/58
Clubs: Manchester United

"He was the best player I have ever seen, the best footballer I have played with for United or England, the only player who ever made me feel inferior," Bobby Charlton once confessed. "As good as anyone… mature beyond his years," remarked Bill Foulkes. And to many United fans Duncan Edwards is still the greatest ever player to wear a United shirt. When his rivals for the accolade are lined up in a Red Devils shirt, it makes the statement all the more remarkable.

The fact that Edwards would die 15 days after the Munich air crash on 6 February 1958 at the age of just 21 makes the statement tragic. Less than five seasons in the first team, only 177 games and a mere 21 goals, the young man from Dudley in the West Midlands was still in the formative years of his career. So

Above: 5 January 1954. Duncan Edwards training after being selected for England's Under-23 team at the age of just 17 years.

Right: 22 February 1958. A wreath is carried aboard the aeroplane transporting the body of Edwards from Munich to Manchester.

much talent and so revered by his teammates, it makes his premature death one of football's most heart-rending stories.

Edwards was born on 1 October 1936 and played for Dudley schoolboys at the age of eleven, when his precocious talent was clear to see; his then sports teacher predicted he would one day play for England. Meanwhile, the youngster turned out for England schoolboys and, during his school days in Wolverhampton, nearby Wolverhampton Wanderers tried to sign him. Edwards wanted to join United and was prepared to wait until they came knocking. Busby, who had been tipped off about the lad from one of his own scouts, Jack O'Brien, ensured the deal was done. On 31 May 1952, "Manboy" – his nickname because of his huge physique – joined the Reds (newly crowned First Division champions) and in just under a year had made his first team debut.

Edwards was only 16 years and 185 days old when he started in the match against Cardiff City in April 1953. He was one of the youngest players ever recorded to play in the English First Division and while it was his only appearance that season, and the match was lost 4-1, Busby knew he had found a star.

The manager did not start Edwards again until the end of October in the following season of 1953-54. But from that moment on the teenager was a fixture in the now-forming Busby Babes line-up. He played 24 games that season and the Red Devils finished a creditable fourth in

the league. Busby often used Edwards at left back in the early days, but half back would be the position he would grow into, and it was not long in coming.

The potential and future legendary status of Edwards was already starting to emerge, beginning with his effect on the United youth team who would win the Youth Cup three times in succession with Edwards as their star player. At such a young age, he seemed to have so much: the ability to pass and control the ball with both feet; a raging desire to give everything in every game; a crunching tackle; and a wonderfully level-headed temperament. This was a man who knew that there was more to life than football. He even took on an apprenticeship as a carpenter when he signed as a professional because he wanted financial security as well as the plaudits. "It's what you have in the bank when you have finished the game that cheers a footballer most of all," he once said. In fact, Edwards was to become one of the first players to work with product sponsors and also earned money from a book he wrote called *Tackle Soccer This Way*.

In 1953-54 and still a teenager, Edwards was central to the team's success because although Stan Pearson was the highly respected team captain and Tommy Taylor would score bags of goals, everyone knew Edwards was the most talented player. Another season passed and Edwards helped United to fifth in the league. In April 1955 Edwards made his England debut against Scotland

aged 18 years and 183 days – setting a post-war record as the youngest international. A few months later he began his compulsory national service, stationed in army barracks in Shropshire along with Bobby Charlton.

Although they turned out for the army team on occasion, both players were allowed to play for United in the 1955-56 breakthrough season. Edwards played 33 games (he missed two months of the season with influenza) and scored three goals as United won the league title by a massive eleven points. The following season both player and team were just as impressive and another title was secured, while a foray into Europe was a new and exciting experience (United made the European Cup semi-finals).

Edwards' football life was thoroughly enjoyable: he loved the club and his team-mates with whom he had grown up in the youth team; more United trophies

were a near-certainty because of his unstoppable power and total dedication to the game; the England captain's job was likely to be his in a few seasons; and a trip to the World Cup in Sweden in the summer of 1958 was looming. Still only 21 years old and with a young fiancée, the whole world stretched out before him.

Then came the Munich air crash in February 1958 and Edwards was killed along with seven other players. That he held on to life for 15 days after the crash made his story yet more heart-rending. He had suffered multiple injuries – leg and rib fractures and severe kidney damage – but doctors were hopeful of his eventual recovery. A kidney transplant, however, only caused more problems with internal bleeding. He drifted in and out of consciousness for days and at one point was thought to be improving dramatically. Edwards died on 21 February in Rechts der Isar Hospital in Munich. His grave in Dudley is still a

place of pilgrimage for football fans.

Even after his death, the tributes to Edwards continued. Contemporaries talked of his versatility, his dynamism, his stamina and his skill in any position. When asked about Edwards, one of England's all-time greats Stanley Matthews said he was, "Like a rock in a raging sea."

Above: 3 April 1957. England's Stanley Matthews, Duncan Edwards and captain Billy Wright train at Highbury before a match against Scotland.

Left: 1 February 1958. Duncan Edwards signs an autograph for a young fan on the Highbury pitch just before the kick-off against Arsenal. United won 5-4.

Above: 16 April 2011. Patrice Evra of United clashes with Mario Balotelli of Manchester City.

ADAM JAMES ECKERSLEY
Country: England
Born: 7 Sep 1985
Debut: 26 Oct 2005 v Barnet
Position: Full back
Appearances: 1 **Goals scored:** 0
Seasons: 2005/06
Clubs: Manchester United, Royal Antwerp (*loan*), Brondby (*loan*), Barnsley (*loan*), Port Vale (*loan*), Horsens, AGF

RICHARD JON ECKERSLEY
Country: England
Born: 12 Mar 1989
Debut: 24 Jan 2009 v Tottenham Hotspur
Position: Defender
Appearances: 0 (4) **Goals scored:** 0
Seasons: 2008/09
Clubs: Manchester United, Burnley, Plymouth Argyle (*loan*), Bradford City (*loan*), Bury (*loan*), Toronto FC (*loan*)

ALFRED 'ALF' EDGE
Country: England
Born: Oct 1864 **Died:** 11 Apr 1941
Debut: 3 Oct 1891 v Manchester City
Position: Inside forward
Appearances: 3 **Goals scored:** 3
Seasons: 1891/92

Clubs: Stoke, Newton Heath, Stoke, Northwich Victoria, Ardwick, Macclesfield

HUGH EDMONDS
Country: Scotland
Born: 1884 **Died:** Unknown
Debut: 11 Feb 1911 v Bristol City
Position: Goalkeeper
Appearances: 51 **Goals scored:** 0
Seasons: 1910/11 – 1911/12
Clubs: Linfield, Bolton Wanderers, Manchester United, Glenavon, Linfield, Jarrow

PAUL FRANCIS EDWARDS
Country: England
Born: 7 Oct 1947
Debut: 19 Aug 1969 v Everton
Position: Defender
Appearances: 66 (2) **Goals scored:** 1
Seasons: 1969/70 – 1972/73
Clubs: Trainee, Manchester United, Oldham (*loan*), Oldham, Stockport County (*loan*), Stockport County

DAVID ELLIS
Country: Scotland
Born: 2 Mar 1900 **Died:** Unknown
Debut: 25 Aug 1923 v Bristol City
Position: Outside right
Appearances: 11 **Goals scored:** 0
Seasons: 1923/24
Clubs: Airdrieonians, Maidstone United, Manchester United, St Johnstone, Bradford City, Arthurlie

FREDERICK CHARLES 'FRED' ERENTZ
Country: Scotland
Born: Mar 1870 **Died:** 6 Apr 1938
Debut: 3 Sep 1892 v Blackburn Rovers
Position: Defender
Appearances: 310 **Goals scored:** 9
Seasons: 1892/93 – 1901/02
Clubs: Dundee Our Boys, Newton Heath

A Scotsman with a Danish father, Erentz played at either full back or half back in the final ten years when the club was known as Newton Heath. He was an ever present for many years and once rejected a move to Tottenham Hotspur where his brother Harry played. He was forced to retire following a knee injury.

HENRY BERNT 'HARRY' ERENTZ
Country: Scotland
Born: 17 Sep 1874 **Died:** 19 Jul 1947
Debut: 18 Jan 1898 v Arsenal
Position: Right back
Appearances: 9 **Goals scored:** 0
Seasons: 1897/98
Clubs: Dundee Our Boys, Oldham County, Newton Heath, Tottenham Hotspur, Swindon Town

GEORGE EVANS
Country: Unknown

Born: Unknown **Died:** Unknown
Debut: 4 Oct 1890 v Higher Walton
Position: Forward
Appearances: 1 **Goals scored:** 1
Seasons: 1890/91
Clubs: Newton Heath

JONATHAN GRANT 'JONNY' EVANS

Country: Northern Ireland
Born: 2 Jan 1988
Debut: 26 Sep 2007 v Coventry City
Position: Centre back
Appearances: 77 (10) **Goals scored:** 0
Seasons: 2006/07 - present
Clubs: Manchester United, Royal
Antwerp (*loan*), Sunderland (*loan*)

SIDNEY EVANS

Country: England
Born: 1893 **Died:** Unknown
Debut: 12 Apr 1924 v Crystal Palace
Position: Forward
Appearances: 6 **Goals scored:** 2
Seasons: 1923/24 – 1924/25
Clubs: Cardiff City, Manchester United, Pontypridd

PATRICE LATYR EVRA

Country: France
Born: 15 May 1981
Debut: 14 Jan 2006 v Manchester City
Position: Left back
Appearances: 225 (21) **Goals scored:** 3
Seasons: 2005/06 - present
Clubs: Paris Saint-Germain, Marsala, Monza,
Nice, AS Monaco, Manchester United

Following a tough debut in 2006 against Manchester City, Patrice Evra recovered to become a key member of United's starting eleven. Athletic and attacking, he is every inch the modern day full back. He has won four titles with United to date and has captained both club and country on a number of occasions.

JOSEPH WILLIAM FALL

Country: England
Born: 1872 **Died:** Unknown
Debut: 2 Sep 1893 v Burnley
Position: Goalkeeper
Appearances: 27 **Goals scored:** 0
Seasons: 1893/94
Clubs: Middlesbrough Ironopolis,
Newton Heath, Small Heath

ALFRED H FARMAN

Country: England
Born: Apr 1869 **Died:** Unknown
Debut: 18 Jan 1890 v Preston North End
Position: Forward
Appearances: 61 **Goals scored:** 28
Seasons: 1889/90 – 1894/95

Clubs: Birmingham Excelsior, Aston Villa,
Bolton Wanderers, Newton Heath

Some sources suggest he scored the first penalty in history of football for Newton Heath against Blackpool (others say it was a Wolves player).

JOHN IGNATIUS 'SONNY' FEEHAN

Country: Ireland
Born: 17 Sep 1926 **Died:** 11 Mar 1995
Debut: 5 Nov 1949 v Huddersfield Town
Position: Goalkeeper
Appearances: 14 **Goals scored:** 0
Seasons: 1949/50
Clubs: Waterford, Manchester United,
Northampton Town, Brentford, Headington United

GEORGE FELTON

Country: England
Born: 1859 **Died:** Unknown
Debut: 25 Oct 1890 v Bootle Reserves
Position: Half back
Appearances: 1 **Goals scored:** 0
Seasons: 1890/91
Clubs: Unknown

RIO GAVIN FERDINAND

Country: England
Born: 7 Nov 1978
Debut: 27 Aug 2002 v Zalaegerszeg
Position: Defender
Appearances: 356 (5) **Goals scored:** 7
Seasons: 2002/03 - present
Clubs: West Ham United, AFC Bournemouth
(*loan*), Leeds United, Manchester United

When Rio Ferdinand moved from Leeds United to Manchester United in 2002 for £30 million he became the world's most expensive defender for the second time. He justified his price tag immediately as United won the Premier League in his first season. However, the following season he missed a drugs test and was banned from playing for eight months. Since returning he has provided a powerful, classy presence at the heart of the defence. Despite numerous injuries, he has captained the side many times and forged a formidable partnership with Nemanja Vidic. Having already won four further league titles, the FA Cup and the Champions League, he has represented England on 81 occasions.

DANIEL FERGUSON

Country: Wales
Born: 25 Jan 1903 **Died:** Oct 1971
Debut: 7 Apr 1928 v Burnley
Position: Forward
Appearances: 4 **Goals scored:** 0
Seasons: 1927/28
Clubs: Rhyl Athletic, Manchester United,
Reading, Accrington Stanley, Chester, Halifax
Town, Stockport County, Macclesfield Town

DARREN FERGUSON

Country: Scotland
Born: 9 Feb 1972
Debut: 26 Feb 1991 v Sheffield United
Position: Midfield
Appearances: 22 (8) **Goals scored:** 0
Seasons: 1990/91 – 1993/94
Clubs: Manchester United, Wolverhampton
Wanderers, Sparta Rotterdam,
Wrexham, Peterborough United

The son of Sir Alex Ferguson, he is currently the manager of Peterborough United.

Left: 14 May 2011. Rio Ferdinand during the match against Blackburn Rovers at Ewood Park when United secured a record 19th league title.

JOHN JOSEPH FERGUSON

Country: England
Born: 12 Dec 1904 **Died:** 1981
Debut: 29 Aug 1931 v Bradford Park Avenue
Position: Forward
Appearances: 8 **Goals scored:** 1
Seasons: 1931/32
Clubs: Grimsby Town, Workington, Spen Black and White, Wolverhampton Wanderers, Watford, Burton Town, Manchester United, Derry City

RONALD JOHNSON FERRIER

Country: England
Born: 26 Apr 1914 **Died:** 11 Oct 1991
Debut: 4 Sep 1935 v Charlton Athletic
Position: Forward
Appearances: 19 **Goals scored:** 4
Seasons: 1935/36 – 1938/39
Clubs: Grimsby Wanderers, Grimsby Town, Manchester United, Oldham Athletic

WILLIAM JOHN FIELDING

Country: England
Born: 17 Jun 1915 **Died:** May 2006
Debut: 25 Jan 1947 v Nottingham Forest
Position: Goalkeeper
Appearances: 7 **Goals scored:** 0
Seasons: 1947/48
Clubs: Broadbottom YMCA, Hurst FC, Cardiff City, Bolton Wanderers, Stockport County, Bolton Wanderers, Manchester United

JAMES FISHER

Country: Scotland
Born: 1876 **Died:** Unknown
Debut: 20 Oct 1900 v Walsall
Position: Forward
Appearances: 46 **Goals scored:** 3
Seasons: 1900/01 – 1901/02
Clubs: East Stirlingshire, St Bernard's, Aston Villa, King's Park, Newton Heath

JOHN FITCHETT

Country: England
Born: Apr 1880 **Died:** Unknown
Debut: 21 Mar 1903 v Leicester City
Position: Full back
Appearances: 18 **Goals scored:** 1
Seasons: 1902/03 and 1904/05
Clubs: Bolton Wanderers, Southampton, Manchester United, Plymouth Argyle, Manchester United, Fulham, Exeter

GEORGE ARTHUR FITTON

Country: England
Born: 30 May 1902 **Died:** 10 Sep 1984
Debut: 26 Mar 1932 v Oldham Athletic
Position: Forward
Appearances: 12 **Goals scored:** 2
Seasons: 1931/32 – 1932/33
Clubs: Kidderminster Harriers, West Bromwich Albion, Manchester United, Preston North End

JOHN HERBERT NORTON FITZPATRICK

Country: Scotland
Born: 18 Aug 1946
Debut: 24 Feb 1965 v Sunderland
Position: Defender/Midfielder
Appearances: 141 (6) **Goals scored:** 10
Seasons: 1964/65 – 1972/73
Clubs: Manchester United

DAVID FITZSIMMONS

Country: Scotland
Born: 1875 **Died:** Unknown

Debut: 7 Sep 1895 v Crewe Alexandra
Position: Half back
Appearances: 31 **Goals scored:** 0
Seasons: 1895/96 and 1899/1900
Clubs: Annbank, Newton Heath, Fairfield FC, Wigan County

THOMAS FITZSIMMONS

Country: Scotland
Born: 21 Oct 1870 **Died:** Unknown
Debut: 19 Nov 1892 v Aston Villa
Position: Forward
Appearances: 30 **Goals scored:** 6
Seasons: 1892/93 – 1893/94
Clubs: Annbank, Newton Heath, Annbank

DARREN BARR FLETCHER

Country: Scotland
Born: 1 Feb 1984
Debut: 12 Mar 2003 v Basel
Position: Midfield
Appearances: 233 (59) **Goals scored:** 21
Seasons: 2002/03 - present
Clubs: Manchester United

Darren Fletcher came through the youth ranks at United. As a central midfielder it took some time for him to become a fixture in the team. Known more for reliability than spectacular skills, he has nonetheless scored several crucial goals. In May 2004 he became Scotland's youngest captain in more than 100 years.

PETER FLETCHER

Country: England
Born: 2 Dec 1953
Debut: 14 Apr 1973 v Stoke City
Position: Forward
Appearances: 2 (5) **Goals scored:** 0
Seasons: 1972/73 – 1973/74
Clubs: Manchester United, Hull City, Stockport County, Huddersfield Town

ALAN FOGGON

Country: England
Born: 23 Feb 1950
Debut: 21 Aug 1976 v Birmingham City
Position: Forward
Appearances: 0 (3) **Goals scored:** 0
Seasons: 1976/77
Clubs: Newcastle United, Cardiff City, Middlesbrough, Hartford Bi-Centennials, Rochester Lancers, Manchester United, Sunderland, Southend United, Hartlepool (*loan*), Consett

GEORGE FOLEY

Country: England
Born: 1875 **Died:** Unknown
Debut: 17 Mar 1900 v Barnsley
Position: Forward
Appearances: 7 **Goals scored:** 1
Seasons: 1899/1900
Clubs: Ashford FC, Newton Heath

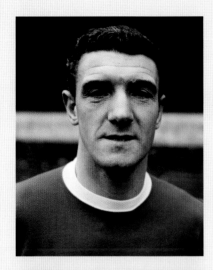

WILLIAM ANTHONY 'BILL' FOULKES

Country: England
Born: 5 Jan 1932
Debut: 13 Dec 1952 v Liverpool
Position: Centre back
Appearances: 685 (3) **Goals scored:** 9
Seasons: 1952/53 - 1969/70
Clubs: Manchester United

There are many remarkable things about the career of Bill Foulkes. The defender with a granite-like countenance that was a true reflection of the measure of his bravery played 688 times for United, was the rock of the defence for nearly 20 years, survived the Munich air crash, but was capped only once by England.

Born in 1932 into a rugby league family in St Helens in Lancashire, Foulkes chose football as his preferred sport and made his name as a teenager with a nearby junior team, Whiston Boys Club, while also working at the local colliery.

United signed him as an 18-year-old and Foulkes turned professional 18 months later, making his first team debut in December 1952 at just 20. He continued to work part-time at the colliery, as his prospective professional football career remained uncertain. Foulkes played just two matches for United's first team in his debut season, but the following year became a regular team member with 32 appearances. Now he could give up his colliery job.

In his early days, Foulkes was a right back and was seen as the natural replacement for long-time United skipper Johnny Carey. He actually played his one and only game for England in the position just under two years after making his debut for United.

By 1957 Foulkes had won two league championships with United as right back and may well have gone to the 1958 World Cup. However, the fateful trip to Belgrade and the Munich air crash almost ended his career. Foulkes was only 26 at the time and was playing in a card school with other United players – including Roger Byrne, Liam Whelan and David Pegg (who would all die in the crash) – when the plane tried to take off. Apart from a bottle of gin falling from the luggage rack and hitting him on the head, Foulkes was miraculously unscathed. The plane had broken around him, but he escaped while eight teammates died.

In the immediate aftermath of Munich, Foulkes captained the team and moved to centre half, a position on the field where he remained for the rest of his career. Along with manager Matt Busby and fellow crash survivor Bobby Charlton, Foulkes continued to work towards returning United to greatness.

By the mid-sixties, Foulkes (nicknamed 'Cowboy' by his teammates) had become a highly respected defender, pocketing an FA Cup winner's medal in 1963 and two more league title honours in 1965 and 1967. He had players like George Best and Denis Law in front of him and all that was missing was a European Cup triumph. That came in 1968, with Foulkes playing the unlikely role of key goalscorer in the second leg of the semi-final against Real Madrid. The rugged centre half scoring the third goal in the 3-3 draw after a lung-bursting run from defence is part of Red Devil legend.

Although ready to retire after the European triumph, Foulkes stayed on and played his last game in August 1969 before serving as a youth team coach for five years.

Left: Circa 1960. Bill Foulkes was originally signed by United as a forward, but an injury meant he was moved into the defence – and stayed there.

Below: 29 May 1968. Matt Busby is hugged by Pat Crerand and Bill Foulkes (l) after their historic European Cup win at Wembley.

JOSEPH BERTRAM FORD
Country: England
Born: 7 May 1886 **Died:** Unknown
Debut: 31 Mar 1909 v Aston Villa
Position: Forward
Appearances: 5 **Goals scored:** 0
Seasons: 1908/09 – 1909/10
Clubs: Witton Albion, Crewe Alexandra, Manchester United, Nottingham Forest, Goole Town

DIEGO FORLAN CORAZO
Country: Uruguay
Born: 19 May 1979
Debut: 29 Jan 2002 v Bolton Wanderers
Position: Forward
Appearances: 37 (61) **Goals scored:** 17
Seasons: 2001/02 – 2004/05
Clubs: Club Atletico Penarol, Danubio Futbol Club, Club Atletico Independiente, Manchester United, Villarreal, Atletico Madrid

THOMAS 'TOMMY' FORSTER
Country: England
Born: Apr 1894 **Died:** 6 Feb 1955
Debut: 8 Nov 1919 v Burnley
Position: Full back
Appearances: 36 **Goals scored:** 0
Seasons: 1919/20 – 1921/22
Clubs: Northwich Victoria, Manchester United, Northwich Victoria

ALEXANDER 'ALEX' FORSYTH
Country: Scotland
Born: 5 Feb 1952
Debut: 6 Jan 1973 v Arsenal
Position: Right back
Appearances: 116 (3) **Goals scored:** 5
Seasons: 1972/73 – 1977/78
Clubs: Arsenal, Partick Thistle, Manchester United, Glasgow Rangers, Motherwell, Hamilton Academicals, Queen of the South

QUINTON FORTUNE
Country: South Africa
Born: 21 May 1977
Debut: 30 Aug 1999 v Newcastle United
Position: Midfield
Appearances: 88 (38) **Goals scored:** 11
Seasons: 1999/2000 – 2005/06
Clubs: RCD Mallorca, Atletico Madrid, Manchester United, Bolton Wanderers, Brescia, Tubize, Doncaster Rovers

BENJAMIN ANTHONY 'BEN' FOSTER
Country: England
Born: 3 Apr 1983
Debut: 15 Mar 2008 v Derby County
Position: Goalkeeper
Appearances: 23 **Goals scored:** 0
Seasons: 2007/08 – 2009/10
Clubs: Racing Club Warwick, Stoke City, Bristol City (loan), Tiverton Town (loan), Stafford Rangers (loan), Kidderminster Harriers (loan), Wrexham (loan), Manchester United, Watford (loan), Birmingham City, WBA

THOMAS FRAME
Country: Scotland
Born: 5 Sep 1902 **Died:** 17 Jan 1988
Debut: 1 Oct 1932 v Preston North End
Position: Half back
Appearances: 52 **Goals scored:** 4
Seasons: 1932/33 – 1935/36
Clubs: Cowdenbeath, Manchester United, Southport, Rhyl Athletic, Bridgnorth Town

STANLEY GALLIMORE
Country: England
Born: 14 Apr 1910 **Died:** Sep 1994
Debut: 11 Oct 1930 v Wrexham
Position: Forward
Appearances: 76 **Goals scored:** 20
Seasons: 1930/31 – 1933/34
Clubs: Witton Albion, Manchester United, Altrincham

CHARLES 'DICK' GARDNER
Country: England
Born: 22 Dec 1913
Debut: 28 Dec 1935 v Plymouth Argyle
Position: Forward
Appearances: 18 **Goals scored:** 1
Seasons: 1935/36 – 1936/37
Clubs: Evesham Town, Notts County, Stourbridge, Manchester United, Sheffield United

WILLIAM 'BILLY' GARTON
Country: England
Born: 15 Mar 1965
Debut: 26 Sep 1984 v Burnley
Position: Defender/Full back
Appearances: 47 (4) **Goals scored:** 0
Seasons: 1984/85 – 1988/89
Clubs: Manchester United, Salford City, Witton Albion, Hyde United

JAMES GARVEY
Country: England
Born: Jan 1878 **Died:** Unknown
Debut: 1 Sep 1900 v Glossop North End
Position: Goalkeeper
Appearances: 6 **Goals scored:** 0
Seasons: 1900/01
Clubs: Wigan County, Manchester United, Middleton FC

DAVID GASKELL
Country: England
Born: 5 Oct 1940
Debut: 24 Nov 1956 v Manchester City
Position: Goalkeeper
Appearances: 119 (1) **Goals scored:** 0
Seasons: 1956/57 – 1966/67
Clubs: Manchester United, Wrexham, Arcadia Shepherds

RALPH GAUDIE
Country: England

Born: Jan 1876 **Died:** Unknown
Debut: 5 Sep 1903 v Bristol City
Position: Forward
Appearances: 8 **Goals scored:** 0
Seasons: 1903/04
Clubs: South Bank, Sheffield United, Aston Villa, Woolwich Arsenal, Manchester United

COLIN GIBSON
Country: England
Born: 6 Apr 1960
Debut: 30 Nov 1985 v Watford
Position: Full back/Midfield
Appearances: 89 (6) **Goals scored:** 9
Seasons: 1985/86 – 1989/90

Clubs: Aston Villa, Manchester United, Leicester City, Blackpool, Walsall

DARRON GIBSON

Country: Republic of Ireland
Born: 25 Oct 1987
Debut: 26 Oct 2005 v Barnet
Position: Midfield
Appearances: 35 (23) **Goals scored:** 10
Seasons: 2005/06 – present
Clubs: Manchester United, Royal Antwerp (loan), Wolverhampton Wanderers (loan)

DON GIBSON

Country: England

Born: 25 Oct 1987
Debut: 26 Aug 1950 v Bolton Wanderers
Position: Half back
Appearances: 115 **Goals scored:** 0
Seasons: 1950/51 – 1954/55
Clubs: Manchester United, Sheffield Wednesday, Leyton Orient

RICHARD GIBSON

Country: England
Born: Feb 1889 **Died:** Unknown
Debut: 27 Aug 1921 v Everton
Position: Winger
Appearances: 12 **Goals scored:** 0
Seasons: 1921/22

Clubs: Sultan FC, Birmingham City, Manchester United

TERRY GIBSON

Country: England
Born: 23 Dec 1962
Debut: 2 Feb 1986 v West Ham United
Position: Striker
Appearances: 27 **Goals scored:** 1
Seasons: 1985/86 – 1986/87
Clubs: Tottenham Hotspur, GAIS, Coventry City, Manchester United, Wimbledon, Swindon Town, Peterborough United, Barnet

Left: Circa 1970. Former United's goalkeeper David Gaskell (then with Wrexham) with his hands full of cabbages outside his general stores. In more than a decade at United, he was rarely first-choice keeper, but he did appear in the 1963 FA Cup final and remains the youngest player ever to appear for United, aged 16 years and 19 days, when he was called out of the crowd to replace the injured Ray Wood in the 1956 Charity Shield.

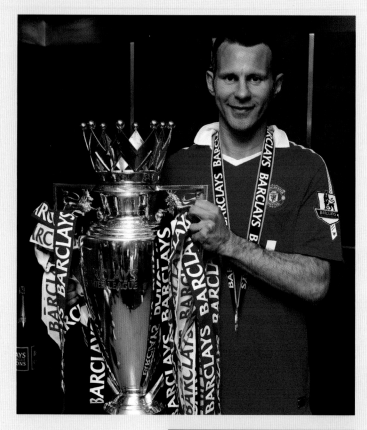

RYAN GIGGS

Country: Wales
Born: 29 Nov 1973
Debut: 2 Mar 1991 v Everton
Position: Midfield/Winger
Appearances: 747 (129) **Goals scored:** 159
Seasons: 1990/91 - present
Clubs: Manchester United

Above: 22 May 2011. Ryan Giggs in the dressing room at Old Trafford with the Barclays Premier League trophy.

Right: 2 March 1991. Team sheet showing Ryan Giggs' first appearance.

Opposite Top: 9 May 2010. Ryan Giggs scores United's second goal during the Premier League match against Stoke City at Old Trafford. Former Red Danny Higginbotham can do nothing about it.

In early 2011, United conducted a worldwide poll of the club's fans in order to crown its greatest ever player. In a club redolent with history, and with a roll call of illustrious names equal to that of any club in football, one player stood out above the rest. With 21 seasons at United and more honours than any other Red Devil in history, that player was Ryan Giggs.

By the end of the 2010-11 season, Giggs' remarkable fact sheet at United looked like this: 876 appearances, 159 goals, 12 Premier League titles, four FA Cup winners medals, four League Cups, eight Community Shields, two Champions Leagues, one European Super Cup, an Intercontinental Cup, a World Club Cup and many individual awards.

Born in Cardiff, Giggs moved to Manchester at the age of six. Even though he would go on to become a hero at Old Trafford, it was with Salford boys and at Manchester City's School of Excellence that the Welshman's football education began. Fortunately for the Reds, Alex Ferguson soon became aware of the teenage prodigy and a personal visit, on his 14th birthday, to the soon-be-Red by the manager was enough to persuade young Ryan to sign.

He turned professional on 29 November 1990, his 17th birthday, and made his first team debut on 2 March 1991 against Everton. Fittingly for a United legend his first goal came soon after – against cross-town rivals City on 4 May 1991, a deflected strike that secured a 1-0 victory.

It would not be until the following season that Giggs became a first team regular, but then he did not have to wait long for his first piece of silverware. United picked up the European Super Cup in 1991 with Giggs as a 71st minute substitute in the game.

By now Giggs' trickery and pace were marking him out as one to watch. His mature displays would soon pave the way for a new generation of talented youngsters to break into the first team. Giggs would be tagged as one of Fergie's Fledglings, tasting success captaining the under-eighteen side to the FA Youth Cup in May 1992 – alongside David Beckham, Nicky Butt and Gary Neville.

Also playing in the first team, Giggs grabbed another senior medal as United beat Nottingham Forest in the League Cup final. Giggs set up Brian McClair for the only goal of the game and the Welshman went on to receive individual recognition, named the Professional Footballers' Association Young Player of the Year, an honour he would win the following season as well.

It was during the 1992-93 campaign that Giggs' and United's march to supremacy really began. The side contained experienced campaigners such as Mark Hughes and Paul Ince, and Ferguson added Eric Cantona mid-season. The Reds clinched the league for the first time since 1967. A league and cup double followed in 1993-94 and another two years later. In fact, this was the Giggs story for the almost every season that followed: United would win trophies and the flying Welshman would be play a prominent role in the story.

Having now played an integral part in two double-winning sides, Giggs added further to his already impressive trophy cabinet with a fourth Premier League medal in the 1996-97 season, but there was a significant gap in his list of achievements – a Champions League winners' medal.

The 1998-99 season would not only fill the gap, but supply the most extraordinary story. Inevitable injuries and Ferguson's reluctance to over play such a vital player had limited Giggs starting appearances. While he had made 40 or even 50 appearances in his first five full seasons, Giggs had scaled down his number of starts in the past three. However, this year his form and fitness was good. He started 44 games and would score seven goals, but it was his overall influence on the team that was now so important. At 25, he had matured

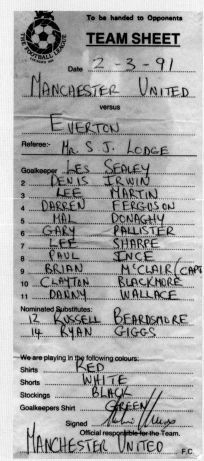

into a player of grace as well as pace, but also one with a play-for-the-team mentality.

United would win a glorious treble this season and Giggs was at the centre of the action, but his greatest moment came in the FA Cup semi-final at Villa Park against Arsenal. Down to ten men and desperately holding on to a 1-1 scoreline, Giggs picked up a loose pass inside his own half and then drove at the heart of the Gunners' backline, slaloming past defenders and slamming the ball high into the net for the winning goal. The image of Giggs wheeling away, chest bared as he whirled his shirt over his head in celebration provided perhaps the most iconic image of his career.

Over the following seasons as many of the treble-winning team retired or were sold, Giggs remained. Fears that the success of the treble had dulled his appetite were quelled as United picked up three more Premier League titles over the next four seasons, Giggs playing a

pivotal role. A testimonial in 2001 celebrated his ten-year anniversary at Old Trafford and Giggs was named in the team of the season and the team of the decade.

In 2007, Giggs won a record ninth league winners medal and that year also witnessed two further landmarks. One was with a view to extending his club career when he retired from international football with 64 caps and 12 goals, but the other was a huge personal honour, the award of an OBE.

It is one of football's great 'what-could-have-beens' that Giggs never played in a World Cup. However, Wales' loss was United's gain, and in the 2007-08 season he won another league title and also passed Bobby Charlton's 758 game appearance record – against Chelsea in the Champions League final victory in Moscow.

A change of position from left wing to a more central role saw Giggs continue to flourish. In 2009-10 he scored his

150th goal for United with a strike against German side Wolfsburg in the Champions League, only the ninth United player to reach this milestone. And it made for a record-equalling 14 Champions League seasons in which he had scored. In November 2009 just before his 36th birthday, Giggs scored his 100th Premier League goal. In December that year Giggs was voted BBC Sports Personality of the Year.

At the start of the 2010-11 season Giggs kept up his record of scoring in every Premier League season. Since Giggs has scored in the final two seasons of the old Football League First Division, he has now scored in 21 successive top division campaigns.

It was fitting that United's most decorated player, boasting an appearance record unlikely to ever be beaten, should be part of the team to overhaul Liverpool title record earning United's 19th and his 12th league winners medal in 2010-11.

1991	Makes league debut as substitute against Everton
1992	Wins the FA Youth Cup as captain of team containing Beckham, Butt, and Gary Neville
1994	Wins second consecutive PFA Young Player of the Year Award
1996	Wins second double with United and nominated for goal of the season
1999	Wins goal of the season for a wonder goal in FA Cup Semi final against Arsenal
2002	Scores 100th league goal in draw with Chelsea at Stamford Bridge
2004	Appointed captain of Wales
2005	Inducted into English Football's Hall of Fame in recognition of contribution to the game
2008	Comes on as substitute in Champions League final to break Bobby Charlton's appearance record
2010	Scores against Newcastle to maintain record of scoring in every Premier League season

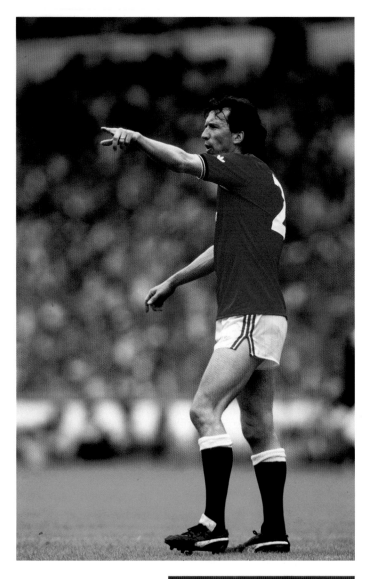

JOHN GIDMAN

Country: England
Born: 10 Jan 1954
Debut: 29 Aug 1981 v Coventry City
Position: Full back
Appearances: 116 (4) **Goals scored:** 4
Seasons: 1981/82 - 1985/86
Clubs: Aston Villa, Everton, Manchester United, Manchester City, Stoke City, Darlington

A stylish attacking full back, John Gidman was born in Liverpool and began by playing for Liverpool's youth team, but never made a first-team appearance. Released by his home-town side in 1971, he was snapped up by then Third Division Villa. He stayed with the club for eight years as they progressed through the divisions, returning to the First Division in the 1975-76 season. He moved to Everton for £650,000 in 1979. In 1981 he became recently arrived

United manager Ron Atkinson's first signing, as part of a £450,000 swap deal with Mickey Thomas going the other way. Although Gidman helped United win the FA Cup in 1983 and 1985, injuries meant his appearances in the United shirt became increasingly sporadic. After scoring four goals in 120 games he left the club for Manchester City in 1986. Gidman was capped by England just once in 1977.

MICHAEL JOHN 'JOHNNY' GILES

Country: Republic of Ireland
Born: 6 Nov 1940
Debut: 12 Sep 1959 v Tottenham Hotspur
Position: Midfield
Appearances: 115 **Goals scored:** 13
Seasons: 1959/60 - 1963/64
Clubs: Manchester United, Leeds United, West Bromwich Albion, Philadelphia Fury, Shamrock Rovers

TONY GILL

Country: England
Born: 6 Mar 1968
Debut: 3 Jan 1987 v Southampton
Position: Midfield/Full back
Appearances: 7 (7) **Goals scored:** 2
Seasons: 1986/87 - 1988/89
Clubs: Manchester United, Bath City

KEITH GILLESPIE

Country: Northern Ireland
Born: 18 Feb 1975
Debut: 5 Jan 1993 v Bury
Position: Winger
Appearances: 14 **Goals scored:** 2
Seasons: 1992/93 - 1994/95
Clubs: Manchester United, Newcastle United, Blackburn Rovers, Wigan Athletic, Leicester City, Sheffield United, Charlton Athletic, Bradford City, Glentoran

MATTHEW GILLESPIE

Country: Scotland
Born: 24 Dec 1869 **Died:** Unknown
Debut: 28 Nov 1896 v Birmingham City
Position: Forward
Appearances: 89 **Goals scored:** 21
Seasons: 1896/97 - 1899/1900
Clubs: Glasgow Thistle, Blackburn Rovers, Lincoln City, Newton Heath

THOMAS GIPPS

Country: England
Born: Jan 1888 **Died:** Unknown
Debut: 25 Dec 1912 v Chelsea
Position: Half back
Appearances: 23 **Goals scored:** 0
Seasons: 1912/13 - 1914/15
Clubs: Walthamstow FC, Tottenham Hotspur, Barrow, Manchester United

DANIEL JOSEPH 'DON' GIVENS

Country: Republic of Ireland
Born: 9 Aug 1949
Debut: 9 Aug 1969 v Crystal Palace
Position: Forward
Appearances: 5 (4) **Goals scored:** 1
Seasons: 1969/70
Clubs: Manchester United, Luton Town, Queens Park Rangers, Birmingham City, Bournemouth, Sheffield United, Neuchatel Xamax

GEORGE GLADWIN

Country: England
Born: 28 Mar 1907 **Died:** Unknown
Debut: 27 Feb 1937 v Chelsea
Position: Midfield
Appearances: 28 **Goals scored:** 1
Seasons: 1936/37 - 1938/39
Clubs: Doncaster Rovers, Manchester United (Note played for Barnsley, Doncaster Rovers, West Ham United and Wrexham during WW2)

GILBERT GODSMARK

Country: England
Born: Jan 1877 **Died:** Feb 1901
Debut: 3 Feb 1900 v Sheffield Wednesday
Position: Forward
Appearances: 9 **Goals scored:** 4
Seasons: 1899/1900
Clubs: Ashford FC, Newton Heath

ERNEST 'ERNIE' GOLDTHORPE

Country: England
Born: 8 Jun 1898 **Died:** 5 Nov 1929
Debut: 11 Nov 1922 v Leyton Orient
Position: Forward
Appearances: 30 **Goals scored:** 16
Seasons: 1922/3 - 1924/5
Clubs: Bradford City, Leeds United, Bradford City, Manchester United, Rotherham United

Played for Tottenham Hotspur during the First World War.

WILLIAM 'BILLY' GOODWIN

Country: England
Born: Jan 1892 **Died:** 9 Jul 1951
Debut: 28 Aug 1920 v Bolton Wanderers
Position: Striker
Appearances: 7 **Goals scored:** 1
Seasons: 1920/21 - 1921/22
Clubs: Exeter City, Manchester United, Southend United

FREDERICK GOODWIN

Country: England
Born: 28 Jun 1933
Debut: 20 Nov 1954 v Arsenal
Position: Midfield
Appearances: 107 **Goals scored:** 8
Seasons: 1954/55 - 1959/60
Clubs: Manchester United, Leeds United, Scunthorpe United

ANDY GORAM

Country: Scotland
Born: 13 Apr 1964

Debut: 14 Apr 2001 v Coventry City
Position: Goalkeeper
Appearances: 2 **Goals scored:** 0
Seasons: 2000/01
Clubs: Oldham Athletic, Hibernian, Glasgow Rangers, Notts County, Sheffield United, Motherwell, Manchester United, Hamilton Academical, Coventry City, Oldham Athletic, Queen of the South, Elgin City

JAMES GOTHERIDGE
Country: England
Born: 1863 **Died:** Unknown
Debut: 30 Oct 1886 v Fleetwood Rangers
Position: Forward
Appearances: 1 **Goals scored:** 0
Seasons: 1886/87
Clubs: Newton Heath

JOHN GOURLAY
Country: Scotland
Born: 1879 **Died:** Unknown
Debut: 18 Feb 1899 v Loughborough Town
Position: Defender
Appearances: 1 **Goals scored:** 0
Seasons: 1898/99
Clubs: Annbank, Newton Heath

ALAN GOWLING
Country: England
Born: 16 Mar 1949
Debut: 30 Mar 1968 v Stoke City
Position: Forward
Appearances: 77 (10) **Goals scored:** 21
Seasons: 1967/68 - 1971/72
Clubs: Manchester United, Huddersfield Town, Newcastle United, Bolton Wanderers, Preston North End

ARTHUR GRAHAM
Country: Scotland
Born: 26 Oct 1952
Debut: 20 Aug 1983 v Liverpool
Position: Winger
Appearances: 52 **Goals scored:** 7
Seasons: 1983/84 - 1984/85
Clubs: Aberdeen, Leeds United, Manchester United, Bradford City

DEINIOL GRAHAM
Country: Wales
Born: 4 Oct 1969
Debut: 7 Oct 1987 v Hull City
Position: Striker
Appearances: 1 (3) **Goals scored:** 1
Seasons: 1987/88 - 1989/90
Clubs: Manchester United, Barnsley, Preston North End, Carlisle United, Stockport County, Scunthorpe United, Halifax Town, Dagenham and Redbridge

GEORGE GRAHAM
Country: Scotland
Born: 30 Nov 1944
Debut: 6 Jan 1973 v Arsenal
Position: Midfield
Appearances: 44 (2) **Goals scored:** 2
Seasons: 1972/73 - 1974/75

Clubs: Aston Villa, Chelsea, Arsenal, Manchester United, Portsmouth, Crystal Palace, California Surf

JOHN GRAHAM
Country: England
Born: 1873 **Died:** Unknown
Debut: 11 Nov 1893 v Wolverhampton Wanderers
Position: Forward
Appearances: 4 **Goals scored:** 0
Seasons: 1893/94
Clubs: Blyth FC, Newton Heath

WILLIAM 'BILLY' GRASSAM
Country: Scotland
Born: 20 Nov 1878 **Died:** Unknown
Debut: 3 Oct 1903 v Arsenal
Position: Forward
Appearances: 37 **Goals scored:** 14
Seasons: 1903/04 - 1904/05
Clubs: Redcliffe Thistle, Glasgow Maryhill, Burslem Port Vale, West Ham United, Glasgow Celtic, Manchester United, Leyton FC

DAVID GRAY
Country: Scotland
Born: 4 May 1988
Debut: 25 Oct 2006 v Crewe Alexandra
Position: Full back
Appearances: 1 **Goals scored:** 0
Seasons: 2006/07
Clubs: Manchester United, Preston North End

IAN GREAVES
Country: England
Born: 26 May 1932 **Died:** 2 Jan 2009
Debut: 2 Oct 1954 v Wolverhampton Wanderers
Position: Full back
Appearances: 75 **Goals scored:** 0
Seasons: 1954/55 - 1959/60
Clubs: Manchester United, Lincoln City, Oldham Athletic

ROBERT EDWARD 'EDDIE' GREEN
Country: England
Born: Jan 1912 **Died:** Unknown
Debut: 26 Aug 1933 v Plymouth Argyle
Position: Forward
Appearances: 9 **Goals scored:** 4
Seasons: 1933/34
Clubs: Bournemouth and Boscombe Athletic, Derby County, Manchester United, Stockport County

BRIAN GREENHOFF
Country: England
Born: 28 Apr 1953
Debut: 8 Sep 1973 v Ipswich Town
Position: Midfield/Defender/Full back
Appearances: 268 (3) **Goals scored:** 17
Seasons: 1973/74 - 1978/79
Clubs: Manchester United, Leeds United, Rovaniemen Palloseura, Rochdale

Born in Barnsley, Brian Greenhoff was a hard-working defender and sometime midfield player. The younger of the two

Greenhoff brothers (Jimmy was almost seven years older) to play for United, he joined United as a youth player in 1968. Progressing through the Reds' youth system, he made his first team debut in 1973. He would develop into a centre back of international class and secured a FA Cup winners medal in 1977 with United before being transferred to Leeds United for £350,000 in 1979. He was capped by England 18 times.

JIMMY GREENHOFF
Country: England
Born: 19 Jun 1946
Debut: 20 Nov 1976 v Leicester City
Position: Striker
Appearances: 119 (4) **Goals scored:** 36
Seasons: 1976/77 - 1980/81
Clubs: Leeds United, Birmingham City, Stoke City, Manchester United, Crewe Alexandra, Toronto Blizzard, Port Vale, Rochdale

Jimmy Greenhoff arrived at Manchester United in 1976. He helped the Reds win the 1977 FA Cup, scoring the winner at Wembley, in so doing famously denying Liverpool the treble. He made 123 appearances for the club before being sold to Crewe Alexandra in 1980.

Above: 1976. Jimmy Greenhoff is challenged for the ball by Alan Woollett of Leicester City on his debut for United. He quickly developed a superb strike partnership with Stuart Pearson.

JONATHAN GREENING

Country: England
Born: 2 Jan 1979
Debut: 28 Oct 1998 v Bury
Position: Midfield
Appearances: 13 (14) **Goals scored:** 0
Seasons: 1998/99 – 2000/01
Clubs: York City, Manchester United, Middlesborough, West Bromwich Albion, Fulham

WILSON GREENWOOD

Country: England
Born: Jul 1871 **Died:** Jan 1943
Debut: 20 Oct 1900 v Walsall
Position: Forward
Appearances: 3 **Goals scored:** 0
Seasons: 1900/01
Clubs: Blue Star, Brierfield, Accrington Stanley, Sheffield United, Rossendale FC, Nelson, Rochdale Athletic, Warmley, Grimsby Town, Newton Heath

HENRY 'HARRY' GREGG

Country: Northern Ireland
Born: 25 Oct 1932
Debut: 21 Dec 1957 v Leicester City
Position: Goalkeeper
Appearances: 247 **Goals scored:** 0
Seasons: 1957/58 – 1966/67
Clubs: Doncaster Rovers, Manchester United, Stoke City

The Northern Irishman joined United from Doncaster Rovers three months before the Munich air crash for a then world record amount for a goalkeeper of £23,000. He survived the tragedy with just a bloody nose and heroically staged a remarkable series of rescues. Among those he helped were Vera Lukić, the pregnant wife of a Yugoslav diplomat and her daughter, Vesna, as well as his badly injured manager Matt Busby and some of his teammates including Bobby Charlton and Dennis Viollet. He was capped by Northern Ireland 25 times and during the 1958 World Cup was voted the best keeper of the tournament. A shoulder injury almost forced early retirement in 1962, but he continued another four years before trying his hand as a manager at several clubs. He was awarded an MBE in 1985.

BILLY GRIFFITHS

Country: England
Born: 1877 **Died:** Unknown
Debut: 1 Apr 1899 v Arsenal
Position: Half back
Appearances: 175 **Goals scored:** 30
Seasons: 1898/99 – 1904/05
Clubs: Berry's Association FC, Newton Heath (Manchester United from 1902), Atherton Church House

Above: 17 September 1962. United and Northern Ireland goalkeeper Harry Gregg is pictured relaxing at home.

CLIVE GRIFFITHS

Country: Wales
Born: 22 Jan 1955
Debut: 27 Oct 1973 v Burnley
Position: Half back
Appearances: 7 **Goals scored:** 0
Seasons: 1973/74
Clubs: Manchester United, Tranmere Rovers, Chicago Sting, Chicago Sting, Tulsa Roughnecks

JOHN 'JACK' GRIFFITHS

Country: England
Born: 15 Sep 1908 **Died:** 1 Jan 1975
Debut: 17 Mar 1934 v Fulham
Position: Full back
Appearances: 173 **Goals scored:** 1
Seasons: 1933/34 – 1938/39
Clubs: Fenton Boys Brigade, Shirebrook FC, Wolverhampton Wanderers, Bolton Wanderers, Manchester United

ASHLEY GRIMES

Country: Republic of Ireland
Born: 2 Aug 1957
Debut: 20 Aug 1977 v Birmingham City
Position: Midfield/Winger
Appearances: 77 (30) **Goals scored:** 11
Seasons: 1977/78 – 1982/83
Clubs: Stella Maris, Bohemians, Manchester United, Coventry City, Luton Town, CA Osasuna, Stoke City

ANTHONY GRIMSHAW

Country: England
Born: 8 Dec 1957
Debut: 10 Sep 1975 v Brentford
Position: Midfield
Appearances: 0 (2) **Goals scored:** 0
Seasons: 1975/76
Clubs: Manchester United, Mossley

JOHN GRIMWOOD

Country: England
Born: 25 Oct 1898 **Died:** 26 Dec 1977
Debut: 11 Oct 1919 v Manchester City
Position: Midfield
Appearances: 205 **Goals scored:** 8
Seasons: 1919/20 – 1926/27
Clubs: Marsden Colliery School, Marsden Rescue FC, Marsden PM, South Shields Parkside, Manchester United, Aldershot Town

JOHN GRUNDY

Country: England
Born: 1873 **Died:** Unknown

Debut: 28 Apr 1900 v Chesterfield
Position: Winger
Appearances: 11 **Goals scored:** 3
Seasons: 1899/00 - 1900/01
Clubs: Wigan County, Newton Heath

WILLIAM GYVES
Country: England
Born: Jul 1867 **Died:** Unknown
Debut: 25 Oct 1890 v Bootle Reserves
Position: Goalkeeper
Appearances: 1 **Goals scored:** 0
Seasons: 1890/91
Clubs: Newton Heath

JOHN 'JACK' HACKING
Country: England
Born: 22 Dec 1897 **Died:** 31 May 1955
Debut: 17 Mar 1934 v Fulham
Position: Goalkeeper
Appearances: 34 **Goals scored:** 0
Seasons: 1933/34 - 1934/35
Clubs: Blackpool, Fleetwood, Oldham Athletic, Manchester United, Accrington Stanley

JOHN 'JACK' HALL
Country: England
Born: Jan 1905 **Died:** Unknown
Debut: 6 Feb 1926 v Burnley
Position: Outside right
Appearances: 3 **Goals scored:** 0
Seasons: 1925/26 - 1926/27
Clubs: Lincoln City, Accrington Stanley, Manchester United

JOHN JACK HALL
Country: England
Born: 23 Oct 1912 **Died:** Aug 2000
Debut: 30 Sep 1933 v Oldham Athletic
Position: Goalkeeper
Appearances: 73 **Goals scored:** 0
Seasons: 1932/33 - 1935/36
Clubs: Manchester United, Tottenham Hotspur, Stalybridge Celtic, Runcorn

PROCTOR HALL
Country: England
Born: Jan 1884 **Died:** Unknown
Debut: 26 Mar 1904 v Grimsby Town
Position: Forward
Appearances: 8 **Goals scored:** 2
Seasons: 1903/04 - 1904/05
Clubs: Oswaldtwistle Rovers, Manchester United, Brighton & Hove Albion, Aston Villa, Bradford City, Luton Town, Chesterfield, Hyde, Preston North End

HAROLD 'HARRY' JAMES HALSE
Country: England
Born: 1 Jan 1886 **Died:** 25 Mar 1949
Debut: 23 Mar 1908 v Sheffield Wednesday
Position: Forward
Appearances: 125 **Goals scored:** 56
Seasons: 1907/08 - 1911/12
Clubs: Clapton Orient, Southend United, Manchester United, Aston Villa, Chelsea, Charlton Athletic

Harry Halse was the first player to appear in FA Cup finals for three different clubs. He also scored twice on his England debut, but was never again selected. He also once scored six goals in a game for United, against Swindon Town in the 1911 Charity Shield, one of only two men ever to do so for United.

REGINALD LLOYD 'REG' HALTON
Country: England
Born: 11 Jul 1916 **Died:** 17 Mar 1988
Debut: 12 Dec 1936 v Middlesbrough
Position: Forward
Appearances: 4 **Goals scored:** 1
Seasons: 1936/37
Clubs: Stafford Rangers, Buxton, Manchester United, Notts County

MICHAEL 'MICKEY' HAMILL
Country: Ireland
Born: 19 Jan 1889 **Died:** 23 Jul 1943
Debut: 16 Sep 1911 v West Bromwich Albion
Position: Wing half
Appearances: 60 **Goals scored:** 2
Seasons: 1911/12 - 1914/15
Clubs: Belfast Celtic, Manchester United, Belfast Celtic, Celtic (loan), Manchester City, Fall River Marksmen, Boston SC, New York Giants, Belfast Celtic

JOHN JAMES 'JIMMY' HANLON
Country: England
Born: 12 Oct 1917 **Died:** 12 Jan 2002
Debut: 26 Nov 1938 v Huddersfield Town
Position: Forward
Appearances: 69 **Goals scored:** 22
Seasons: 1938/39 - 1948/49
Clubs: Manchester United, Bury

CHARLES 'CHARLIE' HANNAFORD
Country: England
Born: 8 Jan 1896 **Died:** Jul 1970
Debut: 28 Dec 1925 v Leicester City
Position: Forward
Appearances: 12 **Goals scored:** 0
Seasons: 1925/26 - 1926/27
Clubs: Maidstone United, Millwall, Charlton Athletic, Clapton Orient, Manchester United

JAMES 'JIMMY' HANSON
Country: England
Born: 6 Nov 1904 **Died:** Unknown
Debut: 15 Nov 1924 v Hull City
Position: Forward
Appearances: 147 **Goals scored:** 52
Seasons: 1924/25 - 1929/30
Clubs: Stalybridge Celtic, Manchester United

HAROLD PAYNE HARDMAN
Country: England

Born: 4 Apr 1882 **Died:** 9 Jun 1965
Debut: 19 Sep 1908 v Manchester City
Position: Midfield
Appearances: 4 **Goals scored:** 0
Seasons: 1908/09
Clubs: Blackpool, Everton, Manchester United, Bradford City, Stoke

Harold Hardman won four England amateur caps and an Olympic gold medal for the Great Britain football team when the Games came to London in 1908. He was normally an outside left, but could also turn up on the right wing. Hardman became a club director and then United chairman in 1951. He served the club for over 50 years.

OWEN LEE HARGREAVES
Country: England
Born: 20 Jan 1981
Debut: 19 Aug 2007 v Manchester City
Position: Midfield
Appearances: 26 (13) **Goals scored:** 2
Seasons: 2007/08 - 2010/11
Clubs: Bayern Munich, Manchester United

FRANCIS 'FRANK' EDGAR HARRIS
Country: England
Born: 17 Dec 1899 **Died:** Dec 1983
Debut: 14 Feb 1920 v Sunderland
Position: Full back
Appearances: 49 **Goals scored:** 2
Seasons: 1919/20 - 1922/23
Clubs: Manchester United

THOMAS 'TOM' HARRIS
Country: England
Born: 18 Sep 1905 **Died:** Mar 1985
Debut: 30 Oct 1926 v West Ham United
Position: Forward
Appearances: 4 **Goals scored:** 1
Seasons: 1926/27 - 1927/28
Clubs: Skelmersdale United, Wigan Borough, Manchester United

Below: 21 September 2008. Injury plagued Owen Hargreaves takes on Ashley Cole of Chelsea. The England midfielder made fewer than 40 appearances in four seasons at United, but was part of the 2008 Champions League-winning team.

CHARLES HARRISON
Country: England
Born: Unknown **Died:** Unknown
Debut: 18 Jan 1890 v Preston North End
Position: Full back
Appearances: 1 **Goals scored:** 0
Seasons: 1889/90
Clubs: Newton Heath

WILLIAM EWART HARRISON
Country: England
Born: 27 Dec 1886 **Died:** Aug 1948
Debut: 23 Oct 1920 v Preston North End
Position: Outside right
Appearances: 46 **Goals scored:** 5
Seasons: 1920/21 – 1921/22
Clubs: Crewe Alexandra, Wolverhampton
Wanderers, Manchester United,
Port Vale, Wrexham

ROBERT HARROP
Country: England
Born: 25 Aug 1936 **Died:** 8 Nov 2007
Debut: 5 Mar 1958 v West Bromwich Albion
Position: Half back
Appearances: 11 **Goals scored:** 0
Seasons: 1957/58 - 1959/60
Clubs: Manchester United,
Tranmere Rovers, Margate

WILLIAM HARTWELL
Country: England
Born: 1880 **Died:** Unknown

Debut: 30 Apr 1904 v Leicester City
Position: Forward
Appearances: 4 **Goals scored:** 0
Seasons: 1903/04 – 1904/05
Clubs: Kettering Town, Manchester
United, Northampton Town

GEORGE HASLAM
Country: England
Born: 23 Mar 1898 **Died:** 13 Aug 1980
Debut: 25 Feb 1922 v Birmingham City
Position: Full back
Appearances: 27 **Goals scored:** 0
Seasons: 1920/21 – 1927/28
Clubs: Darwen, Manchester
United, Portsmouth

ANTHONY 'TONY' HAWKSWORTH
Country: England
Born: 15 Jan 1938
Debut: 27 Oct 1956 v Blackpool
Position: Goalkeeper
Appearances: 1 **Goals scored:** 0
Seasons: 1956/57
Clubs: Manchester United, Bedford
Town, Rushden Town

RONALD HAWORTH
Country: England
Born: 10 Mar 1901 **Died:** Oct 1973
Debut: 28 Aug 1926 v Liverpool
Position: Inside forward
Appearances: 2 **Goals scored:** 0
Seasons: 1926/27
Clubs: Hull City, Manchester United, Darwen

TOM HAY
Country: England
Born: Jul 1858 **Died:** 10 Jan 1940
Debut: 18 Jan 1890 v Preston North End
Position: Goalkeeper
Appearances: 1 **Goals scored:** 0
Seasons: 1889/90
Clubs: Staveley FC, Bolton Wanderers,
Great Lever FC, Halliwell FC, Burslem
FC, Newton Heath, Accrington Stanley

FRANK HAYDOCK
Country: England
Born: 29 Nov 1940
Debut: 20 Aug 1960 v Blackburn Rovers
Position: Central defender
Appearances: 6 **Goals scored:** 0
Seasons: 1960/61 – 1962/63
Clubs: Manchester United, Charlton
Athletic, Portsmouth, Southend United

JAMES 'VINCE' HAYES
Country: England
Born: Apr 1879 **Died:** Unknown
Debut: 25 Feb 1901 v Walsall
Position: Full back
Appearances: 128 **Goals scored:** 2
Seasons: 1900/01 – 1910/11
Clubs: Newton Heath Athletic, Brentford,
Newton Heath, Manchester United, Bradford

Below: 26 November 2006.
Argentine international Gabriel
Heinze quickly became a firm
favourite with the Old Trafford
crowd, and won a Premier
League title medal in 2007.

JOE HAYWOOD
Country: England
Born: Apr 1893 **Died:** Unknown
Debut: 22 Nov 1913 v Sheffield United
Position: Half back
Appearances: 26 **Goals scored:** 0
Seasons: 1913/14 – 1914/15
Clubs: Hindley Central, Manchester United

DAVID HEALY
Country: Northern Ireland
Born: 5 Aug 1979
Debut: 13 Oct 1999 v Aston Villa
Position: Forward
Appearances: 0 (3) **Goals scored:** 0
Seasons: 1999/00 – 2000/01
Clubs: Manchester United, Port Vale, Preston
North End, Norwich City, Leeds United,
Fulham, Sunderland, Ipswich Town

JOE HEATHCOTE
Country: England
Born: Jan 1878 **Died:** Unknown

Debut: 16 Dec 1899 v Middlesbrough
Position: Inside forward
Appearances: 8 **Goals scored:** 0
Seasons: 1899/00 – 1901/02
Clubs: Berry's Association FC, Newton Heath

GABRIEL HEINZE

Country: Argentina
Born: 19 Apr 1978
Debut: 11 Sep 2004 v Bolton Wanderers
Position: Defender
Appearances: 75 (8) **Goals scored:** 4
Seasons: 2004/05 – 2006/07
Clubs: Newell's Old Boys, Real Valladolid, Sporting CP, Paris Saint-Germain, Manchester United, Real Madrid, Marseille

WILLIAM HENDERSON

Country: Scotland
Born: 1898 **Died:** 1964
Debut: 26 Nov 1921 v Aston Villa
Position: Forward
Appearances: 36 **Goals scored:** 17

Seasons: 1921/22 – 1924/25
Clubs: Airdrieonians, Manchester United

JAMES HENDRY

Country: Scotland
Born: Unknown **Died:** Unknown
Debut: 15 Oct 1892 v Wolverhampton Wanderers
Position: Winger
Appearances: 2 **Goals scored:** 1
Seasons: 1892/93
Clubs: Alloa Athletic, Newton Heath

ARTHUR HENRYS

Country: England
Born: 1870 **Died:** Unknown
Debut: 3 Oct 1891 v Manchester City
Position: Midfield
Appearances: 6 **Goals scored:** 0
Seasons: 1891/92 – 1892/93
Clubs: Notts Jardines, Newton Heath, Leicester Fosse

DAVID HERD

Country: Scotland
Born: 15 Apr 1934
Debut: 19 Aug 1961 v West Ham United
Position: Forward
Appearances: 264 (1) **Goals scored:** 145
Seasons: 1961/62 – 1967/68
Clubs: Stockport County, Arsenal, Manchester United, Stoke City, Waterford United

Son of Manchester City player Alec Herd, this classy forward became a Scottish international at 24 and then joined United for £35,000 from Arsenal. He helped the Reds win an FA Cup and two league titles. Herd broke his leg in March 1967 and his limited appearances thereafter meant he missed out on the European Cup triumph a year later. He moved on to Stoke City in July 1968.

Above: 1964. David Herd outside Old Trafford stadium with his Volvo car. In six years at United, he was never outside the top two scorers in a season, with a best total of 32 in 1965-66. Despite this, he was something of an unsung hero for the Reds.

JAVIER 'CHICHARITO' HERNANDEZ
Country: Mexico
Born: 1 Jun 1988
Debut: 8 Aug 2010 v Chelsea
Position: Forward
Appearances: 27 (18) **Goals scored:** 20
Seasons: 2010/11 – present
Clubs: Guadalajara, Manchester United

TOMMY HERON
Country: Scotland
Born: 31 Mar 1936
Debut: 5 Apr 1958 v Preston North End
Position: Full back/Winger
Appearances: 3 **Goals scored:** 0
Seasons: 1957/58 – 1960/61
Clubs: Queens Park, Portadown, Manchester United, York City, Altrincham

HERBERT HEYWOOD
Country: England
Born: Jul 1913
Debut: 6 May 1933 v Swansea City
Position: Winger
Appearances: 4 **Goals scored:** 2
Seasons: 1932/33 – 1933/34
Clubs: Manchester United, Tranmere Rovers

DANNY HIGGINBOTHAM
Country: England
Born: 29 Dec 1978
Debut: 10 May 1998 v Barnsley
Position: Defender
Appearances: 4 (3) **Goals scored:** 0
Seasons: 1997/98 – 1999/2000
Clubs: Manchester United, Royal Antwerp (loan), Derby County, Southampton, Stoke City, Sunderland

ALEXANDER HIGGINS
Country: England
Born: 1870 **Died:** Unknown
Debut: 12 Oct 1901 v Burton United
Position: Midfield
Appearances: 10 **Goals scored:** 0
Seasons: 1901/02

Clubs: Albion Swifts, Birmingham St. George's, Grimsby Town, Bristol City, Newcastle United, Middlesbrough, Newton Heath, Manchester United

MARK HIGGINS
Country: England
Born: 29 Sep 1958
Debut: 9 Jan 1986 v Rochdale
Position: Defender
Appearances: 8 **Goals scored:** 0
Seasons: 1985/86
Clubs: Everton, Manchester United, Bury, Stoke City

JAMES HIGSON
Country: England
Born: 1876 **Died:** Unknown
Debut: 1 Mar 1902 v Lincoln City
Position: Inside forward
Appearances: 5 **Goals scored:** 1
Seasons: 1901/02
Clubs: Manchester Wednesday, Newton Heath,

CLARENCE 'LAL' HILDITCH
Country: England
Born: 6 Feb 1894 **Died:** 31 Oct 1977
Debut: 30 Aug 1919 v Derby County
Position: Half back
Appearances: 322 **Goals scored:** 7
Seasons: 1919/20 – 1931/32
Clubs: Witton Albion, Altrincham, Manchester United

Popularly known as 'Lal' and born in nearby Cheshire, Hilditch started life as an outside left before converting to half back. He was a star of the team for 12 years, but never secured a winners medal. He became the club's only ever player/manager during the 1926-27 season after manager John Chapman was suspended. He retired in 1932.

GORDON HILL
Country: England

Born: 1 Apr 1954
Debut: 15 Nov 1975 v Aston Villa
Position: Winger
Appearances: 133 (1) **Goals scored:** 51
Seasons: 1975/76 – 1977/78
Clubs: Millwall, Chicago Sting, Manchester United, Derby County, Queens Park Rangers, Montreal Manic, Chicago Sting, Inter-Montreal, FC Twente, HJK Helsinki, Northwich Victoria

One of Tommy Docherty's most effective signings who excited the United fans for just three seasons, yet delivered many great performances and scored plenty of spectacular goals. He formed a two-wing threat with Steve Coppell and won six England caps while at Old Trafford.

CHARLIE HILLAM
Country: England
Born: 6 Oct 1908 **Died:** Apr 1958
Debut: 26 Aug 1933 v Plymouth Argyle
Position: Goalkeeper
Appearances: 8 **Goals scored:** 0
Seasons: 1933/34
Clubs: Clitheroe, Burnley, Manchester United, Leyton Orient

ERNIE HINE
Country: England
Born: 9 Apr 1901 **Died:** 15 Apr 1974
Debut: 11 Feb 1933 v Preston North End
Position: Inside forward
Appearances: 53 **Goals scored:** 12
Seasons: 1932/33 – 1934/35
Clubs: Leicester City, Huddersfield Town, Manchester United, Barnsley

JAMES HODGE
Country: Scotland
Born: 5 Jul 1891 **Died:** 2 Sep 1970
Debut: 17 Apr 1911 v Sheffield Wednesday
Position: Half back
Appearances: 86 **Goals scored:** 2
Seasons: 1910/11 – 1919/20
Clubs: Stenhousemuir, Manchester United, Millwall Athletic

JOHN HODGE
Country: Scotland
Born: Unknown **Died:** Unknown
Debut: 27 Dec 1913 v Sheffield Wednesday
Position: Full back
Appearances: 30 **Goals scored:** 0
Seasons: 1913/14 – 1914/15
Clubs: Stenhousemuir, Manchester United

FRANK HODGES
Country: England
Born: 26 Jan 1891 **Died:** 5 Jun 1985
Debut: 18 Oct 1919 v Manchester City
Position: Inside forward
Appearances: 20 **Goals scored:** 4
Seasons: 1919/20 – 1920/21
Clubs: Birmingham City, Manchester United, Wigan Borough

Right: 23 April 2011. Javier 'Chicharito' Hernandez celebrates scoring against Everton. The Mexican international made an instant impact in his first season with the Reds, beginning with a goal on his debut in the Community Shield.

MARK HUGHES

Country: Wales
Born: 1 Nov 1963
Debut: 26 Oct 1983 v Port Vale
Position: Forward
Appearances: 453 (14) **Goals scored:** 163
Seasons: 1983/84 – 1985/86
and 1988/89 - 1994/95
Clubs: Manchester United, Barcelona, Bayern Munich (*loan*), Chelsea, Southampton, Everton, Blackburn Rovers

The lion-hearted Welshman Mark Hughes was a player who kept things simple: he had a knack for scoring goals; he knew the qualities that made him an intimidating opponent; and he recognised that hard work and total dedication could overcome any perceived shortcomings in his game. In addition, few players return to a club and are more successful the second time around, yet Hughes achieved this and so much more for United during 467 appearances in which he scored 163 goals.

After signing schoolboy forms with the Reds as a 14-year-old, Hughes turned professional three years later in 1980 and spent three seasons in the youth team and reserves. The youngster from Wrexham in north Wales, who played midfield in his early days, was highly regarded from an early age, but had to wait for his debut until a League Cup match in October 1983 – just a few days short of his 20th birthday.

With Ron Atkinson as his manager, Hughes was given 17 appearances up to the end of the season, scoring five goals. By the following campaign he was a starter. It was an attacking team and

Hughes flourished, helping take United to a second FA Cup final victory in three years as well as the quarter-finals of the UEFA Cup.

While the bulldozer that was Hughes often played alongside a more rapier-like strike partner, the Welshman was no slouch at scoring. He top-scored in his first two full seasons and seemed set for a long United career, but when Barcelona came calling, the striker went to Spain in the summer of 1986 for £2.5 million. However, his time with the Catalans was unhappy (he even endured a loan spell at Bayern Munich) and 'Sparky' returned to Old Trafford two years later for £1.5 million – where he would meet his new manager, Alex Ferguson.

For the next seven seasons, Ferguson coaxed great performances and great goals from Hughes, who was named Professional Footballers' Association Player of the Year in the first year of his return. Hughes also helped Ferguson win his first trophy (the FA Cup in

1990) and the following season not only gained a European Cup-Winners' Cup medal, but also scored both goals in the final when United beat his former team, Barcelona. Then, two seasons later, Hughes top scored with 15 goals as United won their first league title for 26 years.

During all these years, Hughes was also a star for the Welsh national team. He would eventually win 72 caps and score nine goals for his country. But by the mid-1990s, Hughes' second period with the Reds was coming to an end, despite his manager's words that he was "the best big game player I have ever known". In the summer of 1995 the striker was sold to Chelsea before moving on to Southampton and also taking on the manager's job for Wales. There were short playing periods at Everton and Blackburn Rovers before the Welshman turned to full-time management with Rovers and later Manchester City and Fulham.

Left: Mark Hughes in action during a match against Liverpool at Anfield.

Below: 18 May 1985. Hughes receives the Young Player of the Year Award from England manager Bobby Robson before the FA Cup final against Everton at Wembley Stadium.

LESLIE HOFTON

Country: England
Born: 3 Mar 1888 **Died:** Jan 1971
Debut: 18 Feb 1911 v Newcastle United
Position: Full back
Appearances: 19 **Goals scored:** 0
Seasons: 1910/11 – 1920/21
Clubs: Worksop Town, Denaby United, Glossop North End, Mexborough Town, Manchester United, Denaby Main

GRAEME HOGG

Country: Scotland
Born: 17 Jun 1964
Debut: 7 Jan 1984 v Bournemouth
Position: Centre back
Appearances: 108 (2) **Goals scored:** 1
Seasons: 1983/84 – 1987/88
Clubs: Manchester United, West Bromwich Albion, Portsmouth, Heart of Midlothian, Notts County, Brentford

DICK HOLDEN

Country: England
Born: 12 Jun 1885 **Died:** Unknown
Debut: 24 Apr 1905 v Blackpool
Position: Full back
Appearances: 117 **Goals scored:** 0
Seasons: 1904/05 – 1912/13
Clubs: Manchester United

EDWARD HOLT

Country: England
Born: 1879 **Died:** Unknown
Debut: 28 Apr 1900 v Chesterfield
Position: Winger
Appearances: 1 **Goals scored:** 1
Seasons: 1899/1900
Clubs: Newton Heath Athletic, Newton Heath

JIM HOLTON

Country: Scotland

Born: 11 Apr 1951
Debut: 20 Jan 1973 v West Ham United
Position: Centre back
Appearances: 69 **Goals scored:** 5
Seasons: 1972/73 – 1974/75
Clubs: Shrewsbury Town, Manchester United, Miami Toros, Sunderland, Coventry City, Detroit Express, Sheffield Wednesday

Jim Holton was a cult hero for the Stretford Enders during his brief time at United.

TOM HOMER

Country: England
Born: Apr 1886 **Died:** Unknown
Debut: 30 Oct 1909 v Arsenal
Position: Forward
Appearances: 25 **Goals scored:** 14
Seasons: 1909/10 – 1911/12
Clubs: Stourbridge, Kidderminster Harriers, Manchester United

BILLY HOOD

Country: Unknown
Born: Unknown **Died:** Unknown
Debut: 1 Oct 1892 v West Bromwich Albion
Position: Forward
Appearances: 38 **Goals scored:** 6
Seasons: 1892/93 – 1893/94
Clubs: Newton Heath

ARTHUR HOOPER

Country: England
Born: Jan 1889 **Died:** Unknown
Debut: 22 Jan 1910 v Tottenham Hotspur
Position: Forward
Appearances: 7 **Goals scored:** 1
Seasons: 1909/10 – 1913/14
Clubs: Kidderminster Harriers, Manchester United, Crystal Palace

FRED HOPKIN

Country: England
Born: 23 Sep 1895 **Died:** 5 Mar 1970
Debut: 30 Aug 1919 v Derby County
Position: Winger
Appearances: 74 **Goals scored:** 8
Seasons: 1919/20 – 1920/21
Clubs: Darlington, Manchester United, Liverpool

JAMES HOPKINS

Country: England
Born: 1876 **Died:** Unknown
Debut: 18 Mar 1899 v New Brighton Tower
Position: Inside forward
Appearances: 1 **Goals scored:** 0
Seasons: 1898/99
Clubs: Berry's Association, Newton Heath

SAMUEL HOPKINSON

Country: England
Born: 9 Feb 1903 **Died:** 9 May 1958
Debut: 17 Jan 1931 v Newcastle United
Position: Forward
Appearances: 53 **Goals scored:** 12
Seasons: 1930/31 – 1933/34
Clubs: Ashton National, Manchester United, Tranmere Rovers

STEWART HOUSTON

Country: Scotland
Born: 20 Aug 1949
Debut: 1 Jan 1974 v Queens Park Rangers
Position: Full back
Appearances: 248 (2) **Goals scored:** 16
Seasons: 1973/74 – 1979/80
Clubs: Chelsea, Brentford, Manchester United, Sheffield United, Colchester United

Stewart Houston helped the Reds back to the First Division in 1975, but missed the 1977 FA Cup final through a late season injury. A solid left back, he won just one Scottish cap and made his debut for United on New Year's Day 1974, the same game that saw George Best play for the last time for the Reds.

TIM HOWARD

Country: USA
Born: 6 Mar 1979
Debut: 10 Aug 2003 v Arsenal
Position: Goalkeeper
Appearances: 76 (1) **Goals scored:** 0
Seasons: 2003/4 – 2005/6
Clubs: North Jersey Imperials, MetroStars, Manchester United, Everton

Above: 22 September 1975. Stewart Houston.

Right: 24 September 1998. Denis Irwin in action against Liverpool at Old Trafford. United won the game 2-0. No other Allex Ferguson signing has made more appearances for the Reds.

JOHN HOWARTH

Country: England
Born: 1899 **Died:** Unknown
Debut: 2 Jan 1922 v Sheffield Wednesday
Position: Full back
Appearances: 4 **Goals scored:** 0
Seasons: 1921/22
Clubs: Manchester City, Darwen, Manchester United

E HOWELLS

Country: Unknown
Born: Unknown **Died:** Unknown
Debut: 30 Oct 1886 v Fleetwood Rangers
Position: Midfield
Appearances: 1 **Goals scored:** 0
Seasons: 1886/87
Clubs: Newton Heath

EDWARD HUDSON

Country: England
Born: Jan 1887 **Died:** Jan 1945
Debut: 24 Jan 1914 v Oldham Athletic
Position: Full back
Appearances: 11 **Goals scored:** 0
Seasons: 1913/14 – 1914/15
Clubs: Walkden Central, Manchester United, Stockport County

AARON HULME

Country: England
Born: Apr 1886 **Died:** Nov 1933
Debut: 25 Apr 1908 v Preston North End
Position: Full back
Appearances: 4 **Goals scored:** 0
Seasons: 1907/08 – 1908/09
Clubs: Newton Heath Athletic, Colne FC, Oldham Athletic, Manchester United, Nelson

GEORGE HUNTER

Country: England
Born: 1885 **Died:** Feb 1934
Debut: 14 Mar 1914 v Aston Villa
Position: Midfield
Appearances: 23 **Goals scored:** 2
Seasons: 1913/14 – 1914/15
Clubs: Aston Villa, Oldham Athletic, Chelsea, Manchester United

REG HUNTER

Country: Wales
Born: 25 Oct 1938
Debut: 27 Dec 1958 v Aston Villa
Position: Winger
Appearances: 1 **Goals scored:** 0
Seasons: 1958/59
Clubs: Colwyn Bay, Manchester United, Wrexham, Bangor City

WILLIAM HUNTER

Country: England
Born: 1888 **Died:** Unknown
Debut: 29 Mar 1913 v Liverpool
Position: Forward
Appearances: 3 **Goals scored:** 2
Seasons: 1912/13

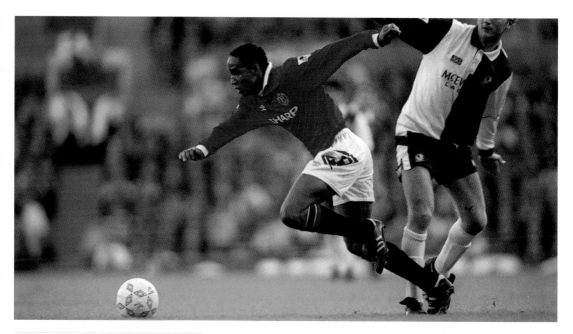

Clubs: Sunderland West End, Liverpool, Sunderland, Lincoln City, Wingate Albion, Airdrieonians, South Shields, Barnsley, Manchester United, Clapton Orient

DANIEL HURST

Country: England
Born: Oct 1876 **Died:** Unknown
Debut: 6 Sep 1902 v Gainsborough Trinity
Position: Winger
Appearances: 21 **Goals scored:** 4
Seasons: 1902/03
Clubs: Black Diamonds FC, Blackburn Rovers, Workington, Manchester City, Manchester United

RICHARD IDDON

Country: England
Born: 22 Jun 1901 **Died:** 26 Feb 1975
Debut: 29 Aug 1925 v West Ham United
Position: Forward
Appearances: 2 **Goals scored:** 0
Seasons: 1925/26 – 1926/27
Clubs: Tarlton FC, Preston North End, Leyland, Chorley, Manchester United, Chorley

PAUL INCE

Country: England
Born: 21 Oct 1967
Debut: 16 Sep 1989 v Millwall
Position: Midfield
Appearances: 276 (5) **Goals scored:** 29
Seasons: 1989/90 – 1994/95
Clubs: West Ham United, Manchester United, Internazionale, Liverpool, Middlesbrough, Wolverhampton Wanderers, Swindon Town, Macclesfield Town

Self-styled 'Guvnor' Paul Ince was the midfield general at United for six seasons after joining from West Ham United in 1989. A tenacious tackler with a ferocious shot, in his first four seasons he won the FA Cup (1990), the European Cup-Winners' Cup (1991), the League Cup (1992) and the Premier League (1993). A domestic double followed in 1994 before he transferred to Inter Milan in 1995.

WILLIAM INGLIS

Country: Scotland
Born: 2 Mar 1894 **Died:** 20 Jan 1968
Debut: 20 Mar 1926 v Everton
Position: Full back
Appearances: 14 **Goals scored:** 1
Seasons: 1925/26 – 1928/29
Clubs: Inverkeithing United, Kirkcaldy United, Raith Rovers, Sheffield Wednesday, Manchester United, Northampton Town

DENIS IRWIN

Country: Republic of Ireland
Born: 31 Oct 1965
Debut: 18 Aug 1990 v Liverpool
Position: Full back
Appearances: 511 (18) **Goals scored:** 33
Seasons: 1990/91 – 2001/02
Clubs: Leeds United, Oldham Athletic, Manchester United, Wolverhampton Wanderers

When Denis Irwin arrived at Manchester United in 1990, they had not won a league title since 1967. By the time he left in 2002, United had added seven league titles, three FA Cups and a UEFA Champions League. Elected to the Premier League Team of the Decade, his steady performances at left-back belied a steely determination that saw him finish his career at United's with 13 winner's medals.

Above: 1994. Paul Ince races past Tim Sherwood of Blackburn Rovers, the club he would later manage.

THOMAS 'TOMMY' JACKSON

Country: Northern Ireland
Born: 3 Nov 1946
Position: Midfield
Debut: 16 Aug 1975 v Wolverhampton Wanderers
Appearances: 22 (1) **Goals scored:** 0
Seasons: 1975/76 - 1977/78
Clubs: Glentoran, Everton, Nottingham Forest, Manchester United, Waterford United

WILLIAM JACKSON

Country: Wales
Born: 27 Jan 1876 **Died:** 25 Mar 1954
Position: Forward
Debut: 2 Sep 1899 v Gainsborough Trinity
Appearances: 64 **Goals scored:** 14
Seasons: 1899/90 - 1901/02
Clubs: Rhyl, Flint, St Helens Recreation, Manchester United, Barrow

STEVE JAMES

Country: England
Born: 29 Nov 1949
Position: Centre back
Debut: 12 Oct 1968 v Liverpool
Appearances: 160 (1) **Goals scored:** 4
Seasons: 1968/69 - 1974/75
Clubs: Manchester United, York City, Kidderminster Harriers

CAESAR JENKYNS

Country: Wales
Born: 24 Aug 1866 **Died:** 23 Jul 1941
Position: Defender
Debut: 1 Sep 1896 v Gainsborough Trinity
Appearances: 47 **Goals scored:** 6
Seasons: 1896/97 - 1897/98
Clubs: Small Heath St Andrews, Walsall Swifts, Unity Gas FC, Small Heath, Woolwich Arsenal, Newton Heath, Walsall

WILLIAM RONALD 'ROY' JOHN

Country: Wales
Born: 29 Jan 1911 **Died:** 12 Jul 1973
Position: Goalkeeper
Debut: 29 Aug 1936 v Wolverhampton Wanderers
Appearances: 15 **Goals scored:** 0
Seasons: 1936/37
Clubs: Walsall, Stoke City, Preston North End, Sheffield United, Manchester United, Newport County

RONNY JOHNSEN

Country: Norway
Born: 10 Jun 1969
Position: Defender
Debut: 17 Aug 1996 v Wimbledon
Appearances: 131 (19) **Goals scored:** 9
Seasons: 1996/97 - 2001/02
Clubs: Stokke IL, Eik Tonsberg, Lyn Oslo, Lillestrom, Besiktas, Manchester United, Aston Villa, Newcastle United, Valerenga

Opposite: 16 April 1957. Centre half Mark Jones in training. Jones would be one of the Busby Babes to die in the Munich air crash.

EDWARD 'EDDIE' JOHNSON

Country: England
Born: 20 Sep 1984
Position: Forward
Debut: 28 Oct 2003 v Leeds United
Appearances: 0 (1) **Goals scored:** 0
Seasons: 2003/04
Clubs: Royal Antwerp (*loan*), Coventry City (*loan*), Crewe Alexandra (*loan*), Manchester United, Bradford City, Chester City, Austin Aztex

SAMUEL 'SAM' JOHNSTON

Country: England
Born: Jul 1881 **Died:** Unknown
Position: Forward
Debut: 20 Mar 1901 v Leicester City
Appearances: 1 **Goals scored:** 0
Seasons: 1900/01
Clubs: Tongue FC, Newton Heath, Heywood FC

WILLIAM JOHNSTON

Country: Scotland
Born: 16 Jan 1901 **Died:** 23 Nov 1964
Position: Forward
Debut: 15 Oct 1927 v Cardiff City
Appearances: 77 **Goals scored:** 27
Seasons: 1927/28 - 1928/29 and 1931/32
Clubs: Huddersfield Town, Stockport County, Macclesfield Town, Manchester United, Oldham Athletic

DAVID JONES

Country: Wales
Born: 10 Jun 1914 **Died:** 30 May 1988
Position: Half back
Debut: 11 Dec 1937 v Bradford Park Avenue
Appearances: 1 **Goals scored:** 0
Seasons: 1937/38
Clubs: Wigan Athletic, Manchester United, Swindon Town

DAVID JONES

Country: England
Born: 4 Nov 1984
Position: Midfield
Debut: 1 Dec 2004 v Arsenal
Appearances: 3 (1) **Goals scored:** 0
Seasons: 2003/04 - 2006/07
Clubs: Preston North End (*loan*), NEC Nijmegen (*loan*), Derby County (*loan*), Manchester United, Derby County, Wolverhampton Wanderers

ERNEST 'ERNIE' JONES

Country: England
Born: 30 Nov 1937
Position: Full back
Debut: 19 Oct 1957 v Portsmouth
Appearances: 1 **Goals scored:** 0
Seasons: 1957/58
Clubs: Manchester United, Wrexham, Stockport County, Altrincham

MARK JONES

Country: England
Born: 15 Jun 1933 **Died:** 6 Feb 1958
Position: Defender

Debut: 7 Oct 1950 v Sheffield Wednesday
Appearances: 121 **Goals scored:** 1
Seasons: 1950/51 - 1957/58
Clubs: Manchester United

Mark Jones was one of the eight United players to lose their lives in the Munich air disaster. He was the club's first choice centre back after Allenby Chilton from 1955, winning two League Championships. The former bricklayer from Barnsley missed the 1957 FA Cup final defeat to Aston Villa through an eye injury, but many felt he was destined for an England call-up if he had not died in the tragedy.

OWEN JONES

Country: Wales
Born: Jul 1871 **Died:** 23 Sep 1955
Position: Forward
Debut: 3 Sep 1898 v Gainsborough Trinity
Appearances: 2 **Goals scored:** 0
Seasons: 1898/99
Clubs: Bangor City, Crewe Alexandra, Chorley, Manchester United, Bangor City, Earlestown, Stalybridge Rovers

PHIL JONES

Country: England
Born: 21 Feb 1992
Debut: 7 Aug 2011 v Manchester City
Position: Defender
Appearances: 0 (1) **Goals scored:** 0
Seasons: 2011/12 - present
Clubs: Blackburn Rovers, Manchester United

The England Under-21 defender joined United as the first recruit of the 2011 summer for a fee reported to be about £16 million.

RICHIE JONES

Country: England
Born: 26 Sep 1986
Position: Midfield
Debut: 26 Oct 2005 v Barnet
Appearances: 3 (2) **Goals scored:** 0
Seasons: 2005/06 - 2007/08
Clubs: Royal Antwerp (*loan*), Colchester United (*loan*), Barnsley (*loan*), Yeovil Town (*loan*), Manchester United, Hartlepool United, Oldham Athletic

THOMAS JONES

Country: Wales
Born: 6 Dec 1899 **Died:** 20 Feb 1978
Position: Full back
Debut: 8 Nov 1924 v Portsmouth
Appearances: 200 **Goals scored:** 0
Seasons: 1923/24 - 1936/37
Clubs: Acrefair, Druids, Oswestry Town, Manchester United, Scunthorpe & Lindsay United

THOMAS JONES

Country: Wales
Born: 6 Dec 1909 **Died:** Unknown
Position: Forward
Debut: 25 Aug 1934 v Bradford City
Appearances: 22 **Goals scored:** 4
Seasons: 1934/35
Clubs: Tranmere Rovers, Sheffield
Wednesday, Manchester United, Watford

JOSEPH 'JOE' JORDAN

Country: Scotland
Born: 15 Dec 1951
Position: Forward
Debut: 20 Jan 1978
Appearances: 125 (1) **Goals scored:** 41
Seasons: 1977/78 - 1980/81
Clubs: Greenock Morton, Leeds United,
Manchester United, AC Milan, Hellas
Verona, Southampton, Bristol City

A strong, fearless and committed player
who had the skills to match and was a
good header of the ball. Joe Jordan is still
fondly recalled as "Jaws" thanks to his
missing front teeth, lost early in his
career and giving him a fearsome aspect.
He played 52 games for Scotland, scoring 11 goals. Now a successful coach at
Tottenham Hotspur.

NIKOLA JOVANOVIC

Country: Yugoslavia
Born: 18 Sep 1952
Position: Defender
Debut: 2 Feb 1980 v Derby County
Appearances: 25 (1) **Goals scored:** 4
Seasons: 1979/80 - 1980/81
Clubs: Red Star Belgrade, FC
Buducnoet, Manchester United

Above: United striker Joe Jordan
showing his missing front
teeth, which earned him the
nickname "Jaws" at the club.

Right: 14 May 1994. Andrei
Kanchelskis at the FA Cup
final. Manchester United
beat Chelsea 4-0.

ANDREI KANCHELSKIS

Country: Ukraine
Born: 23 Jan 1969
Position: Winger
Debut: 11 May 1991 v Crystal Palace
Appearances: 132 (29) **Goals scored:** 36
Seasons: 1990/91 - 1994/95
Clubs: Dynamo Kiev, Shakhtar Donetsk,
Manchester United, Everton, Fiorentina, Glasgow
Rangers, Manchester City (*loan*), Southampton,
Al-Hilal, Saturn Moscow Oblast, Krylia Sovetov

Kanchelskis signed for United for
£650,000 in March 1991. Ferguson hoped
the player would provide him with a quick
resourceful right-sided midfielder. He
would be United's leading scorer in the
1994-95 season with 19 goals in 32 appearances. He was sold to Everton for £5 million at the start of the 1995-96 season.

JAMES KELLY

Country: England
Born: 2 May 1957
Position: Midfield
Debut: 20 Dec 1975 v Wolverhampton Wanderers
Appearances: (0) 1 **Goals scored:** 0
Seasons: 1975/76
Clubs: Manchester United, Chicago Sting, Los
Angeles Aztecs, Tulsa Roughnecks, Toronto Buzzard

FRED KENNEDY

Country: England

Born: 23 Oct 1902 **Died:** 14 Nov 1963
Position: Forward
Debut: 6 Oct 1923 v Oldham Athletic
Appearances: 18 **Goals scored:** 4
Seasons: 1923/24 - 1924/25
Clubs: Rossendale United,
Manchester United, Everton

PATRICK KENNEDY

Country: Ireland
Born: 9 Oct 1934 **Died:** 18 Mar 2007
Position: Full back
Debut: 2 Oct 1954 v wolverhampton Wanderers
Appearances: 1 **Goals scored:** 0
Seasons: 1954/55
Clubs: Johnville, Manchester United, Blackburn
Rovers, Southampton, Oldham Athletic

WILLIAM KENNEDY

Country: Scotland
Born: Unknown **Died:** Unknown
Position: Forward
Debut: 7 Sep 1895 v Crewe Alexandra
Appearances: 33 **Goals scored:** 12
Seasons: 1895/96 - 1896/97
Clubs: Ayr Parkhouse, Newton
Heath, Stockport County

HUGH KERR

Country: Scotland
Born: 1882 **Died:** Unknown
Position: Forward
Debut: 9 Mar 1904 v Blackpool
Appearances: 2 **Goals scored:** 0
Seasons: 1903/04
Clubs: Westerlea, Ayr FC, Manchester United

ROY KEANE

Country: Republic of Ireland
Born: 10 Aug 1971
Position: Midfield
Debut: 7 Aug 1993 v Arsenal
Appearances: 458 (22) **Goals scored:** 51
Seasons: 1993/94 – 2005/06
Clubs: Cobh Ramblers, Nottingham
Forest, Manchester United, Celtic

Roy Keane was the type of player who could inspire a whole team. He could win games with his on-field unarguable leadership and undoubted courage and, on many occasions during his 12 seasons spent at United, he did just that.

Born in Mayfield, Cork, Keane started his football career at Cobh Ramblers in the League of Ireland. His introduction to English football came under the tutelage of Brian Clough after joining Nottingham Forest in 1990. By 1993 his midfield performances attracted the interest of both Blackburn Rovers and United. Despite agreeing a transfer fee and personal terms with Rovers, it was United who eventually secured his signature – for a then British transfer record £3.75 million.

Keane came into a successful side destined to take the place of club legend Bryan Robson. He was to prove an excellent replacement as the Red Devils won the league and FA Cup double in his first season. Over the next three seasons more success followed, with United winning two more league titles before Keane was made club captain in 1997. Ironically, after assuming the captaincy, a cruciate ligament injury against Leeds United saw him miss the majority of the season.

Any thoughts that the injury might diminish his fighting qualities were dispelled on his return the following year. In 1998-99 United romped to the treble, Keane turning in a career-defining performance in the Champions League semi-final second leg against Juventus, scoring United's first goal in a 3-2 win after United had gone two goals behind early on. The fact that a booking in the game would cause him to miss the final must have been a huge disappointment. But his skill and talent did not go unnoticed and in 2000 he was honoured with Player of the Year awards from both his peers and the football writers.

However, alongside on-field recognition there was also controversy. Keane was involved in a number of confrontational incidents during his time at Old Trafford, including coining the term 'the prawn sandwich brigade'. A more unsavoury episode occurred in 2001 when the Irishman received a red card for a bad tackle on Alf Inge Haaland of Manchester City. Keane later admitted in his autobiography that the tackle was intentional, a confession which saw him receive a five-game ban and a £150,000 fine.

It was the same story on the international stage. Keane earned 67 caps and scored nine goals, but he will be best remembered for being sent home from the 2002 World Cup following an altercation with Ireland manager Mick McCarthy.

Keane always set high standards on the field. After leaving United, Keane spent a season at Celtic and then retired from playing and moved into management where his main achievement to date has been taking Sunderland into the Premiership.

Left: 27 July 2004. Roy Keane takes a break during a training session on United's 2004 USA tour.

Below: 15 February 2003. Roy Keane in action during the FA Cup fifth round against Arsenal.

Above: 13 November 1968. Brian Kidd celebrates his goal as United beat Anderlecht 3-0. The Collyhurst-born striker not only played for both Manchester teams, he coached them both, leaving United to become manager of Blackburn Rovers just before the Reds completed the treble.

BRIAN KIDD
Country: England
Born: 29 May 1949
Position: Forward
Debut: 12 Aug 1967 v Tottenham Hotspur
Appearances: 257 (9) **Goals scored:** 70
Seasons: 1967/68 – 1973/74
Clubs: Manchester United, Arsenal, Manchester City, Everton, Bolton Wanderers, Atlanta Chiefs (loan), Fort Lauderdale Strikers, Minnesota Strikers

Brain Kidd was schooled in the United youth team. He came to prominence when, in his first full season, he played in the 1968 European Cup final and scored in the game on his nineteenth birthday.

Kidd won two England caps and was later United assistant manager from 1991 to 1998. He now has the same role at Manchester City.

JOSHUA KING
Country: Norway
Born: 15 Jan 1992
Position: Forward
Debut: 23 Sep 2009 v Wolverhampton Wanderers
Appearances: (0) 1 **Goals scored:** 0
Seasons: 2009/10 – present
Clubs: Manchester United, Preston North End (loan)

JOSEPH KINLOCH
Country: England
Born: Jan 1864 **Died:** Unknown

Position: Forward
Debut: 29 Oct 1892 v Nottingham Forest
Appearances: 1 **Goals scored:** 0
Seasons: 1892/93
Clubs: Newton Heath

ALBERT KINSEY
Country: England
Born: 19 Sep 1945
Position: Forward
Debut: 9 Jan 1965 v Chester City
Appearances: 1 **Goals scored:** 1
Seasons: 1964/65 – 1965/66
Clubs: Manchester United, Wrexham

JOSE PEREIRA KLEBERSON
Country: Brazil
Born: 19 Jun 1979

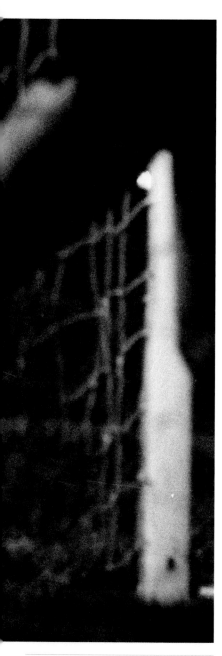

Position: Midfield
Debut: 27 Aug 2003 v Wolverhampton Wanderers
Appearances: 24 (6) **Goals scored:** 2
Seasons: 2003/04 – 2004/05
Clubs: Atlético Paranaense, Manchester United, Besiktas, Flamengo

FRANK KNOWLES
Country: England
Born: Apr 1891 **Died:** 20 Jan 1951
Position: Half back
Debut: 30 Mar 1912 v Aston Villa
Appearances: 47 **Goals scored:** 1
Seasons: 1911/12 – 1914/15
Clubs: Stalybridge Celtic, Manchester United, Arsenal, Hyde Park, Oldham Athletic, Sandbach Ramblers, Hartlepool United

FRANK KOPEL
Country: Scotland
Born: 28 Mar 1949
Position: Full back
Debut: 9 Sep 1967 v Burnley
Appearances: 10 (2) **Goals scored:** 0
Seasons: 1967/68 – 1968/69
Clubs: Manchester United, Blackburn Rovers, Dundee United

TOMASZ KUSZCZAK
Country: Poland
Born: 20 Mar 1980
Position: Goalkeeper
Debut: 17 Sep 2006 v Arsenal
Appearances: 56 (5) **Goals scored:** 0
Seasons: 2006/07 - present
Clubs: Hertha BSC, West Bromwich Albion, Manchester United

JOSEPH LANCASTER
Country: England
Born: 28 Apr 1926
Position: Goalkeeper
Debut: 14 Jan 1950 v Chelsea
Appearances: 4 **Goals scored:** 0
Seasons: 1949/50 – 1950/51
Clubs: Manchester United, Accrington Stanley

THOMAS LANG
Country: Scotland
Born: 3 Apr 1905 **Died:** Unknown
Position: Winger
Debut: 11 Apr 1936 v Bradford Park Avenue
Appearances: 13 **Goals scored:** 1
Seasons: 1935/36 – 1936/37
Clubs: Newcastle United, Huddersfield Town, Manchester United, Swansea Town

LEN LANGFORD
Country: England
Born: 30 May 1899 **Died:** 26 Dec 1973
Position: Goalkeeper
Debut: 22 Sep 1934 v Norwich City
Appearances: 15 **Goals scored:** 0
Seasons: 1934/35 – 1936/37
Clubs: Nottingham Forest, Manchester City, Manchester United

HUBERT 'HARRY' LAPPIN
Country: England
Born: 16 Jan 1879 **Died:** May 1925
Position: Forward
Debut: 27 Apr 1901 v Chesterfield
Appearances: 27 **Goals scored:** 4
Seasons: 1900/01 – 1902/03
Clubs: Oldham Athletic, Newton Heath, Grimsby Town

HENRIK LARSSON
Country: Sweden
Born: 20 Sep 1971

Position: Forward
Debut: 7 Jan 2007 v aston Villa
Appearances: 10 (3) **Goals scored:** 3
Seasons: 2006/07
Clubs: Högaborg, Helsingborg, Feyenoord, Celtic, Barcelona, Manchester United (*loan*), Helsingborg

REGINALD LAWSON
Country: England
Born: Nov 1880 **Died:** Unknown
Position: Forward
Debut: 1 Sep 1900 v Glossop
Appearances: 3 **Goals scored:** 0
Seasons: 1900/01 – 1901/02
Clubs: Cheshire College, Newton Heath, Bolton Wanderers

Below: 28 February 2010. Tomasz Kuszczak with the Carling Cup trophy after United had beaten Aston Villa 2-1. In his first five seasons at the club, he was often kept in reserve behind Edwin van der Sar.

DENIS LAW

Country: Scotland
Born: 24 Feb 1940
Position: Forward
Debut: 18 Aug 1962 v West Bromwich Albion
Appearances: 398 (6) **Goals scored:** 237
Seasons: 1962/63 - 1972/73
Clubs: Huddersfield Town, Manchester City, Torino, Manchester United, Manchester City

Over the course of football history, every player has been given a label that identifies his position or role in the team. For example, there are full backs, centre midfielders, inside forwards or strikers. But Denis Law was different. For all his 404 appearances for United, the Scot could be described most accurately as 'goalscorer'. That was Law's job – score for the team by any means possible. Using his natural predatory instincts, Law did just that. Goals defined his career: 237 for the Red Devils in eleven seasons, including a phenomenal 46 in 1963-64 alone. Little wonder that United fans referred to Law by another name as well – The King.

The youngest of seven children, Law was born in Aberdeen, son of a local fisherman. The boy went barefoot for

Above: 5 September 1964. Denis Law photographed at Craven Cottage.

Right: 15 July 1962. Denis Law arrives at Old Trafford, to sign for Manchester United from Italian club Torino.

most of the first 12 years of his young life as the family scraped a living, but he developed a passion for football and even turned down the chance of a better education at a rugby-playing grammar school to continue his playing football. Originally a full back and suffering from a serious squint, Law was eventually switched to inside forward and played for Scotland schoolboys, but his journey to Old Trafford would take some time.

He was first spotted by a Huddersfield Town scout and, much to the surprise of the player himself, was signed in April 1955 aged 15. He was still a skinny teenager, but the club saw something special and, when Law underwent an operation to correct his squint, his confidence grew and his career could really begin.

He made his Huddersfield debut in December 1956 and soon caught the eye of Matt Busby whose £10,000 bid was turned down. Law was also wanted by a number of other teams and would sign for Manchester City in 1960 for a then record fee of £55,000. He stayed at Maine Road for just one season and scored 21 goals and another move, this one to Torino in Italy, did not work out. The patient Busby finally got his man in July 1962 for another British record transfer fee of £110,000.

The move back to Manchester was just what Law needed and he settled quickly into a team still being re-built after the Munich air crash. In his first season, Law helped United win the FA Cup and his 29 goals (including six in the cup) were an important reason why the struggling club remained in the First Division.

When George Best arrived on the scene the following season, Law joined him and club captain Bobby Charlton as a talented trio that would set the English football world on fire. There was nothing more exciting in the game than the famed United Trinity; Best dazzling on the wing, Charlton firing in thunderbolt shots and Law scoring goals with all manner of flying acrobatics. That season the Scot was named European Footballer of the Year. With a spikey blond head of hair, forever clutching the edges of his long shirt sleeves, as if fearing cold weather, Law was an iconic figure whose cheekiness in the penalty box and daring anticipation unsettled defenders. In the 1964-65 campaign United won the league and Law top-scored again with 39 goals. But in October 1965 while on international duty, Law suffered a right knee injury that would plague him for the rest of his career. United missed the title that season, but won it again in 1966-67.

By now Law was an international star of considerable renown, who would eventually gather 55 caps for his country, score 30 goals and play in the 1974 World Cup in West Germany. He was enjoying life at Old Trafford, but it did have its difficult times. In 1966 Law asked manager Busby for a pay rise for his new contract; not only was this summarily refused, but Law was forced to sign a letter of apology that was shown to the media. Law, however, had the last laugh because, as he later claimed, Busby gave him the increase in salary anyway, once all the media interest had quietened down.

The 1967-68 season would ultimately be one of disappointment for Law whose right knee was causing increasing problems. United were on the hunt for the European Cup and would reach the final with little help from the often-injured Scot who played in only three of the ties, scoring two goals. Missing the final while in hospital having undergone a knee operation proved to be a huge regret in his career, even though the manager brought the trophy to his bedside the morning after the victory.

Law would also miss many games through suspension. Often facing defenders of much bigger stature, the Scot's frustrations would gain little sympathy from referees. In one year, he spent two months out of the team through suspensions.

The 1968-69 season saw a re-invigorated Law score 30 times for the Reds, but his final four seasons were mostly stories of injuries rather than glories, and he was given a free transfer to Manchester City in July 1973. United, by this time, had lost Busby as manager and were inexorably heading for the Second Division. Ironically, Law was in the City team at Old Trafford facing United in the penultimate game of the 1973-74 season when relegation was confirmed. The goalscorer supreme even back-heeled the only goal of the game to defeat his former team and famously refused to celebrate, asking to be substituted immediately afterwards. Events elsewhere actually sent United out of the First Division that day, but Law's actions spoke of his feelings for the Red Devils.

After a losers' medal in that season's League Cup final with City and with a World Cup appearance on his resumé that summer, Law retired with his reputation fully intact. He became a TV pundit, but the fact that two statues of him were later unveiled at Old Trafford underlines the love that fans had for the man known as the King of the Stretford End.

Above: 25 May 1963. Leicester City goalkeeper Gordon Banks dives at the feet of Denis Law during the FA Cup final at Wembley. United won 3-1.

NORBERT 'NOBBY' LAWTON

Country: England
Born: 25 Mar 1940
Position: Half back
Debut: 9 Apr 1960 v Luton Town
Appearances: 44 **Goals scored:** 6
Seasons: 1959/60 - 1962/63
Clubs: Manchester United, Preston North End, Brighton & Hove Albion, Lincoln City

EDWIN LEE

Country: England
Born: Jul 1879 **Died:** Unknown
Position: Forward
Debut: 25 Mar 1899 v Lincoln City
Appearances: 11 **Goals scored:** 5
Seasons: 1898/89 - 1899/1900
Clubs: Hurst Ramblers, Newton Heath

KIERAN LEE

Country: England
Born: 22 Jun 1988
Position: Full back/Midfield
Debut: 25 Oct 2006 v Crewe Alexandra
Appearances: 1 (2) **Goals scored:** 1
Seasons: 2006/07 - 2007/08
Clubs: Manchester United, Queens Park Rangers (loan), Oldham Athletic

THOMAS LEIGH

Country: England
Born: Jan 1875 **Died:** Unknown
Position: Forward
Debut: 17 Mar 1900 v Barnsley
Appearances: 46 **Goals scored:** 15
Seasons: 1899/1900 - 1900/01
Clubs: Burton Swifts, New Brighton Tower, Newton Heath

Below: 29 January 2011. Anders Lindegaard in action on his debut during an FA Cup fourth round match.

JAMES 'JIM' LEIGHTON

Country: Scotland
Born: 24 Jul 1958
Position: Goalkeeper
Debut: 27 Aug 1988 v Queens Park Rangers
Appearances: 94 **Goals scored:** 0
Seasons: 1988/89 - 1990/91
Clubs: Dairy Thistle, Aberdeen, Manchester United, Arsenal (loan), Reading (loan), Dundee, Sheffield United (loan), Hibernian, Aberdeen

HENRY LEONARD

Country: England
Born: Jul 1886 **Died:** 3 Nov 1951
Position: Forward
Debut: 11 Sep 1920 v Chelsea
Appearances: 10 **Goals scored:** 5
Seasons: 1920/21
Clubs: Sunderland West End, Grimsby Town, Middlesbrough, Derby County, Manchester United, Leicester Fosse, Heanor Town

EDWARD LEWIS

Country: England
Born: 3 Jan 1935 **Died:** 2 May 2011
Position: Forward
Debut: 29 Nov 1952 v West Bromwich Albion
Appearances: 24 **Goals scored:** 11
Seasons: 1952/53 - 1955/56
Clubs: Manchester United, Preston North End, West Ham United, Leyton Orient, Folkestone Town

LEWIS LIEVESLEY

Country: England
Born: Jul 1911 **Died:** 4 May 1949
Position: Half back
Debut: 25 Mar 1932 v Charlton Athletic
Appearances: 2 **Goals scored:** 0
Seasons: 1931/32 - 1932/33
Clubs: Doncaster Rovers, Manchester United, Chesterfield

WILFRED LIEVESLEY

Country: England
Born: 6 Oct 1902 **Died:** 21 Feb 1979
Position: Forward
Debut: 20 Jan 1923 v Leeds United
Appearances: 3 **Goals scored:** 0
Seasons: 1922/23
Clubs: Derby County, Manchester United, Exeter City

ANDERS LINDEGAARD

Country: Denmark
Born: 13 Apr 1984
Position: Goalkeeper
Debut: 29 Jan 2011 v Southampton
Appearances: 2 **Goals scored:** 0
Seasons: 2010/11 - present
Clubs: Odense Boldklub, Kolding FC, Aalesund FK, Manchester United

OSCAR LINKSON

Country: England
Born: 16 Mar 1888 **Died:** 8 Aug 1916
Position: Full back

Debut: 24 Oct 1908 v Nottingham Forest
Appearances: 59 **Goals scored:** 0
Seasons: 1908/09 - 1912/13
Clubs: Barnet & Alston, The Pirates FC, Manchester United, Shelbourne

GEORGE LIVINGSTONE

Country: Scotland
Born: 5 May 1876 **Died:** 15 Jan 1950
Position: Forward
Debut: 23 Jan 1909 v Manchester City
Appearances: 46 **Goals scored:** 4
Seasons: 1908/09 - 1913/14
Clubs: Sinclair Swifts, Artizan Thistle, Heart of Midlothian, Sunderland, Glasgow Celtic, Liverpool, Manchester City, Glasgow Rangers, Manchester United

ARTHUR LOCHHEAD

Country: Scotland
Born: 8 Dec 1897 **Died:** 30 Dec 1966
Position: Forward
Debut: 27 Aug 1921 v Everton
Appearances: 153 **Goals scored:** 50
Seasons: 1921/22 - 1925/26
Clubs: Heart of Midlothian, Manchester United, Leicester City

WILLIAM LONGAIR

Country: Scotland
Born: 19 Jul 1870 **Died:** 28 Nov 1926
Position: Half back
Debut: 20 Apr 1895 v Notts County
Appearances: 1 **Goals scored:** 0
Seasons: 1894/95
Clubs: Dundee, Newton Heath, Dundee

LONGTON

Country: Unknown
Born: Unknown **Died:** Unknown
Position: Forward
Debut: 30 Oct 1886 v Fleetwood Rangers
Appearances: 1 **Goals scored:** 0
Seasons: 1886/87
Clubs: Newton Heath

THOMAS LOWRIE

Country: Scotland
Born: 14 Jan 1928
Position: Half back
Debut: 7 Apr 1948 v Manchester City
Appearances: 14 **Goals scored:** 0
Seasons: 1947/48 - 1950/51
Clubs: Troon Athletic St Mirran, Manchester United, Aberdeen, Oldham Athletic

GEORGE LYDON

Country: England
Born: 24 Jun 1902 **Died:** 12 Aug 1953
Position: Half back
Debut: 25 Dec 1930 v Bolton Wanderers
Appearances: 3 **Goals scored:** 0
Seasons: 1930/31 - 1932/33
Clubs: Nelson United, Mossley, Manchester United, Southport

MARK LYNCH

Country: England
Born: 2 Sep 1981
Position: Full back
Debut: 18 Mar 2003 v Deportivo de La Coruña
Appearances: 1 **Goals scored:** 0
Seasons: 2002/03
Clubs: Manchester United, St Johnstone (*loan*), Sunderland, Hull City, Yeovil Town, Rotherham United, Stockport County

DAVID LYNER

Country: Northern Ireland
Born: 9 Jan 1893 **Died:** 5 Dec 1973
Position: Forward
Debut: 23 Sep 1922 v Coventry City
Appearances: 3 **Goals scored:** 0
Seasons: 1922/23
Clubs: Glentoran, Manchester United, Kilmarnock

SAMUEL LYNN

Country: England
Born: 25 Dec 1920 **Died:** Jan 1995
Position: Half back
Debut: 3 Jan 1948 v Charlton Athletic
Appearances: 13 **Goals scored:** 0
Seasons: 1947/48 - 1950/51
Clubs: Manchester United, Bradford

GEORGE LYONS

Country: England
Born: Apr 1884 **Died:** Unknown
Position: Forward
Debut: 23 Apr 1904 v Burton United
Appearances: 5 **Goals scored:** 0
Seasons: 1903/04 - 1905/06
Clubs: Black Lane Temperance, Manchester United, Oldham Athletic

LOU MACARI

Country: Scotland
Born: 4 Jun 1949
Debut: 20 Jan 1973 v West Ham United
Position: Forward
Appearances: 374 (27) **Goals scored:** 97
Seasons: 1972/73 - 1983/84
Clubs: Celtic, Manchester United, Swindon Town

Lou Macari joined United in 1973 after

a successful start to his career with Celtic. A debut goal helped him settle in straight away, but his shot that deflected off Jimmy Greenhoff for the winning goal in the 1977 FA Cup final, a goal that ultimately denied Liverpool the European treble, is the one United fans treasure the most. He appeared 24 times for Scotland, moving into management following his retirement from playing.

KEN MACDONALD

Country: Wales
Born: 24 Apr 1898 **Died:** Unknown
Debut: 3 Mar 1923 v Southampton
Position: Forward
Appearances: 9 **Goals scored:** 2
Seasons: 1922/23 - 1923/24
Clubs: Inverness Citadel, Clachnacuddin, Aberdeen, Caerau, Cardiff City, Manchester United, Bradford Park Avenue, Hull City, Halifax Town, Coleraine, Walker Celtic, Blyth Spartans

Above: 14 April 1973. Lou Macari shoots past Stoke City's Mike Pejic during a Division One match at the Victoria Ground. The match finished 2-2. The Scot started his United career as a forward but soon moved back into midfield.

WILLIAM 'BILLY' MEREDITH

Country: Wales
Born: 30 Jul 1874 **Died:** 19 Apr 1958
Debut: 1 Jan 1907 v Aston Villa
Position: Winger
Appearances: 335 **Goals scored:** 36
Seasons: 1906/07 – 1920/21
Clubs: Chirk, Northwich Victoria, Manchester City, Manchester United, Manchester City

Billy Meredith's name will never be forgotten as long as people remain fascinated by United's history. Perhaps the first football superstar, he was one of the most famous men in the country at the start of the twentieth century. An intriguing character who starred in the game for over 30 seasons, Meredith played with a toothpick in his mouth, supposedly to assist his concentration, and then unpicked defences on a regular basis. All this made Meredith, known as the Welsh Wizard (and also known as Old Skinny because of his slender frame), a Reds legend who helped bring the first major trophies to the club. His crosses from the right wing were as just as effective as those of David Beckham, another United icon of many decades later.

Meredith was born in Black Park, north Wales, in 1874 and began work in the local mine as a pit pony driver at the age of 12. The Meredith family was replete with footballing talent, and a young Billy was no different. Chirk was a top amateur team in the area and he made his first team debut for them in 1890, winning the Welsh Cup in 1894, while playing at the time for an English team, Northwich Victoria. But it was a move to Manchester City that began Meredith's irresistible rise to football fame. He joined City in 1894 against his mother's advice, because she wanted him to stay in Wales, work in the mines and only play football for fun. But the 20-year-old defied his parent's wishes and signed for the club, although as an amateur – he would continue to work as a miner for another year.

Meredith made an immediate impact at City, finishing top scorer in his first two seasons and helped them to the FA Cup in 1904. But controversy was looming, something the player would continue to face for much of his career. It all began the following season after the cup triumph when he was found guilty of trying to bribe an opponent and given a lengthy ban, although Meredith declared his innocence. He was punished again by the authorities for trying to (illegally) obtain monies from the club while still suspended.

The Football Association was investigating City for a host of illegal payments, and the authorities eventually forced the Sky Blues to sell 17 of their players. One City player was banned for life and some critics said Meredith was lucky not to receive the same punishment. The scandal led to Meredith and three of his City colleagues signing for United. Meredith was the first player to join (he was registered with the Reds in October) for a £500 fee.

The transfers happened just a few years after the United had been saved from financial extinction, and with so much talent (particularly the inimitable Meredith) now on board, there was an air of anticipation and real hope that better times were ahead for the Reds. Manager Ernest Mangnall gave Meredith his debut along with the three other ex-Sky Blues on 1 January 1907 and the win on the day was an omen that United were about to become a real force in football.

Meredith led United's charge to their first silverware the very next season. He played in all but one league match (37) and scored 10 goals as the Red Devils took their first ever First Division championship, and the following season the Reds won the FA Cup for the first time with their Welsh star awarded man of the match. It was no surprise that United won another league championship in 1910-11, again with Meredith as a leading figure (35 games and five goals).

The thing about Meredith was that, with his trim haircut and moustache, he was the ultimate provider of goals and a team leader par excellence. He had great pace, despite his bandy legs, and a facial

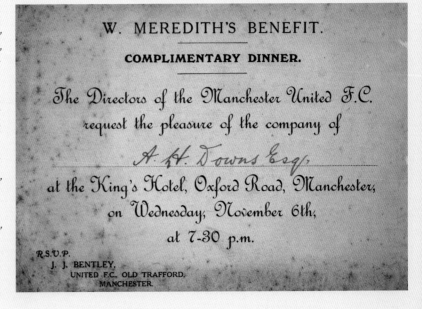

W. MEREDITH'S BENEFIT.

COMPLIMENTARY DINNER.

The Directors of the Manchester United F.C. request the pleasure of the company of

A. H. Downs Esq

at the King's Hotel, Oxford Road, Manchester, on Wednesday, November 6th, at 7-30 p.m.

R.S.V.P.
J. J. BENTLEY,
UNITED F.C. OLD TRAFFORD,
MANCHESTER.

Above: Circa 1908. William "Billy" Meredith.

Right: An invitation to Billy Meredith's Benefit dinner.

pallor that was positively ghostly. His leadership qualities meant he would be one of the instigators of the players' union at a meeting in December 1907. Meredith had seen colleagues unable to provide for their families and treated carelessly by their clubs. At the time, footballers were restricted to a £4 maximum wage, and Meredith chaired meetings around the country to demand the ceiling be abolished. The battle between the union and the FA came to a climax in 1909 when Meredith, along with his United teammates, were banned. But the defiant Welshman would not give up and the team trained on their own: a photograph of them under the name Outcasts FC exists. A settlement was reached just before the following season,

but Meredith was to face his own financial problems when a sports shop that he own burned down, almost leading him into bankruptcy.

Despite all this, the Welshman played on regardless and by the time First World War broke out he was 40 years old and still a United regular. During the conflict, Meredith played in unofficial club matches (once he even guested for an opponent against United) and still had two more seasons left in him when league football returned.

On 7 May 1921, a crowd of 10,000 saw Meredith – now aged 47 years and 285 days – play his 335th and final match as a Red. He had scored just 36 goals in eleven seasons, but had assisted on many, many more.

Rebellious to the end, Meredith was still fighting for higher player salaries at the time, and he left Old Trafford angry that this issue had not been solved. He returned to Manchester City in the July of 1921 and stayed for three more years, playing his last professional match aged 49 years 245 days. In fact, he had finished playing for Wales only four years earlier, totalling 48 caps and 11 goals.

Once retired, Meredith turned to coaching and was involved in starting a new club, Manchester Central, in 1928. Despite earlier acrimony, Meredith and United came together again in 1931 when he worked for the club as a scout and he stayed close to Old Trafford until he died at his home in Withington, Manchester, in 1958 aged 84.

Above: 29 August 1908. Billy Meredith (l) during the first ever FA Charity Shield match against Queens Park Rangers. Following a 1-1 draw, United won this replay 4-0.

TED MACDOUGALL
Country: Scotland
Born: 8 Jan 1947
Debut: 7 Oct 1972 v West Bromwich Albion
Position: Forward
Appearances: 18 **Goals scored:** 5
Seasons: 1972/73
Clubs: Liverpool, York City, Bournemouth, Manchester United, West Ham United, Norwich City, Jewish Guild, Southampton, Weymouth, Bournemouth, Detroit Express, Blackpool, Salisbury, Poole Town, AFC Totton, Gosport Borough, Floreat Athena, St George Budapest, Andover

FEDERICO MACHEDA
Country: Italy
Born: 22 Aug 1991
Debut: 5 Apr 2009 v Aston Villa
Position: Forward
Appearances: 13 (14) **Goals scored:** 4
Seasons: 2008/09 - present
Clubs: Manchester United, Sampdoria (*loan*)

CHARLES MACKIE
Country: Scotland
Born: 1882 **Died:** Unknown
Debut: 3 Sep 1904 v Port Vale
Position: Forward
Appearances: 7 **Goals scored:** 4
Seasons: 1904/05
Clubs: Aberdeen, Manchester United, West Ham United, Lochgelly United

GIULIANO 'JULES' MAIORANA
Country: England
Born: 18 Apr 1969
Debut: 14 Jan 1989 v Millwall
Position: Left Winger
Appearances: 2 (6) **Goals scored:** 0
Seasons: 1988/89 - 1993/94
Clubs: Histon, Manchester United, Ljungskile, Newmarket Town

THOMAS RONALD 'TOM' MANLEY
Country: England
Born: 7 Oct 1912 **Died:** 4 Jul 1988
Debut: 5 Dec 1931 v Millwall
Position: Forward
Appearances: 195 **Goals scored:** 41
Seasons: 1931/32 - 1938/39
Clubs: Manchester United, Brentford

Originally joined United as an amateur in 1930, and was given his debut a year later. Manley was a versatile player who could play at half back or in the forward line. He scored two goals in the 2-2 draw that clinched promotion for the Reds back to the First Division in the 1935-36 season. During the war years, while playing for Brentford, he guested for Manchester United and continued to play professionally until he was 40.

FRANK MANN
Country: England
Born: 17 Mar 1891 **Died:** Jul 1966
Debut: 17 Mar 1923 v Bradford City
Position: Half back
Appearances: 197 **Goals scored:** 5
Seasons: 1922/23 - 1929/30
Clubs: Aston Villa, Huddersfield Town, Manchester City, Manchester United, Mossley

HERBERT MANN
Country: England
Born: 30 Dec 1907 **Died:** 24 Apr 1977
Debut: 29 Aug 1931 v Bradford Park Avenue
Position: Forward
Appearances: 13 **Goals scored:** 2
Seasons: 1931/32 - 1933/34
Clubs: Griff Colliery, Derby County, Grantham Town, Manchester United, Ripley Town

THOMAS MANNS
Country: England
Born: Jan 1911 **Died:** Unknown
Debut: 3 Feb 1934 v Burnley
Position: Wing half
Appearances: 2 **Goals scored:** 0
Seasons: 1933/34
Clubs: Burnley, Manchester United, Clapton Orient

MATEUS ALBERTO CONTREIRAS 'MANUCHO' GONCALVES
Country: Angola
Born: 7 Mar 1983
Debut: 23 Sep 2008 v Middlesbrough
Position: Forward
Appearances: 0 (3) **Goals scored:** 0
Seasons: 2008/09
Clubs: Benfica de Luanda, Petro Atletico, Manchester United, Panathinaikos, Hull City, Real Valladolid, Bucaspor, Manisaspor

PHILIP MARSH
Country: England
Born: 15 Nov 1986
Debut: 25 Oct 2006 v Crewe Alexandra
Position: Forward
Appearances: 1 **Goals scored:** 0
Seasons: 2006/07
Clubs: Manchester United, Blackpool, Northwich Victoria, Hyde United, Leigh Genesis, FC United of Manchester, Stalybridge Celtic

ARTHUR MARSHALL
Country: England
Born: Oct 1881 **Died:** Unknown
Debut: 9 Mar 1903 v Woolwich Arsenal
Position: Full back
Appearances: 6 **Goals scored:** 0
Seasons: 1902/03
Clubs: Everton, Chester, Crewe Alexandra, Leicester Fosse, Stockport County, Manchester United, Portsmouth

LEE MARTIN
Country: England
Born: 5 Feb 1968
Debut: 9 May 1988 v Wimbledon
Position: Full back
Appearances: 84 (25) **Goals scored:** 2
Seasons: 1987/88 - 1993/94
Clubs: Manchester United, Glasgow Celtic, Bristol Rovers, Huddersfield Town

LEE MARTIN
Country: England
Born: 9 Feb 1987
Debut: 26 Oct 2005 v Barnet
Position: Midfield
Appearances: 3 **Goals scored:** 0
Seasons: 2005/06 - 2008/09
Clubs: Manchester United, Royal Antwerp, Rangers, Stoke City, Plymouth Argyle, Sheffield United, Nottingham Forest, Ipswich Town, Charlton Athletic

MICHAEL 'MICK' MARTIN
Country: Republic of Ireland
Born: 9 Jul 1951
Debut: 24 Jan 1973 v Everton
Position: Midfield
Appearances: 36 (7) **Goals scored:** 2
Seasons: 1972/73 - 1974/75
Clubs: Bohemians, Manchester United, West Bromwich Albion, Newcastle United, Vancouver Whitecaps, Willington

Athletic, Cardiff City, Peterborough United, Rotherham United, Preston North End

WILLIAM MATHIESON
Country: Scotland
Born: 1870 **Died:** Unknown
Debut: 3 Sep 1892 v Blackburn Rovers
Position: Forward
Appearances: 10 **Goals scored:** 2
Seasons: 1892/93 – 1893/94
Clubs: Glasgow Thistle, Clydesdale FC, Newton Heath, Rotherham Town

DAVID MAY
Country: England
Born: 24 Jun 1970
Debut: 14 Aug 1994 v Blackburn Rovers
Position: Defender
Appearances: 98 (20) **Goals scored:** 8
Seasons: 1994/95 – 2002/03
Clubs: Blackburn Rovers, Manchester United, Huddersfield Town, Burnley

NEIL MCBAIN
Country: Scotland
Born: 15 Nov 1895 **Died:** 13 May 1974
Debut: 26 Nov 1921 v Aston Villa
Position: Half back
Appearances: 43 **Goals scored:** 2
Seasons: 1921/22 – 1922/23
Clubs: Hamilton Academical, Ayr United, Manchester United, Everton, St. Johnstone, Liverpool, Watford, New Brighton

JAMES 'JIM' MCCALLIOG
Country: Scotland
Born: 23 Sep 1946
Debut: 16 Mar 1974 v Birmingham City
Position: Midfield
Appearances: 37 (1) **Goals scored:** 7
Seasons: 1973/74 – 1974/75
Clubs: Chelsea, Sheffield Wednesday, Wolverhampton Wanderers, Manchester United, Southampton, Chicago Sting, Lyn Oslo, Lincoln City

PATRICK MCCARTHY
Country: Wales
Born: Apr 1888 **Died:** Unknown
Debut: 20 Jan 1912 v West Bromwich Albion
Position: Forward
Appearances: 1 **Goals scored:** 0
Seasons: 1911/12
Clubs: Chester, Skelmersdale United, Manchester United

JOHN MCCARTNEY
Country: Scotland
Born: 1866 **Died:** 18 Jan 1933
Debut: 8 Sep 1894 v Burton Wanderers
Position: Full back
Appearances: 20 **Goals scored:** 1
Seasons: 1894/95
Clubs: Cartvale FC, Thistle FC, Glasgow Rangers, Cowlairs FC, Newton Heath, Luton, Barnsley

WILLIAM MCCARTNEY
Country: Scotland

Born: Unknown **Died:** Unknown
Debut: 5 Sep 1903 v Bristol City
Position: Forward
Appearances: 13 **Goals scored:** 1
Seasons: 1903/04
Clubs: Rutherglen Glencairn, Ayr FC, Hibernian, Manchester United, West Ham United

BRIAN MCCLAIR
Country: Scotland
Born: 8 Dec 1963
Debut: 15 Aug 1987 v Southampton
Position: Forward
Appearances: 398 (73) **Goals scored:** 127
Seasons: 1987/88 – 1997/98
Clubs: Aston Villa, Motherwell, Celtic, Manchester United

'Choccy', as Brian McClair is known, formed half of a potent striking partnership with Mark Hughes at United in the late 80s and early 90s. Four times a league winner at the club, he had a habit of picking up decisive goals, including the winner in the 1992 League Cup final. In the 1990-91 European Cup-Winners' Cup he scored in every round on the way to the final before a Hughes double strike sealed a memorable victory against Barcelona. At the end of the 1997-98 season, McClair was given a free transfer to Motherwell, where he spent six months before announcing his retirement. He returned to United to join the coaching staff, and is now director of the Academy.

JAMES MCCLELLAND
Country: Scotland
Born: 11 May 1903 **Died:** Unknown
Debut: 2 Sep 1936 v Huddersfield Town
Position: Forward
Appearances: 5 **Goals scored:** 1
Seasons: 1936/37
Clubs: Rosslyn, Raith Rovers, Southend United, Middlesbrough, Bolton Wanderers, Preston North End, Blackpool, Bradford Park Avenue, Manchester United

JAMES MCCRAE
Country: Scotland
Born: 2 Sep 1894 **Died:** 3 Sep 1974
Debut: 16 Jan 1926 v Arsenal
Position: Midfield
Appearances: 13 **Goals scored:** 0
Seasons: 1925/26
Clubs: Clyde, West Ham United, Bury, Wigan Borough, New Brighton, Manchester United, Watford

DAVID MCCREERY
Country: Northern Ireland
Born: 16 Sep 1957
Debut: 15 Oct 1974 v Portsmouth

Position: Midfield
Appearances: 57 (53) **Goals scored:** 8
Seasons: 1974/75 – 1978/79
Clubs: Manchester United, Queens Park Rangers, Tulsa Roughnecks, Newcastle United, GIF Sundsvall, Heart of Midlothian, Hartlepool United, Coleraine, Carlisle United

WILLIAM MCDONALD
Country: Scotland
Born: 9 Jul 1905 **Died:** Unknown
Debut: 23 Apr 1932 v Bradford City
Position: Forward
Appearances: 27 **Goals scored:** 4
Seasons: 1932/33 – 1933/34
Clubs: Coatbridge FC, Law Scotia FC, Dundee United, Broxburn United, Armadale, Airdrieonians, Manchester United, Tranmere Rovers

ROBERT 'BOB' MCFARLANE
Country: Scotland
Born: Unknown **Died:** Oct 1898
Debut: 3 Oct 1891 v Manchester City
Position: Full back
Appearances: 3 **Goals scored:** 0
Seasons: 1891/92
Clubs: Airdrieonians, Bootle, Sunderland Albion, Manchester United

NOEL MCFARLANE
Country: Republic of Ireland
Born: 20 Dec 1934 **Died:** Unknown
Debut: 13 Feb 1954 v Tottenham Hotspur
Position: Forward
Appearances: 1 **Goals scored:** 0
Seasons: 1953/54
Clubs: Manchester United, Waterford, Altrincham, Hyde United

DAVID MCFETTERIDGE
Country: Scotland
Born: Unknown **Died:** Unknown
Debut: 13 Apr 1895 v Newcastle United
Position: Forward
Appearances: 1 **Goals scored:** 0
Seasons: 1894/95
Clubs: Cowlairs, Bolton Wanderers, Newton Heath, Derby County

SCOTT MCGARVEY
Country: Scotland
Born: 22 Apr 1963
Debut: 10 Sep 1980 v Leicester City
Position: Forward
Appearances: 13 (12) **Goals scored:** 3
Seasons: 1980/81 – 1982/83
Clubs: Manchester United, Wolverhampton Wanderers, Portsmouth, Carlisle United, Grimsby Town, Bristol City, Oldham Athletic, Wigan Athletic, Mazda, Aris Limassol, Derry City, Barrow, Witton Albion

PATRICK MCGIBBON
Country: Northern Ireland
Born: 6 Sep 1973
Debut: 20 Sep 1995 v York City

Above: 13 February 1987. Alex Ferguson with Paul McGrath (l) and Bryan Robson at Old Trafford.

Right: 9 March 1976. Sammy McIlroy celebrates after scoring a goal in the FA Cup sixth round replay against Wolverhampton Wanderers in his most prolific season, when he scored 13 goals.

Opposite: Future United manager Wilf McGuinness (l) and Jackie Blanchflower in the 1950s.

Position: Defender
Appearances: 1 **Goals scored:** 0
Seasons: 1995/96
Clubs: Portadown, Manchester United, Swansea City, Wigan Athletic, Scunthorpe United, Tranmere Rovers, Glentoran

CHARLES MCGILLIVRAY

Country: Scotland
Born: 5 Dec 1912
Debut: 26 Aug 1933 v Plymouth Argyle
Position: Forward
Appearances: 9 **Goals scored:** 0
Seasons: 1933/34
Clubs: Ayr United, Glasgow Celtic, Manchester United, Motherwell, Dundee

JOHN MCGILLIVRAY

Country: England
Born: Apr 1886 **Died:** Unknown
Debut: 11 Jan 1908 v Blackpool
Position: Midfield
Appearances: 4 **Goals scored:** 0
Seasons: 1907/08 - 1908/09
Clubs: Berry's Association, Manchester United, Southport Central, Stoke, Dartford

WILLIAM MCGLEN

Country: England
Born: 27 Apr 1921
Debut: 31 Aug 1946 v Grimsby Town
Position: Full back/Midfield
Appearances: 122 **Goals scored:** 2
Seasons: 1946/47 - 1951/52
Clubs: Manchester United, Lincoln City, Oldham
Died: 23 Dec 1999

CHRISTOPHER MCGRATH

Country: Northern Ireland
Born: 29 Nov 1954
Debut: 23 Oct 1976 v Norwich City
Position: Midfield
Appearances: 15 (19) **Goals scored:** 1
Seasons: 1976/77 - 1980/81
Clubs: Tottenham Hotspur, Millwall, Manchester United, Tulsa Roughnecks, South China

PAUL MCGRATH

Country: Republic of Ireland
Born: 4 Dec 1959
Debut: 10 Nov 1982 v Bradford City
Position: Defender
Appearances: 192 (7) **Goals scored:** 16
Seasons: 1982/83 - 1988/89
Clubs: St. Patrick's Athletic, Manchester United, Aston Villa, Derby County, Sheffield United

McGrath was a powerful, composed central defender. He led by example and was unlucky to suffer several serious injuries throughout his career. He was voted Man of the Match as United won the 1985 FA Cup final. After United he joined Aston Villa where he won two League Cups. He won 83 caps for the Republic of Ireland between 1985 and 1997.

WILFRED 'WILF' MCGUINNESS

Country: England
Born: 25 Oct 1937
Debut: 8 Oct 1955 v Wolverhampton Wanderers

Position: Wing half
Appearances: 85 **Goals scored:** 2
Seasons: 1955/56 - 1959/60
Clubs: Manchester United

Wilf McGuinness struggled to get into the United side before Munich, because he was battling against Duncan Edwards for his place. Afterwards, he went on to win two England caps before his career was ended by a broken leg. He became a coach, and worked with England during the 1966 World Cup before succeeding Sir Matt Busby as United manager in 1969.

SAMUEL 'SAMMY' MCILROY

Country: Northern Ireland
Born: 2 Aug 1954
Debut: 6 Nov 1971 v Manchester City
Position: Midfield
Appearances: 391 (28) **Goals scored:** 71
Seasons: 1971/72 - 1981/82
Clubs: Manchester United, Stoke City, Manchester City, Orgryte IS, Bury, Admira Wacker, Preston North End, Northwich Victoria

In November 1971 an explosive debut from 17 year-old Sammy McIlroy in the Manchester derby game guaranteed him an immediate place in the hearts of United faithful. He went on to play 419 games, scoring 71 times along the way. Although he appeared in three FA Cup finals he tasted victory just once, United's 2-1 victory over Liverpool in the 1977 Wembley showpiece. He won 88 caps and scored five goals for Northern Ireland, playing in all of the country's matches during both the 1982 and 1986 World Cups, captaining the side in the latter tournament.

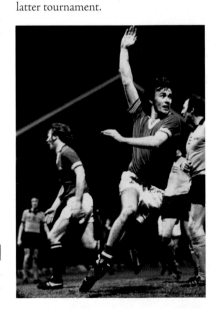

Above: Circa 1979. Gordon McQueen works out in the gym.

EDWARD JOSEPH MCILVENNY
Country: USA
Born: 21 Oct 1924 **Died:** 18 May 1989
Debut: 19 Aug 1950 v Fulham
Position: Midfield
Appearances: 2 **Goals scored:** 0
Seasons: 1950/51
Clubs: Morton, Wrexham, Philadelphia Nationals, Manchester United, Waterford United, Headington United

WILLIAM 'BILL' MCKAY
Country: Scotland
Born: 24 Aug 1906 **Died:** Unknown
Debut: 17 Mar 1934 v Fulham
Position: Midfield
Appearances: 182 **Goals scored:** 15
Seasons: 1933/34 - 1938/39
Clubs: East Stirlingshire, Hamilton Academicals, Bolton Wanderers, Manchester United, Stalybridge Celtic

COLIN MCKEE
Country: Scotland
Born: 22 Aug 1973
Debut: 8 May 1994 v Coventry City
Position: Forward
Appearances: 1 **Goals scored:** 0
Seasons: 1993/94
Clubs: Manchester United, Bury, Kilmarnock, Partick Thistle, Falkirk, Queen of the South, Ross County, Stirling Albion, Vikingur, Queen's Park, Fauldhouse United

GEORGE MCLACHLAN
Country: Scotland
Born: 21 Sep 1902 **Died:** Unknown
Debut: 21 Dec 1929 v Leeds United
Position: Winger
Appearances: 116 **Goals scored:** 4
Seasons: 1929/30 - 1932/33
Clubs: Queen's Park Strollers, King's Park Strollers, Cardiff City, Manchester United, Chester, Le Havre

HUGH MCLENAHAN
Country: England
Born: 23 Mar 1909 **Died:** May 1988
Debut: 4 Feb 1928 v Tottenham Hotspur
Position: Midfield
Appearances: 116 **Goals scored:** 12
Seasons: 1927/28 - 1936/37
Clubs: Blackpool, Stockport County, Manchester United, Notts County

SAMUEL MCMILLAN
Country: Northern Ireland
Born: 20 Sep 1941
Debut: 4 Nov 1961 v Sheffield Wednesday
Position: Forward
Appearances: 15 **Goals scored:** 6
Seasons: 1961/62 - 1962/63
Clubs: Manchester United, Wrexham, Southend United, Chester, Stockport County, Oswestry Town

WALTER MCMILLEN
Country: Northern Ireland
Born: 24 Nov 1913 **Died:** 11 May 1987
Debut: 16 Sep 1933 v Brentford
Position: Midfield
Appearances: 29 **Goals scored:** 2
Seasons: 1933/34 - 1934/35
Clubs: Carrick Fergus Distillery, Cliftonville Strollers, Cliftonville Olympic, Manchester United, Chesterfield

JAMES MCNAUGHT
Country: Scotland
Born: 8 Jun 1870 **Died:** Mar 1919
Debut: 2 Sep 1893 v Burnley
Position: Midfield
Appearances: 162 **Goals scored:** 12
Seasons: 1893/94 - 1897/98
Clubs: Linfield, Newton Heath, Tottenham Hotspur, Maidstone United

THOMAS MCNULTY
Country: England
Born: 30 Dec 1929 **Died:** Apr 1979
Debut: 15 Apr 1950 v Portsmouth
Position: Full back
Appearances: 60 **Goals scored:** 0
Seasons: 1949/50 - 1953/54
Clubs: Manchester United, Liverpool

FRANCIS MCPHERSON
Country: England
Born: 14 May 1901 **Died:** 5 Mar 1953
Debut: 25 Aug 1923 v Bristol City
Position: Forward
Appearances: 175 **Goals scored:** 52
Seasons: 1923/24 - 1927/28
Clubs: Barrow, Manchester United, Manchester Central, Watford

GORDON MCQUEEN
Country: Scotland
Born: 26 Jun 1952
Debut: 25 Feb 1978 v Liverpool
Position: Centre back
Appearances: 229 **Goals scored:** 26

Seasons: 1977/78 - 1983/84
Clubs: St. Mirren, Leeds United, Manchester United, Seiko SA

Straight-talking and a robust centre back who joined United for £450,000 from Leeds United, a record for a defender. On signing he famously remarked that "ninety nine per cent of players want to play for Manchester United and the rest are liars." McQueen scored the first goal in the ill-fated 3-2 FA Cup defeat in 1979, but grabbed a FA Cup winners medal in 1983 against Brighton. He lost his place to Paul McGrath in 1985 and left the club shortly after.

HENRY 'HARRY' MCSHANE
Country: Scotland
Born: 8 Apr 1920
Debut: 13 Sep 1950 v Aston Villa
Position: Winger
Appearances: 57 **Goals scored:** 8
Seasons: 1950/51 - 1953/54
Clubs: Blackburn Rovers, Huddersfield Town, Bolton Wanderers, Manchester United, Oldham Athletic, Chorley, Wellington Town, Droylsden

THOMAS MEEHAN
Country: England
Born: Jun 1896 **Died:** 18 Aug 1924
Debut: 1 Sep 1919 v Sheffield Wednesday
Position: Midfield
Appearances: 53 **Goals scored:** 6
Seasons: 1919/20 - 1920/21
Clubs: Rochdale, Manchester United, Chelsea

JOHN MELLOR
Country: England
Born: Jul 1906 **Died:** Unknown
Debut: 15 Sep 1930 v Huddersfield Town
Position: Full back
Appearances: 122 **Goals scored:** 0
Seasons: 1930/31 - 1936/37
Clubs: Witton Albion, Manchester United, Cardiff City

ALEXANDER MENZIES
Country: Scotland
Born: 25 Nov 1882 **Died:** Unknown
Debut: 17 Nov 1906 v Sheffield Wednesday
Position: Forward
Appearances: 25 **Goals scored:** 4
Seasons: 1906/07 - 1907/08
Clubs: Blantyre Victoria, Heart of Midlothian, Motherwell, Arluthie, Manchester United, Luton Town

JOHN WILLIAM 'JACK' MEW
Country: England
Born: 30 Mar 1889 **Died:** 16 Jan 1963
Debut: 26 Oct 1912 v Middlesbrough
Position: Goalkeeper
Appearances: 199 **Goals scored:** 0
Seasons: 1912/13 - 1925/26

Clubs: Marley Hill United, Manchester United, Barrow

Relatively short for a goalkeeper at 5ft 8ins, but was highly respected nonetheless. Mew won a Central League championship with the reserves before breaking into the first team where he missed just four games in four seasons. He played once for England at the age of 31 and later became a coach in Belgium.

ROBERT MILARVIE

Country: Scotland
Born: 1864 **Died:** Nov 1912
Debut: 4 Oct 1890 v Higher Walton
Position: Forward
Appearances: 1 **Goals scored:** 0
Seasons: 1890/91
Clubs: Hibernian, Stoke City, Bursley Port Vale, Derby County, Newton Heath, Ardwick

GEORGE MILLAR

Country: Scotland
Born: 1874 **Died:** Unknown
Debut: 22 Dec 1894 v Lincoln City
Position: Forward
Appearances: 7 **Goals scored:** 5
Seasons: 1894/95
Clubs: Glasgow Perthshire, Newton Heath, Chatham Town

JAMES MILLER

Country: Scotland
Born: Unknown **Died:** Unknown
Debut: 15 Mar 1924 v Hull City
Position: Forward
Appearances: 4 **Goals scored:** 1
Seasons: 1923/24
Clubs: Port Glasgow Athletic, Blantyre Victoria, Hamilton Academicals, St. Mirren, Morton, Grimsby Town, Manchester United, York City, Boston Town, Shirebrook

LIAM MILLER

Country: Republic of Ireland
Born: 13 Feb 1981
Debut: 11 Aug 2004 v Dinamo Bucharest
Position: Midfield
Appearances: 11 (11) **Goals scored:** 2
Seasons: 2004/05 - 2005/06
Clubs: Glasgow Celtic, AGF Aarhus, Manchester United, Leeds United, Sunderland, Queens Park Rangers, Hibernian, Perth Glory

THOMAS MILLER

Country: Scotland
Born: 30 Jun 1890 **Died:** 3 Sep 1958
Debut: 25 Sep 1920 v Tottenham Hotspur
Position: Forward
Appearances: 27 **Goals scored:** 8
Seasons: 1920/21
Clubs: Larkhall Hearts, Glenview, Third Lanark, Larkhall United, Hamilton Academical, Liverpool, Manchester United, Heart of Midlothian

RALPH MILNE

Country: Scotland
Born: 13 May 1961
Debut: 19 Nov 1988 v Southampton
Position: Winger
Appearances: 26 (4) **Goals scored:** 3
Seasons: 1988/89 - 1989/90
Clubs: Dundee United, Charlton Athletic, Bristol City, Manchester United, West Ham United, Sing Tao

ANDREW MITCHELL

Country: Scotland
Born: Unknown **Died:** Unknown
Debut: 10 Sep 1892 v Burnley
Position: Full back
Appearances: 61 **Goals scored:** 0
Seasons: 1892/93 - 1893/94
Clubs: Airdrieonians, Manchester United, Burton Swifts

ANDREW MITCHELL

Country: England
Born: 20 Apr 1907 **Died:** 3 Dec 1971
Debut: 18 Mar 1933 v Notts County
Position: Winger
Appearances: 1 **Goals scored:** 0
Seasons: 1932/33
Clubs: Coxhoe Albion, Ferryhill Athletic, Crook Town, Sunderland, Cockfield, Notts County, Darlington, Manchester United, Hull City

J MITCHELL

Country: Unknown
Born: Unknown **Died:** Unknown
Debut: 30 Oct 1886 v Fleetwood Rangers
Position: Full back
Appearances: 3 **Goals scored:** 0
Seasons: 1886/87 and 1890/91
Clubs: Bolton Wanderers, Newton Heath

CHARLES 'CHARLIE' MITTEN

Country: England
Born: 17 Jan 1921 **Died:** 2 Jan 2002
Debut: 31 Aug 1946 v Grimsby Town
Position: Winger
Appearances: 162 **Goals scored:** 61
Seasons: 1946/47 - 1949/50
Clubs: Manchester United, Santa Fe, Fulham

While he signed with the club in 1936, Mitten's first professional appearance did not come until 1946 because of the Second World War. Playing on the wing, Mitten would help the club win the FA Cup in 1948. In 1950 he was approached to play for Independiente Santa Fe in Bogotá. In accepting the money to play, Mitten was nicknamed "The Bogotá Bandit." A year later on his return to England, United, who still owned the player, and Matt Busby suspended him for six months before selling him to Fulham.

HENRY 'HARRY' MOGER

Country: England
Born: Sep 1879 **Died:** 16 Jun 1927
Debut: 10 Oct 1903 v Barnsley
Position: Goalkeeper
Appearances: 266 **Goals scored:** 0
Seasons: 1903/04 - 1911/12
Clubs: Freemantle, Southampton, Manchester United

Tall and lean, Harry Moger joined United in 1903 and would stay with the club until 1912 when he retired. In a career spanning 266 appearances, he picked up two league championships – in 1907-08 and 1910-11, and the FA Cup in 1909. He died at the age of 47.

IAN MOIR

Country: Scotland
Born: 30 Jun 1943
Debut: 1 Oct 1960 v Bolton Wanderers
Position: Winger
Appearances: 45 **Goals scored:** 5
Seasons: 1960/61 - 1964/65
Clubs: Manchester United, Chester City, Wrexham, Shrewsbury Town, Arcadia Shepherds, Oswestry Town, Colwyn Bay

ARCHIBALD MONTGOMERY

Country: Scotland
Born: 27 Jan 1873 **Died:** 5 Jan 1922
Debut: 16 Sep 1905 v Glossop
Position: Goalkeeper
Appearances: 3 **Goals scored:** 0
Seasons: 1905/06
Clubs: Glasgow Rangers, Bury, Manchester United

Left: February 1949. "The Bogotá Bandit" Charlie Mitten in action.

JAMES MONTGOMERY
Country: England
Born: 1890 **Died:** 14 Nov 1960
Debut: 13 Mar 1915 v Bradford City
Position: Half back
Appearances: 27 **Goals scored:** 1
Seasons: 1914/15 - 1920/21
Clubs: Glossop, Manchester United

JOHN MOODY
Country: England
Born: 1 Nov 1904 **Died:** 23 Apr 1963
Debut: 26 Mar 1932 v Oldham Athletic
Position: Goalkeeper
Appearances: 51 **Goals scored:** 0
Seasons: 1931/32 - 1932/33
Clubs: Arsenal, Bradford Park Avenue, Doncaster Rovers, Manchester United, Chesterfield

CHARLES WILLIAM 'CHARLIE' MOORE
Country: England
Born: 3 Jun 1898 **Died:** 9 Mar 1966
Debut: 30 Aug 1919 v Derby County
Position: Full back
Appearances: 328 **Goals scored:** 0
Seasons: 1919/20 - 1920/21
and 1922/23 - 1929/30
Clubs: Hednesford Town, Manchester United

Joining United in 1919, Moore was a reliable right back – often playing opposite left back Jack Silcock – for a decade, yet he was never lucky enough to win a medal with United or an England cap – although both were deserved. A recurring injury initially forced his retirement from the game in 1921, but a year later he succeeded in making a comeback, and would play on for eight more years.

GRAHAM MOORE
Country: Wales
Born: 7 Mar 1941
Debut: 9 Nov 1963 v Tottenham Hotspur
Position: Forward
Appearances: 19 **Goals scored:** 5
Seasons: 1963/64
Clubs: Cardiff City, Chelsea, Manchester United, Northampton Town, Charlton Athletic, Doncaster Rovers

KEVIN MORAN
Country: Republic of Ireland
Born: 29 Apr 1956
Debut: 30 Apr 1979 v Southampton
Position: Centre back
Appearances: 284 (5) **Goals scored:** 24
Seasons: 1978/99 - 1987/88
Clubs: Manchester United, Sporting Gijon, Blackburn Rovers

Right: 18 May 1985. Kevin Moran shields the ball from Everton's Trevor Steven and Graeme Sharp during the FA Cup final. He had also been on the winning side in 1983.

Kevin Moran is probably best remembered for being the first player to be sent off in an FA Cup final. He played Gaelic football prior to joining United in 1978 and spent ten seasons in Manchester, playing 289 games and scoring 24 goals. Following his retirement he opened football agency Proactive Sports Management that went on to represent United stars Wayne Rooney and Andy Cole.

HUGH MORGAN
Country: Scotland
Born: 1875 **Died:** Unknown
Debut: 15 Dec 1900 v Lincoln City
Position: Forward
Appearances: 23 **Goals scored:** 4
Seasons: 1900/01
Clubs: Harthill Thistle, Airdrieonians, Sunderland, Bolton Wanderers, Newton Heath, Manchester City, Accrington Stanley, Blackpool

WILLIAM 'BILLY' MORGAN
Country: England
Born: 1878 **Died:** Unknown
Debut: 2 Mar 1897 v Darwen
Position: Midfield
Appearances: 152 **Goals scored:** 7
Seasons: 1896/97 - 1902/03
Clubs: Horwich FC, Newton Heath, Bolton Wanderers, Watford, Leicester Fosse, New Brompton

WILLIAM 'WILLIE' MORGAN
Country: Scotland
Born: 2 Oct 1944
Debut: 28 Aug 1968 v Tottenham Hotspur
Position: Winger
Appearances: 293 (3) **Goals scored:** 34
Seasons: 1968/69 - 1974/75
Clubs: Burnley, Manchester United, Bolton Wanderers, Chicago Sting, Minnesota Kicks, Blackpool

Morgan started his career by replacing United-bound John Connelly at Burnley and then came to the Reds in 1968 to replace Connelly again. He played in the World Cup for Scotland in 1974 and the Reds' promotion team a year later. Playing usually on the right wing, he won 21 caps for Scotland as well as the Division Two title with United.

KENNETH 'KENNY' MORGANS
Country: Wales
Born: 16 Mar 1939
Debut: 21 Dec 1957 v Leicester City
Position: Winger
Appearances: 23 **Goals scored:** 0
Seasons: 1957/58 - 1960/61
Clubs: Manchester United, Swansea Town, Newport County

Kenny Morgans played in the European Cup quarter-final against Red Star Belgrade on 5 February 1958 and survived the Munich air crash, returning to the side two months later.

JOHN MORRIS
Country: England
Born: 27 Sep 1923 **Died:** 6 Apr 2011
Debut: 26 Oct 1946 v Sunderland
Position: Forward
Appearances: 93 **Goals scored:** 35
Seasons: 1946/47 - 1948/49
Clubs: Manchester United, Derby County, Leicester City, Corby Town

RAVEL MORRISON
Country: England
Born: 2 Feb 1993
Debut: 26 Oct 2010 v Wolverhampton Wanderers
Position: Midfield
Appearances: 0 (1) **Goals scored:** 0
Seasons: 2010/11 - present
Clubs: Manchester United

Position: Midfield
Appearances: 93 (5) **Goals scored:** 18
Seasons: 1982/83 – 1984/85
Clubs: Volendam, Ajax Amsterdam, FC Twente, Ipswich Town, Manchester United

PHILIP MULRYNE
Country: Northern Ireland
Born: 1 Jan 1978
Debut: 14 Oct 1997 v Ipswich Town
Position: Midfield
Appearances: 4 (1) **Goals scored:** 0
Seasons: 1997/98 – 1998/99
Clubs: Manchester United, Norwich City, Cardiff City, Leyton Orient, King's Lynn

ROBERT MURRAY
Country: Scotland
Born: 27 Mar 1915 **Died:** Unknown
Debut: 28 Aug 1937 v Newcastle United
Position: Forward
Appearances: 4 **Goals scored:** 0
Seasons: 1937/38
Clubs: Heart of Midlothian, Manchester United, Bath City

GEORGE MUTCH
Country: Scotland
Born: 21 Nov 1912 **Died:** 30 Mar 2001
Debut: 25 Aug 1934 v Bradford City
Position: Forward
Appearances: 120 **Goals scored:** 49
Seasons: 1934/35 – 1937/38
Clubs: Arbroath, Manchester United, Preston North End, Bury, Southport

JOSEPH MYERSCOUGH
Country: England
Born: 8 Aug 1893 **Died:** 29 Jul 1975
Debut: 4 Sep 1920 v Bolton Wanderers
Position: Forward
Appearances: 34 **Goals scored:** 8
Seasons: 1920/21 – 1922/23
Clubs: Lancaster Town, Manchester United, Bradford Park Avenue

'NANI' LUIS CARLOS ALMEIDA DA CUNHA
Country: Portugal
Born: 17 Nov 1986
Debut: 5 Aug 2007 v Chelsea
Position: Winger
Appearances: 123 (33) **Goals scored:** 29
Seasons: 2007/08 - present
Clubs: Sporting Lisbon, Manchester United

Joined United from Sporting Lisbon, Nani is a winger of pace and trickery, who is also an established international with Portugal, scoring nine goals in 45 appearances for his country. He was voted the United Players' Player of the Year in 2011.

THOMAS MORRISON
Country: Northern Ireland
Born: 16 Dec 1874 **Died:** 26 Mar 1940
Debut: 25 Dec 1902 v Manchester City
Position: Forward
Appearances: 36 **Goals scored:** 8
Seasons: 1902/03 – 1903/04
Clubs: Glentoran, Burnley, Glasgow Celtic, Manchester United, Colne FC

BENJAMIN MORTON
Country: England
Born: 28 Aug 1910 **Died:** Nov 1962
Debut: 16 Nov 1935 v West Ham United
Position: Forward
Appearances: 1 **Goals scored:** 0
Seasons: 1935/36
Clubs: Stourbridge FC, Wolverhampton Wanderers, Manchester United, Torquay United, Swindon Town

REMI MARK MOSES
Country: England
Born: 14 Nov 1960
Debut: 19 Sep 1981 v Swansea City
Position: Midfield

Appearances: 188 (11) **Goals scored:** 12
Seasons: 1981/82 – 1987/88
Clubs: West Bromwich Albion, Manchester United

Joined United along with Bryan Robson as ex-West Bromwich Albion manager Ron Atkinson came to Old Trafford and brought in his former players. Moses was the first black player to score for the Reds. He was unlucky to miss the 1983 and 1985 FA Cup finals, the first through injury and the second due to a suspension. Moses was a key defensive midfielder during the 1980s, but suffered a succession of serious injuries that eventually forced him out of the team. At 28, he retired from the game during the 1988-89 season.

ARNOLD MUHREN
Country: Netherlands
Born: 2 Jun 1951
Debut: 28 Aug 1982 v Birmingham City

Above: 12 March 1983. Remi Moses in action during the sixth round FA Cup tie against Everton, which United won 1-0. Moses played in every round bar the final.

Above: 14 April 1979. Jimmy Nicholl heads the ball during a First Division game against Liverpool. He had helped beat the Merseysiders in the 1977 FA Cup final, and won 73 caps for Northern Ireland between 1976 and 1986. He was sold by Ron Atkinson after the arrival of John Gidman.

DANIEL NARDIELLO
Country: England
Born: 22 Oct 1982
Debut: 5 Nov 2001 v Arsenal
Position: Forward
Appearances: 1 (3) **Goals scored:** 0
Seasons: 2001/02 – 2003/04
Clubs: Manchester United, Swansea City, Barnsley, Queens Park Rangers, Blackpool, Hartlepool United, Bury, Oldham Athletic, Exeter City

PHILIP 'PHIL' NEVILLE
Country: England
Born: 21 Jan 1977
Debut: 28 Jan 1995 v Wrexham
Position: Full back, Midfield
Appearances: 301 (85) **Goals scored:** 89
Seasons: 1994/95 – 2004/05
Clubs: Manchester United, Everton

Philip Neville is the younger brother of United stalwart Gary Neville. Despite not always being a regular starter, Phil Neville picked up six Premier League titles, three FA Cups and a UEFA Champions League medal during his United career. He was mainly used at left back, but was a versatile player who could deputise in midfield. In 2005, ten years after making his Old Trafford bow, Neville moved to Everton where took up a central midfield role, becoming club captain in 2007. He has been capped by England 59 times.

GEORGE NEVIN
Country: England
Born: 16 Dec 1907 **Died:** Jan 1973
Debut: 6 Jan 1934 v Lincoln City
Position: Full back
Appearances: 5 **Goals scored:** 0
Seasons: 1933/34
Clubs: Newcastle United, Sheffield Wednesday, Manchester United, Burnley, Lincoln City

ERIK NEVLAND
Country: Norway
Born: 10 Nov 1977
Debut: 14 Oct 1997 v Ipswich Town
Position: Forward
Appearances: 2 (4) **Goals scored:** 1
Seasons: 1997/98 – 1998/99
Clubs: Viking FK, Manchester United, IFK Goteborg, FC Groningen, Fulham

PERCY NEWTON
Country: England
Born: Jan 1904 **Died:** Unknown
Debut: 3 Feb 1934 v Burnley
Position: Defender
Appearances: 2 **Goals scored:** 0
Seasons: 1933/34
Clubs: Sandbach Ramblers, Manchester United, Tranmere Rovers

JAMES 'JIMMY' NICHOLL
Country: Northern Ireland
Born: 28 Feb 1956
Debut: 5 Apr 1975 v Southampton
Position: Full back
Appearances: 235 (13) **Goals scored:** 6
Seasons: 1974/75 – 1981/82
Clubs: Manchester United, Sunderland, Toronto Blizzard, Glasgow Rangers, West Bromwich Albion, Dunfermline Athletic, Raith Rovers, Bath City

JAMES NICHOLSON
Country: Northern Ireland
Born: 27 Feb 1943
Debut: 24 Aug 1960 v Everton
Position: Midfield
Appearances: 68 **Goals scored:** 6
Seasons: 1960/61 – 1962/63
Clubs: Manchester United, Huddersfield Town, Bury, Mossley, Stalybridge Celtic

GEORGE NICOL
Country: Scotland
Born: 14 Dec 1903 **Died:** 18 Dec 1968
Debut: 11 Feb 1928 v Leicester City
Position: Forward
Appearances: 7 **Goals scored:** 2
Seasons: 1927/28 – 1928/29
Clubs: Saltcoats Victoria, Manchester United, Brighton and Hove Albion, Glenavon, Gillingham, RC Roubaix

ROBERT 'BOBBY' NOBLE
Country: England
Born: 18 Dec 1945
Debut: 9 Apr 1966 v Leicester City
Position: Full back
Appearances: 33 **Goals scored:** 0
Seasons: 1965/66 – 1966/67
Clubs: Manchester United

JOSEPH NORTON
Country: England
Born: Jul 1890 **Died:** Unknown
Debut: 24 Jan 1914 v Oldham Athletic
Position: Forward
Appearances: 37 **Goals scored:** 3
Seasons: 1913/14 – 1914/15
Clubs: Stockport County, Manchester United, Leicester City, Bristol Rovers, Swindon Town

ALEXANDER NOTMAN
Country: Scotland
Born: 10 Dec 1979
Debut: 2 Dec 1998 v Tottenham Hotspur
Position: Forward
Appearances: 0 (1) **Goals scored:** 0
Seasons: 1998/99
Clubs: Manchester United, Aberdeen, Sheffield United, Norwich City, King's Lynn, Boston United, Wrexham, Formartine United

THOMAS NUTTALL
Country: England
Born: Jan 1889 **Died:** Oct 1963
Debut: 23 Mar 1912 v Liverpool
Position: Forward
Appearances: 16 **Goals scored:** 4
Seasons: 1911/12 – 1912/13
Clubs: Heywood United, Manchester United, Everton

GARY NEVILLE

Country: England
Born: 18 Feb 1975
Debut: 16 Sep 1992 v Torpedo Moscow
Position: Full back
Appearances: 566 (36) **Goals scored:** 7
Seasons: 1992/93 – 2010/11
Clubs: Manchester United

There was no player more passionate about Manchester United in the modern era than Gary Neville. The rugged full back wore his heart on his sleeve and, in so doing, won the hearts of the supporters. During his 19-year career at Old Trafford – including five seasons as club captain – and 602 games, there were many more skilful players in red, but Neville brought that extra amount of desire that help feed his teammates with an outstanding will to win.

Neville signed with United straight from school in 1991 aged just 16, and was part of a successful youth team that included his younger brother Phil and future greats David Beckham, Ryan Giggs and Paul Scholes. His elevation to the first team came at the tender age of 17 1/2 in September the following year, as a substitute in a UEFA Cup match at Old Trafford. Early in the 1994-95 season he got his chance to be the club's regular right back after injuries plagued the United's defence, but it took until the spring before he made the position his own. Neville eventually played in all the crucial end-of-season games that season including the FA Cup final, which United lost 1-0 to Everton.

The young Red Devil had now been a squad member for three seasons, but had won no medals, a situation that was remedied over the next 16 years as Neville became a fixture in the side, racking up 19 winners' medals.

He was first picked for his country in 1995 and was first choice right back by the time of the Euro 96 championships, staged in England. Neville would eventually play in the 1998 World Cup (he missed out in 2002 with a broken foot) and the 2000 and 2004 European Championship – compiling a total of 85 international appearances.

During his halcyon days in the late 1990s and early 2000s, it was Neville's partnership with his good friend David Beckham on the team's right-hand side that proved to be a major force for the Reds. Their understanding and Neville's selfless running and overlapping were a constant threat, while the defender also tackled like a terrier.

His unrestrained passion for United also brought controversy – most typically in a goal celebration directly in front of Liverpool fans in the January 2006 match at Old Trafford. Neville ran from the halfway line to show his joy, but the FA fined him £5,000 for the privilege, while the player countered that it was better than players acting "like robots".

Into his mid-30s, Neville was increasingly troubled by a variety of injuries, making just one substitute appearance in 2007-08. Bravely he kept returning to first team action, albeit on increasingly rare occasions and made just 52 starts in his last three seasons as his playing career wound down.

Always much-loved by the fans, Neville – called "the best English right back of his generation" by Sir Alex Ferguson – stands fifth in the all-time list of United player appearances. He retired in February 2011 and moved into TV punditry.

Left: 1 August 2000. A portrait of Gary Neville.

Below: 26 May 2009. At a United training session before the Champions League final against Barcelona at the Stadio Olimpico in Rome.

GABRIEL OBERTAN
Country: France
Born: 26 Feb 1989
Debut: 27 Oct 2009 v Barnsley
Position: Winger
Appearances: 13 (15) **Goals scored:** 1
Seasons: 2009/10 - 2010/11
Clubs: Bordeaux, Lorient, Manchester United

GEORGE O'BRIEN
Country: England
Born: Unknown **Died:** Unknown
Debut: 7 Apr 1902 v Middlesbrough
Position: Winger
Appearances: 1 **Goals scored:** 0
Seasons: 1901/02
Clubs: Newton Heath

LIAM O'BRIEN
Country: Republic of Ireland
Born: 5 Sep 1964
Debut: 20 Dec 1986 v Leicester City
Position: Midfield
Appearances: 17 (19) **Goals scored:** 2
Seasons: 1986/87 - 1988/89
Clubs: Bohemians, Shamrock Rovers, Manchester United, Newcastle United, Tranmere Rovers, Cork City

PATRICK O'CONNELL
Country: Republic of Ireland
Born: 8 Mar 1887 **Died:** 27 Feb 1959
Debut: 2 Sep 1914 v Oldham Athletic
Position: Defender
Appearances: 35 **Goals scored:** 2

Seasons: 1914/15
Clubs: Sheffield Wednesday, Hull City, Manchester United, Dumbarton, Ashington

JOHN O'KANE
Country: England
Born: 15 Nov 1974
Debut: 21 Sep 1994 v Port Vale
Position: Full back
Appearances: 5 (2) **Goals scored:** 0
Seasons: 1994/95 - 1996/97
Clubs: Manchester United, Bury, Bradford City, Everton, Burnley, Bolton Wanderers, Blackpool, Hyde United

ROBERT LESLIE 'LES' OLIVE
Country: England
Born: 27 Apr 1928 **Died:** 20 May 2006
Debut: 11 Apr 1953 v Newcastle United
Position: Goalkeeper
Appearances: 2 **Goals scored:** 0
Seasons: 1952/53
Clubs: Manchester United

Although he had only a brief playing career for United, Les Olive was assistant secretary at Old Trafford at the time of the Munich disaster, and would succeed Walter Crickmer, who died in the crash as secretary. He worked for the club until 2005.

JESPER OLSEN
Country: Denmark
Born: 20 Mar 1961
Debut: 25 Aug 1984 v Watford
Position: Winger
Appearances: 149 (27) **Goals scored:** 24
Seasons: 1984/85 - 1987/88
Clubs: Naestved, Ajax Amsterdam, Manchester United, Bordeaux, Caen

THOMAS O'NEIL
Country: England
Born: 25 Oct 1952 **Died:** May 2006
Debut: 5 May 1971 v Manchester City
Position: Full back
Appearances: 68 **Goals scored:** 0
Seasons: 1970/71 - 1972/73
Clubs: Manchester United, Blackpool, Southport, Tranmere Rovers, Halifax Town

T O'SHAUGHNESSY
Country: Unknown
Born: Unknown **Died:** Unknown
Debut: 25 Oct 1890 v Bootle Reserves
Position: Forward
Appearances: 1 **Goals scored:** 0
Seasons: 1890/91
Clubs: Newton Heath

JOHN O'SHEA
Country: Republic of Ireland
Born: 30 Apr 1981
Debut: 13 Oct 1999 v Aston Villa
Position: Defender, Midfield

Appearances: 301 (92) **Goals scored:** 15
Seasons: 1999/00 - 2010/11
Clubs: Waterford Bohemians, Manchester United, Bournemouth (*loan*), Royal Antwerp (*loan*), Sunderland

Irishman John O'Shea spent 13 seasons at United as a reliable and flexible squad player. During his time at Old Trafford he operated in both full back slots, as well as centre back, central midfield, striker and even on one occasion deputising as goalkeeper. After winning five league titles and numerous other honours he transferred to Sunderland in July 2011. He has played for the Republic of Ireland on 70 occasions.

GEORGE OWEN
Country: Wales
Born: 1865 **Died:** 29 Jan 1922
Debut: 18 Jan 1890 v Preston North End
Position: Forward
Appearances: 1 **Goals scored:** 0
Seasons: 1889/90
Clubs: Chirk, Newton Heath, West Manchester

JOHN OWEN
Country: Wales
Born: 1866 **Died:** Unknown
Debut: 18 Jan 1890 v Preston North End
Position: Midfield
Appearances: 6 **Goals scored:** 0
Seasons: 1889/90 - 1891/92
Clubs: Chirk, Newton Heath

MICHAEL OWEN
Country: England
Born: 14 Dec 1979
Debut: 9 Aug 2009 v Chelsea
Position: Forward
Appearances: 15 (33) **Goals scored:** 14
Seasons: 2009/10 - present
Clubs: Liverpool, Real Madrid, Newcastle United, Manchester United

WILLIAM 'BILL' OWEN
Country: Wales
Born: Unknown **Died:** Unknown
Debut: 15 Oct 1898 v Birmingham City
Position: Winger
Appearances: 1 **Goals scored:** 0
Seasons: 1898/99
Clubs: Newton Heath

WILLIAM OWEN
Country: England
Born: 17 Sep 1906 **Died:** 26 Mar 1981
Debut: 22 Sep 1934 v Norwich City
Position: Forward
Appearances: 17 **Goals scored:** 1
Seasons: 1934/35 - 1935/36
Clubs: Northwich Victoria, Macclesfield Town, Manchester United, Reading

P

LOUIS PAGE

Country: England
Born: 27 Mar 1899 **Died:** 11 Oct 1959
Debut: 25 Mar 1932 v Charlton Athletic
Position: Forward
Appearances: 12 **Goals scored:** 0
Seasons: 1931/32 - 1932/33
Clubs: Stoke City, Northampton Town, Burnley, Manchester United, Port Vale, Yeovil and Petters United

ALBERT PAPE

Country: England
Born: 13 Jun 1897 **Died:** 18 Nov 1955
Debut: 7 Feb 1925 v Leyton Orient
Position: Forward
Appearances: 18 **Goals scored:** 5
Seasons: 1924/25 - 1925/26
Clubs: Rotherham County, Notts County, Clapton Orient, Manchester United, Fulham, Rhyl Athletic, Hurst, Darwen, Manchester Central, Hartlepool United, Halifax Town, Burscough Rangers, Horwich RMI, Nelson

JI-SUNG PARK

Country: South Korea
Born: 25 Feb 1981
Debut: 9 Aug 2005 v Debrecen
Position: Midfield
Appearances: 127 (50) **Goals scored:** 24
Seasons: 2005/06 - present
Clubs: Kyoto Purple Sanga, PSV Eindhoven, Manchster United

Ji-Sung Park is the most decorated Asian player in history of the game, and is the first Asian player to win a Champions League medal. He had moved to PSV Eindhoven when South Korea team manager, Guus Hiddink, took up the reins at the club. Sir Alex Ferguson signed him for £4 million. Park can play anywhere in the midfield and is renowned for his work rate, fitness and team-minded approach. He has won 100 caps for South Korea including an appearance in the 2002 World Cup semi-final. Park retired form international football after the Asian Cup in 2011.

PAUL PARKER

Country: England
Born: 4 Apr 1964
Debut: 17 Aug 1991 v Notts County
Position: Full back
Appearances: 137 (9) **Goals scored:** 2
Seasons: 1991/92 - 1995/96
Clubs: Fulham, Queens Park Rangers, Manchester United, Derby County, Sheffield United, Chelsea

Along with Peter Schmeichel, Parker was the last piece in the defensive jigsaw that would form the basis of Alex Ferguson's first great United side: Schmeichel, Parker, Irwin, Bruce and Pallister were the bedrock of his first two title-winning sides. After winning the double in 1994, injury and then the emergence of Gary Neville limited his appearances, and Parker was then sold on to Derby County.

SAMUEL PARKER

Country: Scotland
Born: 1872 **Died:** Unknown
Debut: 13 Jan 1894 v Sheffield Wednesday
Position: Forward
Appearances: 12 **Goals scored:** 0
Seasons: 1893/94
Clubs: Hurlford FC, Newton Heath, Burnley,

THOMAS PARKER

Country: England
Born: 22 Nov 1906 **Died:** 11 Nov 1964
Debut: 11 Oct 1930 v West Ham United
Position: Defender
Appearances: 17 **Goals scored:** 0
Seasons: 1930/31 - 1931/32
Clubs: Manchester United, Bristol City, Carlisle United, Stalybridge Celtic

ROBERT PARKINSON

Country: England
Born: 27 Apr 1873 **Died:** Unknown
Debut: 11 Nov 1899 v Barnsley
Position: Forward
Appearances: 15 **Goals scored:** 7
Seasons: 1899/00
Clubs: Rotherham Town, Luton Town, Blackpool, Warmley, Nottingham Forest, Newton Heath, Watford, Swindon Town

EDWARD 'TEDDY' PARTRIDGE

Country: England
Born: 13 Feb 1891 **Died:** Jun 1970
Debut: 9 Oct 1920 v Oldham Athletic
Position: Winger
Appearances: 160 **Goals scored:** 18
Seasons: 1920/21 - 1928/29
Clubs: Ebbw Vale FC, Manchester United, Halifax Town

STEVEN WILLIAM 'STEVE' PATERSON

Country: Scotland
Born: 8 Apr 1958
Debut: 29 Sep 1976 v Ajax Amsterdam
Position: Defender
Appearances: 5 (5) **Goals scored:** 0
Seasons: 1976/77 - 1979/80
Clubs: Nairn County, Manchester United, Sheffield United, Hong Kong Rangers, Yomiuri

ERNEST PAYNE

Country: England

Born: 23 Dec 1884 **Died:** 10 Sep 1961
Debut: 27 Feb 1909 v Nottingham Forest
Position: Winger
Appearances: 2 **Goals scored:** 1
Seasons: 1908/09
Clubs: Worcester City, Manchester United

STEPHEN PEARS

Country: England
Born: 22 Jan 1962
Debut: 12 Jan 1985 v Coventry City
Position: Goalkeeper
Appearances: 5 **Goals scored:** 0
Seasons: 1984/85
Clubs: Manchester United, Middlesbrough, Liverpool, Hartlepool United

MARK PEARSON

Country: England
Born: 28 Oct 1939
Debut: 19 Feb 1958 v Sheffield Wednesday
Position: Forward
Appearances: 80 **Goals scored:** 14
Seasons: 1957/58 - 1962/63
Clubs: Manchester United, Sheffield Wednesday, Fulham, Halifax Town, Bacup Borough

Below: March 1994. Paul Parker.

STANLEY 'STAN' PEARSON
Country: England
Born: 11 Jan 1919 **Died:** 20 Feb 1997
Debut: 13 Nov 1937 v Chesterfield
Position: Forward
Appearances: 343 **Goals scored:** 148
Seasons: 1937/38 - 1953/54
Clubs: Manchester United, Bury, Chester City

Unlucky to spend most of his peak years in the army during the Second World War, Stan Pearson was nonetheless a fabulously successful goalscorer, netting six hat-tricks as a Red. He scored in the 1948 FA Cup final win and collected a league championship medal in 1952. Pearson played on until he was 40.

STUART PEARSON
Country: England
Born: 21 Jun 1949
Debut: 17 Aug 1974 v Leyton Orient
Position: Forward
Appearances: 179 (1) **Goals scored:** 66
Seasons: 1974/75 - 1978/79
Clubs: Hull City, Manchester United, West Ham United

Known as Pancho, Pearson was brought to Old Trafford to help the team escape from the Second Division, and his 17 league goals in 1974-75 did the trick. It was Pearson's shot from Jimmy Greenhoff's pass that gave United their first goal against Liverpool as they went on to win the 1977 FA Cup final. He was capped by England on 15 occasions.

JACK PEDDIE
Country: Scotland
Born: 3 Mar 1876 **Died:** 20 Oct 1928
Debut: 6 Sep 1902 v Gainsborough Trinity
Position: Forward
Appearances: 121 **Goals scored:** 58
Seasons: 1902/03 and 1904/05 - 1906/07
Clubs: Newcastle United, Manchester United, Plymouth Argyle, Manchester United, Heart of Midlothian

JOHN PEDEN
Country: Northern Ireland
Born: 11 Mar 1865 **Died:** Sep 1944
Debut: 2 Sep 1893 v Burnley
Position: Winger
Appearances: 32 **Goals scored:** 8
Seasons: 1893/94
Clubs: Linfield, Newton Heath, Sheffield United, Distillery

DAVID PEGG
Country: England
Born: 20 Sep 1935 **Died:** 6 Feb 1958
Debut: 6 Dec 1952 v Middlesbrough
Position: Winger
Appearances: 150 **Goals scored:** 28
Seasons: 1952/53 - 1957/58
Clubs: Manchester United

David Pegg was a young left winger of outstanding potential when he was killed in the Munich air crash; he had fatally moved to the back of the plane just before take-off. On leaving school, Pegg was signed by United in 1950 and made his first team debut at the age of 17. He and Albert Scanlon vied to succeed Jack Rowley as outside left after he finished in 1954-55. Yorkshireman Pegg was the trickier of the two, while Scanlon was more direct. Pegg had recently lost his place to Scanlon at the time of the disaster, but had picked up two league title medals the previous two seasons, and in 1957 had just won his first England cap; it was thought by many that he was the natural replacement in the national team for the great Tom Finney. He was buried in Redhouse Cemetery near the village of Highfields where he was born.

ERNEST 'DICK' PEGG
Country: England
Born: Jul 1878 **Died:** 11 Jun 1916
Debut: 6 Sep 1902 v Gainsborough Trinity
Position: Forward
Appearances: 51 **Goals scored:** 20
Seasons: 1902/03 - 1903/04
Clubs: Loughborough Town, Kettering, Reading, Preston North End, Manchester United, Fulham, Barnsley

JAMES KENNETH PEGG
Country: England
Born: 4 Jan 1926 **Died:** 25 Aug 1999
Debut: 15 Nov 1947 v Derby County
Position: Goalkeeper
Appearances: 2 **Goals scored:** 0
Seasons: 1947/48
Clubs: Manchester United, Torquay United

FRANCIS PEPPER
Country: England
Born: Jul 1875 **Died:** Unknown
Debut: 10 Dec 1898 v Blackpool
Position: Defender
Appearances: 8 **Goals scored:** 0
Seasons: 1898/99
Clubs: Sheffield United, Newton Heath, Barnsley

GEORGE PERRINS
Country: England
Born: 24 Feb 1873 **Died:** Unknown
Debut: 3 Sep 1892 v Blackburn Rovers
Position: Half back
Appearances: 98 **Goals scored:** 0
Seasons: 1892/93 - 1895/96
Clubs: Birmingham St. George's, Newton Heath, Luton Town

JAMES PETERS
Country: England
Born: Unknown **Died:** Unknown
Debut: 8 Sep 1894 v Burton Wanderers
Position: Winger
Appearances: 51 **Goals scored:** 14
Seasons: 1894/95 - 1895/96
Clubs: Heywood Central, Newton Heath, New Brompton, Sheppey United

MICHAEL 'MIKE' PHELAN
Country: England
Born: 24 Sep 1962
Debut: 19 Aug 1989 v Arsenal
Position: Defender/Midfield
Appearances: 127 (19) **Goals scored:** 3
Seasons: 1989/90 - 1993/94
Clubs: Burnley, Norwich, Manchester United, West Bromwich Albion

Mike Phelan followed Steve Bruce from Norwich to United for £750,000 in July 1989. A right back who also played on the right or in the centre of midfield, his playing career at United was largely ended by the arrival of a new generation of young players, and in 1994 he moved to West Bromwich Albion. After retiring from playing and a period in management, Phelan took up a role with United's Centre of Excellence and was promoted to first-team coach in 2001. Following Carlos Queiroz's departure, he was appointed assistant manager in 2008.

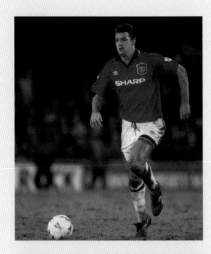

GARY PALLISTER

Country: England
Born: 30 Jun 1965
Debut: 30 Aug 1989 v Norwich City
Position: Defender
Appearances: 433 (4) **Goals scored:** 15
Seasons: 1989/90 – 1997/98
Clubs: Middlesbrough, Darlington (*loan*), Manchester United, Middlesbrough

United's history is filled with countless superb goalscorers and forward talent, but there is also a long list of outstanding defenders, and Gary Pallister's name is always mentioned near the top. Brought to Old Trafford by Alex Ferguson as one of the last pieces of his league-winning jigsaw, Pallister provided size, steadiness and ability both in the air and on the ground.

Although born in Kent, Pallister was raised in the north-east and was spotted playing for Billingham Town by scouts from nearby Middlesbrough, the team he supported as a boy. At the start of the 1985-86 season, Pallister made his Boro debut and would play for the club for four seasons through increasingly troubled times (financially, the club was within hours of going out of business at one point) – eventually ending up in the Third Division with them.

Under manager Bruce Rioch the team had pulled together winning an automatic return to the Second Division and then back to the First Division the following season. However, while starting well back in the top flight, a mid-season slump meant they were relegated back to the Second Division and Pallister was sold to Manchester United for a then national record transfer fee of £2.3 million.

His new manager Alex Ferguson was still waiting to win his first trophy at Old Trafford and the arrival of Pallister proved to be crucial to the FA Cup win against Crystal Palace that came at the end of the season. Still, the centre back needed to improve and the United backroom staff put their new star defender on a weight training regime that helped put muscle on his relatively skinny 6 ft 5 in frame.

The improved body weight helped enormously and, along with his centre back partner Steve Bruce, Pallister became a lynch pin of the defence. In fact, the pair became nicknamed Dolly and Daisy. Pallister was also a model of consistency and during three seasons from 1992 to 1995, when United began winning multiple trophies, he missed only one league game. During this era Ferguson relied on his centre backs to provide the platform to launch their attacks and to win a first league championship in 26 years.

The partnership with Bruce lasted for seven seasons, but by 1996-97 other centre backs came along to pair with Pallister, who himself lasted only one more season at Old Trafford.

As well as winning four Premiership title medals, three FA Cups and a European Cup-Winners' Cup, Pallister was honoured as the Professional Footballers' Association Player of the Year in 1992. There was also international recognition with a total of 22 caps, starting in 1988 when he was still with Boro. For United he scored 15 goals and fans with a memory of the 1996-97 Premiership title still recall his brace against Liverpool in April of that season that brought a 3-1 win and helped clinch another title.

After nine years in Manchester and 437 appearances, Pallister moved back to Middlesbrough in a transfer that cost the north-east club £2.5 million, £200,000 more than his selling price. But after three seasons undermined by injury, Pallister retired from the game – firstly to become a media pundit and then, in 2010, he was appointed operations director at Darlington FC, a club where he had spent a short loan spell early in his career.

Left: 7 March 1995. United central defender Gary Pallister who won 22 England international caps.

Below: 3 May 1993. Gary Pallister celebrates his goal during the league match against Blackburn Rovers at Old Trafford. United won 3-1 to become Premier League Champions.

Above: Circa 1952. Albert Quixall is pictured repairing and cleaning his football boots in his early days at Sheffield Wednesday.

JOHN PICKEN
Country: Scotland
Born: 1880 **Died:** 31 Jul 1952
Debut: 2 Sep 1905 v Bristol City
Position: Forward
Appearances: 122 **Goals scored:** 46
Seasons: 1905/06 - 1910/11
Clubs: Bolton Wanderers, Plymouth Argyle, Manchester United, Burnley, Bristol City

KEVIN PILKINGTON
Country: England
Born: 8 Mar 1974
Debut: 19 Nov 1994 v Crystal Palace
Position: Goalkeeper
Appearances: 6 (2) **Goals scored:** 0
Seasons: 1994/95 - 1997/98
Clubs: Manchester United, Rochdale (loan), Rotherham United, Glasgow Celtic (loan), Port Vale, Aberystwyth Town, Mansfield Town, Notts County, Luton Town

MICHAEL PINNER
Country: England
Born: 16 Feb 1934
Debut: 4 Feb 1961 v Aston Villa
Position: Goalkeeper
Appearances: 4 **Goals scored:** 0
Seasons: 1960/61
Clubs: Aston Villa, Sheffield Wednesday, Queens Park Rangers, Manchester United, Chelsea, Swansea City, Leyton Orient, Lisburn Distillery

GERARD PIQUE
Country: Spain
Born: 2 Feb 1987
Debut: 26 Oct 2004 v Crewe Alexandra
Position: Defender
Appearances: 14 (9) **Goals scored:** 2
Seasons: 2004/05 - 2007/08
Clubs: Manchester United, Real Zaragoza (loan), Barcelona

KAREL POBORSKY
Country: Czech Republic
Born: 30 Mar 1972
Debut: 11 Aug 1996 v Newcastle United
Position: Winger
Appearances: 28 (20) **Goals scored:** 6
Seasons: 1996/97 - 1997/98
Clubs: Ceske Budejovice, Viktoria Zizkov, Slavia Prague, Manchester United, Benfica, Lazio, Sparta Prague

WILLIAM PORTER
Country: England
Born: Jul 1905 **Died:** 28 Apr 1946
Debut: 19 Jan 1935 v Barnsley
Position: Full back
Appearances: 65 **Goals scored:** 0
Seasons: 1934/35 - 1937/38
Clubs: Oldham Athletic, Manchester United, Hyde United

RODRIGO POSSEBON
Country: Brazil
Born: 13 Feb 1989
Debut: 17 Aug 2008 v Newcastle United
Position: Midfield
Appearances: 3 (5) **Goals scored:** 0
Seasons: 2008/09
Clubs: Manchester United, Sporting Braga (loan), Santos

ARTHUR POTTS
Country: England
Born: 26 Jun 1888 **Died:** Jan 1981
Debut: 9 Jan 1915 v Sheffield Wednesday
Position: Forward
Appearances: 29 **Goals scored:** 5
Seasons: 1913/14 - 1919/20
Clubs: Willenhall Swifts, Manchester United, Wolverhampton Wanderers

JOHN POWELL
Country: Wales
Born: 25 Mar 1860 **Died:** 16 Mar 1947
Debut: 30 Oct 1886 v Fleetwood Rangers
Position: Full back
Appearances: 4 **Goals scored:** 0
Seasons: 1886/87 - 1890/91
Clubs: Druids, Bolton Wanderers, Newton Heath

JOHN PRENTICE
Country: Scotland
Born: 19 Oct 1898 **Died:** 28 Jun 1966
Debut: 2 Apr 1920 v Bradford Park Avenue
Position: Winger
Appearances: 1 **Goals scored:** 0
Seasons: 1919/20
Clubs: Manchester United, Swansea City

STEPHEN PRESTON
Country: England
Born: 1879 **Died:** Unknown

Debut: 7 Sep 1901 v Gainsborough Trinity
Position: Forward
Appearances: 34 **Goals scored:** 14
Seasons: 1901/02 – 1902/03
Clubs: Newton Heath, Manchester
United, Stockport County

ALBERT PRINCE

Country: England
Born: 1895 **Died:** Unknown
Debut: 27 Feb 1915 v Everton
Position: Forward
Appearances: 1 **Goals scored:** 0
Seasons: 1914/15
Clubs: Manchester United, Stafford Rangers

D PRINCE

Country: Unknown
Born: Unknown **Died:** Unknown
Debut: 4 Nov 1893 v Darwen
Position: Winger
Appearances: 2 **Goals scored:** 0
Seasons: 1893/94
Clubs: Newton Heath

WILLIAM PRUNIER

Country: France
Born: 14 Aug 1967
Debut: 30 Dec 1995 v Queens Park Rangers
Position: Defender
Appearances: 2 **Goals scored:** 0
Seasons: 1995/96
Clubs: Auxerre, Marseilles, Bordeaux, Manchester
United, Copenhagen, Montpellier, Napoli, Heart
of Midlothian, KV Kortrijk, Toulouse, Al-Siliya

DANIEL 'DANNY' PUGH

Country: English
Born: 19 Oct 1982
Debut: 18 Sep 2002 v Maccabi Haifa
Position: Midfield
Appearances: 3 (4) **Goals scored:** 0
Seasons: 2002/03 – 2003/04
Clubs: Manchester United, Leeds United,
Preston North End, Stoke City

JAMES PUGH

Country: England
Born: Jul 1891 **Died:** Unknown
Debut: 29 Apr 1922 v Cardiff City
Position: Full back
Appearances: 2 **Goals scored:** 0
Seasons: 1921/22 – 1922/23
Clubs: Brighton and Hove Albion, Hereford
United, Bridgend Town, Abertillery,
Manchester United, Wrexham

JOHN QUINN

Country: Scotland
Born: 1890 **Died:** Unknown
Debut: 3 Apr 1909 v Sheffield Wednesday
Position: Forward

Appearances: 2 **Goals scored:** 0
Seasons: 1908/09 – 1909/10
Clubs: Higher Broughton, Cheatham Hill,
Manchester City, Manchester United, Nelson F.C.

ALBERT QUIXALL

Country: England
Born: 9 Aug 1933
Debut: 20 Sep 1958 v Tottenham Hotspur
Position: Forward
Appearances: 184 **Goals scored:** 56
Seasons: 1958/59 – 1963/64
Clubs: Sheffield Wednesday, Manchester United,
Oldham Athletic, Stockport County, Altrincham

While at Sheffield Wednesday, Quixall
was a star of English football. He was
signed by Matt Busby in September
1958 for a then British record fee of
£45,000. Busby saw Quixall as a key part
of his post-Munich team re-building.
During his first season Quixall helped
the team go on a run of only two losses
in 23 matches to end the campaign as
runners-up in the First Division. He
would score 56 goals in 184 games for
United, but his only medal with the club
was the FA Cup in 1963. He was capped
five times for England.

PAUL RACHUBKA

Country: England
Born: 21 May 1981
Debut: 31 Oct 2000 v Watford
Position: Goalkeeper
Appearances: 1 (2) **Goals scored:** 0
Seasons: 1999/00 – 2000/01
Clubs: Manchester United, Royal Antwerp
(loan), Oldham Athletic (loan), Charlton Athletic,
Burnley, Milton Keynes Dons, Northampton Town,
Huddersfield Town, Peterborough United, Blackpool

GEORGE RADCLIFFE

Country: England
Born: Unknown **Died:** Unknown
Debut: 12 Apr 1899 v Luton Town
Position: Winger
Appearances: 1 **Goals scored:** 0
Seasons: 1898/99
Clubs: Newton Heath

CHARLES RADFORD

Country: England
Born: 19 Mar 1900 **Died:** 14 Jul 1924
Debut: 7 May 1921 v Derby County
Position: Full back
Appearances: 96 **Goals scored:** 1
Seasons: 1920/21 – 1923/24
Clubs: Walsall, Manchester United

DANIEL ROBERTSON 'ROBERT' RAMSAY

Country: England
Born: Oct 1864 **Died:** Unknown
Debut: 4 Oct 1890 v Higher Walton
Position: Defender
Appearances: 1 **Goals scored:** 0
Seasons: 1890/91
Clubs: Stoke City, Newton Heath
West Manchester FC

CHARLES RAMSDEN

Country: England
Born: 11 Jun 1904 **Died:** 16 Feb 1975
Debut: 24 Sep 1927 v Tottenham Hotspur
Position: Winger
Appearances: 16 **Goals scored:** 3
Seasons: 1927/28 – 1930/31
Clubs: Rotherham Town, Stockport County,
Manchester United, Manchester North End

WILLIAM RATTIGAN

Country: England
Born: Apr 1868 **Died:** Unknown
Debut: 25 Oct 1890 v Bootle Reserves
Position: Midfield
Appearances: 1 **Goals scored:** 0
Seasons: 1890/91
Clubs: Newton Heath

WILLIAM ERNEST 'BILL' RAWLINGS

Country: England
Born: 3 Jan 1896 **Died:** 25 Sep 1972
Debut: 14 Mar 1928 v Everton
Position: Forward
Appearances: 36 **Goals scored:** 19
Seasons: 1927/28 – 1929/30
Clubs: Southampton, Manchester United, Port
Vale, New Milton, Newport (Isle of Wight)

THOMAS HERBERT 'BERT' READ

Country: England
Born: Unknown **Died:** Unknown
Debut: 6 Sep 1902 v Gainsborough Trinity
Position: Full back
Appearances: 42 **Goals scored:** 0
Seasons: 1902/03 – 1903/04
Clubs: Stretford F.C., Manchester
City, Manchester United

WILLIAM REDMAN

Country: England
Born: 29 Jan 1928 **Died:** Dec 1994
Debut: 7 Oct 1950 v Sheffield Wednesday
Position: Full back
Appearances: 38 **Goals scored:** 0
Seasons: 1950/51 – 1953/54
Clubs: Manchester United, Bury, Buxton

HUBERT REDWOOD

Country: England
Born: Jul 1913 **Died:** 28 Sep 1943
Debut: 21 Dec 1935 v Tottenham Hotspur
Position: Full back
Appearances: 93 **Goals scored:** 4
Seasons: 1935/36 – 1938/39
Clubs: New Brighton, Manchester United

THOMAS REID
Country: Scotland
Born: 15 Aug 1905 **Died:** Jul 1972
Debut: 2 Feb 1929 v West Ham United
Position: Forward
Appearances: 101 **Goals scored:** 67
Seasons: 1928/29 – 1932/33
Clubs: Clydebank, Liverpool, Oldham
Athletic, Manchester United, Barrow, Rhyl

CLATWORTHY 'CHARLIE' RENNOX
Country: Scotland
Born: 25 Feb 1897 **Died:** 1967
Debut: 14 Mar 1925 v Portsmouth
Position: Forward
Appearances: 68 **Goals scored:** 25
Seasons: 1924/25 – 1926/27
Clubs: Dykehead, Wishaw, Clapton Orient,
Manchester United, Grimsby Town

FELIPE RICARDO
Country: Spain
Born: 30 Dec 1971
Debut: 18 Sep 2002 v Maccabi Haifa
Position: Goalkeeper
Appearances: 3 (2) **Goals scored:** 0
Seasons: 2002/03
Clubs: Atletico Madrid, Valladolid, Manchester
United, Racing Santander, Osasuna

CHARLES RICHARDS
Country: England
Born: 9 Aug 1885 **Died:** Unknown
Debut: 6 Sep 1902 v Gainsborough Trinity
Position: Forward
Appearances: 11 **Goals scored:** 2
Seasons: 1902/03
Clubs: Gresley Rovers, Newstead Byron, Notts
County, Nottingham Forest, Grimsby Town, Leicester
Fosse, Manchester United, Doncaster Rovers

WILLIAM 'BILLY' RICHARDS
Country: England
Born: 6 Oct 1874 **Died:** 12 Feb 1926
Debut: 21 Dec 1901 v Port Vale
Position: Forward
Appearances: 9 **Goals scored:** 1
Seasons: 1901/02
Clubs: West Bromwich Albion, Manchester
United, Leicester Fosse

KIERAN RICHARDSON
Country: England
Born: 21 Oct 1984
Debut: 23 Oct 2002 v Olympiakos
Position: Winger/Midfield
Appearances: 44 (37) **Goals scored:** 11
Seasons: 2002/03 – 2006/07
Clubs: Manchester United, West
Bromwich Albion (loan), Sunderland

LANCE RICHARDSON
Country: England
Born: Apr 1899 **Died:** 22 Sep 1958
Debut: 1 May 1926 v West Bromwich Albion
Position: Goalkeeper

Appearances: 42 **Goals scored:** 0
Seasons: 1925/26 – 1928/29
Clubs: South Shields, Chopwell,
Manchester United, Reading

WILLIAM RIDDING
Country: England
Born: 4 Apr 1911 **Died:** 1981
Debut: 25 Dec 1931 v Wolverhampton Wanderers
Position: Forward
Appearances: 44 **Goals scored:** 14
Seasons: 1931/32 – 1933/34
Clubs: Manchester City, Manchester United

JOSEPH RIDGWAY
Country: England
Born: 25 Apr 1873 **Died:** Unknown
Debut: 11 Jan 1896 v Rotherham United
Position: Goalkeeper
Appearances: 17 **Goals scored:** 0
Seasons: 1895/96 – 1897/98
Clubs: West Manchester F.C., Newton
Heath, Rochdale Town

JOHN JAMES 'JIMMY' RIMMER
Country: England
Born: 10 Feb 1948
Debut: 15 Apr 1968 v Fulham
Position: Goalkeeper
Appearances: 45 (1) **Goals scored:** 0
Seasons: 1967/68 – 1972/73
Clubs: Manchester United, Swansea City (loan),
Arsenal, Aston Villa, Hamrun Spartans, Luton Town

ANDREW 'ANDY' RITCHIE
Country: England
Born: 28 Nov 1960
Debut: 26 Dec 1977 v Everton
Position: Forward
Appearances: 32 (10) **Goals scored:** 13
Seasons: 1977/78 – 1980/81
Clubs: Manchester United, Brighton
and Hove Albion, Leeds United,
Oldham Athletic, Scarborough

JOHN ROACH
Country: England
Born: Unknown **Died:** Unknown
Debut: 5 Jan 1946 v Accrington Stanley
Position: Full back
Appearances: 2 **Goals scored:** 0
Seasons: 1945/46
Clubs: Manchester United

DAVID ROBBIE
Country: Scotland
Born: 6 Oct 1899 **Died:** 4 Dec 1978
Debut: 28 Sep 1935 v Southampton
Position: Winger
Appearances: 1 **Goals scored:** 0
Seasons: 1935/36
Clubs: Renton, Bury, Plymouth
Argyle, Manchester United

ROBERT ROBERTS
Country: England
Born: 1892 **Died:** Unknown

Debut: 27 Dec 1913 v Sheffield Wednesday
Position: Full back
Appearances: 2 **Goals scored:** 0
Seasons: 1913/14
Clubs: Altrincham, Manchester United

W A ROBERTS
Country: Unknown
Born: Unknown **Died:** Unknown
Debut: 18 Feb 1899 v Loughborough Town
Position: Winger
Appearances: 10 **Goals scored:** 2
Seasons: 1898/99 – 1899/00
Clubs: Newton Heath

ALEXANDER ROBERTSON
Country: Scotland
Born: Unknown **Died:** Unknown
Debut: 5 Sep 1903 v Bristol City
Position: Winger
Appearances: 34 **Goals scored:** 10
Seasons: 1903/04 – 1904/05
Clubs: Hibernian, Fair City
Athletic, Manchester United

ALEXANDER 'SANDY' ROBERTSON
Country: Scotland
Born: 1878 **Died:** Unknown
Debut: 5 Sep 1903 v Bristol City
Position: Half back
Appearances: 35 **Goals scored:** 1
Seasons: 1903/04 – 1905/06
Clubs: Dundee, Middlesbrough, Manchester
United, Bradford Park Avenue

THOMAS ROBERTSON
Country: Scotland
Born: 1875 **Died:** Unknown
Debut: 5 Sep 1903 v Bristol City
Position: Forward
Appearances: 3 **Goals scored:** 0
Seasons: 1903/04
Clubs: East Benhar Heatherbell, Motherwell,
Fauldhouse, Heart of Midlothian, Liverpool,
Dundee, Manchester United,

WILLIAM ROBERTSON
Country: Scotland
Born: 20 Apr 1907 **Died:** 1980
Debut: 17 Mar 1934 v Fulham
Position: Midfield
Appearances: 50 **Goals scored:** 1
Seasons: 1933/34 – 1935/36
Clubs: Stoke City, Manchester United, Reading

MARK ROBINS
Country: England
Born: 22 Dec 1969
Debut: 12 Oct 1988 v Rotherham United
Position: Forward
Appearances: 27 (43) **Goals scored:** 17
Seasons: 1988/89 – 1991/92
Clubs: Manchester United, Norwich City,
Leicester City, Copenhagen (loan), Reading
(loan), CD Ourense, Panionios, Manchester City
(loan), Walsall, Rotherham United, Bristol City
(loan), Sheffield Wednesday, Burton Albion

CHARLES 'CHARLIE' ROBERTS

Country: England
Born: 6 Apr 1883 **Died:** 7 Aug 1939
Debut: 23 Apr 1904 v Burton United
Position: Half back
Appearances: 302 **Goals scored:** 23
Seasons: 1903/04 - 1912/13
Clubs: Bishop Auckland, Grimsby Town,
Manchester United, Oldham Athletic

For many reasons, Charlie Roberts can be thought of as having been born ahead of his time – with his on-field clothing, his fight for a footballers' union and his dedication to his trade. All these things looked eccentric in the early 20th century, but would later be regarded as visionary.

Born in Darlington in 1883, Roberts was only a teenager when he starred for Bishop Auckland, one of the best amateur teams in the north-east of England. Grimsby Town then signed him as a professional at the age of 20, but after only 31 games the much-admired Roberts was on his way to Manchester.

The Second Division club had re-invented itself under the name of Manchester United after more than two decades as Newton Heath and, with new owners spending new-found cash, Roberts was seen as a key acquisition. The six-foot tall Roberts made his debut for United at the tail end of the 1903-04 season and two years later helped the Reds back into the First Division. However, the player started courting trouble with Football Association – bizarrely, by wearing shorts that were cut high up on the thigh (1970s style) rather than fashionably covering the knee. Although the FA passed a law banning Roberts' style of shorts, he carried on wearing them regardless.

With United in the First Division, Roberts was joined by Billy Meredith and a host of ex-Manchester City players who then took the Red Devils to their first ever league title in 1907-08 and repeated the feat in 1910-11, and winning the FA Cup in between.

Despite enjoying a frosty relationship with the football authorities, Roberts was capped for England three times, becoming United's first England international player. The centre half famed for his tackling, stamina and attacking style also played for the prestigious Football League XI on nine occasions. His battles the football law makers and custodians of the game was clearly ingrained, and in 1907 Roberts was one of the players who helped form the first ever Players' Union.

The union was highly unpopular with club owners and the FA, and it is not unsurprising that Roberts never played for England again despite his natural strength and speed (he could run the 100-yard dash in eleven seconds). When the Association Football Players Union (AFPU) came to an end in 1909, Roberts said: "As far as I am concerned, I would have seen the FA in Jericho before I would have resigned membership of that body, because it was our strength and right arm, but I was only one member. To the shame of the majority, they voted the only power they had away from themselves and the FA knew it."

Aged just 30 and still a star for United, Roberts was transferred in August 1913 to near neighbours Oldham Athletic for a phenomenal £1,750. He played there for just two seasons and managed the club for one season after the war, but without much success. In 1928, he joined up again with Billy Meredith and formed another local club, Manchester Central, but it lasted only four years. After complaining for many years of dizzy spells, Roberts died in hospital in Manchester after a cranial operation in 1939 aged 56.

Left: Circa 1908. Charlie Roberts, United centre half who won three England international caps in 1905.

Below: 2 September 1912. A modern-looking player with his 1970s style shorts that caused so many problems. Seen here before kicking off against Arsenal.

BRYAN ROBSON

Country: England
Born: 11 Jan 1957
Debut: 7 Oct 1981 v Tottenham Hotspur
Position: Midfield
Appearances: 437 (24) **Goals scored:** 99
Seasons: 1981/82 - 1993/94
Clubs: West Bromwich Albion,
Manchester United, Middlesbrough

In the great tradition of United number 7s, Bryan Robson was a leader among men. As an inspirational captain with endless stamina, the ability to score key goals, pick pinpoint passes and defend heroically, he embodied the spirit that typified the Reds during his 13 seasons at Old Trafford. In a career marred by serious injury, he led club and country on many occasions with a never-say-die attitude that lifted those around him.

Robson was one of a long line of great footballers to come out of the north-east of England. Born in Chester-le-Street, he began his career aged 15 as an apprentice at West Bromwich Albion in 1972. He signed professional forms in the summer of 1974 and made his debut towards the end of that season in a 3-1 victory over York City.

He started his career playing variously at left back and centre half, but as a combative ball winner Robson's natural position was centre midfield. However, he was soon to succumb to the type of injury jinx that would beset him throughout his career. Three broken legs in the space of a single season threatened his future, but against the odds he made a full recovery.

He played at The Hawthorns under Ron Atkinson and when Big Ron moved to United, the manager took Robson with him in October 1981 for the then British record fee of £1.5 million. The player's debut came in a 1-0 League Cup defeat to Tottenham Hotspur in October 1981. Three days later he made his league debut wearing the number 7 shirt that was to become his own in a goalless draw with Manchester City.

His first season at Old Trafford ended with 32 appearances and five goals as he also became a regular in Ron Greenwood's England side. At the 1982 World Cup, Robson wrote himself into the record books with a goal after just 27 seconds against France, a mark that stood for 20 years.

The following season Robson was made Red Devils club captain. Despite injuring ankle ligaments in a League Cup semi-final victory, he returned to inspire United to victory in the FA Cup final, scoring twice in the replayed final against Brighton & Hove Albion. He selflessly declined the opportunity of a Cup final hat-trick, allowing regular penalty taker Arnold Muhren to convert the spot-kick which sealed a 4-0 win.

For many people, his finest hour in a United shirt came the next season, when United took on Barcelona – Maradona and all – in the European Cup-Winners' Cup quarter-final. Behind 2-0 after the first leg in Spain, he led a stunning fightback at Old Trafford, scoring twice in front of a passionate crowd of over 58,000.

In 1985 Robson led United to another FA Cup triumph as the Reds defeated league champions Everton 1-0 thanks to a Norman Whiteside winner. Now as captain of the national side, Robson and England went to Mexico in 1986 for the World Cup with high hopes. However a shoulder injury in the group stages against Morocco ruled him out of the tournament.

In the same year, Atkinson was sacked as United manager, but new boss Alex Ferguson kept faith with Robson as captain. He was awarded an OBE for services to football in January 1990. That year he would lift another trophy as United beat Crystal Palace 1-0, once again in an FA Cup final replay. Injury restricted him to just 20 league appearances with United in that season and the club finished 13th, but the following summer he captained England for a second time in the World Cup. Once again injury curtailed his tournament, when Achilles tendon and toe injuries flared up.

After a testimonial in 1990, Robson picked up his first European silverware in 1991, helping United beat Barcelona in the Cup-Winners' Cup. He continued to lead by example as the Reds then mounted a challenge for the league in 1991-92, only to be overhauled by Leeds United. In the same season, Robson was absent through injury when United won their first League Cup title, beating Nottingham Forest 1-0 at Wembley.

By now, Robson's influence was diminishing and the following season, 1992-93, he was blighted by back and hamstring problems, restricting him to just 14 appearances. Yet this was the season that saw United's 26-year wait for the league title come to an end. Robson made only six starts, but the season finished on a personal high as he scored

Above: 18 May 1985. United captain Bryan Robson clutches his winner's medal during the lap of honour after his team's victory over Everton in the FA Cup final.

Right: 1 January 1994. Bryan Robson in action against Leeds United during his final season with the Reds.

against Wimbledon on the final day of the season to seal the first league championship medal.

The next season was to be Robson's last at Old Trafford. Ferguson had gathered a large squad and the club skipper was playing only a limited role. Nevertheless, he made enough appearances to pick up a second championship medal, his final game coming at home in a 0-0 draw with Coventry. His had been a career at United of great credit and, in addition to domestic league titles and cups, he picked up three Charity Shields along with the Super Cup in 1991. For England, Robson won 90 caps and scored 26 goals.

During his 13 seasons Bryan Robson made 461 appearances and scored 99 goals. In May 1994 he moved to Middlesbrough, taking on the role of player manager and led the club from the First Division to the Premier League in his first season. Marquee signings such as Brazilian star Juninho followed as Boro reached both domestic finals in 1997. Yet they fell at the last hurdle in both finals and were to suffer the added pain of relegation. They won promotion back at the first time of asking, but after being relegated once again in 2001, Robson left the club by mutual consent.

Managerial spells with Bradford City, Sheffield United and West Bromwich

Albion followed before a return to United in 2008 in an ambassadorial capacity. In 2009 Robson was then offered his first international manager's post, taking charge of the Thai national team.

In March 2011 it as revealed that Robson had undergone a successful operation for throat cancer and in June that year he resigned as manager of Thailand.

Compared to more recent United heroes, Robson's career honours might seem minimal, yet his inspirational displays and role as powerhouse and motivator during a period of Liverpool dominance made the man christened Captain Marvel a heroic presence in the distinguished history of United leaders.

Above: 3 October 1981. United chairman Martin Edwards, secretary Les Olive and manager Ron Atkinson watch as Bryan Robson completes his £1,5 million transfer to Old Trafford from West Bromwich Albion.

JAMES ROBINSON
Country: Northern Ireland
Born: 8 Jan 1898 **Died:** Unknown
Debut: 3 Jan 1920 v Chelsea
Position: Forward
Appearances: 21 **Goals scored:** 3
Seasons: 1919/20 – 1921/22
Clubs: Manchester United, Tranmere Rovers

MATTHEW ROBINSON
Country: England
Born: 21 Apr 1907 **Died:** Aug 1987
Debut: 26 Sep 1931 v Chesterfield
Position: Winger
Appearances: 10 **Goals scored:** 0
Seasons: 1931/32
Clubs: Cardiff City, Manchester United, Chester City

LEE ROCHE
Country: England
Born: 28 Oct 1980
Debut: 5 Nov 2001 v Arsenal
Position: Full back
Appearances: 2 (1) **Goals scored:** 0
Seasons: 2001/02 – 2002/03
Clubs: Manchester United, Wrexham, Burnley, Droylsden

PATRICK 'PADDY' ROCHE
Country: Republic of Ireland
Born: 4 Jan 1951
Debut: 8 Feb 1975 v Oxford United
Position: Goalkeeper
Appearances: 53 **Goals scored:** 0
Seasons: 1974/75 – 1981/82
Clubs: Shelbourne, Manchester United, Brentford, Halifax Town

MARTYN ROGERS
Country: England
Born: 26 Jan 1960 **Died:** 1992
Debut: 22 Oct 1977 v West Bromwich Albion
Position: Full back
Appearances: 1 **Goals scored:** 0
Seasons: 1977/78
Clubs: Manchester United, Queens Park Rangers

GIUSEPPE ROSSI
Country: Italy

Born: 1 Feb 1987
Debut: 10 Nov 2004 v Crystal Palace
Position: Forward
Appearances: 6 (8) **Goals scored:** 4
Seasons: 2004/05 – 2005/06
Clubs: AC Parma (*loan*), Manchester United, Newcastle United (*loan*), Villarreal

CHARLES ROTHWELL
Country: England
Born: Unknown **Died:** Unknown
Debut: 2 Dec 1893 v Everton
Position: Forward
Appearances: 3 **Goals scored:** 3
Seasons: 1893/94 – 1896/97
Clubs: Newton Heath

HERBERT ROTHWELL
Country: England
Born: 1880 **Died:** Unknown
Debut: 25 Oct 1902 v Arsenal
Position: Full back
Appearances: 28 **Goals scored:** 0
Seasons: 1902/03
Clubs: Glossop North End, Manchester United, Manchester City

WILLIAM GEORGE ROUGHTON
Country: England
Born: 11 May 1909 **Died:** 7 Jun 1989
Debut: 12 Sep 1936 v Manchester City
Position: Full back
Appearances: 92 **Goals scored:** 0
Seasons: 1936/37 – 1938/39
Clubs: Huddersfield Town, Manchester United

ELIJAH ROUND
Country: England
Born: Jan 1882 **Died:** Unknown
Debut: 9 Oct 1909 v Liverpool
Position: Goalkeeper
Appearances: 2 **Goals scored:** 0
Seasons: 1909/10
Clubs: Barnsley, Oldham Athletic, Manchester United

JOCELYN ROWE
Country: England
Born: Unknown **Died:** Unknown
Debut: 5 Mar 1914 v Preston North End

Position: Full back
Appearances: 1 **Goals scored:** 0
Seasons: 1913/14
Clubs: Manchester United, Bohemians

HENRY ROWLEY
Country: England
Born: 23 Jan 1904 **Died:** 19 Dec 1985
Debut: 27 Oct 1928 v Huddersfield Town
Position: Forward
Appearances: 180 **Goals scored:** 55
Seasons: 1928/29 – 1931/32 and 1934/35 – 1936/37
Clubs: Shrewsbury Town, Manchester United, Manchester City, Oldham Athletic, Burton Albion

EZRA ROYALS
Country: England
Born: Jan 1882 **Died:** Unknown
Debut: 23 Mar 1912 v Liverpool
Position: Goalkeeper
Appearances: 7 **Goals scored:** 0
Seasons: 1911/12 - 1913/14
Clubs: Chesterton White Star, Manchester United, Northwich Victoria

JAMES 'JIMMY' RYAN
Country: Scotland
Born: 12 May 1945
Debut: 4 May 1966 v West Bromwich Albion
Position: Winger
Appearances: 24 (3) **Goals scored:** 4
Seasons: 1965/66 – 1969/70
Clubs: Manchester United, Luton Town, Dallas Tornado

S

DAVID SADLER
Country: England
Born: 5 Feb 1946
Debut: 24 Aug 1963 v Sheffield Wednesday
Position: Forward/Defender
Appearances: 328 (7) **Goals scored:** 27
Seasons: 1963/64 - 1973/74
Clubs: Maidstone United, Manchester United, Preston North End

David Sadler could play in defence, midfield or attack and was the team's utility player for a decade. He helped the club win the 1965 and 1967 First Division championships and took injured Denis Law's place in the team for the European Cup semi-final second leg (he scored the second goal in the 3-3 draw against Real Madrid) and the final in 1968. He left the club in 1974 to join Bobby Charlton-managed Preston North End. He was capped four times by England and is secretary of the Manchester United Former Players' Association.

Right: David Sadler is very proud of his car in a photograph taken outside Old Trafford.

CRISTIANO RONALDO

Country: Portugal
Born: 5 Feb 1985
Debut: 16 Aug 2003 v Bolton Wanderers
Position: Winger
Appearances: 244 (48) **Goals scored:** 118
Seasons: 2003/04 - 2008/09
Clubs: Sporting Lisbon, Manchester United, Real Madrid

It was obvious from an early age that Cristiano Ronaldo was destined to be a great footballer. Blessed with searing pace, trickery with the ball and an eye for goal, at the age of 12 the young Portuguese was using his skills to beat fully grown defenders at local amateur club Andorinha. Ronaldo turned professional in 2001 with Sporting Lisbon and, in the summer of 2003 aged 18, played in a friendly match against United. Ronaldo produced such an impressive performance that some Reds players urged Sir Alex Ferguson sign him there and then.

Ferguson did the deal for £12.24 million and Ronaldo drew rave reviews for his debut in August 2003 when he came on as a substitute against Bolton Wanderers in the first match of the season. Wearing the iconic number 7 shirt that had just beeen vacated by David Beckham, the young winger eventually attracted some criticism for excessive and unproductive showboating, but helped United win the FA Cup in his first season, scoring two goals in the final against Millwall.

In the same summer that he joined United, Ronaldo won his first international cap, and was named player of the tournament at the 2004 European Championships in his home country, where Portugal lost 2-1 to Greece in the final.

In 2006 the fast-maturing Ronaldo helped United win the League Cup, scoring in the final as opponents Wigan Athletic were put to the sword in a 4-0 drubbing.

But it was the next three seasons at Old Trafford that solidified Ronaldo's reputation as one of the world's great players as he scored an incredible 91 goals in all competitions during which United won no fewer than eight trophies. The highlights included three Premiership titles and a Champions League victory over Chelsea in 2008.

The partnership with teammate Wayne Rooney was blossoming and Ronaldo was now becoming the complete attacking weapon himself, by translating his trademark tricks and flicks into more goalscoring conversions. He was also building a reputation as a taker of ferocious free kicks, and could score headed goals with the best centre forwards. Ronaldo sufferd an ankle injury that would require surgery in the summer of 2008, but individual awards came thick and fast. He had already won all the top individual awards in English football when in December 2008, Ronaldo became the first United player since George Best to win the prestigious Ballon D'Or, and in 2009 became the first Premiership player to win the FIFA World Player of the Year.

But by 2008, there were also signs that Ronaldo's time in Manchester was coming to an end. Real Madrid were anxious to sign him and when the Spanish team offered a world record £80 million for his services in June 2009, United felt obliged to accept, in the knowledge that Ronaldo was hankering after a move to the club he had wanted to play for since he was a boy. CR7, as he had become known, left Old Trafford after 292 United appearances and 118 goals. His reputation as a relatively short-lived but much revered great United player secure for all time.

Left: 21 February 2009. Cristiano Ronaldo in typical pose as he lines up a free-kick against Blackburn Rovers.

Below: 30 November 2003. Cristiano Ronaldo in action during a league match against Chelsea.

Born: 10 Oct 1935 **Died:** 22 Dec 2009
Debut: 20 Nov 1954 v Arsenal
Position: Winger
Appearances: 127 **Goals scored:** 35
Seasons: 1954/55 - 1960/61
Clubs: Manchester United, Newcastle United, Lincoln City, Mansfield Town, Belper Town

ALFRED SCHOFIELD
Country: England
Born: 1873 **Died:** Unknown
Debut: 1 Sep 1900 v Glossop
Position: Winger
Appearances: 179 **Goals scored:** 35
Seasons: 1900/01 - 1906/07
Clubs: Everton, Newton Heath, Manchester United

GEORGE SCHOFIELD
Country: England
Born: 6 Aug 1893 **Died:** unknown
Debut: 4 Sep 1920 v Bolton Wanderers
Position: Forward
Appearances: 1 **Goals scored:** 0
Seasons: 1920/21 - 1921/22
Clubs: Southport Junior Football, Manchester United, Crewe Alexandra

CHARLES SAGAR
Country: England
Born: 28 Mar 1878 **Died:** 4 Dec 1919
Debut: 2 Sep 1905 v Bristol City
Position: Forward
Appearances: 33 **Goals scored:** 24
Seasons: 1905/06 - 1906/07
Clubs: Bury, Manchester United

Along with Wayne Rooney, he is the only player to have scored a hat-trick on his debut.

LOUIS SAHA
Country: France
Born: 8 Aug 1978
Debut: 31 Jan 2004 v Southampton
Position: Forward
Appearances: 76 (48) **Goals scored:** 42
Seasons: 2003/04 - 2008/09
Clubs: FC Metz, Newcastle United (*loan*), Fulham, Manchester United, Everton

GEORGE SAPSFORD
Country: England
Born: 10 Mar 1896 **Died:** 17 Oct 1970
Debut: 26 Apr 1920 v Notts County
Position: Forward
Appearances: 53 **Goals scored:** 17
Seasons: 1919/20 - 1921/22
Clubs: Manchester United, Preston North End

CARLO SARTORI
Country: Italy
Born: 10 Feb 1948
Debut: 9 Oct 1968 v Tottenham Hotspur
Position: Midfield
Appearances: 40 (16) **Goals scored:** 6
Seasons: 1968/69 - 1971/72
Clubs: Manchester United, Bologna, Lecco, SPAL 1907, Rimini, Trentino

WILLIAM SARVIS
Country: Wales
Born: Jul 1898 **Died:** 22 Mar 1968
Debut: 23 Sep 1922 v Coventry City
Position: Forward
Appearances: 1 **Goals scored:** 0
Seasons: 1922/23
Clubs: Aberdare Athletic, Merthyr Town, Manchester United, Bradford City, Walsall

JAMES SAUNDERS
Country: England
Born: Oct 1878 **Died:** Unknown
Debut: 26 Dec 1901 v Lincoln City
Position: Goalkeeper
Appearances: 13 **Goals scored:** 0
Seasons: 1901/02 - 1904/05
Clubs: Glossop, Middlesbrough, Newton Heath, Manchester United, Nelson

ROBERT EDWARD 'TED' SAVAGE
Country: England
Born: Jan 1912 **Died:** 30 Jan 1964
Debut: 1 Jan 1938 v Newcastle United
Position: Midfield
Appearances: 5 **Goals scored:** 0
Seasons: 1937/38
Clubs: Lincoln City, Liverpool, Manchester United, Wrexham

THOMAS SAWYER
Country: Unknown
Born: Unknown **Died:** Unknown
Debut: 14 Oct 1899 v Birmingham City
Position: Forward
Appearances: 6 **Goals scored:** 0
Seasons: 1899/1900
Clubs: Newton Heath, Chorley

ALBERT SCANLON
Country: England

JOSEPH SCHOFIELD
Country: England
Born: 1881 **Died:** unknown
Debut: 26 Mar 1904 v Grimsby Town
Position: Forward
Appearances: 2 **Goals scored:** 0
Seasons: 1903/04
Clubs: Brynn Central, Ashton Town, Manchester United, Stockport County

PERCY SCHOFIELD
Country: England
Born: Apr 1893 **Died:** 20 Jun 1968
Debut: 1 Oct 1921 v Preston North End
Position: Forward
Appearances: 1 **Goals scored:** 0
Seasons: 1921/22
Clubs: Eccles Borough, Manchester United, Eccles United

JOHN 'JACKIE' SCOTT
Country: Northern Ireland
Born: 22 Dec 1933 **Died:** Jun 1978
Debut: 4 Oct 1952 v Wolverhampton Wanderers
Position: Forward
Appearances: 3 **Goals scored:** 0
Seasons: 1952/53 - 1955/56
Clubs: Manchester United, Grimsby Town, York City, Margate

JOHN SCOTT
Country: Scotland
Born: unknown **Died:** unknown
Debut: 27 Aug 1921 v Everton
Position: Half back
Appearances: 24 **Goals scored:** 0
Seasons: 1921/22
Clubs: Hamilton Academicals, Bradford Park Avenue, Manchester United, St Mirren

Above: Circa 1950. Albert Scanlon and David Pegg battled over the left-wing position in the Busby Babes side of the mid-1950s, but by the time of the Munich disaster the shirt was Scanlon's. Both were on that fateful flight, but only Scanlon survived, eventually recovering from his injuries sufficiently to start playing again the following season, when he played every game and scored 16 goals.

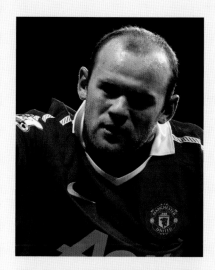

WAYNE ROONEY

Country: England
Born: 24 Oct 1985
Debut: 28 Sep 2004 v Fenerbahce
Position: Forward
Appearances: 289 (34) **Goals scored:** 147
Seasons: 2004/05 - present
Clubs: Everton, Manchester United

In 2002, a 16-year-old Everton player announced himself to the football world by scoring a stunning winner that brought to an end Arsenal's 30-game unbeaten run. "Remember the name," implored a prescient TV commentator. Since then the name Wayne Rooney has become as well known as any player on the planet and he has earned the reputation as one of the most naturally talented footballers of his generation.

Born in the Croxteth district of Liverpool, a young Rooney set record after record as a schoolboy, scoring a remarkable 99 goals in one season before being spotted by an Everton scout. Despite a trial at Liverpool, at the age of nine Rooney signed schoolboy forms for the team he and his family had always supported. In 1995-96 at the Everton Centre of Excellence, he scored an amazing 114 goals in 29 games for the under 11s. His senior debut came on 17 August 2002, shortly followed by his crushing goal against Arsenal.

Just two seasons later he rejected a new contract offer from the Merseysiders, instead joining United for £20 million – the highest fee ever paid for a teenager. Yet any worries that the price tag might weigh down the youngster were swiftly dashed by a spectacular hat-trick on debut in front of 67,000 at Old Trafford in a Champions League match. The season ended trophyless for Rooney and United, but the player had the personal satisfaction of being named Young Player of Year by his peers.

Rooney's first United trophy came the next season (2005-06) as he produced a man of the match performance with two goals in the 4-0 League Cup final victory against Wigan Athletic. The season saw further individual recognition with Rooney picking up the Professional Footballers' Association Player of the Year award. Rooney helped the Reds win a league title the following year; by now the teenager had matured into a tireless, highly skilled player, seen as the beating heart of the team, and capable of scoring quite magnificent goals.

At just 17 years 111 days, on 12 February 2003, Rooney had become the youngest player ever to play for England and would lead the attack in European Championships a year later. Just before the 2006 World Cup, the nation held its breath as the striker tried to recover from an injury. He played in the tournament, but was never in top form and was ultimately sent off for allegedly stamping on a Portuguese player during England's quarter-final exit. Rooney's return to domestic football was potentially complicated by the need to re-establish his relationship with striking partner Portuguese Cristiano Ronaldo, who had been peripherally involved in the sending off. Fortunately, the two United players continued a remarkable partnership

In 2009-10 Rooney had his most productive season for the Red Devils, scoring 34 goals before injury interrupted his progress. Then after a slow start to the following season, there were unwanted headlines when Rooney announced he would leave Old Trafford, with rivals Manchester City touted as likely buyers. Quickly matters were resolved and the player signed a new long-term contract. In short order he won back the adoration of the fans by scoring the goal that clinched United's record 19th league title. At the end of the 2010-11 season his 102 United goals in 217 Premier League appearances suggests that Rooney is set to become one of the club's greatest players of all time.

Left: 27 November 2010. Wayne Rooney in action for United against Blackburn Rovers at Old Trafford.

Below: 12 March 2011. On the ball in the quarter-final of the FA Cup against Arsenal, the man widely believed to be the best English player of his generation.

LESLIE 'LES' JESSE SEALEY

Country: England
Born: 29 Sep 1957 **Died:** 19 Aug 2001
Debut: 14 Apr 1990 v Queens Park Rangers
Position: Goalkeeper
Appearances: 55 (1) **Goals scored:** 0
Seasons: 1989/90 - 1990/91 and 1993/94
Clubs: Coventry City (*loan*), Luton Town, Plymouth Argyle (*loan*), Manchester United, Aston Villa, Coventry City, Birmingham City (*loan*), Blackpool, West Ham United, Leyton Orient, Bury (*loan*)

MAURICE EDGAR SETTERS

Country: England
Born: 16 Dec 1936
Debut: 16 Jan 1960 v Birmingham City
Position: Half back
Appearances: 194 **Goals scored:** 14
Seasons: 1959/60 - 1964/65
Clubs: Exeter City, West Bromwich Albion, Manchester United, Stoke City, Coventry City, Charlton Athletic

Maurice Setters brought steel and experience to the post-Munich United defence, and won an FA Cup medal in the 1963 final. He played 434 games in his whole career and was assistant manager for the Republic of Ireland team under Jack Charlton, attending the 1990 and 1994 World Cups.

LEE STUART SHARPE

Country: England
Born: 25 May 1971
Debut: 24 Sep 1988 v West Ham United
Position: Left-winger/Full back/Midfield
Appearances: 213 (50) **Goals scored:** 36
Seasons: 1988/89 - 1995/96
Clubs: Torquay United, Manchester United, Leeds United, Sampdoria (*loan*), Bradford City, Portsmouth (*loan*), Exeter City, Grindavik, Garforth Town

Not many players have celebrations named after them but Lee Sharpe's 'shuffle' became the stuff of legend at Old Trafford. A skilful left winger, he played an important role in the club's rise in the early nineties. He won three league titles, scoring many important goals including a memorable hat-trick in a 6-2 League Cup win over Arsenal in 1990.

WILLIAM SHARPE

Country: England
Born: Unknown **Died:** Unknown
Debut: 4 Oct 1890 v Higher Walton
Position: Forward
Appearances: 2 **Goals scored:** 0
Seasons: 1890/91 - 1891/92
Clubs: Newton Heath

RYAN JAMES SHAWCROSS

Country: England
Born: 4 Oct 1987
Debut: 25 Oct 2006 v Crewe Alexandra
Position: Defender
Appearances: 0 (2) **Goals scored:** 0
Seasons: 2006/07 - 2007/08
Clubs: Manchester United, Royal Antwerp (*loan*), Stoke City (*loan*), Stoke City

JOHN SHELDON

Country: England
Born: Jan 1887 **Died:** 19 Mar 1941
Debut: 27 Dec 1910 v Bradford City
Position: Forward
Appearances: 26 **Goals scored:** 1
Seasons: 1909/10 - 1913/14
Clubs: Nuneaton FC, Manchester United, Liverpool,

ARNOLD SIDEBOTTOM

Country: England
Born: 1 Apr 1954
Debut: 23 Apr 1973 v Sheffield United
Position: Defender
Appearances: 20 **Goals scored:** 0
Seasons: 1972/73 - 1974/75
Clubs: Manchester United, Huddersfield Town, Halifax Town

Although his United career was a brief one, Sidebottom also played cricket for Yorkshire at the same time and went on to play one Test for England in 1985.

JOHN 'JACK' SILCOCK

Country: England
Born: 15 Jan 1898 **Died:** 28 Jun 1966
Debut: 30 Aug 1919 v Derby County
Position: Full back
Appearances: 449 **Goals scored:** 2
Seasons: 1919/20 - 1933/34
Clubs: Manchester United, Oldham Athletic

In 15 seasons between the wars, Jack Silcock made 449 appearances at full-back for United. Known for his accurate distribution and strong, skilful style he scored twice during his time at Old Trafford. Despite not earning any silverware he was capped three times by England before moving on to Oldham Athletic.

Below: 25 May 1963. Manchester United beat Leicester City 3-1 to win the FA Cup final. David Herd, Denis Law and Maurice Setters celebrate in the dressing room.

JOHN 'JACK' ROWLEY

Country: England
Born: 7 Oct 1920 **Died:** 27 Jun 1998
Debut: 23 Oct 1937 v Sheffield Wednesday
Position: Forward
Appearances: 424 **Goals scored:** 211
Seasons: 1937/38 - 1954/55
Clubs: Bournemouth, Manchester
United, Plymouth Argyle

In his 12 seasons as one of United's most consistent goalscorers, Jack Rowley scored 211 times in 424 appearances in all competitions, and remains one of the club's most respected marksmen, still ranking third in the all-time list. But, oh what a record Rowley would have had if seven years of his playing career had not been denied by the Second World War.

Born in 1920 in Wolverhampton, Rowley played as a 15-year-old in the Birmingham and District League for Cradley Heath. It was regarded as one of the tougher amateur leagues and in the same year he signed for his local team, Second Division Wolverhampton Wanderers. However, Rowley never made a first team appearance with Wolves and instead in 1937 went to Bournemouth and Boscombe Athletic for regular outings. Twelve goals in 22 games later, the 17-year-old was spotted by United's scouts and brought to Manchester for the princely sum of £3,000.

It took Rowley just eight months with the Reds before he played for the first team in October 1937. He did not score that day against Sheffield Wednesday, but in his second start on the left wing in December, he grabbed four goals in a 5-1 win against Swansea. Rowley had arrived

and now helped United win promotion back to the First Division. He finished the season with nine goals from 29 appearances and in his second full season brought ten more goals from 39 appearances. The young Midlander was set for inevitable stardom.

But it was 1939 and war was imminent. Jack Rowley's life, like millions of others, changed irrevocably. He joined the South Staffordshire Regiment and, would take part in the Normandy landings on D-Day. During the war years he guested for a variety of teams and is recorded as having scored 102 War League goals.

After the war Rowley was de-mobbed and returned to United. He became part of Matt Busby's first successful team. Now known as "Gunner" because of his war exploits, Rowley was almost 26-years-old when he re-started his career and took his place among the Famous Five forward line that won the FA Cup in 1948. Rowley, now playing at

centre forward, scored two goals in the final. It was Rowley's partnership with Scotsman Jimmy Delaney that troubled defences most of all and would eventually bring the Englishman six caps for his country. He scored six goals for England including four against Ireland in a 9-2 win in 1949.

Rowley also won a league championship medal with United when his 30 goals during the 1951-52 season equalled his own club record set three years earlier. In fact, he was United's top scorer for five out of the six full seasons immediately after the war. But as he entered his 30s, manager Busby had ideas for a younger team and Rowley was transferred to Plymouth Argyle in February 1955 where he was made player/manager. The star forward spent two seasons in the west country before going on to manage a number of other clubs including Oldham Athletic and Ajax of Amsterdam. He died in June 1998 aged 77.

Left: November 1950. Striker Jack Rowley in action.

Below: 7 February 1948. Charlton Athletic goalkeeper Sam Bartram makes a save from Jack Rowley during an FA Cup fifth round match held at Huddersfield due to bomb damage at Old Trafford.

MIKAEL SILVESTRE

Country: France
Born: 9 Aug 1977
Debut: 11 Sep 1999 v Liverpool
Position: Defender
Appearances: 326 (35) **Goals scored:** 10
Seasons: 1999/2000 – 2007/08
Clubs: Rennes, Internazionale, Manchester United, Arsenal, Werder Bremen

French international Mikael Silvestre signed for United from Inter Milan in 1999. He was a solid and dependable defender, able to play at both centre back and left back. During his time at United he had numerous defensive partners but always proved reliable. He won four league titles, one FA Cup and the Champions League. He moved to Arsenal for the 2008-09 season and joined German side Werder Bremen in 2010.

DANIEL 'DANNY' SIMPSON

Country: England
Born: 4 Jan 1987
Debut: 26 Sep 2007 v Coventry City
Position: Defender
Appearances: 4 (4) **Goals scored:** 0
Seasons: 2007/08
Clubs: Manchester United, Royal Antwerp (loan), Sunderland (loan), Ipswich Town (loan), Blackburn Rovers (loan), Newcastle United

JOHNNY SIVEBAEK

Country: Denmark
Born: 25 Oct 1961
Debut: 9 Feb 1986 v Liverpool
Position: Midfield
Appearances: 32 (2) **Goals scored:** 1
Seasons: 1985/86 – 1986/87
Clubs: Vejle, Manchester United, Saint-Etienne, AS Monaco, Pescara, AGF Aarhus

J F SLATER

Country: Unknown
Born: Unknown **Died:** Unknown
Debut: 4 Oct 1890 v Higher Walton
Position: Goalkeeper
Appearances: 4 **Goals scored:** 0

Seasons: 1890/91 – 1892/93
Clubs: Newton Heath

TOM SLOAN

Country: Northern Ireland
Born: 10 Jul 1959
Debut: 18 Nov 1978 v Ipswich Town
Position: Midfield
Appearances: 4 (8) **Goals scored:** 0
Seasons: 1978/79 – 1980/81
Clubs: Ballymena United, Manchester United, Chester City, Linfield, Coleraine, Raglan Homers

CHRIS SMALLING

Country: England
Born: 22 Nov 1989
Debut: 8 Aug 2010 v Chelsea
Position: Defender
Appearances: 24 (10) **Goals scored:** 2
Seasons 2010/11 - present
Clubs: Maidstone United, Fulham, Manchester United

ALAN SMITH

Country: England
Born: 28 Oct 1980
Debut: 8 Aug 2004 v Arsenal
Position: Forward/midfield
Appearances: 61 (32) **Goals scored:** 12
Seasons: 2004/05 – 2006/07
Clubs: Leeds United, Manchester United, Newcastle United

ALBERT SMITH

Country: Scotland
Born: 1905 **Died:** Unknown
Debut: 22 Jan 1927 v Leeds United
Position: Forward
Appearances: 5 **Goals scored:** 1
Seasons: 1926/27
Clubs: Petershill FC, Manchester United, Northampton Town

RICHARD 'DICK' SMITH

Country: England
Born: Unknown **Died:** Unknown
Debut: 8 Sep 1894 v Burton Wanderers
Position: Forward
Appearances: 101 **Goals scored:** 37
Seasons: 1894/95 – 1900/01
Clubs: Halliwell Rovers, Wigan County, Newton Heath, Bolton Wanderers

JOHN 'JACK' SMITH

Country: England
Born: 7 Feb 1915 **Died:** 21 Apr 1975
Debut: 2 Feb 1938 v Barnsley
Position: Forward
Appearances: 41 **Goals scored:** 15
Seasons: 1937/38 – 1945/46
Clubs: Huddersfield Town, Newcastle United, Manchester United, Port Vale, Macclesfield Town

Played in the Wartime League scoring 160 goals, which, of course, remain unrecognised in the official league records.

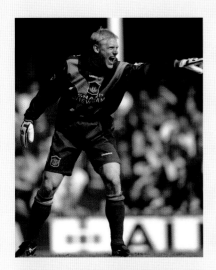

PETER SCHMEICHEL

Country: Denmark
Born: 18 Nov 1963
Debut: 17 Aug 1991 v Notts County
Position: Goalkeeper
Appearances: 398 **Goals scored:** 1
Seasons: 1991/92 - 1998/99
Clubs: Gladsaxe-Hero, Hvidovre, Brøndby, Manchester United, Sporting Lisbon, Aston Villa, Manchester City

Known as the Great Dane, Peter Schmeichel is most fans' choice as the best goalkeeper ever to wear a United shirt. During eight spectacular seasons with the 6ft 4in penalty-box-dominating Dane between the posts, the Reds won every conceivable trophy; it was only on his departure immediately after the 1999 treble-winning season that his immense value to the side became truly apparent. Finding the replacement for Schmeichel, who gave such confidence to his defence, took several seasons and cost the club many millions of pounds.

Signed by Alex Ferguson in August 1991 for £500,000 at the age of 27, Schmeichel had already been a notable success at Brøndby IF in Denmark, winning three league championships and two cup medals. He came to Manchester after a season in which Les Sealey had finally secured the starting job from three other goalkeepers – Gary Walsh, Mark Bosnich and Jim Leighton. But Sealey was not seen as the long-term answer and the incoming Dane had an immediate effect on the Reds. His first four games were clean sheets and his defence conceded just four goals in his first 14 matches. Not only did Schmeichel make dozens of spectacular saves, he was also a leader: effectively marshalling the troops in front of him, particularly at set pieces. He was a master at intimidating opposing strikers with both his size (he weighed over 16 stones) and his massive XXXL gloves making the goal seem small.

United won the League Cup and Super Cup in his first season in goal, but more importantly the Reds took their first league championship title in 26 years the following season – Schmeichel played in every league game and conceded just 31 goals in 42 games.

During the treble-winning season Schmeichel played in more games than any other United player (56) and his saves helped win many matches that might easily have been lost, including the Champions League final when only his giant presence seemed to keep the English team in the match at one time. "He was tremendous value, he had an immense presence. Defenders had to get used to the verbal volleying he would give them, but he only did that because his heart was in it and he was always an absolute winner," Sir Alex Ferguson said after the Dane left.

In his United career, Schmeichel won five Premiership medals, three FA Cups, one League Cup, four FA Charity Shields, one Super Cup and, best of all, the Champions League title in 1999. After the famous victory against Bayern Munich, Schmeichel moved on to Sporting Lisbon in Portugal, Aston Villa and Manchester City before retiring from the sport in 2003. He won 129 caps for Denmark and was part of the European Championship-winning Danish team in 1992. There were individual honours too as he was UEFA goalkeeper of the year four times and awarded the MBE in 2000.

Left: 13 Apr 1996. Closing in on the title, Peter Schmeichel organises his defence.

Below: 14 May 1994. Peter Schmeichel the ultimate shot-stopper, but not on this occassion; he is well beaten by Gavin Peacock's shot, which hits the crossbar and rebounds to safety during the FA Cup final.

PAUL SCHOLES

Country: England
Born: 16 Nov 1974
Debut: 21 Sep 1994 v Port Vale
Position: Midfield/Forward
Appearances: 552 (124) **Goals scored:** 150
Seasons: 1994/95 - 2010/11
Clubs: Manchester United

If the mark of a great player is not just the awards he receives and the trophies he collects, but the regard in which he is held by fellow professionals, then Paul Scholes is up there with the very best to have graced the game. Undoubtedly one of the finest passers and strikers of a ball in the Premiership era, Scholes has attracted praise from many of the greats of the game, like former FIFA World Player of the Year France's Zinedine Zidane, who said: "Scholes is undoubtedly the best midfielder of his generation."

Born in Salford, Scholes signed for United on 8 July 1991 and played alongside Phil Neville in the FA Youth Cup final in 1993, before making his first team debut in the League Cup against Port Vale in September 1994, scoring both goals in a 2-1 win. A naturally attack-minded player, Scholes began to make an impression on the United first team during his debut season, even coming on as substitute in the FA Cup final loss to Everton in May 1995.

With Mark Hughes sold and Eric Cantona suspended, Scholes began the 1995-96 season as a support striker to Andy Cole. His effectiveness was immediately apparent, weighing in with 14 goals in all competitions as United won the Premiership and FA Cup double. The following year he picked up a second league winners' medal and when Roy Keane suffered a season-ending knee injury in 5 September 1997 Scholes moved back into midfield.

Initially he took time to adapt to his new position; United ending a season trophyless for only the second time in the 1990s. However, Scholes was to play a key role a season later as the Reds won a historic treble, scoring in the 2-0 FA Cup final win over Newcastle United. Unfortunately, suspension kept him out of the Champions League final. He had scored a crucial goal against Internazionale in the quarter-final, but coming on as a substitute against Juventus in the semi-final, he picked up a yellow card that ruled him out of the biggest game of the season. In spite of all his gifts, yellow and red cards would plague him. Scholes picked up 90 yellows and four reds in the Premiership plus 32 yellow cards in the Champions League making him the most booked player ever in the competition.

More Premiership glory followed, with titles in 2000, 2001 and 2003, the latter season seeing Scholes finish with a career-high 20 goals in all competitions. While Scholes picked up a second FA Cup winner's medal in 2004, his uncharacteristically missed penalty in the 2005 final shootout was to cost United victory against Arsenal.

Capped by England 66 times, scoring 14 international goals and playing in World Cups in 1998 and 2002, Scholes retired early from international football in August 2004, citing family life and extending his club career as reasons. An eye problem restricted his contribution in 2005-06. However, Scholes came firing back the following year to help the Reds reclaim their Premiership title and one of his many personal highlights was a thunderous trademark volley against Aston Villa which won him United's goal of the season award.

Above: 22 May 1999. Paul Scholes scores in the FA Cup final against Newcastle United. It means the match finishes in a 2-0 win for United and they achieved the double for the third time in six years.

Right: 8 October 1994. A young Paul Scholes who would win 66 England international caps between 1997 and 2004.

If 2006-07 had been a successful year domestically, the next season offered catharsis for Scholes on the European front. United once again wrapped up the league title and it was a classic Scholes strike in the semi-final of the Champions League against Barcelona that helped United book their place in the final. Even though he picked up an almost customary yellow card and was subbed in the 87th minute of the Moscow final, Scholes picked up his much-sought after winners' medal from European competition.

Despite a continued reluctance to give press interviews or promote his own role in the team, significant recognition of his contributions started to come the following summer as Scholes was inducted into the English Football Hall of Fame. Then an injury lay-off at the start of 2008-09 kept him out until Christmas, but on his return, his effectiveness was proved with a thumping volley from a corner against Fulham in February 2009. A hat-trick of titles provided Scholes with his ninth league winner's medal and while his goals contribution had waned somewhat, he still possessed the ability to control the tempo of matches.

A feature of Scholes' game throughout his career had been his ability to contribute big goals in big games. This came to the fore once again in 2009-10 as Scholes scored in a 3-2 Champions League win in Milan to give the Reds their first ever away win against the Rossoneri. Then in April he netted a 93rd-minute winner against Manchester City at Eastlands to keep United in the hunt for the title.

On 31 May 2011, after helping United to a record-breaking 19th league title and playing in his third Champions League final, Scholes announced his retirement. He finished with 150 goals and an incredible 676 appearances in a Red Devils shirt, behind only Ryan Giggs, Bobby Charlton and Bill Foulkes in the all-time list.

Scholes had never rocked the boat at United, never courted controversy and always preferred to let his football do the talking. His reticence was perhaps why the player never received the individual recognition of others around him. In spite of his fantastic ability and his contributions to such a successful team, Scholes received few nominations for prestigious individual awards. However, the esteem in which his colleagues hold him says everything about what he brought to the game. 2010 FIFA World Player of the Year nominee Xavi Hernandez offered a telling insight: "In the last 15 to 20 years the best central midfielder that I have seen is Paul Scholes. If he had been Spanish then maybe he would have been valued more." Not surprisingly, the one-club-man Scholes has stayed with at Old Trafford after retirement as a player where he will help coach the club's reserves.

1994	Makes professional debut for United in League Cup against Port Vale
1996	Adopts the number 18 shirt which he wears until his retirement
1997	Makes international debut under Glenn Hoddle against South Africa
1999	Sent off for first time in career (against Chelsea)
2000	Scores both goals for England in 2-0 play-off win over Scotland
2003	Nets career-high 20 goals as United win 15th league title
2004	Retires from international football to concentrate on family and United
2006	Makes 500th appearance for United
2008	Inducted into English Football Hall of Fame
2011	Announces retirement from football and joins United coaching staff

Above: 28 May 2011. The Champions League final between Barcelona and Manchester United at Wembley Stadium brings the curtain down on the playing career of one United's greatest servants.

LORENZO SMITH
Country: England
Born: Jul 1878　**Died:** Sep 1912
Debut: 22 Nov 1902 v Leicester Fosse
Position: Forward
Appearances: 10 **Goals scored:** 1
Seasons: 1902/03
Clubs: Newton Heath, New Brampton

THOMAS GABLE SMITH
Country: England
Born: 18 Oct 1900　**Died:** 21 Feb 1934
Debut: 19 Jan 1924 v Fulham
Position: Forward
Appearances: 90 **Goals scored:** 16
Seasons: 1923/24 - 1926/27
Clubs: Marsden Villa, Whitburn FC, South
Shields, Leicester City, Manchester
United, Northampton Town

WILLIAM 'BILL' SMITH
Country: England
Born: Unknown　**Died:** Unknown
Debut: 14 Sep 1901 v Middlesbrough
Position: Forward
Appearances: 17 **Goals scored:** 0
Seasons: 1901/02
Clubs: Stockport County, Manchester
City, Newton Heath

JOHN SNEDDON
Country: Unknown
Born: Unknown　**Died:** Unknown
Debut: 3 Oct 1891 v Manchester City
Position: Forward
Appearances: 3 **Goals scored:** 1
Seasons: 1891/92
Clubs: Newton Heath

JONATHAN SPECTOR
Country: USA
Born: 1 Mar 1986
Debut: 25 Aug 2004 v Dinamo Bucharesti
Position: Defender
Appearances: 4 (3) **Goals scored:** 0
Seasons: 2004/05 - 2005/06
Clubs: Chicago Sockers, Manchester United,
Charlton Athletic (*loan*), West Ham United

Above: 21 May 1983. Frank Stapleton celebrates after scoring United's first goal during the FA Cup final.

Right: Circa. 1912. George Stacey won three honours while at United, but after retiring from the game he returned to his Yorkshire pit village and worked down the mines as well as running a sweet shop.

CHARLES 'CHARLIE' SPENCER
Country: England
Born: 4 Dec 1899　**Died:** 9 Feb 1953
Debut: 15 Sep 1928 v Liverpool
Position: Defender
Appearances: 48 **Goals scored:** 0
Seasons: 1928/29 - 1929/30
Clubs: Newcastle United, Manchester United,
Tunbridge Wells Rangers, Wigan Athletic

WALTER SPRATT
Country: England
Born: Oct 1892　**Died:** Unknown
Debut: 6 Feb 1915 v Sunderland
Position: Full back
Appearances: 13 **Goals scored:** 0
Seasons: 1914/15 - 1919/20
Clubs: Rotherham Town, Brentford,
Manchester United

GEORGE STACEY
Country: England
Born: Apr 1881　**Died:** Unknown
Debut: 12 Oct 1907 v Newcastle United
Position: Full back
Appearances: 270 **Goals scored:** 9
Seasons: 1906/07 - 1914/15
Clubs: Sheffield Wednesday, Thornhill
United, Barnsley, Manchester United,

Stacey, who could play in both full back positions, joined United from Barnsley in 1907 for a £200 fee. Winning the league title in his first season, he was a member of the 1909 FA Cup-winning side and helped United win the First Division championship in 1910-11 by a solitary point. He remained at the club until the outbreak of the First World War, playing for his local Rotherham County club during the war years. He retired from the game at the end of the final War League season of 1918-19.

HARRY STAFFORD
Country: England
Born: 1869　**Died:** 1940
Debut: 3 Apr 1896 v Darwen
Position: Full back
Appearances: 200 **Goals scored:** 1
Seasons: 1895/96 - 1901/02
Clubs: Southport Central, Crewe
Alexandra, Newton Heath

Captain of Newton Heath and a noted snappy dresser, he was both hero and villain of the club. He helped bring John Henry Davies on board as its financial saviour and became a director of the newly renamed United. But was suspended a year later for making illegal payments to players.

JAAP STAM
Country: Netherlands
Born: 17 Jul 1972
Debut: 9 Aug 1998 v Arsenal
Position: Centre back
Appearances: 125 (2) **Goals scored:** 1
Seasons: 1998/99 - 2001/02
Clubs: FC Zwolle, Cambuur Leeuwarden,
Willem II, PSV Eindoven, Manchester
United, Lazio, AC Milan, Ajax

The Dutch defender was a vital recruit at the start of the 1998-99 season, replacing Gary Pallister. He helped United to the treble that season, and won two further Premier League titles with the Reds.

FRANCIS 'FRANK' ANTHONY STAPLETON
Country: Republic of Ireland
Born: 10 Jul 1956
Debut: 29 Aug 1981 v Coventry City
Position: Forward
Appearances: 267 (21) **Goals scored:** 78
Seasons: 1981/82 - 1986/87
Clubs: Arsenal, Manchester United, Ajax,
Anderlecht (*loan*), Derby County, Le Havre
AC, Blackburn Rovers, Aldershot, Huddersfield
Town, Bradford City, Brighton & Hove Albion

When he scored United's 55th minute equaliser against Brighton in 1983, Frank Stapleton made history by becoming the first player to score for two different clubs in FA Cup finals (having previously netted for Arsenal against United in the 1979 final). As an old-fashioned centre forward he was particularly good in the air. He scored 78 goals in total for the Reds across 288 appearances and played 71 times for his country.

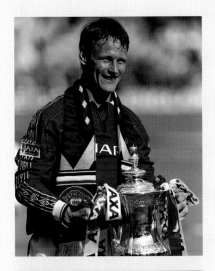

EDWARD PAUL 'TEDDY' SHERINGHAM

Country: England
Born: 2 Apr 1966
Debut: 10 Aug 1997 v Tottenham Hotspur
Position: Forward
Appearances: 101 (52) **Goals scored:** 46
Seasons: 1997/98 – 2000/01
Clubs: Millwall, Aldershot (*loan*), Djurgaarden (*loan*), Nottingham Forest, Tottenham Hotspur, Manchester United, Tottenham Hotspur, Portsmouth, West Ham United, Colchester United

Described by all who came into contact with him as the model professional, perhaps the pinnacle of his playing career came when he scored the equaliser and supplied the assist for United's winning goal in the final moments of the 1999 Champions League final. A win that gave the Reds the treble. At 16, Sheringham began his professional career at Millwall in 1982 after impressing during a youth team game against Millwall while playing for a non-league side. He quickly became a first team choice and would be the club's top goal scorer over four seasons. In all, Sheringham scored 111 goals in all competitions in his eight years at the club. Now 25, he was sold to Nottingham Forest for £2 million to partner Nigel Clough. In August 1992 he would score the first ever Premiership goal (against Liverpool) shown on Sky Sports, but was promptly sold to Tottenham Hotspur a few days later. Sheringham would prove immensely popular with the Spurs fans and was acknowledged as one of the best strikers in the Premiership, but by the mid 1990s was 31 and without major honours in the game. In June

1997, Sheringham was signed by Alex Ferguson for £3.5 million to replace the retiring Eric Cantona. After a slow start in his first season (he scored 14 goals in all competitions) his relationship with strike partner Andy Cole apparently soured. The arrival of Dwight Yorke from Aston Villa meant his appearances would be limited in future, but he managed to play in enough Premiership games to qualify for a title winner's medal at the end of the season. Finally, at the age of 33, he had won a major trophy. A week later he scored one of United's two goals in the FA Cup final to claim his second honour. Then came the Champions League final in Barcelona. The player without a medal to his name

on leaving Spurs now had won every top-level trophy in the club game. In 2000–01 Sheringham had one of his best seasons, his form ensuring precedence over Dwight Yorke and finishing as United's top scorer with 21 goals in all competition as well as being voted Player of the Year by both the Professional Footballers' Association and the Football Writers' Association. In 2001 his tenure at United came to an end and he returned to Tottenham as one of Glenn Hoddle's first signings. He would go on to play for a further seven seasons, retiring from competitive football at the end of the 2007–08 season at the age of 42. He was capped by England 51 times, scoring 11 goals.

Left: 22 May 1999: Goal scorer Teddy Sheringham with the FA Cup trophy after United beat Newcastle United. The win meant United completed the double for the third time in six years.

Below: 26 May 1999. Teddy Sheringham celebrates his equaliser during the Champions League Final against Bayern Munich.

Alex Stepney made more appearances than any other goalkeeper in the club's history. His career started at Millwall and he joined United in 1966, playing under five different managers during his time with the club. He won a league championship in 1967, the European Cup in 1968, and was an FA Cup winner nine years later. After more than a decade in goal he left Manchester to continue his career in the North American Soccer League.

ALFRED STEWARD
Country: England
Born: 18 Sep 1896 **Died:** Unknown
Debut: 23 Oct 1920 v Preston North End
Position: Goalkeeper
Appearances: 326 **Goals scored:** 0
Seasons: 1920/21 - 1926/27
Clubs: Manchester United, Manchester North End

Steward learned his football playing in the army during the First World War, and signed for United as an amateur to cover for incumbent Jack Mew. He became a regular in 1923-24 and played every game of the promotion campaign the following year. He also played cricket for Lancashire.

MICHAEL STEWART
Country: Scotland
Born: 26 Feb 1981
Debut: 31 Oct 2000 v Watford
Position: Midfield
Appearances: 7 (7) **Goals scored:** 0
Seasons: 2000/01 - 2002/03
Clubs: Manchester United, Royal Antwerp (loan), Nottingham Forest (loan), Heart of Midlothian, Hibernian, Genclerbirligi, Charlton Athletic

WILLIAM S STEWART
Country: Scotland
Born: 11 Feb 1872 **Died:** Jun 1945
Debut: 4 Oct 1890 v Higher Walton
Position: Half back
Appearances: 87 **Goals scored:** 5
Seasons: 1890/91 - 1894/95
Clubs: Warwickshire County, Newton Heath, Luton Town

WILLIAM 'WILLIE' STEWART
Country: Scotland
Born: 29 Apr 1910 **Died:** Unknown
Debut: 19 Nov 1932 v Fullham
Position: Forward
Appearances: 49 **Goals scored:** 7
Seasons: 1932/33 - 1933/34
Clubs: Larne FC, Cowdenbeath, Manchester United, Motherwell

R STEPHENSON
Country:
Born: Unknown **Died:** Unknown
Debut: 11 Jan 1896 v Rotherham United
Position: Forward
Appearances: 1 **Goals scored:** 1
Seasons: 1895/96
Clubs: Talbot FC, Newton Heath

ALEXANDER 'ALEX' CYRIL STEPNEY
Country: England
Born: 18 Sep 1942
Debut: 17 Sep 1966 v Manchester City
Position: Goalkeeper
Appearances: 539 **Goals scored:** 2
Seasons: 1966/67 - 1977/78
Clubs: Tooting & Mitcham United, Millwall, Chelsea, Manchester United, Dallas Tornados, Altrincham (loan)

Above: 20 August 1985.Gordon Strachan along with Jesper Olsen, formed one of the smaller wide midfield partnerships for United.

During his time at Manchester United,

HERBERT STONE
Country: England
Born: Apr 1873 **Died:** Unknown
Debut: 26 Mar 1894 v Blackburn Rovers
Position: Midfield
Appearances: 7 **Goals scored:** 0
Seasons: 1893/94 - 1894/95
Clubs: Newton Heath, Ashton North End

IAN STOREY-MOORE
Country: England
Born: 17 Jan 1945
Debut: 11 Mar 1972 v Huddersfield Town
Position: Forward
Appearances: 43 **Goals scored:** 12
Seasons: 1971/72 - 1973/74
Clubs: Nottingham Forest, Manchester United

GORDON DAVID STRACHAN
Country: Scotland
Born: 9 Feb 1957
Debut: 25 Aug 1984 v Watford
Position: Midfield
Appearances: 196 (6) **Goals scored:** 38
Seasons: 1984/85 - 1988/89
Clubs: Dundee, Aberdeen, Manchester United, Leeds United, Coventry City

What Gordon Strachan lacked in height he more than made up for in heart. The diminutive Scotsman was an industrious, skilful midfielder with an eye for a defence-splitting pass. He won the FA Cup in 1985 and appeared at two World Cup finals for Scotland. From United he joined Leeds where he was voted 1990-91 Football Writers' Association Footballer of the Year.

ERNEST STREET
Country: England
Born: 1878 **Died:** Unknown
Debut: 7 Feb 1903 v Liverpool
Position: Forward
Appearances: 3 **Goals scored:** 0
Seasons: 1902/03
Clubs: Sale Homefield, Manchester United

JOHN SUTCLIFFE
Country: England
Born: 14 Apr 1868 **Died:** 7 Jul 1947
Debut: 5 Sep 1903 v Bristol City
Position: Goalkeeper
Appearances: 28 **Goals scored:** 0
Seasons: 1903/04
Clubs: Bolton Wanderers, Millwall Athletic, Manchester United, Plymouth Argyle

ERIC SWEENEY
Country: England
Born: 3 Oct 1903 **Died:** Oct 1968
Debut: 13 Feb 1926 v Leeds United
Position: Forward
Appearances: 32 **Goals scored:** 7
Seasons: 1925/26 - 1929/30
Clubs: Manchester United, Charlton Athletic

OLE GUNNAR SOLSKJAER

Country: Norway
Born: 26 Feb 1973
Debut: 25 Aug 1996 v Blackburn Rovers
Position: Forward
Appearances: 216 (150) **Goals scored:** 126
Seasons: 1996/97 - 2006/07
Clubs: Clausenengen, Molde, Manchester United

The term 'super sub' was first coined in English football during the seventies, but while in his playing career at United, Ole Gunnar Solskjaer took the concept to a whole new level. Over eleven seasons the slightly built Norwegian striker was a substitute for 150 of his 366 appearances, which means he started just 216 games or 41 percent of his appearances were cameos from the bench.

Yet his 126 career goals ranks him 16th in the United all-time list. Of those goals, a record 28 were scored after he came off the bench. But beyond statistics, there was something special about Solskjaer's United career. His singular talent for scoring crucial goals, often having only just come on to the pitch as a substitute, won the fans' hearts.

Solskjaer arrived at Old Trafford for £1.5 million in July 1996 aged 23 having scored 31 times in 42 appearances for Molde in Tippeligaenthe, the Norwegian Premier League. Fittingly, on his debut against Blackburn Rovers in the fourth game of the 1996-97 season, Solskjaer came on as substitute and scored in the 2-2 draw. That first season in the English Premiership, he made only 25 league starts and eight appearances as substitute yet still finished as the club's top scorer with 18 goals. It would be a

pattern that continued throughout his career and earned Solskjaer the nickname The Baby-faced Assassin.

Manager Alex Ferguson understood Solskjaer's special quality and saw how the player would study the game from the bench and then put that knowledge to good use on the pitch – for example when he came on as substitute against Nottingham Forest in February 1999 for just 12 minutes and scored four times.

His place in United folklore was secured later that season. Solskjaer was not the Reds' preferred striker at this time; Andy Cole and Dwight Yorke were first choice while Teddy Sheringham vied with the Norwegian for the role of first-change forward. In the Champions League final against Bayern Munich in May 1999, Solskjaer scored an unlikely winning goal after coming off the bench with just nine minutes remaining in the match.

His willingness to adopt the role of professional substitute demonstrated a

degree of selflessness combined with a dedication to the United cause, something Solskjaer confirmed two seasons later when he chased back to commit a professional foul in a key game against Newcastle United, knowing he would be sent off, yet still protecting the result for the team. There was always a lot more to Solskjaer than met the eye.

Despite relatively few starting appearances, Solskjaer helped United win eleven trophies including five Premierships. Injuries restricted his football in his last few seasons and he missed the entire 2004-05 season and most of the following one with a serious knee injury before retiring in August 2007. He stayed initially in the United family in a coaching capacity and as a club ambassador. In 2008, Solskjær became Manchester United's first full-time reserve team manager since 2006. He left the club in 2011 to manage his former club Molde.

Left: 1 December 2002. Ole Gunnar Solskjaer super sub and model professional.

Below: 26 May 1999. Ole Gunnar Solskjaer scores the second and winning goal for United deep in injury time during the European Champions League final against Bayern Munich in the Nou Camp Stadium. The win secured United the treble of League, FA Cup and European Cup.

T

MASSIMO TAIBI
Country: Italy
Born: 18 Feb 1970
Debut: 11 Sep 1999 v Liverpool
Position: Goalkeeper
Appearances: 4 **Goals scored:** 0
Seasons: 1999/2000
Clubs: Licata, Trento, AC Milan, Como, Piacenza, Venezia, Manchester United, Reggina, Atalanta, Torino, Ascoli Calcio

NORMAN TAPKEN
Country: England
Born: 21 Feb 1913 **Died:** Jun 1996
Debut: 26 Dec 1938 v Leicester
Position: Goalkeeper
Appearances: 16 **Goals scored:** 0
Seasons: 1938/39
Clubs: Newcastle United, Manchester United, Darlington

CHRISTOPHER TAYLOR
Country: England
Born: 18 Oct 1899 **Died:** 16 Mar 1972
Debut: 17 Jan 1925 v Coventry City
Position: Forward
Appearances: 30 **Goals scored:** 7
Seasons: 1923/24 - 1931/32
Clubs: Redditch United, Manchester United, Hyde United

ERNEST 'ERNIE' TAYLOR
Country: England
Born: 2 Sep 1925 **Died:** 9 Apr 1985
Debut: 19 Feb 1958 v Sheffield Wednesday
Position: Midfield
Appearances: 30 **Goals scored:** 4
Seasons: 1957/58 - 1958/59
Clubs: Hilton Colliery, Newcastle United, Plymouth Argyle, Blackpool, Manchester United, Sunderland, Altrincham, Derry City

WALTER TAYLOR
Country: England
Born: 1901 **Died:** Unknown
Debut: 2 Jan 1922 v Sheffield United
Position: Forward
Appearances: 1 **Goals scored:** 0
Seasons: 1921/22
Clubs: New Mills FC, Manchester United

CARLOS TEVEZ
Country: Argentina
Born: 5 Feb 1984
Debut: 15 Aug 2007 v Portsmouth
Position: Forward
Appearances: 73 (26) **Goals scored:** 34
Seasons: 2007/08 - 2008/09
Clubs: Boca Juniors, Corinthians, West Ham United, Manchester United, Manchester City

HENRY 'HARRY' THOMAS
Country: Wales
Born: 28 Feb 1901 **Died:** Unknown
Debut: 22 Apr 1922 v Oldham Athletic
Position: Winger

Appearances: 135 **Goals scored:** 13
Seasons: 1921/22 - 1929/30
Clubs: Swansea City, Porth FC, Manchester United, Merthyr Town

MICHAEL 'MICKEY' THOMAS
Country: Wales
Born: 7 Jul 1954
Debut: 25 Nov 1978 v Chelsea
Position: Midfield
Appearances: 110 **Goals scored:** 15
Seasons: 1978/79 - 1980/81
Clubs: Wrexham, Manchester United, Everton, Brighton & Hove Albion, Stoke City, Chelsea, West Bromwich Albion, Derby County (loan), Wichita Wings, Shrewsbury Town, Leeds United, Stoke City, Wrexham

JOHN 'ERNIE' THOMPSON
Country: England
Born: 21 Jun 1909 **Died:** 28 Dec 1985
Debut: 21 Nov 1936 v Liverpool
Position: Forward
Appearances: 3 **Goals scored:** 1
Seasons: 1936/37 - 1937/38
Clubs: Newbiggin, Ashington, Stakeford United, Carlisle United, Bristol City, Bath City, Blackburn Rovers Manchester United, Gateshead

WILLIAM THOMPSON
Country: Scotland
Born: Unknown **Died:** Unknown
Debut: 21 Oct 1893 v Burnley
Position: Forward
Appearances: 3 **Goals scored:** 0
Seasons: 1893/94
Clubs: Dumbarton, Aston Villa, Newton Heath

ARTHUR THOMSON
Country: England
Born: Jul 1903 **Died:** Unknown
Debut: 26 Jan 1929 v Bury
Position: Forward
Appearances: 5 **Goals scored:** 1
Seasons: 1928/29 - 1930/31
Clubs: West Stanley, Craghead United, West Stanley, Morecambe, Manchester United, Southend United

ERNEST THOMSON
Country: England
Born: 1884 **Died:** Unknown
Debut: 14 Sep 1907 v Middlesbrough
Position: Midfield
Appearances: 4 **Goals scored:** 0
Seasons: 1907/08 - 1908/09
Clubs: Darwen, Manchester United, Nelson

JAMES THOMSON
Country: Scotland
Born: Unknown **Died:** Unknown
Debut: 13 Dec 1913 v Bradford City
Position: Forward
Appearances: 6 **Goals scored:** 1
Seasons: 1913 /14
Clubs: Clydebank, Renton, Manchester United, Dumbarton Harp

J. SPENCE, Manchester United.

JOSEPH 'JOE' SPENCE

Country: England
Born: 15 Dec 1898 **Died:** 31 Dec 1966
Debut: 30 Aug 1919 v Derby County
Position: Forward
Appearances: 510 **Goals scored:** 168
Seasons: 1919/20 – 1932/33
Clubs: Scotswood, Manchester United, Bradford City, Chesterfield

"Give it to Joe" was the regular cry heard from the terraces during the 14-year career of one of United's most talented forwards of the first half of the 20th century, Joe Spence. Geordie Joe was an England international who could play in any position along the forward line. He made a total of 510 appearances for the club, was six times the leading scorer and was known as 'Mr Soccer' in Manchester for much of the 1920s and the early 1930s. Spence was a real local hero, but unfortunately played in United teams that were not of a highest standard. In fact, he spent five of his 14 seasons with the club in the Second Division.

Nevertheless, he was a remarkable player. Born in 1898, Spence was brought up in Northumberland and began work as a collier at just 13 years of age. He made his name on the local football scene playing for Blucher Juniors,

scoring 42 goals out of the team's total of 49 during one season alone. Conscripted into the army at 17 during the First World War, he served as a machine gunner, yet still managed to play football regularly, his battalion winning the Army Cup during the years of the conflict. After the war he played briefly for local side Scotswood before signing for United in 1919.

Once a United player, Spence quickly showed his potential. Before league matches restarted, Spence scored four goals on his Lancashire Cup debut, and would go on to be the team's top scorer with 14 goals in the 1919-20 First Division season.

Usually playing on the right wing, Spence was a stocky figure with a winger's trickery and a level of consistency that made him a relentless goalscoring threat. Injury restricted his appearances in his second season and in 1921-22, despite his 15 goals, United were relegated to the Second Division. It would take the team and Spence three seasons to gain promotion, but the return to the

top flight would launch the winger's most productive period.

In the next three seasons back in the First Division, Spence scored 54 league and cup goals and was capped twice for England. Unfortunately, more international recognition failed to materialise and United were once again relegated in 1930-31.

Spence continued to work his magic along the forward line, but he would not see the Reds promoted and was transferred to Bradford City in the summer of 1933. His 510 league and cup appearances stood as a record for a United player for the next 31 years while his total of 168 goals still ranks sixth in the all-time list and was not surpassed until 1952.

After leaving Old Trafford, Spence eventually lifted his only footballing silverware with Chesterfield in 1936 when they won the Third Division North title. Spence would eventually return to United in 1945 under Matt Busby as a coach and also work as a scout. He died aged 68 in 1966.

Left: "Give it to Joe." A cigarette card of one United's most popular players during the 1920s and early 1930s.

Below: 1921-22. A Manchester United team photograph. Joe Spence is fourth from the left in the first seated row.

Presented with ALL SPORTS, November 5th, 1921.

MANCHESTER UNITED FOOTBALL CLUB, 1921-2
Ground : Warwick Road North, Old Trafford, Manchester. Colours : Shirts red, knickers white.

Left to right (back row) : Morrison, W. Goodwin, J. Montgomery, T. Forster, S. Bennion, F. Harris, J. Robinson, G. Schofield. Third row : Puller (trainer), H. Roebuck, A. Stewart, C. Radford, J. Grimwood, Barlow, J. Silcock (*E), G. Haslam, G. Bissett, Jones (assistant trainer). Second row : P. Schofield, W. Harrison, F. Brett, J. Spence, G. Sapsford, J. Scott, J. Mew (*E), C. Hilditch (*E), Lockhead. Front row : R. Gibson, E. Partridge, J. Myerscough.

Players starred are Internationals.

Photo by Tuson, Manchester.

BENJAMIN 'BEN' LINDSAY THORNLEY

Country: England
Born: 21 Apr 1975
Debut: 26 Feb 1994 v West Ham United
Position: Winger
Appearances: 6 (8) **Goals scored:** 0
Seasons: 1993/94 – 1997/98
Clubs: Manchester United, Stockport County (*loan*), Huddersfield Town (*loan*), Huddersfield, Aberdeen, Blackpool, Bury, Halifax, Bacup Borough, Salford City, Wilmslow Albion, Witton Albion

PAUL TIERNEY

Country: England
Born: 15 Sep 1982
Debut: 3 Dec 2003 v West Bromwich Albion
Position: Midfield
Appearances: 1 **Goals scored:** 0
Seasons: 2003/04
Clubs: Manchester United, Crewe Alexandra (*loan*), Colchester United (*loan*), Bradford City (*loan*), Livingston, Blackpool, Stockport County (*loan*), Altrincham

MADS TIMM

Country: Denmark
Born: 31 Oct 1984
Debut: 29 Oct 2002 v Maccabi Haifa
Position: Forward
Appearances: 0 (1) **Goals scored:** 0
Seasons: 2002/03
Clubs: Manchester United, Viking (*loan*), Lyn (*loan*), Walsall (*loan*), Odense, Lyngby

GRAEME TOMLINSON

Country: England

Born: 10 Dec 1975
Debut: 5 Oct 1994 v Port Vale
Position: Forward
Appearances: 0 (2) **Goals scored:** 0
Seasons: 1994/95
Clubs: Bradford City, Manchester United, Luton Town (*loan*), Bournemouth (*loan*), Millwall (*loan*), Macclesfield Town, Exeter City, Stevenage Borough, Kingstonian, Bedford Town, St Albans City, Billericay Town, Stotfold, Dunstable Town

WILLIAM 'BILLY' TOMS

Country: Ireland
Born: 19 May 1895 **Died:** Unknown
Debut: 4 Oct 1919 v Middlesbrough
Position: Forward
Appearances: 14 **Goals scored:** 4
Seasons: 1919/20 – 1920/21
Clubs: Manchester United, Plymouth Argyle

HENRY TOPPING

Country: England
Born: 27 Oct 1908 **Died:** Jan 1977
Debut: 5 Apr 1933 v Bradford Park Avenue
Position: Full back
Appearances: 12 **Goals scored:** 1
Seasons: 1932/33 – 1934/35
Clubs: Horwich RMI, Manchester United, Barnsley

ZORAN TOSIC

Country: Serbia
Born: 28 Apr 1987
Debut: 24 Jan 2009 v Tottenham Hotspur
Position: Winger
Appearances: 0 (5) **Goals scored:** 0
Seasons: 2008/09 – 2009/10

Clubs: Proleter Zrenjanin, Banat Zrenjanin, Partizan, Manchester United, FC Cologne (*loan*), CSKA Moscow

WILFRED TRANTER

Country: England
Born: 5 Mar 1945
Debut: 7 Mar 1964 v West Ham United
Position: Defender
Appearances: 1 **Goals scored:** 0
Seasons: 1963/64
Clubs: Manchester United, Brighton & Hove Albion, Baltimore Bays, Fulham, St Louis Stars

GEORGE TRAVERS

Country: England
Born: 4 Nov 1888 **Died:** 31 Aug 1946
Debut: 7 Feb 1914 v Tottenham Hotspur
Position: Forward
Appearances: 21 **Goals scored:** 4
Seasons: 1913/14 – 1914/15
Clubs: Bilston United, Rowley United, Wolverhampton Wanderers, Birmingham, Aston Villa, Queen's Park Rangers, Leicester Fosse, Barnsley, Manchester United, Swindon Town

JAMES 'JIMMY' TURNBULL

Country: Scotland
Born: 23 May 1884 **Died:** Unknown
Debut: 28 Sep 1907 v Chelsea
Position: Forward
Appearances: 78 **Goals scored:** 45
Seasons: 1907/08 – 1909/10
Clubs: Dundee, Falkirk, Rangers, Preston North End, Leyton, Manchester United, Bradford Park Avenue, Chelsea

ALEXANDER 'SANDY' TURNBULL

Country: Scotland
Born: 1884 **Died:** 3 May 1917
Debut: 1 Jan 1907 v Aston Villa
Position: Forward
Appearances: 247 **Goals scored:** 101
Seasons: 1906/07 – 1914/15
Clubs: Manchester City, Manchester United

Sandy Turnbull was one of the four Manchester City players, including Billy Meredith, who transferred to United at the beginning of 1907 when the ban that had been imposed on the City squad (for illegal payments made to players) was lifted. He helped the club to their first championship in 1908 and to lift the 1909 FA Cup, scoring the only goal in the final against Bristol City. He also scored the first goal at Old Trafford, a low header against Liverpool on 19 February 1910. In May 1917, while serving in the East Surrey Regiment, Turnbull died at Arras, France aged 32. He had received a life-long ban from football, along with several other players, in 1915 for match fixing. The ban was posthumously rescinded in 1919.

Below: 24 January 2009. Zoran Tosic is challenged by Giovani Dos Santos of Tottenham Hotspur during the FA Cup fourth round match.

NORBERT 'NOBBY' STILES

Country: England
Born: 18 May 1942
Debut: 1 Oct 1960 Bolton Wanderers
Position: Midfield/Defender
Appearances: 395 **Goals scored:** 19
Seasons: 1960/61 - 1970/71
Clubs: Manchester United,
Middlesbrough, Preston North End

The gap-toothed grin, the bone-crunching tackle, the unyielding competitiveness – all these things and more were what made Nobby Stiles such a favourite at Old Trafford for eleven seasons. In the era of Best, Law and Charlton, the Reds needed a fixer, a tough guy, someone to win the ball for the benefit of the talented goalscorers and Stiles was that man. He was the team's defensive midfielder who protected his back four with a passion and provided the ball to his more creative team-mates.

Born Norbert Stiles in May 1942 in the north-east part of Manchester, the young United supporter joined the club's youth set-up in 1957 aged 15, having been talented enough to play for England Schoolboys. However, Stiles was small and relatively slight of build (he would eventually grow to be only 5ft 6ins tall), so the chances of him ever making the first team seemed as slim as his youthful frame. He also looked older than his years with an early receding hairline and dentures that he took out while playing to reveal the absence of front teeth. But manager Matt Busby was convinced by his on-field tenacity, and gave Stiles his professional debut in 1960 at the age of 18. The teenager was so impressive that he kept his place for the rest of the season, making 26 appearances.

For the next eight seasons, barring injury, Stiles was as much a fixture in the team as his more illustrious teammates. He was hugely disappointed not to be picked for the FA Cup final team in 1963, but would win two league championship medals in 1965 and 1967.

Stiles was a key part of Alf Ramsey's England team and played in the World Cup-winning side in 1966. After the game, with his toothless grin and holding the Jules Rimet trophy, Stiles performed the now-famous jig that was about as much as his exhausted body could stand.

This period saw Stiles at his most effective: his reputation as a fearless tackler meant other midfield players took his presence seriously; although sent off several times when his enthusiasm got the better of him, there was never a doubt that this was an honest player who knew his role in the team. Best of all as a United player, Stiles helped the team win the European Cup in 1968, having been given the responsibility of marking Benfica's best player Eusébio in the final.

In May 1971 after 395 appearances for United, Stiles was sold to Middlesbrough for £200,000. He played there for two seasons and two more at Preston North End before becoming the Lancashire club's manager in 1977. He also managed Vancouver Whitecaps in the North American Soccer League and West Bromwich Albion back in England then left the football world for good in 1986. His 28 England caps, World Cup winners' medal and starring role at United all contributed to his MBE awarded in 2000.

Top Left: 30 July 1966. England manager Alf Ramsey celebrates his team's 4-2 victory in extra time over West Germany in the World Cup final at Wembley Stadium. With him are captain Bobby Moore – holding the Jules Rimet Trophy – and Nobby Stiles.

Left: Nobby Stiles' 1966 FIFA World Cup winner's medal.

Below: 23 May 1968. Nobby Stiles receives treatment on his knee from the club physiotherapist Ted Dalton a few days before the Europen Cup final.

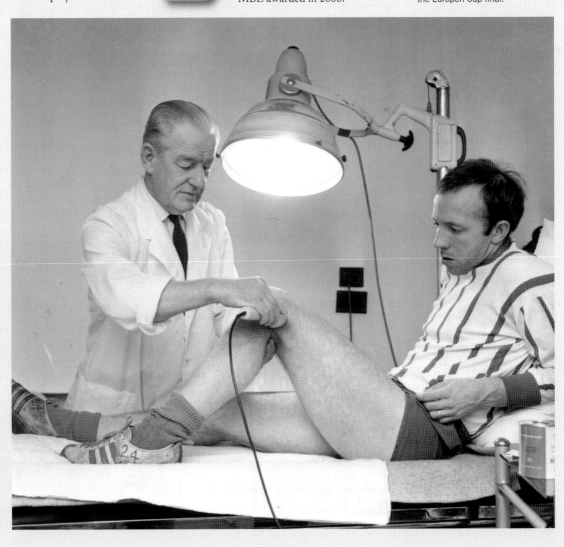

TURNER
Country: Unknown
Born: Unknown **Died:** Unknown
Debut: 25 Oct 1890 v Bootle Reserves
Position: Forward
Appearances: 1 **Goals scored:** 0
Seasons: 1890/91
Clubs: Newton Heath

CHRISTOPHER 'CHRIS' ROBERT TURNER
Country: England
Born: 15 Sep 1958
Debut: 14 Dec 1985 v Aston Villa
Position: Goalkeeper
Appearances: 79 **Goals scored:** 0
Seasons: 1985/86 – 1987/88
Clubs: Sheffield Wednesday, Lincoln City (loan), Sunderland, Manchester United, Leeds United (loan), Leyton Orient

JOHN TURNER
Country: England
Born: Unknown **Died:** Unknown
Debut: 22 Oct 1898 v Loughborough Town
Position: Half back
Appearances: 4 **Goals scored:** 0
Seasons: 1898/99
Clubs: Gravesend United, Newton heath

ROBERT TURNER
Country: England
Born: 1877 **Died:** Unknown
Debut: 8 Oct 1898 v Port Vale
Position: Defender
Appearances: 2 **Goals scored:** 0
Seasons: 1898/99
Clubs: Newton Heath, Brighton United

MICHAEL TWISS
Country: England
Born: 26 Dec 1977
Debut: 25 Feb 1998 v Aston Villa
Position: Midfield
Appearances: 1 (1) **Goals scored:** 0
Seasons: 1997/98 – 1999/2000
Clubs: Manchester United, Sheffield United (loan), Port Vale, Leigh RMI, Chester City, Morecambe, Stalybridge Celtic, Altrincham

SIDNEY TYLER
Country: England
Born: 7 Dec 1904 **Died:** 25 Jan 1951
Debut: 10 Nov 1923 v Leicester City
Position: Full back
Appearances: 1 **Goals scored:** 0
Seasons: 1923/24
Clubs: Manchester United, Wolverhampton Wanderers

JOHN FRANCOMBE 'IAN' URE
Country: Scotland
Born: 7 Dec 1939

Debut: 23 Aug 1969 v Wolverhampton Wanderers
Position: Defender
Appearances: 65 **Goals scored:** 1
Seasons: 1969/70 – 1970/71
Clubs: Dundee, Arsenal, Manchester United, St Mirren

ANTONIO VALENCIA
Country: Ecuador
Born: 4 Aug 1985
Debut: 9 Aug 2009 v Chelsea
Position: Winger
Appearances: 52 (17) **Goals scored:** 10
Seasons: 2009/10 – present
Clubs: El Nacional, Villarreal CF, Recreativo (loan), Wigan Athletic, Manchester United

BOB VALENTINE
Country: England
Born: Unknown **Died:** Unknown
Debut: 25 Mar 1905 v Blackpool
Position: Goalkeeper
Appearances: 10 **Goals scored:** 0
Seasons: 1904/05 – 1905/06
Clubs: Manchester United

JAMES VANCE
Country: England
Born: 1877 **Died:** Unknown
Debut: 3 Feb 1896 v Leicester City
Position: Forward
Appearances: 11 **Goals scored:** 1
Seasons: 1895/96 – 1896/97
Clubs: Annbank, Newton Heath, Fairfield

RAIMOND VAN DER GOUW
Country: Netherlands
Born: 24 Mar 1963
Debut: 21 Sep 1996 v Aston Villa

Position: Goalkeeper
Appearances: 48 (12) **Goals scored:** 0
Seasons: 1996/67 – 2001/02
Clubs: Go Ahead Eagles, Vitesse, Manchester United, West Ham United, RKC Waalwijk, AGOVV Apeldoorn

EDWIN VAN DER SAR
Country: Netherlands
Born: 29 Oct 1970
Debut: 9 Aug 2005 v Debreceni
Position: Goalkeeper
Appearances: 266 **Goals scored:** 0
Seasons: 2005/06 – 2010/11
Clubs: Ajax, Juventus, Fulham, Manchester United

Edwin van der Sar joined United from Fulham in 2005 and spent the remainder of his career at Old Trafford. He was known for his reliability and excellent ball distribution. Calm and consistent, he inspired confidence in his defence and in 2008-09 went a record 1,311 minutes without conceding a goal in the Premier League. He won four Premier League titles during his time at United, but he will be best remembered for his save against Nicolas Anelka in the penalty shoot-out that decided the 2008 Champions League final in favour of the Reds.

JUAN SEBASTIAN VERON
Country: Argentina
Born: 9 Mar 1975
Debut: 19 Aug 2001 v Fulham
Position: Midfield
Appearances: 75 (7) **Goals scored:** 11
Seasons: 2001/02 – 2002/03
Clubs: Estudiantes, Boca Juniors, Sampdoria, Parma, Lazio, Manchester United, Chelsea, Internazionale (loan), Estudiantes

Right: 4 May 2011. Antonio Valencia scores the opening goal during the Champions League semi-final against Schalke 04. The Ecuadorian international was signed to replace Cristiano Ronaldo on the right flank of United's attack, and provided great service for Wayne Rooney in his first season. His second campaign was disrupted by a badly broken leg, but he returned to win his first league title with the Reds.

THOMAS 'TOMMY' TAYLOR
Country: England
Born: 29 Jan 1932 **Died:** 6 Feb 1958
Debut: 7 Mar 1953 v Preston North End
Position: Forward
Appearances: 191 **Goals scored:** 131
Seasons: 1952/53 – 1957/58
Clubs: Barnsley, Manchester United

United's list of centre forwards down the years is studded with truly great names, but many believe the greatest of all – despite having played only 191 games for the club – was Thomas 'Tommy' Taylor. Bought by Matt Busby from Barnsley for a then-record transfer fee of £29,999, Taylor had size and strength, a good touch and a goal scorer's natural instinct for finding the net. The fact that he was one of the eight United players killed in the Munich air crash at the age of 26 makes his achievements in five years at the club all the more remarkable.

Taylor was born in the Yorkshire mining town of in Barnsley in 1932 and worked in the colliery from the age of 14. He was spotted by Second Division Barnsley scouts as a 16-year-old playing for a local colliery team and made his debut for Barnsley's first team in October 1950 at the age of 18. In his second match he scored a hat-trick; in total Taylor scored 26 times in 44 league appearances in under three seasons. It was the kind of goalscoring ratio that he would continue throughout his short career. Two years of national service disrupted Taylor's footballing life in Yorkshire when he joined the Royal Artillery and was posted to a base in Shropshire.

Yet his reputation had grown so fast that by March 1953 Matt Busby was keen to sign him. Busby, anxious to avoid saddling the young man with the label of the first £30,000 player, handed over £1 of the transfer fee to a lady serving refreshments in his office as the deal was being finalised. Or at least so the story goes.

Taylor, still only 21-years-old, did not seem to care what price United paid because he immediately started scoring goals with the same passion for the Reds. In his first, shortened season at Old Trafford, Taylor scored seven times in eleven games including two on his debut. In the same year he began his England international career and ultimately played 19 times for his country, scoring 16 goals.

Taylor was a magnificent header of the ball, was two-footed with a splendid first touch. He fitted into the Busby style of play as if to the manor born. He top-scored for the club in his first full season with 23 goals and achieved the same status both in 1955-56 and 1956-57 seasons (25 and 34 goals respectively) when he also won league championship medals.

As United began winning matches in Europe, Taylor's reputation widened. The great Alfredo Di Stefano of Real Madrid, regarded by many as the best player of his time, called him 'Magnifico' as the Reds reached their first European Cup semi-final in 1957. That same year, Busby refused a world record amount of £65,000 for Taylor from Internazionale of Milan.

Such stories would only add to the legend of the player who lost his life on the runway in Munich in February 1958. He died instantly, leaving behind a young fiancée and the adoration of United fans. Taylor scored two goals in every three games for United, and his 131 goals still puts him 14th in the list of all-time scorers.

Left: England and Manchester United forward Tommy Taylor.

Below: Circa 1957. Tommy Taylor, David Pegg and Roger Byrne.

NEMANJA VIDIC
Country: Serbia
Born: 21 Oct 1981
Debut: 25 Jan 2006 v Blackburn Rovers
Position: Centre back
Appearances: 227 (7) **Goals scored:** 18
Seasons: 2005/6 – present
Clubs: Red Star Belgrade, Spartak Subotica (*loan*), Spartak Moscow, Manchester United

Since his arrival in England, Nemanja Vidic has developed into one of the toughest, most uncompromising centre backs in the league. He started his career with Red Star Belgrade and after a spell at Spartak Moscow, joined United in 2006. In his first full season he won the league title, forming a solid defensive pairing with Rio Ferdinand. He has gone on to win three more league titles as well as the Champions League and three League Cups. In 2008-09 he helped United to a record 14 consecutive clean sheets and was voted Barclays Player of the Season. In 2010-11 he was named team captain and again elected Barclays Player of the Season.

ERNEST VINCENT
Country: England
Born: 28 Oct 1910 **Died:** 2 Jun 1978
Debut: 6 Feb 1932 v Chesterfield
Position: Midfield

Below: 17 May 1990. Danny Wallace during the FA Cup final replay at Wembley. Manchester United beat Crystal Palace 1-0.

Appearances: 65 **Goals scored:** 1
Seasons: 1931/32 – 1933/34
Clubs: Southport, Manchester United, Queens Park Rangers

GEORGE VOSE
Country: England
Born: 4 Oct 1911 **Died:** 20 Jun 1981
Debut: 26 Aug 1933 v Plymouth Argyle
Position: Defender
Appearances: 209 **Goals scored:** 1
Seasons: 1933/34 – 1938/39
Clubs: Peasley Cross Athletic, Manchester United, Runcorn

COLIN WALDRON
Country: England
Born: 22 Jun 1948
Debut: 4 Oct 1976 v Sunderland
Position: Defender
Appearances: 4 **Goals scored:** 0
Seasons: 1976/77
Clubs: Bury, Chelsea, Burnley, Manchester United, Sunderland, Tulsa Roughnecks, Philadelphia Fury, Atlanta Chiefs, Rochdale

DENNIS WALKER
Country: England
Born: 26 Oct 1944
Debut: 20 May 1963 v Nottingham Forest
Position: Midfield
Appearances: 1 **Goals scored:** 0

Seasons: 1962/63
Clubs: Manchester United, York City, Cambridge United

ROBERT WALKER
Country: Unknown
Born: Unknown **Died:** Unknown
Debut: 14 Jan 1899 v Glossop
Position: Defender
Appearances: 2 **Goals scored:** 0
Seasons: 1898/99
Clubs: Newton Heath

GEORGE WALL
Country: England
Born: 20 Feb 1885 **Died:** Apr 1962
Debut: 7 Apr 1906 v Leyton Orient
Position: Winger
Appearances: 319 **Goals scored:** 100
Seasons: 1905/06 – 1914/15
Clubs: Barnsley, Manchester United, Oldham Athletic, Hamilton Academicals, Rochdale

A fast and tricky left winger who made United such a threat, along with Billy Meredith on the right flank, during the club's first two league championship seasons and the 1909 FA Cup triumph. Wall served in the Black Watch regiment in the First World War and won seven England caps, scoring two international goals.

DANIEL LLOYD 'DANNY' WALLACE
Country: England
Born: 21 Jan 1964
Debut: 20 Sep 1989 v Portsmouth
Position: Winger
Appearances: 53 (18) **Goals scored:** 11
Seasons: 1989/90 – 1992/93
Clubs: Southampton, Manchester United, Millwall (*loan*), Birmingham City, Wycombe Wanderers

RONALD 'RONNIE' WALLWORK
Country: England
Born: 10 Sep 1977
Debut: 25 Oct 1997 v Barnsley
Position: Midfield
Appearances: 10 (18) **Goals scored:** 0
Seasons: 1997/98 – 2001/02
Clubs: Manchester United, Carlisle United (*loan*), Stockport County (*loan*), Royal Antwerp (*loan*), West Bromwich Albion, Bradford City (*loan*), Barnsley (*loan*), Huddersfield Town (*loan*), Sheffield Wednesday

GARY WALSH
Country: England
Born: 21 Mar 1968
Debut: 13 Dec 1986 v Aston Villa
Position: Goalkeeper
Appearances: 62 (1) **Goals scored:** 0
Seasons: 1986/87 – 1994/95
Clubs: Manchester United, Airdrieonians (*loan*), Oldham Athletic (*loan*), Middlesbrough, Bradford City (*loan*), Bradford City, Middlesbrough (*loan*), Wigan Athletic

RUUD VAN NISTELROOY

Country: Netherlands
Born: 1 Jul 1976
Debut: 12 Aug 2001 v Liverpool
Position: Forward
Appearances: 200 (19) **Goals scored:** 150
Seasons: 2001/02 – 2005/06
Clubs: Den Bosch, SC Heerenveen, PSV Eindhoven, Manchester United, Real Madrid, Hamburg, Malaga

Joining United a year after a career-threatening ruptured cruciate ligament injury and tasked with replacing Blackburn Rovers-bound Andy Cole, Ruud van Nistelrooy's job did not appear to be an easy one before the 2001-02 season started. Yet it is a measure of his character and predatory eye for goal that he was able to settle in immediately and go on to score a remarkable 150 goals in 200 starts across five successful seasons at Old Trafford.

Improbably for such a prolific striker, van Nistelrooy – born in 1976 – started his football life as a central defender at Dutch Second Division outfit FC Den Bosch. After conversion to centre forward, the goals began to flow and before long he moved to PSV Eindhoven via SC Heerenveen for a Dutch record fee of €6.3 million. A pair of Dutch league titles later, coupled with two seasons as the leading scorer in the Dutch top flight and Europe's leading clubs came calling.

United were about to sign him in April 2000, but he failed the medical and days later suffered a freak knee injury in training that delayed the move for a year. The delay did not faze the Dutchman, who eventually signed for £19 million, as he scored 36 goals in 49 matches in his first season, including an impressive haul of ten in the Champions League that saw him named Professional Footballers' Association Player of the Year.

In his second season, a further 44 goals in 52 matches left him top scorer in the Premier League. His contribution helped propel United to their fourth title in five years as van Nistelrooy became one of Europe's most feared strikers. Surprisingly, considering his rich goal scoring haul in a red shirt, it turned out to be United's only league title during van Nistelrooy's time in Manchester.

Characteristically, United fans were not slow to recognise his contribution and he was voted Matt Busby Player of the Year in both 2002 and 2003. Then in 2004 he played a vital role in winning United their eleventh FA Cup with two goals in a 3-0 win over Millwall at Cardiff's Millennium Stadium.

The 2004-05 season was marred by injury, yet van Nistelrooy still managed a season's best eight Champions League goals, overtaking Denis Law's previous club record of 28 European goals in the process. He was by now a fixture in the Dutch national team and would go on to win 70 caps and score 35 goals for his country.

More United silverware was to follow in the shape of the 2006 League Cup, although van Nistelrooy was an unused substitute and there were media reports of disharmony. He was sold to Real Madrid for £12.3 million in July 2006 to the bemusement of many United fans.

Ruud van Nistelrooy's career continued to flourish and in the Spanish capital he scored a hat-trick in only his second league appearance and would pick up more trophies. After spending the 2010-11 season in Germany with Hamburg, he recently completed a move back to Spain with Malaga.

Above: 12 Aug 2001. Ruud van Nistelrooy scores during the Charity Shield encounter between Liverpool and United at The Millennium Stadium, Cardiff.

Below: 5 Dec 2001. Ruud van Nistelrooy scores a goal in the Champions League against Boavista. Always a prolific goalscorer, his record in this competition was even better than his overall record: 38 goals in 47 appearances.

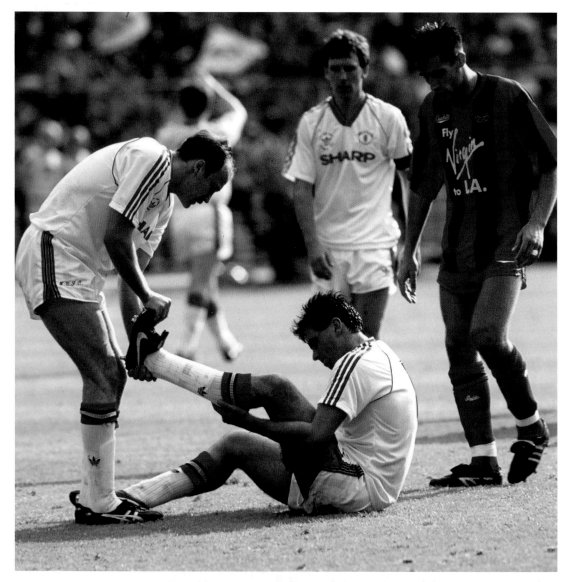

Above: 12 May 1990. Neil Webb receives attention for cramp from Michael Phelan during the FA Cup final. He missed much of his first season at United with an Achilles injury.

JOSEPH 'JOE' WALTON
Country: England
Born: 5 Jun 1925 **Died:** 31 Dec 2006
Debut: 26 Jan 1946 v Preston North End
Position: Forward
Appearances: 23 **Goals scored:** 0
Seasons: 1945/46 – 1947/48
Clubs: Manchester United, Preston North End, Accrington Stanley

JOHN WALTON
Country: England
Born: 21 Mar 1928 **Died:** 17 Jul 1979
Debut: 29 Sep 1951 v Preston North End
Position: Forward
Appearances: 2 **Goals scored:** 0
Seasons: 1951/52
Clubs: Bury, Manchester United, Burnley, Coventry City, Chester, Kettering Town

ARTHUR WARBURTON
Country: England
Born: 30 Oct 1903 **Died:** 21 Apr 1978
Debut: 8 Mar 1930 v Aston Villa
Position: Forward
Appearances: 39 **Goals scored:** 10
Seasons: 1929/30 – 1933/34
Clubs: Manchester United, Burnley

JOHN 'JACK' WARNER
Country: Wales
Born: 21 Sep 1911 **Died:** 4 Oct 1980
Debut: 5 Nov 1938 v Aston Villa
Position: half back
Appearances: 116 **Goals scored:** 2
Seasons: 1938/39 – 1949/50
Clubs: Swansea Town, Manchester United, Oldham Athletic

JAMES 'JIMMY' WARNER
Country: England
Born: 15 Apr 1865 **Died:** 7 Nov 1943
Debut: 3 Sep 1892 v Blackburn Rovers
Position: Goalkeeper
Appearances: 22 **Goals scored:** 0
Seasons: 1892/93 – 1893/94

Clubs: Milton FC, Aston Villa, Newton Heath, Walsall Town Swifts

JOHN 'JACKIE' WASSALL
Country: England
Born: 11 Feb 1917 **Died:** Apr 1994
Debut: 9 Nov 1935 v Swansea City
Position: Forward
Appearances: 47 **Goals scored:** 6
Seasons: 1935/36 – 1938/39
Clubs: Wellington Town, Manchester United, Stockport County

WILLIAM 'WILLIE' WATSON
Country: Scotland
Born: 4 Dec 1949
Debut: 26 Sep 1970 v Blackpool
Position: Fullback
Appearances: 14 **Goals scored:** 0
Seasons: 1970/71 – 1972/73
Clubs: Manchester United, Miami Toros, Motherwell

JEFFREY 'JEFF' WEALANDS
Country: England
Born: 26 Aug 1951
Debut: 2 Apr 1983 v Coventry City
Position: Goalkeeper
Appearances: 8 **Goals scored:** 0
Seasons: 1982/83 – 1983/84
Clubs: Wolverhampton Wanderers, Northampton Town (loan), Darlington, Hull City, Birmingham City, Manchester United, Oldham Athletic (loan), Preston North End (loan), Altrincham, Barrow

NEIL WEBB
Country: England
Born: 30 Jul 1963
Debut: 19 Aug 1989 v Arsenal
Position: Midfield
Appearances: 105 (5) **Goals scored:** 11
Seasons: 1989/90 – 1992/93
Clubs: Reading, Portsmouth, Nottingham Forest, Manchester United, Nottingham Forest, Swindon Town (loan), Grimsby Town, Aldershot Town

DANIEL VAUGHN 'DANNY' WEBBER
Country: England
Born: 28 Dec 1981
Debut: 28 Nov 2000 v Sunderland
Position: Striker
Appearances: 3 **Goals scored:** 0
Seasons: 2000/01 – 2002/03
Clubs: Manchester United, Port Vale (loan), Watford (loan), Watford, Sheffield United (loan), Sheffield United, Portsmouth

COLIN WEBSTER
Country: Wales
Born: 17 Jul 1932 **Died:** 1 Mar 2001
Debut: 28 Nov 1953 v Portsmouth
Position: Striker
Appearances: 79 **Goals scored:** 31
Seasons: 1953/54 – 1958/59
Clubs: Cardiff City, Manchester United, Swansea Town, Newport County

DENNIS SYDNEY VIOLLET

Country: England
Born: 20 Sep 1933 **Died:** 6 Mar 1999
Debut: 11 Apr 1953 v Newcastle United
Position: Forward
Appearances: 293 **Goals scored:** 179
Seasons: 1952/53 - 1961/62
Clubs: Manchester United, Stoke
City, Baltimore Bays, Linfield

Of all the young men blessed to play for the Busby Babes, Dennis Viollet looked the least likely in terms of his physical make-up. The Manchester-born striker was scrawny and looked pale and under-strength when compared to his counter-parts, and yet his role as a phenomenal scorer of goals – 179 in just 293 games – marks Viollet out from those around him. He left the robustness of forward play to men like Tommy Taylor and, instead, brought his innate attributes of positioning, acceleration and marksman-ship to the team. At 5ft 8ins and just over 10½ stones in weight, the inside forward was more of a threat than his size indicated. He remains perhaps the most underrated of United's forwards in the post-war era.

Viollet joined United as a trainee in 1949 aged 16 and turned professional a year later. In 1952-53 he made his debut, making three appearances and scoring one goal. The following year he made his way into the team as the Babes were starting to take shape.

His partnership with Taylor was an almost immediate success as United began building towards their consecu-tive league championships in 1955-56 and 1956-57. Viollet scored 46 goals in

all competitions during those two title-winning seasons and would eventually top score for the club on three occasions.

Miraculously, Viollet survived the Munich air crash in February 1958. He was sitting next to Bobby Charlton on the plane and was thrown clear of the wreckage, suffering only minor head injuries. He recovered in time to take his place in the United team that reached the FA Cup final at Wembley in May against Bolton Wanderers, picking up a runners-up medal – just as he had done the previous year when the Reds lost to Aston Villa.

Despite losing so many teammates, Viollet had two more incredible goal-scoring seasons at Old Trafford. His total of 32 league goals in 1959-60 was a record for a United player that remains unbeaten. Such prodigious scoring did not go unnoticed and won him two England caps. However, Matt Busby now wanted change, and in January 1962, Viollet was transferred to Stoke City for

£25,000, a move that surprised many fans and pundits.

At Stoke, Viollet teamed up with Stanley Matthews and helped the Potters to the Second Division title in his first season. He moved away from English football in 1967 and headed for America where he played in the nascent North American Soccer League (NASL), but returned after two years for spells at Witton Albion and Linfield where he won the Irish Cup in 1970 in his final season as a player.

Viollet's attempts at coaching with Preston North End and management with Crewe Alexandra were failures, so he returned to America, joining up with ex-teammate Noel Cantwell again in the NASL. Viollet was altogether more suc-cessful in America and settled in Florida – continuing to coach in Jacksonville, where he was extremely well-respected. He was given the freedom of the city not long before his death from a brain tumour in 1999 aged 65.

Left: 1 October 1956. Dennis Viollet at Old Trafford.

Below: Circa 1956. A rare colour photograph of United's phenomenal goal scorer.

FRANK WEDGE
Country: England
Born: 28 Jul 1876 **Died:** Unknown
Debut: 20 Nov 1897 v Leicester City
Position: Forward
Appearances: 2 **Goals scored:** 2
Seasons: 1897/98
Clubs: Manchester Talbot, Newton Heath, Chorlton-cum-Hardy

DANIEL 'DANNY' WELBECK
Country: England
Born: 26 Nov 1990
Debut: 23 Sep 2008 v Middlesbrough
Position: Striker
Appearances: 16 (9) **Goals scored:** 5
Seasons: 2008/09 – present
Clubs: Manchester United, Preston North End (loan), Sunderland (loan)

RICHARD WELLENS
Country: England
Born: 26 Mar 1980
Debut: 13 Oct 1999 v Aston Villa
Position: Midfield
Appearances: 0 (1) **Goals scored:** 0
Seasons: 1999/2000
Clubs: Manchester United, Blackpool, Oldham Athletic, Doncaster Rovers, Leicester City

ENOCH 'KNOCKER' WEST
Country: England
Born: 31 Mar 1886 **Died:** Sep 1965
Debut: 1 Sep 1910 v Arsenal
Position: Forward
Appearances: 181 **Goals scored:** 80
Seasons: 1910/11 – 1914/15
Clubs: Nottingham Forest, Manchester United

JOSPEH 'JOE' WETHERELL
Country: England
Born: 1880 **Died:** Unknown
Debut: 21 Sep 1896 v Walsall
Position: Goalkeeper
Appearances: 2 **Goals scored:** 0
Seasons: 1896/97
Clubs: Newton Heath

ARTHUR WHALLEY
Country: England
Born: 17 Feb 1886 **Died:** 23 Nov 1952
Debut: 27 Dec 1909 v Sheffield Wednesday
Position: Half back
Appearances: 106 **Goals scored:** 6
Seasons: 1909/10 – 1919/20
Clubs: Wigan Town, Blackpool, Manchester United, Southend United

HERBERT 'BERT' WHALLEY
Country: England
Born: 6 Aug 1912 **Died:** 6 Feb 1958
Debut: 30 Nov 1935 v Doncaster Rovers
Position: Defender
Appearances: 38 **Goals scored:** 0
Seasons: 1935/36 – 1946/47
Clubs: Stalybridge Celtic, Manchester United

Bert Whalley played for Bolton Wanderers, Liverpool, and Oldham Athletic during the war. Afterwards Matt Busby appointed him first-team coach. He was killed in Munich air crash.

ANTHONY WHELAN
Country: Republic of Ireland
Born: 23 Nov 1959
Debut: 29 Nov 1980 v Southampton
Position: Defender
Appearances: 1 **Goals scored:** 0
Seasons: 1980/81
Clubs: Bohemians, Manchester United, Shamrock Rovers, Cork City, Bray Wanderers, Shelbourne

WILLIAM 'LIAM' WHELAN
Country: Republic of Ireland
Born: 1 Apr 1935 **Died:** 6 Feb 1958
Debut: 26 Mar 1955 v Preston North End
Position: Forward
Appearances: 98 **Goals scored:** 52
Seasons: 1954/55 – 1957/58
Clubs: Manchester United

Billy Whelan was just 22 years old when he died in the Munich air crash. A devout Roman Catholic, he was not a confident flyer and is reputed to have said on boarding the fateful aircraft: "Well, if this is the time, then I'm ready." He made 98 appearances for United, scoring 52 goals and was capped four times by the Republic of Ireland.

JEFFERY WHITEFOOT
Country: England
Born: 31 Dec 1933
Debut: 15 Apr 1950 v Portsmouth
Position: Midfield

Appearances: 95 **Goals scored:** 0
Seasons: 1949/50 – 1955/56
Clubs: Manchester United, Grimsby Town, Nottingham Forest

At 16 years 105 days, Jeff Whitefoot is the youngest outfield player ever to play for United. The wing half went on to win the FA Cup with Nottingham Forest.

JAMES WHITEHOUSE
Country: England
Born: Apr 1873 **Died:** 7 Feb 1934
Debut: 15 Sep 1900 v Burnley
Position: Goalkeeper
Appearances: 64 **Goals scored:** 0
Seasons: 1900/01 – 1902/03
Clubs: Albion Swifts, Birmingham St. George, Grimsby Town, Aston Villa, Bedminster, Grimsby Town, Newton Heath, Manchester City

WALTER WHITEHURST
Country: England
Born: 7 Jun 1934 **Died:** 7 Jun 1934
Debut: 14 Sep 1955 v Everton
Position: Midfield
Appearances: 1 **Goals scored:** 0
Seasons: 1955/56
Clubs: Manchester United, Chesterfield, Crewe Alexandra

KERR WHITESIDE
Country: Scotland
Born: 1887 **Died:** Unknown
Debut: 18 Jan 1908 v Sheffield United
Position: Midfield
Appearances: 1 **Goals scored:** 0
Seasons: 1907/08
Clubs: Irvine Victoria, Manchester United, Hurst FC

NORMAN WHITESIDE
Country: Northern Ireland
Born: 7 May 1965
Debut: 24 Apr 1982 v Brighton & Hove Albion
Position: Midfield/Forward
Appearances: 256 (18) **Goals scored:** 67
Seasons: 1981/82 – 1987/88
Clubs: Manchester United, Everton

Norman Whiteside became the youngest player to represent United since Duncan Edwards when he made his debut, as a substitute, in April 1982 – two weeks before his 17th birthday. A few weeks later he became United's youngest ever scorer as the Reds beat Stoke 2-0 at Old Trafford. In 1983 he became the youngest ever FA Cup final scorer as United beat Brighton. As if that wasn't enough he also became the youngest to score in a League Cup final, in 1983, while the previous year he had set the record as the youngest player ever to appear in the World Cup finals, beating Pelé. In 1985 he scored the winner in the FA Cup final against Everton. In all the powerfully built Irishman scored 67 goals in 274 appearances at Old Trafford. He retired prematurely at 26 due to persistent knee injuries.

JOHN WHITNEY

Country: England
Born: 1874 **Died:** Unknown
Debut: 29 Feb 1896 v Burton Wanderers
Position: Midfield
Appearances: 3 **Goals scored:** 0
Seasons: 1895/96 and 1900/01
Clubs: Newton Heath

WALTER WHITTAKER

Country: England
Born: 20 Sep 1878 **Died:** 2 Jun 1917
Debut: 14 Mar 1896 v Grimsby Town
Position: Goalkeeper
Appearances: 3 **Goals scored:** 0
Seasons: 1895/96
Clubs: Molyneaux F.C., Newton Heath, Grimsby Town

JOHN WHITTLE

Country: England
Born: 29 Jun 1910 **Died:** 31 Jul 1987
Debut: 16 Jan 1932 v Swansea City
Position: Winger
Appearances: 1 **Goals scored:** 0
Seasons: 1931/32
Clubs: Manchester United, Rossendale United

NEIL WHITWORTH

Country: England
Born: 12 Apr 1972
Debut: 13 Mar 1991 v Southampton
Position: Defender
Appearances: 1 **Goals scored:** 0
Seasons: 1990/91
Clubs: Wigan Athletic, Manchester United, Preston North End (loan), Barnsley (loan), Rotherham United (loan), Blackpool (loan), Kilmarnock, Wigan Athletic (loan), Hull City, Exeter City, Southport, Radcliffe Borough (loan)

TOM WILCOX

Country: England
Born: 1879 **Died:** 10 Sep 1963
Debut: 24 Oct 1908 v Nottingham Forest
Position: Goalkeeper
Appearances: 2 **Goals scored:** 0
Seasons: 1908/09
Clubs: Norwich City, Blackpool, Manchester United, Carlisle United

RAY WILKINS

Country: England
Born: 14 Sep 1956
Debut: 18 Aug 1979 v Southampton
Position: Midfield
Appearances: 191 (3) **Goals scored:** 10
Seasons: 1979/80 – 1983/84

Clubs: Chelsea, Manchester United, Milan, Paris St. Germain, Rangers, Queens Park Rangers, Crystal Palace, Wycombe Wanderers, Hibernian, Millwall, Leyton Orient

The record signing of the England midfielder from Chelsea for £777,777 in August 1979 was a great move by manager Dave Sexton, who had coached Ray Wilkins as a 15-year-old at the London club. He was already captain of the Blues, and was expected soon to take that role both for United and for England, as proved to be the case. While never a prolific goalscorer himself, he had superb vision and was a great distributor of the ball. Eventually he was sold to AC Milan for about £1.5 million after five seasons with the Reds. He won just one honour in his time at United: the 1983 FA Cup.

HENRY 'HARRY' WILKINSON

Country: England
Born: 1883 **Died:** Unknown
Debut: 26 Dec 1903 v Burton United
Position: Winger
Appearances: 9 **Goals scored:** 0
Seasons: 1903/04
Clubs: Athletic, Hull City, West Ham United, Haslingden FC

IAN WILKINSON

Country: England
Born: 2 Jul 1973
Debut: 9 Oct 1991 v Cambridge United
Position: Goalkeeper
Appearances: 1 **Goals scored:** 0
Seasons: 1991/92
Clubs: Manchester United, Stockport County, Crewe Alexandra

WILLIAM 'BILL' WILLIAMS

Country: Unknown
Born: Unknown **Died:** Unknown
Debut: 7 Sep 1901 v Gainsborough Trinity
Position: Forward
Appearances: 4 **Goals scored:** 0
Seasons: 1901/02
Clubs: Everton, Blackburn Rovers, Bristol City, Newton Heath

Above: 2 August 1981. Ray Wilkins in action during a pre-season friendly against West Ham United. He formed a superb midfield partnership with Bryan Robson for club and country.

Above: January 1958. Ray Wood during a training session.

FRANK WILLIAMS
Country: England
Born: 1908 **Died:** Unknown
Debut: 13 Sep 1930 v Newcastle United
Position: Midfield
Appearances: 3 **Goals scored:** 0
Seasons: 1930/31
Clubs: Stalybridge Celtic, Manchester United, Altincham

FREDERICK 'FRED' WILLIAMS
Country: England
Born: 1873 **Died:** Unknown
Debut: 6 Sep 1902 v Gainsborough Trinity
Position: Forward
Appearances: 10 **Goals scored:** 4
Seasons: 1902/03
Clubs: Hanley Swifts, South Shore, Manchester City, Manchester United

HARRY WILLIAMS
Country: England
Born: 1899 **Died:** Unknown
Debut: 28 Aug 1922 v Sheffield Wednesday
Position: Forward
Appearances: 5 **Goals scored:** 2
Seasons: 1922/23
Clubs: Chesterfield, Manchester United, Brentford

HARRY 'HENRY' WILLIAMS
Country: England
Born: 1883 **Died:** Unknown
Debut: 10 Sep 1904 v Bristol City
Position: Forward
Appearances: 37 **Goals scored:** 8
Seasons: 1904/05 - 1907/08
Clubs: Bolton Wanderers, Burnley, Manchester United, Leeds City

JOSEPH 'JOE' WILLIAMS
Country: England
Born: 1873 **Died:** Unknown
Debut: 25 Mar 1907 v Sunderland
Position: Forward
Appearances: 3 **Goals scored:** 1
Seasons: 1906/07
Clubs: Macclesfield, Manchester United

REES WILLIAMS
Country: Wales
Born: Jan 1900 **Died:** 30 Dec 1963
Debut: 8 Oct 1927 v Everton
Position: Winger
Appearances: 35 **Goals scored:** 2
Seasons: 1927/28 - 1928/29
Clubs: Sheffield Wednesday, Manchester United, Thames Association

JOHN WILLIAMSON
Country: England
Born: 1893 **Died:** Unknown
Debut: 17 Apr 1920 v Blackburn Rovers
Position: Midfield
Appearances: 2 **Goals scored:** 0
Seasons: 1919/20
Clubs: Manchester United, Bury

DAVID WILSON
Country: England
Born: 20 Mar 1969
Debut: 23 Nov 1988 v Sheffield Wednesday
Position: Midfield
Appearances: 0 (6) **Goals scored:** 0
Seasons: 1988/89
Clubs: Manchester United, Lincoln City (loan), Charlton Athletic (loan), Bristol Rovers, RoPS, Ljungskile, Haka, HJK Helsinki, Ljungskile, Rosseröd

EDGAR WILSON
Country: Unknown
Born: Unknown **Died:** Unknown
Debut: 18 Jan 1890 v Preston North End
Position: Forward
Appearances: 1 **Goals scored:** 0
Seasons: 1889/90
Clubs: Newton Heath

JOHN THOMAS 'JACK' WILSON
Country: England
Born: 8 Mar 1897 **Died:** Unknown
Debut: 4 Sep 1926 v Leeds United
Position: Half back
Appearances: 140 **Goals scored:** 3
Seasons: 1926/27 - 1931/32
Clubs: Leadgate United, Newcastle United, Leadgate Park, Durham City, Stockport County, Manchester United, Bristol City

MARK WILSON
Country: England
Born: 9 Feb 1979
Debut: 21 Oct 1998 v Brondby IF
Position: Midfield
Appearances: 6 (4) **Goals scored:** 0
Seasons: 1998/99 - 1999/2000
Clubs: Manchester United, Wrexham (loan), Middlesbrough, Stoke City (loan), Swansea City (loan), Sheffield Wednesday (loan), Doncaster Rovers (loan), Livingston (loan), FC Dallas, Doncaster Rovers, Tranmere Rovers (loan)

THOMAS CARTER 'TOMMY' WILSON
Country: England
Born: 20 Oct 1877 **Died:** 30 Aug 1940

Debut: 15 Feb 1908 v Blackburn Rovers
Position: Winger
Appearances: 1 **Goals scored:** 0
Seasons: 1907/08
Clubs: Ashton-in-Makerfield FC, West Manchester FC, Ashton Town, Ashton North End, Oldham County, Swindon Town, Blackburn Rovers, Swindon Town, Millwall Athletic, Aston Villa, Queen's Park Rangers. Bolton Wanderers, Leeds City, Manchester United

WALTER WINTERBOTTOM
Country: England
Born: 31 Jan 1913 **Died:** 16 Feb 2002
Debut: 28 Nov 1936 v Leeds United
Position: Half back
Appearances: 27 **Goals scored:** 0
Seasons: 1936/37 - 1937/38
Clubs: Mossley FC, Manchester United

Born in Oldham, Winterbottom trained as a teacher and qualified as a physical education instructor in 1933. He was a keen amateur footballer and was signed by United, joining the team that won promotion to the First Division in 1937-38. Injury would bring an early end to his playing career. In 1946 the FA appointed him as national team manger – he is the only England manager to have had no prior management experience. Winterbottom managed the England team for its first four World Cup competitions in 1950, 1954, 1958 and 1962. He remains the only manager to have taken England to more than two World Cup finals.

RICHARD 'DICK' WOMBWELL
Country: England
Born: Jul 1877 **Died:** Jul 1943
Debut: 18 Mar 1905 v Grimsby Town
Position: Winger
Appearances: 51 **Goals scored:** 3
Seasons: 1904/05 - 1906/07
Clubs: Derby County, Bristol City, Manchester United, Heart of Midlothian

JOHN WOOD
Country: Scotland
Born: 17 Sep 1894 **Died:** 9 Sep 1971
Debut: 26 Aug 1922 v Crystal Palace
Position: Winger
Appearances: 16 **Goals scored:** 1
Seasons: 1922/23
Clubs: Dumbarton, Manchester United, Lochgelly United

NICHOLAS ANTHONY 'NICKY' WOOD
Country: England
Born: 6 Jan 1966
Debut: 26 Dec 1985 v Everton
Position: Winger
Appearances: 2 (2) **Goals scored:** 0
Seasons: 1985/86 - 1986/87
Clubs: Manchester United

RAYMOND ERNEST 'RAY' WOOD
Country: England
Born: 11 Jun 1931 **Died:** 7 Jul 2002
Debut: 3 Dec 1949 v Newcastle United
Position: Goalkeeper
Appearances: 208 **Goals scored:** 0
Seasons: 1949/50 - 1958/59
Clubs: Darlington, Manchester United, Huddersfield Town, Bradford City, Barnsley

Ray Wood, a strong agile man, could have been a professional sprinter, but chose football instead. He joined United in December 1949 after a brief period at Darlington. Wood is particularly remembered for the 1957 FA Cup final, where he was the victim of (a legal) shoulder charge by Villa's Peter McParland that left him with a broken jaw. In the era before substitutes, his forced departure from the field severely handicapped United, who would lose the game 2-1. However, he would win two league championship medals during his time in Manchester. He survived the Munich air crash, but played for United just once more, losing his place in the team to Harry Gregg. Wood moved to Huddersfield Town in 1958 where he would spend seven seasons.

WILFRED 'WILF' WOODCOCK
Country: England
Born: 15 Feb 1892 **Died:** Oct 1966
Debut: 1 Nov 1913 v Liverpool
Position: Forward
Appearances: 61 **Goals scored:** 21
Seasons: 1913/14 - 1919/20
Clubs: Stalybridge Celtic, Manchester United, Manchester City

HAROLD 'HARRY' WORRALL
Country: England
Born: 19 Nov 1918 **Died:** 5 Dec 1979
Debut: 30 Nov 1946 v Wolverhampton Wanderers
Position: Full back
Appearances: 6 **Goals scored:** 0
Seasons: 1946/47 - 1947/48
Clubs: Winsford United, Manchester United, Swindon Town

PAUL WRATTEN
Country: England
Born: 29 Nov 1970
Debut: 2 Apr 1991 v Wimbledon
Position: Midfield
Appearances: 0 (2) **Goals scored:** 0
Seasons: 1990/91
Clubs: Manchester United, Hartlepool United, York City, Bishop Auckland

WILLIAM 'BILLY' WRIGGLESWORTH
Country: England

Born: 12 Nov 1912 **Died:** 8 Aug 1980
Debut: 23 Jan 1937 v Sheffield Wednesday
Position: Forward
Appearances: 34 **Goals scored:** 9
Seasons: 1936/37 - 1946/47
Clubs: Frickley Colliery, Chesterfield, Wolverhampton Wanderers, Manchester United, Bolton Wanderers, Southampton, Reading, Burton Albion, Scarborough

WILLIAM YATES
Country: England
Born: 1883 **Died:** Unknown
Debut: 15 Sep 1906 v Sheffield United
Position: Forward
Appearances: 3 **Goals scored:** 0
Seasons: 1906/07
Clubs: Aston Villa, Brighton & Hove Albion, Manchester United, Heart of Midlothian

DWIGHT YORKE
Country: Trinidad & Tobago
Born: 3 Nov 1971
Debut: 22 Aug 1998 v West Ham United
Position: Forward
Appearances: 120 (32) **Goals scored:** 66
Seasons: 1998/99 - 2001/02
Clubs: Aston Villa, Manchester United, Blackburn Rovers, Birmingham City, Sydney F.C., Sunderland

The Smiling Assassin, so-called because of his goalscoring prowess and ever-grinning demeanour, played most of his career for Aston Villa. Discovered by Villa (and future England) manager Graham Taylor on a tour of the West Indies in 1989, Yorke appeared in a team that played a friendly match against them. Taylor was impressed enough to offer Yorke a trial and subsequently a permanent contract. Over nine years he would appear for Aston Villa on 231 occasions, scoring 97 goals. His departure to Manchester United for £12.6 million was controversial at the time, but in his first season he proved he would be a key United player, helping guide the club to a unique treble. He formed a terrific partnership with Andy Cole, finishing that season as top goalscorer in the league. He was a member of the 1999-2000 Premier League-winning side. Limited appearances in the 2001-02 season led to his move to Blackburn Rovers for £2 million.

ANTHONY YOUNG
Country: England
Born: 24 Dec 1952
Debut: 29 Aug 1970 v West Ham United
Position: Fullback/Midfield
Appearances: 79 (18) **Goals scored:** 1
Seasons: 1970/71 - 1975/76
Clubs: Manchester United, Charlton Athletic, York City, Runcorn

ARTHUR YOUNG
Country: Scotland
Born: unknown **Died:** unknown
Debut: 27 Oct 1906 v Birmingham City
Position: Midfield/Defender
Appearances: 2 **Goals scored:** 0
Seasons: 1906/07
Clubs: Hurlford Thistle, Manchester United

ASHLEY YOUNG
Country: England
Born: 9 Jul 1985
Debut: 7 Aug 2011 v Manchester City
Position: Winger
Appearances: 1 **Goals scored:** 0
Seasons: 2011/12 -
Clubs: Watford, Aston Villa, Manchester United

The England international and winner of the 2009 PFA Young Player of the Year Award joined United from Aston Villa in the summer of 2011. He can play either on the wing or up front.

Left: 14 April 2001. Dwight Yorke celebrates after scoring one his 66 goals for United.

4

The Competitions

1888 | The Football League is formed of 12 clubs, with Preston North End triumphing as the first champions, undefeated in 22 games.

1892 | Division Two is created as the league expands to accommodate more clubs.

1898 | Both divisions expand to 18 clubs as the Football League begins to eclipse the existing Northern and Southern Leagues.

1908 | United are crowned champions of Division One for the first time, with Sandy Turnbull scoring 25 goals.

1915 | The league is suspended due to the First World War.

1920 | Third Division added which quickly becomes Division Three South and Division Three North.

1923 | Further expansion sees 88 clubs playing league football in total.

1931 | Arsenal begin a sustained period of success winning the first of five titles in eight years under the guidance of Herbert Chapman.

1939 | The league is suspended at the advent of the Second World War.

1952 | After finishing runners-up four times since the resumption of the league, Manchester United become English champions for the third time in their history.

1956 | The first floodlit game takes place between Portsmouth and Newcastle United, creating the possibility of midweek evening matches.

1958 | After winning consecutive titles and developing into one of England's finest teams, Matt Busby's United side is ripped apart by the Munich air disaster which claims the lives of eight players.

1965 | The use of substitutes is permitted for the first time to replace injured players and the following season is relaxed further to allow for tactical changes.

1967 | Denis Law scores 23 goals as United claim their seventh league title less than a decade since the Munich disaster

1977 | For the first time, separating teams who finish level on points by goal difference is introduced. In a bid to encourage attacking play, if goal difference is level priority is given to the highest scoring team.

1979 | Trevor Francis becomes the first million pound player when he transfers from Birmingham City to Nottingham Forest.

1981 | The decision is made to award three points for a win instead of two in a further effort to increase attacking play.

The League

THE SPORT OF football grew up when formal league structures came into being during the late 19th century. Before then the game had been played for hundreds of years in England without nationally recognised rules and even when the first amateur clubs were formed they played games against each other that often went unrecorded. Nor were the clubs part of any organised alliance. Games were one-offs or friendlies with usually little more than pride or local bragging rights at stake.

As professional football emerged, not unnaturally the teams wanted some means by which they could judge themselves in a more structured way; the Football League was the result. It was formed in 1888 with 12 founding clubs and is the oldest football league in the world. The FA Cup may be slightly older (it was first staged in 1871-72 season) and its knockout formula certainly promised more glamour to the participants and winners in its early years, but professional footballers from any era will acknowledge that to win their national league title is the ultimate accomplishment.

Newton Heath (the club was not known as Manchester United until 1902) was not one of the original 12 Football League teams. Instead, the Heathens first joined a new league called The Combination in 1888-89 and when that folded spent the next three seasons in the Alliance League, which was set up for clubs not quite ready for the Football League. Newton Heath's best finish was second in 1891-92.

In time for 1892-93, the Football League and the Alliance League merged to create the Football League Second Division and Newton Heath's runners-up position of the prior season allowed them to actually join the First Division of the Football League. It was a status that lasted just two years. The Heathens then spent seven seasons in the Second Division, finishing runners-up in 1896-97, but failing to gain promotion via the test matches (latter day play-offs) against First Division opponents.

All those 14 seasons as Newton Heath were a precursor to the birth of Manchester United FC in 1902, after the original club ran into financial problems. As United, the club began life in the Football League Second Division – but with more money and, very soon, better players. It led to promotion to the First Division in 1905-06 after a runners-up finish in the lower league.

1985 A fire at Bradford City's Valley Parade kills 56 and injures a further 265 spectators in one of the worst disasters in English football history.

1987 Play-offs are introduced to determine promotion places in a bid to make more clubs eligible for promotion at the end of the season.

1992 The Premier League is formed when the top 22 English clubs break away from the Football League to become more profitable and to make more impact on the European stage.

1993 Twenty six years after their previous title, Manchester United finally claim their eighth League Championship win and begin a period of rich success at the head of English football.

1999 United win the first of a hat-trick of titles, clinching the league over Arsenal with a last-day win against Tottenham Hotspur.

2003 After surrendering their crown to Arsenal the previous year, United regain the title as Ruud Van Nistelrooy top scores with 25 goals.

2008 With Cristiano Ronaldo in prolific form, United clinch title number 17 as they close in on Liverpool's record of 18 titles.

2011 Having equalled the 18-title milestone just two years earlier, Sir Alex Ferguson and United seal a record-breaking 19th title in the penultimate game of the season.

United's new-found impetus climaxed with their inaugural First Division championship in 1907-08, just six years after almost going out of existence. Three years later there was a second league title as the Reds established themselves as one of the outstanding teams of the pre-First World War era.

In the inter-war years, however, United were much less successful. In the 20 full seasons between 1919 and 1939, the Reds spent 11 seasons in the First Division and nine in the Second, suffering three relegations, but also three promotions, including a Second Division championship in 1935-36.

When the Second World War began in 1939, United were in the First Division and that was their status when league football resumed in 1946; it was the time for the second great period of United to begin. Under new manager Matt Busby a different sort of United team was taking to the pitch: thoroughly prepared local youngsters rather than bought-in ready-made star players. The Reds finished runners-up in four of the five immediate post-war seasons. Busby's first league title came in 1951-52 (his sixth season in charge). Meanwhile a new side was emerging on the training pitch under the watchful eye of Jimmy Murphy and four seasons later, the Busby Babes won the first of two consecutive titles.

In the February of the 1957-58 season, United were in third place in the First Division and ready for another springtime push towards a hat-trick of championships. However, the Munich air crash claimed the lives of eight Babes, changing the history of the club forever. Although Busby's first efforts to rebuild the team brought a remarkable runners-up spot in 1958-59, it was the mid-sixties before United returned to the league's top spot. This third Busby era brought two titles in three seasons between 1964 and 1967 as well as two runners-up spots, but when the manager retired the club's fortunes again dipped and relegation to the Second Division followed in 1973-74.

New boss Tommy Docherty took United to the Second Division title (the second in the club's history) the next season, but it took 18 years and the sixth post-Busby manager before there was another First Division championship. In fact, by the time Alex Ferguson won the Reds' eighth title in 1992-93, the First Division had become the FA Premiership.

Sir Alex's reign has been the most successful of any manager, not just in United's history, but in the annals of English football's league competitions. In total the Scot has led United to 12 Premierships, six runners-up spots and three third places in 24 full seasons in the manager's seat. In fact, since the 1991-92 season United have not finished outside the top three places in the league, which is a span of exactly 20 seasons.

The 2010-11 championship was significant because it was United's 19th First Division or Premiership title in their history, taking the club past Liverpool's record of 18. The club with the next most championships is Arsenal with 13. The Reds' other league record is 14 runners-up spots, two more than the next best (Liverpool with 12).

Top Left: 15 May 1967. Bobby Charlton, Denis Law, George Best and Bill Foulkes show off the cup.

Top Right: 27 March 1969. In a 2-2 draw against Fulham, Denis Law sends the ball goalwards watched by Tony Macedo during the match at Craven Cottage.

Opposite: 16 May 1999. Players celebrate winning the title after the final match against Tottenham Hotspur at Old Trafford. The match finished in a 2-1 win for United.

1907/08

> "A man of big shoulders and active feet and active brain, Sandy is a great player, and a more unselfish inside man I never saw. A great opportunist with class written all over his football."
>
> *Manchester Evening News* reporter 'Wanderer' describes Sandy Turnbull.

> "When (Billy) Meredith lifts the ball across the goal there are invariably three of his partners in a line ready to receive it."
>
> A *Manchester Guardian* reporter pays tribute to United's most famous player of the day.

Above: United defender Richard Holden photographed in 1908, when the Reds won the First Division title for the first time.

Division One Champions

TO GET OFF to the kind of start in the league that United managed this season is the stuff that dreams are made of: three wins against good teams (Aston Villa 4-1 away, Liverpool 4-0 at home and Middlesbrough 2-1 also at home); a sloppy defeat (2-1 again at Middlesbrough); but then ten victories on the trot, including a 6-1 thrashing of the defending champions Newcastle United at St James' Park.

After this sequence of 13 wins in 14 games which took the season to the last week of November, the Reds were in a six-point lead in the league having scored a massive 48 goals. Sandy Turnbull scored an astonishing 19 goals in these games including hat-tricks against Liverpool and Blackburn Rovers, plus all four against Arsenal.

Critics said there was a mid-season disruption for the team after on-field leaders Charlie Roberts and Billy Meredith were the principals in a movement to launch a union for the players. But it would be wrong to blame the union work for what happened next because, after such incredible early season form, even a normal run of results would be disappointing. And, sure enough, a few defeats and a few draws began to litter United's progress to an inaugural First Division title in the spring. The strangest was a 7-4 away defeat to Liverpool in March that reduced the Reds' lead at the top to just five points. However, United still had two games in hand on second placed Newcastle after that loss. Their position was safe because none of their rivals had matched the early season form that had given the Reds such a tremendous start to the campaign. Even a run of two draws and three losses in five games during April could not deny United the title which they eventually won by nine points.

MANCHESTER UNITED 4-1 SHEFFIELD WEDNESDAY

ON 1 JANUARY, United had been ten points clear at the top of the league, but a week before this home match against Sheffield Wednesday, the lead over Newcastle United in second place had been cut to five as they had lost four of the nine games since the year began.

Meanwhile, Wednesday were championship chasers themselves and only a further two points behind in third place. Ernest Mangnall made four changes to the side that had lost the previous game 7-4 at Anfield, bringing in goalkeeper Herbert Broomfield, full back Herbert Burgess, half back Alex Bell and forward Harold Halse.

With only eight of the 38 First Division games left remaining after this one, Meredith and company finally began to gel. Wednesday were no mugs themselves (they had won consecutive league titles earlier in the decade), but they were put to the sword in United's best result during the whole of the second half of the season. Goals from the star winger George Wall (2), Harry Halse (who was making his debut at 22-years-old after a £350 transfer from Southend) and the goal machine Sandy Turnbull were enough to wrap up a victory that put United seven points clear at the top of the table.

MANCHESTER UNITED

1. HERBERT BROOMFIELD
2. GEORGE STACEY
3. HERBERT BURGESS
4. DICK DUCKWORTH
5. ALEX DOWNIE
6. ALEX BELL
7. BILLY MEREDITH
8. JIMMY BANNISTER
9. HAROLD HALSE
10. SANDY TURNBULL
11. GEORGE WALL

SHEFFIELD WEDNESDAY

1. JACK LYALL
2. WILLIE LAYTON
3. SLAVIN
4. TOM BRITTLETON
5. WALTER MILLER
6. BILLY BARTLETT
7. JAMES MAXWELL
8. FRANK BRADSHAW
9. ANDREW WILSON
10. JIMMY STEWART
11. GEORGE SIMPSON

Referee: JH Pearson

MANCHESTER UNITED

MANAGER: ERNEST MANGNALL

SHEFFIELD WEDNESDAY

MANAGER: ARTHUR DICKINSON

Football League Division One

DATE	OPPONENTS	SCORE	GOALSCORERS	ATTENDANCE
Sep 2	Aston Villa	4-1	Meredith 2, Bannister, Wall	20,000
Sep 7	LIVERPOOL	4-0	Turnbull A 3, Wall	24,000
Sep 9	MIDDLESBROUGH	2-1	Turnbull A 2	20,000
Sep 14	Middlesbrough	1-2	Bannister	18,000
Sep 21	SHEFFIELD UNITED	2-1	Turnbull A 2	25,000
Sep 28	Chelsea	4-1	Meredith 2, Bannister, Turnbull A	40,000
Oct 5	NOTTINGHAM FOREST	4-0	Bannister, Turnbull J, Wall, og	20,000
Oct 12	Newcastle United	6-1	Wall 2, Meredith, Roberts, Turnbull A, Turnbull J	25,000
Oct 19	Blackburn Rovers	5-1	Turnbull A 3, Turnbull J 2	30,000
Oct 26	BOLTON WANDERERS	2-1	Turnbull A, Turnbull J	35,000
Nov 2	Birmingham City	4-3	Meredith 2, Turnbull J, Wall	20,000
Nov 9	EVERTON	4-3	Wall 2, Meredith, Roberts	30,000
Nov 16	Sunderland	2-1	Turnbull A 2	30,000
Nov 23	ARSENAL	4-2	Turnbull A 4	10,000
Nov 30	Sheffield Wednesday	0-2		40,000
Dec 7	BRISTOL CITY	2-1	Wall 2	20,000
Dec 14	Notts County	1-1	Meredith	11,000
Dec 21	MANCHESTER CITY	3-1	Turnbull A 2, Wall	35,000
Dec 25	BURY	2-1	Meredith, Turnbull J	45,000
Dec 28	Preston North End	0-0		12,000

DATE	OPPONENTS	SCORE	GOALSCORERS	ATTENDANCE
Jan 1	Bury	1-0	Wall	29,500
Jan 18	Sheffield United	0-2		17,000
Jan 25	CHELSEA	1-0	Turnbull J	20,000
Feb 8	NEWCASTLE UNITED	1-1	Turnbull J	50,000
Feb 15	BLACKBURN ROVERS	1-2	Turnbull A	15,000
Feb 29	BIRMINGHAM CITY	1-0	Turnbull A	12,000
Mar 14	SUNDERLAND	3-0	Bell, Berry, Wall	15,000
Mar 21	Arsenal	0-1		20,000
Mar 25	Liverpool	4-7	Wall 2, Bannister, Turnbull J	10,000
Mar 28	SHEFFIELD WEDNESDAY	4-1	Wall 2, Halse, Turnbull A	30,000
Apr 4	Bristol City	1-1	Wall	12,000
Apr 8	Everton	3-1	Halse, Turnbull A, Wall	17,000
Apr 11	NOTTS COUNTY	0-1		20,000
Apr 17	Nottingham Forest	0-2		22,000
Apr 18	Manchester City	0-0		40,000
Apr 20	ASTON VILLA	1-2	Picken	10,000
Apr 22	Bolton Wanderers	2-2	Halse, Stacey	18,000
Apr 25	PRESTON NORTH END	2-1	Halse, og	8,000

Final Standings

	Pts
Manchester United	52
Aston Villa	43
Manchester City	43
Newcastle United	42

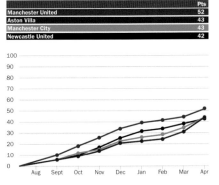

THE MATCH

29 April at Old Trafford, Manchester. Goals: og, Halse (2), Turnbull, West. Attendance: 10,000

MANCHESTER UNITED 5-1 SUNDERLAND

MANCHESTER UNITED

1 HUGH EDMONDS
2 TONY DONNELLY
3 GEORGE STACEY
4 DICK DUCKWORTH
5 ARTHUR WHALLEY
6 JAMES HODGE
7 BILLY MEREDITH
8 HAROLD HALSE
9 ENOCH WEST
10 SANDY TURNBULL
11 SAM BLOTT

SUNDERLAND

1 BILL WORRALL
2 BILLY TROUGHEAR
3 ALBERT MILTON
4 TOMMY TAIT
5 CHARLIE THOMSON
6 HARRY LOW
7 JACKIE MORDUE
8 JIMMY GEMMELL
9 ARTHUR BRIDGETT
10 CHARLIE BUCHAN
11 GEORGE MARTIN

Referee: Unknown

WHAT A SEASON it had been and what a dramatic race for the league championship. With one week remaining United were level on 50 points with Aston Villa, but the Midlands club had two games to play while the Reds only had this home game against third placed Sunderland. In fact, Villa had seemed destined to win the title when they had beaten United 4-2 in Birmingham just a week earlier, putting the championship within their grasp. However, the Midlanders' game in hand ended in a draw, so the final weekend of the season would be the decider; United had to win and hope Villa stumbled. The Birmingham team was playing Liverpool at Anfield at the same time that United and Sunderland would do battle at Old Trafford.

It was the Wearsiders, with the legendary Charles Buchan at inside left, who took the initiative with the opening goal, but then it was time for United's most famous player to step into the spotlight. Winger Billy Meredith, who was the driving force behind United's all-star forward line, had been creating goals all season and, although Harry Halse goes down on the scoresheet for two goals including the equaliser, it was Meredith who turned on the magic by helping set up three of United's goals as they went on to win 5-1. Sandy Turnbull, Enoch West and an own goal were the other scorers. Meanwhile, Villa lost 3-1 at Liverpool to send the championship to Manchester.

MANCHESTER UNITED

MANAGER: ERNEST MANGNALL

SUNDERLAND

MANAGER: BOB KYLE

Division One Champions

IN THEIR PREVIOUS title win, United had sprinted so fast out of the gate at the start of the season that no team could catch them. But this campaign was a different matter, even though there was only one defeat in the first eight games, oddly against a Nottingham Forest team that would be relegated at the end of the season. Certainly their early form was not bad, but by the end of November the Reds were in only third place in the league, having lost three times and scored the fewest goals of the top three, just 25 (at the same point during the 1907-08 championship, United had scored 48 goals). Sunderland were two points ahead at this stage and reigning champions Aston Villa level with United, but with a game in hand.

But this United team was led by some outstanding talent: Charlie Roberts was now in his eighth season at the club leading the defence, and the toothpick-chewing Billy Meredith in attack was both dazzling and dogged.

Although the results were patchy for much of the rest of the season, these Reds kept battling and only once lost two games in a row. However, United always gave their rivals hope because there was an unpredictability about them, beating all their nearest challengers for the championship one week, but losing to poorer teams the next. Then from the beginning of January to mid-March, the Red Devils went unbeaten for nine league games (including a 1-1 draw in the Manchester derby and a 5-0 thrashing of Preston North End at Old Trafford before 25,000 fans) and rose to the top of the league. The drama of the final few weeks thrilled the crowds as United, Sunderland and Villa could all have won the title. In the end it came down to the very last games of United and Villa. (see THE MATCH)

1910/11

"At the end of the game our supporters rushed across the ground in front of the stand to wait for the final news from Liverpool. Suddenly a tremendous cheer rent the air and was renewed again and again and we knew we were the champions once again."

Charlie Roberts speaking to the *Manchester Saturday Post* following United's 5-1 win over Sunderland.

"The ground is situate (sic) at Old Trafford . . . and can be reached by three tram routes. The ground when completed will hold over 100,000 people."

The 1910-11 season was the first time the Reds played at Old Trafford for a whole league campaign and these words are from an invitation in February 1910 to the opening of the new stadium.

Above: The inimitable defensive rock Charlie Roberts.

Football League Division One

DATE	OPPONENTS	SCORE	GOALSCORERS	ATTENDANCE
Sep 1	Arsenal	2-1	Halse, West	15,000
Sep 3	BLACKBURN ROVERS	3-2	Meredith, Turnbull, West	40,000
Sep 10	Nottingham Forest	1-2	Turnbull	20,000
Sep 17	MANCHESTER CITY	2-1	Turnbull, West	60,000
Sep 24	Everton	1-0	Turnbull	25,000
Oct 1	SHEFFIELD WEDNESDAY	3-2	Wall 2, West	20,000
Oct 8	Bristol City	1-0	Halse	20,000
Oct 15	NEWCASTLE UNITED	2-0	Halse, Turnbull	50,000
Oct 22	Tottenham Hotspur	2-2	West 2	30,000
Oct 29	MIDDLESBROUGH	1-2	Turnbull	35,000
Nov 5	Preston North End	2-0	Turnbull, West	13,000
Nov 12	NOTTS COUNTY	0-0		13,000
Nov 19	Oldham Athletic	3-1	Turnbull 2, Wall	25,000
Nov 26	Liverpool	2-3	Roberts, Turnbull	8,000
Dec 3	BURY	3-2	Homer 2, Turnbull	7,000
Dec 10	Sheffield United	0-2		8,000
Dec 17	ASTON VILLA	2-0	Turnbull, West	20,000
Dec 24	Sunderland	2-1	Meredith, Turnbull	30,000
Dec 26	ARSENAL	5-0	Picken 2, West 2, Meredith	40,000
Dec 27	Bradford City	0-1		35,000
Dec 31	Blackburn Rovers	0-1		20,000
Jan 2	BRADFORD CITY	1-0	Meredith	40,000
Jan 7	NOTTINGHAM FOREST	4-2	Homer, Picken, Wall, og	10,000
Jan 21	Manchester City	1-1	Turnbull	40,000
Jan 28	EVERTON	2-2	Duckworth, Wall	45,000
Feb 11	BRISTOL CITY	3-1	Homer, Picken, West	14,000
Feb 18	Newcastle United	1-0	Halse	45,000
Mar 4	Middlesbrough	2-2	Turnbull, West	8,000
Mar 11	PRESTON NORTH END	5-0	West 2, Connor, Duckworth, Turnbull	25,000
Mar 15	TOTTENHAM HOTSPUR	3-2	Meredith, Turnbull, West	10,000
Mar 18	Notts County	0-1		12,000
Mar 25	OLDHAM ATHLETIC	0-0		35,000
Apr 1	LIVERPOOL	2-0	West 2	20,000
Apr 8	Bury	3-0	Homer 2, Halse	20,000
Apr 15	SHEFFIELD UNITED	1-1	West	22,000
Apr 17	Sheffield Wednesday	0-0		25,000
Apr 22	Aston Villa	2-4	Halse 2	50,000
Apr 29	SUNDERLAND	5-1	Halse 2, Turnbull, West, og	10,000

Final Standings

	Pts
Manchester United	52
Aston Villa	51
Sunderland	45
Everton	45

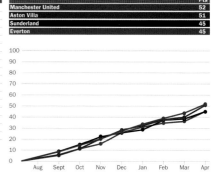

1935/36

Above: Tommy Bamford's 16 goals helped the promotion campaign.

Busby Babe David Pegg is born in Doncaster, Yorkshire, on 20 September. The winger will win one England cap before Munich.

Tommy Bamford is such a legend in Wrexham, they recently named a beer after him.

Half back Bert Whalley, who would go on to be the United team trainer after World War II and then be killed in the Munich air crash, made his debut on 30 November in a 0-0 draw against Doncaster Rovers.

Division Two Champions

THE FINANCIAL CRISIS at the start of 1930s that would result in the club being taken over by a new owner was reminiscent of United's situation in 1902. This time, however, lack of cash had sent the club down to the Second Division and this would be their fifth consecutive season in the lower league; it was a streak that needed to end.

Manager Scott Duncan had been lauded as the saviour when he arrived at the club in 1932 and had spent plenty of the new owner's money on players, but without success. In fact, two seasons previously United had been one point and one place away from the relegation zone. Time was running out for both club and manager.

As so often in the recent past, United's success was tied to excellent home form. Old Trafford was a fortress this season: 16 wins, only two defeats and three draws. But, despite solid results at home, United did not start the season as fast as some of their rivals and, after reaching second place in mid-October, picked up just one win and one draw in seven games to slip back to ninth by early December.

But then the charge to the Second Division title began. The rest of the season was a blur of wins and draws, but only a single defeat (1-0 at Bradford City) in January.

One of the stars during the championship-winning run of form was Tom Manley, who played in many positions during his eight-year United career, and had easily his best season with 15 goals and multiple assists, mostly from the left wing position.

The Reds did not enter the promotion places until mid-April and then vied with Charlton Athletic for the title that was won on the last day of the season when both teams drew their last game.

THE MATCH

14 December at Old Trafford, Manchester. Goals: Bamford (2), Manley, Mutch, Rowley. Attendance: 15,284

MANCHESTER UNITED 5-0 NOTTINGHAM FOREST

MANCHESTER UNITED

1 JACK HALL
2 JACK GRIFFITHS
3 BILLY PORTER
4 JAMES BROWN
5 GEORGE VOSE
6 BILL MCKAY
7 JACK CAPE
8 GEORGE MUTCH
9 TOMMY BAMFORD
10 HARRY ROWLEY
11 TOM MANLEY

NOTTINGHAM FOREST

1 PERCY ASHTON
2 HENRY SMITH
3 FRED WALLBANKS
4 BILLY MCKINLEY
5 TOMMY GRAHAM
6 BOB PUGH
7 ARTHUR MASTERS
8 HENRY RACE
9 JOHNNY DENT
10 TOM PEACOCK
11 WILLIAM SIMPSON

Referee: Mr Clark

UNITED WERE IN lowly ninth place before entertaining Nottingham Forest and had won only one of their last seven games. Although the Reds were only five points behind the league leaders Leicester City, there was a clutch of teams above them all looking more likely to gain promotion. The team needed a spark and when captain and half back James Brown (who was in his first season at the club having arrived from Burnley in August for a fee of £1,000) finally returned after an illness in time for this game, that was enough.

United favoured the long ball against a Forest team that preferred a close passing game. Another returning face to the United team was goalkeeper Jack Hall, who had been dropped for three games. He made a couple of fine early saves to keep the score at 0-0 before United opened the scoring after a cross from Tom Manley on the left wing found Harry Rowley who slotted the ball home.

The second half was only 11 minutes old when George Mutch's hard work was rewarded with a goal and then in their next decent attack Tom Bamford, who had a hand in both the opening two goals, scored himself after the Forest keeper could only half-stop a Rowley shot.

Manley and Bamford both helped themselves to another goal each and United not only moved up two places in the league to seventh, edging a point closer to new leaders Tottenham Hotspur, but had also started a run that would mean only one defeat in the final 24 games of the season.

MANCHESTER UNITED

MANAGER: SCOTT DUNCAN

NOTTINGHAM FOREST

MANAGER: NOEL WATSON

Football League Division Two

DATE	OPPONENTS	SCORE	GOALSCORERS	ATTENDANCE
Aug 31	Plymouth Argyle	1-3	Bamford	22,366
Sep 4	CHARLTON ATHLETIC	3-0	Bamford, Cape, Chester	21,211
Sep 7	BRADFORD CITY	3-1	Bamford 2, Mutch	30,754
Sep 9	Charlton Athletic	0-0		13,178
Sep 14	Newcastle United	2-0	Bamford, Rowley	28,520
Sep 18	HULL CITY	2-0	Bamford 2	15,739
Sep 21	TOTTENHAM HOTSPUR	0-0		34,718
Sep 28	Southampton	1-2	Rowley	17,678
Oct 5	Port Vale	3-0	Mutch 2, Bamford	9,703
Oct 12	FULHAM	1-0	Rowley	22,723
Oct 19	SHEFFIELD UNITED	3-1	Cape, Mutch, Rowley	18,636
Oct 26	Bradford Park Avenue	0-1		12,216
Nov 2	LEICESTER CITY	0-1		39,074
Nov 9	Swansea City	1-2	Bamford	9,731
Nov 16	WEST HAM UNITED	2-3	Rowley 2	24,440
Nov 23	Norwich City	5-3	Rowley 3, Manley 2	17,266
Nov 30	DONCASTER ROVERS	0-0		23,569
Dec 7	Blackpool	1-4	Mutch	13,218
Dec 14	NOTTINGHAM FOREST	5-0	Bamford 2, Manley, Mutch, Rowley	15,284
Dec 26	BARNSLEY	1-1	Mutch	20,993
Dec 28	PLYMOUTH ARGYLE	3-2	Mutch 2, Manley	20,894

DATE	OPPONENTS	SCORE	GOALSCORERS	ATTENDANCE
Jan 1	Barnsley	3-0	Gardner, Manley, Mutch	20,957
Jan 4	Bradford City	0-1		11,286
Jan 18	NEWCASTLE UNITED	3-1	Mutch 2, Rowley	22,968
Feb 1	SOUTHAMPTON	4-0	Mutch 2, Bryant, og	23,205
Feb 5	Tottenham Hotspur	0-0		20,085
Feb 8	PORT VALE	7-2	Manley 4, Rowley 2, Mutch	22,265
Feb 22	Sheffield United	1-1	Manley	25,852
Feb 29	BLACKPOOL	3-2	Bryant, Manley, Mutch	18,423
Mar 7	West Ham United	2-1	Bryant, Mutch	29,684
Mar 14	SWANSEA CITY	3-0	Manley, Mutch, Rowley	27,580
Mar 21	Leicester City	1-1	Bryant	18,200
Mar 28	NORWICH CITY	2-1	Rowley 2	31,596
Apr 1	Fulham	2-2	Bryant, Griffiths	11,137
Apr 4	Doncaster Rovers	0-0		13,474
Apr 10	Burnley	2-2	Bamford 2	27,245
Apr 11	BRADFORD PARK AVENUE	4-0	Mutch 2, Bamford, Bryant	33,517
Apr 13	BURNLEY	4-0	Bryant 2, Rowley 2	39,855
Apr 18	Nottingham Forest	1-1	Bamford	12,156
Apr 25	BURY	2-1	Lang, Rowley	35,027
Apr 29	Bury	3-2	Manley 2, Mutch	31,562
May 2	Hull City	1-1	Bamford	4,540

Final Standings

	Pts
Manchester United	56
Charlton Athletic	55
Sheffield United	52
West Ham United	52

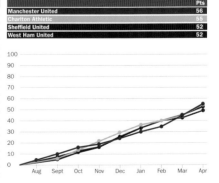

THE MATCH

11 April at Turf Moor, Burnley. Goals: Byrne
Attendance: 38,907

BURNLEY 1-1 MANCHESTER UNITED

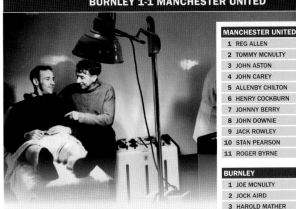

THE HEADLINE NEWS before this game was that Matt Busby had made seven changes, three of them positional, to his team from the previous game, a 1-0 loss at Portsmouth. The return of Reg Allen in goal after recovering from an injury seemed the most important change, while young left back Roger Byrne moving into the forward line at left wing proved to be much more significant in the race for the title. Earlier in the season, the manager had tried to use another defender, John Aston, in attack; he moved the skilful left back to centre forward on two occasions, but each time the Reds were beaten. So moving Aston back to his original position and pushing Byrne forward was another gamble – one that paid off.

The game was played on Good Friday and Byrne scored United's only goal in the 1-1 draw that was enough to keep them top of the league. A second match over Easter at home against Liverpool the next day proved even better for Byrne – he scored twice and United won 4-0. And to cap it all on Easter Monday in the return with Burnley at home, Byrne bagged another two in a 6-1 victory. The *Manchester Evening News* called it a "goal storm".

Second-placed Arsenal clung on to United's coat-tails until the last Saturday of the season when, by chance, the two clubs faced each other. An injury to an Arsenal player during the game helped United establish total supremacy and run out 6-1 winners.

MANCHESTER UNITED
1 REG ALLEN
2 TOMMY MCNULTY
3 JOHN ASTON
4 JOHN CAREY
5 ALLENBY CHILTON
6 HENRY COCKBURN
7 JOHNNY BERRY
8 JOHN DOWNIE
9 JACK ROWLEY
10 STAN PEARSON
11 ROGER BYRNE

BURNLEY
1 JOE MCNULTY
2 JOCK AIRD
3 HAROLD MATHER
4 JIMMY ADAMSON
5 TOMMY CUMMINGS
6 REG ATWELL
7 JOCK CHEW
8 BILLY MORRIS
9 LES SHANNON
10 JIMMY MCILROY
11 ALBERT CHEESEBROUGH

Referee: Unknown

MANCHESTER UNITED
MANAGER: MATT BUSBY

BURNLEY
MANAGER: FRANK HILL

Division One Champions

DURING THE SEASON in which the phrase 'The Busby Babes' was coined, United had hit the top of the league table at the end of December after a 1-0 win at home against Bolton Wanderers and by early March had managed to open up a small lead of three points over Arsenal and Tottenham Hotspur. But then Matt Busby saw his side begin to falter after two defeats in a row (including one to Huddersfield Town who were in one of the relegation places). Before the next match (see THE MATCH), United and Arsenal were level on 47 points with Tottenham on 46 and Portsmouth 45, so the Reds' slide had to be halted.

Busby's team needed inspiration. He had wanted a scoring centre forward all season to help stalwart strikers Jack Rowley and Stan Pearson. The first man he tried was John Aston; twice during the autumn Aston was moved from his normal left back position to wear the No 9 shirt and twice United were beaten. Busby's idea hadn't worked. He tried it again in January in the match against Manchester City and United got a draw; then with Aston still at centre forward the next week at home to contenders Tottenham, the Reds won 2-0, moving to the top of the table. Aston seemed to be the answer, but after a run of five wins in six games, came those two bad defeats.

Finally in a masterstroke Aston's own replacement at left back, Roger Byrne, was moved to the forward line at left wing, with Rowley as the attack leader. The tactic was right, it was just the chosen player who had been wrong. Byrne was a revelation in the forward line, scoring on his debut as a forward against Burnley and then adding another six more as United refused to be pushed off the No 1 spot in the table. Byrne's goals and a rejuvenated team grabbed ten points out of a possible 12 to win the league by four points.

1951/52

"(United) have found new and unexpected wing power from 21-year-old Roger Byrne. His powerful shooting and positional ideas have fitted perfectly into a rejuvenated attack."
Manchester Evening News
15 April.

"It was Matt (Busby) who sorted everything out. I remember he would just put his arm round you and give you a hug, and that's how you knew you'd done all right. I put him in the same vein as Sir Alex Ferguson. I would leave my life with either of them."
Goalkeeper Jack Crompton sums up what made Sir Matt Busby so special.

"The boys deserve it."
Matt Busby, speaking four days after winning the championship as United set off on the ocean liner *Queen Elizabeth* on a tour of the USA and Canada, 29 April.

Above: Left winger Harry McShane, the father of the actor Ian McShane.

Football League Division One

DATE	OPPONENTS	SCORE	GOALSCORERS	ATTENDANCE
Aug 18	West Bromwich Albion	3-3	Rowley 3	27,486
Aug 22	MIDDLESBROUGH	4-2	Rowley 3, Pearson	37,339
Aug 25	NEWCASTLE UNITED	2-1	Downie, Rowley	51,850
Aug 29	Middlesbrough	4-1	Pearson 2, Rowley 2	44,212
Sep 1	Bolton Wanderers	0-1		52,239
Sep 5	CHARLTON ATHLETIC	3-2	Rowley 2, Downie	26,773
Sep 8	STOKE CITY	4-0	Rowley 3, Pearson	48,660
Sep 12	Charlton Athletic	2-2	Downie 2	28,806
Sep 15	Manchester City	2-1	Berry, McShane	52,571
Sep 22	Tottenham Hotspur	0-2		70,882
Sep 29	PRESTON NORTH END	1-2	Aston	53,454
Oct 6	DERBY COUNTY	2-1	Berry, Pearson	39,767
Oct 13	Aston Villa	5-2	Pearson 2, Rowley 2, Bond	47,795
Oct 20	SUNDERLAND	0-1		40,915
Oct 27	Wolverhampton W.	2-0	Pearson, Rowley	46,167
Nov 3	HUDDERSFIELD TOWN	1-1	Pearson	25,616
Nov 10	Chelsea	2-4	Pearson, Rowley	48,960
Nov 17	PORTSMOUTH	1-3	Downie	35,914
Nov 24	Liverpool	0-0		42,378
Dec 1	BLACKPOOL	3-1	Downie 2, Rowley	34,154
Dec 8	Arsenal	3-1	Pearson, Rowley, og	55,451
Dec 15	WEST BROMWICH ALBION	5-1	Downie 2, Pearson 2, Berry	27,584

DATE	OPPONENTS	SCORE	GOALSCORERS	ATTENDANCE
Dec 22	Newcastle United	2-2	Bond, Cockburn	45,414
Dec 25	FULHAM	3-2	Berry, Bond, Rowley	33,802
Dec 26	Fulham	3-3	Bond, Pearson, Rowley	32,671
Dec 29	BOLTON WANDERERS	1-0	Pearson	53,205
Jan 5	Stoke City	0-0		36,389
Jan 19	MANCHESTER CITY	1-1	Carey	54,245
Jan 26	TOTTENHAM HOTSPUR	2-0	Pearson, og	40,845
Feb 9	Preston North End	2-1	Aston, Berry	38,792
Feb 16	Derby County	3-0	Aston, Pearson, Rowley	27,693
Mar 1	ASTON VILLA	1-1	Berry	38,910
Mar 8	Sunderland	2-1	Cockburn, Rowley	48,078
Mar 15	WOLVERHAMPTON W.	2-0	Aston, Clempson	45,109
Mar 22	Huddersfield Town	2-3	Clempson, Pearson	30,316
Apr 5	Portsmouth	0-1		25,522
Apr 11	Burnley	1-1	Byrne	38,907
Apr 12	LIVERPOOL	4-0	Byrne 2, Downie, Rowley	42,970
Apr 14	BURNLEY	6-1	Byrne 2, Carey, Downie, Pearson, Rowley	44,508
Apr 19	Blackpool	2-2	Byrne, Rowley	29,118
Apr 21	CHELSEA	3-0	Carey, Pearson, og	37,436
Apr 26	ARSENAL	6-1	Rowley 3, Pearson 2, Byrne	53,651

Final Standings

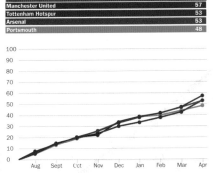

	Pts
Manchester United	57
Tottenham Hotspur	53
Arsenal	53
Portsmouth	48

1955/56

Above: Centre forward Tommy Taylor scored 25 goals this season.

Division One Champions

MATT BUSBY HAD already had one First Division title-winning outfit since his arrival at Old Trafford in 1945, but he had almost immediately begun to re-build and this was the team of his dreams: young, local men brought up through the youth academy, a process that had been started by current secretary and former stand-in manager Walter Crickmer.

The moniker of 'The Busby Babes' (also sometimes referred to as the Busby Boys) had been created by the press and this season would see the stars shine brightly: captain Roger Byrne was a wiser and slightly older head; centre half Mark Jones played in every league game; forwards Tommy Taylor and Dennis Viollet scored 45 goals between them; and the remarkable Duncan Edwards was a dominant force.

However, United were not the only good team in the First Division this season and after three wins and two draws in their first six matches, the Reds were no better than fourth in the league. A couple of defeats and they had dropped to sixth by mid-September.

But then both the goals and the wins started to pile up in good number as Taylor returned to the team after injury. Before the end of the year, United had not only reached the top of the league but had also walloped First Division defending champions Chelsea 3-0 and beaten mighty Wolverhampton Wanderers 4-3, both at Old Trafford.

This team full of twentysomethings was still prone to odd results – like a 5-1 home win over Charlton Athletic on Boxing Day, followed by a 3-0 loss away the very next day – yet they would lose only once from January to the end of the season.

Undefeated at home, with plenty of goals from Busby's brand of attacking football, United's fourth First Division title was won because of defence; no team conceded fewer goals.

MANCHESTER UNITED 2-1 BLACKPOOL

THERE WERE A string of players carrying injuries going into the game, with Dennis Viollet the most doubtful after a kick on the calf in the previous match against Newcastle United. Viollet and the rest of the team actually trained on Blackpool's sea front a few days before the crucial match, something that Matt Busby had organised several times already during this season to relax his players.

However, Busby did not attend the game, rather he kept a promise to his family to attend his mother-in-law's funeral in Lanarkshire, Scotland. Assistant manager Jimmy Murphy was left in charge on the day. It was the final drama in a week of tension after Busby, Murphy and coach Bert Whalley suffered a car accident on the Tuesday before the game. Busby and Murphy suffered knee injuries (Murphy was still limping badly a couple of days afterwards) and Whalley escaped with shock.

The Blackpool side included Stanley Matthews, although full back Jimmy Armfield took a late fitness test. The Seasiders needed to win this and their final two games and hope that United would collapse and fail to win another point this season.

It was a long shot, but Blackpool scored an early goal to make their own dream a possibility. Despite intense United pressure they held onto the lead until half-time, but the Reds refused to panic and improved as the game wore on. A Johnny Berry penalty eventually levelled the scores and a Tommy Taylor goal then won the game and confirmed the championship title.

MANCHESTER UNITED

1	RAY WOOD
2	IAN GREAVES
3	ROGER BYRNE
4	EDDIE COLMAN
5	MARK JONES
6	DUNCAN EDWARDS
7	JOHNNY BERRY
8	JOHN DOHERTY
9	TOMMY TAYLOR
10	DENNIS VIOLLET
11	DAVID PEGG

BLACKPOOL

1	GEORGE FARM
2	JIMMY ARMFIELD
3	TOMMY GARRETT
4	JIM KELLY
5	ROY GRATRIX
6	HUGH KELLY
7	ALAN BROWN
8	STANLEY MATTHEWS
9	JACKIE MUDIE
10	DAVID DURIE
11	BILL PERRY

Referee: Unknown

MANCHESTER UNITED

MANAGER: MATT BUSBY

BLACKPOOL

MANAGER: JOE SMITH

Football League Division One

DATE	OPPONENTS	SCORE	GOALSCORERS	ATTENDANCE
Aug 20	Birmingham City	2-2	Viollet 2	37,994
Aug 24	TOTTENHAM HOTSPUR	2-2	Berry, Webster	25,406
Aug 27	WEST BROMWICH ALBION	3-1	Lewis, Scanlon, Viollet	31,996
Aug 31	Tottenham Hotspur	2-1	Edwards 2	27,453
Sep 3	Manchester City	0-1		59,162
Sep 7	EVERTON	2-1	Blanchflower, Edwards	27,843
Sep 10	Sheffield United	0-1		28,241
Sep 14	Everton	2-4	Blanchflower, Webster	34,897
Sep 17	PRESTON NORTH END	3-2	Pegg, Taylor, Viollet	33,078
Sep 24	Burnley	0-0		26,873
Oct 1	LUTON TOWN	3-1	Taylor 2, Webster	34,409
Oct 8	WOLVERHAMPTON W.	4-3	Taylor 2, Doherty, Pegg	48,638
Oct 15	Aston Villa	4-4	Pegg 2, Blanchflower, Webster	29,478
Oct 22	HUDDERSFIELD TOWN	3-0	Berry, Pegg, Taylor	34,150
Oct 29	Cardiff City	1-0	Taylor	27,795
Nov 5	ARSENAL	1-1	Taylor	41,586
Nov 12	Bolton Wanderers	1-3	Taylor	38,109
Nov 19	CHELSEA	3-0	Taylor 2, Byrne	22,192
Nov 26	Blackpool	0-0		26,240
Dec 3	SUNDERLAND	2-1	Doherty, Viollet	39,901
Dec 10	Portsmouth	2-3	Pegg, Taylor	24,594
Dec 17	BIRMINGHAM CITY	2-1	Jones, Viollet	27,704
Dec 24	West Bromwich Albion	4-1	Viollet 3, Taylor	25,168
Dec 26	CHARLTON ATHLETIC	5-1	Viollet 2, Byrne, Doherty, Taylor	44,611
Dec 27	Charlton Athletic	0-3		42,040
Dec 31	MANCHESTER CITY	2-1	Taylor, Viollet	60,956
Jan 14	SHEFFIELD UNITED	3-1	Berry, Pegg, Taylor	30,162
Jan 21	Preston North End	1-3	Whelan	28,047
Feb 4	BURNLEY	2-0	Taylor, Viollet	27,342
Feb 11	Luton Town	2-0	Viollet, Whelan	16,354
Feb 18	Wolverhampton W.	2-0	Taylor 2	40,014
Feb 25	ASTON VILLA	1-0	Whelan	36,277
Mar 3	Chelsea	4-2	Viollet 2, Pegg, Taylor	32,050
Mar 10	CARDIFF CITY	1-1	Byrne	44,693
Mar 17	Arsenal	1-1	Viollet	50,758
Mar 24	BOLTON WANDERERS	1-0	Taylor	46,114
Mar 30	NEWCASTLE UNITED	5-2	Viollet 2, Doherty, Pegg, Taylor	58,994
Mar 31	Huddersfield Town	2-0	Taylor 2	37,780
Apr 2	Newcastle United	0-0		37,395
Apr 7	BLACKPOOL	2-1	Berry, Taylor	62,277
Apr 14	Sunderland	2-2	McGuinness, Whelan	19,865
Apr 21	PORTSMOUTH	1-0	Viollet	38,417

Final Standings

	Pts
Manchester United	60
Blackpool	49
Wolverhampton	49
Manchester City	46

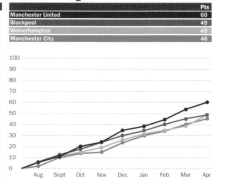

THE MATCH

20 April at Old Trafford, Manchester. Goals: Edwards, Taylor, Whelan (2). Attendance: 58,725

MANCHESTER UNITED 4-0 SUNDERLAND

UNITED HAD LED the First Division for so long this season that by the time the Easter holiday games approached they should probably have already wrapped up the title. However, the pressure of playing in three competitions, including the European Cup, had led to a few too many dropped points and the Reds could still not shake off Preston North End in second place, who were only four points behind United before this home game against Sunderland.

This was the second of three games in just four days over Easter and a victory would all but guarantee the title; United would still need a point to be mathematically secure, but they had three more games to secure it. The other good news was that Eddie Colman was returning from injury while Bobby Charlton was still playing for Dennis Viollet at inside left and the in-form Liam Whelan had just scored a hat-trick in the game against Burnley the day before.

The Wearsiders were no mugs, having just taken 11 points from a possible 14 in their last seven games to ease away from the relegation zone. However, despite the build-up, United ran out easy winners with Whelan firing another two goals, plus one each from Duncan Edwards and Tommy Taylor.

United's confidence knew no bounds and they even secured the championship in front of the entire Real Madrid team, who watched the game before the two teams would play five days later in the European Cup semi-final second leg.

MANCHESTER UNITED

1. RAY WOOD
2. BILL FOULKES
3. ROGER BYRNE
4. EDDIE COLMAN
5. JACKIE BLANCHFLOWER
6. DUNCAN EDWARDS
7. JOHNNY BERRY
8. LIAM WHELAN
9. TOMMY TAYLOR
10. BOBBY CHARLTON
11. DAVID PEGG

SUNDERLAND

1. JOHNNY BOLLANDS
2. JACK HEDLEY
3. JOE MCDONALD
4. DON REVIE
5. GEORGE AITKEN
6. BILLY ELLIOT
7. BILLY BINGHAM
8. STAN ANDERSON
9. CHARLIE FLEMING
10. LEN SHACKLETON
11. COLIN GRAINGER

Referee: Unknown

MANCHESTER UNITED
MANAGER: MATT BUSBY

SUNDERLAND
MANAGER: BILL MURRAY

Division One Champions

THIS MIGHT HAVE been the season when the Busby Babes reached towards the height of their powers in the First Division. The Red Devils roared out of the blocks in August and notched up ten wins in their first 12 games to send them to the top of the table, three points clear of Tottenham Hotspur. The Reds then lost at home to Everton 5-2 after a home European Cup tie against Borussia Dortmund, but pundits attributed that to tiredness and the loss through injury of the rather brittle inside forward Dennis Viollet, who would miss several more games as the season progressed.

A second loss just three games later at Bolton Wanderers allowed Tottenham to take the top spot on goal difference for a week in November, but that was only a minor blip.

United continued to forge ahead and, despite a clumsy 3-1 loss in December to Birmingham City, the Reds ended the year still ahead of Tottenham and the rest of the chasing pack. Into the New Year and the team enjoyed much of the next few weeks scoring 25 league goals in the next six games.

With both FA Cup and European Cup games to play in the spring, there were a few doubts whether the home stretch full of important games would take some of the zip out of United's play. However, despite a run of only two points from four home games in the run-up to Easter, the Reds still had enough class to go on and finish the job with three games to spare. Even United's reserves, who made up the majority of the team in the last three games, were too good for most others in the First Division. They won two and drew the other to stretch United's winning margin in the championship to eight points.

1956/57

"We were good, all right. We were almost certainly going to be the first English team to win the European Cup."

Sir Bobby Charlton reflects on what was next for the Busby Babes after winning the league title.

"I'm not ashamed to admit that the Spaniards had lessons for us – particularly in attack where their forwards never wasted a pass."

Roger Byrne, who led United to league triumph, but knew that European teams still had United's beating; his comments come after Real Madrid's 5-3 aggregate win in the European Cup semi-final.

"Because they were doing things within their limits, they were successful."

Arthur Rowe, manager of Tottenham Hotspur's 1951 championship side.

Above: A portrait of goalkeeper Ray Wood at Old Trafford.

Football League Division One

DATE	OPPONENTS	SCORE	GOALSCORERS	ATTENDANCE
Aug 18	BIRMINGHAM CITY	2-2	Viollet 2	32,752
Aug 20	Preston North End	3-1	Taylor 2, Whelan	32,569
Aug 25	West Bromwich Albion	3-2	Taylor, Viollet, Whelan	26,387
Aug 29	PRESTON NORTH END	3-2	Viollet 3	32,515
Sep 1	PORTSMOUTH	3-0	Berry, Pegg, Viollet	40,369
Sep 5	Chelsea	2-1	Taylor, Whelan	29,082
Sep 8	Newcastle United	1-1	Whelan	50,130
Sep 15	SHEFFIELD WEDNESDAY	4-1	Berry, Taylor, Viollet, Whelan	48,078
Sep 22	MANCHESTER CITY	2-0	Viollet, Whelan	53,525
Sep 29	Arsenal	2-1	Berry, Whelan	62,479
Oct 6	CHARLTON ATHLETIC	4-2	Charlton 2, Berry, Whelan	41,439
Oct 13	Sunderland	3-1	Viollet, Whelan, og	49,487
Oct 20	EVERTON	2-5	Charlton, Whelan	43,151
Oct 27	Blackpool	2-2	Taylor 2	32,632
Nov 3	WOLVERHAMPTON W.	3-0	Pegg, Taylor, Whelan	59,835
Nov 10	Bolton Wanderers	0-2		39,922
Nov 17	LEEDS UNITED	3-2	Whelan 2, Charlton	51,131
Nov 24	Tottenham Hotspur	2-2	Berry, Colman	57,724
Dec 1	LUTON TOWN	3-1	Edwards, Pegg, Taylor	34,736
Dec 8	Aston Villa	3-1	Taylor 2, Viollet	42,530
Dec 15	Birmingham City	1-3	Whelan	36,146
Dec 26	CARDIFF CITY	3-1	Taylor, Viollet, Whelan	28,607
Dec 29	Portsmouth	3-1	Edwards, Pegg, Viollet	32,147
Jan 1	CHELSEA	3-0	Taylor 2, Whelan	42,116
Jan 12	NEWCASTLE UNITED	6-1	Pegg 2, Viollet 2, Whelan 2	44,911
Jan 19	Sheffield Wednesday	1-2	Taylor	51,068
Feb 2	Manchester City	4-2	Edwards, Taylor, Viollet, Whelan	63,872
Feb 9	ARSENAL	6-2	Whelan 2, Berry 2, Edwards, Taylor	60,384
Feb 18	Charlton Athletic	5-1	Charlton 3, Taylor 2	16,308
Feb 23	BLACKPOOL	0-2		42,602
Mar 6	Everton	2-1	Webster 2	34,029
Mar 9	ASTON VILLA	1-1	Charlton	55,484
Mar 16	Wolverhampton W.	1-1	Charlton	53,228
Mar 25	BOLTON WANDERERS	0-2		60,862
Mar 30	Leeds United	2-1	Berry, Charlton	47,216
Apr 6	TOTTENHAM HOTSPUR	0-0		60,349
Apr 13	Luton Town	2-0	Taylor 2	21,227
Apr 19	Burnley	3-1	Whelan 3	41,321
Apr 20	SUNDERLAND	4-0	Whelan 2, Edwards, Taylor	58,725
Apr 22	BURNLEY	2-0	Dawson, Webster	41,321
Apr 27	Cardiff City	3-2	Scanlon 2, Dawson	17,708
Apr 29	WEST BROMWICH ALBION	1-1	Dawson	20,357

Final Standings

	Pts
Manchester United	64
Tottenham Hotspur	56
Preston North End	56
Blackpool	53

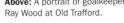

1964/65

Division One Champions

T HIS SEASON WAS a triumph for Busby thanks mainly to a steady squad of just 18 players and almost no injuries to his chosen starting XI. Denis Law missed a few games towards the end of the season, but even he played 36 of the 42 league games (the fewest of the XI), while Shay Brennan, Tony Dunne, Bill Foulkes and John Connelly did not miss a game.

Early form, however, was not good: the Reds were actually 15th after six games with just five points and a single victory. The red giant then woke up and won the next five on the trot to climb to second place, before a draw broke the run. Immediately, another winning run – this time of eight consecutive games – before the end of November put United top of the league, three points ahead of Chelsea and four in front of Leeds.

However, losing 1-0 at home to Leeds on 5 December (George Best was injured just before half-time and unusually ineffective) led to a mini slump as the Yorkshire team would become the Reds' main league rivals.

As Chelsea faded, United and Leeds fought neck and neck for the championship.

While Leeds were distracted by reaching the FA Cup final, the Reds' victory over Blackburn Rovers was the first in another streak of consecutive wins in all competitions, this one running to six. On 26 April United beat Arsenal 3-1 in their penultimate league game while on the same day Leeds could only draw 3-3 with Birmingham City in their last First Division match of the season before the cup final.

Level on points, but slightly ahead on goal average, even a 2-1 loss to Aston Villa could not wrench the title from United's hands. It was a somewhat anticlimatic way to win the championship, but no one at Old Trafford cared.

> "Three newcomers to capture the imagination (this season are) Billy Bremner, Alan Ball and George Best. And I'm not sure the most talented is my teammate George. I have never seen a boy of his age shine so brightly."
>
> Denis Law talks of the league's greatest stars, April 1965

> "Everyone was trying to win for the Munich team. The whole thing was geared to winning the league, it was the only thing we were interested in."
>
> Left-back Tony Dunne explains the motivations behind the first title-winning post-Munich.

Above: Centre forward David Herd has just netted a goal and himself.

THE MATCH

3 April at Ewood Park, Blackburn. Goals: Charlton (3), Connelly, Herd. Attendance: 29,363

BLACKBURN ROVERS 0-5 MANCHESTER UNITED

HAVING JUST LOST a very tough FA Cup semi-final replay to a dour Leeds United team, Matt Busby named an unchanged team for this match. The Red Devils were still only in third place in the league and needed a run of wins if they were to take the title, but there was little evidence that this was on the cards during a sunny but scoreless first half in which United did most of the attacking (often via the brilliance of George Best) but had nothing to show for it. By half-time a small pre-match fight between the fans had been more memorable than the game itself.

But after Busby's half-time team talk United were a different side, particularly Bobby Charlton, who was playing at inside forward rather than on the wing.

It took Charlton just two minutes of the second half to open the scoring by sweeping in a rebound from the Blackburn goalkeeper after a David Herd shot. John Connelly then scored with a header which went into the net off the post, and Herd got the third just after the hour mark from a Tony Dunne left wing cross.

There was still time left for Charlton to get his hat-trick with two classic strikes: the first a typical pile driver in the 65th minute from a Paddy Crerand pass and then a right-foot blaster from outside the penalty area. It was the kind of finishing that had been missing in the cup matches against Leeds, but Busby was happy to see his team's top form return.

MANCHESTER UNITED
1 PAT DUNNE
2 SHAY BRENNAN
3 TONY DUNNE
4 PADDY CRERAND
5 BILL FOULKES
6 NOBBY STILES
7 JOHN CONNELLY
8 BOBBY CHARLTON
9 DAVID HERD
10 DENIS LAW
11 GEORGE BEST

BLACKBURN ROVERS
1 FRED ELS
2 KEITH NEWTON
3 BILLY WILSON
4 MIKE ENGLAND
5 WALTER JOYCE
6 RONNIE CLAYTON
7 MIKE FERGUSON
8 ANDY MCEVOY
9 BRYAN DOUGLAS
10 MIKE HARRISON
11 JOHN BYROM

Referee: Unknown

MANCHESTER UNITED
MANAGER: MATT BUSBY

BLACKBURN ROVERS
MANAGER: JACK MARSHALL

Football League Division One

DATE	OPPONENTS	SCORE	GOALSCORERS	ATTENDANCE
Aug 22	WEST BROMWICH ALBION	2-2	Charlton, Law	52,007
Aug 24	West Ham United	1-3	Law	37,070
Aug 29	Leicester City	2-2	Law, Sadler	32,373
Sep 2	WEST HAM UNITED	3-1	Best, Connelly, Law	45,123
Sep 5	Fulham	1-2	Connelly	36,291
Sep 8	Everton	3-3	Connelly, Herd, Law	63,024
Sep 12	NOTTINGHAM FOREST	3-0	Herd 2, Connelly	45,012
Sep 16	EVERTON	2-1	Best, Law	49,968
Sep 19	Stoke City	2-1	Connelly, Herd	40,031
Sep 26	TOTTENHAM HOTSPUR	4-1	Crerand 2, Law 2	53,058
Sep 30	Chelsea	2-0	Best, Law	60,769
Oct 3	Burnley	0-0		30,761
Oct 10	SUNDERLAND	1-0	Herd	48,577
Oct 17	Wolverhampton W.	4-2	Law 2, Herd, og	26,763
Oct 24	ASTON VILLA	7-0	Law 4, Herd 2, Connelly	35,807
Oct 31	Liverpool	2-0	Crerand, Herd	52,402
Nov 7	SHEFFIELD WEDNESDAY	1-0	Herd	50,178
Nov 14	Blackpool	2-1	Connelly, Herd	31,129
Nov 21	BLACKBURN ROVERS	3-0	Best, Connelly, Herd	49,633
Nov 28	Arsenal	3-2	Law 2, Connelly	59,627
Dec 5	LEEDS UNITED	0-1		53,374
Dec 12	West Bromwich Albion	1-1	Law	28,126
Dec 16	BIRMINGHAM CITY	1-1	Charlton	25,721
Dec 26	Sheffield United	1-0	Best	37,295
Dec 28	SHEFFIELD UNITED	1-1	Herd	42,219
Jan 16	Nottingham Forest	2-2	Law 2	43,009
Jan 23	STOKE CITY	1-1	Law	50,392
Feb 6	Tottenham Hotspur	0-1		58,639
Feb 13	BURNLEY	3-2	Best, Charlton, Herd	38,865
Feb 24	Sunderland	0-1		51,336
Feb 27	WOLVERHAMPTON W.	3-0	Charlton 2, Connelly	37,018
Mar 13	CHELSEA	4-0	Herd 2, Best, Law	56,261
Mar 15	FULHAM	4-1	Connelly 2, Herd 2	45,402
Mar 20	Sheffield Wednesday	0-1		33,549
Mar 22	BLACKPOOL	2-0	Law 2	42,318
Apr 3	Blackburn Rovers	5-0	Charlton 3, Connelly, Herd	29,363
Apr 12	LEICESTER CITY	1-0	Herd	34,114
Apr 17	Leeds United	1-0	Connelly	52,368
Apr 19	Birmingham City	4-2	Best 2, Cantwell, Charlton	28,907
Apr 24	LIVERPOOL	3-0	Law 2, Connelly	55,772
Apr 26	ARSENAL	3-1	Law 2, Best	51,625
Apr 28	Aston Villa	1-2	Charlton	36,081

Final Standings

	Pts
Manchester United	**61**
Leeds United	61
Chelsea	**56**
Everton	**49**

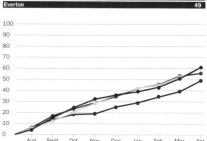

THE MATCH
6 May at Upton Park, London. Goals: Best, Charlton, Crerand, Foulkes, Law (2). Attendance: 38,424

WEST HAM UNITED 1-6 MANCHESTER UNITED

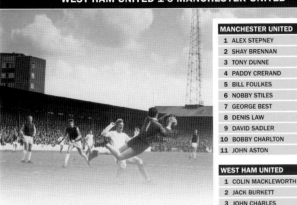

A SINGLE POINT for the title from two games is not always as easy a task as it sounds, but that is what United needed when they took to the field against a West Ham United side that included three of England's recent World Cup winning team (captain Bobby Moore, hat-trick hero Geoff Hurst and midfielder Martin Peters).

With Shay Brennan having successfully returned from injury in the previous game and keeping his place for the trip to London, but still without high scoring David Herd, the Reds needed only to be steady rather than spectacular. However, Matt Busby's team ignored any call for the former and decided on the latter.

Just as their season had begun with a slew of goals, the championship would be clinched in the same way. The United fans who had been at Upton Park from seven o'clock that morning in anticipation of witnessing the crowning of the champions were not disappointed when Bobby Charlton opened the scoring with a rifle-fast shot after just two minutes. Then just four minutes later a cross from the left by John Aston found Paddy Crerand who headed in for the second goal.

United were making life difficult for West Ham's new young goalkeeper Colin Mackleworth and the Reds were 4-0 up by half-time thanks to Bill Foulkes and George Best. The second half was almost a parade by the champions elect and a brace of Denis Law goals brought a 6-1 victory that led to a celebratory pitch invasion.

MANCHESTER UNITED
1 ALEX STEPNEY
2 SHAY BRENNAN
3 TONY DUNNE
4 PADDY CRERAND
5 BILL FOULKES
6 NOBBY STILES
7 GEORGE BEST
8 DENIS LAW
9 DAVID SADLER
10 BOBBY CHARLTON
11 JOHN ASTON

WEST HAM UNITED
1 COLIN MACKLEWORTH
2 JACK BURKETT
3 JOHN CHARLES
4 MARTIN PETERS
5 PAUL HEFFER
6 BOBBY MOORE
7 HARRY REDKNAPP
8 PETER BENNETT
9 RONNIE BOYCE
10 GEOFF HURST
11 JOHN SISSONS

Referee: Unknown

MANCHESTER UNITED
MANAGER: MATT BUSBY

WEST HAM UNITED
MANAGER: RON GREENWOOD

Division One Champions

UNITED SET THEIR stall out early for the title. Four goals in the first 25 minutes in their opening match against West Bromwich Albion told the world they were this season's team to beat. By the beginning of spring the Red Devils looked likely champions as they took over from Liverpool at the top of the table in early March. However, they lost David Herd to a broken left leg in the match against Leicester City on 18 March. Herd was actually returning to the side after missing three games owing to injury and his new injury came while scoring the opening goal after 90 seconds of the match at Old Trafford. In their very next game against Liverpool at Anfield, with United now two points in front of their Mersey rivals, young David Sadler stood in as centre forward and the Reds hung on for a 0-0 draw. That left just nine games to play with the championship still up for grabs.

While others fell to defeats, United stayed unbeaten, fielding a virtually unchanged side for the next several games, with an attack that had to cover for the absence of Herd who had already grabbed 18 goals before his season-ending injury.

Then in their third to last game, United beat a soon-to-be-relegated Aston Villa 3-1 at home despite ex-Red Willie Anderson scoring a goal against his old teammates that gave the Midlands side a 1-0 half-time lead. Ferocious pressure led to three United goals in the second half from John Aston, Denis Law and finally George Best with a beautiful 25-yard curling shot.

The win left United five points ahead of nearest challengers Nottingham Forest who had a game in hand. Just one point from either of their next two matches would be enough for a sixth First Division title and United duly delivered in the very next match beating West Ham United 6-1.

1966/67

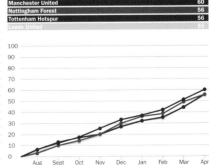

"I feel a pool of 18 players will be necessary in our bid for the European Cup next season. We have won the league several times and the European Cup must now be our sole aim."
Matt Busby after securing the league championship.

"All he did was give me a rollicking and tell me to concentrate on the game."
Nobby Stiles talking about a conversation with Bill Foulkes late in the championship-clinching game against West Ham after he congratulated his no-nonsense teammate a little prematurely on winning a fourth league title.

In an end-of-season tour of Australia, Denis Law swears at a referee in a 7-0 win against West Australian in Perth and is fined 50 Australian dollars.

Above: Bill Foulkes holds the First Division Championship trophy aloft as Matt Busby leads the team on a lap of honour around Old Trafford.

Football League Division One

DATE	OPPONENTS	SCORE	GOALSCORERS	ATTENDANCE
Aug 20	WEST BROMWICH ALBION	5-3	Law 2, Best, Herd, Stiles	41,343
Aug 23	Everton	2-1	Law 2	60,657
Aug 27	Leeds United	1-3	Best	45,092
Aug 31	EVERTON	3-0	Connelly, Foulkes, Law	61,114
Sep 3	NEWCASTLE UNITED	3-2	Connelly, Herd, Law	44,448
Sep 7	Stoke City	0-3		44,337
Sep 10	Tottenham Hotspur	1-2	Law	56,295
Sep 17	MANCHESTER CITY	1-0	Law	62,085
Sep 24	BURNLEY	4-1	Crerand, Herd, Law, Sadler	52,697
Oct 1	Nottingham Forest	1-4	Charlton	41,854
Oct 8	Blackpool	2-1	Law 2	33,555
Oct 15	CHELSEA	1-1	Law	56,789
Oct 29	ARSENAL	1-0	Sadler	45,387
Nov 5	Chelsea	3-1	Aston 2, Best	55,958
Nov 12	SHEFFIELD WEDNESDAY	2-0	Charlton, Herd	46,942
Nov 19	Southampton	2-1	Charlton 2	29,458
Nov 26	SUNDERLAND	5-0	Herd 4, Law	44,687
Nov 30	Leicester City	2-1	Best, Law	39,014
Dec 3	Aston Villa	1-2	Herd	39,937
Dec 10	LIVERPOOL	2-2	Best 2	61,768
Dec 17	West Bromwich Albion	4-3	Herd 3, Law	32,080
Dec 26	Sheffield United	1-2	Herd	42,752
Dec 27	SHEFFIELD UNITED	2-0	Crerand, Herd	59,392
Dec 31	LEEDS UNITED	0-0		53,486
Jan 14	TOTTENHAM HOTSPUR	1-0	Herd	57,366
Jan 21	Manchester City	1-1	Foulkes	62,983
Feb 4	Burnley	1-1	Sadler	40,165
Feb 11	NOTTINGHAM FOREST	1-0	Law	62,727
Feb 25	BLACKPOOL	4-0	Charlton 2, Law, og	47,158
Mar 3	Arsenal	1-1	Aston	63,363
Mar 11	Newcastle United	0-0		37,430
Mar 18	LEICESTER CITY	5-2	Aston, Charlton, Herd, Law, Sadler	50,281
Mar 25	Liverpool	0-0		53,813
Mar 27	Fulham	2-2	Best, Stiles	47,290
Mar 28	FULHAM	2-1	Foulkes, Stiles	51,673
Apr 1	WEST HAM UNITED	3-0	Best, Charlton, Law	61,308
Apr 10	Sheffield Wednesday	2-2	Charlton 2	51,101
Apr 18	SOUTHAMPTON	3-0	Charlton, Law, Sadler	54,291
Apr 22	Sunderland	0-0		43,570
Apr 29	ASTON VILLA	3-1	Aston, Best, Law	55,782
May 6	West Ham United	6-1	Law 2, Best, Charlton, Crerand, Foulkes	38,424
May 13	STOKE CITY	0-0		61,071

Final Standings

	Pts
Manchester United	60
Nottingham Forest	56
Tottenham Hotspur	56
Leeds United	55

1974/75

"This is a hard division. We must capture the right attitude and match the spirit and work rate of our opponents."

Tommy Docherty at the start of the season, after pundits fear his team of ex-First Division stars might not enjoy the rough and tumble of the Second Division.

"Supporters still come up to me now and say 'Thanks, you are the man who took us back into the First Division.' I have to remind them that I was the man who had taken them down in the first place."

Tommy Docherty, Red Devils overseer of both a relegation and a promotion season.

Above: 26 April 1975. Captain Martin Buchan holds the Second Division championship trophy aloft after the presentation at Old Trafford. The presentation took place after United's last home game of the season, against Blackpool, which the Red Devils won 4-0.

Division Two Champions

IT WAS IMPERATIVE that United got off to a good start after several poor seasons in the First Division and the resulting relegation the previous campaign. The team knew that Second Division football required a new, winning attitude and so opening with four consecutive wins and remaining unbeaten in the league until late September was crucial. Manager Tommy Docherty had kept intact the basis of his relegated team and hoped that the addition of Stuart Pearson at centre forward would spark more goals.

The first few games in the Second Division were also important for the fans who dreamed of instant promotion. Average home attendance in the First Division last season had been over 42,000 and when the first home game against Millwall attracted over 44,000 and ended in a 4-0 victory, it was a sign that players and supporters were both pulling in the same direction.

Old Trafford became particularly daunting for visiting sides, and both goals and victories mounted up quickly to take United to the top of the league and keep them there. It was not until February that the Reds lost their one and only game at home.

There were plenty of decent teams in pursuit including Aston Villa, Sunderland, Norwich City and Bristol City yet none of them managed to win as many games as United, whose new confidence had not been so apparent in the previous years.

Losing three consecutive games from the end of January through to early February (two league matches and a League Cup semi-final second leg) created a slight scare and reduced United's lead at the top of the league to three points, but another unbeaten run soon followed and the Reds had guaranteed promotion with four games in hand, taking the championship two weeks later.

THE MATCH
24 August at Old Trafford, Manchester. Goals: Daly (3), Pearson. Attendance: 44,756

MANCHESTER UNITED 4-0 MILLWALL

IN THE OPENING league fixture the previous week, away to Leyton Orient, Tommy Docherty's team displayed all the fighting qualities needed to gain instant promotion, delivering a 2-0 win. But some experts doubted that his players would perform the same way in front of their own fans who were brought up on stylish play rather than simple hard work. The visit of a hardened lower league team like Millwall would be an acid test.

On his home debut, it took only three minutes for Stuart Pearson to score, an opportunist goal after a mistake from an under-pressure Millwall defender trying to make a back pass to his goalkeeper. As United poured forward they missed a few chances before Gerry Daly hooked the ball home after the keeper parried a shot from Mick Martin. Daly then completed a memorable hat-trick with two second-half goals. The relief around Old Trafford was almost palpable.

The Reds had vindicated Docherty's confidence in them by not only scoring plenty of goals, but also playing with a verve and passion that had been missing during the relegation struggle. Skipper Willie Morgan was outstanding on the wing and the new partnership of Stuart Pearson and Sammy McIlroy worked wonders, creating many more chances than the forward line were able to hit home. Meanwhile, the defence, with Martin Buchan and Jim Holton at its heart, looked commanding, allowing keeper Alex Stepney to keep a second consecutive clean sheet, this one against his former team.

MANCHESTER UNITED

1	ALEX STEPNEY
2	ALEX FORSYTH
3	STEWART HOUSTON
4	BRIAN GREENHOFF
6	JIM HOLTON
5	MARTIN BUCHAN
8	WILLIE MORGAN
7	SAMMY MCILROY
9	STUART PEARSON
10	MICK MARTIN
11	GERRY DALY

MILLWALL

1	BRYAN KING
2	DAVE DONALDSON
3	BRIAN BROWN
4	ALAN DORNEY
5	BARRY KITCHENER
6	FRANK SAUL
7	DEREK SMETHURST
8	GORDON HILL
9	MIKE KELLY
10	ALF WOOD
11	BRIAN CLARK

Referee: Unknown

MANCHESTER UNITED

MANAGER: TOMMY DOCHERTY

MILLWALL

MANAGER: BENNY FENTON

Football League Division Two

DATE	OPPONENTS	SCORE	GOALSCORERS	ATTENDANCE
Aug 17	Leyton Orient	2-0	Houston, Morgan	17,772
Aug 24	MILLWALL	4-0	Daly 3, Pearson	44,756
Aug 28	PORTSMOUTH	2-1	Daly, McIlroy	42,547
Aug 31	Cardiff City	1-0	Daly	22,344
Sep 7	NOTTINGHAM FOREST	2-2	Greenhoff, McIlroy	40,671
Sep 14	West Bromwich Albion	1-1	Pearson	23,721
Sep 16	Millwall	1-0	Daly	16,988
Sep 21	BRISTOL ROVERS	2-0	Greenhoff, og	42,948
Sep 25	BOLTON WANDERERS	3-0	Houston, Macari, og	47,084
Sep 28	Norwich City	0-2		24,586
Oct 5	Fulham	2-1	Pearson 2	26,513
Oct 12	NOTTS COUNTY	1-0	McIlroy	46,565
Oct 15	Portsmouth	0-0		25,608
Oct 19	Blackpool	3-0	Forsyth, Macari, McCalliog	25,370
Oct 26	SOUTHAMPTON	1-0	Pearson	48,724
Nov 2	OXFORD UNITED	4-0	Pearson 3, Macari	41,909
Nov 9	Bristol City	0-1		28,104
Nov 16	ASTON VILLA	2-1	Daly 2	55,615
Nov 23	Hull City	0-2		23,287
Nov 30	SUNDERLAND	3-2	McIlroy, Morgan, Pearson	60,585
Dec 7	Sheffield Wednesday	4-4	Macari 2, Houston, Pearson	35,230
Dec 14	LEYTON ORIENT	0-0		41,200
Dec 21	York City	1-0	Pearson	15,567
Dec 26	WEST BROMWICH ALBION	2-1	Daly, McIlroy	51,104
Dec 28	Oldham Athletic	0-1		26,384
Jan 11	SHEFFIELD WEDNESDAY	2-0	McCalliog 2	45,662
Jan 18	Sunderland	0-0		45,976
Feb 1	BRISTOL CITY	0-1		47,118
Feb 8	Oxford United	0-1		15,959
Feb 15	HULL CITY	2-0	Houston, Pearson	44,712
Feb 22	Aston Villa	0-2		39,156
Mar 1	CARDIFF CITY	4-0	Houston, Macari, McIlroy, Pearson	43,601
Mar 8	Bolton Wanderers	1-0	Pearson	38,152
Mar 15	NORWICH CITY	1-1	Pearson	56,202
Mar 22	Nottingham Forest	1-0	Daly	21,893
Mar 28	Bristol Rovers	1-1	Macari	19,337
Mar 29	YORK CITY	2-1	Macari, Morgan	46,802
Mar 31	OLDHAM ATHLETIC	3-2	Coppell, Macari, McIlroy	56,618
Apr 5	Southampton	1-0	Macari	21,866
Apr 12	FULHAM	1-0	Pearson	52,971
Apr 19	Notts County	2-2	Greenhoff, Houston	17,320
Apr 26	BLACKPOOL	4-0	Pearson 2, Greenhoff, Macari	58,769

Final Standings

	Pts
Manchester United	61
Aston Villa	58
Norwich City	53
Sunderland	51

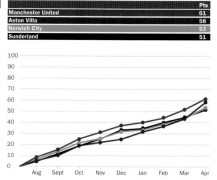

THE MATCH

6 December at Old Trafford, Manchester. Goals: Ince 20', Hughes 73'. Attendance: 44,333

MANCHESTER UNITED 2-1 MANCHESTER CITY

IT IS IMPOSSIBLE for any story of United's first major league title in 26 years not to be linked with the arrival of Eric Cantona. His acquisition by the club has attained mythological status: a chance question by United at the end of a run-of-the-mill phone call about an Old Trafford player's availability for a transfer. So, instead of Denis Irwin moving to Leeds United, the enigmatic Frenchman unexpectedly found his way across the Pennines to the Reds.

Cantona had just helped Leeds win the First Division championship (the last such title before the Premiership was created), but he was not close to the club's Yorkshire manager Howard Wilkinson. The player spent less than a year with Leeds.

Alex Ferguson, however, saw the spark his team needed; Cantona's unnerving unpredictability was something not apparent in Ferguson's teams to date, and the Frenchman's sense of the dramatic was soon evident when he arrived in Manchester right on time to play in the derby game against City.

Cantona had actually donned a United shirt for the first time in a testimonial match for Benfica's great star Eusebio just over a week before turning out against City. But, as league debuts go, it was sublime.

With the Reds in fifth position in the Premiership, Cantona walked on to the Old Trafford pitch as a half-time substitute, and soon sent over a cross for Mark Hughes to score United's first goal in the 2-1 win. The run to the title had truly begun.

MANCHESTER UNITED

1	PETER SCHMEICHEL
2	PAUL PARKER
3	DENIS IRWIN
4	STEVE BRUCE
6	GARY PALLISTER
5	LEE SHARPE
8	PAUL INCE
7	BRYAN ROBSON
9	BRIAN McCLAIR
10	MARK HUGHES
11	RYAN GIGGS 45'

Substitutes

| 12 | ERIC CANTONA 45' |

MANCHESTER CITY

1	TONY COTON
2	ANDY HILL
3	IAN BRIGHTWELL
4	KEITH CURLE
5	TERRY PHELAN
6	FITZROY SIMPSON
7	STEVE MCMAHON
8	DAVID WHITE
9	RICK HOLDEN
10	MIKE SHERON
11	NIALL QUINN

Substitutes

| 12 | PETER REID |
| 13 | GARY FLITCROFT |

Referee: Gerald Ashby

MANCHESTER UNITED

MANAGER: ALEX FERGUSON

MANCHESTER CITY

MANAGER: PETER REID

FA Premiership Champions

1992/93

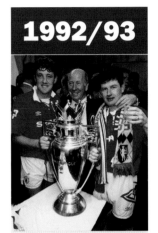

UNITED HAD finished second in last season's title race to a Leeds United team inspired by a certain French import named Eric Cantona, so the start of this campaign lacked a little energy. Two losses and a draw in the first three games was not the start that Alex Ferguson was after in his sixth full season in charge – still without a league championship.

There was a general feeling of relief when new signing Dion Dublin brought the first win of the season in game No 4, away to Southampton, while Peter Schmeichel in his second season between the sticks began marshalling the defensive wall in front of him to good effect; this win was the first of five clean sheets in a row. But to some observers this team was lacking the inner belief of a championship-winning side and they had dropped to seventh in the league by the end of October.

Then in November the very player who had helped Leeds win last year's championship was transferred to Old Trafford and within a few weeks an Eric Cantona-inspired United team were winning games and scoring goals for fun: five against Coventry City, four at home to Tottenham Hotspur. Cantona was at the centre of everything creative and exciting about the team.

From Cantona's debut until the end of the season United lost just twice in the league (tricky away games against Ipswich Town and Oldham Athletic), soaring up the table. They hit the No 1 position in early January and while there was a stutter after the Oldham defeat, which was followed by three successive draws, all of the Reds' final seven games were wins. This unbeaten run in to the end of the season won them the title by ten points; a breakthrough championship for United, the first for Ferguson and the club's eighth in total.

"Excuse me, Mr Ferguson. You are champions."

A fellow golfer informs Alex Ferguson, as the United manager finishes his own game on the links, that his team has won the Premiership because nearest rivals Aston Villa had lost.

"The players knew they were the best and for the most part of the season they demonstrated it where it mattered, on the pitch. The relief was indescribable. For 26 years we had been saying: 'We have to win the league' and the first time was probably the hardest."

Alex Ferguson on his breakthrough title win.

Above: 3 May 1993. Winners from two generations, Steve Bruce, Sir Bobby Charlton and Denis Irwin. The Reds had just been crowned the top team in English league football for the first time in 26 years.

FA Premiership

DATE	OPPONENTS	SCORE	GOALSCORERS	ATTENDANCE
Aug 15	Sheffield United	1-2	Hughes	28,070
Aug 19	EVERTON	0-3		31,901
Aug 22	IPSWICH TOWN	1-1	Irwin	31,704
Aug 24	Southampton	1-0	Dublin	15,623
Aug 29	Nottingham Forest	2-0	Giggs, Hughes	19,694
Sep 2	CRYSTAL PALACE	1-0	Hughes	29,736
Sep 6	LEEDS UNITED	2-0	Bruce, Kanchelskis	31,296
Sep 12	Everton	2-0	Bruce, McClair	30,002
Sep 19	Tottenham Hotspur	1-1	Giggs	33,296
Sep 26	QUEENS PARK RANGERS	0-0		33,287
Oct 3	Middlesbrough	1-1	Bruce	24,172
Oct 18	LIVERPOOL	2-2	Hughes 2	33,243
Oct 24	Blackburn Rovers	0-0		20,305
Oct 31	WIMBLEDON	0-1		32,622
Nov 7	Aston Villa	0-1		39,063
Nov 21	OLDHAM ATHLETIC	3-0	McClair 2, Hughes	33,497
Nov 28	Arsenal	1-0	Hughes	29,739
Dec 6	MANCHESTER CITY	2-1	Hughes, Ince	35,408
Dec 12	NORWICH CITY	1-0	Hughes	34,500
Dec 19	Chelsea	1-1	Cantona	34,464
Dec 26	Sheffield Wednesday	3-3	McClair 2, Cantona	37,708

DATE	OPPONENTS	SCORE	GOALSCORERS	ATTENDANCE
Dec 28	COVENTRY CITY	5-0	Cantona, Giggs, Hughes, Irwin, Sharpe	36,025
Jan 9	TOTTENHAM HOTSPUR	4-1	Cantona, Irwin, McClair, Parker	35,648
Jan 18	Queens Park Rangers	3-1	Giggs, Ince, Kanchelskis	21,117
Jan 27	NOTTINGHAM FOREST	2-0	Hughes, Ince	36,085
Jan 30	Ipswich Town	1-2	McClair	22,068
Feb 6	SHEFFIELD UNITED	2-1	Cantona, McClair	36,156
Feb 8	Leeds United	0-0		34,166
Feb 20	SOUTHAMPTON	2-1	Giggs 2	36,257
Feb 27	MIDDLESBROUGH	3-0	Cantona, Giggs, Irwin	36,251
Mar 6	Liverpool	2-1	Hughes, McClair	44,374
Mar 9	Oldham Athletic	0-1		17,106
Mar 14	ASTON VILLA	1-1	Hughes	36,163
Mar 20	Manchester City	1-1	Cantona	37,136
Mar 24	ARSENAL	0-0		37,301
Apr 5	Norwich City	3-1	Cantona, Giggs, Kanchelskis	20,582
Apr 10	SHEFFIELD WEDNESDAY	2-1	Bruce 2	40,102
Apr 12	Coventry City	1-0	Irwin	24,249
Apr 17	CHELSEA	3-0	Cantona, Hughes, og	40,139
Apr 21	Crystal Palace	2-0	Hughes, Ince	30,115
May 3	BLACKBURN ROVERS	3-1	Giggs, Ince, Pallister	40,447
May 9	Wimbledon	2-1	Ince, Robson	30,115

Final Standings

	Pts
Manchester United	84
Aston Villa	74
Norwich City	72
Blackburn Rovers	71

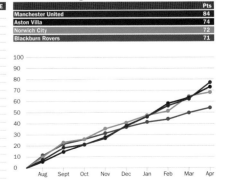

1993/94

> "This club has never won two major trophies in the same season and I feel that would be a tremendous achievement."
>
> Bryan Robson sums up the more confident United this season.

> "I want my players to go out and play the way that Sir Matt would want them to. This game is for his memory."
>
> Alex Ferguson pays tribute to Sir Matt Busby before United's first game after the former manager's death.

FA Premiership Champions

ANY SPORTSMAN will confirm the adage that to win one title requires a supreme effort, but to defend it requires even more of the same. Ferguson knew that he now had a team that was not just talented, but also bursting with confidence. Last season's run of victories at the season's end also confirmed that the choking nerves of previous campaigns were under control, and that he had leaders throughout the team's spine: Schmeichel dominating in goal; Steve Bruce organising the defence; Paul Ince tireless in midfield; and Cantona adding flair to the already talented forward line.

Ferguson's main problem was that success meant more football games. Whereas last year there had been 50 matches to play, this season that total would eventually top 60. Perhaps it was fortunate that the Reds were eliminated by Galatasaray of Turkey in the second round of the European Cup during the first few days of November because the Red Devils went on to make the finals of both domestic cups in the following spring. Just the time when they knew they would also be fighting for the Premiership title as the league season ran into early May.

A fast start in summer continued on into the autumn, and even the winter months of heavier pitches and a constant two-games-a-week schedule could not halt United's quest for another championship. In January the Reds had a 16-point lead over second-placed Blackburn Rovers who had a couple of games in hand.

Eventually the two teams drew level and it took a burst of four straight wins – starting with a 2-0 victory over Manchester City – for United to stretch away and win their second consecutive title, with their first ever league and FA Cup double to follow a week later.

Above: Paul Ince who would make 39 league apperances thiis season, scoring eight goals.

ALEX FERGUSON WAS delighted when his team of defending Premiership champions got off to a flying start this season. The manager did not want the championship of the last campaign to be a one-off after 26 years of waiting and, sure enough, the players responded with confident football that gave them a 14-point lead by the end of the year.

However, before this game kicked off, United had to deal with a number of self-inflicted wounds: Eric Cantona, Peter Schmeichel and Andrei Kanchelskis had all been sent off during the last few games and the League Cup (which the goalkeeper missed through suspension) had been lost. Although winning the FA Cup semi-final against Oldham Athletic had set up the possibility of a league and cup double, the Reds had been caught at the top of the Premiership by Blackburn Rovers. United and Rovers were both on 79 points going into this game, with the Reds having a game in hand.

Coming into a Manchester derby a week after losing a bruising battle with Wimbledon was not ideal preparation, so United needed their best players to step forward. It would have been easy for City to de-rail the Reds' charge to a second successive title, but Eric Cantona - the talisman for the championship win last year - proved he was worth every penny of his £1 million transfer fee once again as he scored both the goals in this 2-0 victory that was the springboard to United winning their first double less than a month later.

MANCHESTER UNITED

1 PETER SCHMEICHEL
2 PAUL PARKER
3 DENIS IRWIN
4 STEVE BRUCE
5 GARY PALLISTER
5 LEE SHARPE 72'
8 PAUL INCE
16 ROY KEANE
14 ANDREI KANCHELSKIS
7 ERIC CANTONA
10 MARK HUGHES

Substitutes
11 RYAN GIGGS

MANCHESTER CITY

25 ANDY DIBBLE
2 ANDY HILL
18 DAVID BRIGHTWELL
5 KEITH CURLE
6 MICHEL VONK
32 STEVE MCMAHON
4 STEVE MCMAHON
31 STEFFAN KARL
7 DAVID ROCASTLE
28 UWE ROSLER
30 PAUL WALSH

Substitutes
12 IAN BRIGHTWELL

Referee: Kelvin Morton

MANCHESTER UNITED

MANAGER: ALEX FERGUSON

MANCHESTER CITY

MANAGER: BRIAN HORTON

FA Premiership

DATE	OPPONENTS	SCORE	GOALSCORERS	ATTENDANCE
Aug 15	Norwich City	2-0	Giggs, Robson	19,705
Aug 18	SHEFFIELD UNITED	3-0	Keane 2, Hughes	41,949
Aug 21	NEWCASTLE UNITED	1-1	Giggs	41,829
Aug 23	Aston Villa	2-1	Sharpe 2	39,624
Aug 28	Southampton	3-1	Cantona, Irwin, Sharpe	16,189
Sep 1	WEST HAM UNITED	3-0	Bruce, Cantona, Sharpe	44,613
Sep 11	Chelsea	0-1		37,064
Sep 19	ARSENAL	1-0	Cantona	44,009
Sep 25	SWINDON TOWN	4-2	Hughes 2, Cantona, Kanchelskis	44,583
Oct 2	Sheffield Wednesday	3-2	Hughes 2, Giggs	34,548
Oct 16	TOTTENHAM HOTSPUR	2-1	Keane, Sharpe	44,655
Oct 23	Everton	1-0	Sharpe	35,430
Oct 30	QUEENS PARK RANGERS	2-1	Cantona, Hughes	44,663
Nov 7	Manchester City	3-2	Cantona 2, Keane	35,155
Nov 20	WIMBLEDON	3-1	Hughes, Kanchelskis, Pallister	44,748
Nov 24	IPSWICH TOWN	0-0		43,300
Nov 27	Coventry City	1-0	Cantona	17,020
Dec 4	NORWICH CITY	2-2	Giggs, McClair	44,694
Dec 7	Sheffield United	3-0	Cantona, Hughes, Sharpe	26,746
Dec 11	Newcastle United	1-1	Ince	36,388
Dec 19	ASTON VILLA	3-1	Cantona 2, Ince	44,499

DATE	OPPONENTS	SCORE	GOALSCORERS	ATTENDANCE
Dec 26	BLACKBURN ROVERS	1-1	Ince	44,511
Dec 29	Oldham Athletic	5-2	Giggs 2, Bruce, Cantona, Kanchelskis	16,708
Jan 1	LEEDS UNITED	0-0		44,724
Jan 4	Liverpool	3-3	Bruce, Giggs, Irwin	42,795
Jan 15	Tottenham Hotspur	1-0	Hughes	31,343
Jan 22	EVERTON	1-0	Giggs	44,750
Feb 5	Queens Park Rangers	3-2	Cantona, Giggs, Kanchelskis	21,267
Feb 26	West Ham United	2-2	Hughes, Ince	28,832
Mar 5	CHELSEA	0-1		44,745
Mar 16	SHEFFIELD WEDNESDAY	5-0	Cantona 2, Giggs, Hughes, Ince	43,669
Mar 19	Swindon Town	2-2	Ince, Keane	18,102
Mar 22	Arsenal	2-2	Sharpe 2	36,203
Mar 30	LIVERPOOL	1-0	Ince	44,751
Apr 2	Blackburn Rovers	0-2		20,886
Apr 4	OLDHAM ATHLETIC	3-2	Dublin, Giggs, Ince	44,686
Apr 16	Wimbledon	0-1		28,553
Apr 23	MANCHESTER CITY	2-0	Cantona 2	44,333
Apr 27	Leeds United	2-0	Giggs, Kanchelskis	41,125
May 1	Ipswich Town	2-1	Cantona, Giggs	22,559
May 4	SOUTHAMPTON	2-0	Hughes, Kanchelskis	44,705
May 8	COVENTRY CITY	0-0		44,717

Final Standings

	Pts
Manchester United	92
Blackburn Rovers	84
Newcastle United	77
Arsenal	71

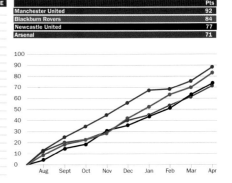

THE MATCH

4 March at St James' Park, Newcastle. Goals: Cantona 51'.
Attendance: 36,584

NEWCASTLE UNITED 0-1 MANCHESTER UNITED

MANCHESTER UNITED

1	PETER SCHMEICHEL
2	GARY NEVILLE
3	DENIS IRWIN
4	STEVE BRUCE
23	PHIL NEVILLE
16	ROY KEANE
5	LEE SHARPE
8	NICKY BUTT
7	ERIC CANTONA
11	RYAN GIGGS
9	ANDY COLE

NEWCASTLE

1	PAVEL SRNICEK
2	WARREN BARTON
27	PHILIPPE ALBERT
6	STEVE HOWEY
3	JOHN BERESFORD
7	ROB LEE
14	DAVID GINOLA
22	DAVID BATTY
8	PETER BEARDSLEY
11	FAUSTINO ASPRILLA
9	LES FERDINAND

Referee: David Elleray

OVER THE LAST few seasons, games between the Reds and Newcastle United had been among the highlights of the Premiership season – as Alex Ferguson battled with his counterpart Kevin Keegan. This year it looked as if Keegan was going to take his first championship trophy, Newcastle leading the league by four points with a game in hand. Earlier in the season the Reds had won the clash between the two teams and now won five games on the trot. It might have seemed a little too early for a championship decider, but that's what this match felt like.

The Reds had slowly been building up the pressure on their increasingly nervous Geordie rivals, who had led them by as many as 12 points at one stage of the season. United had won their last five league games while scoring 14 goals and conceding just two. Newcastle, by contrast, were stumbling slightly, despite having added Colombian Faustino Asprilla to their squad.

The home side certainly attacked with passion and created several excellent first-half chances, yet United goalkeeper Peter Schmeichel was in no mood to concede and kept the game scoreless after 45 minutes. Then, as Newcastle were running out of ideas, United provided the sucker punch and won the match with an Eric Cantona goal from a classic counter attack after 51 minutes. They held on for the win and reduced the Geordies' lead at the top of the table to a single point.

MANCHESTER UNITED

MANAGER: ALEX FERGUSON

NEWCASTLE UNITED

MANAGER: KEVIN KEEGAN

FA Premiership Champions

THIS SEASON WAS loaded with expectation for United fans despite critics, such as the BBC's Alan Hansen, as early as August announcing that Alex Ferguson's young team was simply not good enough to win trophies. The suspended Eric Cantona returned in October following his FA ban (because of last season's kung-fu kick incident) yet, almost immediately, United went out of both European competition and the League Cup to surprise victors (Rotor Volgograd of Russia and York City respectively). Then in October Roy Keane was sent off for the second time this season and Nicky Butt given a three-game suspension for totalling 21 disciplinary points. There seemed little to smile about around Old Trafford.

The domestic league – and later the FA Cup – became Alex Ferguson's focus, but Newcastle United under Kevin Keegan had already roared to the top of the Premiership table with their own brand of high-scoring football and this season looked like it was set to be a disappointing one for the Reds after all.

By Christmas Eve United had clawed their way up to second place, ten points behind Newcastle, who would visit Old Trafford for their next match. Roy Keane was the inspiration in a 2-0 win over the Magpies which gave United renewed optimism that the title was not beyond them.

The glimmer of hope looked to have evaporated in the New Year as United lost 4-1 at Tottenham Hotspur on 1 January and Newcastle won their games in hand to stretch their lead to 12 points. Yet the loss to Spurs was United's last in the league until mid-April and that was enough to reel in Newcastle.

The title was won only on the season's final day and, after so much adversity, it was one of the most satisfying of Ferguson's career.

1995/96

"I always knew our youngsters would deliver."
Alex Ferguson after winning the club's third Premiership.

"Some pundits suggested we couldn't win the title with kids, but they reckoned without the force of a rejuvenated Eric Cantona and the respect and admiration our 'kids' have for him as a footballer."
The manager responds to some pundits'.

"I would love it if we could beat them. Love it. He's gone down in my estimation. Manchester United haven't won this yet, I'd love it if we beat them"
Kevin Keegan's finger-jabbing rant on Sky TV as the 1995-96 title race begins to heat up.

Above: 19 August 1995. David Beckham brought United youthful exuberance against Aston Villa at Villa Park on the opening day of the season.

FA Premiership

DATE	OPPONENTS	SCORE	GOALSCORERS	ATTENDANCE
Aug 19	Aston Villa	1-3	Beckham	34,655
Aug 23	WEST HAM UNITED	2-1	Keane, Scholes	31,966
Aug 26	WIMBLEDON	3-1	Keane 2, Cole	32,226
Aug 28	Blackburn Rovers	2-1	Beckham, Sharpe	29,843
Sep 9	Everton	3-2	Sharpe 2, Giggs	39,496
Sep 16	BOLTON WANDERERS	3-0	Scholes 2, Giggs	32,812
Sep 23	Sheffield Wednesday	0-0		34,101
Oct 1	LIVERPOOL	2-2	Butt, Cantona	34,934
Oct 14	MANCHESTER CITY	1-0	Scholes	35,707
Oct 21	Chelsea	4-1	Scholes 2, Giggs, McClair	31,019
Oct 28	MIDDLESBROUGH	2-0	Cole, Pallister	36,580
Nov 4	Arsenal	0-1		38,317
Nov 18	SOUTHAMPTON	4-1	Giggs 2, Cole, Scholes	39,301
Nov 22	Coventry City	4-0	McClair 2, Beckham, Irwin	23,400
Nov 27	Nottingham Forest	1-1	Cantona	29,263
Dec 2	CHELSEA	1-1	Beckham	42,019
Dec 9	SHEFFIELD WEDNESDAY	2-2	Cantona 2	41,849
Dec 17	Liverpool	0-2		40,546
Dec 24	Leeds United	1-3	Cole	39,801
Dec 27	NEWCASTLE UNITED	2-0	Cole, Keane	42,024
Dec 30	QUEENS PARK RANGERS	2-1	Cole, Giggs	41,890

DATE	OPPONENTS	SCORE	GOALSCORERS	ATTENDANCE
Jan 1	Tottenham Hotspur	1-4	Cole	32,852
Jan 13	ASTON VILLA	0-0		42,667
Jan 22	West Ham United	1-0	Cantona	24,197
Feb 3	Wimbledon	4-2	Cantona 2, Cole, og	25,380
Feb 10	BLACKBURN ROVERS	1-0	Sharpe	42,681
Feb 21	EVERTON	2-0	Keane, Giggs	42,459
Feb 25	Bolton Wanderers	6-0	Scholes 2, Beckham, Bruce, Butt, Cole	21,381
Mar 4	Newcastle United	1-0	Cantona	36,584
Mar 16	Queens Park Rangers	1-1	Cantona	18,817
Mar 20	ARSENAL	1-0	Cantona	50,028
Mar 24	TOTTENHAM HOTSPUR	1-0	Cantona	50,157
Apr 6	Manchester City	3-2	Cantona, Cole, Giggs	29,668
Apr 8	COVENTRY CITY	1-0	Cantona	50,332
Apr 13	Southampton	1-3	Giggs	15,262
Apr 17	LEEDS UNITED	1-0	Keane	48,382
Apr 28	NOTTINGHAM FOREST	5-0	Beckham 2, Cantona, Giggs, Scholes	53,926
May 5	Middlesbrough	3-0	Cole, Giggs, May	29,921

Final Standings

	Pts
Manchester United	82
Newcastle United	78
Liverpool	71
Aston Villa	63

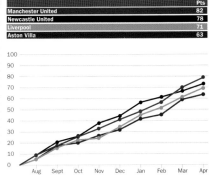

1996/97

> "Eric Cantona's contribution to the Manchester United cause can never be under-estimated – I doubt that I will ever be able to spend £1,000,000 like that again!"
>
> Alex Ferguson weighs up Eric Cantona's United career with a fitting epitaph

> "Our start wasn't incredible and we had that 5-0 defeat at Newcastle. We were neck and neck with Liverpool until we went to Anfield in April and won 3-1, which really killed their hopes."
>
> Gary Pallister pinpoints some key moments from the season.

Above: 11 May 1997. David Beckham and Sir Bobby Charlton celebrate in the dressing room with the FA Premiership trophy after the final match of the season against West Ham United.

FA Premiership Champions

ALEX FERGUSON HAD already signed many top international players before this, his tenth full season as United manager, but two little-known Scandinavians who arrived in time for this season proved to be the keys to a fourth championship in five seasons.

Ronny Johnsen and Ole Gunnar Solskjaer arrived in July, and for modest fees of £1.2 million and £1.5 million respectively. They both made their debuts in August and each brought an extra dimension to the Reds. Johnsen was a steadying influence in the defence, but it was Solskjaer's 18 goals that proved even more vital: the baby-faced assassin had a talent for scoring the goals that mattered.

United looked like the team to beat for long periods of the season, leading the league for most of the second half of the season and Ferguson's personal rivals were no match for him either. Firstly, Newcastle United's Kevin Keegan resigned in January and then Arsenal's new boss Arsene Wenger got into a row with Ferguson as the title race heated up in April when United surprisingly lost 3-2 at home to Derby County.

Fighting for trophies in Europe as well as in the domestic game, Ferguson called for the league schedule to be extended to help ease a fixture pile-up that would mean four games in nine days at the end of the season for his team. When Wenger protested, Ferguson's reaction was blunt. "He has no experience of English football, he's come from Japan and he should keep his mouth shut," said the Scot.

Such a backs-to-the-wall attitude helped the Reds overcome the odds and it was Solskjaer's goal – United's third – in a 3-3 draw against Middlesbrough on 5 May that brought the Reds their fourth Premiership title in five years with two games to spare.

THE MATCH

19 April at Anfield, Liverpool. Goals: Pallister 13', 42', Cole 63'. Attendance: 40,892

LIVERPOOL 1-3 MANCHESTER UNITED

IT WAS TIGHT at the top of the table as the two Lancashire giants faced each other with a handful of Premiership games remaining. United were in first place and two points ahead of Liverpool with a game in hand. A win for the Merseysiders today would put the two clubs almost neck and neck, with Arsenal also in with a chance in third place – a further point behind.

United had nipped past Blackburn Rovers 3-2 away from home the previous week, whereas Liverpool had just been held to a 1-1 draw against cross-town rivals Everton four days earlier. United had good news with the return of Peter Schmeichel in goal, but knew that their record at Anfield over the last nine years (five defeats and just one win) was far from ideal.

In front of a packed crowd of nearly 41,000, tackles flew in fast and furious in the opening minutes as United had the best of the early chances, but it was an unlikely hero who emerged. It was a Gary Pallister header from a corner that put United into the lead only for John Barnes to equalise for the Mersey team, also with a header.

In fact, two more crosses brought two more decisive goals for the Red Devils with Pallister scoring his second of the game (he actually scored only one other goal all season) and Andy Cole nodding in the third at the far post.

This was a game that Liverpool had to win, but ultimately left United five points clear and with the championship fate in their own hands.

MANCHESTER UNITED

1	PETER SCHMEICHEL
2	GARY NEVILLE
12	PHIL NEVILLE
19	RONNY JOHNSEN
6	GARY PALLISTER
16	ROY KEANE
7	ERIC CANTONA
8	NICKY BUTT
10	DAVID BECKHAM
18	PAUL SCHOLES 81'
9	ANDY COLE

Substitutes

13	BRIAN MCCLAIR 81'

LIVERPOOL

1	DAVID JAMES
3	BJORN TORE KVARME
5	MARK WRIGHT
20	STIG INGE BJORNEBYE
12	STEVE HARKNESS
4	JASON MCATEER 51'
16	MICHEAL THOMAS
7	STEVE MCMANAMAN
11	JAMIE REDKNAPP
9	ROBBIE FOWLER
10	JOHN BARNES 67'

Substitutes

8	STAN COLLYMORE 51'
15	PATRIK BERGER 67'

Referee: Graham Poll

MANCHESTER UNITED

MANAGER: ALEX FERGUSON

LIVERPOOL

MANAGER: ROY EVANS

FA Premiership

DATE	OPPONENTS	SCORE	GOALSCORERS	ATTENDANCE
Aug 17	Wimbledon	3-0	Beckham, Cantona, Irwin	25,786
Aug 21	EVERTON	2-2	Cruyff, og	54,943
Aug 25	BLACKBURN ROVERS	2-2	Cruyff, Solskjaer	54,178
Sep 4	Derby County	1-1	Beckham	18,026
Sep 7	Leeds United	4-0	Butt, Cantona, Poborsky, og	39,694
Sep 14	NOTTINGHAM FOREST	4-1	Cantona 2, Giggs, Solskjaer	54,984
Sep 21	Aston Villa	0-0		39,339
Sep 29	TOTTENHAM HOTSPUR	2-0	Solskjaer 2	54,943
Oct 12	LIVERPOOL	1-0	Beckham	55,128
Oct 20	Newcastle United	0-5		36,579
Oct 26	Southampton	3-6	Beckham, May, Scholes	15,253
Nov 2	CHELSEA	1-2	May	55,198
Nov 16	ARSENAL	1-0	og	55,210
Nov 23	Middlesbrough	2-2	Keane, May	30,063
Nov 30	LEICESTER CITY	3-1	Butt 2, Solskjaer	55,196
Dec 8	West Ham United	2-2	Beckham, Solskjaer	25,045
Dec 18	Sheffield Wednesday	1-1	Scholes	37,671
Dec 21	SUNDERLAND	5-0	Cantona 2, Solskjaer 2, Butt	55,081
Dec 26	Nottingham Forest	4-0	Butt, Beckham, Cole, Solskjaer	29,032
Dec 28	LEEDS UNITED	1-0	Cantona	55,256
Jan 1	ASTON VILLA	0-0		55,133

DATE	OPPONENTS	SCORE	GOALSCORERS	ATTENDANCE
Jan 12	Tottenham Hotspur	2-1	Beckham, Solskjaer	33,026
Jan 18	Coventry City	2-0	Giggs, Solskjaer	23,085
Jan 29	WIMBLEDON	2-1	Cole, Giggs	55,314
Feb 1	SOUTHAMPTON	2-1	Cantona, Pallister	55,269
Feb 19	Arsenal	2-1	Cole, Solskjaer	38,172
Feb 22	Chelsea	1-1	Beckham	28,336
Mar 1	COVENTRY CITY	3-1	Poborsky, og 2	55,230
Mar 8	Sunderland	1-2	og	22,225
Mar 15	SHEFFIELD WEDNESDAY	2-0	Cole, Poborsky	55,267
Mar 22	Everton	2-0	Cantona, Solskjaer	40,079
Apr 5	DERBY COUNTY	2-3	Cantona, Solskjaer	55,243
Apr 12	Blackburn Rovers	3-2	Cantona, Cole, Scholes	30,476
Apr 19	Liverpool	3-1	Pallister 2, Cole	40,892
May 3	Leicester City	2-2	Solskjaer 2	21,068
May 5	MIDDLESBROUGH	3-3	Keane, Neville G, Solskjaer	54,489
May 8	NEWCASTLE UNITED	0-0		55,236
May 11	WEST HAM UNITED	2-0	Cruyff, Solskjaer	55,249

Final Standings

	Pts
Manchester United	75
Newcastle United	68
Arsenal	68
Liverpool	68

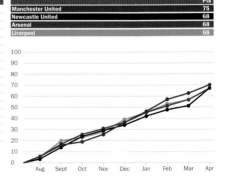

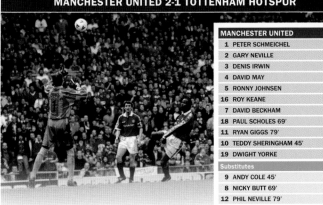

THE MATCH
16 May at Old Trafford, Manchester. Goals: Beckham 42', Cole 47'. Attendance: 55,189

MANCHESTER UNITED 2-1 TOTTENHAM HOTSPUR

MANCHESTER UNITED
1 PETER SCHMEICHEL
2 GARY NEVILLE
3 DENIS IRWIN
4 DAVID MAY
5 RONNY JOHNSEN
16 ROY KEANE
7 DAVID BECKHAM
18 PAUL SCHOLES 69'
11 RYAN GIGGS 79'
10 TEDDY SHERINGHAM 45'
19 DWIGHT YORKE

Substitutes
9 ANDY COLE 45'
8 NICKY BUTT 69'
12 PHIL NEVILLE 79'

TOTTENHAM HOTSPUR
1 IAN WALKER
2 STEPHEN CARR
33 JOHN SCALES 70'
23 SOL CAMPBELL
12 JUSTIN EDINBURGH
4 STEFFEN FREUND
9 DARREN ANDERTON
14 DAVID GINOLA 9'
8 TIM SHERWOOD
18 STEFFEN IVERSEN
10 LES FERDINAND

Substitutes
20 JOSE DOMINGUEZ 9' 76'
32 LUKE YOUNG 70'
22 ANDY SINTON 76'

Referee: Graham Poll

AFTER WEEKS OF topsy-turvy struggle in the league with Arsenal, it was ironically the Londoners' own deadly rivals Tottenham Hotspur who stood in United's way. The Reds had a one-point lead over Arsenal, so only a win would guarantee the title and set up the chance of a treble (the FA Cup and Champions League finals were within the next ten days).

United had been unbeaten in the league since mid-December, but they needed a win against a talented Spurs team. The game began with a comical mistake by Spurs goalkeeper Ian Walker who hit Dwight Yorke with a clearance that nearly cost the visitors a goal. But instead of United being gifted the lead, Les Ferdinand powered through the heart of the Red Devils' defence and chipped over Peter Schmeichel for the opener.

United then pounded at Spurs only to see chances spurned by Paul Scholes and David Beckham. However, the same two players then combined to equalise: Scholes fed Beckham a delightful pass inside the right hand corner of the penalty area and the searing shot went into the top corner. That brought the teams level at half-time while Arsenal were also drawing against Aston Villa. The Reds now had one hand on the trophy.

So when substitute Andy Cole nipped behind the Spurs defence early in the second half to control a difficult through ball and then lob the goalkeeper for 2-1, Old Trafford went wild. Although Arsenal did win their game, United held on for another memorable final-day Premiership victory.

MANCHESTER UNITED
MANAGER: ALEX FERGUSON

TOTTENHAM HOTSPUR
MANAGER: GEORGE GRAHAM

FA Premiership Champions

1998/99

THIS SEASON'S TITLE battle boiled down to a whirlwind five United games in just 16 days in May that took place before the team contested both the FA Cup and Champions League finals. United and Arsenal had been swapping the top spot for the past few weeks and were almost inseparable during the final games. On 1 May, a scorching David Beckham goal from a free-kick almost 30 yards out helped United beat Aston Villa 2-1 and a return to first place. Arsenal's reply was to win their own next game and leap frog the Reds once more.

The drama continued in the midweek games that followed. While Arsenal were winning a north London derby against Tottenham Hotspur, United had gone two goals up against Liverpool (a Dwight Yorke header and a Denis Irwin penalty). But when the Merseysiders converted a penalty of their own and then Irwin was controversially sent off for merely kicking the ball away after he had dribbled it out of play, it was game on. A late Liverpool equaliser from Paul Ince meant United were now three points behind Arsenal but with a game in hand – which they then duly won 1-0 at Middlesbrough four days later thanks to a goal from Yorke.

When the Gunners then lost at Leeds United it meant both teams were on 75 points, while United had a better goal difference by one. The penultimate game for the Reds was against a Blackburn Rovers team managed by ex-Old Trafford star Brian Kidd (who was fighting to keep his team in the Premiership). United's best chance in the match came with a Ryan Giggs header that hit the post, but the 0-0 draw relegated Rovers and left United needing a win in their final match at home. The 2-1 win over Spurs was the first part of the treble that was completed just ten days later.

> "I can't believe it. I can't believe it. Football. Bloody hell."
>
> Sir Alex Ferguson in the immediate aftermath of United's Champions League win.

> "I have a group of players who never cease to surprise me and I'm convinced they are capable of virtually anything. The final weeks of this season will remain with me until the day I die."
>
> Alex Ferguson in a reflective mood after the league, FA Cup and Champions League were won.

> "The last day was typical. We were behind against Spurs but came back to win and clinch the title."
>
> Winger Jesper Blomqvist on the last-day league drama.

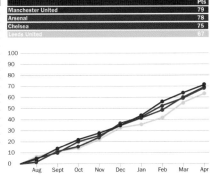

Above: 16 January 1999. Goals by Andy Cole and Dwight Yorke won the Premiership match against Leicester City at Filbert Street. United won 6-2, with Yorke scoring three and Cole two.

FA Premiership

DATE	OPPONENTS	SCORE	GOALSCORERS	ATTENDANCE
Aug 15	LEICESTER CITY	2-2	Beckham, Sheringham	55,052
Aug 22	West Ham United	0-0		26,039
Sep 9	CHARLTON ATHLETIC	4-1	Solskjaer 2, Yorke 2	55,147
Sep 12	COVENTRY CITY	2-0	Johnsen, Yorke	55,198
Sep 20	Arsenal	0-3		38,142
Sep 24	LIVERPOOL	2-0	Irwin, Scholes	55,181
Oct 3	Southampton	3-0	Cole, Cruyff, Yorke	15,251
Oct 17	WIMBLEDON	5-1	Cole 2, Beckham, Giggs, Yorke	55,265
Oct 24	Derby County	1-1	Cruyff	30,867
Oct 31	Everton	4-1	Blomqvist, Cole, Yorke, og	40,079
Nov 8	NEWCASTLE UNITED	0-0		55,174
Nov 14	BLACKBURN ROVERS	3-2	Scholes 2, Yorke	55,198
Nov 21	Sheffield Wednesday	1-3	Cole	39,475
Nov 29	LEEDS UNITED	3-2	Butt, Keane, Solskjaer	55,172
Dec 5	Aston Villa	1-1	Scholes	39,241
Dec 12	Tottenham Hotspur	2-2	Solskjaer 2	36,079
Dec 16	CHELSEA	1-1	Cole	55,159
Dec 19	MIDDLESBROUGH	2-3	Butt, Scholes	55,152
Dec 26	NOTTINGHAM FOREST	3-0	Johnsen 2, Giggs	55,216
Dec 29	Chelsea	0-0		34,741
Jan 10	WEST HAM UNITED	4-1	Cole 2, Solskjaer, Yorke	55,180
Jan 16	Leicester City	6-2	Yorke 3, Cole 2, Stam	22,091
Jan 31	Charlton Athletic	1-0	Yorke	20,043
Feb 3	DERBY COUNTY	1-0	Yorke	55,174
Feb 6	Nottingham Forest	8-1	Solskjaer 4, Cole 2, Yorke 2	30,025
Feb 17	ARSENAL	1-1	Cole	55,171
Feb 20	Coventry City	1-0	Giggs	22,596
Feb 27	SOUTHAMPTON	2-1	Keane, Yorke	55,316
Mar 13	Newcastle United	2-1	Cole 2	36,776
Mar 21	EVERTON	3-1	Beckham, Neville G, Solskjaer	55,182
Apr 3	Wimbledon	1-1	Beckham	26,121
Apr 17	SHEFFIELD WEDNESDAY	3-0	Scholes, Sheringham, Solskjaer	55,270
Apr 25	Leeds United	1-1	Cole	40,255
May 1	ASTON VILLA	2-1	Beckham, og	55,189
May 5	Liverpool	2-2	Irwin, Yorke	44,702
May 9	Middlesbrough	1-0	Yorke	34,665
May 12	Blackburn Rovers	0-0		30,436
May 16	TOTTENHAM HOTSPUR	2-1	Beckham, Cole	55,189

Final Standings

	Pts
Manchester United	79
Arsenal	78
Chelsea	75
Leeds United	67

1999/00

Above: 20 February 2000. Gary Neville gives a characteristic double fist pump during the game against Leeds United.

FA Premiership Champions

COMING OFF AN incredibly draining treble-winning season, the question was how could United top that? The newly knighted Sir Alex Ferguson was in no mood to freewheel. In addition, the Scot had developed a proven tactic of staying calm about the Premiership until well into the New Year; stay in touch until then before staging a push for the finish.

But first, the manager had to settle one area of concern: the goalkeeping position. Peter Schmeichel's departure looked to have been put behind them after the 5-1 end-of-August spanking of Newcastle United at Old Trafford that left the Reds top of the league. The 3-2 victory at Anfield, thanks to two Liverpool own goals helped deflect some of the criticism of an unconvincing display, but in the next two games (both draws against Wimbledon and Southampton), the defence looked increasingly nervous.

Chelsea then scored five unanswered goals as United looked rudderless in defence. New goalkeeper Taibi was quietly dropped and, for the rest of the season, Mark Bosnich and Raimond van der Gouw shared the goalkeeping duties.

Although that spate of games knocked the Reds off the top spot in the Premiership, it is testimony to the strength of the rest of the squad that United were relatively unfazed and dealt with the challenges of Arsenal and Leeds United during the rest of the season. While United were away in Brazil, their rivals all dropped points, so when a refreshed team returned to league action they quickly hit top form.

By the end of January they were top and never looked likely to be caught. Eventually the Reds would lose only three league games all season while winning their sixth Premiership title by a colossal 18 points.

THE MATCH

16 October at Old Trafford, Manchester. Goals: Yorke 39', Cole 42', 50', Irwin 44'. Attendance: 38,164

MANCHESTER UNITED 4-1 WATFORD

AFTER A 5-0 drubbing at Chelsea ten days earlier, Sir Alex Ferguson could wait no longer for his team to return to the treble-winning form of last season. He dropped new keeper Massimo Taibi and recalled Mark Bosnich for this game while also bringing back Ryan Giggs. Roy Keane would be on the bench after his knee injury.

With Premiership newboys Watford still finding their feet in the top division, the prospects looked good for a return to winning ways and so it proved. It took 39 minutes before United broke through the Watford defence, but the goal was well worth waiting for - a spectacular overhead Dwight Yorke kick from a Nicky Butt cross.

Just two minutes later, Andy Cole scored the second with a diving header from another cross, this one from Giggs, and before half-time it was 3-0 after David Beckham was fouled in the penalty area, Denis Irwin scoring from the spot.

More goals seemed inevitable and the next came after 50 minutes when Beckham struck the ball to the far post and Cole finished the move with an over-the-shoulder strike. United were relaxed enough to give substitutes Keane, Jonathan Greening and Ole Gunnar Solskjaer a run-out. Although Watford scored a consolation goal they also had a man sent off near the end in what was the sort of comprehensive win by the Reds their manager was demanding.

The victory restored United's pride and the team's equilibrium. They suffered only two more defeats during the entire season.

MANCHESTER UNITED

1	MARK BOSNICH
12	PHIL NEVILLE
6	JAAP STAM 64'
27	MIKAEL SILVESTRE
3	DENIS IRWIN
18	PAUL SCHOLES
7	DAVID BECKHAM
8	NICKY BUTT
11	RYAN GIGGS 71'
9	ANDY COLE 67'
19	DWIGHT YORKE

Substitutes

16	ROY KEANE 64'
20	OLE GUNNAR SOLSKJAER 67'
34	JONATHAN GREENING 71'

WATFORD

1	ALEX CHAMBERLAIN
16	NIGEL GIBBS
5	STEVE PALMER 83'
4	ROBERT PAGE
32	MARK WILLIAMS
6	PAUL ROBINSON
8	MICAH HYDE 46'
3	PETER KENNEDY
10	RICHARD JOHNSON
14	NORDIN WOOTER
7	MICHEL NGONGE 61'

Substitutes

11	NICK WRIGHT 46'
35	CHARLIE MILLER 61'
17	TOMMY SMITH 83'

Referee: Peter Jones

MANCHESTER UNITED

MANAGER: SIR ALEX FERGUSON

WATFORD

MANAGER: GRAHAM TAYLOR

FA Premiership

DATE	OPPONENTS	SCORE	GOALSCORERS	ATTENDANCE
Aug 8	Everton	1-1	Yorke	39,141
Aug 11	SHEFFIELD WEDNESDAY	4-0	Cole, Scholes, Solskjaer, Yorke	54,941
Aug 14	LEEDS UNITED	2-0	Yorke 2	55,187
Aug 22	Arsenal	2-1	Keane 2	38,147
Aug 25	Coventry City	2-1	Scholes, Yorke	22,024
Aug 30	NEWCASTLE UNITED	5-1	Cole 4, Giggs	55,190
Sep 11	Liverpool	3-2	Cole, og 2	44,929
Sep 18	WIMBLEDON	1-1	Cruyff	55,189
Sep 25	SOUTHAMPTON	3-3	Yorke 2, Sheringham	55,249
Oct 3	Chelsea	0-5		34,909
Oct 16	WATFORD	4-1	Cole 2, Irwin, Yorke	55,188
Oct 23	Tottenham Hotspur	1-3	Giggs	36,072
Oct 30	ASTON VILLA	3-0	Cole, Keane, Scholes	55,211
Nov 6	LEICESTER CITY	2-0	Cole 2	55,191
Nov 20	Derby County	2-1	Butt, Cole	33,370
Dec 4	EVERTON	5-1	Solskjaer 4, Irwin	55,193
Dec 18	West Ham United	4-2	Giggs 2, Yorke 2	26,037
Dec 26	BRADFORD CITY	4-0	Cole, Keane, Fortune, Yorke	55,188
Dec 28	Sunderland	2-2	Butt, Keane	42,026
Jan 24	ARSENAL	1-1	Sheringham	58,293
Jan 29	MIDDLESBROUGH	1-0	Beckham	61,267

DATE	OPPONENTS	SCORE	GOALSCORERS	ATTENDANCE
Feb 2	Sheffield Wednesday	1-0	Sheringham	39,640
Feb 5	COVENTRY CITY	3-2	Cole 2, Scholes	61,380
Feb 12	Newcastle United	0-3		36,470
Feb 20	Leeds United	1-0	Cole	40,160
Feb 26	Wimbledon	2-2	Cole, Cruyff	26,129
Mar 4	LIVERPOOL	1-1	Solskjaer	61,592
Mar 11	DERBY COUNTY	3-1	Yorke 3	61,619
Mar 18	Leicester City	2-0	Beckham, Yorke	22,170
Mar 25	Bradford City	4-0	Yorke 2, Beckham, Scholes	18,276
Apr 1	WEST HAM UNITED	7-1	Scholes 3, Beckham, Cole, Irwin, Solskjaer	61,611
Apr 10	Middlesbrough	4-3	Cole, Giggs, Fortune, Scholes	34,775
Apr 15	SUNDERLAND	4-0	Solskjaer 2, Berg, Butt	61,612
Apr 22	Southampton	3-1	Beckham, Solskjaer, og	15,245
Apr 24	CHELSEA	3-2	Yorke 2, Solskjaer	61,593
Apr 29	Watford	3-2	Cruyff, Giggs, Yorke	20,250
May 6	TOTTENHAM HOTSPUR	3-1	Beckham, Sheringham, Solskjaer	61,629
May 14	Aston Villa	1-0	Sheringham	39,217

Final Standings

	Pts
Manchester United	91
Arsenal	73
Leeds United	69
Liverpool	67

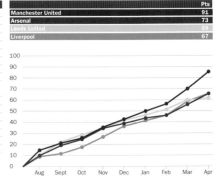

THE MATCH

25 February at Old Trafford, Manchester. Goals: Yorke 3', 18', 22', Keane 26', Solskjaer 38', Sheringham 90'. Attendance: 67,535

MANCHESTER UNITED 6-1 ARSENAL

MANCHESTER UNITED

1	FABIEN BARTHEZ
27	MIKAEL SILVESTRE
6	WES BROWN
6	JAAP STAM
2	GARY NEVILLE
7	DAVID BECKHAM
8	NICKY BUTT
16	ROY KEANE 75'
18	PAUL SCHOLES
20	OLE GUNNAR SOLSKJAER
19	DWIGHT YORKE 75'

Substitutes

36	LUKE CHADWICK 75'
10	TEDDY SHERINGHAM 75'

ARSENAL

1	DAVID SEAMAN
22	OLEG LUZHNY
3	IGOR STEPANOVS
18	GILLES GRIMANDI
16	SILVINHO
29	ASHLEY COLE 46'
15	RAY PARLOUR 68'
4	PATRICK VIEIRA
7	ROBERT PIRES
11	SYLVAIN WILTORD
14	THIERRY HENRY

Substitutes

8	FREDDIE LJUNGBERG 46'
23	NELSON VIVAS 68'

Referee: Paul Durkin

MANCHESTER UNITED

MANAGER: SIR ALEX FERGUSON

ARSENAL

MANAGER: ARSENE WENGER

BEFORE THIS GAME even took place and with 11 league games still to be played, United seemed to have one hand on the Premiership trophy. Arsenal were undoubtedly the nearest challengers to the Reds for the title, but they were a relatively distant second, some 13 points adrift already. United had lost only twice in 27 Premiership matches, but one of those was to the Gunners back on the first day of October: a 1-0 win by the Londoners, with Thierry Henry scoring.

But United hit Arsenal early and hard in this return, with the contest virtually over after the first half, with a Dwight Yorke hat-trick doing much of the damage. Yorke was getting a rare start because of an Andy Cole suspension while Teddy Sheringham was left on the bench. His first goal was a far post tap-in and came after a clever one-two with Paul Scholes in the penalty area just three minutes into the game. Then, after Arsenal equalised, two more well-taken Yorke strikes moved the score to 3-1 with the game still only 22 minutes old.

The striker turned creator when he crossed deftly from the left for Roy Keane to make it 4-1. Ole Gunnar Solskjaer added the fifth with a near post flick from a Nicky Butt cross and sub Sheringham pitched in with the final goal in the second half.

Coming after they had scored just four goals in their last six games in all competitions, the goal-fest was a welcome surprise for the Old Trafford faithful and put United an astonishing 16 points ahead at the top of the table.

FA Premiership Champions

UNITED WERE BEGINNING to dominate English football like no other team in the modern game. The overwhelming supremacy of last season's championship win would be hard to match, but with French World Cup-winning goalkeeper Fabien Barthez confirmed as the new No 1, there was even more confidence flowing through the team.

This was also a United team still scoring plenty of goals by other teams' standards – there would be 79 in all from 15 players – with Teddy Sheringham as the main scorer with 15 from 29 appearances. However, this was well down on last season's 97 and, but for the newly installed Barthez giving more support to the defence that would concede just 31 goals, the fight for the Premiership might have been more of a struggle.

While early season sparring was underway, there was not much evidence that a repeat of last year's dominance was on the cards. United were actually second in the league to Leicester City, with Arsenal third, after eight games. This was after a loss to the Gunners, but the next game was away to Leicester and the 3-0 margin of victory put the Reds on top of the table, sent a season-defining message to the rest of the league and thereafter United never looked like failing to defend their title.

With 11 clean sheets and only two losses from 21 games before the end of December, United were already eight points ahead of Arsenal with little prospect of any other team putting up a significant challenge.

When the Gunners lost so comprehensively at Old Trafford, the Reds needed only 15 points from ten games to record their third Premiership in a row, an achievement confirmed with five games remaining. A relaxed United even lost their last three games yet still finished ten points ahead of Arsenal.

2000/01

"Winning three in a row is something special. Perhaps we're like a great artist whose work is only really appreciated with the passing of time."

Sir Alex on the third of United's hat-trick of titles.

"I'm pleased at the way my partnership with Teddy (Sheringham) is going on the pitch, but it's fair to say that we don't have Sunday lunch together. We are still not talking."

Andy Cole on a lack of dressing room dialogue among the strike force.

"Our main rivals were Arsenal, and during the games there were always fights. I enjoyed them, even the bad words before the games."

United defender Mikael Silvestre, who later went on to play for Arsenal, on the Reds' rivalry with the Gunners.

Above: 5 May 2001. Teddy Sheringham lifts the Premiership trophy after the match against Derby County, which United lost 1-0.

FA Premiership

DATE	OPPONENTS	SCORE	GOALSCORERS	ATTENDANCE
Aug 20	NEWCASTLE UNITED	2-0	Cole, Johnsen	67,477
Aug 22	Ipswich Town	1-1	Beckham	22,007
Aug 26	West Ham United	2-2	Beckham, Cole	25,998
Sep 5	BRADFORD CITY	6-0	Fortune 2, Sheringham 2, Beckham, Cole	67,447
Sep 9	SUNDERLAND	3-0	Scholes 2, Sheringham	67,503
Sep 16	Everton	3-1	Butt, Giggs, Solskjaer	38,541
Sep 23	CHELSEA	3-3	Beckham, Scholes, Sheringham	67,568
Oct 1	Arsenal	0-1		38,146
Oct 14	Leicester City	3-0	Sheringham 2, Solskjaer	22,132
Oct 21	LEEDS UNITED	3-0	Beckham, Yorke, og	67,523
Oct 28	SOUTHAMPTON	5-0	Sheringham 3, Cole 2	67,581
Nov 4	Coventry City	2-1	Beckham, Cole	21,079
Nov 11	MIDDLESBROUGH	2-1	Butt, Sheringham	67,576
Nov 18	Manchester City	1-0	Beckham	34,429
Nov 25	Derby County	3-0	Butt, Sheringham, Yorke	32,910
Dec 2	TOTTENHAM HOTSPUR	2-0	Scholes, Solskjaer	67,583
Dec 9	Charlton Athletic	3-3	Giggs, Keane, Solskjaer	20,043
Dec 17	LIVERPOOL	0-1		67,533
Dec 23	IPSWICH TOWN	2-0	Solskjaer 2	67,597
Dec 26	Aston Villa	1-0	Solskjaer	40,889
Dec 30	Newcastle United	1-1	Beckham	52,134
Jan 1	WEST HAM UNITED	3-1	Solskjaer, Yorke, og	67,603
Jan 13	Bradford City	3-0	Chadwick, Giggs, Sheringham	20,551
Jan 20	ASTON VILLA	2-0	Neville G, Sheringham	67,533
Jan 31	Sunderland	1-0	Cole	48,260
Feb 3	EVERTON	1-0	og	67,528
Feb 10	Chelsea	1-1	Cole	34,690
Feb 25	ARSENAL	6-1	Yorke 3, Keane, Sheringham, Solskjaer	67,535
Mar 3	Leeds United	1-1	Chadwick	40,055
Mar 17	LEICESTER CITY	2-0	Silvestre, Yorke	67,516
Mar 31	Liverpool	0-2		44,806
Apr 10	CHARLTON ATHLETIC	2-1	Cole, Solskjaer	67,505
Apr 14	COVENTRY CITY	4-2	Yorke 2, Giggs, Scholes	67,637
Apr 21	MANCHESTER CITY	1-1	Sheringham	67,535
Apr 28	Middlesbrough	2-0	Beckham, Neville P	34,417
May 5	DERBY COUNTY	0-1		67,526
May 13	Southampton	1-2	Giggs	15,526
May 19	Tottenham Hotspur	1-3	Scholes	36,072

Final Standings

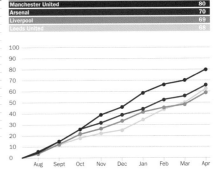

	Pts
Manchester United	80
Arsenal	70
Liverpool	69
Leeds United	68

2002/03

"It's getting tickly now - squeaky-bum time, I call it."

Sir Alex Ferguson describing the tension of the championship run-in.

"My greatest challenge is not what is happening right at this moment, my greatest challenge was knocking Liverpool right off their ****** perch. And you can print that."

Sir Alex Ferguson emphasising his desire to win league titles.

"We played better than any other team in the league from March onwards and you can't beat the kind of momentum we were able to build up."

After wresting the title back from Arsenal, Sir Alex sums up United's strength in the closing stages of the season.

Above: 28 September 2002. Fabien Barthez looks to the footballing gods during the match against Charlton Athletic. The Reds won 3-1.

FA Premiership Champions

TO WRITE OFF United in any title race during the Premiership era would be foolish, and this season proved to be a perfect example of how the team can awaken like a sleeping giant at any moment and surge to another title. The purchase of Rio Ferdinand was key, but the loss of Dwight Yorke before the season started meant a trio of title-winning forwards (the other two being Andy Cole and Teddy Sheringham) had all departed in the last couple of seasons. So this was more work in progress – another new superlative team in the making. Perhaps it was understandable that the early part of the season was dreary, with too few wins, goals or convincing performances.

Liverpool and Arsenal seemed to be battling for the title in the early months of the season and when City won the Manchester derby in early November at Maine Road 3-1, United were fifth in the table and eight points behind the Anfield team.

United went unbeaten in their next five league games, winning four, to lift themselves into second place behind new leaders Arsenal, but two straight defeats followed and the Gunners edged seven points ahead.

Then a routine 2-0 home win over Birmingham City kick-started an 18-game unbeaten run that lasted the rest of the season. Ruud van Nistelrooy played a huge part in the run-in scoring 17 of his 25 league goals in the final 18 matches.

Particularly pleasing were a 4-0 victory over Liverpool and a 6-2 thrashing of Newcastle United.

The streak overhauled Arsenal and also a Chelsea side that had poked their noses in front of United before the New Year. The title was confirmed on the penultimate weekend of the season as United beat Charlton Athletic 4-1 and Arsenal lost to Leeds United.

THE MATCH
16 April at Highbury, London. Goals: van Nistelrooy 24', Giggs 63'. Attendance: 38,164

ARSENAL 2-2 MANCHESTER UNITED

THIS WAS NOT quite a title-decider, but it was awfully close. The Londoners had enjoyed an eight-point lead in early March, but now United were three points ahead, with Arsenal having a game in hand. The build-up was full of tension as the two managers had been swapping salvos in the media for months and both of the teams were expecting another physical confrontation, especially the two captains Roy Keane and Patrick Vieira. A loss for either side would be a huge disadvantage with less than a month of the Premiership season remaining.

The Reds had just beaten Newcastle United 6-2 so were in great form, while Arsenal had Thierry Henry and Dennis Bergkamp back in their side.

it was Ruud van Nistelrooy who opened the scoring after 24 minutes following a pass from Ryan Giggs. Then Vieira had to be substituted because of his recurring knee injury and United's confidence grew. However, Henry deflected an equaliser past Fabien Barthez early in the second half before squeezing Arsenal into a 2-1 lead after 61 minutes.

One minute later, while the Gunners fans were still celebrating, Giggs headed in an equaliser. Arsenal's Sol Campbell was sent off late in the game for elbowing Ole Gunnar Solskjaer, but the score remained at 2-2 after Barthez made a vital last-minute save from Henry.

The Reds travelled home from Highbury in great spirits; they were still top of the table and had managed to repel their most dangerous opponents to make another title more likely.

MANCHESTER UNITED
1	FABIEN BARTHEZ
27	MIKAEL SILVESTRE
6	WES BROWN
5	RIO FERDINAND
22	JOHN O'SHEA 46'
18	PAUL SCHOLES
8	NICKY BUTT
16	ROY KEANE
11	RYAN GIGGS
20	OLE GUNNAR SOLSKJAER
10	RUUD VAN NISTELROOY

Substitutes
2	GARY NEVILLE 46'

ARSENAL
13	STUART TAYLOR
12	LAUREN
3	ASHLEY COLE
5	MARTIN KEOWN
23	SOL CAMPBELL
4	PATRICK VIEIRA 34'
19	GILBERTO SILVA
7	ROBERT PIRES 80'
8	FREDRIK LJUNGBERG
10	DENNIS BERGKAMP 75'
14	THIERRY HENRY

Substitutes
17	EDU 34'
25	KANU 80'
11	SYLVAIN WILTORD 75'

Referee: Mark Halsey

MANCHESTER UNITED
MANAGER: SIR ALEX FERGUSON

ARSENAL
MANAGER: ARSENE WENGER

FA Premiership

DATE	OPPONENTS	SCORE	GOALSCORERS	ATTENDANCE
Aug 17	WEST BROMWICH ALBION	1–0	Solskjaer	67,645
Aug 23	Chelsea	2–2	Beckham, Giggs	41,541
Aug 31	Sunderland	1–1	Giggs	47,586
Sep 3	MIDDLESBROUGH	1–0	van Nistelrooy	67,464
Sep 11	BOLTON WANDERERS	0–1		67,623
Sep 14	Leeds United	0–1		39,622
Sep 21	TOTTENHAM HOTSPUR	1–0	van Nistelrooy	67,611
Sep 28	Charlton Athletic	3–1	Giggs, Scholes, van Nistelrooy	26,630
Oct 7	EVERTON	3–0	Scholes 2, van Nistelrooy	67,629
Oct 19	Fulham	1–1	Solskjaer	18,103
Oct 26	ASTON VILLA	1–1	Forlan	67,619
Nov 2	SOUTHAMPTON	2–1	Forlan, Neville P	67,691
Nov 9	Manchester City	1–3	Solskjaer	34,649
Nov 17	West Ham United	1–1	van Nistelrooy	35,049
Nov 23	NEWCASTLE UNITED	5–3	van Nistelrooy 3, Scholes, Solskjaer	67,625
Dec 1	Liverpool	2–1	Forlan 2	44,250
Dec 7	ARSENAL	2–0	Scholes, Veron	67,650
Dec 14	WEST HAM UNITED	3–0	Solskjaer, Veron, og	67,555
Dec 21	Blackburn Rovers	0–1		30,475
Dec 26	Middlesbrough	1–3	Giggs	34,673
Dec 28	BIRMINGHAM CITY	2–0	Beckham, Forlan	67,640

DATE	OPPONENTS	SCORE	GOALSCORERS	ATTENDANCE
Jan 1	SUNDERLAND	2–1	Beckham, Scholes	67,609
Jan 11	West Bromwich Albion	3–1	Scholes, Solskjaer, van Nistelrooy	27,129
Jan 18	CHELSEA	2–1	Forlan, Scholes	67,606
Feb 1	Southampton	2–0	Giggs, van Nistelrooy	32,085
Feb 4	Birmingham City	1–0	van Nistelrooy	29,475
Feb 9	MANCHESTER CITY	1–1	van Nistelrooy	67,646
Feb 22	Bolton Wanderers	1–1	Solskjaer	27,409
Mar 5	LEEDS UNITED	2–1	Silvestre, og	67,135
Mar 15	Aston Villa	1–0	Beckham	42,602
Mar 22	FULHAM	3–0	van Nistelrooy 3	67,706
Apr 5	LIVERPOOL	4–0	van Nistelrooy 2, Giggs, Solskjaer	67,639
Apr 12	Newcastle United	6–2	Scholes 3, Giggs, Solskjaer, van Nistelrooy	52,164
Apr 15	Arsenal	2–2	Giggs, van Nistelrooy	38,164
Apr 19	BLACKBURN ROVERS	3–1	Scholes 2, van Nistelrooy	67,626
Apr 27	Tottenham Hotspur	2–0	Scholes, van Nistelrooy	36,073
May 3	CHARLTON ATHLETIC	4–1	van Nistelrooy 3, Beckham	67,721
May 11	Everton	2–1	Beckham, van Nistelrooy	40,168

Final Standings

	Pts
Manchester United	83
Arsenal	78
Newcastle United	69
Chelsea	67

THE MATCH

5 May at City of Manchester Stadium, Manchester. Goals: Ronaldo 34' (pen). Attendance: 47,244

MANCHESTER CITY 0-1 MANCHESTER UNITED

THREE DAYS BEFORE this game, United had been knocked out of the Champions League after a bad 3-0 loss to AC Milan in the semi-final. However, the Reds knew that beating City would be a huge step towards the league title they had not won for four years.

In fact, with a league and FA Cup double still to play for, there was no chance to rest players and Sir Alex Ferguson fielded his strongest possible side. Meanwhile, mid-table City had only local pride to play for and were in the doldrums at their Eastlands Stadium: a mere ten goals in 18 Premiership games was a depressing statistic, especially for their fans.

With so much at stake and the normal derby atmosphere on top, the game was a tense affair dominated by Cristiano Ronaldo. The Portuguese was brought down in the penalty area in the 34th minute and converted the spot-kick – after a trademark stutter-step run-up – for the vital lead.

But United fingernails were being bitten in the second half and when City were awarded a penalty of their own (after a foul by Wes Brown), the title celebrations looked like being put on hold.

However, City's Darius Vassell blasted his penalty kick straight at the middle of the goal and the ball hit the knee of Edwin van der Sar to allow the keeper to make the save and protect United's lead. When Chelsea could only draw with Arsenal 24 hours later, United were handed their ninth Premiership title.

MANCHESTER UNITED

1	EDWIN VAN DER SAR
4	GABRIEL HEINZE
6	WES BROWN
5	RIO FERDINAND
15	NEMANJA VIDIC
18	PAUL SCHOLES
16	MICHAEL CARRICK
7	CRISTIANO RONALDO
11	RYAN GIGGS
14	ALAN SMITH 73'
10	WAYNE ROONEY 87'

Substitutes
22	JOHN O'SHEA 87'
24	DARREN FLETCHER 73'

MANCHESTER CITY

1	ANDREAS ISAKSSON
16	NEDUM ONUOHA
3	MICHAEL BALL
22	RICHARD DUNNE
5	SYLVAIN DISTIN
33	MICHAEL JOHNSON
21	DIETMAR HAMANN 46'
24	DAMARCUS BEASLEY 61'
7	STEPHEN IRELAND 69'
9	EMILE LOKANDA MPENZA
11	DARIUS VASSELL

Substitutes
17	SUN JIHAI 46'
28	TREVOR SINCLAIR 61'
14	PAUL DICKOV 69'

Referee: Rob Styles

MANCHESTER UNITED
MANAGER: SIR ALEX FERGUSON

MANCHESTER CITY
MANAGER: STUART PEARCE

FA Premiership Champions

2006/07

NOT HAVING WON the Premiership in three seasons was something Sir Alex Ferguson found deeply unpalatable. Chelsea's billionaire owner Roman Abramovich had changed the landscape of English football by investing huge sums of his own money in the London team, and United had been unable to come up with an immediate response. Until this year that is, when the whole United team could not stop scoring goals – 83 in all from 17 different players.

The Red Devils began the season with a new intensity, losing only two league games between August and December and, at the same time, launching their goalscoring blitz – 47 in all from the first 21 games – while conceding just 13.

It was certainly title-winning form, although defending champions Chelsea, under manager Jose Mourinho, were never going to give up the chase. The Reds' main problem was a congested fixture list with two-leg Champions League knockout games and FA Cup matches (including an unwanted replay in March against Middlesbrough); the relentlessness of the games would take their toll later in the season. What had been a nine-point lead in February was whittled away during the spring and down to three points by 18 April with both teams having five games remaining.

In the first of those run-in games, a 1-1 draw against Middlesbrough looked to have let Chelsea in, but they could get only a point themselves at Newcastle United the next day.

Finally United rose to the Premiership challenge against Everton in their next game; 2-0 down after 50 minutes, the Reds burst back with four unanswered goals to take the match 4-2. Two more Chelsea draws and United had another championship.

> "Chelsea won the last two titles at a canter. We had to do something about it."
>
> Sir Alex Ferguson looks back on breaking Chelsea's period of league dominance.

> "The match against Liverpool in March was vital. I'd got injured towards the end of the game with the score at 0-0. I was sitting in the dressing room with Paul Scholes, who had been sent off. There was a clock in the dressing room so we knew when 90 minutes were up. After about three minutes of added time there was another roar. One of our press officers rushed into the dressing room shouting: "SHAYSIE HAS SCORED!" I couldn't believe it. John O'Shea of all people."
>
> Wayne Rooney was as surprised as anyone at the scorer of one of the season's most vital goals in a 1-0 win over Liverpool at Anfield in March.

Above: 13 May 2007. With 14 and 17 league goals respectively, Rooney and Ronaldo regain the Premiership trophy for United.

FA Premiership

DATE	OPPONENTS	SCORE	GOALSCORERS	ATTENDANCE
Aug 20	FULHAM	5–1	Rooney 2, Ronaldo, Saha, og	75,115
Aug 23	Charlton Athletic	3–0	Fletcher, Saha, Solskjaer	25,422
Aug 26	Watford	2–1	Giggs, Silvestre	19,453
Sep 9	TOTTENHAM HOTSPUR	1–0	Giggs	75,453
Sep 17	ARSENAL	0–1		75,595
Sep 23	Reading	1–1	Ronaldo	24,098
Oct 1	NEWCASTLE UNITED	2–0	Solskjaer 2	75,664
Oct 14	Wigan Athletic	3–1	Saha, Solskjaer, Vidic	20,631
Oct 22	LIVERPOOL	2–0	Ferdinand, Scholes	75,828
Oct 28	Bolton Wanderers	4–0	Rooney 3, Ronaldo	27,229
Nov 4	PORTSMOUTH	3–0	Ronaldo, Saha, Vidic	76,004
Nov 11	Blackburn Rovers	1–0	Saha	26,162
Nov 18	Sheffield United	2–1	Rooney 2	32,584
Nov 26	CHELSEA	1–1	Saha	75,948
Nov 29	EVERTON	3–0	Evra, O'Shea, Ronaldo	75,723
Dec 2	Middlesbrough	2–1	Fletcher, Saha	31,238
Dec 9	MANCHESTER CITY	3–1	Ronaldo, Rooney, Saha	75,858
Dec 17	West Ham United	0–1		34,966
Dec 23	Aston Villa	3–0	Ronaldo 2, Scholes	42,551
Dec 26	WIGAN ATHLETIC	3–1	Ronaldo 2, Solskjaer	76,018
Dec 30	READING	3–2	Ronaldo 2, Solskjaer	75,910
Jan 1	Newcastle United	2–2	Scholes 2	52,302
Jan 13	ASTON VILLA	3–1	Carrick, Park, Ronaldo	76,073
Jan 21	Arsenal	1–2	Rooney	60,128
Jan 31	WATFORD	4–0	Larsson, Ronaldo, Rooney, og	76,032
Feb 4	Tottenham Hotspur	4–0	Giggs, Ronaldo, Scholes, Vidic	36,146
Feb 10	CHARLTON ATHLETIC	2–0	Fletcher, Park	75,883
Feb 24	Fulham	2–1	Giggs, Ronaldo	24,459
Mar 3	Liverpool	1–0	O'Shea	44,403
Mar 17	BOLTON WANDERERS	4–1	Park 2, Rooney 2	76,058
Mar 31	BLACKBURN ROVERS	4–1	Carrick, Park, Scholes, Solskjaer	76,098
Apr 7	Portsmouth	1–2	O'Shea	20,223
Apr 17	SHEFFIELD UNITED	2–0	Carrick, Rooney	75,540
Apr 21	MIDDLESBROUGH	1–1	Richardson	75,967
Apr 28	Everton	4–2	Eagles, O'Shea, Rooney, og	39,682
May 5	Manchester City	1–0	Ronaldo	47,244
May 9	Chelsea	0–0		41,794
May 13	WEST HAM UNITED	0–1		75,927

Final Standings

	Pts
Manchester United	89
Chelsea	83
Liverpool	68
Arsenal	68

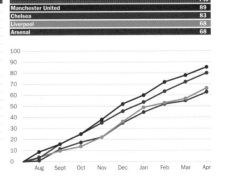

2007/08

"We've expressed ourselves in an entertaining way. The title is well deserved."

With Cristiano Ronaldo and Carlos Tevez racking up the goals, Sir Alex Ferguson reflects on another job well done.

"It was a great feeling to equal Bobby Charlton's appearance record of 758, but winning trophies was more important to me at this stage of my career. That's how it has to be. You can't look back. You have to look forward."

Ryan Giggs shows the attitude that has made him a legend of the modern game.

Above: 15 August 2007. United's new signing Carlos Tevez in action against Portsmouth at Fratton Park. The match was drawn 1-1.

FA Premiership Champions

THIS PREMIERSHIP SEASON would be a classic three-cornered contest between United, Chelsea and Arsenal. The Reds had pushed for the top spot in each of the past two seasons and were not many people's favourites for the title this time around, despite the Blues changing managers (Avram Grant took over from Jose Mourinho after six matches).

An early challenge from Manchester City wore itself out in the New Year, so the trio of big guns did battle alone. All three led the Premiership at some stage of the season and, as March dawned and the run-in began, there was little to choose between them.

Sir Alex Ferguson had long known that this was the most crucial part of the season and the Reds began the period with five consecutive wins without conceding a goal. That left them top and six points clear, but two draws and only one victory in their next three meant that their forthcoming match with second-placed Chelsea would be a pivotal fixture. A 2-1 loss and the two teams were level with two games left, but United were ahead on goal difference while Arsenal had dropped away.

In the penultimate weekend of the season, the Reds overwhelmed West Ham United with four first-half goals and won easily, but Chelsea needed late goals for a 2-0 victory away to Newcastle United.

The deciding games on 11 May would come ten days before United and Chelsea were to meet in the Champions League final, so additional bragging rights were at stake. A Ronaldo penalty against Wigan Athletic after 33 minutes calmed any United nerves and Ryan Giggs scored late in the second half to wrap up the game and take the title back to Manchester, as Chelsea could only draw with Bolton Wanderers.

THE MATCH
23 September at Old Trafford, Manchester. Goals: Tevez 45', Saha 90' (pen). Attendance: 75,663

MANCHESTER UNITED 2-0 CHELSEA

UNITED AND CHELSEA had now been banging heads at the top of the Premiership for several seasons, so every clash between the two teams was important. But this game had special significance because the Londoners had sacked manager Jose Mourinho a few days earlier, a move that had sent shock waves around the the football world – and had surprised Sir Alex Ferguson. Now, even at this early stage of the season, the Reds could do real damage to the confidence of their rivals by securing a convincing win.

Sir Alex Ferguson started all his star names in a match he knew would carry extra significance at the end of the season, but tempers flared in the first half when a studs-up tackle on Patrice Evra by Jon Obi Mikel had the Chelsea player sent off.

Then, just as Chelsea thought they had survived to half-time with only ten men, Ryan Giggs knocked over a cross from the right wing to the near post and Argentine Carlos Tevez glanced in a header for a 1-0 lead.

Despite the paucity of the single-goal lead, United controlled the game in the second half as rain poured down. As injury time began, Louis Saha collected a pass in the penalty area and was brought down as he jinked inside for a shot.

The Frenchman took the spot kick himself and scored; the 2-0 win took United to second place in the league and sent a message to Chelsea's new manager Avram Grant that the Red Devils would go to great lengths to defend their Premiership title.

MANCHESTER UNITED
1	EDWIN VAN DER SAR
3	PATRICE EVRA
6	WES BROWN
5	RIO FERDINAND
15	NEMANJA VIDIC
18	PAUL SCHOLES
16	MICHAEL CARRICK
7	CRISTIANO RONALDO
11	RYAN GIGGS
32	CARLOS TEVEZ 79'
10	WAYNE ROONEY

Substitutes
9	LOUIS SAHA 79'

CHELSEA
1	PETR CECH
20	PAULO FERREIRA
3	ASHLEY COLE
22	TAL BEN HAIM
26	JOHN TERRY
4	CLAUDE MAKELELE
5	MICHAEL ESSIEN
12	JON OBI MIKEL
10	JOE COLE 76'
15	FLORENT MALOUDA 69'
7	ANDRIY SHEVCHENKO 59'

Substitutes
24	SHAUN WRIGHT-PHILLIPS 69'
14	CLAUDIO PIZARRO 76'
21	SALOMON KALOU 59'

Referee: Mike Dean

MANCHESTER UNITED
MANAGER: SIR ALEX FERGUSON

CHELSEA
MANAGER: AVRAM GRANT

FA Premiership

DATE	OPPONENTS	SCORE	GOALSCORERS	ATTENDANCE
Aug 12	READING	0-0		75,655
Aug 15	Portsmouth	1-1	Scholes	20,510
Aug 19	Manchester City	0-1		44,955
Aug 26	TOTTENHAM HOTSPUR	1-0	Nani	75,696
Sep 1	SUNDERLAND	1-0	Saha	75,648
Sep 15	Everton	1-0	Vidic	39,364
Sep 23	CHELSEA	2-0	Saha, Tevez	75,663
Sep 29	Birmingham City	1-0	Ronaldo	26,526
Oct 6	WIGAN ATHLETIC	4-0	Ronaldo 2, Rooney, Tevez	75,300
Oct 20	Aston Villa	4-1	Rooney 2, Ferdinand, Giggs	42,640
Oct 27	MIDDLESBROUGH	4-1	Tevez 2, Nani, Rooney	75,720
Nov 3	Arsenal	2-2	Ronaldo, og	60,161
Nov 11	BLACKBURN ROVERS	2-0	Ronaldo 2	75,710
Nov 24	Bolton Wanderers	0-1		25,028
Dec 3	FULHAM	2-0	Ronaldo 2	75,055
Dec 8	DERBY COUNTY	4-1	Tevez 2, Giggs, Ronaldo	75,725
Dec 16	Liverpool	1-0	Tevez	44,459
Dec 23	EVERTON	2-1	Ronaldo 2	75,749
Dec 26	Sunderland	4-0	Saha 2, Ronaldo, Rooney	47,360
Dec 29	West Ham United	1-2	Ronaldo	34,966
Jan 1	BIRMINGHAM CITY	1-0	Tevez	75,459

DATE	OPPONENTS	SCORE	GOALSCORERS	ATTENDANCE
Jan 12	NEWCASTLE UNITED	6-0	Ronaldo 3, Tevez 2, Ferdinand	75,965
Jan 19	Reading	2-0	Ronaldo, Rooney	24,135
Jan 30	PORTSMOUTH	2-0	Ronaldo 2	75,415
Feb 2	Tottenham Hotspur	1-1	Tevez	36,075
Feb 10	MANCHESTER CITY	1-2	Carrick	75,970
Feb 23	Newcastle United	5-1	Ronaldo 2, Rooney 2, Saha	52,291
Mar 1	Fulham	3-0	Hargreaves, Park, og	25,314
Mar 15	Derby County	1-0	Ronaldo	33,072
Mar 19	BOLTON WANDERERS	2-0	Ronaldo 2	75,476
Mar 23	LIVERPOOL	3-0	Brown, Nani, Ronaldo	76,000
Mar 29	ASTON VILLA	4-0	Rooney 2, Ronaldo, Tevez	75,932
Apr 6	Middlesbrough	2-2	Ronaldo, Rooney	33,952
Apr 13	ARSENAL	2-1	Hargreaves, Ronaldo	75,967
Apr 19	Blackburn Rovers	1-1	Tevez	30,316
Apr 26	Chelsea	1-2	Rooney	41,828
May 3	WEST HAM UNITED	4-1	Ronaldo 2, Carrick, Tevez	76,013
May 11	Wigan Athletic	2-0	Giggs, Ronaldo	25,133

Final Standings

	Pts
Manchester United	87
Chelsea	85
Arsenal	83
Liverpool	76

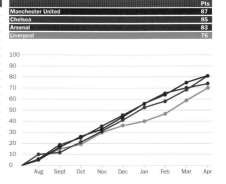

THE MATCH

15 November at Old Trafford, Manchester. Goals: Ronaldo 3', 89', Carrick 45', Berbatov 49' Welbeck 84'. Attendance: 75,369

MANCHESTER UNITED 5-0 STOKE CITY

MANCHESTER UNITED

1	EDWIN VAN DER SAR
3	PATRICE EVRA
23	JONNY EVANS
22	JOHN O'SHEA
15	NEMANJA VIDIC
16	MICHAEL CARRICK
24	DARREN FLETCHER 63'
7	CRISTIANO RONALDO
32	CARLOS TEVEZ 74'
9	DIMITAR BERBATOV
13	JI-SUNG PARK 63'

Substitutes

28	DARREN GIBSON 63'
19	DANNY WELBECK 63'
26	MANUCHO 74'

STOKE CITY

29	THOMAS SORENSEN
25	ABDOULAYE FAYE
3	DANNY HIGGINBOTHAM
2	ANDY GRIFFIN 79'
17	RYAN SHAWCROSS
19	AMDY FAYE
4	SEYI OLOFINJANA 31'
18	SALIF DIAO
24	RORY DELAP
10	RICARDO FULLER 68'
11	MAMADY SIDIBE

Substitutes

28	ANDY WILKINSON 79'
9	RICHARD CRESSWELL 31'
12	DAVE KITSON 68'

Referee: Peter Walton

IN THE FIRST few weeks of the season, it had been a rather limp United defence of their Premiership title. The Reds shone occasionally, but were also prone to average performances, like the 2-1 defeat inflicted by Arsenal at Highbury – as the Gunners had passed their way through the United defence – just before this game. Meanwhile, Liverpool were already eight points ahead of the fourth-placed Reds at the top of the league table.

After just 11 games United really needed to make a statement to the rest of the league and begin a run that would stamp their authority on the title race.

Trying to achieve that against newly promoted Stoke City, who had already beaten Arsenal and were well known for their dangerous long ball and long throw tactics, was potentially a tricky task – a banana-skin moment in the making. . .

The game began as a celebration for Sir Alex Ferguson, who was marking his anniversary of 50 years in football, but it also turned into another kind of celebration as the goals poured in. Firstly, a 30-yard free kick from Cristiano Ronaldo flew into the net for his 100th United goal and further goals came from Michael Carrick and Dimitar Berbatov.

It was 4-0 after ex-youth teamer Danny Welbeck, on his Premiership debut in front of the Stretford End, played a one-two and then hit a right-footed screamer past the Stoke keeper. The Red Devils statement of intent was further underlined when Ronaldo capped the day with his second goal and United's fifth.

MANCHESTER UNITED

MANAGER: SIR ALEX FERGUSON

STOKE CITY

MANAGER: TONY PULIS

FA Premiership Champions

WINNING A THIRD Premiership title on the trot for a second time was Sir Alex Ferguson's ambition at the start of this season, although it was a lacklustre United that began the campaign. The arrival of Dimitar Berbatov from Tottenham Hotspur in September helped lift an early mood of despondency, yet despite the Bulgarian setting up Carlos Tevez for an early lead on his debut against Liverpool, the game still finished in a 2-1 defeat.

United were sitting 11th after the first handful of games as their rivals all made better starts to the season. A 1-1 draw at Chelsea (a late equaliser cancelling out a Ji-Sung Park opener) was good, but then managing only a 4-3 win over newly promoted Hull City was worrying.

Form came after the 5-0 win against Stoke City. Including that game, United had a 16-match run that was remarkable: 14 wins, 28 goals scored and just two goals conceded. Edwin van der Sar's streak of 14 consecutive clean sheets was a Premiership record. Before the run that began in mid-November, United were fourth in the table and eight points behind the leaders; by the time it finished in early March, the Reds were seven points above second-placed Chelsea with a game in hand and just one third of the season to play.

A 4-1 slip-up at home against Liverpool, when Nemanja Vidic was sent off and the entire United defence looked vulnerable, was followed by a surprise 2-0 defeat at Fulham (Paul Scholes and Wayne Rooney were both sent off) this gave the Merseysiders in particular some hope as the Reds' lead at the top was cut to one point after the two losses. But United promptly went on another league-winning unbeaten run of nine games to secure an 18th league title.

2008/09

"The challenge now is to win it next year. A 19th league title would be special."

Having equalled Liverpool's record of 18 titles, Sir Alex Ferguson wastes no time in looking forward to overhauling it.

"This title was as good as any because we used so many players. We had a lot of injuries, and had to change the team quite regularly. (Federico) Macheda won us the league with his late goal in the 3-2 win against Aston Villa and he didn't even get a medal."

Gary Neville gives his verdict on the record-equalling title.

Above: 16 May 2009. Wayne Rooney in action during the Premier League match between United and Arsenal at Old Trafford. The game ended 0-0.

FA Premiership

DATE	OPPONENTS	SCORE	GOALSCORERS	ATTENDANCE
Aug 17	NEWCASTLE UNITED	1-1	Fletcher	75,512
Aug 25	Portsmouth	1-0	Fletcher	20,540
Sep 13	Liverpool	1-2	Tevez	44,192
Sep 21	Chelsea	1-1	Park	41,760
Sep 27	BOLTON WANDERERS	2-0	Ronaldo, Rooney	75,484
Oct 4	Blackburn Rovers	2-0	Brown, Rooney	27,321
Oct 18	WEST BROMWICH ALBION	4-0	Berbatov, Nani, Ronaldo, Rooney	75,451
Oct 25	Everton	1-1	Fletcher	36,069
Oct 29	WEST HAM UNITED	2-0	Ronaldo 2	75,397
Nov 1	HULL CITY	4-3	Ronaldo 2, Carrick, Vidic	75,398
Nov 8	Arsenal	1-2	Rafael	60,106
Nov 15	STOKE CITY	5-0	Ronaldo 2, Berbatov, Carrick, Welbeck	75,369
Nov 22	Aston Villa	0-0		42,585
Nov 30	Manchester City	1-0	Rooney	47,320
Dec 6	SUNDERLAND	1-0	Vidic	75,400
Dec 13	Tottenham Hotspur	0-0		35,882
Dec 26	Stoke City	1-0	Tevez	27,500
Dec 29	MIDDLESBROUGH	1-0	Berbatov	75,294
Jan 11	CHELSEA	3-0	Berbatov, Rooney, Vidic	75,455
Jan 14	WIGAN ATHLETIC	1-0	Rooney	73,917
Jan 17	Bolton Wanderers	1-0	Berbatov	26,021
Jan 27	West Bromwich Albion	5-0	Ronaldo 2, Berbatov, Tevez, Vidic	26,105
Jan 31	EVERTON	1-0	Ronaldo	75,399
Feb 8	West Ham United	1-0	Giggs	34,958
Feb 18	FULHAM	3-0	Berbatov, Rooney, Scholes	75,437
Feb 21	BLACKBURN ROVERS	2-1	Ronaldo, Rooney	75,000
Mar 4	Newcastle United	2-1	Berbatov, Rooney	51,636
Mar 14	LIVERPOOL	1-4	Ronaldo	75,569
Mar 21	Fulham	0-2		25,652
Apr 5	ASTON VILLA	3-2	Ronaldo 2, Macheda	75,409
Apr 11	Sunderland	2-1	Macheda, Scholes	45,408
Apr 22	PORTSMOUTH	2-0	Carrick, Rooney	74,895
Apr 25	TOTTENHAM HOTSPUR	5-2	Ronaldo 2, Rooney 2, Berbatov	75,458
May 2	Middlesbrough	2-0	Giggs, Park	33,767
May 10	MANCHESTER CITY	2-0	Ronaldo, Tevez	75,464
May 13	Wigan Athletic	2-1	Carrick, Tevez	21,286
May 16	ARSENAL	0-0		75,468
May 24	Hull City	1-0	Gibson	24,945

Final Standings

	Pts
Manchester United	90
Liverpool	86
Chelsea	83
Arsenal	72

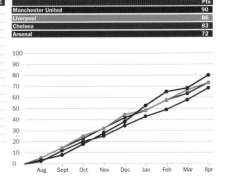

2010/11

FA Premiership Champions

Above: 30 May 2011. Patrice Evra's jacket says it all on the bus during the Premier League winners parade.

Opposite: 8 May 2011. Nemanja Vidic celebrates scoring the second goal during the crucial match against Chelsea at Old Trafford. The Red Devils won 2-1.

THIS WOULD BE one of the most hotly contested Premiership battles for years, as United fought with defending champions Chelsea, title aspirants Manchester City and regular rivals Arsenal throughout the entire season. The top of the table changed on an almost weekly basis as each of the four teams enjoyed periodic supremacy. Chelsea set off the fastest and then Arsenal had their turn to look favourites. City, with their influx of money from new owners, were the outsiders, but also had their moments.

While all this was going on around them, United kept grinding out the victories. It was not always pretty, but the Reds found ways to win and also discovered a new hero in young Mexican Javier Hernandez, whose impish personality and darting runs were providing Wayne Rooney with a perfect striking foil.

United did not hit the top of the league until the end of November after handing out a 7-1 thrashing to Blackburn Rovers at Old Trafford, with Dimitar Berbatov scoring five goals, but it was a significant move because they then beat rivals Arsenal in December and Manchester City a few weeks later. All this time, United kept ahead of the pack and a only a 2-1 loss at Stamford Bridge to Chelsea followed by a 3-1 defeat at Liverpool seemed to shake the Reds.

While many pundits thought this United side was not Ferguson's best, no team was able to catch the Reds and they lost only once in the last nine games – a poor performance against Arsenal that occurred between the two Champions League semi-final games. Three games from the title, a dramatic home win against Chelsea crushed the Reds' nearest rivals and the record-breaking 19th championship was won eventually by a nine-point margin.

THE MATCH

8 May at Old Trafford, Manchester. Goals: Hernandez 1', Vidic 23'. Attendance: 75,445

MANCHESTER UNITED 2-1 CHELSEA

THIS WAS BILLED by the media as a Premiership decider, but the truth was that a Chelsea win would put them and United level on points with only two games remaining, while victory for the Reds would make a 19th league title almost certain; in the event of a win, United would need just one more point for mathematical certainty of the much-prized trophy.

Neither Sir Alex Ferguson nor the under-pressure Carlo Ancelotti wanted a draw, so they were both prepared to attack. However, no one could have predicted the sensational opening as Ji-Sung Park sent Javier Hernandez through to score the first goal after just 26 seconds. New Chelsea centre back David Luiz endured some harsh words from his manager and the London team looked very unsettled. It was less surprising when United scored again, this time after a cross from Ryan Giggs was headed home by Nemanja Vidic in the 23rd minute. Chelsea were reeling and could have conceded more as United looked imperious in the first half. A penalty appeal after a cross from Antonio Valencia hit a Chelsea hand might have put the game beyond Cheslea's reach.

But, with Luiz substituted for the second half, the game became interesting when Frank Lampard stabbed home a goal for the Blues on 68 minutes. United began looking a little nervous, but when Chelsea's midfielder Ramires was sent off, any real hope of a revival by the Londoners left the field with him. The Reds went on to seal the title with a point in their next game.

MANCHESTER UNITED

1	EDWIN VAN DER SAR
22	JOHN O'SHEA 45'
20	FABIO 88'
5	RIO FERDINAND
15	NEMANJA VIDIC
13	JI-SUNG PARK
16	MICHAEL CARRICK
25	ANTONIO VALENCIA
11	RYAN GIGGS
14	JAVIER HERNANDEZ
10	WAYNE ROONEY

Substitutes

23	JONNY EVANS 45'
12	CHRIS SMALLING 88'

CHELSEA

1	PETR CECH
4	DAVID LUIZ 45'
3	ASHLEY COLE
2	BRANISLAV IVANOVIC
26	JOHN TERRY
5	MICHAEL ESSIEN
12	JON OBI MIKEL 45'
8	FRANK LAMPARD
15	FLORENT MALOUDA
11	DIDIER DROGBA
21	SALOMON KALOU 62'

Substitutes

7	RAMIRES 45'
33	ALEX 45'
9	FERNANDO TORRES 62'

Referee: Howard Webb

MANCHESTER UNITED

MANAGER: SIR ALEX FERGUSON

CHELSEA

MANAGER: CARLO ANCELOTTI

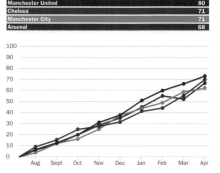

FA Premiership

DATE	OPPONENTS	SCORE	GOALSCORERS	ATTENDANCE
Aug 16	NEWCASTLE UNITED	3-0	Berbatov, Fletcher, Giggs	75,221
Aug 22	Fulham	2-2	Scholes, Hangeland (og)	25,643
Aug 28	WEST HAM UNITED	3-0	Rooney (pen), Nani, Berbatov	75,061
Sep 11	Everton	3-3	Fletcher, Vidic, Berbatov	36,556
Sep 19	LIVERPOOL	3-2	Berbatov (3)	75,213
Sep 26	Bolton Wanderers	2-2	Nani, Owen	
Oct 2	Sunderland	0-0		41,709
Oct 16	WEST BROMWICH ALBION	2-2	Hernandez, Nani	75,272
Oct 24	Stoke City	2-1	Hernandez (2)	27,372
Oct 30	TOTTENHAM HOTSPUR	2-0	Vidic, Nani	75,223
Nov 6	WOLVERHAMPTON WANDERERS	2-1	Park (2)	75,285
Nov 10	Manchester City	0-0		47,679
Nov 13	Aston Villa	2-2	Macheda, Vidic	40,073
Nov 20	WIGAN ATHLETIC	2-0	Evra, Hernandez	74,181
Nov 27	BLACKBURN ROVERS	7-1	Berbatov (5), Park, Nani	74,850
Dec 13	ARSENAL	1-0	Park	75,227
Dec 26	SUNDERLAND	2-0	Berbatov, A. Ferdinand (og)	75,269
Dec 28	Birmingham City	1-1	Berbatov	28,242
Jan 1	West Bromwich Albion	2-1	Rooney, Hernandez	25,499
Jan 4	STOKE CITY	2-1	Nani, Hernandez	73,401
Jan 16	Tottenham Hotspur	0-0		35,828

DATE	OPPONENTS	SCORE	GOALSCORERS	ATTENDANCE
Jan 22	BIRMINGHAM CITY	5-0	Berbatov (3), Giggs, Nani	75,326
Jan 25	Blackpool	3-2	Berbatov (2), Hernandez	15,574
Feb 1	ASTON VILLA	3-1	Rooney (2), Vidic	75,256
Feb 5	Wolverhampton Wanderers	1-2	Nani	28,811
Feb 12	MANCHESTER CITY	2-1	Nani, Rooney	75,322
Feb 26	Wigan Athletic	4-0	Hernandez (2), Rooney, Fabio	18,140
Mar 1	Chelsea	1-2	Rooney	41,825
Mar 6	Liverpool	1-3	Hernandez	44,753
Mar 19	BOLTON WANDERERS	1-0	Berbatov	75,486
Apr 2	West Ham United	4-2	Rooney (3), Hernandez	34,546
Apr 9	FULHAM	2-0	Berbatov, Valencia	75,339
Apr 19	Newcastle United	0-0		49,025
Apr 23	EVERTON	1-0	Hernandez	75,300
May 1	Arsenal	0-1		60,107
May 8	CHELSEA	2-1	Hernandez, Vidic	75,445
May 14	Blackburn Rovers	1-1	Rooney (pen)	29,867
May 22	BLACKPOOL	4-2	Park, Anderson, Evatt (og), Owen	75,400

Final Standings

	Pts
Manchester United	80
Chelsea	71
Manchester City	71
Arsenal	68

FA Cup

AS THE OLDEST football competition in the world, the Football Association (FA) Cup is one of the most prestigious trophies any English football team can win. The first tournament was played in the 1871-72 season (it predates the Football League trophy by more than a decade and a half) and its knockout formula has remained fundamentally unchanged for 140 years. Its final has long been a showcase end to the English football season and its list of champions contains many of the greatest teams ever to play the game. In addition, the focused drama of the one-off, winner-takes-all matches has produced a wealth of stories, both of triumph and tragedy and, most emotive of all, of footballing Davids beating Goliaths.

From its Corinthian beginnings when a team of ex-public schoolboys known as The Wanderers won five of the first seven competitions watched by a few thousand people, the FA Cup has grown into a competition revered and watched by a worldwide audience of tens of millions. The competition's unrivalled history is also part of its prestige and glamour. Other early winners included Old Etonians and Old Carthusians while even Scottish teams once entered (Queen's Park of Glasgow twice made the final in the mid-1880s) and a single winning Welsh team (Cardiff City in 1926-27) took the famous trophy across border. The final itself has been staged at venues as diverse as Wembley (both the new and old), Kennington Oval, Crystal Palace, Goodison Park and outside England at the Millennium Stadium in Cardiff

as well as three times at United's own ground Old Trafford, once for the final itself (1914-15) and twice for replays of the final (1910-11 and 1969-70).

Of all United's remarkable achievements in the world of football, one that is seldom given sufficient prominence is the club's success in the FA Cup. This competition is probably one of the most difficult to win, with its knockout format that pits giants against minnows, a format that can throw up the most untoward results. United have won the FA Cup one

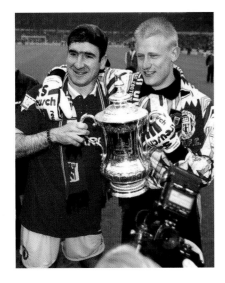

1972 | A rocket from Ronnie Radford helps Hereford of the Southern League defeat First Division Newcastle in one of the cup's great upsets.

1972 | The FA Cup's first penalty shootout takes place as Birmingham City beat Stoke City 4-3 in the third-fourth place play-off.

1973 | Leeds' loss to Sunderland is the only final to use a coloured (orange) ball.

1981 | The 100th FA Cup final sees perhaps its greatest goal as Ricky Villa's mazy run and shot helps Tottenham defeat Manchester City 3-2 in a replay.

1983 | Norman Whiteside becomes the youngest player to score in an FA Cup final at 18 years and 19 days as the Red Devils beat Brighton to win the trophy for the fifth time.

1985 | Manchester United's Kevin Moran makes history as the first player to be sent off in an FA Cup final for a foul on Everton's Peter Reid.

1988 | Dave Beasant becomes the first keeper to save a penalty in a Wembley final as unfancied Wimbledon beat favourites Liverpool 1-0.

1989 | 96 fans die as the result of a crush at Hillsborough at the semi-final between Liverpool and Nottingham Forest.

1994 | Manchester United complete the double courtesy of a 4-0 win over Chelsea at Wembley.

1996 | United become the first side to win the double twice as they beat Liverpool 1-0 a week after clinching the league title.

1999 | United beat Newcastle 2-0 on their way to completing a historic treble of league, FA Cup and Champions League wins.

2001 | The FA Cup final is played outside England for the first time as it is moved to the Millennium Stadium in Cardiff, Liverpool beating Arsenal 2-1.

2004 | Curtis Weston becomes the youngest player to appear in a final, turning out for Millwall against Manchester United at the age of 17 years and 119 days.

2009 | Louis Saha scores the fastest goal in FA Cup final history, netting for Everton against Chelsea after just 25 seconds.

out of every ten attempts: 112 entries into the competition and 11 victories. Not only that, United have won the FA Cup more times than any club in history. In addition, United have been a runner-up in the competition seven times, making a total of 18 FA Cup final appearances another record.

The club's list of FA Cup triumphs started in the 1908-09 season (a 1-0 win against Bristol City at Crystal Palace). That first FA Cup win came during a purple patch for the club (the team also collected two league titles around the same time in 1907-08 and 1910-11), but it took the club almost another four decades to win another; that was a 4-2 triumph against Blackpool in 1947-48.

Perhaps two of the best-known FA Cup finals involving United came in their next two appearances that both ended in defeat. Firstly in 1956-57, the Busby Babes faced Aston Villa, but a controversial goalmouth clash after just six minutes left United keeper Ray Wood unconscious and with a broken cheekbone. At the time no substitutes were allowed on to the field of play, so United played most of the game with 10 men and lost 2-1.

Then, the following season, in February 1958 the Munich air disaster happened – just 13 days before the fifth round tie at home against Sheffield Wednesday. Not only did a depleted and shell-shocked team win that match, but on a wave of emotion United made it to the final where four of the crash survivors played in the team. Whatever the public sentiment, their opponents that day, Bolton Wanderers, were not in a mood to donate a fairy tale ending for United and two Nat Lofthouse goals won the game for the fellow Lancastrians at Wembley.

A third FA Cup final win came in 1962-63, 3-1 against Leicester City, as Matt Busby re-built his team, while in the 1970s, there were three final appearances, but only one win, 2-1 against Liverpool in 1976-77.

There then followed seven wins in just over two decades from the 1982-83 triumph against Brighton & Hove Albion – after only the second ever Wembley replay – through to the club's 11th victory in 2003-04 (against Millwall at the Millennium Stadium). In between, there were wins in 1984-85 against Everton 1-0; 1989-90 against Crystal Palace when a 3-3 draw was followed by a 1-0 victory in the replay; 1993-94 against Chelsea 4-0; 1995-96 against Liverpool 1-0; and 1998-99 against Newcastle United 2-0

During that period came the controversial decision under FA pressure to withdraw from the 1999-00 FA Cup competition and opt instead to play in the inaugural Club World Championship. The fact that United had won the FA Cup the year before made the decision even more upsetting to fans, both those following United and many neutrals.

Nevertheless, United's affinity with the FA Cup was re-established in 2006-07 when the club played in the first final to be staged at the newly re-built Wembley Stadium. Not surprisingly, a 1-0 defeat to Chelsea spoiled the historic day for United fans in the near 90,000 crowd.

Top Left: Eric Cantona and Peter Schmeichel were outstanding in the victory against Chelsea in 1993-94.

Top Right: 25 May 1963. Leicester City goalkeeper Gordon Banks dives at the feet of United's Denis Law during the final.

Opposite: Bryan Robson shows why he was called Captain Marvel.

THE FINAL

United captain Charlie Roberts holds the cup trophy on his knee as the team are greeted by a large crowd of enthusiastic supporters on their return to Manchester.

UNITED HAD FAILED to beat opponents Bristol City in two league matches (actually losing 1-0 at home and drawing 0-0 in the other game), so there was little to choose between the two teams, although United boasted a forward line full of proven goalscorers. The main story was whether the influential inside forward Sandy Turnbull would recover from a knee injury that had kept him out of the team for a month. Turnbull had missed both the league games against Bristol, but on the morning of the final it was still uncertain if he would be selected. "Let him play," captain Charlie Roberts told his manager Ernest Mangnall and added somewhat prophetically, "he might get a goal and, if he does, we can afford to carry him."

So United fielded a full-strength team and Robert's exhortation paid dividends midway through the first half when Turnbull was the first to react in the Bristol goalmouth after a Harold Halse shot hit the crossbar. Turnbull's somewhat scrappy goal was enough to win a disappointing game in which Bristol's Frank Hilton had their best chance athletically saved by United keeper Harry Moger. Eventually, Billy Meredith was judged man of the match and the Reds had their first FA Cup win.

Many rare and rather amusing stories were told after the match, including how the players thought they had lost the trophy after a night out at the theatre, until it was found wrapped in Sandy Turnbull's coat the next morning. Oddly, United's club mascot, a billy goat, took part in the post-final champagne celebrations and unfortunately died soon afterwards. The animal was subsequently stuffed and, decades later, put on display at the Old Trafford museum.

A crowd of around 250,000 fans welcomed the team back to Manchester for a parade through the city that ended in Clayton at their Bank Street ground. Celebrations climaxed with a civic reception to mark the victory.

SEMI-FINALS

27 MARCH 1909		
Manchester United Halse	1-0	Newcastle

27 MARCH 1909		
Bristol City	1-1	Derby County
REPLAY: 31 MARCH 1909		
Derby County	1-2	Bristol City

MANCHESTER UNITED

1	HARRY MOGER
2	GEORGE STACEY
3	VINCE HAYES
4	DICK DUCKWORTH
5	CHARLIE ROBERTS
6	ALEX BELL
7	BILLY MEREDITH
8	HAROLD HALSE
9	JIMMY TURNBULL
10	SANDY TURNBULL
11	GEORGE WALL

BRISTOL CITY

1	HARRY CLAY
2	ARCHIE ANNAN
3	JOE COTTLE
4	PAT HANLIN
5	BILLY WEDLOCK
6	ARTHUR SPEAR
7	FRED STANIFORTH
8	BOB HARDY
9	SAM GILLIGAN
10	ANDY BURTON
11	FRANK HILTON

Referee: J Mason

MANCHESTER UNITED

MANAGER: ERNEST MANGNALL

BRISTOL CITY

MANAGER: HARRY THICKETT

1908/09

24 April 1909 at Crystal Palace, London

Manchester United (1) 1-0 (0) Bristol City

Goals: A. Turnbull 22'

Attendance: 71,401

United were a force in English football by this time, having won the First Division championship the previous season. It was also a team that included a core of highly talented players who played attractive football taken from rivals Manchester City. For the first time the Reds had an extended run in the cup this season, which began in mid-January with relatively low expectations, largely because the team's league form had stalled: four defeats in eight games just before this FA Cup tie had included a 5-0 drubbing a week earlier at Middlesbrough and a 2-0 loss at home to Preston North End the Saturday before that.

But the Reds managed a 1-0 home victory in the first round of the cup against a Brighton & Hove Albion team from the Southern League (they would not enter the Football League for another ten years). The victory was secured thanks to a goal by Harold Halse.

Next up were the more formidable Everton, one of the Football League's founding teams who had won the FA Cup themselves in 1906. The Merseyside team was pushing for the league championship this season, they had already beaten United 3-2 at Goodison Park in the league. A close-fought contest ended in a 1-0 win at home with another Halse goal enough to progress.

Now the competition was starting to get serious as another great team of the early 20th century visited Bank Street, Blackburn Rovers. Another Football League founding team and five times FA Cup winners, Rovers had slipped from their top-most pedestal, but were still considered more than worthy opponents. Yet a rampant United slaughtered their Lancashire rivals 6-1 with both Turnbulls, Sandy and Jimmy, scoring hat-tricks.

The fourth round was where United had failed in the FA Cup last season and, once again, the Reds threatened to fall at the same hurdle as they were losing 1-0 to Burnley at Turf Moor with just 20 minutes remaining. But snow had begun to fall heavily and the referee (ironically, Herbert Bamlett, who would become manager of Manchester United 18 years later) decided to stop the game when he felt the conditions had become unplayable. It turned out that this game had been Burnley's best chance of success; the team was not performing well in the Second Division and the weather had equalised the abilities of the two teams. For United there would be no slip up in the return fixture and the Reds managed a 3-2 win, with Jimmy Turnbull scoring twice and Halse netting yet another cup goal. It was the first time United had progressed this far.

Suddenly United were one game away from the final; standing in their way were Newcastle United. The Geordies were already a candidate for team of the decade, after leaving the Northern League just 15 years earlier. By now Newcastle had won two First Division titles in 1904-05 and 1906-07 and were on their way to a third this season. The semi certainly pitted two of the best teams of the moment together and probably would have been the neutrals' pick for the final.

The two sides had swapped wins when playing each other in the league three months earlier, so they knew each other well and forecasting a winner would be difficult. Again Halse was the Reds' hero, with the only goal of the game played at Bramall Lane in Sheffield in front of just over 40,000 fans.

The FA Cup – still known as the English Cup in 1909 – was regarded by many fans and some media as even more prestigious than a league title and United manager Ernest Mangnall prepared his team for the final with great care and attention. He took the players to a retreat in Essex before the match because Manchester had definitely caught "cup fever" and even had George Robey, one of the most famous music hall comedians of the day, present the team with their game shirts.

1947/48

24 April 1948 at Wembley Stadium, London

Manchester United (1) 4-2 (2) Blackpool

Goals: Shimwell 12' (pen), Mortensen 35', Rowley 28', 70', Pearson 80', Anderson 82'

Attendance: 99,000

In just the second full season of English football since the end of the second World War, United fairly roared through this competition, scoring no fewer than 22 goals in six games. But it was the fact that they beat First Division opposition in every round including the final that stands out; this was undoubtedly a strong United team and a very deserved and hard-won trophy. The goal total points to the team's strength, and an attacking attitude starting with captain and right back Johnny Carey all the way through to a dazzling forward line that starred two ex-servicemen, Jack Rowley (an anti-tank gunner who actually took part in the D-Day landings) and Stan Pearson (who served in the army in India and Burma). In fact, Matt Busby's pre-war veterans proved inspirational.

Nine of the 12 players used during the campaign had signed for United before World War II and several of the team were from Manchester including Pearson, goalkeeper Jack Crompton, full back John Aston and half-backs Henry Cockburn and John Anderson. The team was a classic Busby blend of youth, experience and local players.

It was also a year when United would eventually finish runners-up in the league campaign, although a league and cup double was never particularly close (United ended the season seven points behind Arsenal). However, United did manage to take the same form they showed in the league into their cup run, which began with a remarkable 6-4 win over Aston Villa at Villa Park in the third round.

Despite a Villa goal after 13 seconds (before a United player had touched the ball), the Reds answered with five goals before half-time only to then be pegged back to 5-4 with ten minutes remaining. A Rowley goal eventually gave United the breathing space they needed and the

win. Johnny Morris and Pearson both scored twice that day while Jimmy Delaney got the other goal.

Then Liverpool (the reigning First Division champions) were dispatched 3-0 in the next round with Rowley and Morris again on the score sheet, this time also assisted by one from Charlie Mitten. United's temporary home of Maine Road was being used by Manchester City on the day, so the game was played at Goodison Park, home of Everton.

In the fifth round it was Charlton Athletic who succumbed to the United cup juggernaut 2-0, this time at Huddersfield Town's Leeds Road stadium (again, Maine Road was unavailable). Jack Warner scored his only goal of the season in this game to supplement one from Mitten. An appalling pitch surface of ankle-deep mud negated United's fleet-footed stars early on, as did Charlton goalkeeper Sam Bartram, who held out for an hour despite intense pressure on his goal. The first goal was a freakish affair (sometimes credited as an own goal), but United fully deserved their win against the FA Cup holders from the previous season who had put up a stout defence of the trophy.

The sixth round opposition were fellow Lancastrians Preston North End, this time back at Maine Road, where the first half was goalless. Preston, a solid mid-table First Division club (they would finish seventh in the league this season), were overrun in a second half in which United were rampant and helped themselves to a 4-1 win with two goals from Pearson and one each from Rowley and Mitten.

And it was Pearson again, this time with a hat-trick including two smart headers, who saw off a strong Derby County team (they would finish fourth in the league) 3-1 in the semi-final at Hillsborough in front of 60,000 people in mid-March. United had benefited from a near-unchanged team throughout the competition (Warner had replaced John Anderson at right half in the Charlton game, but that was the only alteration to the team as all the other ten players started every FA Cup game this season).

IT HAD BEEN 39 years since United had appeared in the FA Cup final, but that wouldn't stop this United team from believing they could win the trophy for the second time. However, they faced a formidable Blackpool team featuring England internationals Stanley Matthews and Stan Mortensen.

The two teams had drawn 1-1 in their only league meeting before the final, but this was a much-anticipated game which was later called "Wembley's finest final" by the British press.

Manager Matt Busby could take credit for building his team into a patient and confident group during his three seasons in charge, and those qualities were evident in the final, especially when United went behind to a Blackpool penalty after just 12 minutes. It was a disappointing goal to give away because centre half Allenby Chilton's challenge on Mortensen that prompted the spot-kick was thought by many observers to be outside the penalty box.

Nevertheless, the Red Devils equalised after 28 minutes through centre forward Jack Rowley, who pounced on a loose ball that the Blackpool defence failed to clear. Then a Mortensen goal 10 minutes before half-time put United behind once again; it was a lead that Blackpool held onto until midway through the second half as they dominated the game.

Many neutrals were shouting for Blackpool's Matthews to win his first ever FA Cup winner's medal, but United left back John Aston was keeping him in check. And when Rowley levelled for the second time - this goal was a fantastic diving header - the momentum swung United's way.

Wearing an unfamiliar kit of blue shirts and white shorts, United pressed forward and scored twice in the last 10 minutes - a goal each from Stan Pearson (his eighth in the competition) and John Anderson - to lift the trophy.

MANCHESTER UNITED	
1	JACK CROMPTON
2	JOHNNY CAREY
3	JOHN ASTON
4	JOHN ANDERSON
5	ALLENBY CHILTON
6	HENRY COCKBURN
7	JIMMY DELANEY
8	JOHNNY MORRIS
9	JACK ROWLEY
10	STAN PEARSON
11	CHARLIE MITTEN

BLACKPOOL	
1	JOE ROBINSON
2	EDDIE SHIMWELL
3	JOHN CROSLAND
4	HARRY JOHNSTON
5	ERIC HAYWARD
6	HUGH KELLY
7	STANLEY MATTHEWS
8	ALEX MUNRO
9	STAN MORTENSEN
10	GEORGE DICK
11	WALTER RICKETT

Referee: C.J Barrick

SEMI-FINALS

13 MARCH 1948		
Manchester United	3-1	Derby County
Pearson (3)		Steel

13 MARCH 1948		
Blackpool	3-1	Tottenham Hotspur
Mortensen (3)		Duquemin

MANCHESTER UNITED

MANAGER: MATT BUSBY

BLACKPOOL

MANAGER: JOE SMITH

THE FINAL

His Royal Highness The Duke of Edinburgh shakes manager Matt Busby's hand before the game.

THIS UNITED WERE the youngest team ever to play in an FA Cup final and – watched by the young Queen Elizabeth – soon found their free-flowing, attacking style that had made them the envy of the football world.

But the game changed after just six minutes when an innocuous cross from the Villa right was met by their winger Peter McParland, who headed the ball straight at United keeper Ray Wood. Wood saved easily, but McParland continued his run directly into the goalkeeper and both men ended up on the floor after a sickening collision. Wood was the one who came off much worse; he was carried from the field on a stretcher with a broken cheekbone.

With substitutes not allowed in this era and now down to ten men, United were at a huge disadvantage for the 85 minutes that remained of the game. Jackie Blanchflower went in goal; although a dazed Wood returned as an outfield player, he stood on the right wing unable to really contribute.

There was no score before half-time as, remarkably, United's defence reduced Villa's chances to long-range shots. However, the West Midlanders eventually took advantage of their man advantage. Ironically, McParland was the Villa's hero with two goals midway through the second half. United – with the double at stake – tried everything to get back into the match and Tommy Taylor eventually headed home a late goal after three successive corners.

At this point, the Reds even put Wood back in goal in order to have ten outfield players, but Villa held on to deny United their place in history. The Busby Babes had been denied by ill luck rather than a poor performance. Sadly, it would be the last time the Babes would grace the Wembley turf all together.

SEMI-FINALS

23 MARCH 1957		
Manchester United Berry, Charlton	2-0	Birmingham City
23 MARCH 1957		
Aston Villa McParland (2)	2-2	West Bromwich Albion Whitehouse (2)
REPLAY 27 MARCH 1957		
West Bromwich Albion	0-1	Aston Villa

MANCHESTER UNITED

1. RAY WOOD
2. BILL FOULKES
3. ROGER BYRNE
4. EDDIE COLMAN
5. JACKIE BLANCHFLOWER
6. DUNCAN EDWARDS
7. JOHNNY BERRY
8. LIAM WHELAN
9. TOMMY TAYLOR
10. BOBBY CHARLTON
11. DAVID PEGG

ASTON VILLA

1. NIGEL SIMS
2. STAN LYNN
3. PETER ALDIS
4. STAN CROWTHER
5. JIMMY DUGDALE
6. PAT SAWARD
7. LES SMITH
8. JACKIE SEWELL
9. BILL MYERSCOUGH
10. JOHNNY DIXON
11. PETER MCPARLAND

Referee: F Coultas

MANCHESTER UNITED

MANAGER: MATT BUSBY

ASTON VILLA

MANAGER: ERIC HOUGHTON

1956/57

4 May 1957 at Wembley Stadium, London

Aston Villa (0) 2-1 (0) Manchester United

Goals: McParland 68', 73', Taylor 83'

Attendance: 100,000

This was an entirely different United team to the one that had won the FA Cup nine years earlier. In fact, this was the heart of the era of the Busby Babes, Matt Busby's team of young, local professionals who had grown up together and were now playing some of the most exciting football ever seen from an English team.

Duncan Edwards was the on-field leader and seemingly destined to become recognised as one of the world's great players. Goals flowed from almost every position and especially centre forward Tommy Taylor, a giant of a man at 6ft 4in. While the team also benefited immensely from the calm intelligence of captain Roger Byrne.

This was a team that entered the season as defenders of the league championship and who had already won the FA Charity Shield before the FA Cup run began with a third round match away at Hartlepools United who were pushing hard for promotion from the Third Division North. The north easterners gave a very good account of themselves and lost only 4-3 despite facing a full-strength Reds team. United's goals in an unconvincing performance came from Liam Whelan (two), Johnny Berry and Taylor.

Another away trip to another Third Division North side followed three weeks later, but this time Wrexham's resistance was much less robust and United won easily 5-0. Whelan and Taylor both scored twice and captain Byrne got the other (it would be his only goal of the season).

First Division opposition in Everton were to play the Reds in the fifth round at Old Trafford, although the Mersey team were not having a particularly good season. However, cup football was their best chance of success and so they fought like terriers before Edwards scored the goal to take the tie 1-0.

Luck was with United when the sixth round draw was made because they were plucked out of the hat with Bournemouth & Boscombe Athletic, the only remaining Third Division team in the competition. The south coast outfit had shocked Tottenham Hotspur of the First Division in the last round 3-1 at their own ground of Dean Court and even took out Wolverhampton Wanderers 1-0 at Molineux in the previous round. Wins against such opposition (Tottenham would finish league runners-up this season and Wolves were at the peak of their powers) told United that Bournemouth were the cup giant-killers of the season and should be treated with respect.

Indeed, despite the absence of Taylor from the forward line, United turned in a very professional performance and took the tie 2-1, with Berry getting both goals. Of the four teams now in the semi-finals, all were from the First Division, but three were from the West Midlands. United were drawn against Birmingham City, while Aston Villa played West Bromwich Albion. Taylor was still injured, but United coped admirably and won 2-0 at Hillsborough in front of 65,000 fans with Berry and Charlton on the scoresheet.

It was six weeks to the final and, during this time, United won the league for the second consecutive season but lost the European Cup semi-final to a fine Real Madrid team. That meant the Red Devils would be aiming for a league and cup double against the very team who had last achieved this feat in 1897, Aston Villa. The Midlanders were a decent First Division outfit who finished tenth in the league this season, but who last won a significant trophy in 1920. Villa had lost to United at their own ground 3-1 when Taylor was in the team, but managed a 1-1 draw at Old Trafford when the centre forward was injured. However, the Birmingham men were not forecast to stop the Busby Babes from what many observers felt was their destiny of achieving one of the sport's most difficult feats: winning English football's two major trophies in one season.

1957/58

3 May 1958 at Wembley Stadium, London

Manchester United (0) 0-2 (1) Bolton Wanderers

Goals: Lofthouse 3', 55'

Attendance: 100,000

Everything about this season is overshadowed by the Munich air crash and the FA Cup run is no exception. Just by managing to make an the appearance in the 1957-58 final, the whole club proved its resilience and dignity in the most troubling of times after such great loss and tragedy.

On 25 January 1958, a few days before the fatal crash, United won their fourth round tie in the FA Cup. That day, the Reds easily beat Ipswich Town of the Second Division 2-0 at Old Trafford thanks to two Bobby Charlton goals. The team had already beaten lowly Workington Town of the Third Division North 3-1 in the third round. This was the Busby Babes at their finest, handing out swashbuckling victories to all-comers and fearing no one. In fact, this was almost the same group of players that had missed a chance of the league and cup double last season because of a freak injury to goalkeeper Ray Wood in the cup final, with goalkeeper Harry Gregg the only new recruit. The Babes were imperious again this season and were even more likely to achieve the double this year, according to most pundits. Matt Busby's team was simply that good.

Then on 6 February 1958 while returning from another thrilling European Cup performance – this one against Red Star Belgrade of Yugoslavia – the team's plane crashed at Munich airport and eight players died. Not only that but three backroom staff also lost their lives among the total of 23 deaths, and manager Matt Busby, along with several other players, had to fight hard to recover from dreadful injuries.

The whole of the football world was in shock and United were given time to recover, to recruit new players and to grieve. But a return to action had to come sooner or later and it did so on 19 February when a patched-up team of recovered players (two of them, Harry Gregg and Bill Foulkes), reserves and emergency signings won a highly charged FA Cup fifth round contest 3-0 against Sheffield Wednesday. Old Trafford was jammed with nearly 60,000 tearful fans and the team played with a rare frenzy. Youth team player Shay Brennan made his debut that day (a full back playing on the left wing) and scored twice while reserve forward Alex Dawson got the other goal.

Most people expected United's season to fade away from this point on and, in fact, in the league that is what happened as the champions would go on to finish ninth. But in the FA Cup, the knockout format meant no tomorrows and emotions remained high as First Division West Bromwich Albion were held to a 2-2 draw at The Hawthorns in the sixth round, Dawson and new signing Ernie Taylor from Blackpool scoring the goals. The replay brought a 1-0 win for the Red Devils; Welsh reserve Colin Webster scoring.

Raw emotion was now impelling United on the field of play, but off the field there were also signs of good fortune as the draw for the semi-finals was kind. Instead of burly Bolton Wanderers of the First Division or another Lancashire rival Blackburn Rovers (set to win promotion from the Second Division this season), United were drawn against Fulham, another team from English football's second level and definitely the weakest of the clubs remaining in the competition.

However, the Londoners wanted to make the most of a rare semi-final appearance and were playing a United team still only six weeks after the Munich tragedy. At Villa Park in front of nearly 70,000, Bobby Charlton scored two goals and helped bring about an exciting 2-2 draw.

The replay at Highbury four days later should probably have favoured the London team, but Alex Dawson decided to make this his night to remember, scoring a hat-trick in a 5-3 win; Brennan and Charlton added the other goals. So the bravest and, in some ways, most unlikely FA Cup finalists of all time would walk out onto the Wembley turf in May to face Bolton.

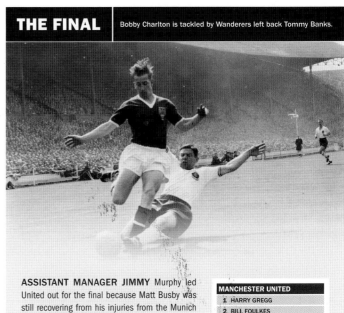

THE FINAL

Bobby Charlton is tackled by Wanderers left back Tommy Banks.

ASSISTANT MANAGER JIMMY Murphy led United out for the final because Matt Busby was still recovering from his injuries from the Munich crash, needing walking sticks to get around. This was just one of the consequences for the final. The most obvious and saddest one was that the team included just four Busby Babes – goalkeeper Harry Gregg, full back Bill Foulkes and forwards Bobby Charlton and Dennis Viollet, who was the latest to return to the team late the previous month.

The team had been somewhat re-built under Murphy and, while league form was disappearing fast, everyone at Old Trafford would cling to the FA Cup as proof that the club would rise once again. Just to reach the final was an incredible achievement and the neutrals obviously wanted a happy ending to this story. However, Bolton Wanderers had not won the FA Cup for almost 30 years and were in no mood to roll over, even in these unique emotional circumstances.

A goal by Wanderers' star centre forward Nat Lofthouse after only three minutes was a measure of Bolton's intent, and put United immediately on the back foot. But the destination of the cup was still uncertain until the 55th minute when, for the second cup final in a row, a United goalkeeper was at the centre of a disputed incident.

Last year Ray Wood suffered a broken cheekbone after being charged into by a player. This year Harry Gregg caught the ball near his own goal line, but was then barged by Lofthouse, dropping the ball into the United net. In an era when goalkeepers received relatively little protection from referees, the Bolton forward's tactic was not judged to be a foul and United were suddenly facing a two-goal deficit, a position that they never recovered from. Finishing as cup runners-up was a sad end to a tragic season.

MANCHESTER UNITED

1	HARRY GREGG
2	BILL FOULKES
3	IAN GREAVES
4	FREDDIE GOODWIN
5	RON COPE
6	STAN CROWTHER
7	ALEX DAWSON
8	ERNIE TAYLOR
9	BOBBY CHARLTON
10	DENNIS VIOLLET
11	COLIN WEBSTER

BOLTON WANDERERS

1	EDDIE HOPKINSON
2	RON HARTLE
3	TOMMY BANKS
4	DEREK HENNIN
5	JOHN HIGGINS
6	BRYAN EDWARDS
7	BRIAN BIRCH
8	DENNIS STEVENS
9	NAT LOFTHOUSE
10	RAY PARRY
11	DOUG HOLDEN

Referee: J Sherlock

MANCHESTER UNITED

MANAGER: JIMMY MURPHY

BOLTON WANDERERS

MANAGER: BILL RIDDING

SEMI-FINALS

22 MARCH 1958		
Bolton Wanderers Gubbins (2)	2-1	Blackburn Rovers Dobing
22 MARCH 1958		
Manchester United Charlton (2)	2-2	Fulham Hill
REPLAY 26 MARCH 1958		
Fulham Stevens, Chamberlain Dwight	3-5	Manchester United Dawson Brennan, Charlton

3 May 1958. The United players are introduced to Prince Philip,
Duke of Edinburgh before the 1958 FA Cup final.

THE FINAL

Matt Busby and team members and wives on the train leaving London for Manchester after their FA Cup victory.

RELEASED FROM THE worry of relegation, finally fulfilling their potential or catching a better team on an off-day – the pundits could choose any one of these reasons or all of them to explain why United, who had performed so poorly on so many occasions for almost two seasons and had not beaten Leicester City in two recent league games, were the victors in this final.

When the Frank McLintock-led Midlands team piled on the pressure in the opening 25 minutes, it was how the formbook suggested the match would play out. But then Denis Law chose the moment to change the whole of United's future by grabbing the opening goal after a pinpoint pass from Paddy Crerard. Leicester's iron wall defence – at the back of which was England goalkeeper Gordon Banks – had been breached and United found a different level of performance on the famously large Wembley pitch.

Law was imperious and after an hour his strike partner David Herd (another recent expensive signing by Matt Busby) grabbed a classic poacher's goal after a Bobby Charlton shot had been parried by Banks. The Red Devils were playing with new-found confidence now and had one hand on their first major trophy in six years.

City, however, were not ready to give up the chance of their first ever FA Cup win and Ken Keyworth scored with a header with ten minutes remaining. The 'league' United might have panicked, but the 'cup' United simply scored another goal – a second by Herd after an Albert Quixall shot was spilled by Banks – and the cup was heading to Manchester.

A first trophy since Munich, a first FA Cup win since 1948 and a vindication of Busby's latest plans to put together another great United team. Now the newspapers had plenty of storylines to explore to explain this win and a new bright future for a Busby designed team seemed inevitable.

MANCHESTER UNITED

1	DAVID GASKELL
2	TONY DUNNE
3	NOEL CANTWELL
4	PADDY CRERAND
5	BILL FOULKES
6	MAURICE SETTERS
7	JOHNNY GILES
8	ALBERT QUIXALL
9	DAVID HERD
10	DENIS LAW
11	BOBBY CHARLTON

LEICESTER CITY

1	GORDON BANKS
2	JOHN SJOBERG
3	RICHIE NORMAN
4	FRANK MCLINTOCK
5	IAN KING
6	COLIN APPLETON
7	HOWARD RILEY
8	GRAHAM CROSS
9	KEN KEYWORTH
10	DAVE GIBSON
11	MIKE STRINGFELLOW

Referee: Ken Aston

MANCHESTER UNITED
MANAGER: MATT BUSBY

LEICESTER CITY
MANAGER: MATT GILLIES

SEMI-FINALS

Southampton

Liverpool

1962/63

25 May 1963 at Wembley Stadium, London
Manchester United (1) 3-1 (0) Leicester
Goals: Law 30', Herd 57', 85', Keyworth 80'
Attendance: 100,000

The early sixties had not been a happy period for United: the spectre of the Munich air disaster still resided in the minds and pysche of many of the players, officials and fans, and the necessary re-building was – not surprisingly – taking time, with no guarantee of the club returning to its former level of greatness. The arrival of Denis Law from the Italian side Torino was a fillip for the team at the start of the season, but this was a group of players lacking in confidence and they needed more than one man to lift them.

In fact, league performances had slumped with each passing season and only a semi-final appearance in last year's FA Cup competition (when Tottenham Hotspur, the eventual winners, beat the Reds) had provided any evidence that Matt Busby's plans to fashion another great team would bear fruit.

So as this season's league form deteriorated to the point that United were involved in a relegation fight, another FA Cup run was a welcome distraction. After all of January and much of February had seen games postponed because of severe snow throughout the country, United's cup campaign began in March when they managed a morale-boosting 5-0 win over Huddersfield Town from the Second Division. Huddersfield was where Denis Law began his professional career and he delighted in scoring a hat-trick against his former club. Johnny Giles and Albert Quixall were the other scorers.

With so much bad weather earlier in the year, FA Cup matches now came thick and fast. A week after the third round victory, Aston Villa of the First Division came to Old Trafford and were beaten with a single goal from Quixall, who had been the Reds' first big money signing after Munich but somehow never developed into a truly dominating player.

However, Busby saw the value of a settled team and the same forward line

took on another Second Division team, Chelsea, again at home, just five days later. The Reds won again – this time 2-1, with yet another Quixall goal and the opener from Law.

Yet with each FA Cup win, United's league position was becoming more dangerous, with relegation looming by the time the Red Devils played their first away fixture in their cup run. The good news for Busby's inconsistent team was that the sixth round was against Division Three side Coventry City, the bad news was that the Midlands team were managed by the inspirational Jimmy Hill (who would eventually become one of the British television's longest-serving football pundits) and the Sky Blues were pushing for promotion while enjoying one of their best ever seasons.

The game had all the hallmarks of a classic FA Cup upset. However, Albert Quixall continued in his role as United's cup talisman and scored for the fourth round in succession while the always threatening Bobby Charlton added two for a 3-1 scoreline.

The semi-final draw then did United a favour by throwing up Southampton as their opponents instead of close rivals Liverpool or high-flying Leicester City. The Hampshire side was the third team from Division Two that United had faced and, although Quixall missed the game through injury, a Law goal 11 minutes into the second half was enough for the Reds to sneak into the final. It had not been a very difficult path to Wembley and the luck of the draw had certainly offered United every chance of progress at each stage, but the players took heart that this all happened while the club's First Division status was threatened.

In fact, between the sixth round match in late March and the eve of the final two months later, United won just four league games out of 14. Only victory in their penultimate league game meant First Division safety this season and it came in time for the team to step more confidently onto the Wembley turf to face a Leicester City side whose fourth place league finish was their highest position for over 30 years.

1975/76

1 May 1976 at Wembley Stadium, London

Manchester United (0) 0-1 (0) Southampton

Goals: Stokes 83'

Attendance: 100,000

It had taken Tommy Docherty just over two seasons to return United to the limelight after a depressing post-European Cup slump that reached its nadir with relegation to the Second Division in 1974. Despite heavy spending, the Doc could not save the Red Devils from the ignominy of descent into the Second Division, but he would oversee the club bouncing back to the First Division after one season, and was now setting off on a Wembley-bound FA Cup run.

In fact, United had even been top of the First Division in the first few weeks of the league season, while that lofty position was tough to maintain, the cup proved more to their liking. The third round match was a gentle introduction to the competition, with the Second Division strugglers Oxford United beaten 2-1 at home by two Gerry Daly goals.

Next up was even easier opposition in Peterborough United of the Third Division; they also travelled to Old Trafford and were dispatched 3-1, with goals coming from Alex Forsyth, Gordon Hill and Sammy McIlroy. In fact, Hill (a November signing from Millwall) was becoming a United icon already with his snappy wing play and would play a key role in the team's ascendancy under Docherty.

The fifth round provided United's first real test in the FA Cup this season, by sending them to Filbert Street to face a solid Leicester City team that had held the Reds to a 0-0 draw at Old Trafford in early October. But with Hill on the left wing now balancing Steve Coppell on the right, United were a different proposition and won 2-1; Daly again and Lou Macari were the scorers.

Another First Division team awaited in the sixth round, Wolverhampton Wanderers. This was a poor relegation-facing Wolves team, who had already lost twice to United in the league. But when the Midlanders battled to a 1-1 draw at

Old Trafford, then it became obvious that the nervousness of Wolves' league performances had been replaced by a determination to reach for salvation in the cup. A Gerry Daly goal helped United force the replay at Molineux, which was played three days later and was full of exciting football. The game eventually went into extra time when the Reds squeezed through 3-2 with Stuart Pearson scoring the winner after goals from Brian Greenhoff and McIlroy.

The draw for the semi-finals would be crucial because only two First Division sides remained, United and the all-powerful Derby County under Dave Mackay, who had taken them to the league championship last season. The other two teams were Southampton of the Second Division (who were managed by Lawrie McMenemy and contained a number of former First Division stars along with a bunch of unknown youngsters) and Crystal Palace of the Third Division, whose boss was the flamboyant Malcolm Allison, the former coach of Manchester City.

The normally lucky Docherty ended up with Derby in the semi-final and joked that this would be the game to decide the destination of the cup. "The other semi-final is a bit of a joke really," he was reported as saying. Indeed, the United-Derby game was a super match with two attacking teams creating plenty of chances.

The younger, less experienced United side settled well; Coppell lifted the best early chance over the bar from a corner, before a curling left-foot shot from Hill flew arrow-like into the Derby net to put the Reds ahead after just 12 minutes. The Londoner would score his second with just six minutes left from a 25-yard free kick that took a slight deflection.

A Wembley appearance in their first season back in the First Division was vindication for Docherty and his strategy of guiding a team mainly made up of youngsters. But in the final they would face the exact opposite, Lawrie McMenemy's Southampton, a side that relied on ex-England internationals like Peter Osgood and Mick Channon – and ex-United star Jim McCalliog.

THE FINAL

United skipper Martin Buchan (l) and Mick Channon (r) of the Saints engage in a friendly game of Subbuteo before the final.

TOMMY DOCHERTY'S WORDS about the Southampton-Crystal Palace semi-final being a bit of a joke would come back to haunt him. But he was not alone in thinking the final could produce only one winner, his United. The bookmakers had made the south coast Second Division team – who had never won any major English trophy in their history - an embarrassing 7/1 against to win. It appeared the younger, fitter, more flamboyant Reds had only to turn up to win.

United's Lou Macari could have scored in the very first minute when the Southampton keeper spilled a Steve Coppell shot, while Gordon Hill missed a one-on-one chance after breaking clear a few minutes later. Almost immediately after that it was Alex Stepney's turn to make a great save, this one with his left foot when Mick Channon ran free for the Saints.

Despite the Channon miss, the opening half hour saw the Reds with the better chances, but still they failed to break the stalemate before half-time. As the second half got underway there were more United missed opportunities when Sammy McIlroy hit the bar from point blank range with a header from an inswinging Hill corner.

As the game edged towards full-time, the Reds seemed far from the team that had won a pulsating semi-final against First Division opposition. Southampton, meanwhile, began to sense a chance of victory. When the decisive goal came from winger Bobby Stokes with just seven minutes to go, there was much irony for Docherty - the player who played the defence-splitting pass was none other than Jim McCalliog, who Docherty had let go just before the season had begun.

The 1-0 win by Southampton was one of the FA Cup final's greatest upsets and the canny Geordie manager Lawrie McMenemy later admitted that he had used Docherty's disparaging words about his team as motivation.

MANCHESTER UNITED

1	ALEX STEPNEY
2	ALEX FORSYTH
3	STEWART HOUSTON
4	GERRY DALY
5	BRIAN GREENHOFF
6	MARTIN BUCHAN
7	STEVE COPPELL
8	SAMMY MCILROY
9	STUART PEARSON
10	LOU MACARI
11	GORDON HILL 66'

Substitute:

12	DAVID MCCREERY 66'

SOUTHAMPTON

1	IAN TURNER
2	PETER RODRIGUES
3	DAVID PEACH
4	NICK HOLMES
5	MEL BLYTH
6	JIM STEELE
7	PAUL GILCHRIST
8	MICK CHANNON
9	PETER OSGOOD
10	JIM MCCALLIOG
11	BOBBY STOKES

Referee: Clive Thomas

SEMI-FINALS

	3 APRIL 1976	
Manchester United Hill (2)	2-0	Derby County

	3 APRIL 1976	
Southampton Gilchrist, Peach	2-0	Crystal Palace

MANCHESTER UNITED

MANAGER: TOMMY DOCHERTY

SOUTHAMPTON

MANAGER: LAWRIE MCMENEMY

THE FINAL

The victory homecoming. United parade the trophy past excited crowds with Martin Buchan and Alex Stepney holding the cup.

THE FEARLESS TOMMY Docherty had promised United fans after last season's FA Cup final loss that his team would be back at Wembley very soon and that they would win the trophy, but the bookmakers could not see how the Doc's prediction might come true. Liverpool were firm favourites against a club that had not won any kind of trophy since the European Cup nine years earlier.

Despite this Red Devils team being relatively inexperienced in terms of major cup finals when compared to their opponents, there was little between the two teams for the first 45 minutes and then a five-minute period from the 50 minute mark saw all three goals scored. First, Stuart Pearson latched on to a lobbed pass from Jimmy Greenhoff and shot United ahead before Jimmy Case equalised for Liverpool with his right foot.

The third, decisive and winning goal typified the good luck that Docherty felt he had had in the competition this season. An off-target snap shot from Lou Macari deflected off the chest of Jimmy Greenhoff who seemed to have been in the way. Instead of flying off to nowhere in particular, the ball looped over Liverpool keeper Ray Clemence and full-back Joey Jones and into the net. It was an extraordinary goal and was enough to secure the trophy for only the fourth time for United in their 99-year history as Docherty's patched-up defence held out.

There are many reasons why fans remember this final: it was the last game Liverpool's Kevin Keegan played in England before moving to Hamburg SV; and United's win also stopped Liverpool achieving the treble that they themselves would manage over two decades later.

For Tommy Docherty, his career at Old Trafford would soon end: it was the last United game he ever managed. Just 44 days later Docherty revealed his affair with Mary Brown, the wife of United's physio, and was sacked.

MANCHESTER UNITED

1	ALEX STEPNEY
2	JIMMY NICHOLL
3	ARTHUR ALBISTON
4	SAMMY MCILROY
5	BRIAN GREENHOFF
6	MARTIN BUCHAN
7	STEVE COPPELL
8	JIMMY GREENHOFF
9	STUART PEARSON
10	LOU MACARI
11	GORDON HILL 81'

Substitute:

12	DAVID MCCREERY 81'

LIVERPOOL

1	RAY CLEMENCE
2	PHIL NEAL
3	JOEY JONES
4	TOMMY SMITH
5	RAY KENNEDY
6	EMLYN HUGHES
7	KEVIN KEEGAN
8	JIMMY CASE
9	STEVE HEIGHWAY
10	DAVID JOHNSON 64'
11	TERRY MCDERMOTT

Substitute:

12	IAN CALLAGHAN 64'

Referee: Robert Matthewson

MANCHESTER UNITED

MANAGER: TOMMY DOCHERTY

LIVERPOOL

MANAGER: BOB PAISLEY

SEMI-FINALS

Leeds United	Clarke (pen)
6	
Liverpool	Neal (pen), Case, Kennedy

1976/77

21 May 1977 at Wembley Stadium, London

Manchester United (0) 2-1 (0) Liverpool

Goals: Pearson 50', J Greenhoff 55', Case 52'

Attendance: 100,000

The FA Cup and Manchester United under Tommy Docherty seemed like a perfect fit. The competition was glamorous, just the word to describe The Doc's teams; to win it needed a degree of good fortune, something that the manager believed he had; and the final was watched live by millions of English football fans and millions more beyond the British Isles, something that appealed to the United boss.

And yet this was only United's second visit to Wembley in almost a decade and a half. Last year's disappointment of defeat in the final to unheralded Southampton had hit Docherty hard. To go one better this season and win the trophy was on the Doc's agenda, but it would not be easy; even with the help of some early, relatively simple draws that proved to be the case.

The opening FA Cup game took place on the second Saturday in January in front of over 48,000 fans at Old Trafford and with only Third Division opposition in Walsall to deal with. By this time the Reds were out of the UEFA Cup in Europe and the League Cup, while it was the blue half of Manchester who were tussling for the league, not the Reds. So with a team lacking in confidence, United made heavy weather of a 1-0 win, with a goal scored by Gordon Hill. An even bigger crowd of 57,000 turned up for another home draw as the Reds played a Queens Park Rangers team managed by Dave Sexton, who would become the boss at Old Trafford six months later. The game also resulted in a 1-0 United win, with Lou Macari getting the goal.

Then came a chance for FA Cup revenge. Southampton were the Reds' fifth round opponents and a 2-2 draw (Hill and Macari scoring) at The Dell was followed by a 2-1 win at home with a brace from Jimmy Greenhoff. The Saints were put to the sword and their surprising win over United in last year's

final was put in its proper context.

Perhaps this was an omen because two more extremely tough opponents would stand between United and a second consecutive FA Cup final. Firstly, Aston Villa (who would eventually finish the season fourth in the league) came to Old Trafford and were dispatched 2-1 thanks to a rare Stewart Houston goal and another one from Macari. Then a semi-final against Leeds United meant another cup bogey team had to be defeated. During the sixties Leeds had seemed to get in the Reds' way all too often in the cup and, while the Yorkshire team's star had dimmed somewhat, it would still be a very tough game.

Before the semi-final Docherty rested several key players (including Martin Buchan and Gordon Hill) as they took on QPR in a league game; United suffered a crushing 4-0 loss. On reflection, it was perhaps not the best preparation strategy.

Under manager Jimmy Armfield, Leeds boasted two future Reds players in Joe Jordan and Gordon McQueen, but in the game, two goals in the opening ten minutes – from Jimmy Greenhoff and Steve Coppell – proved decisive. Although Allan Clarke scored from the penalty spot to bring Leeds back into the tie, those early goals were enough to give United the 2-1 win.

With seven league games before the final, United had only another UEFA Cup place next season to fight for, but their form remained patchy. Then on 7 May left back Stewart Houston broke his ankle. Nineteen-year-old reserve Arthur Albiston had to step in, playing the final three league games in which he and the defence conceded nine goals.

Facing the league champions Liverpool would be a formidable challenge. This was a Merseyside team that would be aiming for a treble, with both the FA Cup and European Cup finals to play in May, while United were still adjusting to life back the First Division.

However, when Liverpool beat United 1-0 in the league just after the semi-final it was highly significant. "We have learned something tonight," said The Doc. "We can beat Liverpool."

1978/79

12 May 1979 at Wembley Stadium, London

Arsenal (2) 3-2 (0) Manchester United

Goals: Talbot 12', Stapleton 43', McQueen 86',

McIlroy 88', Sunderland 89'

Attendance: 100,000

This would be another difficult season for United as manager Dave Sexton struggled to put together a consistently winning team. Liverpool and Nottingham Forest were dominating the league while a spirited young West Bromwich Albion team under Ron Atkinson was adding some sparkle to the First Division, handing out a remarkable 5-3 defeat to United at Old Trafford in December. This was the last game before a big winter freeze halted football in England for a fortnight. United's next game would be in the third round of the FA Cup in mid-January and allowed the manager and players to re-group.

United's main problem at this stage of the season was that a new, young goalkeeper, Gary Bailey, was trying to settle into the side. Sexton had dropped 36-year-old Alex Stepney to the reserves and played Pat Roche in goal instead when the season began. But some poor performances sapped Roche's confidence and Bailey (who had no league experience in England) got the nod when Sexton failed to sign a replacement via the transfer market.

Fortunately, the FA Cup opener would see Chelsea as the visitors and, as a club destined to suffer a pitiful relegation from the First Division, they put up limited resistance. Coppell, Jimmy Greenhoff and Grimes scored the goals in a 3-0 win and Bailey (who had just conceded 11 goals in the previous three league games) managed a clean sheet.

Another London opponent, however, proved more troublesome. Fulham may have been only a mid-table Second Division team, but they held United to a 1-1 draw at Craven Cottage and lost only 1-0 in the replay (Jimmy Greenhoff scored the goals in both these games).

There was still some bad weather and game postponements in February and the Reds did not play another league game before facing Colchester United in the fifth round. United were far from convincing at Colchester's tight ground and it took another Jimmy Greenhoff goal to see them through 1-0.

A third London side, Tottenham Hotspur, were drawn against the Reds in the sixth round at White Hart Lane and one of Sexton's signings, Mickey Thomas, grabbed an equaliser in the 1-1 draw to take the tie back to Old Trafford. At home United put on a much improved performance and goals from Joe Jordan and Sammy McIlroy won the game 2-0.

Each round had seen an increasingly tough opponent for Sexton and the semi-final would provide perhaps the ultimate test for his team against the form team at that time. Liverpool were on their way to a record point-scoring league season and would concede just 16 goals in 42 league matches. The Merseysiders under Bob Paisley were also the current European Cup holders and had easily beaten the Red Devils 3-0 at Anfield in December. No one doubted that Liverpool were the clear favourites in this game.

It would be an epic encounter. The first game at Maine Road would end in a 2-2 draw, but not after plenty of drama. Kenny Dalglish opened the scoring after 20 minutes of the first half, only for Jimmy Greenhoff to cross for Jordan to equalise two minutes later. Then Liverpool missed a penalty before Brian Greenhoff scored his only cup goal of the season, easing United in front in the second half, while Liverpool's Alan Hansen, forced a replay.

Four days later, this time at Goodison Park, United threw everything at their opponents early on only for the Merseysiders to fight back just as hard. Shots rained in on both goals and, although goalposts and crossbars were struck at each end, the first half remained 0-0.

But this had been a United cup run in which Jimmy Greenhoff excelled. He had already scored four cup goals and his fifth – a header from a Thomas cross with ten minutes of the match remaining – was the winner. United again blocked any chance of a Liverpool league and cup double.

THE FINAL | Sammy McIlroy evades the Arsenal defenders before levelling the scores at 2-2 with just 90 seconds remaining.

DAVE SEXTON NEEDED a trophy to quieten the naysayers among the fans who disliked his less-than-dynamic team tactics. The good news for Sexton was that this was a competition in which United had had recent success; it would be the Reds' third Wembley appearance in four seasons.

Having beaten Liverpool in the semi, a fourth London team now stood in United's way – Arsenal, who would finish seventh in the league, just above the Reds in ninth. The two teams had drawn 1-1 at Highbury in September, but Arsenal had won 2-0 at Old Trafford, so the game would be close.

But rather than a tense 90 minutes between two well-matched teams, this would be known as The Five-Minute Final. Arsenal dominated the first 85 minutes and were strolling to the trophy with a 2-0 lead. United were offered only a few fleeting chances as the game moved remorselessly towards an Arsenal victory.

Then with five minutes remaining, Gordon McQueen stabbed home what seemed like a consolation goal for the Reds, only for Sammy McIlroy to dribble through the Arsenal defence and score a second goal within a minute. Celebrations among the United team and on the bench were exuberant as they expected another 30 minutes of extra time to sort out a winner.

However, the very next attack of the game was Arsenal's and a far-post cross went over Gary Bailey's head and found Alan Sunderland, who hit the winner from close range. Up until that point, the game had lacked any real drama, but those three late goals made it one of the most memorable cup finals for many years.

Losing 3-2 in such circumstances was of little comfort to Sexton, but it would sum up the manager's four years in charge: United seemed continually on the edge of a breakthrough that never came.

MANCHESTER UNITED

1	GARY BAILEY
2	JIMMY NICHOLL
3	ARTHUR ALBISTON
4	SAMMY MCILROY
5	GORDON MCQUEEN
6	MARTIN BUCHAN
7	STEVE COPPELL
8	JIMMY GREENHOFF
9	JOE JORDAN
10	LOU MACARI
11	MICKEY THOMAS

ARSENAL

1	PAT JENNINGS
2	PAT RICE
3	SAMMY NELSON
4	BRIAN TALBOT
5	DAVID O'LEARY
6	WILLIE YOUNG
7	LIAM BRADY
8	ALAN SUNDERLAND
9	FRANK STAPLETON
10	DAVID PRICE 83'
11	GRAHAM RIX
Substitute:	
12	STEVE WALFORD 83'

Referee: Ron Challis

MANCHESTER UNITED

MANAGER: DAVE SEXTON

ARSENAL

MANAGER: TERRY NEILL

SEMI-FINALS

31 MARCH 1979		
Manchester United	2-2	Liverpool (aet)
Jordan, B.Greenhoff		Dalglish, Hansen
REPLAY 4 APRIL 1979		
Liverpool	0-1	Manchester United
		J.Greenhoff
31 MARCH 1979		
Arsenal	2-0	Wolverhampton Wanderers
Sunderland, Stapleton		

THE FINAL

Manchester United's Frank Stapleton after scoring his side's first goal in the 2-2 draw that would force a replay.

UNITED SEEMED UNABLE to win a cup competition these days without some kind of desperate last-minute drama. Now it came after they took a 2-1 lead against a Brighton team who were proving better than their relegation form suggested. The south coasters had even taken the lead after 14 minutes through Gordon Smith, but United rallied in the second half and went ahead; first Frank Stapleton scored at the far post after a Mike Duxbury cross and then a curling left-foot shot by Ray Wilkins from 20 yards out found the net. With three minutes left, a nervous United seemed to have done enough, only to allow an equaliser from Gary Stevens after a corner, which set up extra time. Then came the drama.

Tired legs meant few chances in the extra 30 minutes, but in the very final seconds Brighton's Smith was one-on-one with United goalkeeper Gary Bailey; the Scotsman scuffed his shot as the keeper spread himself and managed to block what seemed a certain goal. It would be one of Wembley's most memorable misses and proved to be Brighton's last chance.

A replay at Wembley five days later was a game too far for Brighton, and United ran out very easy winners after a first half in which Bryan Robson scored twice (the first a glorious 20 yard left-foot shot) and Norman Whiteside once. However, it was winger Alan Davies who was the star of the show. The Welshman had played only a handful of first team games before the final and, in fact, would only start eight games in total during his entire United career, but he helped set up the first two goals and even had a hand in the third. A second-half penalty from Arnold Muhren completed the scoring and a 4-0 victory underlined the real gap between the two teams.

The relief of Atkinson and his team was almost palpable after the replay because United had been such heavy favourites.

MANCHESTER UNITED

1	GARY BAILEY
2	MIKE DUXBURY
3	ARTHUR ALBISTON
4	RAY WILKINS
5	KEVIN MORAN
6	GORDON MCQUEEN
7	BRYAN ROBSON
8	ARNOLD MUHREN
9	FRANK STAPLETON
10	NORMAN WHITESIDE
11	ALAN DAVIES

BRIGHTON & HOVE ALBION

1	GRAHAM MOSLEY
2	STEVE GATTING
3	GRAHAM PEARCE
4	TONY GREALISH
5	STEVE FOSTER
6	GARY STEVENS
7	JIMMY CASE
8	GARY HOWLETT
9	MICHAEL ROBINSON
10	GORDON SMITH
11	NEIL SMILLIE

Referee: Alf Grey

MANCHESTER UNITED

MANAGER: RON ATKINSON

BRIGHTON & HOVE ALBION

MANAGER: JIMMY MELIA

SEMI-FINALS

Arsenal	Woodcock
Sheffield Wednesday 3	Mirocevic

1982/83

21 May 1983 at Wembley Stadium, London

Manchester United (0) 2-2 (1) Brighton & Hove Albion

Goals: Smith 14', Stapleton 55', Wilkins 72', Stevens 87'

Attendance: 100,000

R 26 May 1983 at Wembley Stadium, London

Manchester United (3) 4-0 (0) Brighton & Hove Albion

Goals: Robson 25', 44', Whiteside 30', Muhren 62' (pen)

Attendance: 92,000

Just like Tommy Docherty six years earlier, manager Ron Atkinson was building a United team with flair and an attacking sensibility that was best suited to the demands of a knockout cup rather than a league campaign. Like Docherty, Atkinson's first Wembley trip with the Red Devils would end in defeat. That was in March this season when United made the League Cup final only to lose 2-1 to Liverpool. But before then, the FA Cup run had begun in January at home to West Ham United.

Atkinson's team had been among the contenders for the league from the start of the season and the Hammers had also been hovering around the top five in the table, so this game was the pick of the third round ties. A 2-0 win for United, with goals from Steve Coppell and Frank Stapleton, was therefore an excellent start for Atkinson, whose path to the final would include only one team from outside the First Division.

The fourth round saw United travel to Luton Town at a time when United's league challenge was fading. Atkinson now knew that the cup would provide his best chance of silverware for the season.

Luton were less of a test than West Ham; they were struggling to maintain their First Division status because of limited funds, but manager David Pleat had assembled the club's best-ever team and they were certainly seen as no pushovers. However, goals from Remi Moses and Kevin Moran provided a relatively straightforward 2-0 victory.

The fifth round tie against Second Division Derby County took place on the Saturday between two midweek League Cup semi-finals and, when all three games were won, Atkinson's cup band-wagon was rolling. Norman Whiteside, in his first full season with the first team, scored the winning goal after a tight match against County.

Back to First Division opposition for the sixth round and Everton. Under manager Howard Kendall, the Toffees were trying to build a team to challenge Liverpool on a regular basis on all fronts, just like United. Luckily for the Red Devils, another home draw proved decisive and Frank Stapleton's goal settled the tie. Two weeks later, the League Cup would be lost to the other team on Merseyside, Liverpool, but Atkinson would not let the setback disturb his FA Cup run.

The semi-final against Arsenal would be a significant match; a return to Wembley two months after the League Cup disappointment would be the perfect antidote and give more credibility to Atkinson' confident demeanour. In reality it was not the draw either team wanted; the other two semi-finalists, Brighton and Hove Albion (looking favourites for relegation from the First Division) and Sheffield Wednesday (of the Second Division) would have probably proved easier games. Arsenal were not in their pomp this season and would finish just tenth in the league, but they posed much more of a threat.

However, 46,000 fans crammed into Villa Park for the north-vs-south affair that was a repeat of the 1979 final, which Arsenal had won so dramatically 3-2. This game did not have the same memorable ending, but when Tony Woodcock put the Gunners ahead, it was the first goal United had conceded in the competition up to that point.

It did not prove to be the winner, though, because a Bryan Robson header and a Norman Whiteside volley, both in the second half, were the goals that took United to Wembley. By the time the final arrived, Brighton (the conquerors of Wednesday also by a score of 2-1) had been relegated from the First Division. As underdogs in the build-up they would benefit from the support of the neutral fans. United, however, had not won a trophy in six years and were desperate to stop the south coast team winning the FA Cup for the first time ever.

1984/85

28 May 1985 at Wembley Stadium, London

Manchester United (0) 1-0 (0) Everton

Goals: Whiteside 110'

Attendance: 100,000

While the First Division title might have been proving a step too far, the cup competitions would continue to bring Ron Atkinson and his team some comfort, and so it would prove again this season. Winning the FA Cup two seasons earlier had been Atkinson's first United silverware, but last season the defence of the trophy proved one of his most embarrassing moments – a loss in the third round to AFC Bournemouth of the Third Division. That defeat even prompted anti-Atkinson chanting among certain sections of the United fans – another similar cup tie blip had to be avoided this time around.

So when the fates decided to give United a second consecutive third round tie against Bournemouth, there were hearts in mouths. The difference this time, however, was that this FA Cup match was at Old Trafford and Atkinson had strengthened his team this season with the emergence of Mark Hughes and the signing of Gordon Strachan. A 3-0 win for the Reds, with goals from Gordon McQueen, Frank Stapleton and Strachan, was a more realistic measure of the gap in class between the two teams.

Another home draw in the fourth round brought Coventry City to Manchester, and a Hughes goal plus one from Paul McGrath brought a 2-1 win, which was followed by a trip to Blackburn Rovers where 2-0 to United was the scoreline; McGrath and Strachan were the goalscorers.

By now – the beginning of March – United were still involved in the league title race and had a difficult two-leg UEFA Cup quarter-final against Videoton of Hungary in prospect. The first European leg was won at Old Trafford and three days later West Ham United also turned up in Manchester for the FA Cup sixth round tie and were defeated 4-2, with a Norman Whiteside hat-trick and one from Mark Hughes. A European exit on penalties to the

Hungarians, plus Everton stretching out a lead in the league, meant Ron Atkinson's season now rested with the FA Cup run.

Waiting for the semi-final draw to be made, many United fans would have preferred Luton Town to either Everton or Liverpool (who were current league champions and still one of the top sides in Europe). Inevitably, United drew Liverpool and were on their way to Villa Park trying to prevent there being an all-Merseyside final in May.

The tie was fabulously intense with no quarter asked or given, and for 70 minutes the game was scoreless. When a Bryan Robson shot went into the Liverpool net, after a Mark Hughes deflection, the game looked won, but the Merseysiders equalised and the two teams again exchanged goals (Frank Stapleton for United) in extra-time with Liverpool's coming in the final seconds.

A breathless replay followed; a Paul McGrath own goal from a misplaced header in the first half was unrepresentative of United's performance. But with captain Robson almost unstoppable, the Red Devils fought back.

The skipper himself scored to make the game 1-1 and Hughes then muscled past the Liverpool back four to score the winner. The Welshman would be soon named Professional Footballers' Association Young Player of the Year and a goal like this one showed why. In the final, United would face Everton, the latest contenders for a league and cup double. Atkinson's team had no league worries between the semi and the final and the manager rested players as he aimed for his second FA Cup trophy in three years; he knew his side would need all the energy they could muster to beat Everton, who had already handed out a 5-0 drubbing to the Reds earlier in the season.

The fact that this final would be played shortly after the Bradford City stadium fire disaster – it happened on the last Saturday of the league season and left 56 people dead – would make it a game played under a sombre, mournful atmosphere as football came to terms with a new tragedy.

THE FINAL — Goalscorer Norman Whiteside and Kevin Moran (sent off during the game) celebrate the hard-fought victory.

UNITED'S OPPONENTS EVERTON had won the league this season because of a very settled line-up that featured Neville Southall in goal, Kevin Ratcliffe in defence, Peter Reid in midfield and Andy Gray in attack - the most solid spine in English football. By contrast, the Reds were lacking experience. Bryan Robson was a great captain, but Gary Bailey and Mark Hughes were still relatively young.

Kevin Moran and Graeme Hogg had begun the season as the defensive partnership, but then Paul McGrath emerged as the star of the back four and Ron Atkinson had the dilemma of finding him the best partner. In the final, the manager selected Moran, a decision that would create a rather unwanted record for a United player.

The game itself was nip and tuck until ten minutes from the end of normal time, when Everton's Reid burst through for a goal-scoring chance. The midfield player was tripped by Moran, who expected a booking for a professional foul. However, the referee saw things differently and decided to send off the United defender, who became the first player to be dismissed in an FA Cup final.

Yet, the sending off seemed to galvanise the Reds into even more spirited resistance and they took the game to extra time. Early in the second half of the additional 30 minutes, Norman Whiteside darted down the right wing and jinked inside his full back before releasing a fabulous left foot shot towards the far post and into the net.

Winger Jesper Olsen and midfielder Gordon Strachan - both ceaseless runners - were among those to hold United together as Everton piled on the pressure with a man advantage. However, the Red Devils held out for the remaining 25 minutes and took the trophy to the great delight of an initially devastated, but ultimately joyous Moran.

MANCHESTER UNITED	
1	GARY BAILEY
2	JOHN GIDMAN
3	ARTHUR ALBISTON 45'
4	NORMAN WHITESIDE
5	PAUL MCGRATH
6	KEVIN MORAN
7	BRYAN ROBSON
8	GORDON STRACHAN
9	MARK HUGHES
10	FRANK STAPLETON
11	JESPER OLSEN
Substitute:	
12	MIKE DUXBURY 45'

EVERTON	
1	NEVILLE SOUTHALL
2	GARY STEVENS
3	PAT VAN DEN HAUWE
4	KEVIN RATCLIFFE
5	DEREK MOUNTFIELD
6	PETER REID
7	TREVOR STEVEN
8	PAUL BRACEWELL
9	GRAEME SHARP
10	ANDY GRAY
11	KEVIN SHEEDY

Referee: Peter Willis

MANCHESTER UNITED

MANAGER: RON ATKINSON

EVERTON

MANAGER: HOWARD KENDALL

Everton

SEMI-FINALS

13 APRIL 1985		
Manchester United	2-2	Liverpool (aet)
Robson, Stapleton		Whelan, Walsh
REPLAY: 17 APRIL 1985		
Manchester United	2-1	Liverpool
Hughes, Robson		McGrath (og)
13 APRIL 1985		
Everton	2-1	Luton Town (aet)
Mountfield, Sheedy		Hill

THE FINAL

United hero Lee Martin is helped to his feet after scoring the only goal in the replay.

THERE HAD BEEN nothing ordinary or easy about this cup run to date; although Crystal Palace had finished just below United in the league, they had beaten Alex Ferguson's men at Old Trafford back in December, so were going to be no pushovers in the final. This first Wembley showpiece for a Ferguson team was another gripping affair, as had been the semi-final.

The lead would change hands three times and even extra time would not settle the matter. An early Palace lead was negated by a Bryan Robson equaliser on 35 minutes. Mark Hughes put the Reds in front just after the hour, only for the Londoners to bring the teams level again through Ian Wright. An extra 30 minutes brought a goal from each team: Wright seemed to have won it for Palace, but Hughes earned United a draw seven minutes from the end.

United had won every tie so far in the FA Cup this season by a single goal, so it was not entirely surprising that they could not dominate the final either, and so the tie would go to the replay at Wembley five days later.

The pre-match replay drama surrounded the goalkeeping jersey. Jim Leighton took the blame for United's poor defensive display during the first game and was replaced by Les Sealey. As one of Ferguson's signings, from his old club Aberdeen, it was a shock, but confirmed that the manager, ever the pragmatist, would do what was needed to win his first trophy.

Mark Robins had been the unlikely hero of the earlier rounds; Lee Martin would play the role in the replay.

Martin almost did not play in the game because Ferguson had doubts about his fitness, but he popped up unexpectedly in the penalty area after 59 minutes to smash the ball into the roof of the net.

MANCHESTER UNITED

1	LES SEALEY
2	PAUL INCE
3	LEE MARTIN
4	STEVE BRUCE
5	MIKE PHELAN
6	GARY PALLISTER
7	BRYAN ROBSON
8	NEILL WEBB
9	BRIAN MCCLAIR
10	MARK HUGHES
11	DANNY WALLACE

CRYSTAL PALACE

1	NIGEL MARTYN
2	JOHN PEMBERTON
3	RICHARD SHAW
4	ANDY GRAY
5	GARY O'REILLY
6	ANDY THORN
7	PHIL BARBER 64'
8	GEOFF THOMAS
9	MARK BRIGHT
10	JOHN SALAKO 79'
11	ALAN PARDEW

Substitutes:

12	IAN WRIGHT 64'
14	DAVID MADDEN 79'

Referee: Allen Gunn

MANCHESTER UNITED

MANAGER: ALEX FERGUSON

CRYSTAL PALACE

MANAGER: STEVE COPPELL

SEMI-FINALS

8 APRIL 1990

	3-3	Oldham Athletic (aet)
		Barrett, Marshall, Palmer
...990		
...chester United (aet)		
		McClair, Robins
		Liverpool (aet)
		Rush, McMahon, Barnes

1989/90

12 May 1990 at Wembley Stadium, London

Manchester United (1) 3-3 (1) Crystal Palace

Goals: O'Reilly 18', Robson 35', Hughes 62', 113', Wright 72', 92'

Attendance: 80,000

Ⓡ 17 May 1990 at Wembley Stadium, London

Manchester United (0) 1-0 (0) Crystal Palace

Goals: Martin 59'

Attendance: 80,000

The changes at United over the last 22 years had seen seven different managers take charge of hundreds of different players. The FA Cup had been secured three times already during the period, but this season's win would prove to be one of the most significant in the club's history.

The third round match is often seen by many as a key moment in Alex Ferguson's United career. It was at Nottingham Forest's City Ground on Sunday 7 January and was one of the featured ties of the round. Forest's veteran manager Brian Clough was still seen as a continuing success: his two European Cups remained a vivid triumph; the League Cup was won in April 1989; and his side was one of the First Division's strongest.

Ferguson, in contrast, was in only his third full season at United, and his team was struggling. New signings had come and old favourites departed; no trophies had been won; and the Reds were in the middle of a winless run in the league that was causing open fan revolt. And, to make matters more complicated, the unsuccessful takeover bid involving property magnate Michael Knighton had been made public in the autumn – including a bizarre piece of pre-game ball-juggling by Knighton at Old Trafford.

The press were writing Ferguson's obituary and even some players thought another managerial change was possible. After a League Cup exit in October and with no league title in sight, the Forest game was tipped to be the manager's last.

But, from somewhere the United team dug out a dogged performance and young Mark Robins became the latest Reds hero to emerge from the youth team. He scored the only goal of the game and Ferguson was safe, for now. Or

at least so said the press.

The win certainly had no immediate knock-on effect as United lost their next two league games, but the fourth round of the cup against famous giant-killers Hereford United provided another 1-0 away win, with Clayton Blackmore (another ex-youth team player) on the scoresheet.

Newcastle United were next up, a team relegated from the First Division at the end of last season, and another game United could easily have lost, especially at St James' Park. But again the Reds sneaked a close win; an exciting 3-2 victory was achieved with goals by Robins, Brian McClair and Danny Wallace.

Another away tie – they seemed to suit United during this cup run – in the sixth round offered Sheffield United as the Reds' opponents and a tense 1-0 victory (McClair again scoring) was another good result for a team still finding its way. Then came an epic semi-final against an innocuous-seeming Oldham Athletic.

Under their canny manager Joe Royle, this mid-table Second Division team was actually on the rise and would eventually enjoy a period in the top level of English football; this season United's Lancashire neighbours believed that Wembley was their destiny. A pulsating 3-3 draw in the first game, after extra time at Maine Road (goals from Bryan Robson, Wallace and Neil Webb), was great entertainment for the 44,000 crowd, but a nerve-jangling experience for Ferguson, who believed he was now close to a major final.

Some experts thought Oldham's best had been seen in the first game, but the Latics came out again determined to win. United finally found their rhythm, managing a 2-1 win, with Brian McClair getting the first and Robins – off the substitute's bench – claiming the winner in another period of extra time.

United had reached the final without playing a single game at Old Trafford and expected to face arch-rivals Liverpool. But the upstarts Crystal Palace (managed by former Red Steve Coppell) caused a sensation by beating the champions-elect Merseysiders 4-3 in their semi, providing the Reds with unlikely opponents.

1993/94

14 May 1994 at Wembley Stadium, London
Manchester United (0) 4-0 (0) Chelsea
Goals: Cantona 60' (pen), 66' (pen), Hughes
69', McClair 90'
Attendance: 79,634

Overall, this season's competition was one of the most memorable for many years owing to a whole series of shocks and surprises: holders Arsenal lost to Bolton; lowly Luton Town beat Newcastle United; Stockport County dumped out Premiership Queens Park Rangers; and Bristol City did the same to Liverpool. But United avoided falling at several difficult hurdles, although they faced Premiership opposition in four out of the five rounds they had to negotiate to the final.

The FA Cup draws in the third, fourth and fifth rounds were all unkind to United, sending them away from home to face tough Premiership opponents. However, the team responded and progress was achieved each time without conceding a goal.

First up was a match away against Sheffield United, managed by the uncompromising Dave Bassett. The Yorkshire club had beaten United 2-1 in the fifth round of the previous year's FA Cup, a game also played at their Bramall Lane home. This season, Sheffield were struggling to stay in the Premiership and needed an FA Cup run to boost their confidence, but Mark Hughes stole the show. The Welsh centre forward scored the Red Devils' only (and winning) goal, but was later sent off for kicking the Blades' David Tuttle up the backside.

The fourth round game took place just ten days after the death of Sir Matt Busby and the club was still in deep mourning.

The tie itself was forecast to be even tougher than the previous one; it was against Norwich City, a team contesting in European competition, who, in the previous season, had become the only English club to beat Bayern Munich in the Germans' Olympic Stadium. Conveniently, Norwich's manager Mike Walker left the club to take over the reins at Everton just days before United came

to town. A strong Norwich team under new boss John Deehan could not stop their visitors, who won with goals from Eric Cantona and Roy Keane, one in each half.

A third Premiership team in succession faced United in the fifth round: Wimbledon, a club that was enjoying one of its best ever seasons in the top league (it would go on to finish sixth this year). However, United were merciless as Cantona, Paul Ince and Denis Irwin scored in a 3-0 win. The first and only home game in this year's FA Cup campaign took place in the sixth round against Charlton Athletic, one of the strongest sides in the First Division and the team that had already put Premiership title challengers Blackburn Rovers out of the competition. Despite a nervous and goal-less first half, a Hughes strike and two from Andrei Kanchelskis secured a 3-1 win.

The semi-final turned out to be the most dramatic of United's cup run, and important because it came just as United were faltering in the league (Blackburn had drawn level on points when the game was played). United also needed a win after a surprising loss in the League Cup final to Aston Villa less than a fortnight earlier. Now United faced local rivals Oldham Athletic, a team that was charming the football world under manager Joe Royle, while all the time trying to establish itself in the Premiership.

The game took place at Wembley, despite United making strong representation to the Football Association arguing that two Lancashire teams should not have to travel south for the game. However, the Latics loved the idea of playing at the famous ground and were the neutrals' favourites to make their first FA Cup final. Meanwhile United were without the suspended Eric Cantona. With the scores 0-0 after 90 minutes, Oldham went ahead in extra time and only another goal from Hughes with 46 seconds remaining forced a 1-1 draw. Three days later, a convincing 4-1 win in the replay (goals by Ryan Giggs, Irwin, Kanchelskis and Bryan Robson) put United through.

THE FINAL Andrei Kanchelskis and Frank Sinclair battle it out.

ONCE AT WEMBLEY United were far less troubled, although their opponents Chelsea had beaten them twice during the league season, both times 1-0. The Reds had perhaps their best chance ever to win the coveted league and cup double for the first time and, having already sewn up their second Premiership title a week earlier, they were in confident mood. Nothing Chelsea could do seemed to unsettle them.

United were back to full strength, with Eric Cantona returning, although there was some controversy in Alex Ferguson's selection when Bryan Robson did not even make the bench (he would move to Middlesbrough as player/manager next season). The other news for United concerned goalkeeper Peter Schmeichel who was eventually declared fit during the build-up to the game.

The Londoners were the better of the two teams for the first 45 minutes, with Chelsea's Gavin Peacock being denied only by the crossbar. No doubt Chelsea should have led going into half-time, but a rash of United goals after 15 minutes of the second half proved decisive.

The first goal to break the deadlock came after a pass by Ryan Giggs found Denis Irwin who burst into the penalty area; the full back was brought down and a spot-kick awarded. Five minutes later Andrei Kanchelskis was pushed over near Chelsea's goalmouth and a second penalty was awarded. Cantona slotted home the two penalties before a Mark Hughes shot found the net after 69 minutes, and the game was all but over. It was left for Paul Ince to present Brian McClair with a pass for a tap-in fourth goal in the last minute and so launch the celebrations for the club's first league and cup double. United became only the fourth team in the twentieth century to achieve this triumph.

MANCHESTER UNITED
1 PETER SCHMEICHEL
2 PAUL PARKER
4 STEVE BRUCE
6 GARY PALLISTER
3 DENIS IRWIN 84'
14 ANDREI KANCHELSKIS 84'
16 ROY KEANE
8 PAUL INCE
11 RYAN GIGGS
7 ERIC CANTONA
10 MARK HUGHES
Substitutes:
5 LEE SHARPE 84'
9 BRIAN MCCLAIR 84'

CHELSEA
1 DMITRI KHARINE
12 STEVE CLARKE
35 JAKOB KJELDBJERG
5 ERLAND JOHNSEN
6 FRANK SINCLAIR
11 DENNIS WISE
18 EDDIE NEWTON
24 CRAIG BURLEY 68'
10 GAVIN PEACOCK
21 MARK STEIN 78'
7 JOHN SPENCER
Substitutes:
20 GLENN HODDLE 68'
9 TONY CASCARINO 78'

Referee: David Elleray

SEMI-FINALS
9 APRIL 1994		
Chelsea	2-0	Luton Town
Peacock (2)		
10 APRIL 1994		
Oldham	1-1	Manchester United (a.e.t)
Pointon		Hughes
13 APRIL 1994		
Manchester United	4-1	Oldham Athletic
Irwin, Kanchelskis, Robson, Giggs		Pointon

MANCHESTER UNITED
MANAGER: ALEX FERGUSON

CHELSEA
MANAGER: GLENN HODDLE

THE FINAL

The always acrobatic Mark Hughes leaps to avoid Everton midfielder Joe Parkinson's tackle.

UNITED FELT THAT the league and cup double was within their grasp before their last two games of the season – firstly a league match at West Ham United and then the FA Cup final against Everton. But when the West Ham game ended in a 1-1 draw and Blackburn Rovers sneaked the Premiership by a single point, the Reds had to pick themselves up to salvage pride with a trophy from the Everton match six days later.

The Merseysiders under manager Joe Royle had fought off relegation for much of a disappointing season and the club had not won a major trophy for eight years, but they had beaten United at Goodison Park in February, so they were not without hope.

Alex Ferguson made one enforced change for the final as the cup-tied Andy Cole stepped aside for Mark Hughes, while two other key players were also missing: Andrei Kanchelskis was still injured and Eric Cantona suspended. Despite being the clear favourites, the Reds seemed lacklustre in a match with few chances and little drama. That Everton centre back Dave Watson was man of the match tells its own story.

The cup went to Everton thanks to a first-half goal by Paul Rideout, who headed the ball into the net after teammate Graham Stuart had hit the United crossbar with a shot. The goal came after just 30 minutes, and it was Everton's first real chance of the game. There was plenty of time for the Reds to fight back, but Everton goalkeeper Neville Southall coped with everything that came his way.

Bringing on Ryan Giggs at half-time for the injured Steve Bruce only seemed to confuse United rather than inspire them. Royle's team held out for the win. For United then, this was a trophyless season – the first time this state of affairs had occurred in six seasons.

MANCHESTER UNITED

1	PETER SCHMEICHEL
27	GARY NEVILLE
3	DENIS IRWIN
4	STEVE BRUCE 45'
6	GARY PALLISTER
5	LEE SHARPE 72'
16	ROY KEANE
8	PAUL INCE
19	NICKY BUTT
9	BRIAN MCCLAIR
10	MARK HUGHES

Substitutes:

11	RYAN GIGGS '45
24	PAUL SCHOLES 72'

EVERTON

1	NEVILLE SOUTHALL
2	MATT JACKSON
5	DAVE WATSON
26	DAVE UNSWORTH
6	GARY ABLETT
17	ANDERS LIMPAR 69'
18	JOE PARKINSON
10	BARRY HORNE
3	ANDY HINCHCLIFFE
8	GRAHAM STUART
15	PAUL RIDEOUT 51'

Substitutes:

9	DUNCAN FERGUSON 51'
11	DANIEL AMOKACHI 69'

Referee: Gerald Ashby

MANCHESTER UNITED

MANAGER: ALEX FERGUSON

EVERTON

MANAGER: JOE ROYLE

Everton

SEMI-FINALS

9 APRIL 1995		
Tottenham Hotspur Klinsmann	1-4	Everton Jackson, Stuart, Amokachi
9 APRIL 1995		
Manchester United Irwin, Pallister	2-2	Crystal Palace (a.e.t.) Dowie, Armstrong
REPLAY 12 APRIL 1995		
Crystal Palace	0-2	Manchester United Pallister, Bruce

1994/95

20 May 1995 at Wembley Stadium, London

Manchester United (0) 0-1 (1) Everton

Goals: Rideout 30'

Attendance: 79,592

Having magnificently completed their first league and cup double last season (as well as being League Cup finalists), United were favourites for every trophy in English football this season, but fortune did not quite favour the Reds 12 months on – especially as they would be without Andy Cole (who signed from Newcastle United for a British transfer record sum in early January) in the cup campaign as he was cup-tied. At least United's first opponents, Sheffield United, were in Division One. For the second successive season the two clubs would meet in the third round. The result proved to be the same as last time: a 2-0 United win with goals from Eric Cantona and Mark Hughes.

United by now were out of the Champions League, but running neck-and-neck with Blackburn Rovers for the league title and tensions were running high. The Red Devils were lucky to draw a home tie with Wrexham of Division Two the visitors to Old Trafford in late January. All in all, it didn't look too onerous.

Then calamity struck. Three days before the cup game, United played at Crystal Palace in the league and Cantona was sent off. As he walked to the tunnel, a Palace fan hurled abuse at him and the Frenchman responded by leaping into the crowd to kick the man in the chest. The press condemnation was universal. Manchester United immediately fined the player £20,000 and suspended him for the rest of the season.

The Wrexham game was United's first after the incident and while the Reds won easily 5-2, with goals by Denis Irwin (two), Ryan Giggs, Brian McClair plus an own goal, the eyes of the world were on the club for all the wrong reasons.

The visit of Leeds United in mid-February for a fifth round tie came a week after a 3-0 league win in the Manchester derby as United were showing signs of being able to cope with life without Cantona. Leeds were also dismissed with aplomb, 3-1, thanks to goals from Steve Bruce, Mark Hughes and Brian McClair.

A third consecutive home draw against a capable Queens Park Rangers team from mid-table in the Premiership awaited United in the sixth round and another competent performance followed. The Reds won 2-0; Irwin was again on target along with Lee Sharpe.

The football gods have a way of playing tricks on teams, so when the draw for the semi-finals was made it was clear that United wanted to avoid Crystal Palace (the scene of Cantona's transgression). When the two sides were drawn together, Cantona's absence notwithstanding, the press had a field day.

The match at Villa Park offered up more than the usual tension of a cup semi-final and ended in 2-2 draw. United's goals were scored by two defenders, Dennis Irwin again and Gary Pallister.

Palace asked for the replay at the same venue three days later to be postponed (a Palace fan had suffered a fatal accident immediately after the first game). The Football Association refused and, partly as a protest, fewer than 18,000 fans turned up for the second game. Some blamed high ticket prices. Nevertheless, emotions on the pitch were still at fever pitch and violence erupted after a niggly first 45 minutes.

United's Keane had already had stitches in his ankle after a bad tackle by Northern Irish defender Darren Patterson in the first half, so when he was caught again – this time by Gareth Southgate – the United man reacted and stamped on the Villa player as he lay on the ground. A whole gang of players from both teams, then piled in as the Palace defender and Keane exchanged blows. Unsurprisingly both were sent off; Keane's dismissal being the fifth this season for a United player.

When the dust had settled, United had won the match 2-0 (Steve Bruce and Gary Pallister were the scorers), but both games had also left unpleasant memories.

1995/96

11 May 1996 at Wembley Stadium, London

Manchester United (0) 1-0 (0) Liverpool

Goals: Cantona 85'

Attendance: 79,007

Alex Ferguson's team was by now consummate FA Cup contenders, and this would be United's third run to the final in consecutive seasons, but as usual nothing would be straightforward. Eric Cantona had returned to the United line-up earlier in the season after his eight-month suspension, while in the league Kevin Keegan's Newcastle United seemed to be leading the Reds a merry dance.

When the FA Cup campaign opened against Sunderland at Old Trafford in January, United were far from their best and most dominating form; in fact they had lost 4-1 at Tottenham Hotspur five days earlier. A 2-2 draw (goals from Nicky Butt and a late equaliser from Eric Cantona himself) felt like a great escape for the Red Devils against the Wearsiders, but United then managed a 2-1 win at Roker Park in a game that marked the start of a remarkable winning streak in both the cup and the league.

The replay victory was on 16 January and United then won 15 out of the next 16 games, drawing the other. The run would bring a second league and cup double into the cross hairs; the first had been achieved just two years earlier. Of course, in the league, that unbeaten sweet 16 was also devastating for Newcastle, while in the cup it was to progress the team to the final.

After Sunderland, Reading of Division One proved slightly easier opponents, and a 3-0 win with goals from Eric Cantona, Ryan Giggs and Paul Parker conformed to all the pre-match predictions.

The fifth round provided a chance for United to step on Manchester City's toes once again. City were wobbling near the bottom of the Premiership table and would eventually be relegated. But every derby game is hard fought and the manager's inclusion of Steve Bruce in defence and Nicky Butt in midfield was a sure sign that he expected a tough match – so it proved.

The Reds always had a bit too much class for their rivals, who actually took the lead. However, an equalising Cantona penalty plus a goal from Lee Sharpe were enough for a 2-1 win at Old Trafford.

The cup draw again favoured the Reds by bringing Southampton up to Manchester for the sixth round. The south coast team were no pushovers on their home ground The Dell, especially with the dangerous Matt Le Tissier likely to score goals from almost any part of the ground, but at Old Trafford it would be a different story. Again Cantona and Sharpe were the scorers and the winning run was now becoming headline news – it was up to ten.

The spate of victories ended with a draw in the league at Queens Park Rangers, but the winning habit returned in time for the semi-final against a Chelsea team managed by Glenn Hoddle, who was just weeks away from accepting the job as the England manager.

The Londoners were making a habit of falling at the final fence in the chase for trophies and United were in no mood to help them out. Ruud Gullit gave Chelsea a first-half lead and the prospect of a Wembley trip, but United dominated the second half as David Beckham equalised and Andy Cole scored the winner.

It would set up a final against Liverpool, the one team that Ferguson enjoyed beating most of all. Although the Mersey team had not threatened in the league (they would finish third this season), they were still formidable opponents, packed with full internationals.

But United enjoyed the best stimulus when the championship was secured in their last league match of the season at Middlesbrough – just six days before the team stepped onto the Wembley turf. A second league and cup double was now on the cards.

Liverpool had beaten United 2-0 at Anfield in December and forced a draw at Old Trafford two months before that, so the FA Cup final would be eagerly anticipated, a potential classic between two teams at the top of their game.

THE FINAL

Captain and scorer of the winning goal Eric Cantona is greeted by jubilant supporters on his way from Royal Box.

DESPITE SO MUCH talent on show, this final was a dawdling affair replete with mistakes from both sides and evidence of very little creative flair. There was tension and tiredness in the legs of United even though a second league and cup double was at stake. United lost only a single game since 6 January when their FA Cup run started. Liverpool, of course, had an extra incentive: they wanted to deny United the double as they themselves had been denied by the Red Devils at Wembley in 1977.

Despite losing Steve Bruce (injured and replaced by David May), United were still pre-game favourites and certainly won the battle of the pre-match Wembley walkout. Dressed in smart navy blue suits with a red carnation, United's players looked business-like and comfortable compared to the Liverpool team in their now infamous white suits.

But as the showpiece final turned into a dismal display by both teams, with one misplaced pass following another, all the build-up excitement ebbed away. A goalless first half was not unsurprising given the dominance of the defences and the way that the two teams' tactics were cancelling each other out.

Extra time seemed inevitable until David Beckham took a corner in the 85th minute that brought Liverpool keeper David James off his line to punch the ball clear. However, the attempted clearance cannoned off a Liverpool player and fell to Eric Cantona – captain for the day – who twisted and volleyed the bouncing ball through a mass of bodies and into the net.

The bad-boy-turned-hero story was complete when the smiling Frenchman collected the trophy a few minutes later on behalf of the team that had secured another double. The French tricolour was unfurled by celebrating United fans and Alex Ferguson had now won 12 trophies in ten years.

MANCHESTER UNITED

1	PETER SCHMEICHEL
3	DENIS IRWIN
6	GARY PALLISTER
12	DAVID MAY
23	PHIL NEVILLE
24	DAVID BECKHAM '90
16	ROY KEANE
19	NICKY BUTT
11	RYAN GIGGS
7	ERIC CANTONA
17	ANDY COLE 64'

Substitutes:

| 20 | GARY NEVILLE 90' |
| 22 | PAUL SCHOLES 64' |

LIVERPOOL

1	DAVID JAMES
12	JOHN SCALES
5	MARK WRIGHT
6	PHIL BABB
4	JASON McATEER
2	ROB JONES 86'
15	JAMIE REDKNAPP
10	JOHN BARNES
17	STEVE McMANAMAN
23	ROBBIE FOWLER
8	STAN COLLYMORE 74'

Substitutes:

| 16 | MICHAEL THOMAS 86' |
| 9 | IAN RUSH 74' |

Referee: Dermot Gallagher

MANCHESTER UNITED

MANAGER: ALEX FERGUSON

LIVERPOOL

MANAGER: ROY EVANS

SEMI-FINALS

31 MARCH 1996		
Manchester United	2-1	Chelsea
Cole, Beckham		Gullit
31 MARCH 1996		
Liverpool	3-0	Aston Villa
Fowler (2), McAteer		

THE FINAL

Alex Ferguson celebrates the second leg of a magnificent treble as the final whistle blows.

COMPARED TO THE rest of the dramas of this treble-winning season, the final of the FA Cup was viewed as a tame affair, especially given what was going to happen in the Champions League final just four days later. The league title was clinched only on the last weekend, so this game was the latest in a breathless period when almost every game felt like a cup final.

Newcastle United were the opponents and were returning to the final for the second consecutive year. This, however, was not the Kevin Keegan-led team of swashbucklers that had chased United to the league title a few seasons earlier; instead it was a rather more modest team trying to work under Ruud Gullit in his first season as manager, inspired by centre forward Alan Shearer on the field.

United were high on emotion, but the pundits felt that if Newcastle could catch the Red Devils early then the anticipated tiredness of a long season (this was United's 62nd game) could be decisive.

When captain Roy Keane went off injured after just nine minutes, United could have lost their way, but instead Keane's replacement Teddy Sheringham opened the scoring 90 seconds after he joined the action.

The goal settled United, who pressed for a second that would kill off the game. Still 1-0 down at half-time, Gullit brought on striker Duncan Ferguson, replacing a midfield player in an effort to wrench the momentum from United, but the move backfired and Paul Scholes scored nine minutes into the second half with a convincing right-foot shot from Sheringham's set-up.

This one-sided win brought United's tenth FA Cup triumph and provided their third league and cup double, but more importantly it also kept alive the prospect of an unprecedented treble – something that would be completed in four days' time.

SEMI-FINALS

11 APRIL 1999		
Arsenal	0-0	Manchester United

14 APRIL 1999		
Manchester United	2-1	Arsenal (aet)
Beckham, Giggs		Bergkamp

11 APRIL 1999		
Newcastle United	2-0	Tottenham Hotspur
Shearer (2)		

MANCHESTER UNITED

1	PETER SCHMEICHEL
2	GARY NEVILLE
5	RONNY JOHNSEN
4	DAVID MAY
12	PHIL NEVILLE
7	DAVID BECKHAM
18	PAUL SCHOLES 78'
16	ROY KEANE 9'
11	RYAN GIGGS
9	ANDY COLE 60'
20	OLE GUNNAR SOLSKJAER

Substitutes:

6	JAAP STAM 78'
10	TEDDY SHERINGHAM 9'
19	DWIGHT YORKE 60'

NEWCASTLE UNITED

13	STEVE HARPER
38	ANDY GRIFFIN
16	LAURENT CHARVET
34	NIKOS DABIZAS
4	DIDIER DOMI
7	ROB LEE
12	DIETMAR HAMANN 46'
11	GARY SPEED
24	NOLBERTO SOLANO 68'
14	TEMURI KETSBAIA 79'
9	ALAN SHEARER

Substitutes:

10	SILVIO MARIC 68'
17	STEPHEN GLASS 79'
20	DUNCAN FERGUSON 45'

Referee: Peter Jones

MANCHESTER UNITED

MANAGER: ALEX FERGUSON

NEWCASTLE UNITED

MANAGER: RUUD GULLIT

1998/99

22 May 1999 at Wembley Stadium, London
Manchester United (1) 2-0 (0) Newcastle United
Goals: Sheringham 11', Scholes 53'
Attendance: 79,101

By now United were enjoying their most successful ever period of trophy winning. This would be the tenth season since Alex Ferguson broke his silverware duck with the FA Cup in 1989-90, and there had not been a season since then without a cup of some description ending up in the silverware cabinet at Old Trafford. This season's FA Cup final would be the meat in the sandwich of the unique treble – played after United had won the league, but before they would play in the final of the Champions League. Although compared with the European final, it proved to be far less dramatic.

The opening cup game in the campaign, however, was five months earlier, a 3-1 win over Middlesbrough with Andy Cole, Ryan Giggs and Denis Irwin on the scoresheet. Boro were managed by United's former Captain Marvel, Bryan Robson, but there was never room for sentiment at Old Trafford in an FA cup run.

Next up were old rivals Liverpool. The home game for United was won 2-1 with Ole Gunnar Solskjaer and Dwight Yorke getting the goals, but the Old Trafford faithful saw Liverpool score early and had to wait until the last couple of minutes before United hit back twice to snatch the game.

Another home draw brought Fulham to Old Trafford and, although this was a team languishing in Division Two, their manager was now former Newcastle United boss Kevin Keegan. In fact, Fulham were taking their league by storm and the game was an intriguing match-up. It was also a very close affair with only one goal, from United's Cole, deciding the outcome.

A fourth home draw in a row against Chelsea then followed, but the expected victory did not result immediately. The Londoners held out for a 0-0 draw against an under-strength United starting line-up (Cole, Dwight Yorke and Giggs were among those rested), taking the Reds back to Stamford Bridge for an unwanted replay. (The Champions League knockout games were now coming thick and fast.) But, with Cole, Yorke and Giggs restored, United won 2-0, Yorke netting both goals.

The semi-final would be a classic. Arsenal were the FA Cup holders and hard on United's heels in the league, while the Reds had just played the first leg of the Champions League semi-final against Juventus (drawing 1-1 at Old Trafford); talk of the treble was now on everyone's lips. A tense 0-0 draw at Villa Park prompted a replay at the same ground just three days later, and it would be one of the games of the season.

A magnificent David Beckham shot from more than 25 yards opened the scoring in the first half. The goal came after a long kick up field by Peter Schmeichel; it was poorly cleared by the Gunners' defence and landed at Beckham's feet. A quick interchange with Teddy Sheringham and the shot flew past David Seaman's right hand. It took some time before Dennis Bergkamp equalised with a shot of his own in the second half from almost the same distance. Then the drama really began as Nicolas Anelka appeared to have put Arsenal in front only for it to be ruled offside. The let-off seemed to be neutralised when another Roy Keane foul resulted in a second yellow card and the captain left the field, handing the initiative to the Londoners.

So as the pressure built and Phil Neville brought down Ray Parlour to give Arsenal a penalty, the semi-final looked lost. Schmeichel dived to his left to save Bergkamp's spot kick and take the game into extra time. Early on in the added period, the Reds' keeper also pulled off another incredible save from the Bergkamp to keep United's ten-man team in the game.

Then, as the second period of extra time wound down, Giggs picked up a loose Arsenal pass 10 yards inside his own half and sped off on a jinking run that went all the way into the Gunners' penalty area and finished with a rising shot over Seaman. Giggs' individual brilliance made it one of the goals of the season and a fitting way for United to reach Wembley.

2003/04

22 May 2004 at Millennium Stadium, Cardiff

Manchester United (1) 3-0 (0) Millwall

Goals: Ronaldo 44', van Nistelrooy 65' (pen), 81'

Attendance: 71,350

Pundits said United would struggle this season; they had lost Juan Sebastian Veron, Fabien Barthez and David Beckham in the off-season while gaining only Louis Saha and teenager Cristiano Ronaldo. Then star-defender Rio Ferdinand was banned in December for eight months after failing to take an early-season drugs test. From then on the title race was always going to be a difficult one, so the FA Cup campaign that started in January would be a vital element of the season.

A 2-1 third round win at Aston Villa, with Paul Scholes scoring both goals, was the kind of fillip that manager Sir Alex Ferguson wanted. Wes Brown played in place of Ferdinand as the manager rested several players. But when the fourth round tie away at Third Division Northampton Town was played in late January it was known that Ferdinand would be out for the season. Ferguson gave several squad players a start, including Ronaldo (still learning his trade in his first season) and Diego Forlan, who got the opening goal. Mikael Silvestre and a Northampton own goal completed the scoring.

Silvestre was now the most experienced centre back and Brown was competing with John O'Shea to be his regular partner. The Irishman got the nod in the fifth round at home to Manchester City, a game in which Ferguson would never play anything but his strongest team. A 4-2 victory was an excellent result, given the Red Devils had lost at home to Middlesbrough 3-2 three days earlier. Ruud van Nistelrooy scored twice, with Ronaldo and Scholes each getting one. The win came despite a red card for Gary Neville for headbutting Steve McManaman after only 38 minutes. Neville had been denied a penalty and reacted angrily, but the Reds were already 1-0 ahead and were able to power on to the victory. The win over City occurred in February, a month when

both the league season and hopes in Europe would begin to go sour: an unbeaten Arsenal team zoomed past United in the league while Porto won the first leg of the Champions League first round of the knock-out stage in Portugal.

United now needed FA Cup success more than ever and they got it with a sixth round victory over Fulham by 2-1 at Old Trafford, with two more van Nistelrooy goals – who was on his way to a total of 30 for the season in all competitions. The Fulham win, however, was followed by an exit from Champions League after United could only draw against Porto in the second leg at Old Trafford. The semi-final looked even more imposing when Arsenal became the Reds' opponents; the Londoners were heading for an unprecedented unbeaten Premiership season.

The match took place at Villa Park, the same venue for the last semi-final classic between the two rivals in 1999 when a Ryan Giggs wonder goal won a thrilling replay. This time Arsenal were unable to start Thierry Henry (an injury meant he was only a substitute), while the Reds were without van Nistelrooy (who was suffering from fluid on the knee) and cup-tied Louis Saha. Ferguson surprised many people by starting Solskjaer up front along with Giggs, playing in the slot behind him, in the hope that a strong midfield could support them.

Arsenal had the best early chances, but Scholes again scored a decisive goal after 31 minutes and United held out for a 1-0 win. For most neutral observers, this game was the final that they were denied because in the other semi Millwall and Sunderland, both of the First Division, fought for the chance of a rare final appearance.

When the London team won, it meant that United were massive favourites for the final against a team that was able to finish only mid-table in the lower division. Despite being led by former England international Dennis Wise, Millwall's new player/manager, the south London team was given little chance of causing an upset.

WITH LEAGUE AND European glory both long gone, the trip to Cardiff's Millennium Stadium for this final would mean a chance of redemption for the season. Ruud van Nistelrooy was back from injury and both Wes Brown and John O'Shea played in defence while Cristiano Ronaldo was now beginning to assert his talents on the wing.

Against such opposition, Millwall's team of journeymen and young hopefuls looked inexperienced and even awestruck on this glamorous occasion. The Londoners had as many as 16 members of their squad unavailable for the game because of injury or suspension. It was also their first ever cup final appearance and the pressure on them was overwhelming.

United in general and Ronaldo in particular were dazzling in the first half. Roy Keane had a vicious volley tipped over the bar by the Millwall keeper and Ronaldo had a chance cleared off the line. There were innumerable other chances before United actually took the lead after 43 minutes – the goal coming from the Portuguese with a far-post header after a Gary Neville cross from the right.

Any chance of Millwall sneaking a draw, extra time, penalties or any kind of shock result was extinguished after 64 minutes. A mazy run by Giggs ended with him being clumsily fouled near the Millwall six-yard box. Van Nistelrooy took the spot kick and at 2-0 the Red Devils were cruising.

A third goal came as the United players were strolling towards the celebrations that their fans had already begun. A Paul Scholes pass found Giggs who jinked past a defender and sent a cross-come-shot into the goalmouth that was poked into the net by van Nistelrooy for his sixth goal of the competition.

It was United's 11th FA Cup victory, putting them two ahead of the next best in the list of winners (Arsenal with nine) while goalkeeper Tim Howard became the first American to take an FA Cup winner's medal.

MANCHESTER UNITED	
14	TIM HOWARD 84'
2	GARY NEVILLE
6	WES BROWN
27	MIKAEL SILVESTRE
22	JOHN O'SHEA
7	CRISTIANO RONALDO 84'
24	DARREN FLETCHER 84'
16	ROY KEANE
11	RYAN GIGGS
18	PAUL SCHOLES
10	RUUD VAN NISTELROOY
Substitutes:	
13	ROY CARROLL 84'
8	NICKY BUTT 84'
20	OLE GUNNAR SOLSKJAER 84'

MILLWALL	
33	ANDY MARSHALL
25	MARVIN ELLIOT
2	MATTHEW LAWRENCE
12	DARREN WARD
3	ROBBIE RYAN 74'
7	PAUL IFILL
19	DENNIS WISE 89'
8	DAVID LIVERMORE
26	PETER SWEENEY
4	TIM CAHILL
9	NEIL HARRIS 75'
Substitutes:	
37	BARRY COGAN 74'
11	CURTIS WESTON 89'
23	MARK MCCAMMON 75'

Referee: Jeff Winter

MANCHESTER UNITED

MANAGER: SIR ALEX FERGUSON

MILLWALL

PLAYER/MANAGER: DENNIS WISE

SEMI-FINALS		
3 APRIL 2004		
Arsenal	0-1	Manchester United
		Scholes
4 APRIL 2004		
Sunderland	0-1	Millwall
		Cahill

THE FINAL

Paul Scholes can hardly believe that his penalty kick was blocked by Arsenal's Jens Lehmann in the shootout.

IT WAS A rainy Cardiff that provided the venue for the final featuring two of the Premiership's best teams and fiercest rivals. There seemed little love lost between the two managers or the two captains and this was never likely to be a free-flowing encounter with plenty of goals.

Sir Alex Ferguson was, as usual, spoilt for choice about who to include and who to leave out of the starting line-up. Having Ryan Giggs and Gary Neville on the bench was a mark of the class of his current squad. Arsenal, meanwhile, had lost Thierry Henry to injury and manager Arsene Wenger preferred young Philippe Senderos at centre back to Sol Campbell, who had been out with a long-term injury himself.

United had the better chances in a scoreless first half, with Cristiano Ronaldo causing panic in the Gunners defence from his left-wing position. The Red Devils even had a goal disallowed, but the deadlock remained and the second 45 minutes were just as tight. Again, the Reds had chances to win the game, including a Ruud van Nistelrooy header cleared off the line.

Extra time at the end of a long season (this was United's 61st game of the campaign) was always going to test the players, but United were able to bring on Giggs and more openings for United forwards were the result. Yet a breakthrough goal failed to materialise and the second half of the extra period began to descend into a litany of fouls. Just before the final whistle, a foul on Paul Scholes led to Arsenal's Jose Antonio Reyes becoming only the second player to be sent off in an FA Cup final.

By now, a penalty shoot-out was inevitable. Both the opening spot kicks were successful, but the unlucky Scholes surprisingly missed United's second and Arsenal eventually won the penalty contest 5-4, taking a trophy the Reds felt should have been theirs.

MANCHESTER UNITED

- 13 ROY CARROLL
- 22 JOHN O'SHEA 77'
- 5 RIO FERDINAND
- 6 WES BROWN
- 27 MIKAEL SILVESTRE
- 24 DARREN FLETCHER 91'
- 16 ROY KEANE
- 18 PAUL SCHOLES
- 7 CRISTIANO RONALDO
- 8 WAYNE ROONEY
- 10 RUUD VAN NISTELROOY

Substitutes:
- 25 QUINTON FORTUNE 77'
- 11 RYAN GIGGS 91'

ARSENAL

- 1 JENS LEHMANN
- 12 LAUREN
- 28 KOLO TOURE
- 20 PHILIPPE SENDEROS
- 3 ASHLEY COLE
- 15 CESC FABREGAS 86'
- 4 PATRICK VIEIRA
- 19 GILBERTO SILVA
- 7 ROBERT PIRES 105'
- 9 JOSE ANTONIO REYES
- 10 DENNIS BERGKAMP 65'

Substitutes:
- 8 FREDERIK LJUNGBERG 65'
- 17 EDU 105'
- 11 ROBIN VAN PERSIE 86'

Referee: Rob Styles

MANCHESTER UNITED
MANAGER: SIR ALEX FERGUSON

ARSENAL
MANAGER: ARSENE WENGER

SEMI-FINALS

Blackburn

05

Manchester United
van Nistelrooy (2)
Scholes, Ronaldo

2004/05

21 May 2005 at Millennium Stadium Cardiff

Manchester United (0) 0-0 (0) Arsenal (a.e.t)

Goals: United lost on penalties 4-5

Attendance: 71,876

Although United were the FA Cup holders at the start of this season, this was now a competition where squad players would often get a start, especially in the early rounds. With over 60 games facing the Reds between August and May, the risk of rotating the side was balanced by the importance of ensuring that everyone could keep match fit.

So when Exeter City of Division Three came to Old Trafford for the third round tie in early January, Sir Alex used the opportunity to ring the changes. United were already behind both Chelsea and Arsenal in the league and would face Jose Mourinho's team in the first leg of the League Cup semi-final four days after the Devon club came to Manchester.

But with Tim Howard, Phil Neville and Wes Brown as the most senior players in the starting line-up, Exeter thought they had a chance. A 0-0 draw was a great result for the lower league team and an embarrassment for the Reds, who fielded a much stronger starting XI in the replay, winning 2-0 with goals from Cristiano Ronaldo and Wayne Rooney.

In the fourth round at Old Trafford, Middlesbrough met a strong United and a convincing 3-0 win was the result; Rooney scored twice and John O'Shea got the other goal. Then, in early February, there was an off-field distraction when American businessman Malcolm Glazer announced a club takeover bid just as United were building up for the next round of the FA Cup and the Champions League knockout stage.

The financial news did not seem to affect the Reds when they travelled to Everton in the FA Cup fifth round and they duly landed a 2-0 victory with Quinton Fortune and Ronaldo scoring. But as the league title edged further towards Chelsea and when AC Milan triumphed over United in Europe, the sixth round cup tie against Southampton took on major proportions.

In fact, United were given a lucky draw by avoiding more dangerous opponents and having to take on the Hampshire team that was bottom of the Premiership, heading for relegation. At their new St Mary's Stadium, Southampton were no match for United who went a goal up after just two minutes through Roy Keane. Another goal from Ronaldo just before half-time and two from Paul Scholes in the second half cemented an easy win.

United wanted to avoid Arsenal in the semi-final draw and they did so. Instead, they would play Newcastle United now managed by Graeme Souness and with striker Alan Shearer coming towards the end of his playing career. The United team were under fire for a "not acceptable" (according to Sir Alex Ferguson) performance the week before against relegation-bound Norwich City. Not surprisingly, with a few tweaks to the team, the Reds came back strongly. The Geordies proved to be poor opposition and United ran out 4-1 winners, with van Nistelrooy, Ronaldo and Scholes on the scoresheet.

Arsenal would also have a relatively easy passage to the final by beating Blackburn Rovers 3-0, and matching up with the Reds at the Millennium Stadium in Cardiff in May would mean the fifth meeting of the season between the two teams. The Londoners had won the FA Charity Shield back in August, but United were victorious in both league meetings and a League Cup tie at Old Trafford. With Arsenal finishing second and United third in the final Premiership standings (both behind Chelsea), it promised to be a great final.

However, the Glazer takeover returned to the headlines during the big match build-up and five days before the last game of the season took place the American announced he had 75 per cent of the United shares and was now in complete control of the club, but whether this would affect the focus of the players on the game ahead was highly unlikely.

2006/07

19 May 2007 at Wembley Stadium, London

Manchester United (0) 0-1 (0) Chelsea

Goals: Drogba 116'

Attendance: 89,826

With no sign of Sir Alex Ferguson's passion for winning trophies diminishing, the manager had made another bold move in the off-season months before the FA Cup campaign began. Ruud van Nistelrooy had been transferred to Real Madrid to leave room for Wayne Rooney and Cristiano Ronaldo to share the striking responsibilities with Louis Saha. By the time of the third round match at home to Aston Villa, it was clearly proving successful both in the league and Europe.

Ferguson's annual dilemma of which squad players to start in the early rounds of the cup was still causing some worry, but on this occasion he retained much of his strongest side and triumphed 2-1, with goals from Henrik Larsson and substitute Ole Gunnar Solskjaer.

The same tactic was adopted in the fourth round, another home tie against another Premiership team, Portsmouth, and the result was exactly the same as well. A 2-1 win came courtesy of a brace of goals from Rooney.

As mid-February arrived, so did both the fifth round tie at Old Trafford against Reading (managed by former United favourite Steve Coppell) and a run of Champions League knockout games. The last thing the manager wanted was a draw against the Berkshire team, but that is just what he got. Ferguson rested Giggs, Rooney and Ferdinand and paid the price in a 1-1 draw with Michael Carrick scoring United's goal.

The replay was crammed into the schedule 10 days later and provided an exciting encounter that United won 3-2 (Gabriel Heinze, Saha and Solskjaer were the Reds' scorers).

As March arrived, it was clear that United were now fighting alongside Chelsea for the Premiership, the FA Cup and the Champions League; both clubs had a chance of a treble with two months of the season to go. In the sixth

round of the FA Cup, United were drawn to play away at Middlesbrough, yet another Premiership opponent.

An early Rooney goal was cancelled out by two from Boro, one just before half-time and the other a few minutes after. Only goalkeeper Tomasz Kuszczak could be considered a true squad player in this team, so it was no surprise that United had the strength to equalise, which they did from a Ronaldo penalty with 21 minutes left. In the replay at Old Trafford, Boro again fought hard and it was another Ronaldo penalty that proved decisive. The only difference was that this time the Portuguese's spot kick was the only goal and United were into the semi-finals.

By now, the Reds knew that it would be Premiership teams all the way in this year's FA Cup when Watford were drawn as their opponents (they missed Chelsea, who had to play Blackburn Rovers). The Hertfordshire team was on the slippery road to relegation this season and the semi-final would happen four days after United's fabulous 7-1 win in the Champions League quarter-final against Roma. United would stride into the semi full of confidence, despite facing eight matches in the month of April (this was the third of that sequence).

It was a full strength team that proved much too classy for Watford. Rooney got the first goal after just seven minutes. Watford equalised after 25 minutes then the Reds snatched the lead back almost immediately through Ronaldo. Two second-half goals – Rooney again and one from substitute Kieran Richardson – wrapped up the game and set up the encounter with Chelsea that every neutral fan wanted to see.

Both league games between the two teams earlier this season had ended in draws, so the result of the final was not an easy one to forecast and thoughts of a treble for both teams ended with losses in the Champions League semi-finals a few weeks later, although United took the Premiership with two games to spare and so the FA Cup final at least gave the Reds a chance of a fourth double.

THE FINAL

The hard-driving Wayne Rooney is foiled by a brave Petr Cech.

IT WAS THE first time since 1986 that the top two teams in the league would face each other in the season's FA Cup final. This was also a much-anticipated match for another reason: football was coming home as this would be the first FA Cup final to be played at the re-built Wembley Stadium after six years at the Millennium Stadium in Cardiff.

There was a great deal of respect between the managers Sir Alex Ferguson and Jose Mourinho, but neither wanted to concede an inch in the build-up – although both heaped praise on Cristiano Ronaldo who had won both the Professional Footballers' Association Player of the Year and Young Player of the Year awards, a feat never previously achieved.

The game itself was much less glorious than most experts predicted. Both teams looked tired and tense, especially in the opening exchanges, although Chelsea created the most meaningful chances of the first half.

Mourinho then brought on Arjen Robben for Joe Cole at half-time and the game became a little more open, with Wayne Rooney beginning to look dangerous. Half chances would come at both ends in the second 45 minutes, but there was nothing that either team could do to break the deadlock and so came extra time.

Moments later United thought they might have won the match when Ryan Giggs slid into the six-yard box to connect with a Rooney cross. The ball went to Petr Cech in the Chelsea goal and then appeared to cross the goal line. United players appealed vigorously, however the referee waved play on and their best chance had gone. Four minutes before the final whistle Didier Drogba scored to give the Londoners victory and deny the Reds their fourth double.

Sir Alex Ferguson was magnanimous in defeat, saying that, despite this loss, his young team was set for even greater things in the future.

MANCHESTER UNITED

1	EDWIN VAN DER SAR
6	WES BROWN
4	GABRIEL HEINZE
5	RIO FERDINAND
15	NEMANJA VIDIC
16	MICHAEL CARRICK 112'
24	DARREN FLETCHER 92'
18	PAUL SCHOLES
7	CRISTIANO RONALDO
11	RYAN GIGGS 112'
8	WAYNE ROONEY

Substitutes:

22	JOHN O'SHEA 112'
14	ALAN SMITH 92'
20	OLE GUNNAR SOLSKJAER 112'

CHELSEA

1	PETR CECH
20	PAULO FERREIRA
5	MICHAEL ESSIEN
26	JOHN TERRY
18	WAYNE BRIDGE
4	CLAUDE MAKELELE
8	FRANK LAMPARD
12	JOHN OBI MIKEL
24	SHAUN WRIGHT-PHILLIPS 93'
10	JOE COLE 45'
11	DIDIER DROGBA

Substitutes:

3	ASHLEY COLE 108'
16	ARJEN ROBBEN 45'(ON) 108' (OFF)
21	SALOMON KALOU 93'

Referee: Steve Bennett

MANCHESTER UNITED

MANAGER: SIR ALEX FERGUSON

CHELSEA

MANAGER: JOSE MOURINHO

SEMI-FINALS

14 APRIL 2007		
Manchester United	4-1	Watford
Rooney (2), Ronaldo Richardson		Bouazza

15 APRIL 2007		
Blackburn	1-2	**Chelsea**
Roberts		Lampard, Ballack

1961 The League Cup is introduced as a mid-week tournament with semi-finals and finals being played over two legs. The first winners are Aston Villa who defeat Rotherham United 3-2.

1967 In the first single-match final at Wembley, Third Division Queens Park Rangers become the first club outside the top division to win the League Cup.

1970 With UEFA Cup qualification on offer to the winners, all 92 league clubs enter the competition for the first time.

1973 Tottenham Hotspur confirm their reputation as a cup team, beating Norwich City in the final to win the League Cup for the second time in three years.

1977 For the first time the final goes to a replay. Aston Villa needing a second replay to overcome Everton and win the trophy for the third time.

1982 The League Cup joins forces with the Milk Marketing Board to become the Milk Cup, the first of six sponsors to date.

1983 Liverpool win the third of four consecutive League Cups, defeating Manchester United 2-1 after extra-time at Wembley.

1987 Tottenham's Clive Allen sets the record for most goals in one cup campaign with 12.

1988 Andy Dibble saves Nigel Winterburn's penalty as Luton overcome Arsenal thanks to a late Brian Stein winner.

1989 Frankie Bunn of Oldham Athletic scores six goals in one game against Scarborough, a record for the competition.

1992 After defeat the previous season to Sheffield Wednesday, Manchester United finally win their first League Cup following a 1-0 victory over Nottingham Forest.

1995 Liverpool win the League Cup for the fifth time as Ian Rush makes his sixth final appearance, a record he shares with Emile Heskey.

1997 In the last final to go to a replay, Leicester beat Middlesbrough 1-0 after extra time at Hillsborough.

2001 Now called the Worthington Cup, the final moves to the Millennium Stadium while the new Wembley is under construction, Liverpool beat Birmingham on penalties in the first final to be held outside England.

In a decidedly one-sided affair, ...eir second League

League Cup

THE LEAGUE CUP – its full title is the Football League Cup – came into existence in the 1960-61 season and is restricted to the 92 members of the Football League rather than the many hundreds that are members of the Football Association and who enter the much older FA Cup competition.

The tournament began when floodlighting became more widespread among English football grounds, allowing mid-week, evening kick-offs. All League

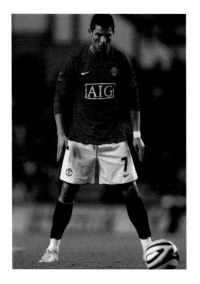

2010 Following victory over Tottenham on penalties the previous year, United retain the League Cup with a 2-1 victory against Aston Villa to win the competition for the fourth time.

Cup games, apart from the final, have always been played mid-week.

As English football's second most significant knockout trophy, the League Cup has suffered a rather chequered history, with some of the top teams not entering in the early years. In addition and more recently, Premiership sides have fielded teams of squad players rather than their first XI because they often consider other silverware – particularly European trophies – more important, taking the decision to rest players rather than select them for the early rounds of the League Cup.

The competition has also had many different sponsors over its 50-year history and has been known by several names: 1982-86 Milk Cup (the Milk Marketing Board were the sponsors); 1986-90 Littlewoods Cup; 1990-92 Rumbelows Cup; 1992-98 Coca-Cola Cup; 1998-2003 Worthington Cup; and 2003-12 Carling Cup.

The current rules state Premiership teams not involved in European competition join the competition in the second round while those who have qualified for Europe from the previous season join in the third round. All ties are one-game-only nowadays, settled by penalties in the case of a draw after extra time, except the semi-finals that have always been two-leg affairs. Winning the final provides a place in European football the following season, which currently means a place in the Europa League.

United entered the very first League Cup competition back in 1960, but exited in the second round against Bradford City and then chose to enter only once (1966-67) in the next eight seasons. However, since 1969-70 the Reds have been part of the competition each year, although they were one of the first clubs to field under-strength teams in the early rounds. Hence it took until 1982-83 for United to make the final (a loss to Liverpool) and, over the years, there have also been embarrassing defeats for the Reds against relatively junior opposition – such as York City and Southend United.

However, in 1990-91 there was another final appearance (although Sheffield Wednesday took the trophy that year) and United finally won the trophy the following season by beating Nottingham Forest; at the time it was Alex Ferguson's third domestic piece of silverware. United did not capture the distinctive three-handled silver cup again until 2005-06 beating Wigan Athletic in the final. The most recent wins were back-to-back in 2008-09 and again in 2009-10; Tottenham Hotspur and Aston Villa were the beaten finalists respectively.

In total United have won the trophy four times with four other appearances in the final. The Reds have also been semi-finalists on five occasions. This means United are the third most successful team in League Cup history behind Liverpool (seven wins) and Aston Villa (five). One significant record is held by a Manchester United player: Norman Whiteside is the youngest ever goalscorer in a final at 17 years 324 days against Liverpool in 1983.

Top Left: 7 January 2009. Cristiano Ronaldo lines up a free kick during the League Cup semi-final first leg match against Derby County.

Top Right: 21 April 1991. Steve Bruce raises his arms in innocence after a challenge on Sheffield Wednesday's Paul Williams.

Opposite: 30 November 1983. Mark Hughes turns to celebrate with Gordon McQueen after scoring in the Football League Cup fourth match against Oxford United Manor Ground in Oxford. ended in a 1-1 draw.

THE FINAL

Gary Bailey is beaten by a curling shot from Liverpool's Ronnie Whelan for the winning goal.

UNITED FOUND THEMSELVES rather on the back foot during the build-up to the final because Bob Paisley had announced his retirement as Liverpool manager and would be leading his team out at a Wembley final for the last time. With Ron Atkinson having won nothing so far with United and his opposite number already a legend in the game, the press focused on Liverpool, talking repeatedly about the likelihood of a sentimental last cup win for Paisley.

When this game was staged, United had just slipped to third place in the league and were a massive 16 points behind Liverpool. United were considerable underdogs for the final, but cup victories were definitely Atkinson's best bet for the first elusive Reds silverware.

Both league matches between the two teams had been tight affairs, ending in draws; so United had no reason to be intimidated. Atkinson put out his best XI and looked to play an attacking game. The tactic worked when Norman Whiteside opened the scoring after just 12 minutes. However, Liverpool were not going to lie down and piled on the pressure in search of an equaliser.

United held on to their lead until 15 minutes before the end when Liverpool full back Alan Kennedy rifled a left-foot shot from 25 yards across Gary Bailey's out-stretched arms and into the net.

As the game went into extra time, Liverpool's experience seemed to pay off. Kennedy was again involved in the build up to the winning goal. Eight minutes in, he made a forward run and passed the ball to Ronnie Whelan who curled a right-foot shot around Bailey. Listening to pundits saying how fitting the Liverpool victory was for Bob Paisley was no consolation for Atkinson and his team.

MANCHESTER UNITED

1	GARY BAILEY
2	MIKE DUXBURY
3	ARTHUR ALBISTON
4	REMI MOSES
5	KEVIN MORAN 69'
6	GORDON MCQUEEN
7	RAY WILKINS
8	ARNOLD MUHREN
9	FRANK STAPLETON
10	NORMAN WHITESIDE
11	STEVE COPPELL

Substitutes:

12	LOU MACARI 69'

LIVERPOOL

1	BRUCE GROBBELAAR
2	PHIL NEAL
3	ALAN KENNEDY
4	MARK LAWRENSON
5	RONNIE WHELAN
6	ALAN HANSEN
7	KENNY DALGLISH
8	SAMMY LEE
9	IAN RUSH
10	CRAIG JOHNSTON 83'
11	GRAEME SOUNESS

Substitutes:

12	DAVID FAIRCLOUGH 83'

Referee: George Courtney

MANCHESTER UNITED

MANAGER: RON ATKINSON

LIVERPOOL

MANAGER: BOB PAISLEY

SEMI-FINALS

1ST LEG 15 FEBRUARY 1983

Arsenal	2-4	Manchester United
Nicholas, Woodcock		Coppell (2), Stapleton, Whiteside

2ND LEG 23 FEBRUARY 1983

1982/83

26 March 1983 at Wembley Stadium, London

Manchester United (1) 1-2 (0) Liverpool (aet)

Goals: Whiteside 12', Kennedy 75', Whelan 98'

Attendance: 100,000

United had already been eliminated from the UEFA Cup in the first round by the time they opened their League Cup campaign this season and Ron Atkinson was still chasing his first trophy as United manager. Atkinson was trying to build a side with flair and pace, but it lacked consistency, so having just lost on aggregate after two games against Valencia of Spain in Europe, it was a relief to face lowly Bournemouth of the Third Division in the League Cup, also over two legs.

A 2-0 win at Old Trafford, with Frank Stapleton opening the scoring and a Bournemouth own goal adding the second, was a decent start for the Reds, but a 2-2 draw in the return leg was anything but convincing by a full-strength team. Steve Coppell and Arnold Muhren provided the goals.

Another Third Division side, Bradford City, also proved to be awkward opponents in the next round. The Reds survived a 0-0 draw at Valley Parade in front of 15,000 fans, which meant a replay, that United then dominated 4-1 (Arthur Albiston, Coppell, Kevin Moran and Remi Moses were the scorers).

Fellow First Division team Southampton were next up on the first day of December and finally United showed their true mettle by dispatching the south coast team 2-0 with goals from Gordon McQueen and Norman Whiteside.

It was six weeks before the quarter-final tie against Nottingham Forest in mid-January and, excluding one blip against Coventry City in the league (a 3-0 loss), the Reds were unbeaten during that period: their defence keeping six clean sheets. So when Forest turned up at Old Trafford and were beaten 4-0, it marked one of United's best performances of the season; McQueen scored two more with Coppell and Bryan Robson adding the others. United were now looking like a good bet in both cup competitions, as they also began beating FA Cup opponents this month and moved up to second place in the league.

The new-found cup confidence was even more in evidence when they took on Arsenal in the semi-finals. Frank Stapleton would be facing his former teammates – an additional incentive for the Irishman to reach another Wembley final. With captain Bryan Robson and Remi Moses controlling the midfield, United shot out of the blocks to a 2-0 half-time lead, with Whiteside and then Stapleton scoring the goals.

With the ineffective under soil heating making the Highbury pitch muddy on one side and frozen on the other, it was fitting that winger Steve Coppell swapped his boots at half-time to get more grip –and scored two goals as a result. At 4-0, United were cruising and could easily have scored even more goals, but failed to close out the game, conceding two late Arsenal consolation goals. However, a 4-2 win was United's best away performance in any competition so far this season and was actually the first time the Red Devils had won at the home of Arsenal since 1968.

United needed a gutsy display in the second leg as Arsenal came to Old Trafford in a determined mood. The bone-hard pitch made good football difficult, but the Reds maintained their concentration as the Gunners' tackles went flying in and following the loss of Robson to an ankle injury after 11 minutes. The game was a scoreless stalemate until Coppell (with his sixth goal of the competition) made it 1-0 after a bold McQueen foray into the attack after 72 minutes. Although a now desperate Arsenal equalised with eight minutes remaining, the Reds were home and dry when Moran scored United's second in the 2-1 win on the night, 6-3 on aggregate.

In the other semi, the League Cup holders Liverpool beat Burnley of the Second Division in their two legs and so English football's top two teams of the season were due to meet in the final.

1990/91

21 April 1991 at Wembley Stadium, London

Manchester United (0) 0-1 (1) Sheffield Wednesday

Goals: Sheridan 37'

Attendance: 77,612

After Alex Ferguson had won his first trophy at United last season (the FA Cup), there was both relief and expectation around Old Trafford at the start of this season. The relief was that the manager would have more time to build his team and the expectation was of more silverware to come. The League Cup was still a trophy that had never appeared on United's list of achievements, with the club appearing in only one final hitherto. This year's run started in the autumn with the two-leg contest against Halifax Town of the Fourth Division, who would go on to finish in 90th place in the entire Football League at the end of the season. And, as should have been the case once United decided to send a full-strength team to The Shay for the first leg, United returned with a convincing 3-1 victory; the scorers were Clayton Blackmore, Brian McClair and Neil Webb. The tie was wrapped up easily enough in the second leg at Old Trafford that ended in a 2-1 win with a rare goal from Viv Anderson and the other from Steve Bruce.

In October, their next opponents could not have been more different – the defending league champions Liverpool. As always, United against Liverpool was a massive draw and over 42,000 turned up at Old Trafford (twice the number that attended the Halifax home League Cup fixture). The crowd witnessed a fine 3-1 United victory, with Bruce, Mark Hughes and Lee Sharpe grabbing the goals and providing some revenge for a 4-0 league loss back in September at Anfield. It was also Liverpool's first defeat of the season in any competition.

While Liverpool at home was a tough fixture, the draw for the next round offered a similarly tough test: Arsenal at Highbury. By this stage of the season – late November – the Reds had won through two rounds of the

European Cup-Winners' Cup, but they were only sixth in the league and looking for signs of better form to come. At Highbury on 28 November, they definitely found it.

The two teams had been hauled in front of the football authorities just a month earlier for a 21-man brawl in the league game at Old Trafford, but this encounter was all about goals. Clayton Blackmore shot the Reds into the lead after just 80 seconds of the match, while Hughes and Sharpe added two more just before half-time to leave the Gunners reeling in front of their own fans.

In a remarkable second half, Arsenal brought the score back to 3-2, but then another slick United attack ended with a Sharpe header for 4-2. The young midfielder completed his hat-trick before Danny Wallace scored the final goal in a 6-2 win.

Another tough First Division opponent was waiting in the quarter-finals, Southampton at The Dell. The hard-fought 1-1 draw that the Red Devils achieved (Hughes again on the scoresheet) was topped in the replay by a 3-2 win and a Hughes hat-trick.

Leeds United then stood in the way of the Reds and only their second League Cup final appearance and Sharpe again took centre stage with a man of the match display in the first leg that ended in a 2-1 win at Old Trafford (Sharpe and McClair the scorers), although Wallace missed a good chance near the end. United held the upper hand for the second leg and they had goalkeeper Les Sealey to thank for an outstanding display that demoralised Leeds so much that the Reds sneaked a winner (Sharpe again) in injury time to win 1-0 on the day and 3-1 on aggregate.

United were in top form and had suffered just one loss between the Arsenal League Cup victory at the end of November and the semi-final triumph in late February. However, it would be another two months before the final against Sheffield Wednesday from the Second Division; there was time for form to change.

THE FINAL

The captains Bryan Robson and Nigel Pearson shake hands prior to the kick-off.

ALEX FERGUSON'S TEAM had dispatched some of the best teams in the country to make the League Cup final: Arsenal would go on to be league champions; Liverpool would finish runners-up; and Leeds United managed fourth spot. Southampton had also been defeated after an away tie at The Dell where the team was often so dangerous. However, finding ex-United manager Ron Atkinson waiting in the final with his Second Division side Sheffield Wednesday was not ideal for Ferguson.

United's current manager had replaced Atkinson at Old Trafford almost five years earlier and the build-up to the game allowed plenty of opportunity for the press to make the most of the comparisons between the two managers' achievements past and present.

United had been in superb form in February when they won their semi-final, but had now gone slightly off the boil as European Cup-Winners' Cup fixtures were mixed with their league games and the anticipation of a rare Wembley visit. There was also the question of fixture congestion for United who were still adjusting to regular European games late in the season; this final took place just three days before the second leg of the European competition quarter-final and it seemed to disturb the Reds.

Meanwhile, the underdogs, Wednesday, were on course for a return to the First Division with promotion at the end of the season. On the day a goal from John Sheridan (a self-confessed Manchester City fan) settled the match; his fierce right-foot shot from just outside the penalty area after 37 minutes was parried by Les Sealey's left hand onto the inside of the post and into the net. It was enough for Atkinson to take the trophy and to deny the Reds a League Cup triumph in the 30th anniversary of the competition.

MANCHESTER UNITED	
1	LES SEALEY
2	DENIS IRWIN
3	CLAYTON BLACKMORE
4	STEVE BRUCE
5	NEIL WEBB 55'
6	GARY PALLISTER
7	BRYAN ROBSON
8	PAUL INCE
9	BRIAN McCLAIR
10	MARK HUGHES
11	LEE SHARPE
Subsitistes:	
14	MIKE PHELAN 55'

SHEFFIELD WEDNESDAY	
1	CHRIS TURNER
2	ROLAND NILSSON
3	PHIL KING
4	JOHN HARKES 87'
5	PETER SHIRTLIFF
6	NIGEL PEARSON
7	DANNY WILSON
8	JOHN SHERIDAN
9	DAVID HIRST
10	PAUL WILLIAMS
11	NIGEL WORTHINGTON
Subsitutes:	
12	LAWRIE MADDEN 87'

Referee: Ray Lewis

SEMI-FINALS

1ST LEG 10 FEBUARY 1991		
Manchester United	2-1	Leeds United
McClair, Sharpe		Whyte

2ND LEG 24 FEBUARY 1991		
Leeds United	0-1	Manchester United
		Sharpe

1ST LEG 24 FEBUARY 1991		
Chelsea	0-2	Sheffield Wednesday
		Shirtliff, Hirst

2ND LEG 27 FEBUARY 1991		
Sheffield Wednesday	3-1	Chelsea
Pearson, Wilson, P Williams		G. Stuart

MANCHESTER UNITED

MANAGER: ALEX FERGUSON

SHEFFIELD WEDNESDAY

MANAGER: RON ATKINSON

THE FINAL

The victorious team. Finally, United win the League Cup for the first time.

HOW WOULD HE win the League Cup for the first time was the relentless question put to Alex Ferguson during the build-up to the game. Ferguson knew that Brian Clough's Nottingham Forest – who had already won this trophy four times including as recently as two years ago – would be anything but easy to beat. United's manager also knew he was dealing with an experienced Wembley manager in Clough and that his United team had lost to Forest 1-0 at the City Ground less than a month earlier. So he made a tactical switch by starting both his wingers, Andrei Kanchelskis and Ryan Giggs, at Wembley when they had both been substitutes for the losing league game. Ferguson also chose a more cautious midfield line-up with defensive-minded Mike Phelan (who had started only one League Cup tie this season up until the final) playing in place of Neil Webb (who was more likely to move up to support his forwards). Webb and the popular Lee Sharpe were on the bench.

It proved to be a brilliant decision, especially when Brian McClair scored for United after just 14 minutes in a simple move: a pass from the halfway line by Gary Pallister straight to McClair, who touched the ball on to Giggs. He ran straight at the centre of the Forest defence before slipping the return pass to the Scot, whose left-foot shot from near the penalty spot easily beat the goalkeeper.

With a goal lead, United were able to gain control of the game, taking the wind out of Forest's sails. The Red Devils' defence held out against a talented forward line led by Teddy Sheringham and supported by midfielder Roy Keane (both future favourites at Old Trafford). United finally had the League Cup to bring to the Old Trafford trophy room and, among others, Giggs got his first winners' medal from this match.

MANCHESTER UNITED

1	PETER SCHMEICHEL
2	PAUL PARKER
3	DENIS IRWIN
4	STEVE BRUCE
5	MIKE PHELAN
6	GARY PALLISTER
7	ANDREI KANCHELSKIS 75'
8	PAUL INCE
9	BRIAN MCCLAIR
10	MARK HUGHES
11	RYAN GIGGS

Substitutes:

12	LEE SHARPE 75'

NOTTINGHAM FOREST

1	ANDY MARRIOTT
2	GARY CHARLES 70'
3	BRETT WILLIAMS
4	DES WALKER
5	DARREN WASSALL
6	ROY KEANE
7	GARY CROSBY
8	SCOT GEMMILL
9	NIGEL CLOUGH
10	TEDDY SHERINGHAM
11	KINGSLEY BLACK

Substitutes:

12	BRIAN LAWS 70'

Referee: George Courtney

MANCHESTER UNITED

MANAGER: ALEX FERGUSON

NOTTINGHAM FOREST

MANAGER: BRIAN CLOUGH

SEMI-FINALS

1ST LEG 4 MARCH 1992		
Manchester United	0-0	Middlesbrough
2ND LEG 11 MARCH 1992		
Manchester United	2-1	Middlesbrough
Sharpe, Giggs		Slaven
1ST LEG 9 FEBRUARY 1992		
Nottingham Forest	1-1	Tottenham Hotspur
Sheringham		Lineker
2ND LEG 1 MARCH 1992		
Tottenham Hotspur	1-2	Nottingham Forest
Lineker		Glover, Keane

1991/92

12 April 1992 at Wembley Stadium, London

Manchester United (1) 1-0 (0) Nottingham Forest

Goals: McClair 14'

Attendance: 76,810

As losing finalists for the second time last season, the League Cup was still the one significant English football trophy that United had never won, despite the competition starting just over three decades ago. It was Alex Ferguson's sixth season in charge and he currently had just one FA Cup and the Cup-Winners' Cup trophy to his name, so picking up more silverware would definitely be a worthy achievement.

This season's campaign began with a two-leg second round contest against Cambridge United, who were enjoying their best ever period in the Football League, playing in the Second Division; they would go one to make the playoffs at the end of this season. However, goals from Steve Bruce, Ryan Giggs and Brian McClair in the first leg really settled the result and a 1-1 draw in Cambridge with a slightly weakened team meant mission accomplished.

Portsmouth were another team challenging for promotion from the Second Division this season and came to Old Trafford looking for at least a draw. But once again United proved too strong, although Mark Robins had to come off the bench to score two goals and Bryan Robson got the other in a 3-1 victory.

Into the last 16 and United faced First Division near neighbours Oldham Athletic in round four. This was a team managed by Joe Royle that caused United considerable torment in the 1990 FA Cup semi-final, but this meeting proved less troublesome and a 2-0 home win, with goals from Andrei Kanchelskis and McClair, put the Red Devils into the quarter-finals.

An away draw at Leeds United was obviously the most anticipated tie of the next round because both clubs were vying for the league championship and matches between them were always going to be a close affair. The two teams had already drawn both this season's

league matches 1-1 and they knew each other well. But Ferguson's players had lost 4-1 at home in the league to Queens Park Rangers a few days before the match and were on the end of a a severe dressing down by the manager. The Leeds League Cup encounter therefore saw a different United attitude and a different result: a 3-1 victory with Clayton Blackmore, Giggs and Kanchelskis on the scoresheet. Leeds would go on to take the First Division title (the last before the introduction of the Premier League) and did not lose a single game at Elland Road while winning this silverware, so given the context, United's League Cup display was an outstanding performance.

The semi-final draw was lucky for United who missed Nottingham Forest and Tottenham Hotspur of the First Division and, instead, were pitched against Middlesbrough of the Second Division. However, the men from the north-east raised their game in the home leg at Ayresome Park, especially as they were facing former star Gary Pallister for the first time since he left for Old Trafford in 1989. Peter Schmeichel had to make several outstanding saves to keep Boro off the scoresheet, while his opposite number Steve Pears (a former United reserve keeper) also kept a clean sheet. Neil Webb had United's best chance but blasted a McClair cross over the bar. The 0-0 draw in that first leg was a good result for United against a team that would go on to finish runners-up in the Second Division.

A week later United could not play Mark Hughes because of suspension, but welcomed back Lee Sharpe from a long-term hernia injury. It was Sharpe who opened the scoring with a vicious shot in the 30th minute, but Boro equalised early in the second half and there was drama when a Pallister goal line clearance stopped Boro taking the lead. However, the deadlock remained unbroken until extra time during which the ever lively Giggs eventually provided the goal for a 2-1 United win that sent Ferguson to Wembley for a third cup final.

1993/94

27 March 1994 at Wembley Stadium, London

Manchester United (0) 1-3 (1) Aston Villa

Goals: Hughes 82', Atkinson 25', Saunders 75', 90' (pen)

Attendance: 77,231

This would be one of the most remarkable United seasons for many years, with drama in all competitions including the League Cup.

The campaign started innocuously enough in the autumn with a tight contest over two legs against Stoke City, a club managed by ex-United star Lou Macari. A 2-1 loss (Dion Dublin scored his first goal since returning from a 12-month injury) to the Potters of the First Division was no disgrace, but a 2-0 win at Old Trafford was more in keeping with the Reds' Premier League form that was already outstanding. Brian McClair and Lee Sharpe were the scorers.

Now into the third round, United were drawn against Leicester City, another First Division team, but the Red Devils totally overpowered the Midlanders 5-1, with Steve Bruce scoring twice and Mark Hughes, McClair and Sharpe getting the other goals.

Away to Everton in the fourth round in November looked tricky, but United were hitting their stride for the season (despite a rare slip-up that put them out of the European Cup earlier in the month). The Goodison outfit were dispatched 2-0 with goals from Ryan Giggs and Mark Hughes.

Portsmouth – the third opponents from the First Division – caused a fright by holding a full-strength United to a 2-2 draw at Old Trafford in the next round (Eric Cantona and Giggs on the scoresheet) and the replay was no easier at Fratton Park. Only another goal from McClair was the difference between the two teams.

Strangely, the two-leg semi-final against Premiership Sheffield Wednesday proved to be easier than the matches against the south coast team. The first leg at Old Trafford was a dull affair, with Wednesday's manager Trevor Francis determined to limit the

damage in the difficult away leg. The Yorkshire team relied on dogged defence and United dealt easily with the rare counter attacks. The Reds won 1-0 thanks to another Giggs goal, this one a masterly piece of anticipation to latch on to a poor back pass, rounding the goalkeeper and squeezing the ball into the net from the tightest of angles, the goal coming after 20 minutes.

The Reds totally controlled the second leg and looked in sparkling form as they eventually ran out 4-1 winners (5-1 on aggregate). There was no Eric Cantona because of injury, but United still had far too much firepower for Wednesday. McClair, who had seen only rare starts in the league, was one of the heroes on the night and he doubled United's aggregate lead after just four minutes, ramming home a cross from Roy Keane. Then Andrei Kanchelskis was on hand at the far post just eight minutes later to make it 2-0. Although Wednesday pulled a goal back, Hughes (nursing ankle and heel injuries) made it 3-1 before half-time. The Welshman was in dominant mood and added the fourth when he volleyed home a pass from McClair with a minute left.

It would be just over three weeks before the final in late March and during that period United lost their first league match since mid-September, but more awkwardly had Peter Schmeichel sent off in an FA Cup tie meaning the Danish goalkeeper would miss the League Cup final that would be against Aston Villa.

The Midlands team had already been beaten twice by the Reds in the league, but the one-off Wembley final would provide new storylines for the press. Firstly, ex-United manager Ron Atkinson had taken over at Villa a few seasons earlier and had another former Red, Paul McGrath, at the centre of his defence.

Add to that the fact that in 1991, a Sheffield Wednesday team also led by Atkinson had beaten Ferguson's United in that year's final of the League Cup and there was always going to be plenty of reasons for fans to enjoy the pre-match build-up.

THE FINAL   Villa's Dalian Atkinson beats United keeper Les Sealey to score the first goal with Steve Bruce and Paul Parker helpless.

THERE WAS NEVER any doubt that this match would be billed as United's current manager Alex Ferguson against his immediate predecessor Ron Atkinson – now in charge of Aston Villa. Ferguson had finally won the League Cup for United two years earlier, as well as last season delivering the club's first league championship for over a quarter of a century. Certainly, neither of the team bosses showed any animosity towards each other in the build-up, but the media loved the idea of the two managers' teams slugging it out, so there was the inevitable extra level of tension in the Wembley atmosphere as the game kicked off.

Outside of this game, United were on their way to a first league and cup double, so they were the pre-match favourites and started the better of the two sides. However, a flick-on just outside his own penalty area caught United's Steve Bruce flat-footed and after 25 minutes Villa went ahead through Dalian Atkinson.

In the second half, United continued to press while Villa were happy to counter attack, but in truth, the Reds created few chances. Then, with just 15 minutes left, a free kick from the left wing swung towards United's goal and Dean Saunders deflected the ball past Les Sealey for 2-0.

There was time for Mark Hughes to get a goal back for the Reds and set up a rousing last eight minutes, but another Villa breakaway led to Andrei Kanchelskis handling a goal-bound shot and conceding a penalty.

To make matters worse for United, referee Keith Cooper decided he had to red card Kanchelskis before Saunders made it 3-1 from the spot and gave Villa an unexpected cup.

MANCHESTER UNITED
13 LES SEALEY
2 PAUL PARKER
4 STEVE BRUCE 83'
6 GARY PALLISTER
3 DENIS IRWIN
14 ANDREI KANCHELSKIS
16 ROY KEANE
8 PAUL INCE
11 RYAN GIGGS 68'
7 ERIC CANTONA
10 MARK HUGHES
Substitutes:
5 LEE SHARPE 68'
9 BRIAN McCLAIR 83'

ASTON VILLA
13 MARK BOSNICH
2 EARL BARRETT
5 PAUL McGRATH
4 SHAUN TEALE
3 STEVE STAUNTON 79'
11 TONY DALEY
25 GRAHAM FENTON
14 ANDY TOWNSEND
6 KEVIN RICHARDSON
10 DALIAN ATKINSON
9 DEAN SAUNDERS
Substitutes:
17 NEIL COX 79'

Referee: Keith Cooper

SEMI-FINALS

1ST LEG 16 FEBRUARY 1994		
Tranmere Rovers	3-1	Aston Villa
Nolan, Hughes, Aldridge		Atkinson

2ND LEG 27 FEBRUARY 1994		
Aston Villa	3-1	Tranmere Rovers
(Villa won 5-4 on penalties)		
Saunders, Teale, Atkinson		Aldridge (pen)

1ST LEG 13 FEBRUARY 1994		
Manchester United	1-0	Sheffield Wednesday
Giggs		

2ND LEG 2 MARCH 1994		
Sheffield Wednesday	1-4	Manchester United
Hirst		McClair, Kanchelskis, Hughes (2)

MANCHESTER UNITED

MANAGER: ALEX FERGUSON

ASTON VILLA

MANAGER: RON ATKINSON

THE FINAL

Mikael Silvestre rises above El Hadji Diouf of Liverpool.

UNITED HAD DEFINITELY enjoyed some significant wins over Liverpool in the last decade with Sir Alex Ferguson as manager, and even won the one league meeting so far this season (a 2-1 victory), partly thanks to a mistake by Liverpool goalkeeper Jerzy Dudek letting in Diego Forlan. The win had demonstrated the current gap between the two teams, but under Frenchman Gerard Houllier, Liverpool had begun winning trophies of their own in recent seasons, and would be dangerous final opponents.

This was the first time Ferguson had faced Houllier in a cup competition since 1999, and was a repeat of the final exactly 20 years earlier.

There was much sparring in the opening minutes of the game, although United had the best of the early exchanges. Ryan Giggs had been one of United's pre-match injury worries, along with Paul Scholes and Wes Brown, but all three eventually started the game, and Giggs nearly helped Ruud van Nistelrooy open the scoring after 20 minutes.

Liverpool then started to push forward and as half-time approached they took an unexpected lead with a slice of good fortune. Steven Gerrard lined up a shot from 25 yards and when it deflected off David Beckham it gave United keeper Fabien Barthez little chance as it looped in over his head.

On the stroke of half-time, Juan Sebastian Veron had a good effort saved and Paul Scholes hit the rebound goalwards only for it to be sensationally blocked on the line. Liverpool keeper Dudek then pulled off a series of great saves from van Nistelrooy twice and Scholes in the second half. The inevitable then happened as United threw men forward, Michael Owen broke free and made the score 2-0 with just four minutes left.

MANCHESTER UNITED

1	FABIEN BARTHEZ
2	GARY NEVILLE
24	WES BROWN 74'
6	RIO FERDINAND
27	MIKAEL SILVESTRE
7	DAVID BECKHAM
16	ROY KEANE
4	JUAN SEBASTIAN VERON
11	RYAN GIGGS
18	PAUL SCHOLES
10	RUUD VAN NISTELROOY

Substitutes:

| 20 | OLE GUNNAR SOLSKJAER 74' |

LIVERPOOL

1	JERZY DUDEK
23	JAMIE CARRAGHER
2	STEPHANE HENCHOZ
4	SAMI HYYPIA
18	JOHN ARNE RIISE
8	EL HADJI DIOUF 90'
16	DIETMAR HAMANN
17	STEVEN GERRARD
13	DANNY MURPHY
10	MICHAEL OWEN
8	EMILE HESKEY 61'

Substitutes:

25	IGOR BISCAN 90'	MF
5	MILAN BAROS 61', 89'	FW
7	VLADIMIR SMICER 89'	MF

Referee: Paul Durkin

MANCHESTER UNITED

MANAGER: SIR ALEX FERGUSON

LIVERPOOL

MANAGER: GERARD HOULLIER

SEMI-FINALS

1ST LEG 7 JANUARY 2003

| Manchester United | 1-1 | Blackburn Rovers |
| Scholes | | Thompson |

2ND LEG 22 JANUARY 2003

| Blackburn Rovers | 1-3 | Manchester United |
| Cole | | Scholes (2), van Nistelrooy |

1ST LEG 8 JANUARY 2003

| Sheffield United | 2-1 | Liverpool |
| Tonge (2) | | Mellor |

2ND LEG 21 JANUARY 2003

| Liverpool | 2-0 | Sheffield United |
| Diouf, Owen | | |

2002/03

2 March 2003 at Millennium Stadium, Cardiff

Manchester United (0) 0-2 (1) Liverpool

Goals: Gerrard 39', Owen 86'

Attendance: 74,500

It had been over ten years since United last won the League Cup as other trophies – particularly the Champions League – had become more important to the club; squad players were now getting a regular chance in the early rounds of this tournament. However, because the club had qualified for European competition this season, the Red Devils were given a bye into the third round, so they were potentially only five games from the final.

This, however, was not on the minds of the United team that took on Leicester City in the third round in early November. The Midlanders were set on promotion from the First Division back into the top level of English football and wanted the chance to prove themselves against the best. Sir Alex Ferguson knew the danger of a hungry Leicester and sent out a strong team at Old Trafford, who won 2-0 with goals from David Beckham (a penalty) and Kieran Richardson in the last ten minutes.

Burnley, also of the First Division, fared no better against the Reds at Turf Moor in the next round, although a capacity crowd created a real Lancashire derby atmosphere. United won 2-0 with goals from Diego Forlan and Ole Gunnar Solskjaer.

Two weeks later, while United were dealing with the end of the group stage fixtures of the Champions League, Chelsea, managed by Claudio Ranieri, were dispatched 1-0 at Old Trafford thanks to another Forlan goal with just ten minutes remaining.

Only Blackburn Rovers – the winners of last year's League Cup final – now stood between Alex Ferguson's team returning to the final themselves. The two-leg semi-final proved to be no easy passage especially against a Rovers squad containing a host of United old boys – Andy Cole, Dwight Yorke, Keith Gillespie, Henning Berg and John Curtis – all of whom wanted to end Ferguson's remarkable run of never having lost a cup semi-final in English football.

The first leg at Old Trafford was a 1-1 draw, but Rovers left the happier team. It was a game of few clear-cut chances, but Ruud van Nistelrooy should have broken the deadlock just before half-time only to shoot weakly at Blackburn keeper Brad Friedel. So a scoreless first half was a frustration for United, a feeling that only grew when van Nistelrooy missed another good chance ten minutes into the second half.

United pressure told three minutes later when Paul Scholes was on hand to stab home a goal from a couple of yards. Reds fans now wanted their team to press for another, but before they had drawn breath, Rovers equalised.

A cross from Gillespie of all people was headed home by David Thompson. Ferguson introduced Forlan and Solskjaer into the United forward line, but Rovers held out for the valuable draw.

Two weeks later at Ewood Park, Rovers were desperate to hang on to the trophy, but instead met a United team in top form. That said, when Cole put Blackburn in front after 12 minutes, the Reds did not look in control of the semi-final. It took a goal from Scholes on the half hour (shooting past Friedel from eight yards) to convert a United period of intense pressure.

The key moment then came just before half-time after Rovers' Damien Duff had been forced to leave the pitch with an injury (Gillespie replaced him) and Scholes turned up again for a second goal; another cross from the right wing and another positive finish.

United continued to look much the better side in the second half and capped a superb performance with a third goal after 77 minutes. Van Nistelrooy was pulled to the ground by keeper Friedel as he was about to score and was given a penalty which the Dutchman dispatched for a 3-1 victory. But Scholes was the man of the moment. "He won the game for us," said Ferguson afterwards.

2005/06

26 February 2006 Millennium Stadium, Cardiff

Manchester United (1) 4-0 (0) Wigan Athletic

Goals: Rooney 33', 61', Saha 55', Ronaldo 59'

Attendance: 66,866

The League Cup had not been a happy hunting ground for United for more than a decade, with only a semi-final appearance last season and a couple of losing finalist appearances dating back to 1994. However, United were coming off a rare trophyless season under Sir Alex Ferguson, so this year would mean a renewed emphasis on the competition. It began with a good draw in the third round (United's entry point into the competition) at home to Barnet of League Two. The advent of such modest opponents meant Ferguson could send out an almost unrecognisable starting XI compared to the previous league game with only goalkeeper Tim Howard, defender Wes Brown and Kieran Richardson in midfield providing any real experience. Nevertheless, the north Londoners helped hand an easy win to United when their goalkeeper was sent off after just four minutes for handling the ball outside his area. Liam Miller scored from the resulting free kick. Sylvan Ebanks-Blake, Richardson and Giuseppe Rossi scored the other goals in a 4-1 victory.

By the time of the next round, United's fans had been rocked by the departure of club captain Roy Keane, but that did not stop another success as the Reds were at home in the fourth round to West Bromwich Albion, who were again struggling in the Premiership despite the best efforts of their manager former United captain Bryan Robson. Early first-half goals from Cristiano Ronaldo (a penalty) and Louis Saha in the first 16 minutes, plus one in the second half from John O'Shea were enough for United, who conceded one late consolation goal, but ran out comfortable 3-1 winners.

There was another Midlands side awaiting the Reds in the quarter-finals, Birmingham City. The match at St Andrew's was scoreless in the first half,

but United pulled away from their opponents with a sudden burst of scoring. Immediately after the break, Saha put United ahead and Ji-sung Park got a second goal four minutes later before the Frenchman slotted in his second on 63 minutes. A late Birmingham goal was never going to take the tie away from United, who won 3-1 for the second round in succession.

Blackburn provided another Premiership opponent for the semi-final, played over two legs, a repeat of the teams' battle at the same stage of the competition three years earlier. Strangely, Rovers were again managed by another ex-United favourite, this time Mark Hughes, who had taken over in September 2004. But despite Hughes' knowledge of all things United, the Reds held on in what turned out to be a hard-fought first match at Ewood Park, which brought eight bookings. Ex-Red Robbie Savage nearly scored for Blackburn in the opening minute before Saha put United ahead after a pass from Ryan Giggs on the half hour. Blackburn managed an equaliser five minutes later and soon afterwards tempers began to fray. Although United were the better side in the second half, they had to be content with a 1-1 draw.

Then in the return at Old Trafford a fortnight later, Ryan Giggs was forced off with an injury after just 13 minutes, but Wayne Rooney took on the starring role – laying on both the goals in a 2-1 win. United started fast and Ruud van Nistelrooy scored after just eight minutes. Rovers equalised again as they did in the first leg, this time after half an hour, before the Reds were awarded a penalty.

The van Nistelrooy spot kick was saved by Brad Friedel. Tempers flared again between the players in the tunnel as they left the field at half-time, with Savage earning a tongue-lashing from the United manager, but it was the Reds who kept their composure in the second half as Saha once again popped up with the winner after 51 minutes with a looping volley. The Frenchman had now scored five goals in four League Cup games.

WIGAN ATHLETIC HAD surprisingly beaten Arsenal in the other semi-final this season to challenge for the first major trophy in their short history. United were huge favourites to see off their Lancashire rivals, who were managed by the personable Paul Jewell and arguably punching above their weight to reach this final. Sir Alex Ferguson sent out a strong team to ensure some silverware came to Old Trafford. Of the squad-based team that opened the cup campaign against Barnet, only Wes Brown was given a starting role, while Tim Howard and Kieran Richardson were on the bench.

But none of these three played as significant a role in the final as Wayne Rooney who scored twice and picked up the man of the match award. United looked at ease at the Millennium Stadium during the early part of the game while Wigan – who lost their starting goalkeeper early on to a groin pull – were left to chase shadows.

Rooney opened the scoring on 33 minutes after two Wigan defenders collided, but they could not increase the lead during the rest of a first half that they dominated. Athletic came more into the game after the break, but Louis Saha got a second in the 55th minute with a second effort after his initial header had been well saved. The Frenchman had now scored in every League Cup game he played this season.

By this time Wigan were looking like a team somewhat deflated, so when Saha put through Cristiano Ronaldo for the third goal four minutes later, the game was effectively over. There was still time for Rooney to grab his second after a Ryan Giggs free kick two minutes later to make the final half hour of the game something of a walk in the park for the Red Devils.

MANCHESTER UNITED	
19	EDWIN VAN DER SAR
2	GARY NEVILLE
27	MIKAEL SILVESTRE 83'
22	JOHN O'SHEA
5	RIO FERDINAND
6	WES BROWN 83'
7	CRISTIANO RONALDO 73'
13	JI-SUNG PARK
9	WAYNE ROONEY
9	LOUIS SAHA
11	RYAN GIGGS
Substitutes:	
23	KIERAN RICHARDSON 73'
3	PATRICE EVRA 83'
15	NEMANJA VIDIC 83'

WIGAN ATHLETIC	
12	MICHAEL POLLITT 14'
2	PASCAL CHIMBONDA
16	ARJAN DE ZEEUW
6	STEPHANE HENCHOZ 62'
26	LEIGHTON BAINES
19	PAUL SCHARNER
11	GRAHAM KAVANAGH 72'
21	JIMMY BULLARD
30	JASON ROBERTS
20	GARY TEALE
7	HENRI CAMARA
Substitutes:	
1	JOHN FILAN 14'
10	LEE McCULLOCH 62'
23	RETO ZIEGLER 72'

Referee: Alan Wiley

SEMI-FINALS		
1ST LEG 11 JANUARY 2006		
Blackburn Rovers	1-1	Manchester United
Pedersen		Saha
2ND LEG 25 JANUARY 2006		
Manchester United	2-1	Blackburn Rovers
Van Nistelrooy, Saha		Reid
1ST LEG 10 JANUARY 2006		
Wigan Athletic	1-0	Arsenal
Scharner		
2ND LEG 24 JANAURY 2006		
Arsenal	2-1	Wigan Athletic (aet)
Henry, van Persie		Roberts

MANCHESTER UNITED

MANAGER: SIR ALEX FERGUSON

WIGAN ATHLETIC

MANAGER: PAUL JEWELL

THE FINAL

Cristiano Ronaldo attempts one of his trademark free kicks.

TOTTENHAM HOTSPUR WERE the League Cup holders, and returning to the final for the second year running – albeit with a different manager in Harry Redknapp – was already quite an achievement. But United also knew how to compete in this tournament even though it was not the top priority when compared with other trophies. Sir Alex Ferguson had used his squad players to get through the opening rounds and now had a chance to win the cup for the second time in four years. He believed the League Cup was a pot worth winning and demanded one hundred percent commitment to the cause by the team. They meant to win the final.

The manager fielded a near-first choice team against Tottenham, with only three of the starters – goalkeeper Ben Foster, midfielder Darron Gibson and striker Danny Welbeck – being considered other than first team regulars. In fact, Foster pulled off a number of good saves during the game to keep United level as neither team was able to make a breakthrough in the rather tentative first half. Both teams' defences continued to rule in the second half. Cristiano Ronaldo had a penalty appeal turned down and also hit the post with a fierce left-foot shot. Even extra time proved fruitless as many of the players started to tire; the penalty shoot-out duly arrived.

As preparations for the spot kicks got underway, United goalkeeping coach Eric Steele was seen discussing goal-saving tactics with Ben Foster as they watched videos of the Spurs penalty takers on an iPod. The last-minute research proved crucial as Foster's goal was breached only once in three attempts by Spurs players, while United's first four spot kickers all scored. Fittingly, the United keeper was named man of the match.

SEMI-FINALS

1ST LEG 6 JANUARY 2009		
Tottenham Hotspur	4-1	Burnley
Dawson, O'Hara Pavlyuchenko, Duff (og)		Paterson

2ND LEG 21 JANUARY 2009		
Burnley	3-2	Tottenham Hotspur
Blake, McCann, Rodriguez		Pavlyuchenko, Defoe

1ST LEG 7 JANUARY 2009		
Derby County	1-0	Manchester United
Commons		

2ND LEG 20 JANUARY 2009		
Manchester United	4-2	Derby County
Nani, O'Shea, Tevez Ronaldo (pen)		Barnes (2, 1 pen)

MANCHESTER UNITED

MANCHESTER UNITED	
12	BEN FOSTER
22	JOHN O'SHEA 76'
23	JONNY EVANS
5	RIO FERDINAND
3	PATRICE EVRA
7	CRISTIANO RONALDO
18	PAUL SCHOLES
28	DARRON GIBSON 91'
17	NANI
32	CARLOS TEVEZ
19	DANNY WELBECK 56'
Substitutes:	
15	NEMANJA VIDIC 76'
8	ANDERSON 56'
11	RYAN GIGGS 91'

TOTTENHAM HOTSPUR	
1	HEURELHO GOMES
22	VEDRAN CORLUKA
20	MICHAEL DAWSON
26	LEDLEY KING
32	BENOIT ASSOU-EKOTTO
7	AARON LENNON 102'
8	JERMAINE JENAS 98'
4	DIDIER ZOKORA
14	LUKA MODRIC
10	DARREN BENT
9	ROMAN PAVLYUCHENKO 65'
Substitutes:	
3	GARETH BALE 98'
5	DAVID BENTLEY 102'
24	JAMIE O'HARA 65'
Referee: Chris Foy	

MANCHESTER UNITED
MANAGER: SIR ALEX FERGUSON

TOTTENHAM HOTSPUR
MANAGER: HARRY REDKNAPP

2008/09

1 March 2009 Wembley Stadium, London
Manchester United (0) 0-0 (0) Tottenham Hotspur (a.e.t) Manchester United win 4-1 on penalty kicks

Attendance: 88,217

As usual, the third round was when United entered the fray for the League Cup this season, but the team that Sir Alex Ferguson sent out against Middlesbrough was a particularly strong one for the early rounds of the Carling Cup. John O'Shea, Anderson, Nemanja Vidic, Wes Brown, Nani, Ryan Giggs and Cristiano Ronaldo all started the game that United soon dominated. However, 18-year-old Ben Amos was in goal making his first ever United appearance, so Ferguson was still keen to use the competition to blood new talent.

Ronaldo opened the scoring after 25 minutes and the Red Devils looked comfortable until a first-time volley from Boro's Adam Johnson levelled the tie 12 minutes after half-time. The match then turned on a sending off and a resulting bad injury to United's Brazilian midfielder Rodrigo Possebon. The young Reds player suffered a nasty gash on his right leg and a ten-man Boro could not hold out after that. Giggs and Nani scored late on to bring a 3-1 victory.

Queens Park Rangers from the Championship were the next opposition and also had to come to Old Trafford. The London team proved difficult to beat, but mostly because they were reluctant to open up the game and it was only after 73 minutes that they had their first shot on goal.

Before then United's re-jigged team (eight changes from the previous league match) had looked disjointed especially in attack, with Wayne Rooney, Cristiano Ronaldo and Dimitar Berbatov all rested. Carlos Tevez was looking the most likely scorer and, indeed, the Argentine did provide the winning goal from the penalty spot after substitute Danny Welbeck had been fouled four minutes after coming on the pitch.

Into the quarter-finals, United faced more Premiership opposition in the form of Blackburn Rovers, but again Old Trafford was the venue. The game turned out to be a goal-fest and another night for Tevez to shine in front of the home fans.

The first 30 minutes of the game was goalless although both teams had chances to score. Tevez was already showing Rovers that he was the danger man and it was no surprise when he was first to put his name on the scoresheet with a headed goal after 36 minutes. The Argentine also helped Nani make it 2-0 before the break during which former United favourite Paul Ince (now manager of Rovers) brought on a new striker, Roque Santa Cruz, who soon helped pull a goal back. However, Tevez would not be denied and scored three more goals in the second half as United ran out deserving 5-3 winners.

In the draw for the semi-finals, there was only one other Premiership team – Tottenham Hotspur – so United were happy to miss them and pick up Derby County of the Championship as their opponents. Any thoughts of an easy ride to the final were removed in the first leg at Pride Park in which the East Midlands team impressed and ran out 1-0 winners.

County were playing in front of manager-to-be Nigel Clough (son of Brian) who was about to take over a team that had won just one of their last eight league games. Facing a club in turmoil should have meant an easy United win, but the Reds' performance was well below par and, even though the starting line-up was not the strongest, the Premiership team should have had enough class not to lose. In fact, Derby had a golden chance late in the game to make the score 2-0 on the night.

But after such a disappointing first leg, it was a much more determined United who came out at Old Trafford. Nani, O'Shea and Tevez scored before half-time and, although the Rams got a goal back with ten minutes to go and another in injury time, Ronaldo scored with a late penalty and the game ended with a 4-2 win to take the Red Devils to Wembley 4-3 on aggregate.

2009/10

28 February 2010 at Wembley Stadium, London

Aston Villa (1) 1-2 (1) Manchester United

Goals: Milner 5' (pen), Owen 12', Rooney 74'

Attendance: 88,596

The opening game of the campaign for the League Cup holders was full of drama as Wolverhampton Wanderers (newly promoted to the Premiership) came to Old Trafford to face a United team that was entirely different from the one that had faced cross-town rivals Manchester City a few days earlier in the league.

Led by Gary Neville in defence, Michael Carrick in midfield and Michael Owen in attack, the Reds did extremely well to eke out a 1-0 win after 18-year-old full back Fabio was sent off for bringing down a Wolves forward who was breaking through for a scoring chance. Even with ten men, United looked impressive and eventually Danny Welbeck, who was making his first start of the season, slotted home the winner from an Owen pass.

It was another team of squad members that took on Championship side Barnsley in the next round at Oakwell and, again, there was a sending off for a United player, this time Gary Neville. The dismissal came after Welbeck had opened the scoring in the sixth minute with a header from a corner, and Owen had already added a second near the hour mark.

There was enough experience in the United team to keep the 2-0 advantage with ten men and Sir Alex Ferguson was able to enjoy his post-game drink with Barnsley manager and ex-United player Mark Robins. It was their first meeting as managers and revived memories of Robins' key moment as a Red when he was widely credited for having saved Ferguson's job back in 1990 by scoring a vital goal to win an FA Cup tie against Nottingham Forest.

The latest batch of young, home-grown talent had taken some criticism before the League Cup quarter-final against Tottenham Hotspur, the team United beat in last season's final. Many of the youngsters had been involved in a poor Champions League performance the previous week that ended in a 1-0 loss that broke a 23-game unbeaten home run in Europe. Ferguson was quick to defend his charges and started them again against Spurs and the resulting 2-0 win quietened the dissenters.

Midfielder Darron Gibson was the star of the show with two well-taken goals in the first half. A full-strength Spurs did not look dangerous after a lively opening period, although United's ex-Tottenham player Dimitar Berbatov also missed an early chance and was substituted after just over an hour. This had been a relatively easy passage to the semi-final where United were drawn to play Manchester City, who had done well to beat Arsenal 3-0 in their own quarter-final.

The first leg belonged to City's Carlos Tevez, who had left the red half of Manchester for the blue half only last summer. The controversial transfer caused the tie to be even more emotional than under normal circumstances, and when Ryan Giggs put United ahead early on, it seemed to be the crucial turning point. Then Tevez scored two goals either side of half-time to give City a 2-1 win. Tevez's celebration near the United technical area after the second was noted by Ferguson and his team.

The whole city was at fever pitch by the time of the return leg at Old Trafford eight days later. A tense first half was scoreless, but then Paul Scholes broke the deadlock on 52 minutes and Carrick added a second after 71. City's new hero Tevez then scored with an outrageous back heel to level the aggregate scores at 3-3. It looked like extra-time and possibly penalties would be needed to split the teams – until Wayne Rooney headed home a corner from Giggs after two minutes of injury time had been played.

Coming four months after United's dramatic 4-3 league victory at home against City back in September, when an Owen goal in the final seconds brought victory, this had been another magnificent piece of entertainment from the two Manchester clubs.

Antonio Valencia is tackled by Villa's Stephen Warnock.

ASTON VILLA UNDER the guidance of manager Martin O'Neill were going to be tough opponents for United, and the match certainly started out in the Midlanders' favour when Gabriel Agbonlahor was brought down by Nemanja Vidic after just four minutes. Many neutrals thought Vidic should have been red carded for the foul as he was the last line of defence, but referee Phil Dowd simply booked the United centre back and awarded a penalty which put the Reds 1-0 down.

United's line-up was a strong one and the team used all its experience to strike back quickly, as Michael Owen latched onto a Dimitar Berbatov pass to score the equaliser after 12 minutes. Now, just before half-time, Owen left the field with an injury, allowing Wayne Rooney to join the action and the change brought the best out of the Reds; it was Rooney who scored the winning goal with 16 minutes left. The impressive Antonio Valencia managed to find a teasing cross that Rooney headed past Villa keeper Brad Friedel.

O'Neill complained bitterly after the game about Vidic being allowed to stay on the pitch, but United had looked the better team for long periods of the game and ran out deserving winners. Rooney had hit the post with another header and although Villa were also denied by the woodwork late in the game, the Reds held on.

This League Cup campaign had been littered with red cards. United's two sendings off in the early rounds had not proved crucial and it was a non-sending off that this final will be remembered for by many. Nevertheless, Sir Alex Ferguson had retained the trophy, a feat not achieved since Brian Clough's Nottingham Forest had done so in 1989 and 1990.

MANCHESTER UNITED	
29	TOMASZ KUSZCZAK
21	RAFAEL 66'
15	NEMANJA VIDIC
23	JONNY EVANS
3	PATRICE EVRA
25	ANTONIO VALENCIA
24	DARREN FLETCHER
16	MICHAEL CARRICK
13	JI-SUNG PARK 85'
7	MICHAEL OWEN 42'
9	DIMITAR BERBATOV

Substitutes:	
2	GARY NEVILLE 66'
28	DARRON GIBSON 85'
10	WAYNE ROONEY 42'

ASTON VILLA	
1	BRAD FRIEDEL
24	CARLOS CUELLAR 80'
29	JAMES COLLINS
5	RICHARD DUNNE
25	STEPHEN WARNOCK
7	ASHLEY YOUNG
8	JAMES MILNER
19	STILIAN PETROV
8	STEWART DOWNING
18	EMILE HESKEY
11	GABRIEL AGBONLAHOR

Substitutes:	
10	JOHN CAREW 80'

Referee: Phil Dowd

SEMI-FINALS

1ST LEG 14 JANUARY 2010		
Blackburn Rovers	0-1	Aston Villa
		Milner

2ND LEG 20 JANUARY 2010		
Aston Villa	6-4	Blackburn Rovers
Warnock, Milner (pen), N'Zonzi (og), Agbonlahor, Heskey, A.Young		Kalanic (2), Olsson, Emerton

1ST LEG 19 JANUARY 2010		
Manchester City	2-1	Manchester United
Tevez (2, 1 pen)		Giggs

2ND LEG 27 JANUARY 2010		
Manchester United	3-1	Manchester City
Scholes, Carrick, Rooney		Tevez

MANCHESTER UNITED

MANAGER: SIR ALEX FERGUSON

ASTON VILLA

MANAGER: MARTIN O'NEILL

1956 At the suggestion of French journalist Gabriel Hanot, the first European Cup is played using a two-legged knockout format. Real Madrid beat Stade de Reims 4-3 in the final.

1957 Having won the previous year's First Division title, Manchester United enter the European Cup for the first time, losing 5-3 on aggregate in the semi-final to eventual winners Real Madrid.

1960 Real Madrid beat Eintracht Frankfurt 7-3 at Hampden Park, securing the fifth of five consecutive titles since the competition's inception and setting a record for the highest scoring final.

1961 Benfica become the first club to win the European Cup with a team consisting solely of players from the club's home nation.

1966 Benfica set the record for the biggest win over two legs, beating Stade Dudelange of Luxembourg 18-0 on aggregate.

1967 Jock Stein's Celtic triumph 2-1 over Helenio Herrera's Inter Milan to become the first and only Scottish side to win the European Cup.

1968 Ten years on from the Munich disaster, Matt Busby's United defeat Benfica 4-1 at Wembley in front of 100,000 spectators to become the first English club to taste success in Europe's premier competition.

1971 Following Feyenoord's win the previous year, a Johan Cruyff-inspired Ajax win the first of three consecutive titles in a golden period for Dutch football.

1978 Liverpool beat Club Brugge 1-0 at Wembley to become the first English team to retain the trophy after beating Borussia Mönchengladbach a year earlier.

1984 Liverpool win the first final to be decided by penalty shootout, overcoming AS Roma 4-2 in front of a partisan crowd in Rome's Stadio Olimpico.

1985 Juventus beat Liverpool 1-0 to win the European Cup but the game is overshadowed by riots and the death of 39 Italian fans. The result is English clubs are banned from European competition for five years.

1991 The European Cup is reformatted as group stages are introduced.

1993 Manchester United take part in Europe's premier competition for the first time since 1969, exiting to Galatasaray on away goals in the 2nd round.

1994 The competition is renamed the UEFA Champions League. Marseille beat Milan 1-0 to win the inaugural Champions League.

European Cup/ Champions League

WHILE THE FIRST official international football match between countries took place in Europe in 1872 (Scotland against England), it took until 1955 for an annual competition to start between European club sides. A tournament in South America between champions of various countries had already begun in 1948, and formed the blueprint for French journalist and editor of *L'Equipe* magazine Gabriel Hanot's suggestion for a Europe version; it was greeted with almost universal approval.

Of the major European football authorities, only the English FA was reluctant to join in, which was something of a surprise because Hanot's idea had been prompted by a *Daily Mail* newspaper article that claimed Wolverhampton Wanderers of the English First Division were the best football team in the world. The claim was made after Wolves won a string of friendly games against top European opposition in the early 1950s. So, taking Hanot's concept to heart, the rest of Europe went ahead without the English and the European Champions Clubs' Cup (a name soon shortened to the European Cup) was staged in 1955-56; Spain's Real Madrid taking the title.

No English representative in the inaugural competition meant United would become the country's first participating club the following season. When the Busby Babes of 1956-57 beat Anderlecht of Belgium 12-0 in their initial two-leg European Cup encounter in September, the club's mark on European football was made early and powerfully.

In fact, United's long-time love affair with the European Cup – these days known as the UEFA Champions League – is a tale of both considerable triumph and unthinkable tragedy. Three times – in 1967-68, 1998-99 and 2007-08 – United have lifted the enormous silver trophy and each of their victorious finals rates among the most dramatic in the competition's history. But always the club remembers the 1957-58 European Cup campaign during which eight of the fabled Busby Babes were killed on a snowy runway in Munich while returning from a quarter-final victory in Belgrade.

The first European Cup win came ten years after the plane crash and was hugely poignant for those players and officials who survived the tragedy. Most famous among the survivors were manager Matt Busby and his captain Bobby Charlton. Their embrace on the Wembley turf after Benfica had been defeated 4-1 after extra time was a bitter-sweet moment: the immense joy of victory was tempered by the sad memories of Munich and the missing faces.

The 1967-68 win has similarities with the 1998-99 competition. There were stars absent from both finals (Denis Law in 1968 and both Paul Scholes and Roy Keane in 1999). The more recent of these two finals is mostly remembered for the injury time period when both United goals were scored in a 2-1 win over Bayern Munich in the Camp Nou, Barcelona.

The 2007-08 victory over Chelsea in the Luzhniki Stadium, Moscow, lives in the memory more for the successful 6-5 penalty shoot-out rather than the game itself, a 1-1 draw after extra time. As a nod to United's tradition and the special connection with the competition, Bobby Charlton led the team onto the podium during the post-match ceremony to collect their medals.

The Red Devils' fourth and fifth appearances in the final of this competition were in 2008-09 and 2010-11, both against Barcelona. Each time, United failed to shine against the Spanish champions, losing 2-0 and 3-1 respectively.

In terms of records, United are the joint seventh most successful club in European Cup and UEFA Champions League history and Sir Alex Ferguson – who is one of very few managers to win the trophy twice – has continually stressed his desire to see United lift Europe's most prestigious trophy as often as possible to secure their place among the pantheon of great clubs in the world.

There is also a wealth of record-breaking detail behind United's three successes in three different decades: first English team to win (1967-68); one of only nine clubs to win without defeat during the campaign and one of only four to achieve this feat twice (1998-99 and 2007-08); more appearances in the group stage of the competition (17 times) than any other team; consecutive number of appearances in the UEFA Champions League (15 from 1996-97 to 2010-11); joint holders of the record victory in the UEFA Champions League knockout stage (7-1 against Roma in the quarter-final 2006-07); the longest run from the start of a campaign without conceding a goal (481 minutes, from September to December 2009-10); most goals scored in the UEFA Champions League group stage (20, 1998-99); most consecutive home wins (12, ended in September 2008 by a 0-0 draw with Villarreal); longest unbeaten run of 25 games, begun with a 1-0 away win against Sporting Club of Portugal in their opening group stage game in 2007-08 and finished with a 3-1 away win against Arsenal in the second leg of the semi-final in 2008-09 (the unbeaten streak was broken by a 2-0 loss to Barcelona in the 2009 final).

Four United players (the joint most from any one club) have made more than 100 appearances in the UEFA Champions League: Ryan Giggs, Paul Scholes, Gary Neville and David Beckham. The first three played only for United in those appearances, while Beckham also played for both AC Milan and Real Madrid.

Among other player records: Wayne Rooney is the youngest player to score a hat-trick in the UEFA Champions League, aged 18 years 335 days on his Champions League and Manchester United debut, in a 6–2 home win against Fenerbahçe on 28 September 2004; and Michael Owen (including one as a United player) is one of only two players to score three hat-tricks in the UEFA Champions League.

1995 At 18 years, 327 days, Patrick Kluivert becomes the youngest player to score in a Champions League final as Ajax beat AC Milan 1-0.

1999 Manchester United come from 1-0 down against Bayern Munich to snatch victory in dramatic fashion with two injury-time goals and with it win their second European crown.

2000 Real Madrid and Valencia take part in the first final to be contested by teams from the same country.

2006 Jens Lehmann becomes the first player to be sent off in a Champions League final as Arsenal lose 2-1 to Barcelona in the Stade de France.

2008 In an all-England final, United seal victory in dramatic fashion once again with a penalty shootout victory over Chelsea in Moscow's Luzhniki Stadium.

2009 Manchester United fail to retain their title as they succumb 2-0 to Barcelona and their unstoppable star Lionel Messi in Rome.

2011 Messi once again torments United as they are beaten by Barcelona, losing 3-1 in front of a packed Wembley and a global audience of millions.

Top Left: 27 May 2009. Wayne Rooney evades Sylvinho of Barcelona in the UEFA Champions League final.

Top Right: 15 May 1968. Bobby Charlton is overcome with emotion after the European Cup semi-final second leg in the Santiago Bernabeu Stadium, Spain. The 3-3 draw with Real Madrid earned the Red Devils their first ever place in a European Cup final.

THE FINAL

David Sadler stretches for a cross before a packed Wembley crowd.

BENFICA, TWICE EUROPEAN Cup champions and a team packed with Portuguese internationals, including one of the world's best in Eusébio, would present the stiffest of tests for United. On the plus side for the Reds, the final was played at the familiar Wembley Stadium, but they would be without Denis Law because of a knee injury. In addition, Munich memories – especially for survivors Matt Busby, Bobby Charlton and Bill Foulkes – would make it a deeply emotional occasion.

After a cagey and scoreless first-half, Busby's team went ahead after 53 minutes with a Charlton header. John Aston on the left wing was creating chances for United to secure the victory, but Benfica refused to lie down, and late into the second half United seemed to visibly tire. With 15 minutes remaining, Jamie Graça equalised for the Portuguese, who then had two chances to win the game, both falling to Eusébio. The opportunities were spurned – one shot hit the bar and the other prompted a magnificent Alex Stepney save – so the game lumbered into extra time.

Then George Best put his mark on the final. It took just two extra minutes for Best to spin past one defender and round the goalkeeper before stroking the ball into the net for a 2-1 lead. As Benfica struggled to reinvigorate themselves, two more United goals by young Brian Kidd (who had replaced the injured Denis Law and was celebrating his 19th birthday) and Charlton wrapped up a 4-1 victory.

Tears flowed freely, particularly from Busby who had carried the burden of Munich for a decade. He said: "The moment Bobby took the Cup...it cleansed me. It eased the pain of the guilt of going into Europe [ten years ago]. It was my justification."

SEMI-FINALS

1ST LEG 24 APRIL 1968		
Manchester United	1-0	Real Madrid
Best		

2ND LEG 15 MAY 1968		
Real Madrid	3-3	Manchester United
Pirri, Gento, Amancio		Zoco (og), Sadler, Foulkes

1ST LEG 9 MAY 1968		
Benfica	2-0	Juventus
Torres, Eusebio		

2ND LEG 15 MAY 1968		
Juventus	0-1	Benfica
		Eusebio

MANCHESTER UNITED

1	ALEX STEPNEY
2	SHAY BRENNAN
3	TONY DUNNE
4	PAT CRERAND
5	BILL FOULKES
6	NOBBY STILES
7	GEORGE BEST
8	BRIAN KIDD
9	BOBBY CHARLTON
10	DAVID SADLER
11	JOHN ASTON

BENFICA

1	JOSE ENRIQUE
2	ADOLFO CASTILLO
3	HUMBERTO FERNANDES
4	JACINTO SANTOS
5	FERNANDO CRUZ
6	JAIME GRACA
7	MARIO COLUNA
8	JOSE AUGUSTO
9	JOSE TORRES
10	EUSEBIO
11	ANTONIO SIMOES

Referee: Concetto Lo Bello

MANCHESTER UNITED
MANAGER: MATT BUSBY

BENFICA
MANAGER: OTTO GLORIA

1967/68

29 May 1968 at Wembley Stadium, London

Manchester United (0) 4-1 (0) Benefica (a.e.t)

Goals: Charlton 53', 99', Best 93', Kidd 94', Graca 75'

Attendance:100,000

This season would mark the 10-year anniversary of the Munich air disaster and result in a European Cup triumph, something that had been the dream of everyone involved in United during the decade. This year's European Cup competition would be just as tough as ever, with some of the all-time great clubs – Real Madrid, Benfica, Ajax, Juventus and the holders Celtic – heavily involved.

United's first round opponents Hibernians of Malta provided little in the way of resistance. An impressive 4-0 win at Old Trafford with two goals each for David Sadler and Denis Law allowed the English champions to coast to a 0-0 draw in the away leg.

In the second round, United faced a trip to Sarajevo in Yugoslavia and had to cope without the suspended Law and an injured Nobby Stiles. A 0-0 draw in the opening away leg provoked a furious reaction from manager Matt Busby, who felt the Yugoslavs were overly aggressive.

However, chiselling out the draw helped United believe in their chances of ultimate European success. The second leg was just as violent and Sarajevo had a man sent off for a foul on George Best. The game finished in a 2-1 United win (an early goal from John Aston and the second just after the hour mark from Best), but never felt easy, especially when Sarajevo scored with three minutes remaining.

The quarter-final draw was relatively kind to United. Górnik Zabrze of Poland had surprised Dynamo Kiev in the previous round and, though not the most prestigious name left in the competition, they were clearly in fine form. Again without Law and Bill Foulkes (both injured) United won a scrappy first leg with an own goal from a deflected Best shot putting United ahead after an hour, and then another in the 90th minute when Brian Kidd touched in a shot from Jimmy Ryan. The 2-0 scoreline gave United some much-needed breathing space as the second leg proved to be another huge test, particularly as the pitch had a thick covering of snow that was packed down rather than swept away. In sub-zero temperatures, United did well to hold on for a goalless first half. With 105,000 fanatical Poles in the stadium, Gornik snatched a goal after 70 minutes, but United defended brilliantly and went through 2-1 on aggregate.

The semi-final against six-time winners Real Madrid would prove to be a true classic; they were a team United had never beaten in the European Cup so far. It was something that did not look likely to change after an opening leg in Manchester that Best settled with a ferocious left-footed volley after 36 minutes. Just a 1-0 lead, though, still left Real as favourites.

The return match at the Bernabeu was as dramatic as the first leg had been nervous. Any thoughts of protecting the lead evaporated as Real went 2-0 up after 41 minutes. Then a sloppy own goal from Madrid defender Zoco put United back in the game only for the Reds to concede a third goal right on half time.

United were hanging on by their finger tips. In fact the first half could have been even worse as Nobby Stiles narrowly escaped being sent off after throwing a punch at a Madrid player. Busby remained calm and told his team at half-time: "You are great players, but you haven't played tonight. Go out now and play and you will win."

Madrid's attacking fury of the opening 45 minutes was not matched in the second half and United began to gain the momentum. A David Sadler headed goal after 73 minutes put United ahead on the away goals rule and when big Foulkes (who had sprinted half the length of the pitch) met a Best cross for another goal five minutes later, the Reds were in the driving seat.

Madrid could not breach the Red Devils' defence. The 3-3 final score meant a 4-3 aggregate win of real quality and the fact that it was capped off by Munich survivor Foulkes made it all the more sweet.

1998/99

26 May 1999 at Estadio Camp Nou, Barcelona

Manchester United (0) 2-1 (1) Bayern Munich

Goals: Sheringham 90+1', Solskjaer 90+3',
Basler 6'

Attendance: 90,000

After finishing runners-up in the English league last season, United needed to play a two-leg qualifying tie in order to progress to the group stage of the Champions League. The Red Devils' opponents were ŁKs Łódź of Poland and a 2-0 home win in the opening leg in early August (just three days after the FA Charity Shield defeat to Arsenal) was a welcome result. A 0-0 draw a fortnight later in Poland was achieved without too much fuss. However, the reward was to be drawn with powerhouses Barcelona of Spain and Bayern Munich of Germany, plus the experienced Danish campaigners Brondby in the group stage.

The opening two games in the group were both draws, firstly at home to Barcelona (a 3-3 thriller) and then a trip to Munich which looked more hopeful until a late own goal by Teddy Sheringham of all people cancelled out goals from Dwight Yorke and Paul Scholes, leaving the score 2-2.

The next two games against Brondby all-but eliminated the Danes while putting pressure on the other teams. A 6-2 away win (Ryan Giggs with two) was followed by a 5-0 triumph at home. United were now top of the group, while Barcelona were in trouble after two losses to Bayern. If United could avoid defeat in the fifth group match against Barça in the Nou Camp, then progress was assured. In one of the key matches of the campaign, United held their nerve with goals from Yorke (two) and Andy Cole in another pulsating 3-3 draw. In their last group match, a fourth draw – 1-1 at home to Munich – left United group runners-up, one point behind the Germans. United had scored far more goals (20) than Bayern (just nine), but four draws meant a tough opponent in the first knockout match.

United faced Internazionale of Milan, a team packed with stars including

Argentina's Diego Simeone, the man involved in David Beckham's recent World Cup red card. However, Beckham won this latest battle between the two men because his two crosses resulted in two first-leg goals for Yorke as United won 2-0 at Old Trafford.

The second leg was a nervy affair, especially when the Italian team scored mid-way through the second half, but a Scholes goal with two minutes left in the tie ensured that United went through. A second consecutive Italian team was waiting for United in the semi-finals – Juventus of Turin, who were aiming for a fourth consecutive Champions League final, something that seemed likely after the first-leg.

A first-half goal by Juve in Manchester allowed the Italian team to play its natural game of strong defence and quick counter attacks. A loss at home would have made a two-leg victory all but impossible, but United refused to accept defeat and kept pressing forward. In the 92nd minute Giggs scored from another Beckham cross.

Of course, the 1-1 draw meant Juve had a vital away goal, making them clear favourites for another final, particularly when United's lack of success in Italy (the Reds needed to win in Turin, but had never beaten an Italian team on their own soil) was taken into account. In the early minutes of the second-leg, United's greatest fears of another Italian disappointment were brought sharply into relief as Filippo Inzaghi scored two goals in the first 11 minutes. But the true mettle of United's team, especially that of captain Roy Keane, was about to be demonstrated.

Keane began the remarkable fight back by scoring with a header after 24 minutes and just 10 minutes later a Yorke header levelled the match and the aggregate score. More significantly, United now held the away goals advantage. Juventus had no alternative but to go on the attack and started to press forward. And yet United's defending, marshalled by Keane, was outstanding. Finally, with six minutes remaining, Cole scored the decisive winning goal and United had beaten both the competition favourites and their Italian jinx.

THE FINAL

Peter Schmeichel does cartwheels as United score their second and winning goal against Bayern Munich.

THE MATCH AT Barcelona's Nou Camp against Bayern Munich will long be remembered for the most dramatic of endings.

United were without the inspirational Roy Keane and Paul Scholes, who were both suspended after bookings in the second leg of the semi-final, so Ryan Giggs was sent to the right wing and Jesper Blomqvist to the left, while David Beckham moved into centre midfield with Nicky Butt. The changes left United as the underdogs and then their German opponents began the match in sublime fashion with a goal from a free kick after just six minutes. Bayern continued to press, hit the woodwork twice and forced United goalkeeper Peter Schmeichel – playing in his final game for the club – to make numerous saves.

With time running out and no sign of a United comeback, manager Alex Ferguson sent on two new strikers – Teddy Sheringham and Ole Gunnar Solskjær. And how the substitutions worked! If anything, Bayern were still looking the most likely to score as the officials signalled there were just three minutes of injury time remaining. Then Beckham went up to take a corner. United were so desperate for an equaliser that Schmeichel galloped into the German penalty area, yet it was Sheringham who swung his boot at the ball as it bounced around the penalty area, his shot somehow finding its way into the Bayern Munich goal.

As the two teams, the crowd of 90,000 and TV's watching millions began mentally preparing themselves for extra time, a last United attack resulted in one of United's most famous goals. This time it was Solskjær who stabbed home an unlikely winner. And so the Cup was United's (see picture overleaf) on the day that would have been the late Sir Matt Busby's 90th birthday.

MANCHESTER UNITED

1	PETER SCHMEICHEL
2	GARY NEVILLE
5	RONNY JOHNSEN
6	JAAP STAM
3	DENIS IRWIN
11	RYAN GIGGS
7	DAVID BECKHAM
8	NICKY BUTT
15	JESPER BLOMQVIST 67'
19	DWIGHT YORKE
9	ANDY COLE 81'

Substitutes:

| 10 | TEDDY SHERINGHAM 67' |
| 20 | OLE GUNNAR SOLSKJAER 81' |

BAYERN MUNICH

1	OLIVER KAHN
10	LOTHAR MATTHAUS 80'
2	MARKUS BABBEL
25	THOMAS LINKE
4	SAMMY KUFFOUR
18	MICHAEL TARNAT
11	STEFAN EFFENBERG
16	JENS JEREMIES
14	MARIO BASLER 90'
19	CARSTEN JANCKER
21	ALEXANDER ZICKLER 71'

Substitutes:

7	MEHMET SCHOLL 71'
17	THORSTEN FINK 80'
20	HASAN SALIHAMIDZIC 90'

Referee: Pierluigi Collina

SEMI-FINALS

1ST LEG 7 APRIL 1999		
Manchester United	1-1	Juventus
Giggs		Conte'
2ND LEG 21 APRIL 1999		
Juventus	2-3	Manchester United
Inzaghi (2)		Keane, Yorke, Cole
1ST LEG 7 APRIL 1999		
Dynamo Kiev	3-3	Bayern Munich
Shevchenko (2), Kosovsky		Tarnat, Effenberg, Jancker
2ND LEG 21 APRIL 1999		
Bayern Munich	1-0	Dynamo Kiev
Basler		

MANCHESTER UNITED

MANAGER: ALEX FERGUSON

BAYERN MUNICH

MANAGER: OTTMAR HITZFELD

THE FINAL

Edwin van der Sar roars with delight after John Terry of Chelsea misses the crucial penalty that keeps United's hopes alive.

UNITED HAD ALREADY played Chelsea three times this season, winning at home in the league, losing the return and drawing in the Charity Shield. The players knew each other well, but Chelsea had lost their charismatic manager Jose Mourinho in September and were now led by Avram Grant.

Sir Alex Ferguson had no major injury worries before the game, but thought carefully about what team would beat his strongest rivals in England. His most difficult decision was who should fill the final midfield place, finally chosing Owen Hargreaves over Ji-sung Park and Ryan Giggs.

The selection seemed to work as the more experienced Reds looked most likely to score early on and then did so through a Cristiano Ronaldo header from a Wes Brown cross. But a second goal would not come and in the last minute of the first half Frank Lampard equalised for a Chelsea team that appeared to be struggling.

The following 45 minutes was a much tighter affair, as chances began to dry up. Then it was an unwanted period of extra time. Both teams were too tired and too cautious for the game to open up and it remained scoreless. Then a clash between United's Carlos Tevez and John Terry of Chelsea resulted in an ugly scrum of players coming together. It ended with Didier Drogba of Chelsea being sent off for slapping United's Nemanja Vidic.

Losing Drogba would prove crucial in the end as the game was decided by penalty kicks. Cristiano Ronaldo missed the third United attempt, but then John Terry slipped and hit the post as he tried to win the cup with Chelsea's fifth spot kick. Both sixth penalties were scored before Giggs netted United's seventh and watched as a weak Nicolas Anelka attempt was saved by Edwin van der Sar to give United the trophy.

MANCHESTER UNITED

1	EDWIN VAN DER SAR
6	WES BROWN 120+5'
5	RIO FERDINAND
15	NEMANJA VIDIC
3	PATRICE EVRA
4	OWEN HARGREAVES
18	PAUL SCHOLES 87'
16	MICHAEL CARRICK
7	CRISTIANO RONALDO
10	WAYNE ROONEY 101'
32	CARLOS TEVEZ

Substitutes:

11	RYAN GIGGS 87'
17	NANI 101'
8	ANDERSON 120+5'

CHELSEA

1	PETR CECH
5	MICHAEL ESSIEN
6	RICARDO CARVALHO
26	JOHN TERRY
3	ASHLEY COLE
4	CLAUDE MAKELELE 120+4'
13	MICHAEL BALLACK
8	FRANK LAMPARD
10	JOE COLE 99'
15	FLORENT MALOUDA 92'
11	DIDIER DROGBA

Substitutes:

35	JULIANO BELLETTI 120+4
21	SALOMON KALOU 92'
39	NICOLAS ANELKA 99'

Referee: Lubos Michel

SEMI-FINALS

	1ST LEG 23 APRIL 2008	
Barcelona	0-0	Manchester United
	2ND LEG 29 APRIL 2008	
Manchester United Scholes	1-0	Barcelona
	1ST LEG 22 APRIL 2008	
Liverpool Kuyt	1-1	Chelsea Riise (og)
	2ND LEG 30 APRIL 2008	
Chelsea Drogba (2), Lampard (pen)	3-2	Liverpool (a.e.t) Torres, Babel

MANCHESTER UNITED

MANAGER: SIR ALEX FERGUSON

CHELSEA

MANAGER: AVRAM GRANT

2007/08

21 May 2008 at Luzhniki Stadium, Moscow	
Manchester United (1) 1-1 (1) Chelsea (a.e.t)	
United win 6-5 on penalty kicks	
Goals: Ronaldo 26', Lampard 45'	
Attendance: 67,310	

Since winning the Champions League final in 1999, United had slipped back as far as European success was concerned. Two semi-final appearances since then were the Red Devils' best achievements and Sir Alex Ferguson was frustrated that as each season passed, European success failed to materialise, sometimes due to unforeseen events or unfancied opponents.

The group stage at the beginning of this year's campaign contained Dynamo Kiev of Ukraine, Roma of Italy and Sporting Lisbon of Portugal, the club from which United signed both Cristiano Ronaldo and Nani. It turned out that none of these teams was in United's class and the Reds won their first five games and drew the sixth to finish on 16 points and easy group winners. Ronaldo scored on his return to Lisbon in a 1-0 win and again in the 2-1 victory over Sporting Lisbon at Old Trafford. But the group highlights were the matches against Kiev, a 4-2 win away and a 4-0 thrashing at Old Trafford. Roma, meanwhile, who had lost 7-1 in Manchester in the quarter-finals the year before, were beaten only 1-0 this time and finished second of the four teams.

Lyon of France were the first round knockout opponents and gave United few chances. The French team went ahead in the first leg at home, but a Carlos Tevez strike after 71 minutes gave United the away goal advantage. The tight second leg was settled by another Ronaldo goal just before half-time and, although Lyon hit the post late on, United squeezed through.

All four English teams had made it through to the quarter-finals and United were given another chance to beat Roma. This was achieved without the élan of last year's crushing win at Old Trafford, but still in a very professional manner. Ronaldo and Wayne Rooney scored a goal in each half in Rome for a 2-0 first

leg win and the return in Manchester was won 1-0 (Tevez), despite some concerns over the defence which had lost Nemanja Vidic to injury and saw the return of Mikael Silvestre after a seven-month absence through knee ligament damage. There was even a 10-minute cameo role for another returnee from injury, Gary Neville, who had been out for 13 months.

So it was a confident United who lined up for the semi-final against the Spanish powerhouse Barcelona, the only other team who had remained unbeaten in the Champions League up to this point. But it was the Reds who made the better start in the first leg in Spain – awarded a penalty after just three minutes for a handball. Ronaldo's spot kick hit the post and Barca breathed again.

Another penalty claim by Ronaldo went unrewarded as United continued to create a few chances despite Barca's superior possession. In the end, Edwin van der Sar had to make a couple of good saves to keep a clean sheet and end the match 0-0.

The second leg began nervously with a Paul Scholes foul on Lionel Messi on the edge of the United box, but Barca could not take advantage and it was Scholes who redeemed himself with an outstanding strike in the 14th minute. After that, Nani could have doubled the lead before half-time, but his header went wide.

In the second half Barcelona again dominated possession and searched for a goal that would send them through, while United's defence showed grim determination, holding on to the end. The 1-0 win was the 12th successive home victory in the Champions League (extending United's own record) and meant an all-English final for the very first time as Chelsea had edged past Liverpool in the other semi.

United had been battling with the Londoners for the Premiership title all season and would clinch that trophy just before the European final in Moscow. However, the Reds had also lost to Chelsea in a league game between the two Champions League semi-finals, so the final would be nothing if not a close-run thing.

2008/09

27 May 2009 at Stadio Olimpico, Rome

Barcelona (1) 2-0 (0) Manchester United

Goals: Eto'o 10', Messi 70'

Attendance: 62,467

As last season's Champions League winners, UEFA gave United top seeding in this season's draw for the group stages. They would not have to face the real cream of Europe – top teams such as Barcelona and Internazionale of Italy – until the knockout stage. In the end, the Reds were favoured with a group featuring another Spanish team, Villarreal, along with Celtic and Aalborg of Denmark. Facing the defending champions meant opponents became extremely defence-minded and United would be constantly confronted with the problem of how to break down over-filled defensive units during the group stage.

Villarreal set the tone by holding out for a 0-0 draw at Old Trafford in the opening match. Many early United chances were squandered and even the introduction of Cristiano Ronaldo in the second half (he was returning from injury) could not produce a United goal.

United did win both their next matches by 3-0. First against Aalborg in Denmark and then at home to Celtic, to take control of the group (Dimitar Berbatov scored four of the six goals and Wayne Rooney the other two). Three more draws to finish the opening phase was a long way short of last season's imperious progress of five wins and a single draw.

Nevertheless, United would progress – although their luck in the draw for the group stage, which had thrown up a relatively weak set of opponents, now ran out. In the knockout stage they were drawn against Internazionale, with old rival and ex-Chelsea boss Jose Mourinho as the Italian team's coach. In the first leg in Milan, the Red Devils created many chances and looked the better side for long periods, yet could not break the deadlock against the well-schooled Italian champions. It would mean a nervous return to Old Trafford – one away goal from Inter could well settle the tie in their favour. Now the press focused on how Sir Alex Ferguson had only ever won one game against Mourinho-managed teams.

However, it took only four minutes before Vidic headed home a Ryan Giggs corner to put United in the driving seat. Inter would hit the bar as half-time approached, but that was before Cristiano Ronaldo nodded in a Wayne Rooney cross. The 2-0 aggregate win was an excellent result for United and gave them great confidence going into the quarter-final against FC Porto of Portugal.

It was a tired performance by the Reds in the first leg against the Portuguese side at Old Trafford. Porto opened the scoring after just four minutes and only a terrible back pass let in Rooney for an equaliser. When Carlos Tevez grabbed a goal with five minutes remaining, United seemed to have escaped, but then they conceded a late goal themselves to end the game 2-2.

It was a rather different story in Porto for the return leg as United used all their experience to eke out a 1-0 win thanks to another Ronaldo strike after just six minutes (this one from almost 40 yards). So, after playing in last year's first ever all-English final in the competition, the Reds now played in their first all-English semi-final against Arsenal.

The Gunners under Arsene Wenger had not enjoyed their best Premiership season (they would go on to finish fourth), but had looked a different team in Europe. United had lost to Arsenal 2-1 in the league match earlier in the season and the two legs were expected to be closely contested.

In the event, United won 1-0 at Old Trafford with a John O'Shea goal from a corner after 17 minutes, having looked much the better team. This was underlined in the return match in London after two goals in the first 11 minutes. Ji-sung Park slotted home a Ronaldo cross to open the scoring and then Ronaldo himself got the second from a long-range free kick. Needing four goals to make the final, Arsenal already looked beaten and a beautifully taken goal by Ronaldo for 3-0 put the tie beyond doubt despite a late Arsenal penalty.

THE FINAL Barcelona's Lionel Messi beats Edwin van der Sar to confirm the Spanish team's victory.

MAKING THE CHAMPIONS League final on a regular basis was one of Sir Alex Ferguson's benchmarks of success for United, so he was delighted to lead out his team at the Stadio Olympico in Rome against Barcelona. In fact, United were the first defending champions to appear in the following final since Juventus in 1997. However, the Reds manager could not have picked a more difficult opponent even though United had beaten the Spanish team over two legs in last season's competition.

Barcelona had looked like the best team in the competition even though they had scraped into the final on away goals thanks to a late-late equaliser against Chelsea in the semi-final. Lionel Messi led a highly talented team that would include ex-United centre back Gerard Pique, but be without suspended defenders Eric Abidal and Dani Alves. Ferguson, meanwhile, left Dimitar Berbatov, Paul Scholes and Carlos Tevez on the bench as he searched for a way to defeat the possession game of the Spanish champions. He also selected Ji-sung Park, making him the first Asian player to begin a Champions League final, while Darren Fletcher was suspended after picking up an unlucky (many would say unjust) late red card against Arsenal in the second leg.

When Barca's Samuel Eto'o scored from their first real chance after just 10 minutes, it looked ominous for the Reds. United never settled into a rhythm and Barca began to grow in confidence as they kept the ball for long periods. Tevez came on for Anderson for the second half, but Messi made it 2-0 to Barcelona after 70 minutes. The introduction of both Scholes and Berbatov caused a few late scares for the Spanish team, but ultimately no joy for United whose challenge ended in frustration and defeat.

MANCHESTER UNITED	
1	EDWIN VAN DER SAR
22	JOHN O'SHEA
5	RIO FERDINAND
15	NEMANJA VIDIC
3	PATRICE EVRA
8	ANDERSON 46'
16	MICHAEL CARRICK
11	RYAN GIGGS 75'
13	JI-SUNG PARK 66'
10	WAYNE ROONEY
7	CRISTIANO RONALDO
Substitutes:	
32	CARLOS TEVEZ 46'
9	DIMITAR BERBATOV 66'
18	PAUL SCHOLES 75'

BARCELONA	
1	VICTOR VALDES
5	CARLES PUYOL
24	YAYA TOURE
3	GERARD PIQUE
16	SYLVINHO
28	SERGIO BUSQUETS
6	XAVI HERNANDEZ
8	ANDREAS INIESTA 90+2'
10	LIONEL MESSI
14	THIERRY HENRY 72'
9	SAMUEL ETO'O
Substitutes:	
15	SEYDOU KEITA 72'
27	PEDRO RODRIGUEZ 90+2'

Referee: Massimo Busacca

SEMI-FINALS		
1ST LEG 29 APRIL 2009		
Manchester United	1-0	Arsenal
O'Shea		
2ND LEG 5 MAY 2009		
Arsenal	1-3	Manchester United
Van Persie (pen)		Park, Ronaldo (2)
1ST LEG 28 APRIL 2009		
Barcelona	0-0	Chelsea
2ND LEG 6 MAY 2009		
Chelsea	1-1	Barcelona
Essien		Iniesta

MANCHESTER UNITED

MANAGER: SIR ALEX FERGUSON

BARCELONA

MANAGER: JOSEP GUARDIOLA

THE FINAL

In the second half United could not halt the incomparable Lionel Messi (below), while goalscorer Wayne Rooney (opposite) gives everything to the Reds' cause.

THIS WOULD BE one of the most anticipated Champions League finals for many years: it involved the best two teams in Europe; they had both ripped through the competition in impressive style while also winning their national leagues; they had each been European champions three times; and were committed to attack. Also, by chance, the game was at the re-built Wembley and the original stadium had been the venue where both teams had won the European Cup for the first time.

Managers Sir Alex Ferguson and Pep Guardiola both looked confident in the build-up and had few selection worries, although Dimitar Berbatov was left out of the Reds' squad altogether (Ferguson felt an extra midfielder was needed on the bench because that area of the game would be so crucial) and Barcelona club captain Carles Puyol was fit enough only to be a substitute.

The game started well for United, who played with their defensive line high up the pitch and had their four-man midfield harass their Barca counterparts. Ji-sung Park led the way for the Reds as the Spanish champions seemed unsettled in the first ten minutes, but gradually the Spaniards' possession game took control, and Barca scored the opening goal after 27 minutes through Pedro. However, United responded and put together their own intricate passing move that Wayne Rooney completed with side-footed shot for the equaliser.

With the scores level at half-time, the next goal would be crucial and Barcelona scored it after 54 minutes from a fine shot by Lionel Messi. Barca now took control and with just over 20 minutes left scored a third goal through David Villa. After the 3-1 loss, Ferguson said: "In my time as manager [at United], it's the best team we've faced."

MANCHESTER UNITED

1	EDWIN VAN DER SAR
20	FABIO 69'
5	RIO FERDINAND
15	NEMANJA VIDIC
3	PATRICE EVRA
25	ANTONIO VALENCIA
16	MICHAEL CARRICK 77'
11	RYAN GIGGS
13	JI-SUNG PARK
10	WAYNE ROONEY
14	JAVIER HERNANDEZ

Substitutes:

17	NANI 69'
18	PAUL SCHOLES 77'

BARCELONA

1	VICTOR VALDES
2	DANIEL ALVES 88'
3	GERARD PIQUE
14	JAVIER MASCHERANO
22	ERIC ABIDAL
16	SERGIO BUSQUETS
6	XAVI HERNANDEZ
8	ANDREAS INIESTA
7	DAVID VILLA 86'
17	PEDRO RODRIGUEZ 90'
10	LIONEL MESSI

Substitutes:

5	CARLES PUYOL 88'
15	SEYDOU KEITA 86'
20	IBRAHIM AFELLAY 90'

Referee: Victor Kassai

SEMI-FINALS

1ST LEG: 26 APRIL 2011		
Schalke	0-2	Manchester United
		Giggs, Rooney
2ND LEG: 4 MAY 2011		
Manchester United	4-1	Schalke
Valencia, Gibson, Anderson (2)		Jurado
1ST LEG: 27 APRIL 2011		
Real Madrid	0-2	Barcelona
		Messi (2)
2ND LEG: 3 MAY 2011		
Barcelona	1-1	Real Madrid
Pedro		Marcelo

MANCHESTER UNITED
MANAGER: SIR ALEX FERGUSON

BARCELONA
MANAGER: JOSEP GUARDIOLA

2010/11

28 May 2011 at Wembley Stadium, London
Barcelona (1) 3-1 (1) Manchester United
Goals: Pedro 27', Messi 54', Villa 69'
Rooney 34'
Attendance: 87,695

By now United were routinely being described as one of the favourites of the competition thanks to their recent history of success (semi-finalists, winners, runners-up and quarter-finalists in the last four seasons); being drawn against Valencia of Spain, Glasgow Rangers of Scotland and Bursaspor of Turkey in the group stage held no immediate fears.

Including an emotional return for Sir Alex Ferguson to Rangers (the club where he starred as a player in the 1960s), the six group games went according to plan with four wins (including all three away games) and two draws that meant United topped the group by three points from Valencia. The loss of winger Antonio Valencia with a broken ankle in the home match against Rangers was the only negative, although scoring only seven goals was a slight worry.

In the draw for the first knockout round, the seeded United avoided awkward opponents such as AC Milan and Bayern Munich and instead were matched with Olympique de Marseille of France. Without an injured Rio Ferdinand for the first leg, United were happy enough with a 0-0 draw. In the second leg, it was Nemanja Vidic's turn to be injured, but two goals by Javier Hernandez, one in each half, put the Reds in control and, despite a nervy last ten minutes after a Wes Brown own goal, the Reds went through 2-1 on aggregate.

An all-English quarter-final against Chelsea was a repeat of the 2008 Champions League final and would be a tough tie because the teams knew each other so well. When United took the first leg at Stamford Bridge 1-0 thanks to a Wayne Rooney goal in the first half and a couple of impressive saves from Edwin van der Sar, it looked decisive.

The second leg saw Chelsea under pressure to score, despite which the Chelsea manager Carlo Ancelotti dropped star-striker Didier Drogba from the starting line-up. When young sensation Hernandez scored at the far post from a Ryan Giggs cross, the Reds began to look more comfortable. Then the sending off of Chelsea's Ramires for two yellow cards seemed to have sealed it. But Drogba had come off the bench and now scored, only for Ji-sung Park to score immediately after and United had won the tie 3-1 on aggregate.

It was a favourable draw for the semi-finals for United, who were paired with the surprise team, Germany's Schalke 04 rather than either Real Madrid or Barcelona. Again, the Reds played the away leg first and put their stamp of authority on the tie. With a full strength team (Valencia had now returned from his broken ankle), United looked in dominating form and scored two goals midway through the second half from Giggs and Rooney. The 2-0 scoreline barely indicated their superiority as the Schalke keeper made save after save.

There was controversy in the second leg as Ferguson rested Rooney, Hernandez, Ferdinand and Vidic. The Reds had just lost 1-0 in a league game to Arsenal and faced Chelsea in a Premiership showdown four days after this second leg tie. The press – and some of the United fans – worried that the manager might rue his selection, but ultimately the much-changed team were equally as impressive in the match.

Antonio Valencia and Darron Gibson got the early goals and although Schalke pulled one back before half-time, United never really looked in trouble; two delightful strikes from Anderson in the second half showed the real gap between the two teams as the Reds reached their fifth European Cup or Champions League final with a 6-1 aggregate win.

By remaining unbeaten in this competition (unlike their final opponents Barcelona who lost one leg of their quarter-final against Arsenal) and then tying up the Premiership with a game to spare, Ferguson could focus on how United were going to overcome Barcelona, as the two teams got ready for a repeat of the 2009 final.

FA Community Shield

THE FOOTBALL ASSOCIATION (FA) Community Shield was first contested in 1908 under the name the FA Charity Shield. It was created as an exhibition match between two of the best teams of the day. Its origins are slightly complicated in that the match actually replaced the Sheriff of London Charity Shield that had been staged for the previous ten years. The Charity Shield came into being only after a rift among the football authorities who, at the time, were trying to fully separate the professional and amateur games. The rift centred on the creation of the Amateur Football Association to oppose the Football Association.

Originally, the game was a challenge match between the best team in professional football (the winners of the First Division) and a champion team of the amateur game (the Southern League winners). The format remained an amateur against professional contest until the First World War, and then, over the next three decades, various different teams contested for the Shield including: FA Cup winners, other top amateur teams, and even representative sides, for example an England World Cup XI who played a Canadian Touring XI in 1950.

Since the early fifties, and with only a few exceptions, the FA Community Shield (it would eventually change its name from the FA Charity Shield following the 2001 game) has been played between the reigning league champions (originally the First Division, but nowadays the Premiership) and the previous season's FA Cup winners. It became

the traditional curtain-raiser for the new season in 1959 and moved to Wembley Stadium as its regular venue in 1974, where it has remained ever since – except during the re-building of the stadium from 2001-06 when the game moved to the Millennium Stadium in Cardiff.

After being crowned champions of the First Division for the first time in 1908, United won the first FA Charity Shield later that year, beating Southern League champions Queens Park Rangers after a replay. The first game in April at Chelsea's Stamford Bridge ended 1-1 with a goal from Billy Meredith. Bizarrely, the replay was not played until August at the same venue. The Reds managed to win the match convincingly 4-0, with a hat-trick from Jimmy Turnbull and one goal from George Wall.

Since then United have won the Shield outright on a total of 15 times – including nine during the reign of Sir Alex Ferguson – and shared it on another four occasions (sharing the trophy occurred until the early nineties instead of penalties). United's total of wins (15) and also their 28 total appearances are both records for the competition.

Another record held by United is to be the highest scorers in a FA Community Shield game. This happened in 1911 when the Reds thrashed Southern League winners Swindon Town 8-4, with Harold Halse scoring six goals (also a record for the match) and Sandy Turnbull and George Wall grabbing the others. Proceeds from that match went to the survivors of the sinking of the *Titanic*.

Opposite: 12 August 1967. Embarrassed Reds goalkeeper Alex Stepney retrieves the ball from his net after his Tottenham Hotspur counterpart Pat Jennings had scored from the opposing end of the pitch direct from a kick out of his hands. The match ended 3-3 and the Shield was shared.

27 APRIL 1908 (FIRST MATCH) AT STAMFORD BRIDGE, LONDON		
Manchester United	1-1	**Queens Park Rangers**
Meredith		Cannon

29 AUGUST 1908 (REPLAY) AT STAMFORD BRIDGE, LONDON		
Manchester United	4-0	**Queens Park Rangers**
J. Turnbull (3), Wall		

25 SEPTEMBER 1911 AT STAMFORD BRIDGE, LONDON		
Manchester United	8-4	**Swindon Town**
Halse (6), A. Turnbull, Wall		Fleming, Wheatcroft, Tout, Jefferson

6 OCTOBER 1948 AT HIGHBURY, LONDON		
Arsenal	4-3	**Manchester United**
Lewis (2), Jones, Rooke		Rowley, Burke, og

24 SEPTEMBER 1952 AT OLD TRAFFORD, MANCHESTER		
Manchester United	4-2	**Newcastle United**
Rowley (2), Byrne, Downie		Keeble (2)

24 OCTOBER 1956 AT MAINE ROAD, MANCHESTER		
Manchester United	1-0	**Manchester City**
Viollet		

22 OCTOBER 1957 AT OLD TRAFFORD, MANCHESTER		
Manchester United	4-0	**Aston Villa**
Taylor (3), Berry (pen)		

17 AUGUST 1963 AT GOODISON PARK, LIVERPOOL		
Everton	4-0	**Manchester United**
Gabriel, Stevens, Vernon (pen), Temple		

14 AUGUST 1965 AT OLD TRAFFORD, MANCHESTER		
Manchester United	2-2	**Liverpool (Shared)**
Best, Herd		Stevenson, Yeats

12 AUGUST 1967 AT OLD TRAFFORD, MANCHESTER		
Manchester United	3-3	**Tottenham Hotspur (Shared)**
Charlton (2), Law		Robertson, Jennings, Saul

13 AUGUST 1977 AT WEMBLEY, LONDON		
Manchester United	0-0	**Liverpool (Shared)**

20 AUGUST 1983 AT WEMBLEY, LONDON		
Manchester United	2-0	**Liverpool**
Robson (2)		

10 AUGUST 1985 AT WEMBLEY, LONDON		
Everton	2-0	**Manchester United**
Steven, Heath		

18 AUGUST 1990 AT WEMBLEY, LONDON		
Manchester United	1-1	**Liverpool (Shared)**
Blackmore		Barnes

7 AUGUST 1993 AT WEMBLEY, LONDON		
Manchester United	1-1	**Arsenal (United won 5-4 on pens)**
Hughes		Wright

14 AUGUST 1994 AT WEMBLEY, LONDON		
Manchester United	2-0	**Blackburn Rovers**
Cantona (pen), Ince		

11 AUGUST 1996 AT WEMBLEY, LONDON		
Manchester United	4-0	**Newcastle United**
Cantona, Butt, Beckham, Keane		

3 AUGUST 1997 AT WEMBLEY, LONDON		
Manchester United	1-1	**Chelsea (United won 4-2 on pens)**
Johnsen		Hughes

9 AUGUST 1998 AT WEMBLEY, LONDON		
Arsenal	3-0	**Manchester United**
Overmars, Wreh, Anelka		

1 AUGUST 1999 AT WEMBLEY, LONDON		
Arsenal	2-1	**Manchester United**
Kanu, Parlour		Yorke

13 AUGUST 2000 AT WEMBLEY, LONDON		
Chelsea	2-0	**Manchester United**
Hasselbaink, Melchiot		

12 AUGUST 2001 AT MILLENNIUM STADIUM, CARDIFF		
Liverpool	2-1	**Manchester United**
McAllister (pen), Owen		van Nistelrooy

10 AUGUST 2003 AT MILLENNIUM STADIUM, CARDIFF		
Manchester United	1-1	**Arsenal (United won 4-3 on pens)**
Silvestre		Henry

8 AUGUST 2004 AT MILLENNIUM STADIUM, CARDIFF		
Arsenal	3-1	**Manchester United**
Gilberto, Reyes, Silvestre (o.g)		Smith

5 AUGUST 2007 AT WEMBLEY, LONDON		
Manchester United	1-1	**Chelsea (United won 3-0 on pens)**
Giggs		Malouda

10 AUGUST 2008 AT WEMBLEY, LONDON		
Manchester United	0-0	**Portsmouth (United won 3-0 on pens)**

9 AUGUST 2009 AT WEMBLEY, LONDON		
Chelsea	2-2	**Manchester United (Chelsea won 4-1 on pens)**
Carvalho, Lampard		Nani, Rooney

8 AUGUST 2010 AT WEMBLEY, LONDON		
Manchester United	3-1	**Chelsea**
Valencia, Hernandez, Berbatov		Kalou

7 AUGUST 2011 AT WEMBLEY, LONDON		
Manchester City	3-2	**Manchester United**
Lescott, Dzeko		Smalling, Nani (2)

European Cup-Winners' Cup

THE FIRST CUP-Winners' Cup competition took place in 1960-61 and was created to provide a European contest for the winners of the previous season's leading domestic knockout cup in each competing country. Only ten teams entered the inaugural competition and Fiorentina of Italy were the winners over Glasgow Rangers.

It was the third pan-European football competition to be formed by UEFA, after the European Cup and the Inter-Cities Fairs Cup (both first contested in 1955). The format was always for two-leg matches on a knockout basis with aggregate scores to count. A one-off final at a neutral venue climaxed the competition and the list of winners is a who's who of European club football including Barcelona (a record four times), AC Milan, Ajax of Amsterdam, Juventus and Bayern Munich.

From 1972 until 1999, the Cup-Winners' Cup champions would play for the Super Cup the following season against the winners of the European Cup (later the Champions League).

However, when the European Cup was replaced by the expanded Champions League in the early nineties, the prestige of the Cup-Winners' Cup was diminished as teams that had won their domestic knockout cup and also finished second in their domestic league started choosing to enter the Champions League. The competition was finally abolished after the 1998-99 season and domestic cup winners were then automatically given a place in the UEFA Cup (later the Europa League).

United entered the competition on five occasions in total, the first time in 1963-64 when they lost in the quarter-finals to Sporting Lisbon of Portugal. It was another 13 years before they featured again and lost for the second time to a Portuguese team, Porto.

A semi-final meeting against Juventus was lost in 1983-84, before United won the trophy for the first and only time in the 1990-91 season. The Reds would beat Barcelona in the final. The defence of their trophy the following season, however, ended quickly with a second round loss against Atletico Madrid.

Apart from the one victory, the most notable United performance in the competition was the quarter-final in 1964. The Reds won the first leg 4-1 thanks to a Denis Law hat-trick and one goal from Bobby Charlton, but the return leg was a complete disaster, a 5-0 drubbing, with all Sporting Lisbon's goals coming in the first 54 minutes. United were playing their 12th match in just over six weeks and ran out of energy in the face of intense Portuguese pressure. That loss remains the worst defeat in Europe in United's history.

Alex Ferguson has won the trophy twice: with United in 1990-91 (his second piece of silverware as manager at Old Trafford), and Aberdeen in 1982-83. Ferguson became only the second manager in the history of the competition (along with Johan Cruyff of the Netherlands) to win the trophy with two different clubs.

United is one of the seven English teams to have won the competition; the others are Chelsea, West Ham United, Arsenal, Manchester City, Tottenham Hotspur and Everton.

Opposite: An inspired Mark Hughes moves past Barcelona captain Jose Alexanko.

1990/91

15 May 1991 at Feyenoord Stadion, Rotterdam

Manchester United (0) 2-1 (0) Barcelona

Goals: Hughes 67', 74', Koeman 79'

Attendance: 50,000

The ban on English clubs playing in Europe was lifted at the start of the season, five years after the tragic deaths of fans at the Heysel Stadium in Belgium before the European Cup final. This was United's fourth entry into the Cup-Winners' Cup competition and their best previous performance was to reach the semi-finals.

The opening round brought United up against Hungary's Pecsi Munkas and a 2-0 home win with early goals from Clayton Blackmore and Neil Webb (both scoring within the first 16 minutes) made the second leg a comfortable proposition that was won 1-0 with a late Brian McClair goal.

United were the subject of all the wrong sort of headlines just before they took on Wrexham in the next round. A mass on-pitch squabble with Arsenal players in a league match meant United were under the spotlight for disciplinary reasons. However, a 3-0 home victory over the Welsh team, who held the game at 0-0 for the first 40 minutes, was perfunctory (Steve Bruce, McClair and Gary Pallister scoring). The 2-0 away win (Bruce again and Mark Robins getting the goals, both in the first half) capped off a capable start to the search for a first European trophy in over 20 years.

The quarter-finals of the competition would not take place for four months, during which time United had shown some good cup form, making the final of the League Cup and only narrowly exiting the FA Cup in the fifth round.

However, against Montpellier in the quarter-final, United were up against a side who had already beaten two of the competition favourites, PSV Eindhoven of the Netherlands and Steaua Bucharest of Romania. The first leg opened spectacularly with a McClair goal after just two minutes, but then Mick Martin put the ball in to his own net just six minutes later and United had a fight on their hands. The Reds were ultimately held to the 1-1 draw and now had to win or force a high-scoring draw in France.

However, with both Steve Bruce and Denis Irwin returning to defensive duties after injury, United looked a more capable team in the second leg and a Blackmore goal direct from a free kick in the first-half injury time gave them the advantage. In the second half, as Montpellier pressed for the goal they now needed, Blackmore was fouled in the penalty area and Bruce netted the vital spot kick to help the Reds to an impressive 3-1 aggregate win.

United actually got through the semi-finals more easily against Legia Warsaw of Poland. It helped that the first leg away from home was won by the Reds 3-1, with Bruce, Hughes and McClair on the scoresheet. That allowed the second leg at Old Trafford to be controlled from the start by United and they duly completed the task with a 1-1 draw (Lee Sharpe the goalscorer) and a 4-2 victory on aggregate.

That would mean a final against Barcelona in the Netherlands which would give Mark Hughes a chance to redeem his reputation in Spain. The Welshman had been a sensation in his first spell at United, but then spent two unhappy seasons with the Catalan giant (even being loaned out to Bayern Munich for a few months) and was eventually told he was not good enough. A return to United had followed and now he had the chance to show the Spanish team they had made a mistake about his talent.

THE FINAL

The atmosphere is explosive during the national anthems.

ANY MEETING BETWEEN two giants of world football such as United and Barcelona is likely to be memorable and so this game proved, especially for Mark Hughes, who was playing in a United team that had performed well in all this season's knock-out competitions and was undefeated throughout the competition so far (unlike Barcelona who had lost twice).

Alex Ferguson was chasing his second trophy after four seasons as United manager and was keen to keep the silverware coming to Old Trafford, and show that the club could compete against the best in Europe. He selected the solid Mike Phelan in midfield while leaving Danny Wallace, Neil Webb and Mark Robins on the bench.

Barcelona manager Johan Cruyff had a side that contained international stars Ronald Koeman of the Netherlands and Michael Laudrup of Denmark, although they were missing star striker Hristo Stoichkov.

The first half was scoreless as the teams probed for an advantage, but as the tension built, a Bryan Robson free kick into the Barca penalty box found Steve Bruce, who sent a header goalwards and was delighted to see Mark Hughes make sure of the opening score. Just seven minutes later Hughes burst forward again and struck a shot into the net with the outside of his foot from a narrow angle.

Although a superb moment of individual skill, it inevitably prompted an immediate Barcelona reply; a Koeman free kick ricocheted off the post and over the line via goalkeeper Les Sealey's legs.

In a frantic final ten minutes, Barca had a goal disallowed for offside and their full back Nando was shown a red card. United, however, maintained their concentration to take only their second ever European trophy back to Manchester.

MANCHESTER UNITED

1 LES SEALEY
2 DENIS IRWIN
3 CLAYTON BLACKMORE
4 STEVE BRUCE
5 MIKE PHELAN
6 GARY PALLISTER
7 BRYAN ROBSON
8 PAUL INCE
9 BRIAN MCCLAIR
10 MARK HUGHES
11 LEE SHARPE

BARCELONA

1 CARLES BUSQUETS
2 NANDO
3 JOSE RAMON ALEXANKO
4 RONALD KOEMAN
5 ALBERT FERRER
6 JOSE MARI BAKERO
7 ANDONI GOIKOETXEA
8 EUSEBIO
9 JULIO SALINAS
10 MICHAEL LAUDRUP
11 TXIKI BEGIRISTAIN

Substitutes:

16 ANTONIO PINILLA

Referee: Bo Karlsson

SEMI-FINALS

1ST LEG 10 APRIL 1991		
Legia Warsaw	1-3	Manchester United
Cyzio		McClair, Hughes, Bruce
2ND LEG 24 APRIL 1991		
Manchester United	1-1	Legia Warsaw
Sharpe		Kowalczyk
1ST LEG 10 APRIL 1991		
Barcelona	3-1	Juventus
Stoichkov (2), Goikoetxea		Casiraghi
2ND LEG 24 APRIL 1991		
Juventus	1-0	Barcelona
Baggio		

MANCHESTER UNITED

MANAGER: ALEX FERGUSON

BARCELONA

MANAGER: JOHAN CRUYFF

UEFA Cup/ Inter-Cities Fairs Cup

AT THE SAME time as the more prestigious European Cup was being dreamt up, the Inter-Cities Fairs Cup was also being formed. Two men – Swiss pools magnate Ernst Thommen and English Football Association general secretary Stanley Rous – were behind the competition, the idea for which derived from the fact that football clubs across Europe often played friendly matches at trade fairs throughout the continent in the immediate post-war years.

In 1955, the first Inter-Cities Fairs Cup was staged, with entry limited to one team per city and would be played over two seasons to avoid clashes with normal league games. Teams entered representing cities including Birmingham, Copenhagen, Frankfurt, Vienna, Cologne, Lausanne, Leipzig, London, Milan, and Zagreb. Barcelona were the eventual winners against London XI, a team that combined players from all the capital's clubs and included Jimmy Greaves (Chelsea), Johnny Haynes (Fulham) and Danny Blanchflower (Tottenham Hotspur).

By 1968, teams were awarded a place in the competition based on their finishing league position in the previous season, rather than by invitation. Three years later UEFA took charge and changed the name to the UEFA Cup as well as abandoning the idea of one-team-per-city rule.

In 1999 the Cup-Winners' Cup was absorbed into the UEFA Cup, while the format changed again in 2009-10 with the creation of league phases and another re-naming to the UEFA Europa League.

United have played in the tournament seven times, starting in the 1964-65 season and, most recently, in 1995-96. Their best performance has been reaching the semi-finals, achieved in their first ever appearance back in the sixties. It began with a comprehensive win over Djurgårdens IF of Sweden, including a 6-1 win at home, with a Denis Law hat-trick.

In the second round, German team Borussia Dortmund were easily dispatched thanks to another 6-1 result, this time in the first leg in Germany, with Bobby Charlton supplying the hat-trick. Fellow English First Division team Everton were then beaten 3-2 on aggregate (it needed a 2-1 second leg away win), while RC Strasbourg of France were overcome 5-0 in the quarter-final.

By now, the only problem with the competition as far as United was concerned was that the two-leg semi-final against Ferencvaros of Hungary would not be completed until 6 June in a season that had started for the Red Devils back in August the previous year. A 3-2 win at home was followed by a 1-0 loss in Hungary, but without an away goals rule, there would have to be a replay. United lost the toss, which meant a return trip to the Népstadion – by now it was mid-June – where a tired team lost 2-1.

The next three appearances (the competition was by now known as the UEFA Cup) were rather short. In 1976-77, United were returning to European football for the first time since 1969. The Reds came up against two powerhouses in succession, beating Ajax of

Amsterdam in the opening round 2-1 on aggregate, with a 2-0 second leg win at home (Lou Macari and Sammy McIlroy scoring the goals). But Juventus of Italy proved too canny for Tommy Docherty's young team and, although United won the first leg 1-0 (Gordon Hill getting the goal), they were outplayed in the second leg and lost it 3-0 to go out 3-1 on aggregate.

In both 1980-81 and 1982-83 under Dave Sexton, United fell at the first hurdle: firstly, to Widzew Łódź of Poland on away goals and then against Valencia of Spain 2-1 on aggregate.

There was a quarter-final appearance in 1984-85 with Ron Atkinson in charge, but after defeating the likes of Scotland's Dundee United and PSV Eindhoven of Holland in exciting two-leg affairs, the Reds went out on penalties to the little-known Videoton FC of Hungary.

The final two UEFA Cup entries were again disappointing, both against Russian teams and both first round defeats. In 1992-93, against Torpedo Moscow neither team could score in the two legs and United went out on penalties. Then in 1995-96 against Rotor Volgograd there was another first leg 0-0 draw before the Russian team forced a 2-2 draw at Old Trafford to progress on away goals; even a rare score from goalkeeper Peter Schmeichel could not save the Reds.

1964/65 – SEMI-FINAL (INTER-CITIES FAIRS CUP)

1ST LEG 31 MAY 1965 AT OLD TRAFFORD, MANCHESTER. ATTENDANCE: 39,902

Manchester United	(1) 3-2 (1)	Ferencvaros TC
Law 34' (pen), Herd 61', 69'		Novak 23', Rakosi 76'

2ND LEG 6 JUNE 1965 AT NEPSTADION, BUDAPEST. ATTENDANCE: 50,000

Ferencvaros TC	(1) 1-0 (0)	Manchester United
Novak 44' (pen)		

PLAY-OFF 16 JUNE 1965 AT NEPSTADION, BUDAPEST. ATTENDANCE: 60,000

Ferencvaros TC	(1) 2-1 (0)	Manchester United
Karaba 44', Fenyvesi 54'		Connelly 86'

1976/77 – SECOND ROUND

1ST LEG 20 OCTOBER 1976 AT OLD TRAFFORD MANCHESTER. ATTENDANCE: 59,000

Manchester United	(1) 1-0 (0)	Juventus
Hill 32'		

2ND LEG 3 NOVEMBER 1976 AT STADIO DELLE ALPI. ATTENDANCE: 66,632

Juventus	(1) 3-0 (0)	Manchester United
Boninsegna 29', 63', Benetti 85'		

1980/81 – FIRST ROUND

1ST LEG 17 SEPTEMBER 1980 AT OLD TRAFFORD, MANCHESTER. ATTENDANCE: 38,037

Manchester United	(1) 1-1 (1)	Widzew Lodz
McIlroy 4'		Surlit 6'

2ND LEG 1 OCTOBER 1980 AT STADIO TKS, LODZ. ATTENDANCE: 40,000

Widzew Lodz	(0) 0-0 (0)	Manchester United
(Lodz won on away goals)		

1982/83 – FIRST ROUND

1ST LEG 15 SEPTEMBER 1982 AT OLD TRAFFORD, MANCHESTER. ATTENDANCE: 46,588

Manchester United	(0) 0-0 (0)	Valencia

2ND LEG 29 SEPTEMBER 1982 AT ESTADIO LUIS CASANOVA, VALENCIA. ATTENDANCE: 35,000

Valencia	(0) 2-1 (1)	Manchester United
Solsana 71' (pen), Roberto 74'		Robson 45'

1984/85 – QUARTER-FINAL

1ST LEG 6 MARCH 1985 AT OLD TRAFFORD, MANCHESTER. ATTENDANCE: 35,432

Manchester United	(0) 1-0 (0)	Videoton FC
Stapleton 60'		

2ND LEG 20 MARCH 1985 AT SOSTOI STADIUM, SZEKESFEHERVAR. ATTENDANCE: 25,000

Videoton FC	(1) 1-0 (0)	Manchester United
Wittman 19'		
(Videoton won 5-4 on penalties)		

1992/93 – FIRST ROUND

1ST LEG 16 SEPTEMBER 1992 AT OLD TRAFFORD, MANCHESTER. ATTENDANCE: 19,998

Manchester United	(0) 0-0 (0)	Torpedo Moscow

2ND LEG 29 SEPTEMBER 1992 AT TORPEDO STADIUM, MOSCOW. ATTENDANCE: 11,357

Torpedo Moscow	(0) 0-0 (0)	Manchester United
(Torpedo Moscow won 4-3 on penalties)		

1995/96 – FIRST ROUND

1ST LEG 12 SEPTEMBER 1995 AT CENTRAL UNION STADIUM, VOLGOGRAD. ATTENDANCE: 33,000

Rotor Volgograd	(0) 0-0 (0)	Manchester United

2ND LEG 26 SEPTEMBER 1995 AT OLD TRAFFORD, MANCHESTER. ATTENDANCE: 29,724

Manchester United	(0) 2-2 (2)	Rotor Volgograd
Scholes 60', Schmeichel 89'		Niederhaus 18', Veretennikov 25'
(Rotor Volgograd won on away goals)		

Above: 6 March 1985. Paul McGrath avoids the challenge from Jozsef Szabo of Videoton FC during the UEFA Cup quarter-final at Old Trafford. United won the match 1-0, but with the aggregate scores level, the unheralded Hungarians would go through on penalties.

European Super Cup

THE EUROPEAN SUPER CUP was created with the idea of putting together the winners of UEFA's top two tournaments (originally, the European Cup and the Cup-Winners' Cup) in a playoff the following season to decide the best team on the continent. It was the idea of a Dutch journalist Anton Witkamp at a time when Dutch football was in its heyday and was prompted by Witkamp's desire to see his nation's champions Ajax of Amsterdam tested by other European teams. In 1973 Ajax (after their second successive win in that competition) played the two-leg Super Cup against Glasgow Rangers, who had won the previous season's Cup-Winners' Cup. However, the Scottish team was serving a 12-month ban because of fan trouble during their victory campaign and UEFA would not acknowledge the initial Super Cup matches, won by the Dutch team. The governing body, however, did see the value of Super Cup and supported the second competition in 1974 that was also won by Ajax, this time beating AC Milan.

Over the years as European-wide competitions have changed names and formats, the two contesting teams in the Super Cup have come from different competitions, but the idea remains to settle the question of who is the best team in Europe. The European Cup has metamorphosed into Champions League and now provides one Super Cup contestant, while their opponents no longer come from the now-extinct Cup-Winners' Cup or its immediate successor the UEFA Cup, but from the winner in the Europa League. The incentive to play is not just a prestigious piece of silverware, but also a first prize of €1.6 million.

Until 1997, the Super Cup was played over two legs, but has now become a single match at a neutral venue. United have taken part on three occasions, winning once. The Reds are one of only five English teams to have won the Super Cup; the others are Aston Villa, Chelsea, Liverpool and Nottingham Forest.

Right: 27 August 1999. This appearance in the Super Cup final in Monaco came after the remarkable treble season, but Teddy Sheringham and the Red Devils could not prolong the magic.

Opposite: (Left) Peter Schmeichel and his son Kasper show off the Super Cup (in the player's right hand) and the League Cup before the 1992-93 season. (Centre) Teddy Sheringham does battle with Paolo Negro of Lazio in the 1999 final. (Right) Paul Scholes, Gary Neville and Rio Ferdinand try to foil a Zenit St Petersburg attack during the 2-1 loss in 2008.

1991/92

19 November 1991 at Old Trafford, Manchester

Manchester United (0) 1-0 (0) Red Star Belgrade

Goals: McClair 67'

Attendance: 22,110

United's first appearance in the European Super Cup came after they had won the 1990-91 Cup-Winners' Cup and faced the previous season's European Cup winners, Red Star Belgrade.

It was meant to be a two-leg affair, but the political situation in war-torn Yugoslavia and the Balkan states reduced the contest to a single match at Old Trafford. Alex Ferguson fielded a full-strength team and the game was settled with a goal by Brian McClair after 67 minutes. The trophy was not the most prestigious on the football calendar at this time and only 22,110 fans turned up, but it was Ferguson's fourth piece of silverware with United and actually the second time he had won the Super Cup (the first was with Aberdeen in 1983).

1999/2000

27 August 1999 at Stade Louis II, Monaco

Manchester United (0) 0-1 (1) Lazio

Goals: Salas 35'

Attendance: 14,461

This would be the last time the winners of the Champions League and the Cup-Winners' Cup faced each other in the competition; next season the UEFA Cup holders would replace the Cup Winners. United were heavy favourites against Lazio of Rome. Andy Cole spurned a good chance early on to put United ahead, while soon afterwards Jaap Stam was involved in a collision with Lazio's Simone Inzaghi, who was replaced by Marcelo Salas, the eventual scorer of the only goal of the game. Roberto Mancini (who would be manager of Manchester City ten years later) almost added a second for Lazio after a mistake from United keeper Raimond van der Gouw, but the Reds could not find a way through the Italian defence.

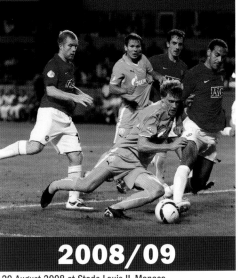

2008/09

29 August 2008 at Stade Louis II, Monaco

Manchester United (0) 1-2 (1) Zenit St Petersburg

Goals: Vidic 73', Pogrebnyak 44', Danny 59'

Attendance: 18,500

Another Champions League triumph in 2008 prompted the Reds' third Super Cup appearance, this time against Zenit St Petersburg of Russia. On a very hot evening, the Russians opened the scoring a minute before half time when the United defence failed to deal with a flick on from a near-post corner. Zenit scored a second just before the hour as United's defence was again opened up by a dribbling Russian forward. The Reds created plenty of chances and, although Nemanja Vidic pulled one back when he forced the ball home from a corner, they could not manage a second goal. Unfortunately, Paul Scholes was sent off in the closing stages when he deliberately handled the ball into the net for a disallowed goal.

MANCHESTER UNITED	RED STAR BELGRADE
1　PETER SCHMEICHEL	1　ZVONKO MILOJEVIC
2　LEE MARTIN 71'	2　DUSKO RADINOVIC
3　DENIS IRWIN	3　GORAN VASILIJEVIC
4　STEVE BRUCE	4　MIODRAG BELODEDICI
5　NEIL WEBB	5　ILIJA NAJDOSKI
6　GARY PALLISTER	6　MIROSLAV TANJGA
7　ANDREI KANCHELSKIS	7　VLADA STOSIC
8　PAUL INCE	8　VLADIMIR JUGOVIC
9　BRIAN MCCLAIR	9　DARKO PANCEV
10　MARK HUGHES	10　DEJAN SAVECEVIC 82'
11　CLAYTON BLACKMORE	11　SINESA MIHAJLOVIC
Substitutes:	Substitutes:
16　RYAN GIGGS 71'	14　ILIJA IVIC 82'

Referee: Mario van der Ende

MANCHESTER UNITED	LAZIO
17　RAIMOND VAN DER GOUW	1　LUCA MARCHEGIANI
2　GARY NEVILLE	2　PAOLO NEGRO
6　JAAP STAM 57'	13　ALESSANDRO NESTA
21　HENNING BERG	11　SINISA MIHAJLOVIC
12　PHIL NEVILLE	15　GIUSEPPE PANCARO
7　DAVID BECKHAM 58'	18　PAVEL NEDVED 66'
16　ROY KEANE	25　MATIAS ALMEYDA
18　PAUL SCHOLES	23　JUAN SEBASTIAN VERON
20　OLE GUNNAR SOLSKJAER	20　DEJAN STANKOVIC
9　ANDY COLE 78'	21　SIMONE INZAGHI 23'
10　TEDDY SHERINGHAM	10　ROBERTO MANCINI 84'
Substitutes:	Substitutes:
13　JOHN CURTIS 57'	9　MARCELO SALAS 23'
14　JORDI CRUYFF 58'	16　ATTILIO LOMBARDO 66'
34　JONATHAN GREENING 78'	14　DIEGO SIMONE 84'

Referee: Ryszard Wojcik

MANCHESTER UNITED	ZENIT ST PETERSBURG
1　EDWIN VAN DER SAR	16　VYACHESLAV MALAFEEV
2　GARY NEVILLE 76'	22　ALEKSANDR ANYUKOV
5　RIO FERDINAND	4　IVICA KRIZANAC 71'
15　NEMANJA VIDIC	28　SEBASTIEN PUYGRENIER 62'
3　PATRICE EVRA	11　RADEK SIRI
24　DARREN FLETCHER 60'	44　ANATOLLY TYMOSHCHUK
18　PAUL SCHOLES	18　KONSTANTIN ZYRYANOV
8　ANDERSON 60'	27　IGOR DENISOV
17　NANI	19　DANNY
10　WAYNE ROONEY	7　ALEJANDRO DOMINGUEZ 46'
32　CARLOS TEVEZ	8　PAVEL POGREBNYAK
Substitutes:	Substitutes:
13　JI-SUNG PARK 60'	10　ANDREI ARSHAVIN 46'
22　JOHN O'SHEA 60'	15　ROMAN SHIROKOV 62'
6　WES BROWN 76'	2　VLADISLAV RADIMOV 71'

Referee: Claus Bo Larsen

MANCHESTER UNITED
MANAGER: ALEX FERGUSON

RED STAR BELGRADE
MANAGER: VLADICA POPOVIC

MANCHESTER UNITED
MANAGER: SIR ALEX FERGUSON

LAZIO
MANAGER: SVEN GORAN ERIKSSON

MANCHESTER UNITED
MANAGER: SIR ALEX FERGUSON

ZENIT ST PETERSBURG
MANAGER: DICK ADVOCAAT

FIFA Club World Cup/ Intercontinental Cup

FIVE YEARS AFTER the creation of the European Cup in 1955 to find the best club team in Europe, the winners of the trophy would be pitched against the club champions of South America (winners of the Copa Libertadores) to play for the Intercontinental Cup. The new cup was played over two legs, home and away, during the subsequent season after the champions had been crowned.

The trophy was originally won on a points system (rather than away goals or penalties), with two points for a win and one for a draw. If the two teams finished level on points after two games then they faced a sudden-death play-off game at a neutral venue. In the inaugural contest in 1960, Real Madrid of Spain played Peñarol of Uruguay, winning by three points to one (that is, a win and a draw). In 1969, the points system was replaced by the more simple method of aggregate scores and penalty kicks in the event of a tie.

The competition was hit by various problems in the early years, including overly aggressive games – in which sendings-off were relatively common – and financial restrictions that caused cancellations (Ajax pulled out in 1973 because of contract disputes over payments). In 1980 the car giant Toyota became the game's sponsors and introduced the name the Toyota Cup to the event, while also insisting its headquarters city of Tokyo would stage the annual single match. The sponsorship took the financial pressure off the competition and the National Stadium in Tokyo staged a total of 22 games up to 2001, while the International Stadium in Yokohama was the venue for three from

2002 to 2004. United entered the Intercontinental Cup on two occasions in 1968 and 1999.

Then in 2005, the Intercontinental Cup merged with the FIFA Club World Cup, a separate competition that had been staged just once (in 2000). FIFA's involvement meant an opportunity for an expanded format, and the Club World Cup brought together not just the continental champions from Europe and South America, but also those from Asia, Oceania, Africa and CONCACAF (North American, Central America and the Caribbean) plus a host country representative. United have entered this competition twice, in 2000 and 2008.

The Reds are one of only five British teams to have taken part in either the Intercontinental Cup or the Club World Cup (the other four are Celtic, Liverpool, Nottingham Forest and Aston Villa), and hold the distinction of being the first British team to win both versions of the competition (the Intercontinental Cup in 1999 and Club World Cup in 2008).

Right: 25 September 1968. A United goal is disallowed (offside) during the first leg of the Intercontinental Cup against Argentinean side Estudiantes de La Plata, in Buenos Aires.

Opposite: 16 October 1968. An Estudiantes de La Plata player ends up injured in the goalmouth during the second leg of the Intercontinental Cup at Old Trafford.

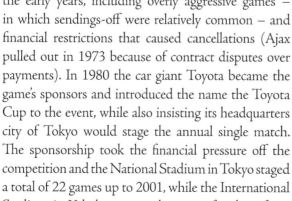

INTERCONTINENTAL CUP 1968/69

United's first appearance in the Intercontinental Cup was an unhappy experience when they met Estudiantes de La Plata of Argentina in 1968. The previous year, Glasgow Celtic had been disturbed by both fans and tactics on the trip to South America and United feared much of the same. Those fears were proved right when a red smoke bomb was set off inside the stadium just before kick-off in the first leg and the Estudiantes players then proceeded to try to kick United off the field – with Nobby Stiles particularly targeted. The midfielder eventually retaliated after being repeatedly fouled, and was sent off. United lost the game 1-0.

The Reds suffered robust treatment from the South American players in the second leg three weeks later, with George Best this time taking the majority of the worst tackles. The second leg started badly for United when they conceded a goal in the seventh minute that allowed Estudiantes to fall back on defence and, although the Reds created chances, they could not score until a Willie Morgan goal in the 89th minute. Before United scored, Best had been sent off along with an Argentinian defender and the match finished 1-1, with United losing 2-1 on aggregate.

1ST LEG

25 September 1968 at Estadio Alberto J. Armando, Buenos Aires

Estudiantes (1) 1-0 (0) Manchester United

Goals: Conigliaro 28'

Attendance: 55,000

MANCHESTER UNITED	ESTUDIANTES
1 ALEX STEPNEY	1 ALBERTO JOSE POLETTI
2 TONY DUNNE	2 OSCAR MALBANAT
3 FRANCIS BURNS	3 RAMON AGUIRRE SUAREZ
4 PADDY CRERAND	4 RAUL MADERO
5 BILL FOULKES	5 JOSE HUGO MEDINA
6 NOBBY STILES	6 CARLOS BILARDO
7 WILLIE MORGAN	7 CARLOS PACHAME
8 DAVID SADLER	8 NESTOR TOGNERI
9 BOBBY CHARLTON	9 FELIPE ROBAUDO
10 DENIS LAW	10 MARCOS CONIGLIARO
11 GEORGE BEST	11 JUAN RAMON VERON

Referee: Hugo Sosa Miranda

2ND LEG

16 October 1968 at Old Trafford, Manchester

Manchester United (0) 1-1 (1) Estudiantes

Goals: Morgan 89', Veron 7'

Attendance: 63,428

MANCHESTER UNITED	ESTUDIANTES
1 ALEX STEPNEY	1 ALBERTO JOSE POLETTI
2 SHAY BRENNAN	2 OSCAR MALBANAT
3 TONY DUNNE	3 RAMON AGUIRRE SUAREZ
4 PADDY CRERAND	4 RAUL MADERO
5 BILL FOULKES	5 JOSE HUGO MEDINA
6 DAVID SADLER	6 CARLOS BILARDO
7 WILLIE MORGAN	7 CARLOS PACHAME
8 BRIAN KIDD	8 NESTOR TOGNERI
9 BOBBY CHARLTON	9 FELIPE ROBAUDO 71'
10 DENIS LAW 43'	10 MARCOS CONIGLIARO
11 GEORGE BEST	11 JUAN RAMON VERON
Substitutes:	**Substitutes:**
12 CARLO SARTORI 43'	12 JUAN ECHECOPAR 71'

Referee: Konstantin Zecevic

MANCHESTER UNITED
MANAGER: SIR MATT BUSBY

ESTUDIANTES
MANAGER: OSVALDO ZUBELDIA

MANCHESTER UNITED
MANAGER: SIR MATT BUSBY

ESTUDIANTES
MANAGER: OSVALDO ZUBELDIA

INTERCONTINENTAL CUP 1999

30 November 1999 at National Stadium, Tokyo

Manchester United (1) 1-0 (0) Palmeiras

Goals: Keane 35'

Attendance: 53,372

In the 38th Intercontinental Cup, known as the Toyota Cup, the Red Devils finally provided Britain with a winner of the competition. United beat the Brazilian and South American champions São Paulo-based Palmeiras, managed by Luis Felipe Scolari (who would later become much better known to English football fans as manager of Portugal's national team and later of Chelsea in the Premiership) and with an attack led by former Newcastle United star Faustino Asprilla.

Palmeiras should have scored early on when Asprilla put through Alex, but Mark Bosnich made a brave save. Then in the 35th minute, a break down the left wing by Ryan Giggs ended in a deep cross which was met by an unmarked Roy Keane, who volleyed into the net. A goal line clearance by Mikael Silvestre kept the score at 1-0 at half-time.

In the second half, the Brazilian team pounded United's goal, but Bosnich was equal to everything, including a point-blank save from substitute Oseas. In the end, the Reds were deserving winners and Giggs was named man of the match.

MANCHESTER UNITED	PALMEIRAS
1 MARK BOSNICH	1 MARCOS
2 GARY NEVILLE	2 FRANCISCO ARCE
6 JAAP STAM	3 JUNIOR BAIANO
27 MIKAEL SILVESTRE	4 ROQUE JUNIOR
3 DENIS IRWIN	6 JUNIOR
7 DAVID BECKHAM	5 CESAR SAMPAO
8 NICKY BUTT	15 GALEANO 54'
16 ROY KEANE	10 ALEX
18 PAUL SCHOLES 75'	11 ZINHO
11 RYAN GIGGS	20 FAUSTINO ASPRILLA 56'
20 OLE GUNNAR SOLSKJAER 46'	7 PAULO NUNES 77'
Substitutes:	**Substitutes:**
10 TEDDY SHERINGHAM 75'	9 OSEAS 56'
19 DWIGHT YORKE 46'	19 EULLER 77'
	17 EVAIR 54'

Referee: Hellmut Krug

MANCHESTER UNITED
MANAGER: SIR ALEX FERGUSON

PALMEIRAS
MANAGER: LUIS FELIPE SCOLARI

CLUB WORLD CHAMPIONSHIP 2000

United made their debut in the inaugural Club World Championship, held in January 2000, representing UEFA against seven other teams who were split into two groups of four with the group winners going forward to a final and the runners-up going to a third place play-off. It was not a successful trip to Brazil for United. The Red Devils' three group games were against Club Necaxa of Mexico, which finished in a 1-1 draw; Vasco da Gama of Brazil, who beat the Reds 3-1; and South Melbourne of Australia, who were beaten 2-0. The poor results put United out of the competition that was eventually won by Corinthians of Brazil.

CLUB WORLD CUP 2008

21 December 2008 at International Stadium, Yokohama

Manchester United (0) 1-0 (0) Liga de Quito

Goals: Rooney 73'

Attendance: 62,619

Eight years after their first Club World Cup appearance, United would perform much better in a shortened version of the competition. As they had in the Intercontinental Cup, the Reds became the first British winners of the competition. They were again competing against seven teams from around the world, however, there were no group games as United were seeded straight into the semi-finals, where they played the Japanese side Gamba Osaka. The Red Devils won 5-3 with two goals from Wayne Rooney and one each from Nemanja Vidic, Cristiano Ronaldo and Darren Fletcher.

The final in the International Stadium in Yokohama three days later was against Liga de Quito of Ecuador, the other seeded team in the competition and the champions of South America. After a scoreless first 45 minutes, Vidic was sent off four minutes into the second half (for elbowing a Quito player). Sir Alex Ferguson re-shuffled his team, bringing on defender Jonny Evans for forward Carlos Tevez.

Until then United had created the best chances and proved to still be the stronger team although reduced to ten men. Rooney eventually scored the only goal of the game midway through the second half. It came after Michael Carrick and Ronaldo set up the striker lurking at the far post and his shot flew back across the goalkeeper and into the net.

MANCHESTER UNITED		LIGA DE QUITO	
1	EDWIN VAN DER SAR	1	JOSE FRANCISCO CEVALLOS
21	RAFAEL 85'	2	NORBERTO ARAUJO
5	RIO FERDINAND	13	NEICER REASCO 82'
15	NEMANJA VIDIC	14	DIEGO CALDERON
3	PATRICE EVRA	23	JAIRO CAMPOS
7	CRISTIANO RONALDO	3	RENAN CALLE 77'
8	ANDERSON 88'	7	LUIS BOLANOS 87'
16	MICHAEL CARRICK	8	PATRICIO URRUTIA
13	JI-SUNG PARK	15	WILLIAM ARAUJO
10	WAYNE ROONEY	21	DAMIAN MANSO
32	CARLOS TEVEZ 51'	16	CLAUDIO BIELER
Substitutes:		Substitutes:	
23	JOHNNY EVANS 51'	4	PAUL AMBROSI 77'
2	GARY NEVILLE 85'	20	PEDRO LARREA 82'
24	DARREN FLETCHER 88'	19	REINALDO NAVIA 87'

Referee: Ravshan Irmatov

MANCHESTER UNITED
MANAGER: SIR ALEX FERGUSON

LDU QUITO
MANAGER: EDGARDO BAUZA

Opposite Top: 30 November 1999. Goalkeepers Mark Bosnich (right) and Massimo Taibi celebrate with the Intercontinental Cup trophy after the 1-0 win over Palmeiras.

Above: 21 December 2008. Wayne Rooney celebrates scoring their winning goal during the FIFA Club World Cup final match against Liga de Quito at the Yokohama International Stadium.

Left: 21 December 2008. Goalscorer Wayne Rooney has another shot on target in the same game.

Opposite Bottom: 11 January 2000. David Beckham gets ready to come on as a substitute against South Melbourne. United beat the Australians 2-0.

5

The Managers

JAMES WEST

Country: England
Born: 26 July 1856 Birkenhead, Cheshire
Died: 26 January 1922
Clubs Managed: Lincoln City, Newton Heath
Took charge: 1 September 1900
To: 26 September 1903

Joining Newton Heath (soon to be re-born as Manchester United) as secretary in 1900 from Lincoln City was something of a poisoned chalice for James West. The 44-year-old born in Birkenhead was coming to a club in decline and, although he also witnessed its re-birth, his stay was short and his team's performances uneventful.

West – who acted as both administrative secretary and football manager (a dual role that the era demanded) – replaced the Heathens' first full-time secretary AH 'Alf' Albut who had overseen seven rather uninspiring seasons in the new Second Division of the Football League. West could do little better and took the Heathens to 10th and 15th in the Second Division during his first two campaigns. But his more important job was about helping salvage the club's finances ahead of the takeover that would be led by John Henry Davies in time for the 1902-03 season to begin. The first season of the takeover would be West's third and last in full charge of the team. After a poor start in 1903-04, West was replaced by Ernest Mangnall whose profile as the then secretary-manager of neighbouring Burnley was a far more attractive proposition to the new United owner.

Overall, West managed the club for 113 games and, considering the fluctuating state of the finances and ownership, he performed remarkably well with 46 wins, 47 losses and 20 draws in just over three seasons.

JAMES ERNEST MANGNALL

Country: England
Born: 4 January 1866 Bolton, Lancashire
Died: 13 January 1932
Clubs Managed: Burnley (1900-03), Manchester United (1903-12), Manchester City (1912-24)
Took charge: 12 October 1903
To: 9 September 1912
Major honours: First Division (2): 1907-08, 1910-11; FA Charity Shield (2): 1908, 1911; FA Cup (1): 1909

Of the three managers to win league championships with Manchester United, undoubtedly the least celebrated of the trio is Ernest Mangnall. Yet his role in United's history cannot be overstated. He was the first ever manager to put major silverware in United's trophy cabinet, taking the club from Division Two obscurity to put them on the footballing map. Inside ten seasons at the club, he won two league titles, two Charity Shields and an FA Cup, and he was instrumental in United moving to Old Trafford stadium.

James Ernest Mangnall was born on 4 January 1866 in Bolton. The son of a joiner, he was educated at Bolton Grammar School and would play football at an amateur level both as goalkeeper and inside-right. His first job in the football world came not as a player or manager, but as director of Bolton. A keen supporter of the club, he was unable to bring success to his boyhood heroes. Bolton were relegated in 1898-99 and Mangnall moved on to become manager of Burnley. Burnley suffered relegation in Mangnall's first season in charge so it came as something of a surprise in 1903-04 when Mangnall, having failed to get Burnley re-promoted, was appointed manager of Divison Two rivals Manchester United.

Fortunately for Mangnall, United's new owner John Henry Davies was on hand to provide ample funds to build a team. Even more fortunately for United, Mangnall opted to spend the money wisely. He bought Charlie Roberts for a record fee of £600. Other key signings included Alex Bell, Charlie Sagar and George Wall. Within three seasons United had won promotion to the First Division having finished runners-up to Bristol City. They scored 90 goals and conceded just 28 in 38 games, with Sagar scoring 16.

United's first season in the top flight (1906-07) was one of consolidation as Mangnall led them to an eighth place finish. His cause was aided greatly that year by the acquisition of a number of key players from rivals Manchester City. City had been embroiled in an illegal payments to players scandal and forced to auction their entire squad. Mangnall wisely grabbed the gifted Billy Meredith along with the talented trio of Jimmy Bannister, Sandy Turnbull and Herbert Burgess.

Mangnall's leadership had long placed emphasis on physical fitness allied with an excellent team spirit. In 1907-08 these twin philosophies came together as a rampant United flew out of the blocks with three wins from their first three matches. A 2-1 defeat next up to Middlesbrough proved to be a mere bump in the road as Mangnall's charges embarked on a ten-game winning streak thereafter, to put daylight between themselves and the rest of the league. Despite a 7-4 reverse to Liverpool on 25 March 1908, United went on clinch the first of 19 titles, finishing nine points clear of Aston Villa.

If Mangnall felt it was job done, there were no signs of complacency in a squad hungry for more success. Even though they were only able to follow up the championship with a mid-table finish, Mangnall took United to the FA Cup final that next season. Having vanquished champions Newcastle in the previous round they met Bristol City in the final at Crystal Palace. In what turned out to be a disappointing game, United (wearing a change strip of white with a red 'V') triumphed 1-0 thanks to a 22nd minute Sandy Turnbull strike. In just two short seasons, Mangnall's team had won two trophies. He had brought success to United for the first time, setting the high standards to which United would adhere for years to come.

Mangnall was to spend three further seasons with United. While he would claim more silverware, arguably the most important event of those years was the relocation of the club to Old Trafford, a move in which Mangnall was instrumental. As early as 1907 owner John Henry Davies decided that the ground at Bank Street was not one befitting a club that was aiming to be the best in the land and commissioned the building of a new stadium. Old Trafford saw its first fixture on 19 February 1910, United losing 4-3 to Liverpool.

Although 1909-10 yielded no trophies, the opening of the new stadium had provided great hopes. In June 1910, Mangnall signed Enoch West from Nottingham Forest to partner Jimmy Turnbull. West proved an instant hit, plundering 19 goals in 35 games as Mangnall's United won the championship for a second time the following season.

Season 1911-12 was to be Mangnall's last at the club. Hit by injuries and illness for the majority of the campaign, the team needed two wins from their final three games to secure First Division safety. Mangnall's team, which had won two Charity Shields in addition to the leagues and the FA Cup, had begun to wane.

In a decision steeped in controversy, Mangnall chose to move on to new pastures across town to manage Manchester City. Ironically his final game in charge of United was the Manchester derby on 7 September 1912. Mangnall watched his future players triumph 1-0. Yet United would have the last laugh as Mangnall would fail to win a single trophy in 12 years at the Blues.

Manchester City moved to Maine Road in 1923 so Mangnall was present to see both Manchester clubs move to new stadia. He eventually retired in 1924. Ernest Mangnall died of a cerebral embolism on 13 January 1932.

W. H. Smith & Son's
SOUVENIR CARD
OF THE
ENGLISH CUP FINAL
1909

W. Memfish
MANCHESTER UNITED v. BRISTOL CITY
PLAYED AT THE
CRYSTAL PALACE
Saturday, April 24th
PRICE : ONE PENNY

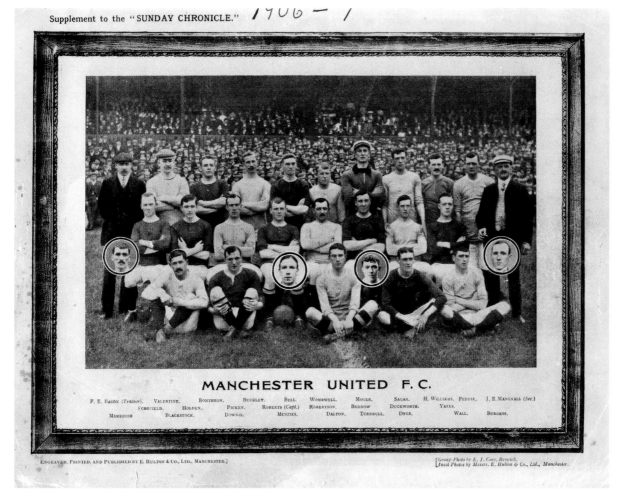

Supplement to the "SUNDAY CHRONICLE." 1906 – 7

MANCHESTER UNITED F. C.

F. E. BACON (Trainer). VALENTINE. BONTHRON. BUCKLEY. BELL. WOMBWELL. MOGER. SAGAR. H. WILLIAMS. PEDDIE. J. E. MANGNALL (Sec.)
SCHOFIELD. HOLDEN. PICKEN. ROBERTS (Capt.) ROBERTSON. BEDDOW. DUCKWORTH. YATES.
MEREDITH. BLACKSTOCK. DOWNIE. MENZIES. DALTON. TURNBULL. DYER. WALL. BURGESS.

ENGRAVED, PRINTED, AND PUBLISHED BY E. HULTON & Co., LTD., MANCHESTER.

[Group Photo by E. J. Care, Berwick.
[Inset Photos by Messrs. E. Hulton & Co., Ltd., Manchester.

Above: Ernest Mangnall took United to their first FA Cup win. This is a contemporary WH Smith souvenir that celebrates the victory.

Below: The 1906-07 United team photograph with a youthful looking Ernest Mangnall on the far right.

JOHN JAMES 'JJ' BENTLEY

Country: England
Born: May 1860 Chapeltown, Lancashire
Died: September 1918
Clubs Managed: Turton FC, Manchester United
Took charge: September 1912
To: 26 December 1914

At the end of the 1911-12 season, United's star had fallen. After the recent haul of silverware, Ernest Mangnall resigned following a poor 13th place league finish and a lack of FA Cup glory. The man who took over needed to be as large a personality as his predecessor and United had one such figure on their board.

John James 'JJ' Bentley had already become one of the most powerful men in the English football world. Before taking on his new role at United, he had been president of the Football League, vice-president of the Football Association, a national newspaper sports columnist and secretary at nearby Bolton Wanderers. During the first decade of the 20th century, his role in the football halls of power put him in conflict with the likes of United stars Charlie Roberts and Billy Meredith, who were fighting to set up the players' union and abolish the maximum wage. This was no professional football lightweight.

So, despite relatively little time in charge of an actual football team, the 52-year-old Bentley replaced Mangnall and set about putting United back on track. In his favour was the fact that he had been a keen footballer in his youth having been born and brought up in Chapeltown, near Darwen in Lancashire, with two older brothers who also enjoyed the game. Bentley made his debut for Turton FC – when the team was a man short – in the Lancashire leagues as a 14-year-old. He played for a total of seven seasons as a half back and also went on to manage the club, which, as a trained accountant, he was well placed to do. Bentley was always more concerned with the administrative running of a club and that is the role he took at United. His playing experience was enough for him to know that the on-field leaders like Roberts and Meredith were better situated than him to spark a revival, which is

what happened. With the players given a freer rein, the mid-tablers of the previous season rose to fourth in the First Division in Bentley's first campaign.

However, when Bentley sold Roberts at the end of the season, it proved a short-sighted and ultimately incorrect decision. Although the club banked a massive and much needed £1,500 cheque for the transfer, United slumped to 14th place in the league the following season, while Roberts and his new team Oldham Athletic finished fourth in the First Division. Now with the benefit of hindsight, Bentley's decisions came under close scrutiny by the club, especially when Oldham thrashed the Reds at Old Trafford 4-1 in front of 55,000 fans in September. In modern parlance,

Bentley had "lost the dressing room" and other results including a 6-0 loss, again at home, to Aston Villa in March were unacceptable to the fans.

In the early months of the 1914-15 season, United won just three games out of 18 and were bottom of the First Division after a 1-1 Boxing Day draw against Liverpool. It was time for Bentley to go. He would never manage another team although he continued in his role at United as secretary for a couple of years. He died in September 1918 aged just 58. In the words of William Pickford, sports writer for the *Manchester Evening Chronicle*: "He could be an autocrat but was rarely unpopular because he drew men towards him like a magnet, once persuaded they were forever loyal."

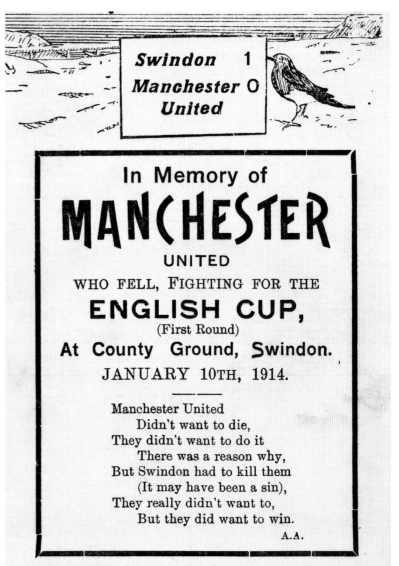

Right: 10 January 1914. A memorial postcard produced to commemorate Swindon Town's victory over Manchester United in the FA Cup first round at the County Ground in Swindon.

JOHN 'JACK' ROBSON

Country: England
Born: 24 May 1860 Gainford, County Durham
Died: 11 January 1922
Clubs Managed: Middlesbrough (1899-1905), Crystal Palace (1905-07), Brighton & Hove Albion (1908-14), Manchester United (1914-21)
Took charge: 1 January 1915
To: 29 October 1921

The 1914-15 season was an ignominious one for both United and for John 'Jack' Robson, who took over from JJ Bentley in the January of the campaign. With the Reds in 20th and last place in the First Division when he took the reins, Robson – who was a football manager rather than a club secretary/administrator like his predecessor – simply needed to avoid relegation to be successful in his first year. He would need all the experience he had gathered in the job over his 15 years with Middlesbrough, Crystal Palace and Brighton & Hove Albion.

Then in April, a huge betting scandal broke out involving three United players and four from Liverpool who were accused of fixing a 2-0 match result between the two teams. Bookmakers smelled a rat when large sums were placed on that exact scoreline at odds of 7/1. The seven players were found guilty and some given life bans from football. Robson lost two key goalscorers – Sandy Turnbull and Enoch West – but somehow pulled the team through. Victories in their last two games lifted United off the bottom of the table and to safety.

The First World War then took away the next four seasons and, when Robson's team re-formed in 1919, they were to prove a solidly mid-table outfit, finishing 12th and 13th in the next two campaigns. Sadly, Robson then had to resign through ill health in October 1921 and died of pneumonia just three months later.

JOHN ALBERT CHAPMAN

Country: Scotland
Born: 1882 Airdrie
Died: Unknown
Clubs Managed: Airdrieonians (1906-21), Manchester United (1921-26),
Took charge: 1 November 1921
To: 2 October 1926

The sudden loss of well-liked John Robson who had resigned led to the arrival of John Chapman at United on 1 November 1921. Chapman had spent 15 years managing Airdieonians in the Scottish leagues and took over a United team in 15th place in the First Division who had just beaten rivals Manchester City 3-1 in Robson's last game. However, the Reds then recorded only one win in Chapman's first 15 games in charge, and were relegated at the end of the season, finishing in 22nd and last place, eight points short of safety.

Nevertheless, the club showed faith in their new manager while in the Second Division and three seasons later, Chapman's Reds won promotion with a second place finish. The next season, United consolidated their position – coming ninth in the First Division – while also reaching the semi-finals of the FA Cup, their best cup showing for a dozen seasons.

A mediocre 1926-27 was not unexpected for the Reds, who were noted, at the time, for following a good campaign with a bad one, but the season was soon dogged by another altogether unforeseen scandal. The Scotsman was approaching his fifth anniversary in charge and had guided the Reds to a comfortable 14th place in the league when the club was notified by the Football Association that Chapman was suspended from the sport and from football management with immediate effect for what they described as "improper conduct as a secretary-manager". No other explanation was given and Chapman left the club, never to return. The full story behind the suspension has remained a mystery ever since.

Above: 25 December 1914. Two pages from the official United programme. On the left new manager John Robson is welcomed to the club – "The engagement of Mr. J. Robson as team manager to the Manchester United Club has elicited the most appreciative notices in the press, and the United directorate and the newcomer have been heartily congratulated on the appointment." Meanwhile right, the news is altogether more ominous.

Left: John Chapman takes United into the First Division at the end of the 1924-25 season. This is the programme for the penultimate game of the season, against Port Vale, that United won 4-0.

GEORGE CLARENCE 'LAL' HILDITCH

Country: England
Born: 2 June 1894 Hartford, Cheshire
Died: 31 October 1977
Clubs Managed: Manchester United (1926-27)
Took charge: 8 October 1926
To: 13 April 1927

In the modern era, football is awash with senior players who also take on the manager's role. In fact, player-managers have won many trophies in English football over the decades, yet United have employed just one man in this role and it happened at a time when it was a truly cutting-edge decision.

Clarence Hilditch – known more often as Clarrie or Lal – was born in the village of Hartford near Northwich in Cheshire in 1894 and would always remain local throughout his football career. In his early playing days turning out for Hartford, Hilditch was a forward, often on the left wing; he would go on to play for two more Cheshire teams, first Witton Albion from 1911 to 1915, where he was a solid inside forward, then nearby Altrincham where he starred for two seasons at left half. While playing War League football, United scouts saw his potential and he joined United in 1916 aged 20. In 1919 with the war ended and league football being played again, Hilditch would play in United's first post-war team at the half back position – having honed his skills in over 100 War League games for the Reds. He played 34 games in that first post-war season.

At 25, he was a stalwart of the team, a defensive half back who represented England in an unofficial international in 1919 and a year later went on tour with the national team to South Africa. In October 1926, when United's manager John Chapman was suddenly suspended by the Football Association for unspecified improper activities, the club turned to Hilditch – now aged 32 – as a short-term answer to the unexpected vacancy. United were in 14th place in the First Division and a player-manager was something of a risk, but new club secretary Walter Crickmer recognised a leader of men and backed the decision.

Lal Hilditch, who had been at the club for seven years and already racked up 200 games, took the title 'player-manager' for the rest of the season. On the field, he was regarded as one of the cleanest tacklers of his age and showed many classic managerial qualities – adaptability, firmness, fairness, confidence and reliability. But as a manager, he was a novice and his first game in charge was a 4-0 defeat to Bolton Wanderers, something of a baptism of fire. His decision-making was questionable given that he often chose to leave himself out of the team (though he was one of the best players) in order to manage.

Hilditch did eventually bring some stability to a difficult season and United finished in 15th place, ten points clear of any relegation worries. The experiment had worked, but Hilditch was not a permanent answer. Herbert Bamlett was appointed for the next season and Hilditch went on to play another five seasons at Old Trafford totalling 322 starts. When he retired from the Reds, he also retired from football and his 33 games in charge of United were his only experience of club management.

Right: A rather serious and young looking Lal Hilditch is featured on the front of this 1917 United programme.

HERBERT BAMLETT

Country: England
Born: 1 March 1882 Gateshead, County Durham
Died: October 1941
Clubs Managed: Oldham Athletic (1914-21), Wigan Borough (1921-23), Middlesbrough (1923-26), Manchester United (1927-31)
Took charge: 18 April 1927
To: 4 April 1931

In the late twenties, United selected a manager like no other before or since – an ex-referee. Herbert Bamlett, a man without any noticeable playing career, joined United in 1927 having won plaudits as a referee, but no trophies as a manager. His main claim to fame was guiding local rivals Oldham Athletic to an unexpected runners-up spot in the First Division.

Bamlett was born in 1882 in Gateshead in the north east of England, a traditional football hotbed, but he never played the game to any notable level. Instead, it was as a referee that he found his calling. In this era, it took an exceptional talent to gain credibility as a referee while in your twenties, but Bamlett did so and was given many high profile games at a young age. He even unwittingly became part of United folklore as a match official. It happened in March 1909 when he was refereeing an FA Cup quarter-final between the Reds and Burnley. United were clear favourites – as the current First Division champions – while their opponents were considered Second Division upstarts. This particular FA Cup match was played at Turf Moor in wintry conditions; deep into the second half, Burnley were ahead 1-0. Referee Bamlett was concerned about worsening weather conditions as snow began falling heavily, and controversially with just 18 minutes remaining, he abandoned the game. A happy United then won the replay 3-2 before going on to reach the final for the first time and taking the trophy. Without Bamlett's intervention, the cup win may never have happened.

This incident in no way diminished Bartlett's refereeing credibility, and by 1914 he had become the youngest official to take charge of an FA Cup final when, ironically, Burnley beat Liverpool 1-0. Having reached his peak in one career, Bamlett immediately tried another as in June 1914 he became secretary-manager of Oldham Athletic, taking them to an outstanding runners-up position in the First Division in his initial season. The First World War halted his immediate successes, but his achievements were noted and, soon after the end of hostilities, Bamlett moved to Wigan Borough and then Middlesbrough before joining United in April 1927.

The Reds already had a secretary in Walter Crickmer, so Bamlett's job was more about working with the team. But his time at United was ill-fated and, although there were some mitigating circumstances (United were experiencing serious financial problems), the team seemed not respond to Bamlett's style of management. In his four seasons in charge, United finished 18th, 12th, 17th and then finally 22nd and bottom of the league (and thus relegated to the Second Division where they would remain for the next five seasons). In that relegation season from the First Division, Bamlett oversaw a record run of 12 consecutive defeats at the very start of the campaign. With four games remaining he was dismissed. Bamlett never managed a football club again and died ten years later aged 59.

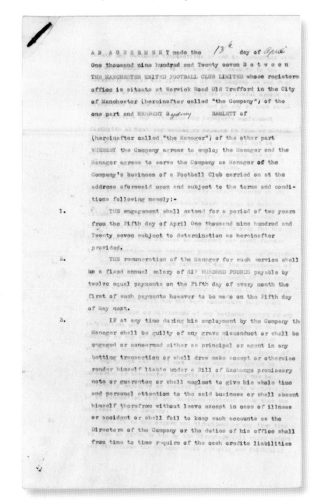

Above: 3 April 1914. Herbert Bamlett in his days as a top referee.

Left: 13 April 1927. The contract between United and Herbert Bamlett.

WALTER CRICKMER

Country: England
Born: 1899
Died: 6 February 1958
Clubs Managed: Manchester United
(1931-32 and 1937-45)
Took charge: first spell 6 April 1931;
second spell 13 November 1937
To: first spell 7 May 1932; second
spell 2 September 1939

Top: Walter Crickmer, the
Manchester United secretary.

Above: 25 March 1932. The Good
Friday match programme against
Charlton Athletic. United lost
2-0 and would finish the season
12th in the Second Division.

Right: 6 February 1958. It is
ironic that Walter Crickmer, who
was so instrumental in securing
permission from the FA for United
to play in the European Cup,
should die in the Munich air crash.

Opposite Top: 1948. Walter Crickmer
(third from right, seated row) in
a photograph taken during the
triumphant FA Cup-winning season.

Opposite Bottom: A letter issued
from Walter Crickmer's office
recalling United season tickets
as league football in Britain
is suspended at the outbreak
of the Second World War.

In the long line of loyal servants of United, Walter Crickmer deserves a special place in the history of the club. This was a man who served the Reds for almost 40 years and was one of the people responsible for setting up the Manchester United Junior Athletic Club that not only helped forge the Busby Babes, but provided many other players for United's first team. Tragically, Crickmer's story would end on a snow-bound runway in Germany when he lost his life in the Munich air crash.

Crickmer was born around the turn of the 20th century, although his actual birthdate remains unrecorded. He joined United the year after First World War ended, working in the administration offices doing various jobs before being made secretary of the club in 1926. This was a difficult time for United as funds were low and a return to the First Division had only just been secured. During the next few seasons under the management of Herbert Bamlett, United fumbled around in the lower half of the First Division before suffering an inevitable relegation at the end of the 1930-31 season. It was a time when money and playing talent was in short supply at the club. Bamlett was fired from his job in April 1931 and, to cut costs, Crickmer was given charge of the

team – heading for the Second Division – on a temporary basis.

Crickmer's intelligence and inclusive managerial style (he would make a point of speaking to fans and even opposition players and officials) provided an immediate lift, though it was too late to avoid relegation. The following campaign would still be a troubled season – the team suffered a 7-0 thrashing away to Wolverhampton Wanderers in December after the players' wages had not been paid at Christmas – but Crickmer kept the team afloat while a new owner was found. United ended the 1931-32 season in 12th position, a respectable finish considering the club faced bankruptcy at one stage.

His job had become much easier during the season with the arrival of new club owner James W. Gibson and Crickmer was finally allowed to return to his role as secretary when a new, permanent manager, Scott Duncan, was appointed for the start of the 1932-33 campaign.

Crickmer and Gibson now worked closely together and, with an eye to the future, put United's youth policy into action in 1938. This strategy was implemented a short while after the resignation of Duncan, a man who had spent

plenty of Gibson's money on players, but to little effect.

In fact, Duncan's sudden resignation in the autumn 1937 meant that Crickmer was forced back into the role of caretaker manager once more. Despite his reluctance to run the team on the training pitch, Crickmer again galvanised the players; as secretary he knew each of them intimately, having had control of much of the business side of the club for over a decade – from making team travel plans to producing player contracts.

With United in 13th place in the Second Division, his first match in charge was a resounding victory, a 7-1 thrashing of Chesterfield. The Reds then won five of the next six matches to end 1937 in fourth place. From there, Crickmer engineered a run at promotion that was worthy of a more experienced football club manager. United lost just four league games from January to May, and won their final match of the season 2-0 at home to Bury to sneak into the runners-up position. The Reds were back in the First Division and Crickmer was a hero.

He continued his secretary-manager role both in the following season, when United finished 14th in the First Division, and during the Second World

War when War League football replaced the official version. Finally in 1945, the chairman of the club found a manager worthy of replacing him in Matt Busby and their partnership would be quite formidable over the next 13 years.

As a leading football administrator in England, Crickmer then became a significant voice in persuading the Football Association to enter a representative team in the European Cup. The Football League Secretary Alan Hardaker believed, at the time, it was in the best interests of English football

and football in general for them not to enter. It is ironic that Crickmer's success in the campaign for participation eventually led to the tragic plane crash at Munich airport in February 1958 when Crickmer and 22 others lost their lives.

Crickmer was a devoted and dedicated United man, often the glue that held the club together. It was a testimony to his influence at Old Trafford that many fans felt his loss on the same level as that of the star players who died alongside him.

ADAM 'SCOTT' DUNCAN

Country: Scotland

Born: 2 November 1888
Dumbarton, Dunbartonshire

Died: 3 October 1976

Clubs Managed: Hamilton Academical (1923-25), Cowdenbeath (1925-32), Manchester United (1932-37), Ipswich Town (1937-55)

First match in charge: 1 August 1932

To: 6 November 1937

Major honours: Second Division (1): 1935-36

The arrival of Scott Duncan at Old Trafford in 1932 marked another significant change for the club, because prior to his appointment – and as was the case for most football clubs in England – the idea of handing over the team to an ex-player was a complete novelty. Managers were originally more club secretaries than team coaches. But this former forward from Dumbarton on the west coast of Scotland was different; at 43 he already had eight years of management experience and was still young enough to be able to relate to the players. His professional playing career in the game was more impressive than any man who had led the team up to that point.

Duncan began his football career after giving up his job as an 18-year-old law clerk to sign for his local team, Dumbarton. So impressive was he on the right wing that two years later he was transferred for £150 to Newcastle United, one of the premier teams in the English First Division at the time. There

he won a league championship in 1908-09 as well as an FA Cup winner's medal the following season. Duncan then joined Glasgow Rangers in 1913 for a £600 fee, but the First World War (in which he served as a signals instructor in the Royal Field Artillery) disrupted his playing career and by 1923, aged 35, he had retired and made a move into management, first at Hamilton Academical and Cowdenbeath in Scotland, and then with United. This was easily the biggest task of Duncan's managerial career to date, as he came to a club that had only recently dropped into the Second Division and just been saved from financial ruin by Manchester businessman James W Gibson. There was an atmosphere of expectation at Old Trafford and also cash to spend, so Duncan spent it, often on players from his native Scotland.

In his first season, 1932-33, a very healthy sixth position in the Second Division augured well, but the following campaign was a near-disaster and relegation to the Third Division was only

avoided on the final day of the season. Despite this, Gibson kept faith with his manager and the signing of George Mutch (from Scotland) helped United to fifth in the league, before a timely promotion in 1935-36.

However, Duncan's team failed to gel and the Reds' return to the First Division lasted just one season. After 14 games back in the Second Division in 1937-38, Duncan left for Ipswich Town who were in the Southern League at the time. The Scot stayed as manager at Ipswich until 1955 (he would remain with the club as secretary for a while longer), only to be replaced by a young Alf Ramsey who would go on to manage the England national team to a World Cup win 11 years later.

Duncan's five seasons in charge of United were definitely eventful, but ultimately unsuccessful, yet, oddly, the notion of the man was right because the next post-war manager of the Reds would be another Scottish-born, ex-player and he would become a one of United's greatest managers.

Right: Circa 1907. Scott Duncan (r) in his playing days at Newcastle United.

they were prepared to give him and instead took up an offer to become manager at United in 1945. It was his first managerial appointment and he was just 36 years old when he took up he position in October after being demobbed. He quickly asserted his authority at the club, demonstrating a tough disciplinary approach and a ruthless streak belied by his amiable exterior.

When he took over, the club was in disarray. Money was short and Old Trafford had been bombed in the war. So Busby began his own rebuilding process. He set up a coherent youth policy at the club and reorganised the scouting system.

His first, and arguably most important signing, was Jimmy Murphy who joined as chief coach. Busby had witnessed Murphy giving a speech to a group of soldiers in Italy, and was so impressed that he made sure Murphy joined the United coaching staff in 1946.

The pair had an immediate impact, United finishing second in the league in 1946-47. They repeated the feat over the next two seasons and proof of progress came in the shape of silverware with the 1948 FA Cup. Busby had put together an exciting team boasting the talents of Johnny Carey, John Aston, Charlie Mitten and Stan Pearson. By the 1951-52 season they were able to mount a sustained challenge, which led them to the league championship, United's first since 1911.

Above: Matt Busby managed the Great Britain football team at the 1948 Olympics. They lost to Yugoslavia 3-1 in the semi-final and then went on to lose the bronze medal play-off to Denmark 5-3. Both games were played at Wembley.

Left: Matt Busby at his desk in 1957.

Below: January 1971. (l-r) Bobby Charlton, Denis Law, George Best, Matt Busby, Brian Kidd, Pat Crerand and David Sadler at Manchester United's Cliff training ground. Busby had returned as team manager after Wilf McGuinness had been sacked.

SIR ALEXANDER MATTHEW 'MATT' BUSBY, CBE, KCSG

Country: Scotland

Born: 26 May 1909 Orbiston, Lanarkshire

Died: 20 January 1994

Clubs Managed: Manchester United (1945-69 and 1970-71)

First match in charge: 27 October 1945

To: 5 May 1971

Major honours: First Division (5): 1951-52, 1955-56, 1956-57, 1964-65, 1966-67; FA Cup (2): 1948, 1963; FA Charity Shield (5): 1952, 1956, 1957, 1965 (shared), 1967 (shared); European Cup (1): 1968

Revered at Manchester United, Sir Matt Busby remains one of the greatest postwar British managers. A select few managers have built great teams, but Matt Busby did more – he built a great club. He joined Manchester United in the aftermath of the Second World War when the ground had been bombed and the club had an overdraft at the bank. He had no managerial experience, yet over the following 26 years, through triumph and tragedy, Busby built a succes-

sion of great teams and forged a dynasty.

Alexander Matthew Busby was born in the mining village of Orbiston, near Bellshill, Lanarkshire, on 26 May 1909 and would escape a life down the coal pit through football. As a teenager he went to Rangers for a trial, but they rejected him after discovering he was Catholic. Then Celtic discovered he had had a trial with Rangers and refused to take him on. But the rejection proved to be a blessing in disguise when he joined Manchester City in 1928 and he won the 1934 FA Cup. At right half, Busby's reputation grew as an intelligent player and a fine passer of the ball. He was sold to Liverpool for £8,000 on 12 March 1936, having made more than 200 appearances for Manchester City, but his playing career came to an abrupt end at the outbreak of the war.

After the war, Busby was offered the assistant manager's job at Liverpool. He decided he wanted more freedom than

His team scored prolifically that season, but Busby knew their time was ending and began building a new team immediately, bringing in talented youth squad players. The era of the 'Busby Babes' was born, with Bobby Charlton, Duncan Edwards, Dennis Viollet, Tommy Taylor and Jackie Blanchflower among them.

Two successive championships followed in 1956 and 1957, after the first of which Busby defied the Football League to enter Manchester United into the European Cup, making them the first English club to take part. Their first foray into Europe took them all the way to the semi-finals where they bowed out to the eventual champions Real Madrid. The second attempt ended with tragic consequences when the team plane crashed on a Munich airfield in 1958 en route home from an encounter with Red Star Belgrade. Eight players were killed and Busby himself was severely injured. He was twice read the last rites in hospital but pulled through, returning to Manchester 71 days after the crash.

The disaster devastated the club and it was only the immense and calm strength of Busby's assistant Jimmy Murphy that kept them together that season, the Welshman brilliantly guiding a makeshift team to an emotionally charged FA Cup final defeat at Wembley.

Busby recovered and took the reins in time for the next season. Just as he had done before, he began rebuilding the team with an iron-willed determination. In 1962-63, Busby took Manchester United back to Wembley where they defeated Leicester City. The win marked the club's third FA Cup and was their first major trophy just five years after the horrors of Munich.

Two more league championships followed, in 1965 and 1967, giving Busby and United the chance to conquer Europe again. First United reached the semi-final of the European Cup in 1966. Then in 1968 they finally realised Busby's dream – beating Benfica 4-1 at Wembley to lift the European Cup, the first English club to win the coveted trophy.

In 1969 Busby retired, although he returned for a spell as caretaker manager a year later. Retirement did not end his association with the club. He remained first as a director for 11 years before being made club president in 1980.

As well as trophies, Busby's managerial reign more than any other left United with a philosophy of how the game should be played. Football was not war by other means; it was a sport to be played for pleasure. His teams were sent out to win, but not for the sake of it. Thanks to Busby, Manchester United became synonymous with a brand of football full of skill, swagger and style.

He summed up his approach to football in a few well-chosen words, 'What matters above all things is that the game should be played in the right spirit, with the utmost resource of skill and courage, with fair play and no favour, with every man playing as a member of his team and the result accepted without bitterness and conceit.'

He was knighted for his services to the game in 1968 and won Manager of the Year the same season. As well as leading United, he coached the 1948 British Olympic team and was in temporary charge of Scotland in 1958, giving a debut to an 18-year-old Denis Law. In 1993 Warwick Road North was renamed Sir Matt Busby Way to honour the man described as 'Mr Manchester United'. On 20 January 1994 after a short illness, Sir Matt Busby died aged 84, having lived long enough to see the club win the league again.

Above: 15 July 1962. Matt Busby and new signing Denis Law under the media spotlight outside Old Trafford following Law's complicated transfer from Italian club Torino.

Right: 22 October 1956. A letter from Matt Busby to Major B. V. Tomlinson at Camp H.Q. Rhine District seeking permission for the United players to "do a little training" on the Army's sports field in preparation for the European Cup second leg match against Borussia Dortmund. Permission was duly granted.

Right: Matt Busby pictured in the Santiago Bernabeu Stadium in Madrid before the European Cup semi-final, second leg match in 1968.

Opposite: Matt Busby with the Manager of the Year Award for 1967-68.

Above: 4 May 1958. The FA Cup final at Wembley against Bolton Wanderers. The United bench in front of the Royal Box prior to kick-off. Jimmy Murphy is the acting manager and behind him is Matt Busby who was still recovering from injuries sustained in the Munich crash.

Opposite: 29 May 1968. The European Cup final at Wembley. At the beginning of extra time, Matt Busby and Jimmy Murphy rally their flagging players.

Inset: 19 February 1958. Just 13 days after the Munich crash, in front of nearly 60,000 grieving fans, United face Sheffield Wednesday in an FA Cup match. Jimmy Murphy is in charge and the official programme cannot name a team in advance.

JAMES PATRICK 'JIMMY' MURPHY

Country: Wales
Born: 8 August 1910 Ton Pentre, Mid Glamorgan
Died: 14 November 1989
Clubs Managed: Manchester United (1958)
First match in charge: 19 February 1958
To: 14 May 1958

While he was never technically 'manager' of Manchester United, it is difficult to overstate the importance of Jimmy Murphy in United's history. Assistant to Matt Busby throughout his years in charge, he served at Old Trafford for 26 years as coach and assistant manager, heroically guiding the team in the tragic aftermath of the Munich disaster.

Murphy was born in Wales and spent most his career as a wing-half at West Bromwich Albion. His playing days were cut short by the Second World War, but it was in Italy during the

conflict that he first met Matt Busby. Busby overheard him talking to some troops about football and, impressed by what he heard, made him his first signing at Manchester United after the war.

From 1945 to 1955 Murphy served as a chief coach at United, then from 1955 to 1971 he held the position of assistant manager. Murphy's great strengths lay in his ability to communicate with and motivate the players. He didn't want to be the focus of attention and much preferred to stay out of the limelight. Yet he had an amazing talent for spotting raw potential and bringing it through to the first team. Many football historians refer to 'Busby's Babes' but Busby himself spoke of 'Murphy's Golden Apples'. Murphy would preach fast, free-flowing football and encourage simplicity ahead

of the 'Hollywood' pass. If he believed a player had the potential he would spend hours on the training pitch, prompting and directing them.

Along with his role at Manchester United, Murphy was also part-time manager of Wales. It was due to international duty that he happened to miss United's match in Belgrade and the ill-fated return flight from Munich. Murphy learned of the tragedy on his return to Old Trafford and when informed by a secretary he openly wept. He flew to Munich to visit the survivors and amid the tragedy and sorrow it was Murphy who stepped forward and got a team together to complete the season.

That team comprised of two survivors, five reserves with barely any experience, two youth players making their debuts and two new signings. Just 13 days after the Munich disaster, Murphy sent out this makeshift side to beat Sheffield Wednesday 3-0 in the FA Cup fifth round. He would lead the team all the way to Wembley that season where they eventually succumbed to Bolton.

Later that year Murphy gladly handed control back to a recovered Busby, to ready the team for the new season. During the summer of 1958 he led Wales in Sweden at their first (and only) World Cup finals where they lost 1–0 in the quarter-finals to Brazil (the eventual winners), to a goal by Pelé. Back at United for the new season he settled into his old role as he and Busby set about rebuilding the club.

People often remember the role of Matt Busby in United's history but Busby paid tribute himself to Murphy, saying, "It needed someone who, though feeling the heartbreak of the situation, could still keep his head and keep the job going. Jimmy was that man."

Murphy continued as assistant to Busby until his retirement in 1971. He died in November 1989, aged 79. In 1990 and to honour such a great servant of the club, Manchester United commissioned the "Jimmy Murphy Young Player of the Year Award", to be given to the best player in the club's youth system in the previous season.

WILFRED 'WILF' MCGUINNESS
Country: England
Born: 25 October 1937 Manchester, Lancashire
Clubs Managed: Manchester United (1969-1970), Aris Salonika (1971-74), Panachaiki (1974-75), York City (1975-77)
First match in charge: 9 August 1969
To: 26 December 1970

The task of replacing Matt Busby would have been an enormously difficult one for a seasoned manager, so for Wilf McGuinness, at 31 years old and with no management experience, it was virtually an impossible mission. That he was Busby's own choice for the role was of little comfort. Appointed on 1 June 1969, McGuinness was never able to inspire United the way his predecessor had, and after 18 months in charge he returned to his previous role of reserve team coach.

As a player, McGuinness had been one of the original Busby Babes. After making his debut aged 17 against Wolves in October 1955 he was part of the league winning sides in 1956 and 1957. His playing career was cut short by a broken leg sustained in a reserve team game, but he stayed on at United, first a youth, then a reserve team coach. Throughout the sixties he worked closely with Busby at United and also with Alf Ramsey and England for a period during the World Cup.

In January 1969 Busby announced that he would be retiring from management at the end of the season. McGuinness was to be promoted from reserve team coach to manager. A new structure was put in place that meant Busby would work as general manager to relieve some of the inevitable pressure on McGuinness. As Busby reflected at the time on the new set-up, "In a year or so, perhaps he [McGuinness] could have full command."

Unfortunately this turned out to be wishful thinking. His first game in charge was away at Crystal Palace. It saw some fine, free-flowing football from a side containing Best, Law, Kidd, Morgan and Charlton, but ended in a 2-2 draw. Things soon got worse, with home defeats to Everton and Southampton and before long Busby felt compelled to

intervene and suggested signing centre-back Ian Ure.

Results picked up slightly and both domestic cup competitions offered a little respite as United made it to the semi-finals of the League and FA Cups. However, they lost to Manchester City in the former and Leeds United in the latter, and finished eighth in the league, though this was actually an improvement on Busby's final season.

Over the summer McGuinness was given the official title of manager (having been chief coach to Busby's general manager the previous season). A poor start to the 1970-71 season left United fifth from bottom heading in to the Christmas period and under real threat of relegation. A 4-4 draw at Derby on Boxing Day forced the board to act and on 29 December, Matt Busby was reluctantly restored as caretaker manager with McGuinness reverting to reserve team coach before leaving the club at the end of the season.

After his time at United, McGuinness spent four years coaching in Greece before returning to England to manage York City. He retains a passion for United and more recently has worked for Manchester United radio, providing expert opinion for the club's media channels.

Right: August 1969. Wilf McGuinness talking to the players during pre-season training at the Cliff.

FRANCIS 'FRANK' O'FARRELL

Country: Ireland

Born: 9 October 1927 Cork, Munster

Clubs Managed: Weymouth (1961-65), Torquay United (1965-68), Leicester City (1968-71), Manchester United (1971-72), Cardiff City (1973-74), Torquay United (1976-77 and 1981-82)

First match in charge: 14 August 1971

To: 16 December 1972

When O'Farrell was appointed manager of United, Matt Busby said, "I look upon Frank O'Farrell as my last great signing, possibly the greatest of the lot." However, just 18 months later, with three and a half years to run on his contract, O'Farrell was dismissed, the second managerial casualty of United's post-Busby years.

As a player, O'Farrell had spent the majority of his career at half-back with West Ham and Preston North End. He represented the Republic of Ireland on nine occasions, scoring two goals, and retired in 1961 following a short spell with Weymouth.

His managerial career started at Weymouth before moving to Torquay then Leicester, with whom he won promotion to the First Division in 1971. It was in June 1971 that United appointed O'Farrell, impressed by his work with the Midlands club.

When O'Farrell took on a talented squad containing the United trinity of Best, Law and Charlton the initial signs looked good. A promising start to the 1971-72 season saw United go on a run of results that would put them top of the table, five points clear approaching Christmas. However, while Best's influence on the pitch was still occasionally

sublime, his behaviour off it was becoming increasingly erratic and difficult to manage. Nearing the end of their careers, Charlton and Law were not quite what they had been. The New Year saw an alarming slump in form as United lost seven straight games to slide down the table. By mid-March they were without a win in 11 league matches and O'Farrell needed to act. He brought in Martin Buchan and Ian Storey-Moore. These additions helped to steady the ship as United rallied to an eighth place finish, but the reprieve was only to be temporary.

A lingering suspicion had set in that O'Farrell was not able to command the loyalty and respect of the players. This was further added to by many of them referring to Busby as 'Boss' in O'Farrell's presence. In the autumn O'Farrell made additions for the new season, signing strikers Ted MacDougall and Wyn Davies. Unfortunately neither managed to sparkle and a fractious dressing room atmosphere did little to help matters on the field.

The final straw came in December 1972. O'Farrell dropped Best for failing to turn up for training three times in a week. On 5 December Best was transfer listed, however a week later, Matt Busby and chairman Louis Edwards agreed to lift the punishment without O'Farrell's knowledge or blessing. Two days later, a Best-less United were thumped 5-0 at Crystal Palace and after three more days O'Farrell was shown the door having refused to resign.

Shy by nature, the sense was that while O'Farrell was a likeable man and well thought of in the game, he was not able to take on a challenge of the magnitude of leading Manchester United. It didn't help that much of the time his authority was questioned. He had been tactically astute enough to win a Second Division title with Leicester, but he wasn't able to make the grade at Old Trafford.

After leaving he managed various other sides including a spell in charge of the Iranian national team.

Left: 11 March 1972. George Best leaves an FA disciplinary hearing in London with Frank O'Farrell ahead of him. Dealing with the wayward star was just one of his problems at United.

THOMAS HENDERSON 'TOMMY' DOCHERTY

Country: Scotland

Born: 24 April 1928 Glasgow, Lanarkshire

Clubs Managed: Chelsea (1961-67), Rotherham United (1967-68), Queens Park Rangers (1968 and 1979-80), Aston Villa (1968-70), Porto (1970-71), Scotland (1971-72), Manchester United (1972-77), Derby County (1977-79), Sydney Olympic (1981 and 1983), Preston North End (1981), South Melbourne (1982-83), Wolverhampton Wanderers (1984-85), Altrincham (1987-88)

First match in charge: 26 December 1972

To: 21 May 1977

Major honours: Second Division (1): 1974-75; FA Cup (1): 1977

Below: Tommy Docherty with his "shooting stars", Steve Coppell (l) and Gordon Hill.

In five years at Manchester United, Tommy Docherty helped the club emerge from the shadow of the sixties and find a new post-Busby identity. The process of reinvention was as colourful as Docherty himself, involving relegation, promotion, two cup finals, legends leaving and a massive 34 new players being signed. The man who once joked he had had 'more clubs than Jack Nicklaus' eventually departed under a cloud, but ultimately he reshaped United and gave them their first major trophy in nearly a decade.

Like many great managers Docherty hailed from Glasgow. His playing career started at Celtic and took him to Preston North End and Arsenal before retiring after a short spell with Chelsea. He moved into management in 1961 at Stamford Bridge with Chelsea where he spent six years in charge, winning the League Cup in 1965.

Following his time at Chelsea he went on to manage Rotherham United, QPR and Aston Villa before taking the top job with Scotland in 1971. At the start of the 1972-73 season, United were in trouble in the league. By December, the decision was taken to relieve Frank O'Farrell of his duties and Tommy Docherty was appointed. He swiftly set about making new signings as Charlton retired and Law was let go at the end of the season. While he was able to keep the club up then, it was clear that United were in a period of transition and the following season they were relegated.

Relegation gave Docherty the chance to overhaul the squad and put his stamp on the club. He got United back up at the first attempt as a new younger team played an attacking brand of football to win the championship by three points.

Back in the top flight, United exceeded Docherty's modest expectations for the season – playing in an attractive style that saw them lead the league at one stage, and eventually finish third. He also took the team to Wembley and the FA Cup final where they suffered something of an upset at the hands of Second Division Southampton. In 1976-77 another solid league campaign ended in a sixth-place finish and a return to Wembley. This time it was United who were unfancied as they faced a treble-chasing Liverpool, but once again the underdogs triumphed, a Jimmy Greenhoff winner putting the seal on a memorable victory.

Then, just as Docherty's position at the club looked secure, it all went wrong. In typical fashion his downfall was in spectacular style, as an affair with the club's physiotherapist's wife came to light. Just six weeks after the high of winning the cup he was sacked.

While he was unhappy at the manner of his departure, he had taken on a club in bad shape and remoulded it, leaving them far better off than when he arrived. His confident, sometimes abrasive style was not to everyone's liking, but he remains a popular figure with the United faithful for creating a new United and moving the club on from the Busby era.

After United he managed numerous other clubs and now works as a speaker on the after dinner circuit and as a football pundit.

DAVID 'DAVE' SEXTON OBE

Country: England

Born: 6 April 1930 Islington, London

Clubs Managed: Leyton Orient (1965), Chelsea (1967-74), Queens Park Rangers (1974-77), Manchester United (1977-81), Coventry City (1981-83)

First match in charge: 13 August 1977

To: 25 April 1981

Major honours: FA Charity Shield (1): 1977 (shared)

Dave Sexton was in charge at United for four seasons between 1977 and 1981. A reserved character, his time in charge saw him take United to a cup final and a second-place league finish. However, he failed to win any trophies during his spell at the club and his management, coming between the more flamboyant reigns of Tommy Doherty and Ron Atkinson, is often, perhaps unfairly, viewed unfavourably.

Sexton spent his playing career as an inside forward for a number of London clubs, along with Brighton and Hove Albion. He cut his managerial teeth as coach at Chelsea before moving to Leyton Orient to take the manager's post in 1965. Bertie Mee brought him to Arsenal as first team coach a year later, but he returned to Chelsea to replace the outgoing Tommy Docherty in 1967.

It was at Chelsea that he had the most successful spell of his career. The Blues won the FA Cup in 1970 and followed that with the European Cup-Winners' Cup in 1971. Defeat in the 1972 League Cup final denied Sexton and Chelsea a hat-trick of cup wins in successive seasons and, after falling out with several senior players, Sexton was shown the door at Chelsea in 1974.

He took over at Queens Park Rangers and led them to within a point of the 1975-76 league title as they were pipped at the post by Liverpool.

In 1977 he was appointed manager of Manchester United, once again following on the heels of Tommy Docherty. His studious, rather shy style was in stark contrast to the outgoing Docherty. Sexton preferred coaching duties and the management of his squad to courting the media. His first game in charge saw United draw 0-0 with Liverpool in the Charity Shield at Wembley, and the 1977-78 season ended in a tenth place league finish.

In 1978-79, Sexton led United out at Wembley for a second time where they lost 3-2 to Arsenal in the last minute of a thrilling FA Cup final. The following year United finished runners-up in the league to Liverpool, but United supporters were not satisfied: either with the lack of trophies or what they considered to be dour, unexciting football.

Even though he won his final seven games in charge, Sexton was dismissed on 30 April 1981. He had been at the helm for 201 matches, winning just over 40 percent of his games in charge.

Despite not picking up any silverware, Sexton made a number of significant signings during his time at United. Ray Wilkins signed from Chelsea in 1979 and went on to have an outstanding career at Old Trafford, as did Joe Jordan, who scored 41 goals after joining in 1978 from Leeds United.

Recognised as a decent football man, Sexton ultimately paid the price at United for failing to land silverware. After United he went on to manage Coventry as well as England's Under-21s.

Above: Dave Sexton listening to a portable radio.

Left: 20 October 1980. Garry Birtles signs for United with Dave Sexton looking on. United's first million-pound transfer was not a success – and the manager took the blame.

with the club. He was also responsible for bringing club legend Bryan Robson to United and nurturing talents like Mark Hughes and Norman Whiteside.

Atkinson's playing days never hit the heights that his managerial career would reach. As a wing-half he captained Oxford United from the Southern League to the Second Division, earning the nickname 'The Tank' for his robust style. Upon retiring he entered management with Kettering at the early age of 32. Success there led to a move to Cambridge United, who he took from the Fourth Division to the brink of the Second Division before taking over at West Bromwich Albion. At West Brom he had great success, leading the relatively small club to third place in the First Division in 1978-79, along with the quarter-finals of the UEFA Cup.

In 1981 his success saw him take the reins at United following the dismissal of Dave Sexton. One of his first moves was to bring dynamic midfielder Robson to United in a deal that saw fellow midfielder Remi Moses join the Reds too. In his first year in charge, he led Manchester United to a third place finish and UEFA Cup qualification.

The end of the 1982 season saw Atkinson give a debut to 16-year-old Norman Whiteside. By the 1982-83 season, Whiteside was a regular starter in Big Ron's first team. Whiteside repaid his manager's faith in him when the young Irishman netted the second goal in the 4-0

replay FA Cup win over Brighton & Hove Albion at the end of the season.

In 1983-84, Atkinson's side finished fourth in the First Division. They also reached the semi-finals of the European Cup-Winners' Cup playing flowing football. Displays such as their 3-0 second leg quarter-final victory against Barcelona thrilled the fans, but what the supporters really craved was the league title.

In 1984-85 United won the FA Cup, but they were denied a place in European football after the tragic events at the Heysel stadium and subsequent ban on English clubs by UEFA from all European competitions. Nor had United still got close to winning the league. Atkinson's side was capable of producing great one-off displays, but without the injury-prone Robson, they lacked the consistency to mount a serious title challenge. That seemed to have changed in 1985-86 when United started the season by winning their first ten games, but when their challenge petered out, disillusionment set in. Atkinson offered his resignation prior to the summer and though he was persuaded to stay on, a poor start to the following season made his departure inevitable.

Atkinson went on to have spells as manager with numerous English clubs, most notably Sheffield Wednesday, Aston Villa and Coventry. He also managed briefly in Spain and then became a well-known TV pundit.

RONALD ERNEST 'RON' ATKINSON

Country: England

Born: 18 March 1939 Liverpool, Lancashire

Clubs Managed: Kettering Town (1971-74), Cambridge United (1974-78), West Bromwich Albion (1978-81 and 1987-88), Manchester United (1981-86), Atlético Madrid (1988-89), Sheffield Wednesday (1989-91 and 1997-98), Aston Villa (1991-94), Coventry City (1995-96), Nottingham Forest (1999), Peterborough United (2006 as caretaker)

First match in charge: 29 August 1981

Last match: 4 November 1986

Major honours: FA Charity Shield (1): 1983; FA Cup (2): 1983, 1985

During his time at Old Trafford, Ron Atkinson was the most successful Manchester United manager since Sir Matt Busby. A larger-than-life character with an easy-going manner, 'Big Ron' gained popularity winning two FA Cups

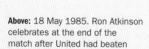

Above: 18 May 1985. Ron Atkinson celebrates at the end of the match after United had beaten Everton 1-0 in the FA Cup final.

Right: 7 October 1981. A worried Ron Atkinson waits to see the extent of the injury sustained by striker Garry Birtles who is being carried off during a League Cup match against Tottenham Hotspur.

Opposite: 29 March 1983. Ron Atkinson takes a training session.

Above: 12 May 1996. Alex Ferguson with the FA Cup and Premiership trophy.

Right: 21 July 2011. Sir Alex Ferguson during a press conference ahead of United's pre-season match against Chicago Fire.

SIR ALEXANDER 'ALEX' FERGUSON CBE

Country: Scotland

Born: 31 December 1941 Glasgow, Lanarkshire

Clubs Managed: East Stirlingshire (1974), St. Mirren (1974-78), Aberdeen (1978-86), Manchester United (1986-present)

First match in charge: 8 November 1986

Major honours: Premier League (12): 1992-93, 1993-94, 1995-96, 1996-97, 1998-99, 1999-2000, 2000-01, 2002-03, 2006-07, 2007-08, 2008-09, 2010-11; FA Cup (5): 1990, 1994, 1996, 1999, 2004; League Cup (4): 1992, 2006, 2009, 2010; FA Charity/Community Shield (10): 1990 (shared), 1993, 1994, 1996, 1997, 2003, 2007, 2008, 2010, 2011; UEFA Champions League (2) 1999, 2008; UEFA Cup-Winners' Cup (1): 1991; UEFA Super Cup (1): 1991; Intercontinental Cup (1): 1999; FIFA Club World Cup (1): 2008

After a relatively unremarkable playing career, Sir Alex Ferguson has gone on to become one of the managerial greats of the game. He is, quite simply, the most successful manager in the history of the British game and has won 37 trophies with United alone. His man-management skills coupled with a fierce will to win have helped him lead United during a period of unprecedented success. He has been honoured both inside and outside the game, and in the pantheon of great United managers he sits proudly at the top.

Yet it was from humble beginnings that Ferguson started his footballing life. Born in 1941 in Govan, Glasgow, Ferguson grew up supporting Rangers. His playing career began aged 16 at amateur club Queen's Park while working at Remington Rand (manufacturer of typewriters), where he would later become a shop steward, and, as a handy striker, would score 170 goals at six clubs during a 17-year career.

In June 1974, shortly after retiring from playing, Ferguson was appointed manager at East Stirlingshire. He was 32. Despite his relative youth, he quickly developed a reputation as a disciplinarian, gaining admiration for his tactical knowledge as the club climbed the table. In October of that year he moved to St Mirren where he oversaw an astounding transformation, as he took the Saints from the second tier to Premier Division in just three years. St Mirren remain the only club to have sacked Ferguson in the course of his disputed move to Aberdeen.

In 1978 he was offered the manager's job at Aberdeen. Ferguson seized the opportunity to shake up Scottish football and break the 'Old Firm' duopoly. At the time Rangers and Celtic had won 14 successive league titles between them, but driven on by an extraordinary hunger for success, Ferguson inspired Aberdeen to the 1980 Premier Division title. Two further championships followed, along with four Scottish Cups and victory over Real Madrid in the 1983 European Cup-Winners' Cup final.

In 1986, Ferguson led Scotland at the World Cup finals (and through the qualifying play-off games) after the sudden death of Jock Stein. Three months later Manchester United asked him to become their manager. After decades of underachievement, England's biggest club were desperate for success. However, on arrival Ferguson found a club beset by a drinking culture and lack of fitness. He set about restoring the club's image, and in his first season hauled the club from 21st position to a respectable 11th place finish.

In his second season United brought in new players such as Viv Anderson and Brian McClair as they pushed on to claim the runner-up spot in the First Division. However, they were still streets behind a dominant Liverpool. Ferguson would later claim it was his greatest mission to, "Knock Liverpool off their perch" – but this was still a distant dream. The next year saw United regress to an 11th place finish and as results dipped, the

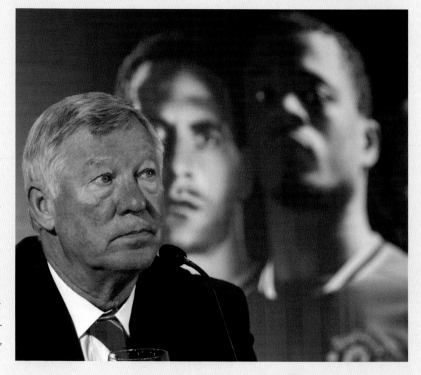

pressure on Ferguson began to intensify.

Big-money signings boosted his squad in 1989-90 but a shaky start to the season saw Ferguson endure calls from some supporters for his removal. Fortunately, the board kept faith with him and Ferguson repaid their belief later that season, winning his first silverware with United, the 1990 FA Cup. This was the spark that United had been waiting for. The Cup-Winners' Cup followed a year later and the League Cup came in 1992, with a 1-0 victory over Nottingham Forest. Then the league title finally returned to Old Trafford in 1993 for the first time in 26 years.

By now Ferguson had a strong squad with an unshakable belief and they would go one better the following season. With Roy Keane signed to replace Bryan Robson and Eric Cantona in scintillating form, United stormed to the league title then thumped Chelsea 4-0 in the FA Cup final securing the first 'double' in the club's history. United went on to add six more league titles and three FA Cups

in the next ten seasons, including another league and FA Cup 'double' in 1996. However, it was the historic 'treble' of 1999 that really established Ferguson among the managerial greats of the game.

Faced with serious challenges in the league, FA Cup and Champions League, Ferguson brilliantly juggled his resources and exhorted his team to play thrilling, attacking football, none more so than that seen at the conclusion of the Champions League final against Bayern Munich, when two goals late in injurytime saw United crowned European champions for the first time since 1968.

Knighted in 1999 for his achievements, Ferguson announced his intention to retire at the end of the 2001-02 season. However, as United faltered he could not resist another challenge and extended his contract, leading his team to another league title in 2003. Freespending Chelsea made success harder to achieve in the early years of the new millennium, but Ferguson led United to victory in the FA Cup in 2004, rebuilding

his team to lift the league title three more times between 2007 and 2009.

European glory was achieved again as Ferguson took United to Moscow in May 2008. There they defeated Chelsea on penalties with Ferguson becoming one of a select band of managers to win two Champions League titles. Twin defeats in the 2009 and 2011 Champions League finals have since followed, but Ferguson's pedigree at the highest level is unquestionable.

Revered by the United faithful and respected throughout the game, Ferguson's career has not been without controversy. There have been media boycotts, the infamous 'hairdryer' treatment has been meted out on countless occasions and players who cross him have been given short shrift. Yet he has won the Manager of the Month more times than anyone in British football history and is the longest serving manager in the history of United. In 2011, he led United to their 19th league title, finally beating Liverpool's old record of 18.

Above: 15 March 1997. Alex Ferguson is Manager of the Month again.

Next Page: 1986. A portrait of Alex Ferguson. The incredible story is just beginning.

7 August 2011. Nani celebrates scoring against Manchester City in the Community Shield, won 3-2 by United to give Sir Alex Ferguson his 37th trophy at United.

Acknowledgements

Produced by Hayden Media Limited, Middlesex, United Kingdom

Creative Director: Jonathan Hayden
Designed by: Marcus Nichols at PDQ Digital Media Solutions Ltd
Contributions by: Ross Biddiscombe, Patrick Curry and Jonathan Hayden
Reproduction by: PDQ Digital Media Solutions Ltd, Bungay, United Kingdom

Acknowledgements
Writing and researching this book has been a team effort:
At Manchester United: media commercial manager James White and curator of the museum, Mark Wylie. Mark has been an important advisor on the club's history and a willing guide to the wealth of materials contained within the museum.
Ian Marshall whose expertise, wealth of knowledge about Manchester United and editorial diligence has been invaluable.
Stephen Bourke, Ned Stratton and Lewis Killeen who helped research the section devoted to United's players.
Richard Baylis who carried out the picture research.
The staff at the British Newspaper Library.
Ray Adler who supplied much of the Manchester United memorabilia featured in these pages and made it a much better book than it might otherwise have been.
Images courtesy of Getty Images, Manchester United and Ray Adler.